# The
# Big
# Time

**Also by Michael MacCambridge:**

*America's Game: The Epic Story of How Pro Football
Captured a Nation*

*Chuck Noll: His Life's Work*

*The Franchise: A History of* Sports Illustrated *Magazine*

*Lamar Hunt: A Life in Sports*

*'69 Chiefs: A Team, A Season, and the Birth of Modern Kansas City*

**Coauthor:**

*More than a Game: The Glorious Present—
and the Uncertain Future—of the NFL*, with Brian Billick

*Red Letters: Two Fervent Liverpool FC Supporters Correspond Through the
Epic Season That Wouldn't End*, with Neil Atkinson

**Contributor:**

*A New Literary History of America*

*NFL 100: A Century of Pro Football*

**Editor:**

*ESPN SportsCentury*

*ESPN College Football Encyclopedia: The Complete History of the Game*

# The Big Time

## HOW THE 1970S TRANSFORMED SPORTS IN AMERICA

## Michael MacCambridge

GRAND
CENTRAL

NEW YORK   BOSTON

Grand Central Publishing
Hachette Book Group
1290 Avenue of the Americas, New York, NY 10104
grandcentralpublishing.com
twitter.com/grandcentralpub

First Edition: October 2023

Grand Central Publishing is a division of Hachette Book Group, Inc. The Grand Central Publishing name and logo is a trademark of Hachette Book Group, Inc.

The publisher is not responsible for websites (or their content) that are not owned by the publisher.

The Hachette Speakers Bureau provides a wide range of authors for speaking events. To find out more, go to hachettespeakersbureau.com or email HachetteSpeakers@hbgusa.com.

Grand Central Publishing books may be purchased in bulk for business, educational, or promotional use. For information, please contact your local bookseller or the Hachette Book Group Special Markets Department at special.markets@hbgusa.com.

Library of Congress Cataloging-in-Publication Data
Names: MacCambridge, Michael, 1963-author.
Title: The big time : how the 1970s transformed sports in America / Michael MacCambridge.
Description: First edition. | New York : Grand Central Publishing, 2023. | Includes bibliographical references and index.
Identifiers: LCCN 2023020956 | ISBN 9781538706695 (hardcover) | ISBN 9781538708040 (ebook)
Subjects: LCSH: Sports—United States—History—20th century. | Sports—Social aspects—United States—History—20th century. | Sports in popular culture—United States—History—20th century. | Discrimination in sports—United States—History—20th century. | Sports for women—United States—History—20th century. | Mass media and sports—United States—History—20th century. | Television broadcasting of sports—United States—History—20th century.
Classification: LCC GV583 .M25 2023 | DDC 796.097309/04—dc23/eng/20230518
LC record available at https://lccn.loc.gov/2023020956

ISBNs: 9781538706695 (hardcover), 9781538708040 (ebook)

Printed in the United States of America

LSC-C

Printing 1, 2023

*For some daughters of Title IX—*
*Laura Pfeifauf,*
*Susan Reckers*
*and Katherine Rivard—*
*athletes from the '70s, friends for life*

# Contents

"That which we do is what we are. That which we remember is, more often than not, that which we would like to have been, or that which we hope to be. Thus our memory and our identity are ever at odds; our history ever a tall tale told by inattentive idealists."

—*Ralph Ellison,* Shadow and Act

"It all happens in sports. Sports, competition, is more important to our lives than some damn U.S. Senate committee hearing or the prime minister of England saying $x$ and then two months later $y$. It matters a great deal."

—Sports Illustrated *managing editor Andre Laguerre*

# PROLOGUE

THE FANS CAME out in record numbers that night, from fervent true believers to dedicated big-game collectors to curious dilettantes. It was one of those peak occasions in American sports in which the gravity of the event dominates the zeitgeist, momentarily transcending everything else going on in the world. As with any long-awaited showdown, the most loyal advocates on each side of the rivalry had gone a bit crazy with the waiting. They arrived in all their brightly colored regalia, cheer buttons, t-shirts, and the inevitable homemade signs. All the trappings were present: network television trucks in the parking lot, a collegiate marching band striding the field in a bustling pregame revelry, VIPs at every turn.

Though the event was absurd on its face—like so much else that happened during the decade—it seemed urgent, necessary, and altogether logical in the moment. On Thursday, September 20, 1973, in the midst of the widespread misery of an oil crisis and a mounting Watergate investigation that threatened Richard Nixon's presidency, more than 45 million Americans gathered around their TV sets to witness the most talked-about sports event of the year.

It wasn't a football game, or a boxing match, or the final of a major tournament. It was a made-for-TV event, a reputed $100,000 "winner-take-all" challenge match between the top-ranked women's tennis player in the world, the twenty-nine-year-old Billie Jean King, and the fifty-five-year-old former Wimbledon men's champion, Bobby Riggs. The crowd that night at the Astrodome in Houston was the largest in history to attend a tennis match, with a record American TV audience for the sport looking on.

Billed as the "Battle of the Sexes" or "the Libber vs. the Lobber," it was also a contest between two visions of what sports should be and, by extension, two visions of what America should be. As both a sports event and a cultural flashpoint, it was an occasion that would have been inconceivable a decade earlier or a decade later. Yet it was consistent with the sensibilities and tone of the era, which is to say that the combatants were carried into the arena by costumed handlers, like floats in a Mardi Gras parade. The tennis hustler Riggs was transported to the court on a rickshaw, borne by a harem of short-skirted beauties ("Bobby's Bosom Buddies"), each wearing a gold t-shirt with the Sugar Daddy candy bar logo, an early sign of the corporate branding that would overrun sports in the coming decades. The defending Wimbledon women's champion King was brought to the court on a palanquin, replete with a rooster-tail of faux-feathered plumage in the back, carried by a group of bare-chested men posing as Roman soldiers, rumored to be members of the Rice University swim team.

Riggs and King were perfect foils, diametrically opposed in all ways, from their gender to their politics to their eyewear. Riggs, slight, flabby, slouching into middle age, sporting the standard-issue, World War II–era black horn-rimmed glasses, already a vestige of the past, a huckster who'd been playing the con so well and for so long that he occasionally forgot it was a con. Then King, at once strong and feminine, resplendent in a sequined multicolored tennis dress (in menthol green and sky blue, created by the tennis devotee/designer Ted Tinling), sporting blue suede tennis shoes, peering out from behind au courant oval wire-rimmed glasses—compact, focused, and deceptively strong.

The event came in the midst of a galvanizing era for women in America. A year earlier, the first issue of *Ms.* magazine hit the newsstands, and the New York congresswoman Shirley Chisholm became the first female to seek a major-party nomination for the presidency. In the summer of 1972, Congress passed the Education Amendments Act, containing Title IX, which promised equality of opportunity for women in high school and college education. Early in 1973, Congress passed the Equal Rights Amendment and the Supreme Court rendered its landmark decision on *Roe v. Wade*, protecting a woman's legal right to abortion.

The resistance to these shifts within the culture was swift and severe. No one better symbolized the backlash than the aging self-proclaimed "male chauvinist pig" Riggs, who'd trounced the previously top-ranked woman Margaret Court earlier that year in "The Mother's Day Massacre." The twice-divorced

Riggs presented himself as a proud troglodyte on gender issues, and at the heart of his persona was a contempt not merely for female athletes but females as a whole. "Women don't have the emotional stability to play," he proclaimed. "They belong in the bedroom and kitchen, in that order." Riggs' acolytes were in attendance that night, many sporting plastic pig snouts in support. One of the night's homemade signs read, "BILLIE JEAN WEARS JOCKEY SHORTS."

By the time they took the court, Riggs vs. King had evolved from a sports event into a cultural proxy war. Las Vegas placed Riggs as the 8–5 favorite; as was his custom, the hustler Riggs was betting on himself with assorted media members. Many within women's tennis, including King's young rival Chris Evert, expected a repeat of Riggs' rout of Court. Others sensed that King was made of sterner stuff, less easily daunted than Court, and more cognizant of all that was at stake.

ABC's live telecast, the first time a full tennis match had ever appeared on prime-time network television in America, treated the event like a heavyweight title fight, with Howard Cosell decked out in a tuxedo and courtside seats going for $100.

During the National Anthem, Riggs was restless while King looked pensive and determined. She'd been training like a boxer in the weeks leading up to the bout, secluding herself, working on the problematic lobs that Riggs loved to put up, which would be all the more difficult under the white ceiling and glaring lights inside the Astrodome.

Over the previous months, she had done the requisite publicity to build interest in the match, and had found herself swept up in the combative vortex of the event, sufficient to understand that beyond trying to beat Riggs, she also carried the pressure of the women's movement on her shoulders. She had won ten Grand Slam singles titles, helped launch the Virginia Slims tour and was in the process of creating the novel concept of World Team Tennis, to debut the following spring. Yet she realized— correctly—that her legacy would be largely defined by the confrontation on the court that night.

Then, in the tense, airless space right before the start of the match, came the moment of clarity. Riggs had stubbornly insisted on wearing his training jacket—it also had the corporate logo for Sugar Daddy—for the warm-up session. Now, as they rested after their warm-up, King glanced over and noticed her voluble opponent was sweating profusely and hyperventilating. Somehow, with the whole world watching, and the perception of the women's liberation movement in the balance, the man was even more nervous than the woman.

In that instant, Billie Jean King *knew*. It had been all circus and bombast in the months leading up to the match, and pure spectacle on the night, but now it was an athletic event, a match like any other. She was younger, fitter, smarter, more prepared. She understood, even as she was toweling off her racket grip and adjusting her glasses, that she was going to win.

What she may not have fully understood in that moment is that the women's movement—and sports in America—would never be the same.

•

"Americans still find it difficult to take the Seventies seriously," wrote the historian Bruce J. Schulman in his account of the decade. Indeed, through the lens of the present day, the era that Thomas Wolfe dubbed "The Me Decade" is primarily noted for possessing the wildest clothes, the stupidest fads, and some of the most ridiculous controversies in the nation's history. The reputation of the '70s has remained resolutely subpar, cut-rate, even fraudulent in the collective imagination since then, perhaps predictably so for any era in which shag carpeting on walls served as a defining characteristic. In popular perception, it was a decade of inconsequential lassitude between the tumult of the '60s and the Reagan Revolution of the '80s. One history of the '70s was titled *It Seemed Like Nothing Happened*.

Yet within the world of American sports, the decade featured a confluence of events that were pivotal and transformative. Every decade brings change, of course, but no decade in American sports history featured such convulsive, conclusive change as the 1970s. A field that had been marginalized and relatively static for decades began to break free of its boundaries, ultimately emerging as something bigger, more serious, and more relevant than before.

So much that we take for granted about sports today either began or reached critical mass in the 1970s: the move of sports into prime time on network television; the dawn of free agency and the beginning of athletes gaining a sense of autonomy for their own careers; integration becoming—at least within sports—more the rule than the exception; and the social revolution prompted by Title IX legislation that brought females into the world of sports in unprecedented numbers, as athletes, administrators, coaches, and spectators.

As the decade moved from the bitter division of the 1960s, settling into the relative comfort of hard-earned social and material freedoms, the people who best defined the American decade were not politicians or movie stars, artists or intellectuals. Instead, the '70s belonged to its most exemplary and prominent athletes. The sweeping changes in American life and culture were most clearly reflected in the collective experience of Billie Jean King and Muhammad Ali, Henry Aaron and Julius Erving, Jack Nicklaus and O. J. Simpson, Kareem Abdul-Jabbar and Chris Evert, among others, who spent the era redefining the role of athletes and athletics in American society.

While the 1960s are widely viewed as the decade of revolution in American history, in the world of American sports that decade was primarily an age of conformity, the last siege before the dam broke. Muhammad Ali and Joe Namath were icons of the '60s, but they were still very much the outliers. The Green Bay Packers' legendary coach Vince Lombardi dominated the decade with his hyper-disciplined persona, and for much of the decade, the crewcut was still the standard hairstyle among ballplayers. The audience for sports was almost entirely male and predominantly white. The key positions on teams—owner, general manager, coach, quarterback, pitcher, catcher—were either exclusively white or nearly so. Professional athletes were essentially indentured servants, though modestly well-paid ones, bound in perpetuity to the clubs that signed them.

The new decade would witness the emergence of spectator sports as an ever-expanding mainstream phenomenon, as well as show remarkable changes in the way athletes were paid, how they played, and how they were perceived. Historically, spectator sports in the U.S. had operated on the margins, a ticket-driven leisure pursuit largely divided from the broader realm of American popular culture. By the end of the 1970s, sports would become a decidedly big business, a microcosm of the larger social fabric, a social glue that crossed all demographic boundaries. One could also begin to see what was to come: sports as a transcendently lucrative profession that would serve as both the last big tent in American popular culture, and a stage upon which many of the nation's more nettlesome issues in morality, ethics, and values would be played out.

•

The broad societal trends and rise of television had created more leisure time and more consumers in the '70s, and presented a horizon full of possibility as well as the freedom to try anything. Over the next ten years, nearly everything was tried.

So much about the decade was marked by *letting things go*—hair, clothing, styles, morality, social conventions, the color of appliances. Writ large, this saw the country acting at times like there *was* no history, no gravity, and no consequences for the present moment of freedom. Psychically, much of the decade had the feeling of third-drink revelry descending into something darker, fourth-drink recklessness bound for a hangover.

In this, the decade in sports closely resembled the American decade as a whole: unruly, unhinged, unpredictable, and in the end, unsustainable. Some breakthroughs proved innovative and resonant, others failed to stand up to time and scrutiny. And they were all mixed together in an indiscriminate mishmash of innovation, novelty, gimmickry, and genuine social progress. The decade in sports brought designated hitters and tearaway jerseys, "wild-card" playoff berths and eligible freshmen, two-fisted backhands in tennis and the three-point line in the NBA, the last all-white national champions in college football and the first Black manager in baseball, a no-hitter pitched while on LSD, a golf shot on the Moon, an attempted rocket jump of the Snake River Canyon, epic heavyweight title fights in Jamaica, Zaire, and the Philippines, made-for-TV competitions like *The Superstars* and the *Battle of the Network Stars*, a thousand winged doves at the Super Bowl, a butterscotch football, an orange baseball, a blue hockey puck, and a red-white-and-blue basketball.

Even the equipment changed: Tennis rackets went from wood to composite materials, jerseys went from wool to cotton to mesh to breathable hybrids, and the decade brought the invention of the aluminum baseball bat, the multicolored tennis ball, the protective flak jacket modified for football, the waffle-trainer running shoe, and, not incidentally, the sports bra.

The universe of sports continued to expand, with upstart leagues in football, basketball, hockey, soccer, and even tennis and volleyball. The era saw the rise and demise of such teams as basketball's San Diego Conquistadors, hockey's California Golden Seals, volleyball's El Paso/Juarez Sol, football's Shreveport Steamers, tennis' Boston Lobsters and soccer's Colorado Caribous, who actually *did* play one season in brown-and-tan game jerseys with a strip of leather fringe across the chest.

No sport was unaffected. The decade that began with the full merger of the National Football League and American Football League also eventually saw two leagues condensed into one in basketball and hockey. While Major League Baseball's structure held, almost nothing else in the sport did, leading one historian to observe that the '70s brought "more changes than the game had known in the first seven decades of the twentieth century." Among the changes that baseball confronted at the beginning—and certainly by the end—of the decade was that it was no longer the national pastime. Pro football had eclipsed the grand old game.

•

It was true that money exploded into sports in the 1970s, but the influx of riches was at once the most obvious and least interesting thing about the decade. The widespread success of sports on TV certainly led to the flood of money that raised the stakes and broadened the scope of sports. But to attribute the change solely to television is to conflate the effect with the root cause.

TV had enjoyed an omnipresence in American life for more than a decade, and by the end of the '60s more homes in America had televisions than had indoor plumbing. Yet the presence of spectator sports was limited to the little-watched TV "ghettos" of Saturday and Sunday afternoons. Football had been ascendant for more than a decade, but was still regarded as too male, too marginal, too parochial to succeed in prime time. What attracted the riches that television offered were the newfound and widespread evidence of the broad appeal of American spectator sports, and the growing size and appetite of its audience.

That development changed the stakes for athletes and owners alike. It was an age of financial and geographic emancipation for many athletes, and the best of them became millionaire celebrities. The athletes were cashing in on the money from television to the owners, staking their claim as the essential part of spectator sports' enduring appeal.

The decade would witness remarkable changes in some instances—and a depressing stasis in others—in how the country grappled with its original sin of racism. The fields and courts slowly became more integrated, setting the pace for the country as a whole.

The most profound change was greeted with the most skepticism at the time. Women had been exercising their right to vote since 1920, but as the decade began, they were still fighting for their right to exercise. While they had started to realize gains in some other segments of society, women were treated with indifference or condescension, or both, in sports.

In the Olympics, prior to 1972, there were no races for women longer than 800 meters because of the conventional wisdom—despite evidence to the contrary—that women couldn't endure the longer distances. Even when girls' sports thrived there were restrictions: Girls' high school basketball was popular in Iowa and Texas, but was played six to a side—with most players confined to the backcourt or the frontcourt on each team—because of the fear that too much running would be dangerous to the delicate constitutions of teen girls. In other states, like Illinois in the '60s, high school girls' sports were prohibited.

Change came slowly and then, in America, very quickly. In 1972, tucked within the larger Education Amendments Act, Congress passed Title IX legislation that outlawed discrimination on the basis of sex in educational institutions. As it turned out, that included interscholastic and intercollegiate sports. The interpretation of this law brought about a different kind of revolution; the Pill had altered the dynamic between men and women in the '60s, and *Roe v. Wade* would change the balance of power further, but Title IX arguably had an even more visible impact, because it affirmed equality for women outside the private spaces of bedrooms and doctors' offices.

·

In the confluence of these sweeping changes came a broad shift in the outlook and habits of American sports fans. The decade began with major media outlets offering sports in small sips—a few pages in the newspaper, one or two games on a weekend day on television, a short sports report, focusing on area teams and high school scores, near the end of the nightly local news. By the end of the decade, sports coverage had become broadly national in scope and had established a foothold in prime-time network television.

During the '70s, the Super Bowl became a civic national holiday, and the most watched TV broadcast of each year; the World Series, the Summer and Winter Olympic Games, and the NCAA basketball championship soon followed *Monday Night Football* into prime time. From the tragedy of the Munich Olympics in 1972 to the Battle of the Sexes a year later, the passion and morality plays in sports were witnessed by some of the largest audiences in American television.

Then, in the fall of 1979, many commentators laughed at the audacious proposition of a cable channel in Bristol, Connecticut, called ESPN, which would consist of nothing but sports, twenty-four hours a day. While it seemed preposterous to many, there was reason to believe it might work. Fans wanted more, and their appetite for news about their favorite teams and favorite sports seemed insatiable.

Because of the reputation of the decade, there is a tendency to reduce everything that happened in the '70s to a shaggy caricature of itself—a no-hitter pitched under the effects of LSD makes that sort of generalizing nearly irresistible. But in the midst of all the ludicrous behavior, stylistic disasters, and excess facial hair, there was a metamorphosis in American sports. By the end of the decade, sports had staked a claim to a central role in the culture.

What emerged from the decade of tumult was an industry poised to enter every living room, nearly every restaurant, and in time every computer and smartphone in the country. Spectator sports had been a sideshow for most of the twentieth century, a distraction primarily for middle-class white males.

By the end of the 1970s, it had become a more pervasive presence, altering holiday schedules, Thanksgiving and Christmas dinner times, shaping attitudes from academia to Wall Street, Madison Avenue to Main Street, imposing its presence in nearly every corner of American life.

Or as Joyce Carol Oates put it, "In the twentieth century, and perhaps most spectacularly in the Seventies, sports has emerged as our dominant American religion."

# ONE

# 1969: THE GATHERING STORM

THE FIRST GLIMPSE of the new decade in American sports appeared early and abruptly, on the morning of March 22, 1969, at the St. Louis Cardinals' spring training site in St. Petersburg, Florida.

In the midst of the usual rites of the season—pitchers in rubber suits trying to get down to weight, half-hearted calisthenics to start the morning—the Cardinals had been summoned by manager Red Schoendienst to a clubhouse meeting in full uniform.

The circumstances were unusual. The team had been gathered for an address by the Cardinals' squat owner, Gussie Busch, who had invited along the beat writers from the *St. Louis Post-Dispatch*, the *St. Louis Globe-Democrat* and other area media outlets for the occasion. The writers sat to the side, within earshot of Busch, taking notes.

The Cardinals were baseball royalty at the time, widely viewed as innovators in race relations, team cohesion, and scouting acumen. They had been in three of the past five World Series and had won two of them. They were coming off back-to-back National League titles and were favored to be among the class of the league again.

But what they were greeted with that day was not a note of congratulation, but rather a stern lecture of Busch's disapproval: "Too many fans are saying our players are getting fat, and they only think of money, and less of the game itself. The fans will be looking at you this year more critically than ever before to watch how you perform and see whether you really are giving everything you have."

Sitting among his teammates, the All-Star pitcher Bob Gibson—the team's highest-paid player—stared at Busch with a look of studied skepticism. It was clear to all present that Busch's message was directed to him. A month earlier, Gibson had been a guest on *The Tonight Show* when Flip Wilson was the guest host. Wilson had asked Gibson about his views on the Major League Baseball Players Association, and Gibson had answered him, touching on the nature of players' modest agenda of putting cost-of-living adjustments into their pension plan.

Now Busch, in the midst of his twenty-five-minute harangue, was criticizing Marvin Miller, head of the union, and player representatives.

"Baseball's union representative made all kinds of derogatory statements about the owners," said Busch. "We suddenly seem to be your greatest enemies. Representatives threw down all sorts of challenges, threats, and ultimatums. Personally, I don't react well to ultimatums."

Neither, it transpired, did Gibson. After Busch finished, to polite applause from the team, the text of his speech was distributed to reporters, who quickly sought out the team leaders for comment. Typical of many other white players on the team, Dal Maxvill complimented Busch's message: "It was first class, typical of an organization that goes first class, that plays first class, and is first class. It was beautiful."

But when Gibson was asked about the speech, he answered, "I have nothing to say about it."

Nor did teammate Curt Flood, who when asked for his reaction, responded, "Comment? I have none. Not when the big boss has spoken."

•

The power dynamic in sports at the end of the 1960s only went one way. For more than a generation, the default position held by both owners and a majority of fans was that athletes were extraordinarily fortunate to receive a salary to play a game.

As early as 1945, owners had groused about runaway payrolls. That year, Daniel F. Reeves, owner of the Cleveland Rams in the National Football League, cracked, "The stars are making so much money now, I call them 'Mister' and they just call me 'Reeves.'"

A generation later, salaries had risen considerably, but a vast majority of players in the four major team sports still found it necessary to work in the off-season. The minimum salary was $9,000 in the NFL, $10,000 in the

National Basketball Association and $12,000 in Major League Baseball. But because the reserve clause bound players to one team, the owners continued to possess all the leverage.

"It is ridiculous to call any discussion we have with our ownership 'negotiation' because they've got all the hammers," said the Pirates' Nelson Briles. "In the final analysis, they can say: 'Take it or leave it.' If you leave it, you don't play and you don't get paid."

Negotiations were more accurately understood as "notifications." When Jon McGlocklin was drafted by the Cincinnati Royals of the NBA in 1965 he received a phone call from the team's general manager, Pepper Wilson, who said, "We're gonna want you to come to rookie camp to see if you can make the team." "Then when I made it," said McGlocklin, "it was, 'Jon, we're gonna give you ten grand, welcome to the Royals.'"

The raises, when they came, were parsimonious. Players negotiating their own deals were often made to feel like college students asking their parents for larger allowances. After his breakout season in 1969, Oakland third baseman Sal Bando went in to negotiate his contract. The A's owner, Charlie Finley, had sent a contract for the same amount as the year prior.

"Mr. Finley, I need more money; I did good," Bando said.

They haggled for a while, and finally Finley said, "I tell you what, I'll give you another couple of thousand, but only because you just got married. You can tell your wife it was a wedding gift."

Even standout athletes, often prominent in their community, still felt the need to supplement their income with off-season work. The Colts' quarterback John Unitas worked for an electronics company, the Chiefs' stellar linebacker Bobby Bell still worked shifts on the assembly line at the Ford plant in Kansas City, the Pistons' Dave Bing worked as a bank teller, and the much-traveled basketball center Caldwell Jones spent his off-seasons laying carpet. A week after winning Game 7 of the World Series in 1971, the Pirates' pitcher Steve Blass was back to work at his off-season job, delivering clean uniforms and picking up dirty ones for an athletic manufacturer servicing area high schools in northwest Connecticut.

Coaches had learned to be frugal as well. It wasn't until 1969, when Chuck Noll was hired as head coach of the Pittsburgh Steelers, that he and his wife, Marianne, allowed themselves two concessions to their new status: No longer would Chuck cut her hair—she could go to a salon now—and no longer would she have to mow the lawn while he was away at training camp.

In every sport but baseball, the preseason was still marked by a barnstorming milk run to medium-sized cities around the region. (The New York Knicks, prior to the 1969–70 regular season, played exhibition games in Saginaw, Grand Rapids, Paterson, Trenton, Bethlehem, Bangor and Utica.)

The regular season offered no great luxury. In Milwaukee, when the Bucks played, there was no training table for the home team. Instead, the All-Pro guard Oscar Robertson would routinely send a ball boy out to the concourse at the Milwaukee Arena for two hot dogs and a Coke, the Big O's pregame meal.

"Our pregame meal was at home," said Steve Blass. "Simple as that. And we would have what Willie Stargell called 'construction meat' after the game, which was bologna, and a really good bread that a friend of the clubhouse manager would bring in to him."

The thriftiness was representative of the larger mindset in professional sports at the time. Every towel was dispensed carefully, every dime was monitored.

A glimpse into the mindset of the era could be found in the uniforms of the New York Knicks, the flagship franchise in the NBA. Each player was issued two uniforms—one white for home games, one blue for road games— for the season. The Knicks' trainer, Danny Whelan, washed the white uniforms weekly when the team was playing at home. But it was left to the players to wash their own uniforms while on the road. Roommates Bill Bradley and Dave DeBusschere were more conscientious than most. They'd wash their jerseys in the bathroom sink of the hotel in which they were staying, then stretch them out over the radiator to dry.

In 1968, when Whelan first decided to sew nameplates with each player's name on the back of the jerseys, he unwittingly ran afoul of the Knicks' infamously parsimonious president Ned Irish, who marched into the Knicks locker room and chewed out Whelan.

"Now that people can see the names," said Irish, "that's going to hurt program sales!"

•

This was the spare, stingy ethos of sports at the end of the 1960s. By any estimation, the decade had been one of growth in American sports. Pro football's universe more than doubled thanks to the rise of the American Football League, Major League Baseball grew from sixteen to twenty-four teams, pro basketball tripled in size from eight to twenty-five teams, while the NHL grew from six to twelve teams. Yet the American sporting establishment still didn't seem to quite know what it was or what it wanted to be.

The sum total of the organizations that made up American spectator sports were aligned more in perception than in fact. The array of sports leagues and governing bodies were competing, unaffiliated, and often uncooperative. There was no sporting equivalent to the umbrella organizations like the Academy of Motion Picture Arts & Sciences or the National Academy of Recording Arts and Sciences.

Each league was mindful of its own priorities. Baseball teams exerted their own grandfathered autonomy; many were the primary occupants of their stadiums, meaning that pro football teams were often at the mercy of Major League Baseball teams in fashioning their schedules. (In all but one year during the period from 1965 to 1971, the Kansas City Chiefs opened each regular season with their first three games on the road.)

While each of the various sports entities were in competition, it was also true that they were allies, part of a loose collective, a federation with competing interests but a common cause. In a society that was increasingly atomized and alienated, they were all competing for something more ineffable but no less important—the time, devotion and money of American sports fans.

For all the grand aspirations, the business of sports remained decidedly low-budget. At five minutes before tip-off time for Chicago Bulls home games, the public address announcer Ben Bentley—also the team's publicist—would take the microphone and announce, "Ladies and gentlemen, would you please stand for our National Anthem." He would then move his microphone toward the speaker of his portable cassette tape recorder, and press play, and the fans in the arena would hear the tinny rendition of a marching band playing "The Star-Spangled Banner." It was cheaper than hiring a real band, and cutting costs was paramount in the NBA. The Bulls were in the third-largest city in the United States, but still had trouble drawing fans for their dates at the Chicago Stadium, managed by their hockey rivals, the Black Hawks, and their owner, Arthur Wirtz. (About whom the baseball owner Bill Veeck once said, "Arthur Wirtz could have twenty wristwatches on, and he still wouldn't give you the right time.") In the 1969–70 season, the Bulls—still dubious if the Chicago market could support a full season of NBA basketball—chose to schedule eight of their home games outside of Chicago, in Kansas City's Municipal Auditorium.

There was little in the way of marketing or business plans. On every team in every league, the focus remained on selling tickets, the historical life-blood of sports franchises. The Bulls' young general manager, an energetic twenty-nine-year-old Veeck protégé named Pat Williams, also had the job of events coordinator. Just to get people out to watch professional basketball in Chicago, Williams came up with every gameday and halftime promotion he could think of: a dance team, Victor the Wrestling Bear, baseball star Richie "Dick" Allen and his doo-wop group the Ebonistics. Some promotions were more successful than others. There was a "blind date night," in which odd-numbered seats in a section would go to single men and even-numbered seats to single women. But when forty-six men and only one woman signed up for the promotion, it was quickly scuttled.

•

In all the major sports, a player was at the mercy of a "reserve clause," which bound him to his team in perpetuity. But in pro basketball, the existence of the upstart American Basketball Association, launched in 1967, gave college seniors preparing to sign their first pro contract a chance to test their true market value.

In the spring of 1969—just a few days after Gussie Busch's scolding of the Cardinals in St. Petersburg—it was about to be Lew Alcindor's time.

Four years earlier, as a generational high school prospect at Power Memorial High School in New York, Alcindor had been besieged by all manner of shadowy agents and oleaginous recruiters. With all the schools in the country to choose from, he'd decided to attend UCLA, mixing the leisure and sunlight of Los Angeles with the firm, decent elegance of John Wooden's teachings in basketball. (While other prospective coaches were unctuous and glib around Alcindor, Wooden was respectful and formal, addressing his player as "Lewis.")

The adjustment from New York to LA was difficult, and Alcindor was stunned when his first practice session under Wooden involved teaching players how to tie their shoes. But he would flourish under Wooden and lead UCLA to three straight national titles (spooked by his instant dominance, the NCAA outlawed the dunk shot after his sophomore season). The sport's profile rose in those years, and when he graduated from UCLA in 1969, he had already proved himself a revolutionary talent. With the ABA desperate for a merger, respect, and a national television contract, Alcindor was the clearest avenue to the new league's survival.

Confident and keenly aware of his bargaining power, Alcindor was transparent about how he would make his decision. He stated that he would have one meeting each with representatives from the two leagues, would receive one offer from each, and then would decide his path. The Milwaukee Bucks, who'd won a coin flip with the Phoenix Suns for the rights to the first pick, had his NBA draft rights. In the ABA, it was Alcindor's hometown New York Nets who owned the draft rights.

The commissioner of the ABA was George Mikan, the bespectacled six-foot-ten-inch legend who'd been a college standout at DePaul and anchored the Minneapolis Lakers during his pro career (the marquee at old Madison Square Garden once billed a game as "George Mikan vs. Knicks"). Mikan had grown comfortable in the public eye and fancied himself a keen businessman. He was pleased that his idea for the new league—a red, white, and blue basketball—was catching on and selling well. Fans loved the flashy colors; coaches loved the ways the multicolored ball allowed one to spot the ball's rotation.

The ABA's owners knew that signing Alcindor could be as critical for the league's future as the AFL's signing of Joe Namath had been in 1965. They'd hatched a yearlong, secret plan, dubbed "Operation Kingfish," designed to lure Alcindor to the ABA. Private investigators went into New York to talk with people who'd known Alcindor in high school, and to Los Angeles, where he was revered mostly at a distance (by his choice) by the student body.

The "Kingfish" study took note of Alcindor's affinity for jazz, his parents' lower-middle-class lifestyle, and the fact that, given his time in New York and Los Angeles, Alcindor would not have been overly enthusiastic about spending his twenties living in Milwaukee, Wisconsin. The study concluded that Alcindor might be impressed with a statement of purpose, so the league owners pitched in and collectively agreed to let Mikan present Alcindor with a certified check in the amount of one million dollars, above and beyond what the New York Nets were offering, if Alcindor would agree to sign with the younger league.

Lew Alcindor grew up the only child of his parents, in the Dyckman Houses in Inwood, on the northern edge of Manhattan, which in the '50s and '60s was a multicultural stew. ("We had the whole world in that project," he would recall later. "We had immigrants from China, Russia, England, Scandinavia, Cuba. There were gypsies, Jews, West Indians, and American blacks.")

"Big Al" Alcindor had attended Julliard on the GI Bill, wound up working with the New York Transit Authority; he was in the police department band that backed Marilyn Monroe when she serenaded President Kennedy on his birthday at Madison Square Garden in 1962. Lew Alcindor was every bit his father's son; quiet and ruminative, with an ear for music and a love of sports. He was shy but watchful as a teen, keenly attuned to the cultural signifiers of his age, and already a student of the jazz scene in which his father was a legitimate, if peripheral, figure. The confluence of elements meant young Lew was inculcated in a kind of urban cool that was cutting edge. Then, for four years at UCLA, he was steeped in the aura of beatnik California existentialism, experimenting with marijuana and LSD, living the entitled life of a movie star in Hollywood, which in a very real sense he was.

In short, Alcindor had led a life that George Mikan was born to not understand.

That week in New York City, Alcindor's cohort made for a curious traveling party: the seven-foot-two star and his six-foot-two father were accompanied by Alcindor's chosen representatives, Sam Gilbert, the longtime UCLA booster, and Ralph Shapiro, a brokerage executive from LA.

On March 24, they met with the NBA and the Bucks owner, the socially conscious self-made millionaire Wesley Pavalon. The Bucks offered Alcindor a $1.4 million, five-year contract, which would instantly make him the highest-paid player in all of professional sports. NBA commissioner Walter Kennedy, who had served as the league's PR director before serving two terms as the mayor of Stamford, Connecticut, attended the meeting.

The next day, the Alcindor group met with the ABA's representatives. Mikan commanded the room, joking about his days in the NBA, and comparing them to what Alcindor could expect. Polite and soft-spoken, Alcindor was cordial yet noncommittal. He knew of and respected Mikan, but he was not one to be sold a used car. In those moments, it seems that Mikan badly misread the room and mistook Alcindor's reserve as naïveté. He thought the young man before him was pliable and easily impressed. He saw no need to proffer the million-dollar bonus check. The Nets' Arthur Brown offered Alcindor the contract that the Nets would pay, which was less than what the Bucks had offered, but made no mention of the league bonus.

After a moment of silence, it was the brusque Gilbert who cut to the chase. "Is that it? Is that the total package? There's no additional bonus or anything?"

"That's it," said Mikan pleasantly. "That's all."

After exchanging a series of knowing looks, Alcindor and his reps politely but firmly declined the offer. Everyone shook hands, and the Alcindor group left, heading to the airport.

Mikan walked down the hall and into another room, where the Kentucky Colonels' co-owner Mike Storen and some ABA executives were nervously waiting. Mikan announced the meeting a success and confidently explained, "We decided it wasn't necessary to give him our best offer. We figure when he comes back to us, then we'll use the check for the second round of talks."

"You did *what*?!" asked an apoplectic Storen.

Mikan assured him that there would be an opportunity to negotiate further.

"You dumb sonofabitch!" Storen shouted. "Why did we spend all that money to find out all this information if you're not going to *use* it?! How could you guys not give him the check?"

As Storen feared, it was already too late.

Shortly after the ABA meeting, Alcindor phoned Walter Kennedy at the NBA offices and told him that he would accept the Bucks' offer.

Alcindor would later concede that he had hoped to sign with the ABA ("the Nets were my first choice"). But when ABA representatives showed up at La Guardia Airport brandishing the million-dollar check, Alcindor wouldn't speak to them. He was a man of his word.

"A bidding war degrades the people involved," Alcindor said later. "It would make me feel like a flesh peddler, and I don't want to think like that."

Mikan, meanwhile, resigned ahead of being fired later that spring. And the ABA offices were finally moved to Manhattan instead of being run out of Mikan's travel agency in Minneapolis.

At the time, no one drew any connections between Busch's peevish speech and Alcindor's big contract, but both of those two incidents hinted at the seismic change that was on the verge of happening in sports.

•

So much was changing in the culture and in the country. But in the world of sports, the power of coaches bordered on the absolute.

In July 1969, as sweltering summer heat enveloped the nation, the United States and much of the rest of the world was focused on the Apollo 11 mission that would attempt to land Americans on the Moon and return them to Earth.

It was also the weekend that the Kansas City Chiefs reported to their training camp, on the campus of William Jewell College in Liberty, Missouri. In the off-season—ahead of Woodstock and the concerts in Harlem later valorized as the "Summer of Soul"—the Chiefs' coach Hank Stram had sent out a letter to his team: "Just so there won't be any misunderstanding regarding my policy on long hair and sideburns, I want to emphasize certain requirements, which I expect everyone to adhere to from this day on. There will be absolutely no mustaches, beards, goatees, or hair on the chin displayed by any member of this club. I also want to emphasize that no one will have sideburns longer than the ones I have."

The Chiefs had picture day on Saturday, July 19, then delayed practice a half hour on Sunday to watch the lunar module detach from the command module. Then they went ahead with the annual tradition at dinner of rookies having to stand before the veterans and sing their college fight song.

But the next morning, July 21, Stram handed down justice.

"I told everybody I wanted them clean-shaven," he reminded his players. "Everybody adhered to the rule—managers, coaches, players, all except one: Otis Taylor, so he will be fined $500."

It was a time of flux, in which Black Power and its accompanying ethos were reaching into the mainstream. Taylor, the splendidly talented wide receiver from Prairie View A&M, had recently married, and his wife, Cheryl, feared he would clash with Stram's policy: "Especially the sideburns—he loved those. He wasn't pleased about it." But in the world of sports in 1969, the coach had the last word. Taylor paid the fine and cut his sideburns.

So it was that in the summer and fall of 1969, the Kansas City Chiefs would look and dress like bankers (players were required to wear tailored black blazers—with the team's logo on the jacket breast—with dress shirts, ties, and houndstooth slacks on road trips).

Stram was right about one thing: His rules did foster team unity. In this case, there was a broad consensus of grumbling. But the Chiefs, entering the final season of the AFL, were determined to go out as the league's first three-time champions. Also, Stram had all the power. So they fell in line.

•

Billie Jean Moffitt and her brother Randy grew up in the center of the middle class in postwar Long Beach, California, the children of a firefighter father and a housewife mother, with all the conveniences of Baby Boom prosperity along with the freedoms of California in the '50s. "Sports was the air we breathed," she said.

Billie Jean was a natural athlete, notwithstanding her 20/400 vision. Steered toward more traditionally feminine sports, she discovered tennis, and after playing the sport for the first time, she breathlessly told her mother that she'd finally found what she wanted to do with her life. She was a natural at the game but slow to master the politesse and protocol for the country club set (she burned with shame on the day when she was excluded from a picture of junior champions because Perry T. Jones, the patron saint of California tennis, forbade her to be included in the picture since she was wearing shorts rather than a proper tennis dress).

She found solace and self-belief on the courts and, in 1961 at the age of seventeen, she took her first overseas flight, where she and her friend Karen Hantze were the surprise winners of the Wimbledon ladies' doubles championship. They were innocents abroad, teenagers who didn't even know how one went about celebrating a Wimbledon title. That night, a garrulous, loudly dressed tennis writer from the *Boston Globe*, Bud Collins, took them out to a celebratory dinner.

Tennis was still ostensibly an amateur sport at the time. "We all deserved Oscars for impersonating amateurs," was how Arthur Ashe would describe it later. In truth, the punning term used to describe it—"shamateurism"—hid the most onerous elements of the arrangement. Under-the-table payments were going on everywhere, and players had to participate in the ruse to remain eligible for the most prestigious tournaments. The hypocrisy could wear on a person. Billie Jean was among the very best in the world at what she did, and yet the rewards were minimal, and technically illegal. The coming years were marked by many envelopes with fifty-dollar bills or, more frequently, twenty-dollar bills. Those elite players who were trying to make a living in a sport that clearly had commercial potential often felt like they were fighting old money in a small town.

While Billie Jean was deeply committed to the American ideal of equality—a product of her patriotic parents—she was not someone who routinely questioned the social norms. Moffitt met a blond, handsome law student named Larry King, and they married in 1965. Billie Jean's feminist awakening began at the behest of her husband. He had been raised by a classic small-c conservative family, staunchly Republican in the Abraham Lincoln tradition. When King was ten, his family drove to a big picnic, but his father turned the family around when he saw the "No Colored Allowed" sign on the campgrounds. "We can't be part of that," King's father said.

So by training and by temperament, he was somewhat more socially aware than his young wife. Later, when both were pursuing studies at Cal State–Los Angeles, Larry pointedly asked Billie Jean, "You realize you're treated like a second-class citizen because you're a girl, right?"

"What do you mean?"

"I'm the seventh man on a six-man tennis team and I'm treated better than you are. You're the best athlete at this school. You should be getting special treatment, not me. And yet you get zero."

It was all supposed to change in 1968 when a century of unseemly hypocrisy was wiped away. The major events in tennis were finally "open" to professionals and a generation of men and women players had high hopes for legitimate athletic careers. Billie Jean King played Virginia Wade in the final of the first genuinely open U.S. Open, on September 8, 1968, with Wade receiving $6,000 for winning. Later that same day, 140 miles to the south, feminists burned bras to protest the Miss America Pageant.

Within a year, it was clear that there were not going to be enough women's tournaments for King or any of her contemporaries to make a living. Larry King—just through law school, but fully committed to supporting his wife's aspirations—wrote a letter outlining the problems. At one of the higher profile stops, tennis legend Jack Kramer's Pacific Southwest tournament, held a week after the U.S. Open, offered $1,200 for the men's champion and $250 for the women's champion. It wasn't enough to live on, even for the winner.

Billie Jean read the letter and complained to her husband about how unfairly women were being treated by the tennis community. He gave her a piece of advice she would eventually heed: "You have to speak up."

•

The most famous athlete in America in 1969 was also the most controversial, and least active. Among individual sports, boxing remained the cesspool of corruption and exploitation it had always been, though it still held the center of the public consciousness, largely because of the inimitable presence of Muhammad Ali. Ali had been born Cassius Marcellus Clay, but had publicly renounced his "slave name" following his stunning upset of Sonny Liston to win the heavyweight title in 1964. Five years later, Ali was still routinely referred to as Clay, in both the media and by his contemporaries. The *New York Times* used the two names interchangeably. And even official sources, like *The Readers' Guide to Periodical Literature*, listed him as Clay rather than Ali.

The undefeated champion had been stripped of his title in 1967 after declining induction into the U.S. Army. At the end of the decade, Ali was beginning his third year in exile, an artist at the height of his powers, but denied his brushes and paints. Among people in both boxing and legal circles, the feeling was that, sooner or later, he would eventually have to serve his five-year prison sentence.

Still in boxing purgatory, Ali was looking for income anywhere he could. Random House advanced him $200,000 for his autobiography. Then he agreed to a preposterous bit of flimflammery, a closed-circuit simulated "fight" against Rocky Marciano. In a studio with a boxing ring, the two had sparred for seventy carefully choreographed rounds in the summer of 1969, with Marciano wearing a toupee and makeup to conceal his age. They were, it was reported, re-creating a computer simulation of what would have happened if the two champions had fought while each was at his peak.

The simulated bout would finally be released on January 20, 1970, in 1,500 closed-circuit theaters around the country—Marciano flooring Ali in the thirteenth round with an unconvincing hook—with the "results" supposedly derived from computations by an NCR315 computer. Ali took the outcome in good spirits. "That computer must have been made in Alabama," he said.

Meanwhile, as his case took its long, serpentine journey through the court system, Ali seemed hemmed in at every turn. He asked why he was refused permission to go to Canada after the activist Abbie Hoffman had been granted permission to travel to Cuba. Within the U.S., Ali was simply hoping for a place to publicly spar. More than seventy communities denied him entrance. At one point, it was rumored Ali might fight in Boley, Oklahoma, an all-Black community of 700 whose original settlers were freed slaves. At the time, Boley only had outside plumbing. "It would be disgraceful for a man of my ability to fight in a place like that," said Ali.

With his generosity and his large entourage, Ali went through money like paper on fire. So he maintained a busy schedule of speaking on college campuses, serving as a symbol of resistance for enlightened liberals and a talisman for Black Americans moving toward a more emphatic self-love. After an appearance at Randolph-Macon College in April 1969, a newspaper account noted that while the content of Ali's address was "standard Black Muslim rhetoric," it remained an entertaining and vibrant talk, so much that "one might, in fact, criticize Ali for making his address so entertaining and amusing that the seriousness of his subject was somewhat obscured." Later, Ali shot an episode of *Firing Line* with the conservative man of letters William F. Buckley Jr., and debated Buckley to a technical draw.

So Ali moved through his days, a talisman, a symbol, an echo. No one knew whether the athletic portion of his story had been fully written.

•

In the sports-mad country, few people were as sports-obsessed as the president of the United States.

In the words of Richard Nixon's biographer Stephen E. Ambrose, "Batting averages, yards gained per carry, earned run averages, pass completion percentage, the whole never-ending stream of numbers was to Nixon what the Western novels were to Eisenhower, the perfect relaxation."

Earlier in 1969, Nixon had phoned Orville Moody after Moody won the U.S. Open. That same summer, he'd hosted both the Senators manager Ted Williams and the Redskins new coach Vince Lombardi, as well as a collection of baseball All-Stars on the eve of the 1969 All-Star Game.

Presidents had been sports fans before, but prior to Nixon, none of them had been quite so avidly involved in the daily discussions and arguments about the games. The gonzo journalist Hunter S. Thompson had given a backhanded endorsement of Nixon's credentials as a fan after interviewing him during the 1968 primaries. Thompson wrote, "Whatever else might be said about Nixon—and there is still serious doubt in my mind that he could pass for Human—he is a goddamn stone fanatic on every facet of pro football." Thompson, in the event, undersold it. Nixon was also a diehard about college football.

In October 1969, a Nixon aide named Harry S. Dent typed up an urgent memo with the sort of enthusiasm political functionaries reserve for eureka moments in which they discover the blindingly obvious. Citing a *New York Times* story, Dent wrote to Nixon aides Dwight Chapin and H. R. "Bob" Haldeman, noting "very truly that football is a religio-social pastime in the South," and Nixon attending a big football game "would be a good way to get him into a key Southern state and get to see many good people from two states, without doing anything political."

On December 6, 1969, the country was facing a myriad of problems. Lt. William Calley was called to testify before a secret panel at the Pentagon on charges that he was responsible for the murder of 109 civilians in the My Lai massacre. At Harvard, 107 Black students had occupied the university's administration building, appealing for greater employment opportunities in a negotiation presided over by the former U.S. solicitor general Archibald Cox. But the president of the United States was not ensconced in the White House or on a diplomatic mission overseas. He was in Fayetteville, Arkansas, doubling down on the previous year's "Southern strategy," and attending the final football game of the 1969 regular season, with No. 1 Texas visiting No. 2 Arkansas.

There may have been unrest throughout much of the rest of the country, but Nixon in Fayetteville was a popular figure. That he was there to present the winner of the game a national championship plaque was much celebrated, as was the presence of another celebrity in attendance—the Rev. Billy Graham, on hand to recite the invocation. ("There had been a lot of presidents," said Texas lineman Bob McKay, "there's only been one Billy Graham.")

There were protesters on the hill near where Nixon's helicopter landed near the stadium. But the conservative college organization Young Americans for Freedom also erected a sign proclaiming "Victory in Vietnam."

During its halftime performance, the University of Texas marching band played a medley of Christmas songs, at one point spelling out the word "TEXAS" on the field, before turning to a rendition of "Hail to the Chief," then moving into an alignment that spelled out "NIXON." After that number, the gray-flannel play-by-play man Chris Schenkel interviewed Nixon in the ABC booth, informing him on national television that "I'm one of the many millions who are glad you won."

Nixon seemed nearly at ease, and mentioned the flak he was getting from Penn State fans for the pregame announcement that he would award a national championship plaque to the winner of the Texas–Arkansas game. "Maybe we ought to have a Super College Bowl," the president suggested.

Then Texas rallied from 14 points down for a thrilling 15–14 win. Afterward, Nixon presented Texas coach Darrell Royal with a plaque declaring the Longhorns national champions and, in doing so, becoming yet another entity that presumed to crown a national champion in the lone sport in America that didn't determine a champion on the field of play.

It wouldn't be the last word from the president on football matters.

•

Alcindor's pro debut in 1969 prompted a wave of new interest in the NBA. For the first time in nine years, the trading card company Topps decided to issue a series of basketball cards for the 1969–70 season. Larry Fleisher, the head of the NBA Players Association—and a man no more popular with basketball owners than Marvin Miller was with baseball owners—had negotiated a deal with Topps that would bring the money to the pension fund.

But even this did not come without a fight.

On the day when pictures of Knicks players for the Topps set were scheduled, Ned Irish announced to the team's player rep, Bill Bradley, that the players would be in violation of their contract.

"The player contract prevents the players from being photographed in anything that identifies them as Knicks players for money!"

"So we can't be photographed with anything that says 'New York' or 'Knicks,' right?" Bradley asked.

"That's right," said Irish, marching away.

Bradley was not a Rhodes Scholar for nothing. He thought quickly. And so the new issue of Topps cards would show Bradley, Willis Reed, Walt Frazier, and their teammates photographed with their Knicks jerseys on *backwards*, so that all that showed was the player's nameplate and number.

It amounted to a silent revolution...and the seeds of a larger change in the future.

·

There was one other bit of foreshadowing at the end of 1969. Back in St. Louis, the repercussions of Gussie Busch's spring training jeremiad were still being felt. The Cardinals did not defend their National League title in 1969, falling to fourth place in the National League East, with an 87–75 record.

For twelve years, the fleet, gifted outfielder Curt Flood had made a living in St. Louis, which still had a reputation within the Black community as a virulently racist city. When Arthur Ashe was a high schooler, he was barred from playing on any public courts and could only play indoors in the winter at the St. Louis Armory. In 1968, *Sports Illustrated* ran a series on "The Black Athlete" and devoted one of the five stories to the racial unrest on the St. Louis Cardinals football team. The city had also seen native musician Chuck Berry sent to prison on a trumped-up Mann Act charge. But Flood had navigated the fraught interpersonal dynamics of the city, earned respect for his range of skills and become something of a fan favorite and a crucial mainstay on the team—he'd been to three All-Star Games, won seven Gold Gloves and had finished fourth in the NL MVP voting in 1968. Flood also managed a nightclub, dabbled in portrait art and owned a photography studio.

So he was wholly unprepared for the news he received on the morning of October 7, 1969, first from a reporter, then from Cardinals GM Bing Devine, informing him that he was part of a seven-player trade that would send him to Philadelphia to play for the downtrodden Phillies, who were shipping outspoken slugger Dick Allen to St. Louis in the deal.

Shocked and saddened, Flood made a snap decision. When the *St. Louis Post-Dispatch* called him for a reaction later in the morning, he informed the paper that he was retiring immediately. "When you spend twelve years with one club, you develop strong ties with your teammates and the fans who have supported you over a period of years."

In the coming weeks, the regret would curdle into a seething resentment. Flood, at thirty-one, still felt he had a few years of prime production ahead of him, but he didn't wish to spend it in Philadelphia. (In Philadelphia, the writer Gerald Early was still a teenager, and remembered the reaction among Blacks in Philadelphia: "How could he not want to come to Philadelphia? Philadelphia couldn't *possibly* be a more racist city than St. Louis!")

In November, Flood made a call to Marvin Miller, who since 1966 had been the executive director of the Major League Baseball Players Association. After serving as an economist for the 1.2 million dues-paying members of the United Steelworkers union, Miller had found the MLBPA to be less enlightened, but he had been speaking to players about the inherent unfairness of the Major Leagues' reserve clause, which bound a player to a team in perpetuity.

Talking privately with his friend and longtime teammate Gibson, Flood shared the same goal. "I knew exactly where he was coming from and I suspected I knew exactly where he was headed," recalled Gibson later.

By December, Flood informed Miller he wanted to challenge the rule in court. "I want to give the courts a chance to outlaw the reserve system," he told Miller. "I want to go out like a man instead of disappearing like a bottle cap."

Miller warned him that challenging the very foundation of Major League Baseball would have severe consequences: Flood would surely be blackballed from any positions in the sport in the future and the case might take two or three years to be decided. And that, owing to baseball's longstanding antitrust exemption, he might well lose.

But Flood remained steadfast and he was invited to a December 13 meeting with all twenty-four player reps at the MLBPA's annual meeting in Puerto

Rico. On the flight from St. Louis to San Juan, he was seated next to the Cardinals' player rep, Dal Maxvill, who told his friend, "Curt, I think you're crazy."

At the meeting in San Juan, Miller introduced Flood, who spent a few minutes talking about why he wanted to challenge Major League Baseball. Flood explained to his peers that his protest was a matter of principle, rather than a negotiating tactic. Then the floor was opened up for questions.

"Does anything about this have to do with asserting Black power?" asked the Dodger catcher Tom Haller.

"There's not much power here," said Flood.

Carl Yastrzemski of the Red Sox remained the most prominent player opposed to Flood's action "because it would ruin the game." With nearly unanimous support, the MLBPA agreed to finance any subsequent legal fees.

In a Christmas Eve letter to Major League Baseball's new commissioner, Bowie Kuhn, Flood wrote that "I do not feel I am a piece of property to be bought or sold irrespective of my wishes."

Kuhn was still new to the job, but his tepid response offered a clue to his blinkered worldview. "I certainly agree with you, as a human being, aren't a piece of property to be bought and sold," replied Kuhn in a letter. "However, I cannot see its applicability to the situation at hand..."

A few weeks later, Flood's lawsuit against Kuhn and Major League Baseball would be filed, and "the applicability of the situation at hand" would be a matter for the courts.

But on Christmas Day 1969, all Curt Flood knew for sure was that his life would be changed forever.

His friend Bob Gibson recognized the same thing. "I knew that there would be no changing his mind once he had made it up, but privately I thought to myself, 'Jesus, Curt, what are you doing?'"

TWO

# THE WHITE HOUSE IS CALLING

AMERICA LURCHED INTO the first day of the 1970s still punch-drunk and hollowed out from the previous decade, still grasping for a way to reconcile multiple assassinations, an apparently unwinnable foreign war, tremendous economic prosperity, deep societal schisms and unimaginable technological triumphs.

Somehow, through the strange and surreal '60s, the impulse among Americans to follow spectator sports—first codified around the dawn of the Industrial Revolution and accelerated into a burgeoning industry by technological advances and urbanization in the first half of the twentieth century—remained resolute.

For American sports fans, the games that began the new decade stood on a threshold stuffed with significant round numerical dates. The bowl games on New Year's Day would complete the one hundredth anniversary season of college football. Major League Baseball had just celebrated the centennial season of professional baseball. In pro football, the National Football League was celebrating its fiftieth season and the American Football League its tenth, before the two leagues would complete their full merger, signed in 1966, that would bring the twenty-six teams together in two thirteen-team conferences in the fall of 1970.

But for all the portentous anniversaries, and the growing profile of spectator sports, what would happen in the following ten years was unforeseeable to most of the athletes who played sports, and almost all of the owners and administrators who ran sports, as well as the tens of millions of fans who followed sports. While the essence of sports would remain unchanged, the context and gravity of the games would be reshaped in the decade ahead.

•

The rush of permissiveness that had begun at the conclusion of World War II and accelerated dramatically in the late '60s was accompanied by a fierce cultural backlash across the country. But at the University of Texas in Austin, the most liberal enclave in that staunchly conservative state, the resistance was more muted.

Most political grievances didn't last past sundown in Austin. The tree-huggers and land-rapers would argue all day long in the City Council and State Legislature, then get drunk and make mischief through the night. On the campus at the University of Texas, coeds skinny-dipped in the fountains, students smoked weed and took LSD at frat parties, and somehow none of it—not a single element of the counterculture and all the questions it posed to conventional norms—punctured the hermetically sealed world of the University of Texas football team, whose unstoppable wishbone offense had led the team to nineteen straight wins. In Austin, the hippies were fans of the football team, and the football coach was tight with the music community; these anomalies owed some to the unique nature of Austin, and a whole lot to the unique nature of Darrell Royal.

Royal had lived through the Depression and World War II, so the deprivations and sacrifices of football seemed entirely natural to him. The players who played for him would marvel for the rest of their lives about Royal's absolute authority. From his elevated coaching tower, he presided with a sharp eye and a quick temper over his massed combatants. John McKay had the same tower at Southern Cal as did Bear Bryant at Alabama. But nobody had quite the numbers that Texas managed. With no strict limits on recruiting, and a seemingly bottomless reservoir of financial support from the alumni, freshman classes going out for football often had 120 students, fully half of them on scholarship. There was a winnowing process each year, with about half of the freshmen dropping out or being cut. But it was not uncommon for Royal to have more than 150 players at a time on a full athletic scholarship. As many as another 100 would walk on just for the distinction of being part of the team.

If Royal came down from the tower during practice, it was because he didn't like what he was seeing. When he turned right, walking toward the defense, the group of players on offense would sigh in relief. When he turned left, the defense would exhale. And while an entire generation of Americans was challenging authority, those impulses did not exist on the Texas football team.

"If Coach Royal told you to do something, well, we didn't ask questions," said the All-American offensive tackle Bob McKay. "If he came down off that tower and he yelled 'Shit!,' there'd be 250 people bent over outside out there making grunting noises."

The process of making the team was brutal and bloody, but those who survived it carried a lasting bond. In the spring and preseason camps, the players were exposed to the punishing "Medina Sessions," run by UT's trainer, the hard-bitten, verbose, possibly sadistic four-foot-ten Cherokee Indian Frank Medina. The macabre workouts exacted a gruesome physical toll, but with the massive number of players on scholarship the human cost was affordable. Toughness was a given. In the spring of 1969, when Steve Worster broke his nose after a collision with Bill Atessis during a preseason blocking drill, a trainer rushed to reset it on the spot, and Worster was back in the rotation—face still covered in blood—without missing a single rep.

All the elements of the program were presided over by the assured Royal, who'd arrived in 1957, his seventh coaching stop in eight years, and proceeded to transform the downtrodden program at UT. He heeded the coaching legend D. X. Bible's advice ("stay away from the Capitol"), and insisted on refurbished facilities and much more ambitious recruiting efforts. Within his first year, he became perhaps the first major-college football coach to hire a dedicated academic advisor—or "brain coach," as they referred to it in Austin—a man named Lan Hewlett, who would serve for eighteen years.

Royal's speech was crisp and resonant, precise and yet leavened by a homespun twang. Men liked him, women were attracted to him and his commanding presence was all the stronger to the people who were closest to him. ("Dammit," the Texas director of publicity Jones Ramsey proclaimed one day. "Darrell is the sexiest man I've ever met!")

By the time the '60s ended, Royal was preeminent among college football demigods. "He's the only coach with his own U.S. president," Clemson's Frank Howard said, and, indeed, Royal counted Lyndon B. Johnson as a personal friend. By 1970, it was perhaps more than one president—Richard Nixon had taken a liking to Royal as well, and called more than once.

What set Royal apart from his equally decorated peers was the impression of levelheadedness. He wasn't a man of hidden obsessions; Royal wasn't going to turn out to be the sort of person who was overly obsessed with the exploits of Civil War generals or a collector of Nazi paraphernalia.

He was, however, a deeply committed country music fan, temperamentally suited to the laid-back vibe of what was emerging in the Austin music scene. When Johnny Cash played a concert at Municipal Auditorium the previous season, Royal had arranged for anyone on the team who was interested (which, in this case, was almost all of his players) to sit at the side of the stage and observe Cash's performance up close. Royal was also tight with Willie Nelson—still sporting short hair and a Nehru jacket at the time; soon to adopt a shaggier look—who'd become a family friend and frequent golfing companion, even something of a confidant. (Later in the '70s, when the two men were playing a game of chess, Nelson asked Royal to promise him that, if the coach ever did decide to get high, he'd do it with Willie. Royal found that an easy promise to make.)

But even kicking back was done with purpose. When one of his musician friends stopped by a Royal gathering and agreed to an impromptu performance, Royal would often begin the music by announcing to the assembled group, "This is an L-and-L deal; either listen or leave. If you want to talk, go do that across the hall."

•

By the time they reached Dallas for the 1970 Cotton Bowl, the Longhorns were ranked number one and had already won the UPI's national championship, as well as President Nixon's. But the Associated Press final poll wouldn't be conducted until after the bowl games.

Royal awoke that January 1, at dawn per usual, and looked out the window of his suite of the Dallas Hilton hotel on the chilled, overcast morning that greeted the new decade. In a season that felt like an epic quest, he'd arrived at the final obstacle.

The identity of Texas' Cotton Bowl opponent was itself a sign of the changing times. The most hallowed name in all of college football, the Notre Dame Fighting Irish, were there at the behest of the school president, Father Theodore Hesburgh, who—growing increasingly comfortable with the school's identity as a football school—had finally agreed to end the Irish's forty-five-year moratorium on participating in bowl games.

In so many ways, the 1970 Cotton Bowl pregame festivities captured perfectly the schizophrenic zeitgeist of the moment, veering between reverence and irreverence, high and low culture meeting in the middle, the ways of the past colliding with the sensibilities of the future. The performance featured four different Texas high school marching bands performing themed odes to: political protests, miniskirts ("Can't Take My Eyes Off of You"), heart transplants, plane hijacking, nudity onstage, the newfound popularity of credit cards ("Big Spender"), and the Apollo moon shot. At various times during the performance, the bands marched into the formation of protest signs, shortening skirts, male and female gender symbols, and even spelled out "HIJACK" before dissolving into "HI CUBA" during the performance of "Come Fly with Me." That would be followed by a performance from the traveling cast of the saccharine singing group Up with People, which would be heard from again before the decade was out.

The game itself proved less frenetic but more absorbing. In an era when intersectional games were still relatively rare in college football, Notre Dame–Texas provided a mouthwatering contrast of styles and strategies. The Irish were bigger and faster than Texas, but the Longhorns and their as-yet-unsolvable wishbone offense had a tactical advantage. Inculcated in Royal's system was an unerring focus on the next play, and a strictly regimented process that had been honed to a fine perfection. Texas didn't spend a lot of time on scouting reports. As with Lombardi's Packers in the '60s, there was an assumption that if every man executed his assignment, it wouldn't matter what the other team did.

All season long that gave the Longhorns a rare composure under pressure. Texas had trailed both Oklahoma and Arkansas by 14 points, and in the bitter chill of unseasonably cold Dallas, would need to rally against the Fighting Irish to secure their uncontested national title. Texas was trailing 10–7 when it got the ball in the third quarter and commenced a relentless, error-free, eighteen-play drive to go ahead. When Notre Dame answered with its own sustained drive to retake the lead, the Longhorns found their backs against the wall again. And they responded as they had all season. What followed was a seventeen-play drive, including two fourth-down conversions, in a stirring 21–17 victory.

After the come-from-behind win, former president Lyndon B. Johnson was in the Texas locker room to congratulate the Longhorns and express gratitude for their dream season. Royal was gracious but sheepish, standing in his thermal underwear when the former leader of the free world walked in to congratulate him.

Then the phone rang in the Texas locker room, and Royal was summoned. It was the White House.

"You played like champions," said Richard Nixon.

"Well, Mr. President," said Royal, "I'm glad we didn't embarrass your selection."

After the Cotton Bowl win, Texas would be named the unanimous national champions and close out the sport's centennial season on a twenty-game win streak. It was an inescapable fact—not often mentioned, but very much noticed—that the Longhorns had done it all without a single African American football player.

•

If the all-white composition of Texas' national champions harkened to sports' segregated past, then the game played ten days later—Super Bowl IV, the Minnesota Vikings vs. the Kansas City Chiefs at Tulane Stadium in New Orleans—provided a glimpse of the future.

It would be the last game before the National Football League and American Football League fully merged. The differences between the Vikings and Chiefs were stark, in both composition and approach. Neither team had existed ten years earlier; the Vikings didn't debut in the NFL until 1961, after reneging on a commitment to play in the start-up American Football League; the Chiefs were originally the Dallas Texans, and moved to Kansas City only in 1963 after AFL founder Lamar Hunt realized—after three years of war with the NFL's Cowboys—that Dallas would never be big enough for both teams.

The Vikings were fundamentalists, coached by the flinty Bud Grant, a man so completely a product of the Great White North that he didn't allow heaters on the Vikings sideline, because he felt that body temperature was really just a state of mind. Grant's charges used an exceedingly simple playbook, not much more than the scant handful of plays that the Packers ran under Vince Lombardi.

The Chiefs, by contrast, were innovators, as the preening bantam of a head coach Hank Stram was convinced that the game's future would require not only physical dominance but also intellectual superiority. "Hank Stram's Wild West Variety Show," as one writer dubbed it, was infused with trickery, sleight of hand, and dozens of variations on a simple theme: If defenses couldn't easily identify the direction or nature of a play, that split second it took them to react could be crucial. Defensively, Stram flipped the tables, using his triple stack defense that disguised which gaps each linebacker was responsible for by having them line up directly behind a defensive lineman.

There was one other significant distinction. The Vikings had Black players on both sides of the ball; many of them were trained in the Big Ten, and all came from major colleges. The Chiefs were far more deeply integrated—the first team in pro football history in which a majority of the twenty-two starters were Black—but it went beyond that. Minnesota had zero players from historically Black colleges and universities. The Chiefs, over the course of the 1969 season, had fourteen different players from HBCUs, largely a product of the efforts of Lloyd Wells, the boisterous, blasphemous raconteur who was pro football's first full-time Black scout.

That created an unusually diverse group of players in Kansas City. "You could have men from the South, men from Alabama, and you would have some from the West Coast, where Huey Newton was gaining prominence, and you had some of us from the East, who were perhaps a little more elitist," said Willie Lanier, the team's All-Pro middle linebacker, and the first Black player to start at the position in pro football. "But you had all of that coming together, and people got along. People allowed whatever political philosophies to be left at the door, and to become part of this thing called the Kansas City Chiefs, and the objective was to win and be better than anyone else and to get to this important step, which was the Super Bowl. I can't really remember any racial strife at all. No error of somebody uttering something that, oops, they apologized for. I mean zero."

The players both respected and feared their leader Stram, whom many players referred to as "Little Caesar," but to a man they respected his fairness. One day after practice, an integrated group of players was discussing the racial problems on the St. Louis Cardinals football team and marveling at the absence of such tension on the Chiefs.

"Well, shit—*of course* we ain't got no problems here," said Otis Taylor, with a rueful smile. "'Cause Hank treats us *all* like niggas."

The Vikings entered the game as a two-touchdown favorite, but the contest turned into a rout for Kansas City. The Chiefs dominated the first half, 16–0, behind a suffocating defense, soccer-style kicking specialist Jan Stenerud's three field goals, and a fumble recovery that led to a second-quarter touchdown (on a play Stram called—65 Toss Power Trap—immortalized in the official Super Bowl documentary produced by NFL Films). After Minnesota clawed back to 16–7 midway through the third quarter, the Chiefs put the game out of reach when Len Dawson hit Taylor on a hitch pass, and he eluded the tackle of cornerback Earsell Mackbee. High-stepping down the sidelines, amid the din of 80,000 roaring fans, Taylor could make out the resonant, high-pitched shout of his own mother in the corner of the end zone exclaiming, "That's my baby!" The Chiefs' comprehensive 23–7 win left the AFL square with the NFL, with two wins apiece from the first four Super Bowls, and also earned the younger league a measure of grudging respect at the very instant that the AFL ceased to exist.

In the postgame locker room celebration inside the old Tulane Stadium, as he was answering questions from the press, the Super Bowl MVP Dawson was summoned.

"Hey, Lenny, come here," said Bobby Yarborough, the Chiefs' equipment manager. "The phone—it's the president."

"The president of *what*?" said Dawson.

"The president," said Yarborough. "*Nixon.*"

It was not Richard Nixon's first call of the day. He'd rung up Stram that morning to tell him that he, and the Justice Department, knew there was nothing to the allegations linking Dawson to a gambling ring that had been exposed days earlier.

An operator asked Dawson to spell his last name, which he dutifully did. Then the president was patched through. "I certainly appreciate that, Mr. President, but it wasn't only me," Dawson said. "It was the whole team."

•

Amid the bustle of reporters, athletes, and dignitaries in the Chiefs' locker room after Super Bowl IV was a dapper, fifty-year-old African American with processed hair and a tailored suit, who moved easily through the raucous scene, giving out congratulations and greeting old friends. Eddie Robinson— who in 1970 had already been the head football coach at Grambling State University for more than half his life—was looking at both the past and the future.

He understood, better than almost anyone, the forces at play in both Darrell Royal's New Year's Day triumph with Texas and Hank Stram's Super Bowl IV win with the Chiefs. Robinson was friends with both men. He and his Grambling staff had for years been visiting Royal at Texas spring practices. And he was close enough with Stram to meet with him privately later that day to talk about the future of one of his former players.

Robinson was the son of a third-generation Louisiana sharecropper and a domestic, and had caught the football fever early. As a youth, he was once caught and beaten for trying to sneak into an LSU football game. As he matured and realized he wanted to coach, he treated the study of the game as an academic discipline to be mastered. Robinson began coaching Grambling in 1941, for a salary of $63 a month, and lived through years when he and his wife had to pack sandwiches for road trips because he knew the team would not be able to eat in any of the public facilities on the way to a game in the Jim Crow South. In 1958, Robinson went to Iowa to study Forest Evashevski's Wing-T offense. He'd already mastered the art of recruiting by then, and spent the '60s persuading some of the best high school football players in the South to come play for him.

Robinson's recruiting pitch was both simple and successful. "Mrs. Harris," he said to the mother of James "Shack" Harris in 1965, "I just want you to know, if you allow me to coach your son, I'll coach him, and I'll also make sure he goes to church on Sunday, and gets his college degree and he'll make a difference in society."

Starting in the mid-'60s, Robinson and his staff began visiting Austin each spring to watch Royal run his troops through spring practices. Royal and Robinson had a kinship based on their belief that coaches were primarily teachers, and their dislike of preening players—or coaches.

Robinson wasn't much interested in the Wishbone offense—he still adhered to a more modernized, pass-heavy version of Evashevski's Wing-T. What fascinated him was the defensive philosophy and the sheer scale of the Texas organization.

That and the meat freezer. Robinson and his aides were dazzled by the immense resources at UT, especially the alumni contributions that allowed Royal to provide a steady diet of steak dinners to his vast roster of players. "We used to tease them," said Robinson's longtime assistant, Doug Porter, "because of the fact that they had all those freezers full of steaks. And we used to tell 'em, we ought to take some of those steaks back to Grambling with us."

A decade earlier, Grambling was little known outside of the group of historically black colleges and universities that dotted the Southeastern United States, where the remnants of segregation meant that Blacks were routinely denied entrance to state colleges they were otherwise qualified to attend.

More than fifteen years after the Supreme Court had overruled the "separate but equal" fiction in *Brown v. Board of Education*, parts of the nation were still heavily segregated. Southern powers like Alabama and Texas had yet to have a varsity player who was Black, and the University of Mississippi fans still waved Confederate flags in support of their football team, nicknamed the Rebels, with a caricature of a plantation owner on their helmets.

But Robinson had profited from that discrimination. His Grambling Tigers were one of the most talented teams in the country and were developing a national following. Grambling's president, Ralph Waldo Emerson Jones—the revered and respected "Prez"—had himself helped the university prosper, winning more than 800 games as a baseball manager and also writing the school alma mater. He had given Robinson and the school's sports information director, Collie Nicholson, nearly free rein to raise Grambling's national profile in any way possible.

It was Jones who paid for the travel expenses so that Grambling's marching band could play during the first Super Bowl. The writer Jerry Izenberg had profiled Robinson and his "football factory" in rural Louisiana, then in turn convinced Howard Cosell and ABC to produce a documentary, *Grambling College: 100 Yards to Glory,* which had aired throughout the country in July 1968 as a lead-in to that summer's College All-Star Game. Nicholson was that very January developing a network of syndicated television outlets to show condensed replays of Grambling games on Sunday mornings around the country, joining Notre Dame as the only two colleges whose games were regularly replayed from coast to coast. A year later, in 1971, Grambling's game against Morgan State would be the first live national telecast of a game involving two historically Black schools.

Though he lacked the imposing tower of Royal and Bryant, Robinson didn't want for authority. He was a striver who developed strivers—a principled football coach who insisted his players graduate, and remained adamant about their ethics and comportment. As a coach, he'd perfected a persona of near-constant scolding distress. "Coach Rob wouldn't swear," recalled Shack Harris. "But he wore *damn* and *hell* out."

As Robinson left the victorious Chiefs' locker room and headed out into the night, where the Grambling staff would share their own celebratory dinner that night at Dooky Chase's, he knew that Grambling's reputation would continue to grow throughout the country. Talent was the coin of the realm in football, and Robinson understood it was the crucial component to Grambling's success.

Just seventeen days after Super Bowl IV, the 1970 NFL Draft was conducted. Robinson's tiny college of Grambling had nine players selected. That was more players than were taken from the high-profile Cotton Bowl combatants, Texas and Notre Dame, combined.

But Robinson was also keenly aware that time was running out on his pipeline of prime talent. One of the things that was changing—Royal knew it, Stram knew it, Robinson knew it—was that soon Texas and other Southern schools would be more actively recruiting Black players. Some schools in the south had started to recruit Blacks; Jerry Levias had starred at SMU, Warren McVea at Houston, and Joe Greene—recruited to North Texas State—had been the fourth player taken in the 1969 NFL draft. Once the big schools started in, the circumstances for Grambling and other HBCUs would necessarily change.

During the entire history of their relationship, Royal and Robinson had never been after the same player. Now that was about to change.

"That was a topic we didn't really discuss much," said the Grambling assistant Doug Porter. "That was better left unsaid."

All three coaches—Royal, Stram, and Robinson—were riding different parts of a social wave. Royal knew he'd have to change to maintain the Longhorns' supremacy, and the case could be made that he already waited too long to do so.

Stram knew that the advantages the Chiefs had enjoyed in the '60s were dissipating as other NFL teams became more cognizant of the talent at historically Black colleges. The Steelers would soon hire the *Pittsburgh Courier* sportswriter Bill Nunn as a scout, and under Chuck Noll the team would scout extensively in HBCUs.

And what was true at Texas was true in much of the country. In what was said and what was left unsaid, race remained in many ways the single most galvanizing issue in sports at the beginning of the decade. Some people whispered about it, others joked about it, but everyone seemed acutely aware of it.

For Robinson, there remained a personal challenge. While he was still getting some of the best players in the country, could he break the final positional barrier and send a successful Black quarterback to the NFL? For all the Grambling players that had gone to the pros, none of his quarterbacks had made it in the NFL, and before 1969, when Buffalo took Shack Harris in the eighth round, none had ever been drafted.

"We have to develop a quarterback," Robinson had vowed, "who can make it in the NFL on his merits." The glamour position was the most cerebral in the game, and many white scouts—to say nothing of white coaches, general managers, and owners—were convinced that Black quarterbacks lacked the necessary intelligence, composure, and leadership skills to excel in the NFL.

Harris was Robinson's project to prove the doubters wrong. "Coach Rob, that was his crusade, to make sure that James had the opportunity to play quarterback in the NFL," recalled Porter. "Sometimes scouts would come in and talk about, 'He could make a great tight end.' And Rob wasn't having it, he would not even put a moment's time on that. 'No, he is a quarterback.'"

At one of his workouts, a scout wanted to "warm up" Harris by playing catch with him. As the two men threw the ball back and forth, Harris kept noticing the scout's throws were consistently awry. Harris thought, *This is the worst passer I've ever seen; he's throwing balls all over the place.* Then he realized the scout was surreptitiously seeing if Harris might make a decent receiver.

Heading to Buffalo, Harris knew that he needed to succeed both on the field and off it, and that his coaches and teammates would be looking at him with an exacting scrutiny.

"James was extremely intelligent," said Porter. "And he did not delude himself into believing things that were not factual. He knew it was gonna be a struggle. He knew there were going to be a lot of eyes on him that he had to conduct himself in a way that would not allow anybody to find any fault with the way his personal life was carried out."

During his exhibition debut in '69, Harris ran onto the field for his first series. As he kneeled in the huddle to call the first play, he had the fleeting thought that it was the very first time in his life he'd given orders to a group of white people. (Conversely, in 1971, Archie Manning would complete his storied career at the University of Mississippi without ever once playing alongside a Black player.)

Historians would point to the game in September of 1970—when Sam "Bam" Cunningham scored two touchdowns to lead USC and its all-Black backfield to a 42–21 rout of all-white Alabama—as the *Brown v. Board of Education* game in college football, the one that busted open the doors to integration in the south. (In fact, Alabama had already recruited Wilbur Jackson, who was a freshman in 1970.) But even walking out of Tulane Stadium after Super Bowl IV nine months earlier, Robinson knew the change was coming.

That fall of 1970, the sophomore Julius Whittier would become the first Black letterman on the Texas football team, with a handful of other Black players joining the incoming freshman class. But a blinkered perspective still informed the perceptions. "This whole race question is very complicated," Royal would say later in 1970. "A bunch of Negro boys came to me a while ago and said I could solve all possible difficulties by hiring a black coach. Now that would be fine for them but I've got to look at the other side. I'd have a whole lot of white boys on the team coming to me saying they couldn't play for a black coach. The family atmosphere of the team would be destroyed. And don't kid yourself. A lot of these Northern teams—professional and college, in all sports—that brag about their integration aren't getting along at all. Once the club harmony and spirit begin to deteriorate, I don't care what kind of talent you have, you won't win."

•

At the end of World War II, there were no Blacks in any of the professional team sports in America. By 1971, 330 out of the 1,040 players in pro football were Black, 153 out of 280 players in basketball were Black, and 150 out of 600 players in Major League Baseball were Black. While sports remained closer to a meritocracy than virtually any other institution in the United States, gains for Blacks were still limited. In pro football at the time, there were no regular Black starting quarterbacks or centers and only one Black middle linebacker. There were no African American head coaches in either baseball or football, though Bill Russell had opened the door—as a player-coach—for Blacks to coach basketball. The NBA still seemed acutely sensitive to its racial makeup. Since the mid-'60s, the question of Blacks' incursion into the NBA was perceived as a problem by some in the league. One anonymous coach told *Sport* magazine, "Nobody wants to say anything, but, of course, the owners are worried. How are you guys going to draw with eleven colored players on your team?"

"You didn't want to have too large a number of Black athletes, the thinking was that white fans would be offended or wouldn't want to go see the games," said Pat Williams, a general manager in Chicago and later in the decade Philadelphia. "So it turns out that many of your guys at the very end of the bench in those years were white."

Much of the racism that existed was so routine and so pervasive, it was never reported. When the Celtics veteran center Wayne Embry walked onto the court in Philadelphia for Game 7 of the 1968 Eastern Division finals, he sat down on the bench and a 76ers fan came from his seat and thrust a banana in Embry's face, shouting, "Here you go, you big ape!"

On the eve of Super Bowl IV in New Orleans, a group of writers drove to Baton Rouge to watch LSU's phenomenal scorer Pete Maravich face Auburn. That night, the ugly scene at LSU's Parker Agricultural Museum (known as "the Cow Palace" to students) focused on Auburn's Henry Harris, the first Black scholarship athlete at Auburn. Harris, playing his first season with the varsity, was the focal point of the LSU crowd and heard a chorus of shouts of

"Leroy!"—a common racial epithet of the era—any time he handled the ball throughout the game.

In the aftermath of the assassinations of Malcolm X and Martin Luther King Jr.—and the widespread riots after King was slain—race remained both a charged and prominent topic in America. The Supreme Court decision that struck down miscegenation laws—*Loving v. Virginia*—had only been handed down in 1967. The United States was still very much a case of two separate Americas. And there was evidence it was getting worse. When Nixon took office in January 1969, fifteen years after the *Brown v. Board of Education* decision, 68 percent of the Black students in the South still attended all-Black schools. And even in the face of widespread affirmative action programs meant to help rescue the underclass, the Black family median income as compared to whites declined from 61 percent in 1969 to 58 percent in 1973.

The remnants of racism were still remarked upon, especially in basketball where a rueful joke, which Bill Russell was fond of repeating, held that teams could play "two Blacks at home, three on the road, four when we're behind." One school referred to its interracial team's makeup as "four dots and a dash," while Marquette's coach Al McGuire compared it to a checkerboard, before joking ruefully that "I'm the only coach in the country with white problems."

But the divide couldn't be bridged with jests and one-liners.

"There are so many forces," said the Knicks' African American guard Dick Barnett. "You have the environmental force, you have the forces of culture, you know, you got so many things. Like I want to see Sly & the Family Stone. Like, the white players, they aren't hip to that, that's not in their world, you know, they're apart from it. They might go see Johnny Cash, I can't dig him. There are so many things. Like, most white players don't dance, they don't know how to dance...I mean, like, it's what do you have in common except playing basketball?"

The new decade witnessed Black Americans asserting themselves in ways that had heretofore been unimaginable, and the impact could be felt throughout the popular culture, from James Brown's declamation, "Say It Loud (I'm Black and I'm Proud)," which hit the charts in 1968, to something as prosaic as the "Black ABC's," flashcards popular with African American families ("A is for Afro," "N is for Natural," "S is for Soul Sister").

But the racial schism was felt throughout the games and butted up against the absolute authority that football coaches had traditionally possessed. The University of Wyoming head coach T. K. Eaton dropped fourteen Black players from his team in 1969 because they took part in a demonstration against the racial policies of Brigham Young University. "They came in together and they came wearing armbands," Eaton complained. "It was simply a matter of discipline. Black or white, it didn't matter to me. They broke the rule and I told them they were no longer members of the team." (One of Wyoming's Black players, Joe Williams, had a different version: "He said our very presence defied him. He said he has had some good Neee-gro *boys.* Just like that.")

That same year, nine of the ten Black players on Syracuse's football team refused to report for spring practice, in protest to what they felt was Ben Schwartzwalder's broken promise that he would hire a Black assistant coach.

"Nobody wants to talk about football anymore," said Schwartzwalder. "All they want to talk about is that. Some young kid I never saw before came into my office today. He asked me about that. I told him that I didn't talk to Communists, draft dodgers, flag burners, or people trying to destroy our country. He assured me he was none of those things so I sat down and talked with him. I don't know what's happening anymore. I'm not supposed to be a football coach, I'm supposed to be a sociologist or something."

For the athletes growing up in this environment, the messages from a prideful Black community couldn't be clearer. Reflecting on the inflection point in history, the wondrous basketball player Julius Erving—attending the University of Massachusetts at the time—remembered his mindset: "There is a war in Vietnam. There are riots on the streets of Newark. There are those who tell me that I need to make a choice. That the Black man in America has been oppressed. That what is needed is nothing less than a revolution, a new society, or, even more confusing, that we need to return to Africa, to rediscover our culture and ourselves. And, man, some brothers are telling me I need to say if I'm with the Man, or against him."

•

For all the simmering resentment, there was also progress, instances where history was being made without many even realizing it. On September 1,

1971, the Pittsburgh Pirates took the field for a game against the St. Louis Cardinals. Dave Cash moved over to third base to start for the injured Richie Hebner. Shortstop Gene Alley was out, so Jackie Hernandez replaced him.

In the third or fourth inning, as the Pirates were working their way a second time through their batting order, Cash and Al Oliver were sitting next to each other in the dugout when Oliver said, "You know what? We got all brothers out there, man."

It was the first game in the history of Major League Baseball in which a team was fielded entirely made up of people of color. Oliver, remembering the conversation years later, said, "We kind of chuckled because it was no big deal to us. We had no idea that history was being made."

Even when the progress was noted, the distinction could be a burden; the breakthroughs came at a cost. "Every time I look around, somebody's asking me, 'How does it feel to be the first black this and the first black that?'" said Eddie McAshan, the first Black starting quarterback at Georgia Tech.

Those questions, as it transpired, were only just beginning. In the midst of all the change, Eddie Robinson still had a message he was convinced could resonate.

"Black parents and white high school coaches often discourage the top black stars from coming to us," he said in 1970. "And the fact that integration is phasing out a lot of black schools and black coaches are being demoted when they are reassigned to integrated schools, disrupts our supply line. But I got to hang in there with the black athlete, because he's missed so much. There are things that he's got to be told every day, and hell, I want to tell him. I not only want to make a football player out of him. I want to make him a man, a fighter, a producer. I want to tell him about the kind of country we're living in and what it really takes to make it. I feel I can tell him these things better than the white man. I don't know, I'm silly enough to feel that the black athlete needs me. He needs me to teach him these things."

# THREE

# THE WORKING PRESS

GAME 7 OF the 1970 NBA Finals was winding down and a pulsating Madison Square Garden—which had become the place to be seen in Manhattan during the New York Knicks' dream season—was incandescent.

The deciding game between the Knicks and Los Angeles Lakers had long ago been settled. In the final minute, after Bill Bradley grabbed an offensive rebound, he dished back out to Walt "Clyde" Frazier, and the five Knicks moved the ball around with a kind of gleeful insouciance, part fundamentals, part Globetrotters. Nate Bowman sank the last basket for New York before the Lakers scored once more. As the final seconds ticked off on New York's 113–99 win, jubilant Knicks fans rushed the floor.

By that time, the group of newspaper and magazine writers covering the game, including the young reporter Bob Ryan of the *Boston Globe*, had already been ushered into the Knicks' locker room. The scribes were waiting for the new champions when the Knicks came off the floor and into the locker room, led by Frazier, who'd had the game of his life—36 points, 19 assists, and 7 rebounds, and proclaimed, "Man, I need a beer!" a line which Ryan worked into his game story.

The game was nationally televised—it was the first time in history that every game of the NBA Finals had been broadcast live—but the ABC crew that handled the broadcast received no preferential postgame treatment, and wasn't even allowed in the Knicks' locker room.

Instead, ABC set up its camera in the vacant New York Rangers locker room across the hall, and Frazier and his teammates were brought over individually for live interviews with ABC's Howard Cosell, who explained the stillness of the surroundings by noting, "We've not been granted access to the Knicks' locker room because of its diminution in size."

The real reason was simpler: the longtime primacy of print over electronic media in the world of sports. At Madison Square Garden, the newspaper and magazine reporters usually got five minutes in the locker room with players before the TV and radio crews were allowed in. And the ink-stained wretches generally viewed the TV and radio reporters as interlopers at best and charlatans at worst. At Shea Stadium in the aftermath of the 1969 World Series, the cantankerous *New York Daily News* columnist Dick Young almost came to blows with Cosell, who was recording interviews for his radio show. In postgame locker rooms, jockeying for position with electronic media, Young often threatened, "Back up or I'll put *fuck*s on your audio."

To those who came of age in the streaming, video-on-demand, round-the-clock world of sports television in the twenty-first century, it's almost impossible to explain how completely print dominated the world of sports media at the beginning of the 1970s, or how much of an effort it could be to get even the score of an out-of-town game the night of the event. All over the country in 1970, fans of every sport and every stripe spent an inordinate amount of time just trying to find out what was going on in the rest of the sporting world.

"One thing I have such a hard time explaining to my kids was how in the dark we were all the time," wrote Joe Posnanski about growing up in the '70s. "We couldn't get scores. We couldn't get news. We had to wait for the newspaper."

The reason print journalism was so important was because so few sports events were actually televised. The constellation of spectator sports was still a loose amalgam of events witnessed only by those in attendance. The games were real; following them was often an exercise in projection. One would read a wire-service story and its scant detail and have to visualize Brigham Young's Gary Sheide throwing for 310 yards; or look at a box score and picture the Pirates' slugger Willie Stargell going 3-for-4 with two doubles; or try to imagine what someone named Fly Williams—playing at someplace called Austin Peay State University—might actually look like scoring 26 points in a NCAA tournament win over Jacksonville. Serious fans could envision it, but they rarely saw a single play of any of it. Some of the greatest moments in the history of sports were similarly evanescent. There were no film crews in Hershey, Pennsylvania, the night that Wilt Chamberlain scored 100 points against the Knicks in 1962. All fans knew was that it actually happened. You had to be there.

Sports coverage on television and radio was scant and, for the most part, slavishly local. It wasn't that TV didn't exist or wasn't considered important. It was that the primacy of the press had been baked into the DNA of sports for decades.

"Print was number one," said Bill Hancock, who started as an assistant sports information director at Oklahoma and later moved to the Big Eight offices in Kansas City. "Print was number one, two, three and four. And then radio and television. Part of that was because the newspapers were so big and so influential. And so chock full of advertising and such a powerful business enterprise and, furthermore, so much better able to get up close to bring people, figuratively, into the locker room."

It was easy to find out what the home team was doing. People walking down the street in Baltimore could hear Chuck Thompson calling the Orioles games on WBAL-AM, while natives of Pittsburgh grew accustomed to the sound of Bob Prince calling Pirates games on KDKA-AM.

But for those trying to follow the entire universe of sports—a holiday invitational in college basketball, a tennis tournament in Europe, a World Cup qualifying match in South America, even a baseball game on the West Coast—sports was often an elusive, indistinct thing, the sound of a train in the distance.

Those who had no reliable radio source for information had to wait until the next morning's—or even the next afternoon's—paper for West Coast results, as those games didn't finish in time for the next morning's paper. Instead, a fan in Kansas City opening the *Times* the next morning would not find a game story on the hometown Royals but instead a small box labeled "BULLETIN" on the front page of the sports section. "The Royals led the California Angels, 3–2 in the sixth inning, when the *Times* went to press." There was even less information about other teams. A line below the major league standings would include final scores of early games, and then, for West Coast games, just the perfunctory "Milwaukee at Oakland, night."

For fans who absolutely, positively had to have a score—and this wasn't only the gamblers, but also the true believers following a pennant race or the dislocated loyalists like a UCLA alum living in Chicago or a Los Angeles Lakers fan residing in Nashville—there was often no recourse other than calling the sports desk of the local newspaper, where a harried, surly copyeditor might grudgingly provide a score before hanging up.

But the rest of the world of sports, for those who wanted to follow it, was consumed via sporadic radio updates late at night or two-paragraph wireservice stories or a series of agate box scores in seven-point Franklin Gothic condensed typeface in the newspaper.

One reason for the continued power of print media was the scant coverage provided in sports reports on local TV stations. With the exception of WGN in Chicago, which offered the country's longest sports reports on its nightly news shows, most major stations included a perfunctory four to five minutes, almost all of it devoted to local news.

The announcer Gil Stratton of KNXT-TV in Los Angeles viewed it as a product of ignorance for those who didn't understand sports. "There is no doubt in my mind," he said in 1972, "that there is a lot of built-in resentment, nationwide, among news directors when it comes to sports. They view all sports as one story, not as several stories. Baseball, football, and basketball are all one to them. They don't consider politics, business, and entertainment all one, but they do sports."

Even the scores, when they came, were doled out sparingly. The Knicks' public address announcer John Condon knew that fans at Madison Square Garden were eager for other scores, and gamblers were particularly attuned to out-of-town results. "When I'd introduce a score you could hear a pin drop in the place if the money was big on it," Condon recalled. "They never knew whether I'd give the loser or the winner first. I'd say, 'Here is an NBA score from Philadelphia… at the end of the third quarter, Philadelphia 71…' then a good long pause to let them mull it over '…and Boston 83.' Man, those guys wanted to kill me."

Much of the country remained relatively provincial. Even people within the world of sports weren't always aware of what they were watching. In 1970, a sixth-grader named Larry Joe Bird left his home in French Lick, Indiana, and traveled with a cousin to Louisville to watch a game. "I guess I didn't get it straight," Bird recalled later, "because I thought he had told me it was a college game."

Only later did young Larry Bird realize that he hadn't watched the University of Kentucky Wildcats, but had actually been at an American Basketball Association game between the Kentucky Colonels and the Virginia Squires. "Why didn't you tell me?" he asked his cousin later. "I would have watched it closer."

Bird was hardly unique in his insular worldview. When Nebraska's stellar defensive lineman Larry Jacobsen was informed he'd won the Outland Award in 1971—presented every year to the outstanding lineman in college football—Jacobsen had never heard of the honor. He had to ask his defensive coordinator, Monte Kiffin, to spell out the name of the award.

•

No one understood the power of the press better than the commissioner of the National Football League, Pete Rozelle, who'd once been the public relations director of the Los Angeles Rams. Rozelle had helped the NFL eclipse Major League Baseball in the '60s in part because of how sophisticated NFL teams were in courting the media. At the time, the NFL still sent "advance men" from visiting teams to the next opponent's city to help increase interest in ticket sales for the upcoming weekend's games. The PR men, like Ernie Accorsi in Baltimore (later to become general manager of the Colts), would make the rounds to newspaper and TV stations, with black-and-white glossy photographs and 16 mm film clips.

In Boston, where the *Boston Globe* had one of the best and largest sports sections in the country, the press credentials and parking passes for the *Globe*'s coverage of the Patriots home games were regularly delivered on Friday mornings to the sports editor's office by the Patriots *owner*, William "Billy" Sullivan.

Within almost every city, it was the columnists and beat writers at newspapers who set the agenda. In Miami, when the phone rang in the sports department, it was sometimes Muhammad Ali, calling from Angelo Dundee's gym in Miami Beach, to take issue with one of Edwin Pope's columns in the *Miami Herald*. In Boston, where the *Globe* still didn't send their beat writer Bob Ryan on the road with the team, the Celtics coach Tom Heinsohn dutifully called Ryan late after every road game to provide him quotes and detail for his story in the next afternoon's paper.

Preeminent among all the entities, often trumping even the revered and feared local sports columnist, were the writers at *Sports Illustrated* which, after an uncertain beginning—the magazine launched in 1954 and lost money for ten straight years—eventually gave way to a new vision, articulated by the managing editor Andre Laguerre, who took over in 1960 and repositioned *SI* as a weekly newsmagazine devoted to sports.

"I'm developing a strong hunch that pro football is our sport," Laguerre wrote to Time, Inc. founder Henry Luce in 1962. "We have grown with it, and each of us is a phenomenon of the times." So it proved as *SI*'s circulation and influence grew with each passing year, and the workmanlike Hamilton "Tex" Maule chronicled the pro game for millions of upscale, literate readers.

In the meantime, college football—on the back of ABC's national TV coverage—grew in popularity as well. *SI*'s writers dominated the scene. It was a writer, not a TV reporter—*Sports Illustrated*'s Dan Jenkins—who'd driven with Darrell Royal around Fayetteville on the eve of 1969's "Game of the Century" between Arkansas and Texas. So it was Jenkins in the car, there to witness Royal getting his game face on, declaring his disdain for the entire state: "Arkansas! All they do here is sell jelly and cider by the side of the road." *SI*'s basketball writer Frank Deford was once invited into the Kentucky locker room at halftime of the national championship game.

There were other factors helping print. At the beginning of the '70s, as the FCC declared a moratorium on cigarette advertising on TV, print media was strengthened, and TV entities grew more anxious. Both Major League Baseball and the NFL were concerned about the effect of the Federal Trade Commission's ban on cigarette advertising on television and radio (which took effect at midnight, January 2, 1971). Tobacco companies sponsored more than a quarter of Major League Baseball's telecasts and, by one estimate, accounted for a fifth of baseball's TV and radio advertising revenue in 1969. Cigarettes had provided a sixth of NFL advertising. In the short term, it strengthened the advertising power of print media.

In 1970, the aging *Boston Globe* sports editor Ernie Roberts advised his bosses to hire Dave Smith, the sports editor at the *Fort Lauderdale Sun-Sentinel*, to become his heir apparent. Smith had been a sports obsessive from an early age, and recognized early in the '60s that because there were so many transplants living in the area, his sports page had to be more national in its outlook. Among his early innovations was taking all of the statistical minutiae that used to run with game stories—box scores, scoring summaries, standings, and other statistics—and grouping them together over the better part of the interior page of a sports section, and calling that page "Scoreboard." That freed up the rest of the paper for larger pictures, other design innovations and, eventually, longer and more writerly stories.

First in the pages of the *Globe*'s Sunday sports section, and then throughout the week, Smith assembled an arsenal of writers and made the Sunday section an innovative, one-stop destination for sports news. By 1971, he'd started weekly "notes columns" in major and minor sports; Will McDonough in football, Peter Gammons in baseball, Ryan in basketball, the glib, florid Bud Collins in tennis and, eventually, Jack Craig covering the TV and radio beat all wrote regular columns reporting not just on local news but national developments. Each was a quality writer, but what they had in common beyond that was an indefatigable reportorial work ethic, honed by Smith's demanding leadership.

•

There was an art to how you treated the press that went beyond hot food and accurate stat sheets in the press box. Especially in college football, there was a standard operating procedure for big schools on the eve of home games.

"There was the press party, quote unquote, on Friday night," said Bill Hancock. "Dinner and drinks, and, for those interested, some chicanery after dinner and drinks." On the eve of Oklahoma home games, writers were feted at Fuzzy's lounge, famous for its tabouli, in Oklahoma City. When writers traveled to Lincoln, Nebraska, for a Nebraska game, it was Misty's Lounge, renowned for its prime rib.

Few had the system down to more of a science than the University of Texas. On Friday nights before games and Saturday nights after games, the Texas sports information director Jones Ramsey booked suite 2001 at the Villa Capri Hotel close to campus.

"How you hittin' 'em?" was Ramsey's standard greeting before welcoming an out-of-town reporter. Typically, radio and television people weren't invited to these fetes, so the writers received extra attention.

When the formidable and respected *Dallas Times-Herald* columnist

Blackie Sherrod flew to Austin the week before 1969's Texas-Arkansas showdown, Jones Ramsey met him at his gate as he deplaned and, walking through the terminal, explained apologetically that he wouldn't be able to arrange an interview with quarterback James Street because Street needed to concentrate on the big game. Then Ramsey walked Sherrod out to the curb where a car was waiting to drive him into town. The driver behind the wheel of the car, wearing a chauffeur's cap, was James Street.

A year earlier, one of the Villa Capri's meet-ups was responsible for naming the new formation that the Longhorns began using, the triple-option attack cooked up by Royal and his assistant, Emory Bellard. A writer asked Royal what they called their new alignment.

"We don't call it anything. The backfield is in the shape of a Y. How about that?"

The spry *Houston Post* columnist Mickey Herskowitz perked up. "That's not very original. Your backfield is in the shape of a wishbone. Why don't you call it that?"

"There you go," said Royal. And with that, the Wishbone was named.

At the Villa Capri, there was a cooler iced down with beer after the games and a cart with liquor. Royal always stopped by after his postgame shower. There were no pens and notebooks, because everything was off the record. There were no cameras because it was almost exclusively print media that was invited.

Implicit in all of it was a recognition that the writers covering the University of Texas football program could shape public opinion. "I found out real early in coaching that I needed the press," said Royal. "The press had a job to do, and I had a story to tell, so we needed to work together."

•

But even the world of sports was not immune from the societal changes in the '60s. For decades, the actual shenanigans and idiosyncrasies of being an athlete remained behind a scrim of implicit agreement. "It wasn't unusual for athletes or managers or coaches or whatever to be in a bar or a restaurant, and writers coming in and they sit down together and have beers together," said Dave Smith. "You could almost use the word 'camaraderie.' And it was interesting because, you know, the boundaries were understood."

As the new decade dawned, that cloak of anonymity was being torn down in American life. Its fall in sports was inevitable as well.

"Look here," said the Knicks guard Dick Barnett to the writer Phil Berger in 1969, "most of the things that happen when you're a ballplayer, you really can't tell about because most of it has to do with broads and chicks and most of it isn't…if you really want the best seller in the world, if you really ran it down like that, you'd have a hell of a story."

Barnett's observation would prove prescient by the spring of 1970.

The journeyman pitcher Jim Bouton had been keeping a journal of observations and experiences throughout the 1969 season, as a member of the expansion Seattle Pilots and later, after a trade, the Houston Astros. Teaming up with the acerbic writer Leonard Schechter, Bouton offered an unvarnished look at life in the major leagues. When *Look* magazine ran an excerpt from the book in May of 1970, what got the most attention was not Bouton's account of his struggles in 1969, but instead his recollection of his time with the New York Yankees, especially the drinking and hijinks of Mickey Mantle, whom he regarded (accurately, as it turned out) as a gifted player who squandered much of his talent through alcohol.

The book was released in June to largely positive reviews, but many writers sensed the backlash that had already started. Writing in the *Washington Post*, David Markham called *Ball Four* "a wry, understated, honest and memorable piece of Americana, by a good man they will clobber because of it."

Nowhere was the exposé treated with more derision than in the Office of the Commissioner, where the new commissioner, Bowie Kuhn—who already possessed the self-seriousness of someone who fancied himself the conscience of the game—was apoplectic. After reading *Ball Four*, he ordered Bouton into his office. "I told him it was a poor thing to write," said Kuhn. "It was inconsistent with his standard of playing. It is not proper for one in baseball to criticize baseball. In the entertainment business, it's not in the best interest to criticize the quality of the product."

That marked perhaps the first instance in which a commissioner stated that baseball was, in fact, in the "entertainment business." But Kuhn's opposition wasn't based on Bouton's standard of playing as much as his level of candor. The book sold 200,000 copies, landed on the bestseller lists, and changed the way sports was reported forever. Breaking the traditional code of silence about off-field behavior engendered resentment from teammates and opponents alike. Before a game against the Cincinnati Reds, Bouton was greeted with a volley from the Reds' dugout, where Pete Rose shouted, "Fuck you, Shakespeare!"

*Ball Four* opened the floodgates. Within two years, Dan Jenkins' raucous, bawdy *Semi-Tough*, a fictional exposé of pro football, made the *New York Times* bestseller list and earned Jenkins a guest spot on *The Tonight Show* with Johnny Carson. Shortly thereafter, former Cowboy receiver Peter Gent published *North Dallas Forty,* a darker, grittier fictional takedown of the Dallas Cowboys.

It was going to be difficult going back to the way it used to be, especially since the tenor of the age was bringing about a change in the way sportswriters did their work.

The dividing line between sports and the real world had grown more and more blurry. The cases of Muhammad Ali and Curt Flood winding up on the Supreme Court docket meant that the job was more demanding. "Because of Flood," observed the writer Allen Barra, "sports journalism no longer simply required a writer to be knowledgeable about the subjects of batting averages and ERAs. You had to be a part-time economist, sociologist, and labor-relations historian."

But it went beyond an awareness of the way sports intersected with other parts of society. There was a sense that the athletes in question were more interesting as fallible humans than as mythic heroes. "I stopped Godding up the players," was how Shirley Povich at the *Washington Post* put it.

•

For sports fans, the beginning of the Sunday evening time slot often signaled the beginning of a desert of five days before any more sports appeared on TV. There were scant exceptions—some baseball road games in certain cities, or in the rare instance a local hockey or basketball team's road game was telecast back to the home market. Saturday would typically include one college football game with, earlier in the fall, a baseball game of the week or, later in the fall, a regional college basketball telecast. Sunday offered typically one or two football games—though never the home games of the local team, as the

NFL's blackout rules meant that in NFL cities where a game was playing at home, there would be no telecasts on at that time.

But in the main, during the week, there was nothing. "The thought of watching a game during the week, it just didn't happen," said the announcer Mike Breen, then a teenager growing up in Yonkers. "There were no games during the week so you waited for the weekend. And you couldn't wait, because it was the one game that you could actually see."

As the '70s began, it had been nearly a decade since any sports were regularly on prime time on American network television (boxing, having strangled its own popularity through overexposure, saw *Friday Night Fights* canceled on NBC in 1960). None of the previous 493 World Series games had ever been played in the evening, nor had any NFL Championship Games nor any of the Super Bowls.

In short, sports were still cordoned off in American society in 1970, in the "toy department" of newspapers and the Saturday and Sunday "afternoon ghetto" of network television when overall viewership was low.

Though the televised games were by now routinely offered in color, they were often not experienced that way. America was a country whose homes were still populated largely by box fans and black-and-white television sets. "The New York Knicks are wearing the dark blue or, if you're not in color, the dark shirts," Keith Jackson explained to ABC's viewers prior to a 1970 Knicks–Bucks game, because so many American TV watchers still had black-and-white sets. It wasn't until 1972 that color televisions outsold black-and-white models. Virtually all newspapers ran photographs in black-and-white, and most preseason annuals featured only black-and-white photography inside. (While *Sports Illustrated* had promoted the use of "fast color" in the late '60s, there was still a strict limit on its use, and color editorial pages were so rare and expensive that *Time* magazine still listed its two to four pages of color in the table of contents.)

Then there was the tepid aesthetic of sports on television. Since the early days of the form, leagues had been heavy-handed in trying to manage the game, typically insisting on approval of all network announcers. The result of this was a pervasive blandness in the way the games were presented.

NBC's broadcast of Game 1 of the 1970 World Series was emblematic.

There was little narrative thrust; no mention in the opening that the Orioles—playing in their third World Series in five years—were trying to redeem themselves from the upset loss to the Amazin' Mets in 1969; no mention that the Reds hadn't been to the World Series in nine years.

The only person the network interviewed on field before the game, oddly, was the actor Tony Martin, who was slated to sing the national anthem the *following* day, before Game 2. He joked with on-field reporter Tony Kubek about struggling to remember the words to the song. The feature that took the most time during the pregame were shots of Cincinnati's new Riverfront Stadium, which had opened the previous June.

Later, a PA announcer introduced the Lemon-Monroe High School band to play the National Anthem before Game 1, and the group that would sing the song. After the performance the singers were identified by NBC's play-by-play man Curt Gowdy as "that great young mod group, the Jackson Five."

Typical of much live coverage in the era, the broadcast lacked any real sense of history in the setup or narrative arc in the presentation. The implicit job of the telecast was to promote and present an event, never to explain it, contextualize, or criticize it.

The man who would soon change all that was Roone Pinckney Arledge, the head of ABC Sports. He'd grown up on Long Island, the son of an insurance executive, captivated by news and sports in an age of reading and listening. He encountered television for the first time as an eight-year-old visiting the 1939 World's Fair. By 1960, he had started working with the New York City sports broadcasting pioneer Edgar J. Scherick, and when Scherick sold his company, Sports Program, Inc., to ABC, Arledge was on the ground floor of the distant third major network.

Arledge, red-haired, red-faced, sharply intelligent, possessed a sense of wonder about what sports could be. Like so many kids shuttled to the sideline, he viewed the games as taking place on a higher plane, elusive and fascinating. He wanted cameras to pierce the veneer of distance that surrounded television sports. Throughout the '60s, under Arledge, ABC had carved out a niche as an innovator in both live and recorded sports telecasts.

A fanatic about intimacy and a sense of place, Arledge had introduced handheld sideline shots (which he dubbed the "peepy-creepy" camera) during the early days of the American Football League and later in the '60s when ABC got the NCAA's college football package. He was the mastermind behind the anthology series *Wide World of Sports,* which had dominated Saturday afternoons in the '60s with a wide array of mostly prerecorded segments of all manner of sporting competitions. On *Wide World,* Arledge focused on the personalities of the athletes to further underscore the stakes and the competition. To ABC Sports staffers, the segments were known as "Up Close and Personals," or simply UCAPS.

"Arledge taught us that without context, you're going to be hard-pressed to give any sort of meaning or perspective," said his protégé at ABC, Geoff Mason. "And the best way to provide context is to, a) lead off with 'where are we?' and show it, and b) more importantly, dive into who these people are."

*Wide World* had little competition over the weekends in American sports in the '60s. ABC's college football game—the only football telecast in the country each Saturday—was the lead-in. By the end of the '60s, Arledge was already regarded as something of a television visionary. What he still needed was a larger stage to exhibit his mastery of the form.

•

Those who knew—and liked and sometimes feared—Pete Rozelle had learned to look for the tells. For the still youthful commissioner of the NFL—forty-two and seemingly always tan—there were no obvious ones like fidgeting or perspiration. In his outward countenance, Rozelle remained composed, relaxed and impeccably dressed. But in times of stress, or from a weaker bargaining position, he might smoke his cigarettes slightly faster, might fidget with his gold-plated lighter for an extended period. On this day, though, in the midtown Manhattan restaurant "21", there was no rush, not even a deep drag on his Camel cigarette. Just slow, relaxed puffs.

Which is how Arledge, invited out to lunch with the NFL commissioner, knew that Rozelle wasn't bluffing when he said he really would sell his proposed package of prime-time games, *Monday Night Football,* to the Hughes Television Network if the NFL couldn't get its series on the air with ABC.

Rozelle was already the dominant administrator in American professional sports, but he had a vision that transcended its present boundaries. Congressional edicts prevented the NFL from staging games either on Fridays during the high school football season or on Saturdays during the college football season. But Rozelle was convinced that the broader audience of prime time would embrace a weekly football game on Monday nights.

By that point, both CBS and NBC had already passed on the proposed series. ("What? And pre-empt Doris Day?" asked an incredulous CBS exec. NBC, for its part, didn't want to alienate Johnny Carson by having games delay the start of *The Tonight Show*). When the package was offered to ABC, Arledge and the ABC execs were originally tepid about it. He told at least two co-workers that he was skeptical whether a regular diet of football in prime time could work.

But it was apparent to Arledge that Rozelle's determination to establish the series meant that ABC *had* to buy the package or risk, as the number three network, losing affiliates on Monday nights during the fall, which might lead to a precipitous and irreversible slide. Rozelle was armed with pocket aces, and his strong hand would, in time, revolutionize both television and American sports. Though the maverick network being put together by Howard Hughes offered more money for the package, Rozelle stuck with the more established ABC.

His commercial instincts proved unerring. By May, a full four months before *Monday Night Football*'s debut, Arledge announced that ABC had sold out its ad inventory for the season. The advertisers included Ford, Goodyear, United Air Lines, Philip Morris (burning through its last TV ads before the cigarette ban took effect), and Firestone.

Before ABC signed the deal with the NFL, Arledge pointedly insisted that the league would not have approval over ABC's announcers for the series. His choice was Howard Cosell, already a controversial figure for his public defense of Muhammad Ali (even for his continued, pointed insistence to call Ali by his chosen name). But Cosell was primarily seen on weekend afternoons, on ABC's *Wide World of Sports*, and by limited audiences in boxing matches. In a sports broadcasting field populated by amiable, beige Midwestern voices, Cosell stood out for his staccato vocal delivery, his deep vocabulary, and his unmistakable ethnicity. To parts of America at that point, he was "that loud Jew on TV."

Sports was in uncharted territory. By the beginning of the 1970s, the prime-time television audience was the biggest congregation in the American marketplace, and one of its characteristic features was that it was a majority female. The central challenge for Arledge was how to get more viewers to watch. If ABC could only attract the audience the NFL had for Sunday after-noons on Monday evenings, the series could crater.

Arledge knew he needed something more than attractive matchups and the gravitas of Howard Cosell. First there was "Dandy" Don Meredith, the homespun retired Cowboys' quarterback who'd flirted with an entertain-ment career even before his playing days were up. For the first time in sports TV, Arledge went with a three-person announcing booth, with veteran play-by-play man Keith Jackson joining Meredith and Cosell.

In late August, Jackson sternly assured a reporter about his new *Monday Night Football* booth colleague Cosell, "He will not be the dominant per-sonality on the broadcast." Jackson would become a television legend in col-lege football over the coming decades, but in this case he was spectacularly wrong.

The challenge facing Arledge would be markedly different from the one on *Wide World of Sports*. It was one thing to film a cliff-diving tournament or a ski-jumping competition from halfway around the world and package it a week or two later into a tightly formatted thirty-minute segment with the key jumps and "UCAP" segments culminating in what the show's opening montage described as "the thrill of victory, the agony of defeat."

But it was more daunting to do that live, on a three-hour telecast, for a national prime-time audience comprised of both casual fans who didn't know the game well and knowledgeable fans who were passionate and opin-ionated about the sport.

As it happened, ABC and Arledge had already shown the ability to deliver that very thing.

On Friday evening, May 8, 1970, in that Game 7 of the NBA Finals—the one that found Cosell demoted to the hockey locker room for basketball postgame reporting—the network had presented the Arledge vision in nearly perfect composition.

Earlier that week, Game 5 had been played in a cloud of uncertainty and mourning, occurring the same day that four Kent State student protesters had been shot and killed by National Guardsmen. Only late in the afternoon was the game green-lighted. The Knicks team captain and 1970 league MVP Willis Reed was injured in the game, but the inspired Knicks rallied without their leader and won, taking a 3–2 lead in the series. Suffering from a torn thigh muscle, Reed didn't make the trip to Los Angeles for Game 6, where Wilt Chamberlain was unstoppable and the Lakers won easily.

That set up Game 7, back in New York, as the fans in Madison Square Garden and the world of pro basketball waited to see if Reed would even be able to play.

The game announcers—Chris Schenkel doing play-by-play with former All-Star Jack Twyman as the analyst—set the stage, and ABC quickly cut to a pregame interview from earlier in the evening, with Cosell questioning the Knicks coach Red Holzman about Reed's injury. As the shot went back to live pregame coverage, with Schenkel and Twyman discussing the challenge at hand, Twyman noted a ripple of activity around the tunnel leading out of the Knicks' locker room, and the next shot showed a hobbled Reed emerging from the catacombs, intent but limping, to a standing ovation. Moments later, Twyman informed the TV audience that Reed had been injected with 200 ccs of cortisone.

Reed strode to the free throw line and took a few flat-footed set shots, his small Sacred Heart medal bouncing on a chain around his neck. At the other end of the court, the Lakers' shootaround stuttered, with players moving haltingly and sneaking looks at the Knicks' game but wounded captain.

When the game started, Chamberlain won the tip—Reed didn't even try to elevate—but on the Knicks' first trip down the floor, Reed sank a jumper from near the foul line before dragging his numb right leg back down to the other end. Moments later, Reed got an open shot from sixteen feet and sank his second jumper. The Garden crowd reached another crescendo, and the Knicks were off and running.

Reed scored no more, but he didn't need to; his presence roused the crowd and his teammates, and fazed the Lakers. New York led by as many as 29 points on the way to the decisive win.

But in a way that it hadn't been before, the event was framed, contextualized and dramatized by ABC. Not incidentally, it would be remembered for decades for the very elements—the game warrior Reed limping onto the court to a standing ovation, the crucial early baskets—that ABC's broadcast had emphasized.

Could Arledge and his team deliver that kind of vividness and intimacy on a weekly basis, and was there a large enough audience in prime time to sustain it?

•

On September 21, 1970, *Monday Night Football* made its premiere. Unlike every other game broadcast in television history beforehand, this telecast began with a self-referential scene set inside a TV control booth, and the voice of a director urgently counting down, "Five seconds to air, four, three, two, and... *take tape!*" A jazzy keyboard riff—from "Killing Me Softly with His Song" composer Charles Fox—surged forward, and the opening titles of *Monday Night Football* took to the air.

As the first telecast began, Cosell was down on the field. "It is a hot, sultry, almost windless night here," he said, by way of scene-setting, before interviewing the Jets' star quarterback Joe Namath.

"Of course, Weeb Ewbank has characterized this Jets team as superior even to the Super Bowl champions of January 12, 1969," Cosell said to Namath. "Do you agree with that assessment?"

"Um, no, I don't," said Namath. "But I hope Weeb's right. At this stage, it's too difficult to tell... The '68 team proved itself, and this '70 team has to go out and prove itself." It was a small but significant moment, perhaps the first time that an athlete in a team sport had contradicted his head coach on live national television.

Very soon, as the game began, in front of a sold-out crowd at Cleveland's Municipal Stadium, the striking visual qualities of football at night became apparent. The green grass was more vivid, the shiny helmets positively gleamed under the high-wattage arc lights, and the many close-ups—ABC had more cameras than had ever been used for a football telecast before—added a grandeur, amplified by the shortened depth-of-focus in the night setting. There was also a simple, ineluctable truth: Sports *felt* different when it was on at night, and more people were watching it.

The way it was covered was different as well. Play-by-play man Keith Jackson's role was to call the game and direct the traffic of commentary. In the opener, the statement that Cosell made that elicited the most outrage was his observation, late in the second half, that "Leroy Kelly has not been a compelling factor in this game." The All-Pro Kelly, Cleveland's most reliable offensive threat, had been held to 62 yards on twenty carries, far below his average.

"When the games came on that first season, a lot of the people, especially advertisers, hated Howard," said ABC producer Dennis Lewin. "Howard was this monstrous rebel that came along and broke the mold. And he broke the mold forever."

Don Meredith's charge was to simplify the increasingly complex game and use his finely tuned, Southern-fried persona to pull in casual fans and women alike. There was a sly transgressiveness to his humor. When the Browns' wide receiver Fair Hooker was cited in the first Monday game, Meredith waited a beat and said, "Fair Hooker...well, I haven't met one yet."

When Namath and the Jets got the ball, trailing by three points, with forty-seven seconds left in the game, the NFL and ABC got what they'd wanted—the scene set for a classic finish. Namath dropped back and fired a pass to the center of the field, but it was intercepted by Cleveland's Billy Andrews, who ran it back for a touchdown. And in that moment, amid the crowd's joyous roar, there was a long isolation shot of Namath, hands on his hips, head bowed, frozen in self-castigation. It wasn't merely an indelible sports moment. It was *good television*.

"We knew that the audience needed to change, and we wanted to do *Monday Night Football* in a very different manner," said ABC's Lewin. "Everything from how it was presented in the booth with our announcers, to bringing in celebrities into the booth to keep amplifying that idea that it was also entertainment, to how we presented the game technologically, because we took it to a different level. But I don't want to lose sight of the fact that a lot of the things we did to make *Monday Night Football* what it became stemmed from our *Wide World of Sports* show."

Arledge put more cameras in more places and brought a college football innovation—a portable camera on a golf cart with a flatbed trailer, moving up and down the sidelines as drives progressed, so as to always have a shot down the line of scrimmage—to the pro game.

Then there was Cosell. If the cameras and close-ups and Meredith's slangy analysis put you into the huddle, Cosell's pontificating—and it was certainly that—painted the bigger picture, the larger narrative.

Instantly, the ABC crew knew what they had. Not by the praise, but by the vituperative complaints. Or, as Geoff Mason would put it, "the first time we saw a headline in the *Chicago Tribune* or wherever that a bunch of people in Cornpone, Nebraska, were shooting the lights out of a TV set because they got so pissed off at Howard Cosell. We began to realize when we read that and other things, that this was indeed going beyond the normal bounds."

One of the features of the series that had the greatest impact was the package of halftime highlights that debuted in week one and became a staple. Americans, used to switching channels or heading to the kitchen when presented with marching bands at halftime, suddenly became even more rapt as halftime approached. Children pleaded to stay up past their bedtime to see the highlights of the previous day's games, which normally weren't available until later in the week on the syndicated telecasts of *This Week in the NFL*.

The packaged highlights from NFL Films were rushed from stadiums to NFL Films' offices and then flown to New York, where they were shown live, while Cosell read off of a shot sheet. It was the sort of thing ABC had been doing for years with its Sunday morning college football highlights show; but this was different—football highlights in prime time, in front of an audience of tens of millions of people.

In Oakland, the coach John Madden started having an assistant alert him when the Monday night game reached the half. At that point the Raiders staff would take their dinner break and watch the highlights.

"If you were not included, you called the network to complain," said Ernie Accorsi, the PR man for the Colts in 1970. "I remember calling Dennis Lewin, and I said, 'How could you not have our game with the Dolphins?' You wanted to be on there—that was a huge deal."

But *Monday Night Football*'s other phenomenon was that it became required viewing for most of the other players in the league, who rarely had the chance to watch their peers at work.

"Wherever I was, whatever I was doing, I had to be someplace that I could catch *Monday Night Football*," said the Steelers' Joe Greene. "The halftime highlights, because you couldn't get that anywhere else, and that would give you a recap of everything that happened that weekend. And, I must admit, Howard Cosell brought a lot to this."

There was no greater proof of *Monday Night Football*'s immediate impact than the grousing of other networks.

"ABC has lost sight of the fact that pro football is a game, not a show for three TV stars," complained CBS's Bill MacPhail. "What should we do, follow them with a team of Don Rickles, Milton Berle, and Mickey Rooney?"

Arledge, unfazed by the criticism, recognized that the technical brilliance with which the games were presented was beyond criticism. Those who disliked *Monday Night Football*, or claimed to, could only charge that it was a three-ring circus.

"Sport is a business, not a religion, and there is no sacred way things must be done," said Arledge. "The games aren't played in Westminster Abbey."

He wasn't finished. In 1971, he replaced Keith Jackson as play-by-play man with the player-turned-announcer Frank Gifford, who was generally popular with male viewers and plainly adored by female viewers.

Gifford, the subject of obsession in Frederick Exley's "fictional memoir" *A Fan's Notes*, had a golden aspect about him. He was assured without being overly polished. He was so attractive, so clearly comfortable in his own skin, that he conveyed the demeanor of a man who had nothing to prove.

There was something else. Gifford, though schooled at USC and having lived for more than a decade in New York City, still exuded a kind of Midwestern charm and politesse. There were no leering asides nor the choked urgency that so many announcers brought to bear. Gifford lacked the sharp precision of truly great play-by-play announcers like Dick Enberg, but fans of both genders liked him and forgave him.

By its second season, *Monday Night Football* had brought on a host of other viewers, like women and children, who'd not been exposed to the game before. The show merged a simulacrum of journalism (Cosell's mantra of "Tell it like it is") with elements of pure entertainment and show business—near the end of games, when the outcome was no longer in doubt, Meredith would serenade the TV audience with the strains of Willie Nelson's "(Turn Out the Lights) The Party's Over."

One measure of the cultural footprint of *Monday Night Football* came in 1972, when *The Bob Newhart Show* on CBS aired an episode called "Don't Go to Bed Mad," in which Bob and his wife, Emily, argue over his desire to watch *Monday Night Football*.

Almost all of the innovations were an expression of Arledge's sensibilities. And that made a difference. As the writer Ron Powers noted in his sports television history *Supertube,* "One of the most striking features of Arledge's TV-sports motif has been his attention to nuance, to subtle drama, to color and style, to all the various human relationships that unfold with the stadium—items of interest normally ascribed to a feminine sensibility."

So it wasn't surprising that, from the start, more than a third of the audience for *Monday Night Football* was female. That meant two things: 1) Sports really could succeed on prime-time television, and 2) to reach this larger, more casual audience, the broadcasts of the games would be packaged, dramatized, shaped into a coherent narrative structure. Sports would, forever more, become something else—entertainment as well.

By the end of the 1970 season, it was clear that the gamble had paid off for both ABC and the NFL, which was earning $41.6 million in television revenues, divvied among the twenty-six teams, each season.

The explosion in television money and the extinguishing of the war between the leagues had caused franchise values to grow exponentially. The Jets, purchased for $1 million in 1963, had sold for $20 million in 1968.

Rozelle was among the first to recognize that pro football wasn't merely successful, it was increasingly upscale. "Our demographics are such that an advertiser who pays a higher cost-per-1,000 for sponsoring pro football really has a better buy than if he paid much less for another program," he noted.

The Rubicon had been crossed. In the spring of 1971, Major League Baseball renewed its contract with NBC, adding a stipulation that Game 4 of the 1971 World Series, a Wednesday game, would be played at night, and broadcast in prime time. It earned an estimated audience of 61 million viewers, and along with the NFL's success, offered further proof that a major sports event could succeed in prime time.

And it followed from there. In 1972, the Olympics from Munich would dominate two weeks of prime-time coverage, creating a ratings juggernaut that wiped out all other competitors. In 1973, the NCAA national championship basketball game moved to prime time, as did "same-day coverage" of the Indianapolis 500.

Even as print still dominated, television's growing importance was recognized everywhere. After the ABA announced a contract with CBS to telecast their 1970 All-Star Game, New Orleans Buccaneers owner Maurice Stern said, "This will have a psychological effect on our fans. They realize when you get on TV it means somebody has enough faith in the league to sponsor it."

And as the money from the networks increased, as television's millions gravitated to the owners in various leagues, the players looked on, growing increasingly skeptical of the owners' perennial cries of poverty.

## FOUR

# DOWN TO BUSINESS

IN THE 1970 preseason, the Steelers' wide receiver Roy Jefferson was traded to the Baltimore Colts, who were on an extended road trip, training that week in Golden, Colorado. The deal was considered a coup for the Colts; Jefferson was a coveted difference-maker who'd led the NFL in receiving yards in 1968 and had been named All-Pro in 1969. But he'd also gained a reputation as a difficult player, and had been run out of Pittsburgh when the Steelers' coach Chuck Noll decided Jefferson was a poor influence on the team's younger players.

After flying to Colorado to meet the team, Jefferson showed up in shorts but not full pads to his first practice. An age-old custom in pro football held that newly acquired players were always timed in the forty-yard dash.

"Hey, Blub," Colts' head coach Don McCafferty said to assistant Dick "Blub" Bielski at the end of practice. "Go time him."

A few minutes later, McCafferty was back in his dorm room when an exasperated Bielski knocked on the door and said, "Um, Don? Yeah, he told me to go to hell."

Just then, as McCafferty was pondering his next move, John Mackey, the Colts' all-pro tight end and newly elected president of the NFL Players Association, ducked his head in McCafferty's door. "Coach," Mackey said, "Room him with me."

John Mackey would make sure Jefferson wouldn't be a problem.

With the Colts having lost the consummate wide receiver Raymond Berry to retirement a year earlier, the acquisition of Jefferson was pivotal. Rooming with Mackey in training camp, he soon adapted to his new surroundings and went on to have a standout season, playing an instrumental role in

Baltimore's resurgence and march toward a world championship in Super Bowl V.

Those on the Colts recognized the crucial role that Mackey performed in defusing the early situation. Voted the league's all-time tight end on the NFL's fiftieth anniversary team, he was as respected as he was liked. His open, oval face seemed to quickly take the measure of any scene he surveyed, and his engaging manner and willingness to listen made him both popular and influential with teammates.

"I never met a greater leader," said Ernie Accorsi of the Colts. "I never met a more charismatic leader. Everybody respected him to the utmost. Mackey was everything you'd want in a teammate."

Mackey had been elected president of the enlarged NFLPA (which now included all of the former AFL players) just days before Curt Flood filed his lawsuit in the beginning of 1970.

He understood that representing his fellow players would be a particularly challenging task; the culture of collective bargaining was not deeply ingrained in the NFL and the Players Association had traditionally earned little respect from the owners. The first meeting that summer in which Mackey met with NFL management as president of the NFLPA offered a portent of things to come. Both sides came to New York for a meeting that was originally scheduled for Westchester Country Club until it was brought to the league's attention that the club still didn't allow Black guests. Instead, the meeting was moved to the City Squire Hotel in Manhattan.

Tex Schramm, the gruff, domineering president of the Dallas Cowboys—generally heard before seen—was heading the owners' side of the negotiation, and their initial encounter that day fairly encapsulated both the generation gap and the racial divide in contemporary American life.

Schramm showed up dressed in his usual suit and tie. Mackey arrived resplendent in a purple velour jumpsuit.

There were no formalities.

"What the *hell* are you doing," Schramm demanded of Mackey, "showing up for this meeting in a purple jumpsuit?"

"I don't know, Tex," replied Mackey coolly, then pointed to Schramm's feet. "I could ask you what *you're* doing showing up for this meeting in white socks."

Schramm looked down at his feet and snorted. "I *like* white socks."

"Well, I like purple jumpsuits," replied Mackey. "Let's get on with it."

The ensuing negotiation was predictably unproductive, over some nominal changes to the players' pension fund, but it marked an early effort by the newly enlarged NFLPA to push for recognition and a toehold at collective bargaining.

"We thought if we could get *any* kind of agreement," said Bill Curry, the Colts' player rep, "that would be recognition that we were no longer going to be chattel, and we were not always going to be told where we were going to work every single year and on every single occasion."

At the time, the traditional beginning of the football season was the late-July matchup between the defending Super Bowl champion and a team of college All-Stars, comprised entirely of NFL rookies. In 1970, that was threatened by the owners locking the players out of training camp, and the players saying they wouldn't have reported anyway. (Mackey and the NFLPA gave the Chiefs special dispensation to play the game.)

At heart, the fight was about the pension plan; Major League owners contributed $5.4 million annually to their players' pension fund (with 600 active players each year), while owners in the enlarged NFL were scheduled to contribute only $2.8 million (with 1,040 active players each year). Three days after the College All-Star Game, the players and the owners settled. The agreement, concluding a twenty-two-hour negotiating session, called for a four-year deal with $19.1 million in pension and other benefits.

But they did so without finalizing the conditions. "I'm almost ashamed," said the Packers' Ken Bowman later in the fall. "Any union man will tell you that you don't put the workers back in the plant until it's all in black and white, with signatures from both sides. I'm fed up. I think John is as irate as I am. If it isn't settled, we would withhold our services again." (The grievance wound up going to the National Labor Relations Board, which ruled that the league must sign the agreement; after further machinations, the league eventually complied.)

•

The essential debate—not only about how much an athlete was worth, but what an athlete's rights should be—had been a point of contention since nearly the beginning of organized professional sports.

Yet in each of the four major team sports, a player under contract to a team was bound to that team for the duration of his playing career. Rookies had some bargaining power in the first half of the '60s in football when the AFL challenged the NFL. The same was true in basketball starting in 1967, when the ABA challenged the NBA. But those challenges by other leagues were unsustainable, and by the end of the '60s, each league had a players' association that endeavored to engage in collective bargaining.

So the heads of these associations started out with modest goals—securing a legitimate pension plan, increasing per diems and minimum salaries. Throughout the late '60s, the prospect of genuine free agency remained elusive.

"The idea that players were tied to their teams for life, like modern-day serfs, was so ingrained in professional sports that no one seriously sought to challenge it in court or at the bargaining table," said the lawyer Jim Quinn, who would serve as counsel to union leaders in multiple sports.

In baseball, the reserve rule—what Curt Flood went to court to protest—was backed up by Major League Baseball's antitrust exemption. Flood filed his suit against Major League Baseball on January 16, 1970, asking for $1.4 million in damages and for baseball to scrap its reserve clause.

When players reported for spring training in Florida and Arizona in February, Flood was in Copenhagen, corresponding with close friends like Bob Gibson and waiting for his trial.

While many old-school writers (and fans) saw Flood as an ungrateful egoist, *Sports Illustrated* was more circumspect. "The outcome of the lawsuit seems inevitable," predicted Robert W. Creamer in the magazine's Scorecard section. "The reserve clause in its present form will disappear."

As the case worked its way through the courts, the people in baseball remained keenly aware of the implications. "It was conceptual and theoretical at that point," recalled John Schuerholz, then in the Royals system. "But it was also frightening. Anyone who worked in baseball and said they weren't frightened is being disingenuous."

What they were frightened of, by then, was not only Flood, but the formidable Marvin Miller. On July 1, 1966, the Major League Baseball Players Association hired Miller as its first full-time executive director, straight from his job as an economist for the United Steelworkers. Miller had been born with a withered hand, but still exuded an air of urbane sophistication. Sporting the trim mustache, dapper style, and twinkling eyes of a '40s movie star, he was an instantly galvanizing presence.

When, in an early meeting with the commissioner Gen. William Eckert, in 1966, Miller bemoaned the minimum salary of $6,500, Eckert replied, "Why I know families of four in Japan that live quite comfortably on that amount."

Historically, the culture at the players' association had been one of accommodation (to the point that the owners had traditionally had veto power over the MLBPA's chief). Miller knew it would take time to help the players' views evolve. In the meantime, he began to work at the margins. In the spring of 1967, he coordinated a better deal with the Topps Company that had been printing baseball cards. The deal called for $250 per player, plus 8 percent of all sales up to $4 million, and 10 percent thereafter.

Even in these early pursuits, the owners disparaged Miller.

"The owners called him nothing but a one-armed bandit," said outfielder Ralph Garr. "But we knew he was the right man for the job."

Around the world of sports, Flood's stand was noted and discussed. "It was a stunning thing," said Bill Curry, center for the Colts. "We knew what a big deal it was, and what was being sacrificed. I'm not sure any of us understood he was sacrificing everything."

Though Flood would later be celebrated as a heroic pioneer, not a single active major league player testified on his behalf in the trial, which began in May 1970. Hall of Famers Jackie Robinson and Hank Greenberg did, as did the once and future owner Bill Veeck. Federal district court judge Irving Ben Cooper ruled in favor of Major League Baseball.

The original verdict was upheld by the U.S. Circuit Court of Appeals on April 7, 1971, by which time Flood had been traded again, this time to the Washington Senators. He'd agree to sign a contract with the stipulation that doing so would in no way affect his case against Major League Baseball.

But the layoff had been too long, the psychological stress on Flood too great, and before the end of April, he'd left the team and flown back to Europe, later sending a telegram to the Senators' owner, Robert Short, in which he said, "I tried. A year and a half is too much. Very serious problems mounting every day. Thanks for your confidence and understanding."

The case was eventually argued in front of the Supreme Court on March 20, 1972. It was a shockingly poor performance by Flood's lawyer Arthur Goldberg, the former Supreme Court justice, in front of his erstwhile peers on the court. He seemed curiously unprepared and ill-informed, and bumbled through his oral argument as Flood looked on in bewilderment.

Throughout, Major League Baseball had held firm to its position. "The reserve clause is reasonable," said commissioner Bowie Kuhn. "The court has no jurisdiction. It boils down to a collective bargaining process and not an antitrust action."

In the end, when the decision was handed down on June 19 of that year, the court ruled by a five-to-three margin in favor of Major League Baseball, though the decision also described baseball's antitrust exemption as "aberrant," and Chief Justice Warren Burger joined the majority with "grave reservations."

But Flood's stand, and Miller's direction, had galvanized the players' association. In the two years that the case wound its way through the courts, the players had grown more unified. Prior to the 1972 season, Miller and the owners were negotiating for new terms in the players' pension plan, for which Miller was asking for an increase commensurate with the cost-of-living increases over the previous years.

In the days leading up to the strike deadline, the Cards' owner, Gussie Busch, was heard from again. "We voted unanimously to take a stand," he said of his fellow owners. "We're not going to give them another goddamn cent! If they want to strike, let them strike."

By that point, sixteen of the previous year's twenty-four player reps had been cut or traded, but Miller had his troops in line. He had counseled caution—even asked the player reps to consider delaying a strike for another year—but the reps and their deputies voted 47–0 in favor of the strike action, to start April 1, just five days before the scheduled opening day.

"I'll never forget his stance, standing up there," said the Pirates' Steve Blass. "Marvin would stand up and he had a birth defect, so he had a withered arm. And he would have small pieces of paper, maybe half the size of a yellow legal tablet, kind of wrapped around his hand, and he worked from those notes for about an hour. He said, 'This can work, guys—this can work for us and it can work for the owners too. So we need to be strong because it is the right thing to do.' And we believed him because he had made some strides. And so in '72, it was the same kind of theme. He said, 'This is not going to wreck baseball. They're saying this is going to wreck baseball, but it's not.' He had his act together."

After the strike vote, Miller was on a late connecting flight through Baltimore to New York, when he encountered the New York Knicks, fresh off an overtime loss in Game 1 of their conference semifinal series against the Baltimore Bullets. "The Knicks greeted us with cries of 'Right on!'" recalled Miller. Several of the players commiserated with Miller on the flight, and Bill Bradley followed up a few days later with a letter to the editor of the *New York Daily News*, refuting a Dick Young column critical of Miller.

On April 1, 1972, the strike began, the first ever in American sports to cause the cancellation of games. In *The Sporting News*, editor C. C. Johnson Spink described the strike as "the darkest day in sports history." The Braves' GM Paul Richards said, "Tojo and Hirohito couldn't stop baseball but Marvin Miller could."

Then, not for the last time, the owners blinked.

The strike ended twelve days later with a settlement that provided an additional $490,000 to the players' pension plan. The owners were sullen and embittered. Gussie Busch ordered the front office to announce that Cardinals players would no longer be able to room alone on the road, but instead would be roomed in pairs so the club could save $10,000. When Bob Gibson got into a jam in the first inning of the opener against Montreal, one fan yelled, "Hurry up, I've got to go to a union meeting!"

For baseball's owners, there were only dark skies. "We have reached the saturation point insofar as our player payroll is concerned," said Cubs president John Holland. "If it goes any higher, we just can't make it."

•

Throughout the '60s, even as the Celtics were dominating the NBA with their string of titles, few people questioned who the best all-around player in basketball was. Though he was outgunned at every turn by playing on the poorly run, underfunded Cincinnati Royals, the phenomenal Oscar Robertson—a six-foot-five guard who could muscle with forwards and rebound with centers—was an astonishingly effective hybrid player.

Robertson had the great player's tetchy impatience, which meant he was not only respected but also feared by his teammates. During the 1969–70 season, even as he labored through a season of discontent playing for Bob Cousy in Cincinnati, he also met regularly with Larry Fleisher, the executive director of the National Basketball Players Association.

As Marvin Miller's opposite number in pro basketball, Lawrence "Larry" Fleisher, a graduate of Harvard Law, was just as idealistic, though somewhat less confrontational than Miller. Miller was crisply refined; Fleisher tended toward a more rumpled look. His father, Morris, had run a print shop in Manhattan and was a proud, card-carrying Communist in the '30s, but the son was more practical, and developed a love for sports, from stickball to basketball.

In 1962, he became the president of the players' association and later represented Bill Bradley when he finished his Rhodes Scholarship and signed with the Knicks.

"It was unbelievable to me when I came to the NBA there was no pension, no health benefits, meal money maybe eight dollars," Bradley said. "Larry was the lawyer for my first contract and a friend. We would strategize about what could be done. Larry was so important in everything that happened."

Fleisher realized that the association needed to act quickly in the spring of 1970 when rumors started spreading that a secret committee of ABA and NBA owners were hammering out a deal, with ten ABA teams moving into the NBA (save for the Virginia Squires, who were deemed too close to the Baltimore Bullets' territory). Each of the ABA teams would pay the NBA $125,000 a year for ten years, a total entry fee of $12.5 million.

That's when Fleisher huddled with The Big O. Robertson was as devoted to Fleisher as Fleisher was to the players' association. "[W]henever Larry called me and said, 'O, hey, we need a meeting,' I was there," wrote Robertson in his autobiography. "Larry used to say that I had the one great talent necessary for an effective labor negotiator: always distrust the other side."

Robertson was the lead plaintiff in a suit filed on April 16, 1970, against the NBA, in the same courthouse in the Southern District of New York that Flood had filed his suit. All fourteen of the other player reps—including the Celtics' John Havlicek, Robertson's Bucks teammate Jon McGlocklin, the Suns' Paul Silas and the Knicks' Dave DeBusschere—were also listed in the suit, which claimed that the proposed merger between the leagues would make pro basketball a monopoly and would be a violation of the Sherman Antitrust Act.

The request for a temporary restraining order would eventually be upheld by Judge Robert L. Carter, who'd served on Thurgood Marshall's legal team in the epochal *Brown v. Board of Education* case in 1954.

With the merger on hold, the ABA was struggling to merely survive. After George Mikan resigned (rather than be fired) in the aftermath of the Lew Alcindor debacle, the ABA hired Jack Dolph, former director at CBS Sports, figuring that Dolph's connections would lead to a TV contract.

Dolph did get the 1971 ABA All-Star Game televised on CBS, but that same weekend, in a conference room with writers in attendance, Dolph absentmindedly left his briefcase open, and reporters saw signed contracts with Villanova's Howard Porter and Western Kentucky's Jim McDaniels, both of whom were still in college. Porter and McDaniels would lead their teams to the NCAA Final Four that season, but Dolph's bit of executive buffoonery meant both schools eventually had to forfeit their tournament prize money because signing the contracts had rendered Porter and McDaniels ineligible.

The ABA was already in court over having signed the gifted power forward Spencer Haywood before his college eligibility ran out. In March 1971, the Supreme Court ruled 7–2 that Haywood shouldn't be prohibited from pursuing a pro career until his college class graduated. Just as in the previous decade, when the AFL and NFL battled over rookies, the bidding wars brought cash-strapped teams on both sides to the negotiating table.

In the meantime, the proposed merger agreement would be vetted by the Senate Subcommittee on Antitrust and Monopoly, chaired by Sam Ervin, the magisterial North Carolinian who would soon become a key player in the Watergate hearings. While the committee approved in theory a merger between the leagues on September 8, 1972, it also stipulated that the reserve clause, as presently written, couldn't be part of an agreement.

With that avenue cut off, and the Robertson case still in court, the two sides faced a prolonged stalemate.

At one of the merger meetings with owners from both leagues present, the idea was floated that the reserve clause should be dropped so the ABA–NBA merger would have the blessing of Congress.

But the Knicks' president Ned Irish remained adamant. "We'll never give up the reserve clause."

After he stormed out of the meeting, Dick Tinkham of the ABA's Pacers asked the Sonics' owner Sam Schulman to talk to Irish. "He won't change his mind," Schulman said. "Besides, whatever the Knicks want, the NBA will do."

This was perhaps not literally true, but close enough as to make no difference. The NBA offices at the time were located in the building above Madison Square Garden, at 2 Penn Plaza. That made the league, technically, the tenant of the Knicks.

•

The NFL nominally allowed player movement, but with a crippling caveat. After playing out his option, a player could sign with another team, but then the original team must be compensated. When teams couldn't agree on fair compensation—which was essentially all the time—commissioner Pete Rozelle would decide on the compensation.

The league's compensation rule, known throughout football circles as "The Rozelle Rule," had a predictably chilling effect. When the 49ers' wide receiver Dave Parks signed with the Saints prior to the 1968 season, he was coming off an injury-plagued year in which he caught 26 passes for 313 yards. Rozelle awarded the 49ers two first-round draft choices (which became Ted Kwalick, seventh overall in 1969, and Cedrick Hardman, tenth overall in 1970) as compensation. Due to awards like that, teams in the NFL almost never signed free agents, because the consequences invariably weakened the team doing the signing.

Within three years, John Mackey would file a lawsuit against the NFL seeking the same thing that Curt Flood sought in baseball and that Oscar Robertson sought in basketball: the opportunity for a veteran player, at some point, to have the option to test his value on the open market. Each player wound up staking his career on a lawsuit that challenged the reserve rule in professional sports. All three players were All-Stars. All three were consummate team leaders. And all three were African American.

In retrospect, this seems not a coincidence.

"Black players, who are the leaders and form the majority of the union, found it easy to doubt the lofty promises offered by owners as substitutes for meeting player demands," Bill Bradley wrote in his playing days memoir *Life on the Run*, though his analysis applied in other team sports as well. "Many white players, accustomed to father/son relationships with white coaches, general managers, and owners, hesitated at first but then slowly realized that major gains were possible only if everyone stayed together."

The Steelers' defensive tackle Joe Greene, a one-year vet when the 1970 strike began, had already noticed a trend.

"Anything that had anything to do with taking away my freedom," said Joe Greene, "it was the black athletes that spoke out. And I wonder why. Maybe because we didn't have enough sense to be afraid of what the repercussions were? No, that's too easy. We were probably more tuned in to the things that would rob us of our freedom or our rights."

And so those three men—Flood, Robertson and Mackey—would risk it all to press their case. "The reality is that, virtually simultaneously, because the Flood suit and the Robertson suit were filed within a few months of each other, and the Mackey suit was filed later, but they were all going simultaneously," said Jim Quinn. "And they were all seeking essentially the same thing, which was some level of freedom, in the sense of economic freedom, so that they could cash in on what their *actual* value was."

•

In the wake of the protracted debate, there was ample evidence in another realm of the sports world that athletes deserved a bigger share of the vast amount of money fans were paying.

The political scientist Andrew Hacker somewhat prematurely announced 1970 as "the end of the American era," arguing that the United States was no longer a nation, but instead a collection of "two hundred million egos." The grandest ego in the country may well have belonged to Muhammad Ali, whose unignorable presence in the previous decade carried over into the next.

Fully six years after converting to Islam, Ali remained a divisive figure, facing the prospect of five years in a federal prison for refusing induction into the military. The case was still on appeal in 1970 when promoters found a way around the strictures that most state boxing commissions placed against licensing. Ali would return to the ring for an October 26 fight against Jerry Quarry in Atlanta, Ali's first bout since the spring of 1967.

Ali's comeback featured a landmark moment in American history, the mainstream acknowledgment of Atlanta as a fount of Black culture. "From every corner of the country and world they came," wrote Mark Kram in *Sports Illustrated,* "in brilliant plumage, the most startling assembly of black power and black money ever displayed."

Ali's entourage for the fight was tour bus–sized, and left from an Atlanta hotel. (Coretta Scott King, slated to ride on the bus, was running late and was left behind.) Sidney Poitier stopped by Ali's dressing room in the minutes before the fight.

Waiting for Ali in the ring was the latest, not-so-great white hope, the brawny Jerry Quarry from California. Then to raucous applause, stepping through the ropes in white satin trunks with black trim, appearing like an apparition, 1,314 days after his last fight, there at last was Ali.

That night also marked the return of the man who served an essential but ineffable role in the Ali universe, Drew "Bundini" Brown, the confidant, consigliere, and cheerleader for which there had never really been an analog in the history of professional sports; Ben Hogan never had a hype man.

Ali showed rust in the return bout but retained the core of his remarkable skills. Bundini, from the first round on, resumed regularly scheduled programming after the three-and-a-half-year interruption, shouting, "We here all night!" every time Ali tagged Quarry with a left jab in the first round, which was often. The fight ended by the fourth round, with Quarry's face reduced to a bloody mess.

There was one more tune-up, against the awkward, difficult Argentine Oscar Bonavena, who accused Ali of cowardice ("You chicken...you no go in Army") at the weigh-in, and lasted into the fifteenth round before Ali scored a TKO. At ringside, the heavyweight champion Joe Frazier described the fight as "the dullest I ever saw."

By that time, Frazier and Ali were already inextricably linked, two fighters on a collision course that spoke to the anguished, conflicted moment in American history.

Joe Frazier often had the expression of a man just realizing that something important in his life wasn't quite working out. The 1964 Olympic heavyweight champion was easily stereotyped—by both the media and by Ali—but had already surmounted a series of forbidding obstacles and emerged his own man. His father, a sharecropper in South Carolina, lost an arm in a farming accident. Joe toiled on the farm before eventually taking a Greyhound bus up north, settling in Philadelphia, where he began his amateur boxing career. After winning the gold in Tokyo, he turned pro and worked his way up the rankings. In Ali's absence, Jimmy Ellis had won a tournament sponsored by the World Boxing Association to fill the vacated heavyweight championship. Frazier, who'd declined to compete in the tournament to protest the WBA's decision to strip Ali of his title, defeated Ellis in four rounds to assume the title in February 1970.

Frazier understood better than anyone that he needed to beat Ali to be considered a true champion. The two men had been circling each other for years, wary but friendly while preparing for a confrontation that they both wanted.

While Frazier was often depicted as a rural country bumpkin, he in fact had his own measure of flamboyance; he was seriously intent on pursuing a singing career, and routinely sported a pinky ring with a three-and-a-half-carat diamond. As the Ali fight neared, Frazier even ventured toward a design innovation. Discussing a new boxing robe with a seamstress in 1970, Frazier ordered, "Make me a good one this time. I want it green because that's my color and I'm going to stick with it, and I want gold flecks on it. What's flecks? You know how Liberace has his jackets made? That's flecks."

By the end of the year, the stage was set for the first-ever confrontation between two undefeated heavyweight champions—"The Fight of the Century"—between Ali and Frazier on March 8, 1971, in Madison Square Garden.

The appeal of the fight was obvious. So, too, was the degree to which the promise of Ali–Frazier transcended sports. Here was the boastful, draft-dodging Black Muslim Ali representing much of the new stridency of modern American culture. He was matched against the sullen but respectful Frazier, a man of more conventional bent. Whom you were rooting for often said something about the sort of person you were.

The top bid for the bout was an unthinkable $2.5 million guaranteed to each boxer from a consortium led by the longtime MCA agent and entrepreneur Jerry Perenchio and the Los Angeles Lakers' owner Jack Kent Cooke. "I knew right away I wanted it," Perenchio said. "This was the sort of thing I'd been training twenty years for."

Perenchio had lived a riches-to-rags adolescence. The son of A. J. Perenchio, co-owner of Sunnyside Winery, he went to private schools, only to see his father go broke once the son started at UCLA. So the younger Perenchio hustled, booking bands for frat parties and dances up and down the West Coast, later rising through MCA as an agent and protégé of chairman Lew Wasserman. He opened his own talent agency, Chartwell Artists, whose clients included Glen Campbell, Henry Mancini and Andy Williams. In 1968, he bought the Chartwell Estate that had been used as the location for the 1960s sitcom *The Beverly Hillbillies*.

"This one transcends boxing," promised Perenchio in the buildup. "It's a show business spectacular. You've got to throw away the book on this fight. It's potentially the greatest grosser in the history of the world."

With a keen eye to the deal, he and Cooke recognized that a big guarantee would likely earn the trust of Ali and Frazier, and also give the promoters more latitude to keep the profit from the closed-circuit broadcast rights.

"Once Jerry put $2.5 million out there for each fighter, it was closed," said the boxing promoter Bob Arum. "That blew everyone's mind. No fighter had ever made anything like that in the history of boxing, not Jack Dempsey, not Gene Tunney, not Louis, nobody!"

In fact, nobody in the history of sports had made that kind of money. Ali–Frazier was an event that hinted at the riches sports could bring. The cultural resonance was what made the fight so wildly discussed, but it was the purse that landed the two boxers on the cover of *Time* magazine, under the headline, "The $5,000,000 Fighters."

With Perenchio's direction, the event was billed like a major movie premiere—"THE FIGHT" read the billing on the match program, with profile shots of Ali and Frazier beneath a shot of Madison Square Garden's glimmering ceiling.

It was the kind of fight for which the writer George Plimpton would throw a pre-bout party at Elaine's, attended by Norman Mailer, Pete Hamill, Bruce

Jay Friedman and dozens of other luminaries from the world of literature and the arts.

While Ali was still an undeniably polarizing figure, his constituency had grown considerably since he was stripped of his title. College students, white intellectuals, anti-war protesters—an odd alliance of acolytes—had rallied to his cause. It helped that the Vietnam War was far less popular than it had been in 1967, and a consensus was building that Ali's anti-war stance was sincere. But there was something more at work—a sense within much of the culture that his declamations weren't disrespectful so much as celebratory. Ali hadn't changed his message considerably; what was beginning to change was America.

While Ali's popularity in the Black community was a given, there was complexity even to that. Growing up in Philadelphia, the writer Gerald Early remembered identifying with Frazier even as he preferred Ali.

"If you want to look at it in a certain way, Ali represented the new black person, and Frazier was the old Negro," said Early. "So there it was. I had a certain kind of sympathy with that, and Frazier reminded me of my uncles, and the black men I grew up with in the neighborhood. I kind of knew people like Joe Frazier. I had never known *anybody* like Muhammad Ali."

On the eve of the fight, visited by writers to his hotel suite at the New Yorker, Ali doubled down on his framing of Frazier as an Uncle Tom and the white man's choice. "Frazier's no real champion," Ali charged. "Nobody wants to talk to him. Oh, maybe Nixon. Nixon will call him if he wins. I don't think he'll call me."

On the night of March 8, 1971, people flocked by the tens of thousands to halls and arenas, auditoriums and stadiums, to watch the closed-circuit broadcast. In Memphis, a sold-out crowd at Ellis Auditorium was packed, and included the Ali supporter Elvis Presley, decked out in a $10,000 gold belt for the occasion.

And at Madison Square Garden on the night was... well, everybody. "Stars of stage and screen" doesn't really begin to do it justice. Frank Sinatra was at ringside, shooting photographs for *Life* magazine. Burt Lancaster was doing color commentary for the closed-circuit broadcast. Miles Davis sat close to the ring. The French actor Jean-Paul Belmondo accompanied the Italian actress Antonella Lualdi. Isaac Hayes was there, as was Duke Ellington. Joe

Namath attended. Sammy Davis Jr. was there, as were Jack Nicholson, Robert Redford and Barbra Streisand. So was Diana Ross, sporting black hot pants. The Bruins' Bobby Orr, longtime Ali fan, was close to ringside. So were Bob Dylan and Diane Keaton. The Knicks had the night off, so Walt "Clyde" Frazier was in attendance, as was the fanatical Knick follower Woody Allen. Dustin Hoffman and Hugh Hefner were there, the latter with Barbi Benton, who got more attention due to her see-through blouse. Perhaps never before had such a wide swath of American culture—high, low, Black, white, movies, music, sports—ever assembled for a single event.

If the fight was unprecedented, then so was the fashion. And it wasn't only the crowd that dressed up. For decades boxing matches paired fighters in two of three different hues of trunks: white, black, or blue. But in this instance, on this stage, in this decade, nothing so mundane would have sufficed. So Ali arrived, for the first time in his career, in red trunks with white trim, sporting red tassels on his white boxing boots. Frazier's designer had accommodated Smokin' Joe's request for "flecks," and he sported trunks in a jazzy print of green and gold.

The fight itself somehow lived up to the impossible hype, a perfect blend of styles. Ali's flowing movement, and his lightning jab from his superior height and reach, meant he was always within striking distance. Frazier, coiled but relentless, bobbed and weaved. Even though he was shorter and slower than Ali, his deceptive, crablike movements made him a surprisingly elusive target. Cutting off the ring from Ali, he burrowed into the previous champ's midsection, and from close quarters, fired off his dreaded left hook.

The battle ebbed back and forth. Ali could still move, but Frazier was implacable. Absorbing punishment in the face from Ali's jabs, he kept moving in, punishing Ali with body blows and finally connecting with a fierce hook that knocked Ali down in the fifteenth round. It was a startling moment, as shocking to the crowd as it was to Ali himself.

The fight had been close, but Frazier's stamina and the late knockdown made the decision inevitable. In the commotion after the bell to end the fight, as the fighters moved unsteadily to their respective corners, having survived the draining spectacle, "Bundini" Brown was already in tears, in the forefront of the Ali partisans who'd experienced the unthinkable, watching their prince defiled.

The unanimous decision brought a sense of vengeful glee to the pro-Frazier cohort in the crowd. Just a few feet away from the ring, the German actor Curd Jürgens stood with his wife, the model Simone Bicheron, and, glaring at Ali, said, "He deserved it. He *deserved* that beating."

And at the White House that night, the inveterate sports fan Richard Nixon, who'd arranged to have the closed-circuit broadcast screened at his residence, celebrated Frazier's decision over "that draft dodger asshole."

In the aftermath of the fight, Frazier sat for the press with a face that was a collage of bumps and bruises. He was at once proud of his accomplishment and respectful of Ali. "Let me go and straighten out my face," he said in concluding his post-fight press conference. "I ain't really quite this ugly." Though Frazier had won, the punishment he endured was enough to keep him hospitalized for an extended stay.

"End of the Ali Legend," blared one headline—but rumors of Ali's demise would prove premature. In the hours and days that followed, something curious happened. Ali, the malcontent that white America wanted silenced, became gracious, nearly gallant, in defeat. Like all the great champions before him, he recognized the greatness of his opponent.

Ali's case had been appealed all the way to the Supreme Court where, on April 19, 1971, oral arguments were heard in the case of *Cassius Marsellus Clay, Jr. v. United States*. (Ali had not legally changed his name when converting to Islam in the '60s.) On the morning of June 28, 1971, the decision came down, with the court deciding in a unanimous opinion to overturn the conviction.

In this, too, the hyperkinetic Ali seemed atypically serene and at peace. He cast no aspersions. "They only did what they thought was right," he said. "That was all. I can't condemn them."

Another reporter started to ask a question. "Champ—" he said, but Ali cut him off.

"Don't call me the champ," he said quietly. "Joe's the champ now."

Somehow, Frazier, for so long hailed the white man's hope to quiet the loud Black Muslim, became smaller, not larger, in victory. The call from the president never did come that night. And the white America that had seemed to embrace him beforehand suddenly cooled. Embarking on a concert tour of the U.S. with his soul backing band the Knockouts, Frazier played in front of fewer than 100 people at San Francisco's Winterland.

Things did not improve during the European tour in the spring of 1971 that had been scheduled as a victory lap for Frazier, proof that he was every bit the multi-talented hyphenate that the writer-debater-poet-actor Ali wanted to be. But Frazier, who now had the rightful claim to be the undisputed heavyweight champion of the world, didn't have that ineffable appeal that Ali would forever possess. There were more than 6,000 empty seats in the 7,000-seat Pellikaan Hall near Amsterdam, and just 250 people buying tickets in Cologne. Frazier sold just 28 tickets for a show in a 3,000-seat hall in Copenhagen. Upon his return to the U.S., Frazier said, "Man, you can't club people over the head to make them come out."

•

Jack Kent Cooke and Jerry Perenchio made out gloriously well, reaping as much as $20 million in profits from the closed-circuit deals they struck. But Ali–Frazier was a commercial success because it had transcended boxing and sports and every other rail and boundary in American culture.

"If there had never been a Vietnam War, and if Ali had not been stripped of his crown, he would most likely have taken on Frazier in 1968 or 1969," wrote Michael Arkush in his book *The Fight of the Century*. "They would not have done a commercial for Vitalis hair products. They would not have appeared on the covers of *Time* and *Life*. Ali vs. Frazier would not have been the fight of the century or even the fight of the decade. But there was a war, which tore two countries apart."

In the aftermath of the fight that night in New York, at the end of the post-fight party hosted by Jerry and Jacquelyn Perenchio, after Burt Lancaster had booted out his drunken friend Patrick O'Neal, Perenchio was still hyper with the heady thrill of it all.

"Do you think I'll ever do anything as big again?" he asked his wife.

The answer, it turned out, would be yes, and it would come two and a half years later, in another encounter that Perenchio would promote as the battle for the ages.

That event wouldn't involve Ali, but instead another athlete who was in attendance that night at Madison Square Garden.

Her name was Billie Jean King. Like Ali, she had a cause.

# FIVE

# A WOMAN'S PLACE

HALF THE HUMAN race is female," wrote Elizabeth Janeway in *Saturday Review* in 1969. "It is sometimes difficult to remember this, even for a female; and never more difficult than when reading history."

As the new decade dawned with a greater awareness of the double standards in American life, the condition of women still lagged behind. The median salary for women was 48 percent of that for men, and they received 40 percent less pay than men for identical jobs. Forty-three states limited the number of hours that women could work a week, preventing them from getting overtime pay. It remained exceedingly difficult for a woman to get a credit card unless a male authority figure—a husband, a father, a boss—signed for it. Even New York governor Nelson Rockefeller sheepishly admitted that the laws were "more often protective of men," a fairly massive understatement.

Women in prominent positions weren't just rare; they were becoming rarer. There hadn't been a woman cabinet member since 1955, and there were only eleven female members of Congress, down from seventeen in 1960. The number of women on college faculties had actually declined, from 28 percent in 1939 to 18 percent in 1966.

But throughout the country at the beginning of the '70s, to a degree that the mainstream culture was not yet equipped to deal with, women were experiencing an epiphany—the "initial feminist understanding," in the words of *Village Voice* columnist Vivian Gornick.

"We have suddenly and shockingly perceived the basic disorder," wrote *Ms.* magazine co-founder Jane O'Reilly, "in what has been believed to be the natural order of things."

What was true in the general society was even more true for the universe of American sports, where women were not so much marginalized as ignored, less overlooked then simply invisible.

"I had gotten quite angry by that time," said Peg Burke, physical education professor at the University of Iowa, "because I had realized how discriminated against I had been, and how much discrimination I had allowed to be visited on my students. And once you cross that bridge of seeing the inequality, it's a one-way bridge, you can't re-cross it."

And yet, beneath the radar of mainstream sports, a seismic shift had already commenced.

•

The revolution began with an heiress.

Doris Duke was, for a time in the 1930s, not merely "the richest girl in the world," but also, quite possibly, the richest athlete in the world. The daughter of James Buchanan Duke—for whom Duke University was renamed upon his death in 1924—she grew up athletic and adventuresome, possessing both financial clout and the casual impertinence about the flouting of social norms that would inspire made-for-TV movies and dishy *Vanity Fair* profiles long after her death in 1993.

In the course of her life, she became a champion swimmer and canoe racer, learned surfboarding in Hawaii from Olympic gold medalist Duke Kahanamoku and his brother Sam, fell into and out of love with Duke, may or may not have had affairs with Gen. George Patton, Marlon Brando, and Errol Flynn, and donated millions to Margaret Sanger and the cause of women's reproductive rights.

On one of her philanthropic binges, in 1960, she donated $500,000 to the United States Olympic Committee in an effort to improve the performance of American women in Olympic sports. In the heart of Cold War competitiveness, and in the face of Soviet success in Olympic sports, the USOC became more focused on training a new generation of elite female athletes.

A half million dollars went a long way in the '60s and was allocated toward a handful of weeklong gatherings called "The National Institute on Girls' Sports." From the first National Institute—held in 1963 at the University of Oklahoma and focused on gymnastics and track and field—the gatherings were designed not to identify exceptional female athletes, but rather to find a new generation of coaches and teachers. The Institutes aimed to inculcate the best practices for teaching sports to hundreds of women, who in turn would teach and coach the next generation of female Olympic medalists. Female physical education teachers, coaches and administrators from around the country were invited to take part, with the understanding that, following a week of intensive hands-on practice and instruction, each would go back to her state and conduct her own series of clinics. "Each one teach one" was the motto, with the idea that, across the years and many different sports, the Institutes would be the catalyst for future excellence.

Billie Moore might have been Exhibit A. She had grown up a tomboy in the northeast Kansas town of Westmoreland, playing basketball and baseball with her brothers. She was tall, strong, and smart, and she absorbed the ethos of sports from her father, who coached the boys' high school basketball team in town. She learned a jump shot early playing with the boys, and became a terror in softball.

But things changed when the family moved to the bigger city of Topeka. Like a lot of American cities in postwar America, where cultural norms about gender roles were more rigid, there was little infrastructure for girls' team sports. Moore's love for sports didn't diminish, but it no longer had an outlet in a school setting. By her high school years, she had joined an elite women's team in the Amateur Softball Association. She stayed in Topeka and went to Washburn University. After graduation, she got a job in Topeka, teaching physical education classes at Boswell Junior High School.

Then one day in the fall of 1966, her principal told Moore she'd been invited to attend the Fourth National Institute on Girls' Sports, held December 3–10 at Indiana University in Bloomington. As the afternoon bell rang at Boswell that Friday afternoon, December 2, Moore loaded up her car and drove the eight hours to Bloomington.

The Fourth Institute was devoted to basketball and volleyball, and in each discipline, invites had been sent out, usually to two women from each of the fifty states. On that first Saturday, they posed for a group picture and then dressed out for the on-court sessions. For the next week 100 women were drilled in the finer points of basketball and, elsewhere on the IU campus, another 100 women studied the modern techniques of coaching volleyball.

On the basketball side, the different groups were divided up by names of characters from Charles Schulz's *Peanuts*, the popular comic strip already recognized among careful readers as being sympathetic to the idea of women's athletics (Charlie Brown's baseball team was co-ed, and a new character, the tomboy athlete Peppermint Patty, had been introduced the previous summer). The women received a week's worth of on-court instruction and blackboard sessions, all dedicated to the deeper understanding of basketball and its tactics. There were weave drills and in-depth discussions of free throw and jump ball situations, lessons on zone defense—with and without a chaser—and how to use screens to free up shooters. At the end of the day's sessions, there were scrimmages. At night, in the dorms, the sound of weary chatter and the smell of Ben-Gay pervaded the hallways.

One of the women in Billie Moore's assigned group was Charlotte West, a robust, athletic shooter with a wry sense of humor, who matched Moore in both competitiveness and prior knowledge. West had a questing spirit. She had grown up in Florida, smart and inquisitive and absolutely liberated by playing sports. After graduating from Florida State, she earned a master's degree from North Carolina–Greensboro and a doctorate from Wisconsin–Madison. Along the way, she landed as a professor at Southern Illinois, where she saw with clarity that she wanted to devote her life to the idea of women's enlightenment through athletics and physical education. At SIU she taught classes in math and education, served as the women's athletic director, and coached the women's teams in basketball, golf and softball.

They were kindred spirits. Moore liked West's no-nonsense competence—she was comfortable on the court—and West immediately noticed that Moore was confident in her abilities and possessed a true jump shot (the set shot still being de rigueur in much of the women's game).

Both women found, as the week progressed, they shared a set of assumptions. They reveled in the seriousness of sports, which was unusual enough for American women in 1966. Beyond that, neither felt the need to apologize for that passion, which was virtually unheard of at the time.

For Moore, the week offered a revelation, a sense of a possible world that stretched far beyond square-dance lessons and games of dodgeball for junior high schoolers in Topeka. For her part, West was impressed with Moore's competitiveness, tempered by her Midwestern politesse. "We had a couple of women who wanted to tell us how to do everything," said West. "And Billie's disdain for that was the same as mine."

At the end of the week, West made the pitch to Moore: Come to SIU, work on an advanced degree, be my assistant coach for the basketball team. In the fall of 1967, Moore made the leap, moved to Carbondale, and began working on her master's thesis on self-teaching the jump shot.

"I remember being so impressed with her approach to physical education and athletics," said Moore. "I had never separated those things out, always just thought of physical education. But in their world, athletics—this competitive side—was something completely different. And for me, when I was at Washburn my four years there, competition was not something you were supposed to be proud of. At Southern Illinois, that was a very vital and important part of what they were doing, and that was an eye-opening experience for me."

In later years, Moore would often say that if she'd never gone to the National Institute and met West, she'd have spent her whole career as a PE teacher in Topeka. At SIU, she realized that her true desire was to follow her father into coaching. She understood something else intuitively: She wasn't going to be coaching *women*. She was going to do just what her father did; she was going to be coaching *basketball*.

•

The National Institutes were pushing against some long-established cultural forces.

Throughout much of American society at the end of the 1960s, the conventional wisdom held that sports was something that only boys and grown men did, as well as something that only boys and grown men watched.

This was reflected in countless ways, most visibly in the wide range of resources devoted to men's and women's sport at major colleges. One school district in Texas allotted $250,000 for boys' athletics, compared to $970 for girls. At the University of Michigan, the men's athletic budget was $1 million. For women it was $0.

Historically, female physical educators tended to frown on overly competitive pursuits. At the Wellesley College gymnasium, across the top of the wall read the epigraph, "Ever gentle and soft as a lady." Those were fighting words to women like Carole Oglesby, another elite softball player and academic who attended the Fourth National Institute to study volleyball. During her time at Purdue in the late '60s, she had volunteered to coach volleyball and softball, about which she was an expert, as well as gymnastics and swimming, about which she was a novice. "We had no money, no time, no support, no expertise," she'd recall later. "It was a really difficult situation."

Women in high schools or colleges seeking athletic outlets often had to settle for "play days," a female variant of field days in which schools would gather and play a variety of games, with the emphasis always on participation rather than competition. One of the characteristics of play days—and one of the reasons women athletes like Charlotte West despised them—was that the schools didn't compete, but were divvied up with different women from different schools forming temporary teams. This reflected a common aversion, in much of women's physical education, to anything that even remotely resembled competition.

In 1970 in the U.S., only one girl out of every twenty-seven participated in organized high school team sports. In Illinois, and several other states, high school team sports for girls weren't merely discouraged, they were prohibited. It was written in the bylaws of Little League Baseball and the National Collegiate Athletic Association specified those organizations were for males only.

Such was the challenge facing Charlotte West. "Our players were coming out of high school with zero—I mean, zero—competitive experience," she said. "If our Carbondale Community High School players would go eight miles and play the Murfreesboro High School then the men would be disqualified from their state championship."

Governance for women's athletics, such as it was, belonged to the Division for Girls and Women's Sport (DGWS), a group within the American Alliance for Health, Physical Education and Recreation (AAHPER), a nationwide organization of physical education professionals who were exceedingly fond of acronyms, and viewed with suspicion anything that smacked of competition.

Yet within DGWS there was a new generation of women who recognized the need for greater athletic opportunities for elite female athletes. In 1966, the cohort founded the Commission on Intercollegiate Athletics for Women (CIAW), whose purpose was to explore the sanctioning of intercollegiate competition and national championships.

Among the women who organized the CIAW was the charismatic

academic Katherine "Tyke" Ley, who viewed athletics for women as an essential outlet too long denied. As chair of the department of physical education at the State University of New York, Cortland campus, she was one of the intellectual lodestars of the movement, and a key figure in the push to give elite female athletes an arena of competition.

By 1969, CIAW was sponsoring national events in gymnastics and track and field. That same year, Carol Eckman, the coach of the women's basketball team at West Chester University in Pennsylvania, decided to organize a women's national basketball tournament, to be recognized by the CIAW. One of the sixteen teams that qualified, by winning a state tournament of Illinois colleges, was Charlotte West's Southern Illinois squad.

The women's game had developed at a maddeningly slow pace—continuous dribbling wasn't allowed until 1966, and coaching from the sidelines wasn't permitted until 1968. Throughout the '60s, the games were played six players to a side, two stationed in the backcourt, two in the frontcourt, and two "rovers" allowed to run the full length of the court.

"Oh, I thought it was quite atrocious," said Peg Burke at Iowa. "It was such a limitation on girls—this idea that they couldn't run the full length of the court without their womb dropping out, basically."

The "six-on-six" game was wildly popular in Iowa high schools and extensively played in Texas, but it was based on the assumption that full-court basketball was too strenuous for most teenage girls. Defending the ponderous half-court game a few years later, one Texas high school administrator explained, "See, this way even the heavyset girls can play." An administrator in Iowa claimed the rules were "really important because it isn't feminine to sweat."

There were other nettlesome issues around women's sports, among the most prominent being whether women could be athletes and still be considered sufficiently feminine. One of Charlotte West's players at Southern Illinois, the aggressive rover Jennifer Stanley, learned to be careful about mentioning her love of sports on dates. "I would wait a while," she said. "The first thing out of my mouth on a date wasn't 'I'm majoring in physical education' or that 'I play basketball.' It was let me get to know you first so you can see I'm *really a girl* because yes, it was there. It was most definitely there."

On a second date, a young man told Stanley that women weren't athletes and that she could find a better use of her time. She decided then that she could find a better use of her time than going on a third date.

Of course, there was no budget for travel to a national tournament. After SIU qualified in 1969, West "literally begged" a university vice president for the money to take her team to West Chester. She got authorization for two university cars to drive from Carbondale to Pennsylvania, where Eckman's West Chester State College team was both host and favorite. West and Moore were in the process of cutting their fifteen-woman squad down to ten so she and Moore could each drive a car with five players when her team captains came to her and pleaded to take eleven players, vowing "we'll ride with four in the backseat." And so they did. "All I remember," said Moore, "is that no one complained."

At the Hollinger Field House on the West Chester campus, the SIU players wore their belted one-piece white tunics with numbered pinnie vests. ("They called us 'the chariot riders' or the 'nursing corps,'" recalled one player.) Many teams played in even more uncomfortable attire, thick one-piece dresses with bloomers underneath. SIU had it better than most. "We had two different sets of pinnies—maroon and white," said SIU's Marie Ballard. "We were *uptown.*"

The women on the sixteen teams spent the whole weekend playing and watching basketball; there were winners' and losers' brackets, so all sixteen teams got to play at least two games. At the end, West Chester—the rare school with two African American starters—won the tournament. It received virtually no coverage in the press, but for West and Moore, it was proof of progress and an embrace of competition—exactly what they were striving for.

Later that year, Billie Moore got her own coaching offer—to become a physical education instructor and the women's basketball coach at Cal State–Fullerton. By then, she was spending her summers playing for the Raybestos Brakettes, the Connecticut-based softball dynasty, led by legendary pitcher Joan Joyce. Some of the women on the Fullerton basketball team—Sue Sims, Cec Ponce and Rosie Adams—were part of the softball team the Orange Lionettes, and knew Moore because they had played against her when the Lionettes defeated the Brakettes for the 1969 Amateur Softball Association (ASA) national championship.

When Moore got to California, she had another discovery. Instead of having to coax women into competitiveness, as at Southern Illinois, she was coaching a group of women for whom all that came naturally. "These women have played sports all their lives," Moore told West. "I don't have to *teach* them to be aggressive."

The goal was the same—a spot among the best sixteen teams in the country at the CIAW championship invitational. Then came the news that the 1970 tournament, to be held at Northeastern University in Boston, would be the first to be played by traditional five-on-five basketball rules. Moore felt redeemed: "I thought, *Finally*. We're going to get to play the game the way it should be played."

Moore's 1969–70 Cal State–Fullerton team was fast, fit, and disciplined and earned an at-large berth to the second tournament, financed through washing cars, working concession stands at the men's basketball games, and the inevitable candy-bar sales (though Moore ruefully noted that the best customers for the candy-bar sales were her own players). "We ate a lot of chocolate," said Cec Ponce. "I remember some of us having to write a check out for the box of bars that were half-eaten."

In mid-March, they flew to Boston for the tournament at Northeastern University. It was the sport's future meeting its past. Most of the other fifteen teams were still decked out in tunics or skirts, while Moore's Titans team ran the court in shorts, paced by point guard Rosie Adams. After winning the first two games, Fullerton dealt with the slowdown tactics of Western Carolina in a 38–31 semifinal win. In the final on Sunday, March 15, in front of hundreds of people on the Northeastern campus, Fullerton trailed at halftime, before Sue Sims went on a shooting tear in the second half, and Fullerton edged defending national champion West Chester State, 50–46.

Even after the victory, Moore was contained; she was not for big celebrations. Her star players—including Sims and Ponce and Patty Meyers— got a car and headed to Chinatown to drink Singapore Slings. Louise "Lou" Albrecht, the former Fullerton coach and Moore's softball teammate on the Brakettes, had showed up to cheer her former charges on and helped the seniors smuggle a bottle of champagne back to the hotel.

The next morning, the *Boston Globe* carried an eight-page sports section. There wasn't a story, or a picture, or a box score, or even a final score. Back in

California, the *Los Angeles Times* sports section had two pictures on a local handball tournament, and write-ups on the Pacific Indoor Rodeo, the Teutonia Soccer Club of San Francisco beating Alemania of Los Angeles in an amateur soccer match, and agate summaries of yacht racing, trapshooting and the Desert Conference junior college track meet. But no mention of a national championship won by an area team. As with the previous year's tournament, unless you were a direct participant, or related to one, you wouldn't have known the event occurred. But for Moore and her players, and the growing universe of women's college basketball, *they knew.* For the time being, that was enough.

•

The individual sports had developed more quickly than team sports for women, though save for the Olympics, most elite female athletes competed in obscurity. Prior to the '70s, the best-known women athletes in America were figure skaters, but they rarely crossed the national consciousness outside of Olympic years. The Ladies Professional Golf Association tour had been in existence since 1950, but was rarely seen on TV. The CIAW championships were little seen and even less reported.

By the beginning of the '70s, the best-known female athletes were tennis players. They had an advantage that the golfers didn't: The four major tournaments in the sport—the Australian Open, the French Open, Wimbledon, and the U.S. Open—were two-week tournaments in which both the best men and the best women competed.

Yet even here, the best women's tennis players were treated as second-class. Even the bigger names in women's tennis were often stationed on the isolated outer courts at Wimbledon and the U.S. Open. This was reflected as well in television coverage. When the Australian Margaret Court completed her grand slam of winning all four majors at the U.S. Open in Forest Hills in 1970, CBS showed only the last ten minutes of her three-set championship match with Rosie Casals.

By the fall of 1970, tennis had been openly professional for two years, but the promise of the money was almost entirely on the men's side. That prompted two women pros, Ceci Martinez and Esmé Emmanuel, to distribute a questionnaire to fans attending the U.S. Open at Forest Hills, which—unscientific though the survey group may have been—seemed to show a healthy interest in the women's game (49 percent of the men surveyed expressed interest in watching the women play), drastically contradicting the dismissive attitude of the male pros, such as Clark Graebner, that "the women are going to disappear because they don't draw flies."

The retired tennis legend Jack Kramer's high-profile Pacific Southwest Tournament, held in late September in Los Angeles, was one of the tournaments that offered brackets for both the men and the women. In 1970, the Pacific Southwest announced a $65,000 purse for the men ($12,500 for the winner), compared to $7,500 for the women ($1,500 for the winner).

The extreme disparity rankled the women, none more so than Billie Jean King. She sought out *World Tennis* publisher Gladys Heldman to broker a fairer deal for the women.

Heldman was an American original, a smart, tough, chain-smoking, scotch-drinking woman in a man's world. She had a master's degree in medieval history from Cal–Berkeley, was the mother of touring pro Julie Heldman, and had become the de facto den mother to the women's players on the tour. After meeting with King and Casals, she reluctantly agreed to talk to Kramer and try to persuade him to provide a more reasonable payout for the women. When Heldman returned to the women's locker room at Forest Hills after her conversation, she wore an annoyed expression. "Jack Kramer," she announced, "is an ass."

Heldman agreed to organize a rival event for women in Houston the same week as the Pacific Southwest tournament. She soon recruited the avid tennis fan Joe Cullman, the Philip Morris CEO who had just rolled out a new brand of cigarettes catering to women called Virginia Slims. With that, the First Houston Women's International Tennis Tournament became the Virginia Slims of Houston.

With Cullman handling much of the financing and Heldman overseeing the organizational details, the women broke from the United States Lawn Tennis Association (USLTA), and later in 1970 announced the Virginia Slims/*World Tennis* women's tour for 1971. "You've heard of Women's Lib?" said Heldman. "This is Women's Lob."

The irony of a women's tennis tour being sponsored by a product that caused lung cancer was not lost on King, who confronted the two-pack-a-day smoker Heldman, saying, "We're athletes. This bothers me."

"You want a tour or not?" asked Heldman.

The mere existence of a breakaway tournament for women ran afoul of the USLTA, which threatened to bar the women from the U.S. Open and international competition. Among "The Original Nine" women who signed on with the Slims tour, the consequences were varied. Australians Judy Dalton and Kerry Melville weren't merely barred from the Australian Open, they were forbidden from playing on any tennis court in the country when they returned home that winter.

But the women stood their ground and stuck with Heldman and the Slims tour. In 1971, the tour held tournaments in nineteen cities, with $309,100 in purses. By 1972, the prize money grew to more than $500,000 and, in 1973, to $775,000.

"To our great surprise and delight, the public adored the women," Heldman said. "They still enjoy the longer rallies, the greater variation and consistency of the women's matches compared with the men's."

It was Cullman who suggested that the Slims tour hire the dress designer and tennis gadfly Ted Tinling, the bald, British, six-foot-five bundle of kinetic energy and dishy gossip. Tinling was an artist with the same sense of mission as King—get women tennis pros noticed—and possessed an elegant sense of style and a zesty love of transgression. "I put sin into tennis," he liked to say.

Tinling sensed, in a way that the businessmen and marketing types didn't, that tennis "had to turn into a spectacle, and you must pay your debts to the spectators who keep it alive. They don't want to do that here, but that's part of my job." In Tinling's case, the job was designing graceful dresses that, without fail, accentuated each player's femininity.

•

There were no antecedents for Billie Jean King. Despite her habitually bad knees, she was a kinetic presence both on and off the court, and possessed a kind of grit that was still rare in the country-club sport. One of the few elite professionals to wear glasses, she moved with a kind of headstrong purposefulness. She lacked the dainty pirouettes and elegant flowing forehands of other top women players. King attacked the ball, attacked the net, attacked her opponent. Even her speech consisted of an aggressive set of slangy expressions, many of them being Southern California idioms of broken Spanish—a late choke was an "el foldo," when she gained too much weight, she would refer to herself as "el flabbo," while a parsimonious tipper would be tagged as "el cheapo."

She also had a keen sense for the larger narrative. In American sports—and to a great extent, in American culture—the magic figure was $100,000 a year. The best baseball players were making six figures, and the round number had become a yardstick of excellence in individual sports like tennis and golf.

Which is why King conducted a punishing schedule in 1971, playing nearly all the Virginia Slims events, but also a wide range of other tournaments, in hope of becoming the first woman athlete to reach the $100,000 mark for yearly earnings. As she plotted her schedule that spring and summer, she grew increasingly excited about the prospect. Not for the money itself so much as what the accomplishment would signify.

King finally pushed over the line with a 7–5, 6–1 win over Rosie Casals at the Thunderbird Tournament in Phoenix on October 3.

That prompted a press conference the next day at the Philip Morris headquarters in New York, when Richard Nixon called in to offer congratulations on passing the milestone.

"Hello, Mr. President," King said.

"Yes, I just wanted to congratulate you for your great successes this year," Nixon told her. "I'm glad to see a fellow Californian get over $100,000."

"Well, it proves that women can earn a respectable living in sports," she said. "It'll open up more avenues for women in other sports."

"Well, that's the most important thing," Nixon said.

While King's earnings were gaining attention—"You girls are making some real bread!" exclaimed Reggie Jackson, who met King at a Bay Area sports awards dinner at the end of the year—she also recognized that the key to the sport's long-term success was finding new faces whom the sports public viewed as compelling.

Earlier that fall, at the U.S. Open, King was sure she'd seen the future of tennis, in the person of a sixteen-year-old from Florida named Chris Evert, who arrived on the scene with a preternatural sense of poise.

Evert (even then, everyone called her Chrissie) was one of five children, raised in a three-bedroom—and, eventually, four-bedroom, and, finally, five-bedroom—ranch-style home in Fort Lauderdale, the daughter of the teaching pro Jimmy Evert, who presided over the nearby public court Holiday Park, where Chrissie Evert, from an early age, showed an unshakable capacity for concentration.

Evert burst onto the national scene at the '71 U.S. Open, an indomitable competitor in ribbons and bows. In her first-round match at Forest Hills, she fought off six match points before rallying to win. She advanced to the semifinals, playing on center court to ever more enthusiastic crowds fascinated by the teenager's maturity and comportment. Her on-court cool became an instant calling card. "The Ice Princess" or "The Ice Maiden" were early nicknames. In Evert's honey-blond good looks King recognized an ambassador for the sport, the girl next door who could captivate the imagination of both women and men.

Evert was stoic and shy and, well, sixteen. "I think the older players were slow to warm to her," said the pro Judy Dalton. "She was reserved and aloof and cold."

At one point during the tournament, King gathered some of the veteran women on the tour and made an impassioned plea for them to be kinder to Evert. "Listen, you guys, Chris Evert is the greatest thing that could happen to us," King implored. "Look at her—she is *it!* She's our next superstar and you're going to be passing the baton to her. So, I don't even care if you like her. We've got to make her feel welcome. It's not about 'like.' It's about doing the right thing."

One of the players mentioned to King that Evert wasn't particularly friendly to them, either. "Guys, she's *sixteen!*" pleaded King.

King had defended Evert, and now she had to defeat her. Evert had thus far avoided the full Virginia Slims tour and was playing only the rival USLTA-sanctioned events. King recognized that an Evert victory over her at Forest Hills might delegitimize the whole Virginia Slims tour.

On their walk to the court before the semifinal at Forest Hills, King counseled Evert to savor her arrival in the spotlight. Then she disposed of Evert in straight sets.

Asked in the winter of 1972 if she was growing tired of the focus on her callow youth, Evert replied, "Well, it would be nice if some writer would get around to describing me as sexy."

In the event, she wouldn't have to wait long. The attention generated by Evert and the indigenous Australian Evonne Goolagong, twenty-one, reflected their grace and promise, but at times seemed beyond what their court accomplishments had to that date merited.

In the summer of 1972, the elfin Goolagong had been the subject of illicit attention from the *Sun*, the tawdriest of London's Fleet Street tabloids, which published a sketch imagining what she would look like playing in the nude. It wasn't the sort of thing Johnny Unitas ever had to deal with.

•

Thanks largely to King's crusade, there was a growing awareness of the obvious inequities in prize money, publicity, and conditions. Covering Donna Caponi's win at the U.S. Women's Open golf tournament in 1970, the *Sports Illustrated* writer Bil Gilbert compared Caponi's prize money ($5,000) to the check for the men's Open winner, Tony Jacklin ($30,000). Gilbert, like many sympathetic male writers at the time, argued for the relevance and excitement of women's sports. But, also like many male writers at the time, he emphasized pulchritude over competitiveness:

> And a lithe, emotionally expressive girl in a short skirt generally makes a more attractive spectacle than a paunchy, balding male who, for reasons of masculine tradition and ego, usually wears a frozen, I-am-stalking-a-lion, do-not-disturb mask.
>
> There is a deep-rooted attitude at large in the nation that the Girl Next Door ought to damn well stay there—symbolically, at least—and that girls who don't are some kind of freaks. And any girl who moves away to play golf for money is doubly freaky, if not downright kinky.
>
> Touring women professionals, it is true, do not look exactly like the girl next door, being as a rule more tanned, fit, and muscular. Their lifestyle is nomadic and therefore suspect. When, as Joe Ann Prentice once put it, they come to town and then go out on it, they are stigmatized as swingers; when they stay in their motels and relax, they raise other sorts of questions.

And this was the essence of the contradiction. Despite the growing prominence of women's tennis, what inevitably got the most coverage in sports pages and sports magazines were cheerleaders, buxom fans and young women in bikinis.

At the Army–Navy football game in 1970, in front of 95,000 fans at JFK Stadium in Philadelphia, a go-go dancer from Pittsburgh ran onto the field during the opening coin toss and kissed both captains. That photo made a lot of newspapers the next day. The exotic dancer Morganna had started her tour of ballpark interruptions in 1969, running onto the field to kiss, at different times in different cities, Pete Rose, Frank Howard, Clete Boyer, and others.

In 1970, *Sports Illustrated* published a two-page pictorial story about a game at the Tarrant County Convention Center in Fort Worth, an opening act to a Dallas Chaparrals ABA game, that matched flight attendants from Frontier Airlines against hostesses from Las Vegas' Desert Inn, the Pzazz-ers. The teams held practices by a hotel pool, wearing bikinis for uniforms, serving champagne during the action. Two years later, the ABA's Kentucky Colonels scheduled a halftime exhibition game between a team of Playboy bunnies and local TV, print, and radio correspondents covering the team.

In baseball, major league teams began featuring teenage ball girls, often dressed in hot pants. In Oakland, they were simply called the Athletics' ball girls, in Chicago they were the "Soxettes," and in Philadelphia, they were the "Liberty Belles."

Each of these incidents received more press coverage than the first and second CIAW women's national championship tournaments in basketball.

•

Ever since its formation, Katherine Ley and the other foremothers of CIAW recognized its insufficiency for the growth of women's intercollegiate sports. In 1969, a group of women representing CIAW and DGWS traveled to Kansas City to meet with Walter Byers, the head of the National Collegiate Athletic Association, to see if the NCAA would conduct championships in women's sports.

"No, ladies, we are not interested," Byers told the women during the meeting. "We are an organization run by men for men. And we will stand ready to help you ladies in any way that you'd like."

And so the women decided to create a full-fledged membership organization expressly designed to govern women's intercollegiate sports. While still under the auspices of DGWS and AAHPER, the new organization would be called the Association for Intercollegiate Athletics for Women, to replace CIAW in 1971. Beginning with a charter membership of 278 schools, AIAW sponsored their first championships in the 1972–73 school year, in the same seven sports that the CIAW had sponsored: basketball, golf, gymnastics, track and field, badminton, swimming and diving, and volleyball.

The women who started AIAW dreamed of creating a utopian new organization. Almost to a person, they loved sports and disapproved of what it had slouched toward in major-college athletics—overly monied, overly commercialized, often exploiting student-athletes for commercial gain, frequently separated from the larger academic mission.

Ley was on the forefront, a cerebral idealist who could rally a crowd with the clarity of her vision and the purity of her principles.

"She was one of the most dynamic professors and speakers that I've ever heard," said Sharon E. Taylor, who heard Ley speak about CIAW and the future of women's athletics in 1969 (three years before Taylor launched her field hockey dynasty at Lock Haven State College). "She's the person who really introduced this and we sat there with our chins hanging off, touching the desk, listening to what she was telling us about this organization and how it was going to function and everything like that."

When the women formed AIAW, there was more of a consensus about what they *didn't* want their new organization to be as what they did.

The new group would endeavor to expand competitive opportunities for the highly skilled female athlete, and do so while maintaining a constant balance between academics and athletics, and ensure that the governmental oversight of women would be handled by women.

While there was broad agreement that the women did not want women's intercollegiate sports to develop in the way that men's sports had, there were broadly divergent views on the nature and value of competition.

Carole Oglesby had been the director of competition for the CIAW and, in part because she was young, indefatigable, and among the leaders in both athletic and academic pursuits, she was elected the first president of the AIAW. As a professor at the University of Massachusetts Amherst, Oglesby would describe herself in "a feminist foxhole." Her office walls included positive epigrams, including the Irina Dunn proclamation—often erroneously attributed to Gloria Steinem—that "a woman needs a man like a fish needs a bicycle." Some of the visitors to her office would blanch at the signs, which only reinforced Oglesby's belief that the signs were doing their job.

Like Billie Moore at Cal State–Fullerton, Peg Burke at Iowa and Charlotte West at Southern Illinois, Oglesby took on extra coaching and professional duties on a volunteer basis, working punishing hours and still finding the time for softball on the weekends, academic papers, AIAW executive board meetings, and other events.

The AIAW's bylaws, in the words of the scholar Diane Williams, "became this kind of aspirational document of saying, if we were to take seriously the ideas in women's physical education, that athletics and physical education should be connected to a student's educational experience and that athletics cannot draw away from a student's education, but instead enhance these kinds of principles…what would this look like?"

What it looked like was a stark departure from NCAA norms. There would be no athletic scholarships offered (because the AIAW leaders feared that would upend the academic and athletic balance) and there would be no recruiting done off-campus. They didn't want student-athletes to be subservient to the commercial dictates of the marketplace.

Its official statement noted, "DGWS does not approve of awarding scholarships, financial awards, or giving financial assistance for women participants in intercollegiate sports competition…[women should] choose their campus on the basis of academic worth, free from pressure recruiting and performer exploitation."

A later AIAW policy statement would codify this mindset: "The enrichment of the life of the participants is the focus and reason for the existence of any athletic program. All decisions should be made with this fact in mind."

Like absolute socialism and perfect love, the idea of sports organized around the "enrichment of the life of the participants" was easier to grasp as a theoretical construct than it was to codify in the real world. The AIAW was officially formed in October of 1971. The first complaint to the AIAW about recruiting violations occurred later that month.

•

Old attitudes died hard. Until 1970, the Amateur Athletic Union, the governing body for track and field events, would not recognize women distance runners for any distance longer than one and a half miles.

When Roberta Gibb applied to run in the Boston Marathon in 1966, she received a rejection from race organizers informing her that "women are physiologically incapable of running 26.2 miles." Gibb turned up for the race anyway and, disguised in a blue hoodie, started with the rest of the runners and completed the course in 3 hours 21 minutes 40 seconds. A year later, Gibb again completed the race, again without an official number. That same year, the nineteen-year-old Syracuse journalism student Kathrine Switzer entered under the name K. V. Switzer. Early in the race, she was spotted by marathon organizer John "Jock" Semple, who charged her on the course, trying to rip her numbered bib off, only to be shoulder-checked away by Switzer's boyfriend, hammer thrower Tom Miller. Despite the evidence that women runners could complete the race—in some cases faster than most men—it was five more years before Boston officially allowed female entrants.

The notion of women being anywhere in the realm of male athletes seemed alien to some. When the golfer Shirley Englehorn tried to enter the PGA's 1970 Los Angeles Open, she was rejected by Joe Day, president of the PGA's Tournament Players Division. The touring pro Billy Casper agreed to play a round with her at Los Coyotes Golf Club in Orange County, shooting 70 to Englehorn's 79. Asked what would have happened if Englehorn had won the round, Casper said, "We'd have both set golf back fifty years."

Women were even barred from competition by an organization called the World Marbles Board of Control, whose representative Sean O'Geary explained, "They look ridiculous when they crouch. Miniskirts are a disaster for marbles. Even in trousers or maxi-skirts their bottoms are not suitable for the game."

It wasn't only the men who were bewildered. There was still a tremendous amount of cultural ambivalence about the notion of women as athletes, even among some of the athletes themselves.

Chris Evert's father had recognized his daughter's excellence early in her teenage years, but was still from another time. "Chrissie, I want you to be a good tennis player, have a lot of fun and work hard. But what would make me most happy is if you would lead a normal life and get married and have children."

Evert remained conflicted at the time about the entire proposition. "I never felt like an athlete," she said of those teen years. "I was just *someone who played tennis matches.* I still thought of women athletes as freaks, and used to hate myself, thinking I must not be a whole woman."

Billie Jean King was a whole woman, keenly aware of the rising profile of women in sports and the attendant pressure surrounding it. She was also a pragmatist who would become famous during a decade noted for its howling contradictions. It was understandable that Billie Jean King would become the best-known women athlete in the country. But she was not quite ready, yet, to call herself a feminist. She preferred to call the Virginia Slims "the broads' tour."

"Women's lib can be so negative, so defensive, so narrow-minded," she said in 1971. "They think their thing is the only thing in the world for everybody. I have to do things my own way." Others on the tour were equally reluctant to align themselves with feminism. "The majority of players didn't want to know about women's lib," said Julie Heldman. "People kept laying women's lib on us instead of laying it on them."

•

On June 23, 1972, at the Queen's Club tournament in London—the traditional warm-up prior to Wimbledon—Evert defeated Wendy Overton, 5-7, 6-2, 6-1, in a semifinal match. On the same day, back in the U.S., President Nixon signed into law the Education Amendments of 1972, a broad education bill which authorized nearly $19 billion in aid for the country's institutions of higher learning over the following three years.

The fanatical sports fan Nixon didn't know it at the time (to be fair, almost no one else did, either), but he'd just made his most substantial contribution to sports in America.

Within the Education Acts signed into law that day was Title IX, which stated, "No person in the United States shall, on the basis of sex, be excluded from participation in, be denied the benefits of, or be subjected to discrimination under any educational program or activity receiving Federal financial assistance." That Friday night, in Washington, D.C., a woman named Bernice

"Bunny" Sandler came home and reported to her family that "something big" had happened that day. "Title IX is now official," she said, "and women are going to get more power and equality." Sandler had been the catalyst for Title IX. After getting a doctorate in counseling and personnel services, she was passed over repeatedly for a full-time teaching position at her alma mater, the University of Maryland. For three years, Sandler had worked ceaselessly to document the widespread gender discrimination in education, working with one of the few women in Congress, Rep. Edith Green, to advocate for federal legislation to outlaw the quotas and discriminatory practices. The low-key, well-organized effort had also been aided in the House by Representative Patsy Mink of Hawaii, and in the Senate by Birch Bayh of Indiana. But it wasn't only Democrats. The Alaska senator Ted Stevens, a Republican, was a co-sponsor of the bill as well.

That Friday evening, Sandler felt profound satisfaction, and was convinced that the new law would help women get into more professions, like engineering and medicine. Even after the passage of the law, Sandler herself wasn't clear on its athletic implications. "I remember saying, 'Oh, isn't this nice, it's covering athletics—it means on field day the girls will have more activities.'"

As it turned out, it would come to mean a lot more than that. The fact of the law, and the broad way it was interpreted, would forever change the boundaries, makeup, and character of American sports. But it would be more than a year later before the key figures in American sports—or nearly anyone else—realized that.

# SIX

# AMATEUR ACTS

By THE BEGINNING of the '70s, the social conventions in American workday life were melting away, with business suits and dresses giving way to more casual clothing, from leisure suits to fringed vests to paisley mini-skirts. In American offices, the more relaxed environment was populated with irony and self-referential humor, as empty and whimsical as smiley-face buttons and pet rocks.

But those touchstones of the era—in fact the entire ethos that character-ized life in the early '70s—ceased to exist upon passing through the front door of the National Collegiate Athletic Association offices.

The NCAA offices of the '70s weren't so much in a time warp as a parallel universe. The bright, disciplined, and hardworking staffers who inhabited the organization's offices abided by a strict dress code, and most of them still worked six days a week, with everyone at their desks for Saturday's half-day shift. Men wore suits and ties in the NCAA offices and did not take their suit jackets off while there. After a long day, they could loosen the top button of their dress shirt. "And that was as far as the dress code ever wavered," said one longtime staffer. Women employees wore dresses and heels, in accordance with Rule 6.1.1 in the *NCAA Office Policies and Procedures* booklet. Mary Tyler Moore may have been wearing pantsuits in the '70s, but such minor departures from social norms were still not allowed at the NCAA offices, nor were personal pictures or artifacts of any kind on employees' desks.

Nor, for that matter, were food and drink. Staffers' desks were pristine. There was no conversation by the water cooler because there was no water cooler. There was no kibitzing over coffee because there was no kibitzing full stop. "If you wanted to have coffee," said NCAA enforcement director David

Berst, "you were supposed to show up before work and have it down in the break room." Even the break room was something of a misnomer because for a time there were no breaks. "I thought it was a good idea, but people abused them," said the longtime secretary Marge Fieber. Cigarettes could be smoked in the lunchroom, but nowhere else.

All of this order and discipline came at the behest of the NCAA's executive director, Walter Byers. While the commissioners of the major sports leagues and the heads of the sports divisions of the major television networks were regarded as the power players in sports in the '70s, each had checks on their autonomy; the commissioner of each league had a group of strong-willed owners to answer to and the network sports executives still had to tangle with the heads of news and entertainment divisions for their power.

But for Byers, who'd been in the position for twenty years by 1971, there were no true rivals, within or without. He ruled a growing collegiate sports empire with absolute authority. Enrollment at American colleges and universities had quadrupled from 2.1 million to 8.6 million since he took office. The former United Press reporter had been named the NCAA's first executive director in 1951, at a time when the NCAA was little more than an athletic record-keeping organization, renting space in the Big Ten offices in Chicago. Shortly thereafter, he'd moved the offices to downtown Kansas City, where Byers had grown up, and built the NCAA into the broadly powerful governance organization for intercollegiate sports.

It was an irony noted by both critics and employees that the executive director of the NCAA never actually graduated from college. Byers started at Rice, then transferred to Iowa, then quit school to enlist in the Army in 1943, only to be discharged a year later because of strabismus, also known as "lazy eye."

Byers sported sideburns and cowboy boots along with—in the words of Jim Host, who would work with Byers in the '70s to market the NCAA's basketball tournament—"the worst toupee I'd ever seen in my life."

As a result of his journalism background, Byers wielded a sharp red pencil, resulting in an atmosphere of painstaking punctiliousness in NCAA communications, with all press releases and in-house publications copyedited down to a bland precision.

"I think he was trying to establish a climate of excellence," said his longtime lieutenant, NCAA executive vice president Tom Hansen. "He didn't want sloppy conduct of any nature and he was demanding in that way. And he was a perfectionist so he criticized things that weren't to his liking."

There were a lot of things that weren't to Byers' liking, from ending a sentence with a preposition (this would merit some of his heaviest red marks) to Marquette University's horizontally striped "bumblebee" uniforms (which Byers ordered outlawed after the 1971 season on the grounds that they were "distracting" to opponents).

After two decades of rapid growth when the offices were in downtown Kansas City, the NCAA broke ground in 1972 on a 26,900-square foot office in suburban Mission, Kansas, just across the state line from Kansas City, in Johnson County. The NCAA loomed so large that ABC televised the new building's April 28, 1973, official opening on *Wide World of Sports*.

By that time, Roone Arledge and ABC had developed a symbiotic relationship with Byers and the NCAA. Arledge would note later that the NCAA in this era "had a cozy deal going. Walter organized his favorite athletic directors (meaning everybody except Notre Dame, it sometimes seemed) into committees, and the committees got to go off on junkets to decide the important things, like the next season's schedule, and television paid handsomely for all of it. Walter could hide behind his committees on one hand, and manipulate them on the other, and he managed to do it successfully for a number of years."

•

It was Byers who crafted the term "student-athlete" and turned it into a common phrase around college athletics. The rules at the NCAA were clear: "No student shall represent a college or university in any intercollegiate game or contest...who has at any time received, either directly or indirectly, money or any other consideration."

Trying to enforce those rules at a time when recruiting had grown venomously competitive, when there were more than 100 schools across the country playing major-college football and twice as many playing major-college basketball, when inducements and under-the-table payments had become part of the culture, was virtually impossible. That Byers remained committed to that principle—and acted as though he believed it could be adequately policed—was one of the things his critics found maddening.

At the same time, the NCAA's decision to approve an eleventh regular-season football game starting in 1970, at the behest of major powers eager for the windfall of one more home game, increased the perception that the big business of football had overtaken the consideration of a proper balance between academics and athletics.

It didn't stop there. At the Diplomat Hotel in Hollywood, Florida, in 1972, the NCAA voted to undo the sixty-year-old policy of declaring freshmen ineligible for intercollegiate athletic competition. Later, at a special convention in August of 1973, the NCAA divided into three divisions: Division I, for major colleges; Division II, for smaller colleges that still offered scholarships; and Division III, which prohibited awarding athletic scholarships. The division allowed the major-college schools—the football and basketball powerhouses—to legislate themselves.

Critics said the changes would hasten more recruiting violations and lead to lower academic standards. As the NCAA was allowing students to start participating in sports sooner in their college careers, a federal court judge was ruling that athletes could leave colleges for the pros earlier. The 1971 case of the University of Detroit's Spencer Haywood dealt a blow to the NCAA's legal standing, when the federal court ruled that it was legally permissible for Haywood to sign with a pro team before the typical four-year waiting period after his high school graduation.

Faced with the continuing push for more revenue, and the prospect that some of the NCAA's brightest stars might be leaving early, one anonymous college commissioner told *Sports Illustrated*, "We could always go back to using students as athletes."

•

The most buttoned-down of organizations was presiding over the most unruly, disorganized, irrational sport on the American landscape. College football was unlike anything else in American sports. It was the only American sport that didn't end its season with a champion decided on the field of play. Instead, a loose affiliation of holiday bowls had been gradually tacked on to the end of the regular-season schedule and grown in stature and importance as the sport's popularity grew. And even their meaning was amorphous.

As the decade began, the two major polls that decided the mythical national championship were divided on the issue. In the United Press International poll, a board of coaches would vote for the top twenty teams, and conduct its final poll to crown its national champion at the end of the regular season and prior to the bowls. Meanwhile, in the Associated Press poll, a board of writers would vote for its final top twenty and crown *its* national champion after the bowls were played. Some fans thought it absurd that a sport as popular as college football didn't have a championship tournament; others loved the messy ambiguity and endless arguments sparked by the disarray.

Thanks to the innovations of Arledge's work at ABC, and the stalwart writing of Dan Jenkins covering big games throughout the country in the pages of *Sports Illustrated,* the college game had grown in scope and popularity by the beginning of the '70s.

Sunday sections in big-city newspapers had for decades been full of in-depth stories on the closest major-college team. But they were largely focused on a particular region of the country. What *SI* did was make the audience much more conscious of the game nationally. Jenkins, arriving in 1963 from a newspaper career in Fort Worth and Dallas, had explained to managing editor Andre Laguerre, "You know, there's this thing called No. 1, there's a race for No. 1—that should guide our football coverage. We go to the biggest game every week, we all drive toward a goal, the goal is 'Who's Number One?'" Jenkins well understood the obsessive interest in the sport (as indicated by the title of his 1970 collection, *Saturday's America: The Chronic Outrage and Giddy Passion of College Football*). The chronic outrage was baked into the sport.

The first NCAA football deal was signed in 1952 with NBC, for a dozen "Game of the Week" broadcasts for a rights fee of slightly more than $1 million. It was indicative of how sports was viewed at the time that when NBC's sports chief Tom Gallery started his job, the head of sales at NBC sat him down and said, "I want to straighten you out. We don't want any goddamn baseball or football on this network. We don't have any clients that would buy it. And don't you be bringing it in."

But since 1966, when Arledge and ABC had shrewdly won the bid for the NCAA football package, the sport had enjoyed steady growth. Arledge had appealed to Byers' resentment (or jealousy) of pro football by noting that, at ABC, the NCAA would get the best of the best rather than the leftovers of CBS and NBC, which both devoted the lion's share of their sports resources to pro football.

With ABC, the appeal of the sport had grown despite the highly limited exposure being offered. In 1970, ABC showed a total of seventeen games over the thirteen-week span of the regular season (eleven nationally televised, six more regional telecasts). Most Saturdays, only one football game—ABC's national telecast, determined months in advance—would appear on TV sets around the country. Meanwhile, attendance at college football games had exploded in postwar America, from 17.3 million in 1955 to 20.4 million in 1960 to 29.5 million in 1970. As Byers himself concluded, "Television seemed to create *more* interest" in attending games at stadiums.

So Byers was infuriated when ABC announced it was starting the *Monday Night Football* series. When he called to rage at the network, Arledge pointed out that ABC's promise not to show pro football applied only to the first two years of the NCAA contract. Byers peevishly stipulated that ABC could not promote *Monday Night Football* on any of its college football telecasts. Arledge, in turn, committed to promoting NCAA football games during *Monday Night Football*. Finally, Arledge pointed out that the NCAA was still first in ABC's heart—the network in 1970 paid $12.1 million annually for the college football package, and only $8.5 million a year for *Monday Night Football*.

Despite the pending premiere of *Monday Night Football*, ABC moved gingerly into prime time, opening its 1970 NCAA football telecasts with a nationally televised intersectional game with Heisman candidate Jim Plunkett leading Stanford at Arkansas. But the game started at the odd hour of six p.m. Eastern time (in *Sports Illustrated*, Jenkins referred to it as a "twi-night single header") to avoid competing with NBC's telecast of the Miss America Pageant, won that year by Miss Texas, a pianist from Denton named Phyllis George.

•

Much of ABC's schedule was decided in March, a dangerous policy since college football seasons so often followed their own logic. But once in a while ABC managed to scout the field to its own advantage. In 1971, for the first time, Nebraska and Oklahoma moved their annual season-ending Big Eight showdown from the Saturday after Thanksgiving to Thanksgiving Day, where it would compete head-to-head with NFL telecasts on CBS and NBC.

That year, the defending co-champion Nebraska, with its feared "Blackshirts" defense, was ranked number one for much of the season. Its offense was formidable as well, with I-back Jeff Kinney and wingback Johnny Rodgers providing much of the firepower. Meanwhile, resurgent Oklahoma, which had mastered the Wishbone offense, was rolling up preposterous scores (75–28, 58–14) on its way up the polls. To his eventual regret, Darrell Royal had let the Oklahoma coach Chuck Fairbanks come down to spring practice and study the offense, only to have OU rout the Longhorns, 49–27, with faster players operating the Wishbone.

The Huskers and Sooners lacked the natural enmity of rivalries built on proximity like Alabama–Auburn or USC–UCLA, and neither was it a particularly heated border war like Ohio State–Michigan or Georgia–Florida. Instead, throughout the decade, the Nebraska–Oklahoma rivalry—"It was always us or them," said the Sooners' Greg Pruitt—was based on competitive excellence. (Every year from 1962 to 1988 either Nebraska or Oklahoma won or shared the Big Eight title.)

As the Oklahoma–Nebraska showdown neared, ABC publicist Beano Cook reveled in the rare prospect of a college game outpacing an NFL game in the same time slot. "We'll eat the pros alive," he said. "This will be one of the most watched games of all time."

He was right. Number one Nebraska at number two Oklahoma was watched by 55 million people that Thanksgiving; there had never been more viewers for a college football game.

The buildup to the 1971 game began in earnest on October 11, when Oklahoma moved up to number two in the wire-service polls, just behind top-ranked Nebraska. Over the next month and a half the game was previewed on the covers of both *Sports Illustrated* ("Irresistible Oklahoma Meets Immovable Nebraska") and *Life* magazine.

When it finally arrived, the game was a febrile, absorbing classic, with both teams playing spectacularly. After trading touchdowns for much of the afternoon, Nebraska trailed 31–28 midway through the fourth quarter. College football was not a terribly complicated sport in 1971. Before the key drive, Husker coach Bob Devaney's advice to his quarterback Jerry Tagge was simple: "Keep giving the ball to Kinney and, if you get in trouble, throw it to Rodgers." Nebraska rallied late in the fourth quarter for the go-ahead touchdown, winning 35–31.

Afterward there was the big-game staple, President Nixon phoning the winning locker room. "Yes, sir, Mr. President," said Devaney when he was patched through to the White House. "They sold a lot of popcorn today. Nobody left."

Jenkins wrote the most memorable lead from the game: "In the land of the pickup truck and cream gravy for breakfast, down where the wind can blow through the walls of a diner and into the grieving lyrics of a country song on a jukebox—down there in dirt-kicking Big Eight territory—they played a football game on Thanksgiving Day that was mainly for the quarterbacks on the field and for self-styled gridiron intellectuals everywhere."

Dave Kindred, writing in the *Louisville Times*, shared the sentiment more succinctly, describing the game as "A piece of art without flaw, created under pressure without precedent."

At the time, a substantial number of major-college athletic directors were either football coaches or former football coaches. In 1971, when the Big Eight schools Nebraska, Oklahoma and Colorado finished 1-2-3 nationally in the final AP poll, all three head coaches also served as the athletic directors at their schools. In that clubby atmosphere, no one had to justify the massive investment required to conduct a major-college football program. At major state universities, it was what unified the alumni, got them back on campus for homecoming games in the fall, and raised a school's national profile. For all the criticism the comment received, when Dr. George L. Cross, the president of Oklahoma in the early '50s, said, "We want to build a university our football team can be proud of," he was articulating a bottom-line pragmatism. It was a lot easier getting alumni donations for a new library or chemistry lab when a school was winning conference titles and playing in New Year's Day bowl games.

The Big Eight's superiority at the time was no accident. It was already aggressively recruiting Black athletes by the beginning of the '70s, at a time when most schools in the Southeastern and Southwest Conferences remained all-white. Meanwhile, its entry standards were more permissive than those in the Big Ten, which still banned redshirting. (Traditionally the most hidebound of conferences, the Big Ten had a policy barring repeat appearances in the Rose Bowl until 1971, and didn't allow teams to go to any other bowl until 1975.)

The new Big Eight conference commissioner was Chuck Neinas, a smart, rangy go-getter who'd spent a decade as Byers' lieutenant at the NCAA. He landed at the Big Eight just in time for the conference's dream football season. After the 1971 season he printed up bumper stickers that read "1+2+3=The Big Eight," and threw a cocktail party in New York City with the conference's four bowl-winning coaches—Devaney, Fairbanks, Colorado's Eddie Crowder and Iowa State's Johnny Majors—as the Big Eight's reputation grew.

ABC would become synonymous with football during this period. The postgame scoreboard show—*Prudential College Football Scoreboard*—was one of the last major network shows with a corporate sponsor in the title. ABC was devoting an hour on Sunday mornings to a studio show hosted by Bill Flemming, which showed filmed highlights of several of the previous day's games. It was another rushed effort, even more frantic than the network's endeavors to provide filmed NFL highlights for *Monday Night Football*. In 1972, ABC aired a prime-time network special previewing the new season, with the actor Lee Majors narrating the arch script; in a segment on the 1971 season's culminating game, the Orange Bowl between number one Nebraska and then second-ranked and unbeaten Alabama (Nebraska romped, 38–6), Majors intoned that Nebraska and Johnny Rodgers had "turned the Crimson Tide into a polluted pond."

•

While college football possessed a roster of perennial powers, it was different in the NCAA's other commercially viable sport. To a great extent, college basketball at the beginning of the '70s was UCLA. And UCLA was John Wooden, the institution, the coaching legend, a man who paradoxically never urged his team to win and yet won more consistently than any other coach in college basketball history.

The college hardcourt game was the province of control freaks, of coaches stomping on the sidelines, directing every offensive possession and barking out orders on every defensive stand. Wooden was different. In the minutes before his team left the locker room, he would stand among them and say, "Men, I've done my job. The rest is up to you. When the game starts, don't ever look over to me at the sideline. I can't do anything for you."

With the 1971 arrival to the varsity of the highly coveted iconoclastic center Bill Walton from San Diego—regarded as such a prized prospect, Wooden even deigned to make a rare recruiting visit to the Walton home— UCLA's streak of national titles continued.

Outside of the basketball hotbeds, the tournament was little seen. For much of the '60s, a representative in the NCAA office sold the television rights to individual tournament games, primarily the championship, on a market-by-market basis. It wasn't until 1968, when Lew Alcindor and UCLA battled Houston and Elvin Hayes in a regular-season matchup at the Astrodome, that a college basketball game was nationally televised in prime time.

Even as the new decade began, the tournament was a modest, unfocused undertaking. The winners of seven conferences—the Pacific Eight and West Coast Athletic Conference in the West, the Southwest Conference and the Big Eight in the Midwest, the Big Ten and Southeastern Conference in the Mideast, and the Atlantic Coast Conference in the East—received byes into the round of sixteen. The rest of the field consisted of eight other conferences that received automatic berths, and ten schools that received at-large bids, culled from independents and conference champions without an automatic qualification spot.

While there were nominally twenty-five teams in the tournament, it was actually a sixteen-team field after the nine play-in games for independent teams and winners of the smaller conferences staged on the same weekend that the major conferences completed their regular-season schedule.

Distinct from almost all the other conferences, the Atlantic Coast Conference invalidated its regular season standings by playing a postseason conference tournament, the winner of which was automatically placed as the sole ACC entry in the tournament. The system was unforgiving. In 1970, South Carolina went into the ACC tournament ranked third nationally, but after falling to North Carolina State, lost out on the ACC's one and only tournament bid. Meanwhile, Santa Clara, from the West Coast Athletic Conference, got a bye into the second round, even though the Broncos weren't in either wire-service Top 20. In 1971, UCLA went through the regular season with one loss, while crosstown rival (and fellow Pacific Eight school) USC had only two losses, both to UCLA. That gave UCLA an automatic tournament berth and left USC out in the cold.

There had been grumbling for years, since UCLA's run of dominance under Wooden began, that the Bruins had a perpetually easy path to the final. They always got a bye into the round of sixteen, and there was rarely a team in the West region of their caliber. After winning the West regional, they were always matched in the semifinal game with the Midwest Region champion, at a time when the two toughest regions were typically the East and Mideast.

For all of his sage wisdom, careful teaching, and his timeless "pyramid of success," Wooden could seem painfully naïve about the world at large. In May 1972, after Richard Nixon announced the renewed bombing of Hanoi, Walton was arrested at an anti-war rally. A vexed Wooden posted his bail and drove him back to campus. "How can you do this?" he finally asked Walton. "You're letting me down. You're letting UCLA down. You're letting your parents down."

Walton reiterated his opposition to an unjust war and his revulsion at poor kids having to go fight it. He felt he had to protest.

"Getting arrested is not the way to do it," Wooden said. "What you should be doing is writing letters of protest." Walton found that ridiculous, and in response wrote a letter on UCLA stationery, signed by all the players, and sent it to the White House.

Yet in the main, Wooden presided serenely over his dynasty and brooked little compromise on his team. "Bill would test me once in a while," he recalled. "He didn't think I had the right to make him cut his hair or to tell him he couldn't wear a mustache or a beard or a goatee. I told him, 'You're right, Bill. I don't have that right. I do have the right, however, to determine who is going to be on the team. We're going to miss you.' And so he followed the rules."

Through the spring of 1972, on the occasion of UCLA's sixth straight title (led by the sophomore Walton), the tournament—"the UCLA Invitational," as some had taken to calling it—remained a minor event, lacking in profile and clarity.

The NCAA made changes for 1973, moving the semifinals and finals from a Thursday–Saturday format to a Saturday–Monday format, in which both semifinal games were nationally televised, and the national championship game aired on Monday night in prime time.

The semifinal matchups were changed to a rotating system, so that the West region winners weren't always paired with the Midwest winners.

The move into prime time was a risk. Tickets for the 1973 Final Four in St. Louis were still available two weeks beforehand (it finally sold out). In the end of an upset-marred tournament, UCLA rose again, beating Memphis State, 87–66, behind Walton's 21-for-22 shooting performance.

Even in the aftermath of the strong ratings and sold-out Final Four, there was a fear that the sport was on uncertain ground. Speaking to announcer Billy Packer at one point in the early '70s, the producer Eddie Einhorn said, "Billy, you better hope and pray UCLA never goes down, because if they do, college basketball is dead in the water."

Those fears would prove unfounded. As it turned out, dynasties—and the possibility of dynasties falling—are fascinating. A month after the 1973 Final Four, all of the 8,800 seats available for public sale for the 1974 Final Four, to be held in Greensboro, North Carolina, had been sold. More than 120,000 tickets had been requested in the mail lottery.

Football and basketball broadcasting rights were the NCAA's two big moneymakers, but there was no consistency in the way the two sports were handled.

In major-college football, with no championship tournament, the NCAA controlled the rights to the regular-season telecasts. Teams and conferences kept the money from the postseason bowl games, and other than a small sanctioning fee, the NCAA realized no revenue from those games. In the much more diffuse world of college basketball, the regular-season games were out of the NCAA's hands—and in the hands of regional marketers like C. D. Chesney and Einhorn—and the NCAA owned only the rights to the national championship tournament at the end of the season.

•

The NCAA's grip on Olympic sports was much more tenuous and contentious. Often NCAA regulations and events conflicted directly with the long shadow cast by the Amateur Athletic Union. Inevitably, these conflicts waxed and waned, rising to a fever pitch quadrennially around the Olympics. While the AAU had traditionally been the organization that presided over the USA's international efforts, the NCAA had become the home of most elite-level amateur athletes, and the two organizations were constantly sparring for control of the United States Olympic Committee, on which both organizations were represented.

The 1972 Summer Olympic Games would prove to be a turning point in that struggle. Though the University of Indiana swimmer Mark Spitz would win seven gold medals, and the Russian gymnast Olga Korbut would enchant the world with her graceful agility on the uneven parallel bars and pommel horse, the entire fortnight was overshadowed by the Palestinian terrorists of Black September taking hostages and murdering eleven members from Israel's Olympic team, including nine hostages.

At the moment reports of the attack started coming in, Roone Arledge had Olympics host Chris Schenkel sitting in the anchor chair. ABC newsman Peter Jennings—then a correspondent—was also in Munich, as was Howard Cosell, who was imploring Arledge to let him cover it.

Arledge—aware that the entire Olympics Games were now an international incident—turned to his assistant, Geoff Mason, and said: "Get McKay."

At that point, Jim McKay was in a swimming pool at the Munich Sheraton. Mason reached him on the phone and said, "I've never said this to you before, but get your ass over here, *right now.* We've got a situation."

McKay would arrive quickly and spend the next twelve hours on the air, acquitting himself in a time of utter chaos with his poise, calm and decency, as news of the eleven deaths came in. Crucially, Arledge and ABC had previously negotiated with the International Olympic Committee for the use of their own "unilateral camera," which meant they weren't beholden to the Olympics worldwide feed, which was cut off shortly after the crisis began.

Apart from the horror of the murder of Israeli athletes, Americans would remember the Olympics for its shortcomings, none greater than in the men's basketball competition.

A deep, talented and young American men's team was led by the wizened legendary coach Hank Iba, who had piloted the '64 and '68 gold medalists but hadn't coached college basketball since 1970. The reason Iba was coaching—rather than John Wooden, or Al McGuire, or Dean Smith—was that the AAU, forever in a turf war with the NCAA, didn't want an active college coach running the program.

The USA featured a team of freewheeling, fast-breaking stars, but Iba chose to put those same players into a straitjacket of a deliberate, plodding, patterned offense.

The generation gap was acute. "They were funny about the blacks," Olympian Jim Brewer would recall. "Iba couldn't remember anyone's name. He certainly didn't remember mine. The fifteen best basketball players in America and none of us seemed to have names. *'Young-uns,'* he called us. I don't think he much liked the way we dressed, and he hated the stereos. A lot of blacks arrived with stereos."

Constricted into a style that didn't take advantage of its superior speed and transition skills, the U.S. played perfectly into the hands of the taller, heavier, older but less athletic opponents, the Soviet Union, in the gold medal game. The Soviets led by as many as 10 points at one stage, but the U.S. rallied in the second half and, after a hard late foul, Illinois State's Doug Collins sank two free throws to give the U.S. a 50–49 lead with three seconds left.

The chaos at the conclusion of the game would remain confounding decades later. The final three seconds were played three times, the first two deemed insufficient because of confusion over a called time-out, and then because the game clock had been improperly reset. The patron of Olympic basketball, the British eminence R. William Jones, even came out of the stands in the midst of the end-of-the-game confusion (without any official authority to do so) and ordered the officials and timekeeper to reset the clock and replay the final seconds again. On the third opportunity, the Soviet Ivan Edeshko passed the ball the length of the court and Aleksander Belov out-jumped two Americans and laid the ball in as time ran out. Final score, Soviet Union 51, United States 50.

The formal appeal lodged by the U.S. Olympic Committee was denied by a 3–2 vote, with Soviet-bloc countries Poland, Hungary, and Cuba siding with the U.S.S.R. The outraged U.S. team refused to accept its silver medals in protest.

Beyond the basketball debacle, there were a raft of other logistical problems for the USA team. The swimmer Rick DeMont won the 400-meter freestyle, but was stripped of the title by the IOC a day later after a urinalysis showed traces of the banned substance ephedrine. On the medical forms athletes provided prior to the Olympics, DeMont had properly provided notification of the asthma drug he was taking. But in the USOC red tape, the organization had not properly cleared it with the IOC.

The pole vaulter Bob Seagren had set a world record ahead of the Olympics, but his pole, made of flexible composite material, was first banned, then allowed, then banned again, with the USOC hapless in the face of the Olympic bureaucracy. Even the AAU-approved U.S. track and field logo, which was sewn onto the chest of the warm-up jackets, was a heavy nuisance. "When you started jogging," said marathon runner Kenny Moore, "the patch swung back and forth like a pendulum."

Perhaps the most representative failure of all came in the track and field competition, when two U.S. sprinters missed their qualifying heats because their coach, Stan Wright, had misread the schedule (mistaking the military time of 1615 as quarter after six instead of quarter after four).

The *Los Angeles Times* columnist Jim Murray would remember walking into the Olympic broadcasting center and seeing the American sprinters "looking like they had seen a ghost," and behind them, ABC's Howard Cosell muttering, "It's an American tragedy!"

"What is, Howard?" asked Murray.

"These sprinters missed the start time in their heats," said Cosell. "We've handed the hundred to the Russians."

Coming back from Munich, many of the American Olympians expressed a collective dissatisfaction with the USOC. Their interests were not being protected; their voices were not being heard. Donna de Varona, who'd been on the U.S. Olympic swim team in Rome in 1960 and won two golds in Tokyo in 1964, worked for ABC as a commentator in 1972. She came home acutely aware of "how inept our sports system was at representing our athletes internationally. No one was there for our athletes."

Later that year, a garrulous, boisterous former Marine Corps colonel named Mike Harrigan—who'd run track at Penn in the '60s, and had been privy to the AAU–NCAA turf wars himself—was working as a staff assistant in the Nixon White House when he sent a memo to H. R. Haldeman, Nixon's chief of staff. Harrigan proposed a presidential commission to find some remedy to the internecine squabbling among competing amateur organizations that was causing so much consternation in international competition.

Harrigan was uniquely situated to understand the problem. "The athletes for international competitions would come from the NCAA. And the NCAA had no representation in the AAU—none. And the NCAA, quite properly, would say to the AAU, 'We will let you have our athletes, but only if you will allow us to have significant or fair representation in your governing body.' And the AAU would say, 'Fuck you, go away.' And then the NCAA would say, 'Well, you can't have our athletes,' and that in a nutshell was what the AAU–NCAA conflict was about."

The Cold War offered motivation for consolidating and strengthening the Olympic effort. Behind the Iron Curtain, state-sponsored athletes in the Soviet Union and East Germany were de facto pros competing with amateurs of the West. But there was also the unique structural system of the U.S., "the only country in the world which uses the college system as the backbone of athletic development."

It would take nearly three years, two different presidential approvals, and a protracted struggle between the White House and the Office of Management and Budget, but the President's Commission on Olympic Sports was finally convened in 1975 and funded at $569,000. Harrigan would chair the commission—which included de Varona, the sports entrepreneur Lamar Hunt, Olympic gold medalist diver Micki King, Olympic decathlon champion Rafer Johnson, the news announcer Howard K. Smith and retired Oklahoma football coaching legend Bud Wilkinson among others—and eventually try to find a way through the thicket of red tape.

•

College football was growing increasingly expensive and athletic directors were feeling the crunch. Rapidly increasing costs—everything from stadium modernization, increased recruiting expenses (including long-distance phone and postage charges), the widespread custom of putting players up in hotels even the night before home games and switching from black-and-white to color game films—had led to forty-two colleges dropping the sport of football in the previous decade.

By the beginning of 1971, schools were exploring limits to how many scholarships could be offered in a year. There were no limits, which is why schools like Texas and Alabama could offer so many.

"The mandate to cut budgets came from the university presidents," said Doc Councilman, the coach at swimming powerhouse Indiana. "But this is kind of in reverse. Football budgets run about $1 million, minor sports about $30,000 to $50,000. It seems logical to me to cut back in football, where the big money is."

Even Michigan, one of the superpowers, recognized the bind. "We have to start some form of de-escalation or pretty soon we'll go under," said athletic director Don Canham.

•

As the audience for football and basketball was growing, so was the competition in recruiting. For years, Arthur Bergstrom, the NCAA's comptroller, handled all enforcement and eligibility issues.

"The enforcement was basically negligible," said Chuck Neinas. "And so then they picked it up in the '70s."

In 1972, Byers hired David Berst—a physical education instructor and baseball coach at his alma mater, MacMurray College—to beef up the NCAA's enforcement arm, which was increasingly flooded with allegations from schools reporting that other schools were cheating.

Even with the increases in staff, the NCAA had just five investigators to monitor the nearly 200 major-college schools in basketball and the more than 100 major-college schools in football.

While recruiting competition was fierce everywhere, it was particularly fraught in basketball, where one or two blue-chip players could change the course of an entire program. At Marquette, the charismatic Al McGuire had revived the Warriors' fortunes with an aggressive recruiting policy of bringing in Black athletes from Eastern outposts. One prospect in 1974 was the gifted Bronx point guard Butch Lee, the rare blue-chip prospect who was also an honor student, with offers from Penn and other Ivy League schools.

Of his recruiting pitch to Lee, McGuire said, "I told Butch he'd be playing in the Ivy League at 5:15 p.m. in a third-floor walk-up gym against guys with a two-handed dribble and their underwear hanging out. I told him come with me and it'll be SRO every night with balloons and smoke rings, and the band will be playing and the cheerleaders' skirts will be bouncing up and down." Lee chose to attend Marquette.

As the competition intensified, the temptation to finesse the rules became greater. "We've stopped recruiting young men," said Virginia's football coach Sonny Randle, "who want to come here to be students first and athletes second."

Meanwhile, as all this was going on, submerged in the background of all these debates were increased calls for more athletic opportunities for women. Which, at the time in the early '70s, went largely unheeded.

"I don't remember anyone *ever* talking about women's sports," said Bill Hancock, who worked at Oklahoma. "It was not in anyone's consciousness. It should've been. It was a tragedy."

# SEVEN

# STYLE AND SUBSTANCE

ON FRIDAY, OCTOBER 18, 1974, Hubie Brown walked out on the court for his first game as a head coach, leading the Kentucky Colonels of the American Basketball Association onto their home court at Freedom Hall in Louisville. Brown wore the standard basketball coaches' attire —a suit and tie—as did his assistant, Stan Albeck. What he saw next left him speechless.

"So out comes Larry Brown and Doug Moe," said Brown, of the Denver Nuggets head coach and assistant coach. "They have bib overalls on, and 'Mr. B' Billy Eckstine sport shirts, where the collars would go all the way out to the end of your shoulder."

The clothing revolution had come to sports. Even Brown's take on the disco farmer look was far less casual than another ABA coach, Wilt Chamberlain, who was known to show up to coach the San Diego Conquistadors fresh off the beach, sporting shorts and sandals, and still tracking sand onto the side of the court.

There were no such daring stylistic choices from the Pittsburgh Steelers' eminently sensible coach Chuck Noll, but he nonetheless presided over a wide variety of stylistic expression from his players.

"Chuck's rule when we were traveling was, 'no tank tops, no shorts, no sandals,'" said Joe Greene. "But he didn't say anything about those vests, the scarves, the big-collared shirts and the bell-bottoms, the high heels, and the big buccaneer belt buckles. We were just—it was amazing. I attributed that to the Beatles and how they really changed the culture. The audience started dressing like they did."

The sense that almost everyone wanted to be on the cutting edge of fashion was pervasive. Even the retired NFL great Paul Hornung—by now providing color commentary for Notre Dame football—would show up to call games in a distressed denim pullover shirt, with leather laces instead of buttons in the front.

There are periods in American life in which change occurs so rapidly, it can seem for a spell as if nothing from the past particularly pertains anymore. So it was in the early '70s, where many of the old established norms were disintegrating. Single-sex dorms were being phased out for co-ed living; curfews were becoming a thing of the past; and young adults cohabiting before marriage was growing more common. Polyester and plastic and developments in dying and color-fast cottons meant that the palette of acceptable colors exploded into a cornucopia of different hues.

This feverish spell seeped into the world of sports as well. It could be seen in everything from the hairstyles of the athletes to the uniforms they wore to the surfaces they played on. And in that cultural mix, almost anything was possible. It was the sort of decade where the ultra-square afternoon talk show host Mike Douglas would spend an awkward but fascinating week co-hosting the show with Sly Stone. Watching the two men interviewing the guest Muhammad Ali was to witness the multitudes that the country could contain.

Sports had always had its share of flakes, oddballs, and obsessives, but in the new decade they seemed to hit a rich vein of eccentricity. The NBA had Charlie Yelverton, once described as "the league's only black hippie" by Kareem Abdul-Jabbar ("He'd come out during warm-ups and sit at mid-court and meditate. Wore dreadlocks…Made the good impression on the coaches"). In hockey, there was Derek Sanderson, the self-styled hockey maverick who wore flowered bell-bottoms, had a round bed and drove a Rolls-Royce Silver Cloud. In pro football, there was Tim Rossovich, who had perfected a stunt in which he set himself on fire, was fond of chewing glass, and once dove naked into a birthday cake. In baseball, there was Mark "The Bird" Fidrych, the shaggy-haired Tigers pitcher who groomed the mound with his hands and spoke to the baseball he was about to pitch, and Bill "Spaceman" Lee, whose idiosyncrasies—he once claimed to sprinkle marijuana on his buckwheat pancakes—were so pronounced they inspired a Warren Zevon song ("You're supposed to sit on your ass and smile at stupid things/Lord that's hard to do"). Each of them, on his own terms, was unique, but taken together, they spoke to the expanding boundaries of permissible behavior within professional sports.

The Steelers had the sharp-dressing, fast-talking African American running back John Fuqua, who claimed to have been born in a castle outside of Paris, where he ventured out one day with his white poodle, only to have the sun turn his skin a rich chestnut brown. As Fuqua explained, when even his butler Jacques failed to recognize him, "I was banished and had to come to America. The only thing I knew how to do was play soccer. But I found that in America they didn't play soccer. The closest thing was football and so I tried it. My main object was to make enough money so that I could find a specialist to change my complexion back to its natural color and then I could go back and reclaim my castle."

Fuqua finished his career without reclaiming his castle, but he did make a deep impression and land on several best-dressed lists (he was partial to capes), and actually did once wear translucent stacked heels with goldfish swimming in the heels.

Not all of the eccentrics were quite as media-friendly. Before Super Bowl V, the Cowboys' enigmatic running back Duane Thomas was sitting on a stone wall by the Fort Lauderdale hotel the team was staying at, staring out toward the ocean.

Around that time, Frank Luksa of the *Fort Worth Star-Telegram* walked up and asked Thomas what he was looking at.

"New Zealand," said Thomas.

"But Duane, you're looking to the east," Luksa said.

Thomas smiled and said, "It's out there somewhere."

The following year, Thomas went silent for much of the season, refusing to talk with the press until after the Cowboys had won Super Bowl VI. In the postgame bustle, the announcer Tom Brookshier—visibly nervous to be interviewing the player who'd generated so much controversy during the year—stumbled out with an opening question of "Duane, are you really as fast as you appear?"

"Evidently," said Thomas.

•

Among the style mavens, no one could match the two paragons of New York City metropolitan sexuality. The quintessential bachelor quarterback Joe Namath famously wore a mink coat on the sidelines of a Jets game (he was injured and in street clothes) and the Knicks' silky guard Walt "Clyde" Frazier—perhaps along with Fuqua in football—was the first player about whom what he wore to and from the game was news in itself.

Namath's 1969 autobiography, *I Can't Wait Until Tomorrow...'Cause I Get Better-Looking Every Day*, was a more or less conventional athlete's memoir. But in 1973, with Bob Oates Jr., he published a coffee-table book, *Joe Namath: A Matter of Style*, which opened with his own manifesto: "When I come out on the field, I'm ready to roll. And the way I want to do it playing football is the same way I want to be in daily life. I want to be smooth. I want to operate with no excess motion or disturbances. It's a matter of style."

So it was with Frazier, who earned his nickname from the Knicks' trainer, Danny Whelan, who thought he dressed like Warren Beatty's Clyde Barrow in the movie *Bonnie and Clyde*. By 1974, Frazier published his own book, *Rockin' Steady: A Guide to Basketball & Cool*, with Ira Berkow. Like Namath's book, it was a slick, heavily illustrated work that reflected the sensibilities of the book's author. A departure from other athletes' memoirs, Frazier's book spoke to both principles of the game ("when I know I can get my shot off right away, I make my last dribble a hard one to give my body an extra push into the air") and the essentials of cool ("Cool I think is reactions, reflexes, and attitude. You got to feel out the situation.").

Namath and Frazier both exuded a cutting-edge insouciance, a slouchy reserve that in no way dimmed their competitive fire. There were elements of both books showing clear lines of demarcation, of athletes occupying a different social sphere. Namath escorted Raquel Welch to the Academy Awards in 1972; that same year, he appeared on a televised "forum on love" with Dr. Joyce Brothers. At the time, he was signing autographs, "Peace, Joe Namath." Frazier was renowned for his hats and alligator- and lizard-skin shoes; his book was perhaps the first to inform young fans that some players referred to underarm deodorant spray as "pit juice."

Namath and Frazier shared an implicit understanding that, notwithstanding the imperatives of competition, sports was—especially in its modern, telegenic incarnation—a *performing art*. (It was something that Larry Fleisher of the NBPA kept hammering home—in modern professional sports, athletes were entertainers, and needed to be paid accordingly.)

In *A Matter of Style*, Namath observed, "There's been a lot of change in the last ten years. People are feeling a lot more open-minded now about what people wear, how their hair is, what their religion is, what their race is. And it's a good thing, too, because there was a lot of nonsense going on, stuff like if a guy has long hair, he can't work, or if he works at B&W Steel Mill he can't eat at a fancy restaurant, or if he is black he can't choose his seat on the bus. I guess there still is some of that, but things have certainly got better."

•

For all the attention paid to the studied cool of Namath and Frazier, perhaps no athlete better represented the triumph of image than Jack Nicklaus. Forever unstylish in the shadow of the glamorous Arnold Palmer and his devout followers throughout the '60s, Nicklaus played the heavy in the public imagination.

Writing about the differences between the two golfers, the *Los Angeles Times'* Jim Murray once observed, "Arnold Palmer has a belly like a washboard and a back like a chimney. He flies his own plane. Jack Nicklaus has a front like a pile of old clothes and a back like an unmade bed. He gets any heavier, and he'll have to fly as freight."

It was that Nicklaus—"Fat Jack" to the masses in Arnie's Army—who was out on the course at the 1969 Ryder Cup, held at the Royal Birkdale Golf Club in England. Paired with Britain's Tony Jacklin in the final group, Nicklaus exhibited one of the great moments of sportsmanship on the eighteenth green, when he conceded Jacklin's short putt to ensure a draw.

The selfless act would be remembered for decades, but what resonated further was the way Nicklaus felt at the event's conclusion. He had played thirty-six holes that day, and remembering the event later, he said, "I became seriously tired on a golf course for the first time in my life."

It wasn't just the heat and humidity. The prideful champion, who had already won seven professional majors, had grown weary of his own obesity. He was tired of carrying 210 pounds on his five-foot-ten-inch frame. He was tired of being shot from the waist up—or else having the lower half of his body replaced by a body double—in the promotional advertisements for Munsingwear sport shirts he endorsed.

For years, Nicklaus had stoically ignored the jokes, at least in public. But on the flight back to the States, he told his wife, Barbara, that he'd had enough: He was going to lose the weight. With typical Nicklaus commitment he joined Weight Watchers, began running between holes on the golf course and dropped twenty pounds in a matter of weeks.

In the months to follow, Nicklaus would go through what he'd describe as a "metamorphosis." He called the clothier Hart Schaffner Marx and asked them to send down a tailor because he was on his way to needing a new wardrobe. He bought in to the new diet—heavy on cottage cheese and tuna fish—kept the twenty pounds off, then hired consultants and designers to modify his wardrobe. He eschewed his crew cut and his charmless bucket hats, let his golden hair grow longer, allowed his sideburns to creep down below his earlobes. Only weeks later he emerged, at the beginning of 1970, transformed, slimmed down, a newly telegenic presence.

Nicklaus had never spent much time thinking about his appearance and had teased other parents for letting their sons "walk around looking like girls," but when his sons let their hair grow long, he realized he didn't hate it, and he let his own hair grow out as well. "Soon people were telling me I looked younger and less Teutonic and all kinds of nice things," recalled Nicklaus, "and from then on I just kept up with the times in what I wore and how I had my hair cut."

He found the weight loss took a few yards off his drives, but it gave him a better sense of touch around the green. He had more stamina and stopped breathing so heavily during the par fives.

But there was something else: The makeover didn't just make Nicklaus healthier; it radically altered the way he was perceived. Not only for his endorsements and business interests, but on the course and throughout the sports world.

Nicklaus was the same golfer, and his rival and antagonist Palmer hadn't changed. But after a decade of fighting for a public approval that never came, almost overnight it did. Suddenly Fat Jack was...the Golden Bear.

His wife, Barbara, was amused. "My husband, the sex symbol," she said. "You wouldn't believe how much he's enjoying the new fans, the swooning galleries."

The Nicklaus makeover was so complete and so compelling that he soon became an endorsement juggernaut. A single issue of Sports Illustrated in April 1972 included the tanned, blond Golden Bear in four different full-color ads, including a full-page spot for the new Pontiac Grand Prix ("a cut above"), four pages of Nicklaus modeling Hart Shaffner Marx's new line of double-knits, a two-page spread for MacGregor golf clubs, and a spot with Nicklaus behind a Murray lawnmower.

He wasn't the only one to change. The Bruins' superstar Bobby Orr's crew cut was replaced by flowing locks in time for his 1970 season, just in time for his first MVP trophy and a raft of his own endorsements.

Hair was growing everywhere. Oakland's Reggie Jackson showed up to the Oakland Athletics' spring training site in 1971 sporting a mustache—the first major league player with facial hair since before World War II.

Exhibiting his usual mercurial instability, the Oakland owner Charlie Finley originally opposed Jackson's grooming choice before executing a U-turn and deciding that it would earn more attention if the whole team let it all hang out.

"Well, he didn't want to have to tell Reggie to shave," said Sal Bando. "So instead, he'd rather give us all $300 for growing a mustache."

Soon Jackson had a beard, Bando, Joe Rudi, and others were sporting full mustaches, and relief pitcher Rollie Fingers was developing a heavily waxed handlebar mustache that made him look like Snidely Whiplash. The next year, Finley reimagined the Athletics as "The Swingin' A's," with a new logo and new uniforms—a groundbreaking set of mix-and-match V-neck pullovers in white, kelly green and "Fort Knox gold."

By then, people had also taken note of the Indians' outfielder Oscar Gamble, whose afro was an apotheosis of the form, a corona of hirsute flamboyance so large it demanded its own zip code, all the more noticeable in the generally more reserved world of baseball.

Even some of the coaches had come around. Hank Stram had relaxed his rules on facial hair, having been swayed by a meeting with Willie Lanier, in which the linebacker explained the history of facial hair in the African American community and showed Stram that frequent shaving irritated his skin.

When a reporter visited Darrell Royal in his office in 1973 and talked about the changing times, Royal pointed to a can of hairspray on his sink. "I'll tell you how things have changed," he said. "Three years ago I would be hiding this."

There were still coaches who drew a line on long hair, equating conservative hairstyles with mental discipline, but those sorts of strictures elicited more of a pushback in the '70s. The Eagles' Rossovich tangled with Philadelphia's head coach Ed Khayat, who insisted on no long hair or mustaches. Rossovich waited until mere minutes before Khayat's deadline to shave his mustache. "It didn't make sense to me," Rossovich said. "The length of your hair, the width of your lapels or necktie. Did you have a mustache? What did that have to do with playing football?"

It was a question that, by the early '70s, a lot of athletes were asking of a lot of coaches.

"All I know is you can't talk to athletes like you once could," said Penn State coach Joe Paterno. "You can't sit on 'em. They're exposed to too many things. They're too smart, too aware. If they're not convinced that self-discipline is for their own good, they're not going to perform like you want them to."

•

The changes could also be seen on the field as sports uniforms evolved. In 1971, the Pirates and Rawlings debuted their double-knit (cotton and nylon) uniforms, pullover jerseys and beltless pants.

The next year, the A's followed with their green-and-gold ensemble, the Padres wore mustard-yellow uniforms, the White Sox trotted out road uniforms in sky-blue (which soon became league-wide norm). The Texas Rangers—freshly moved from Washington, where the Senators failed to draw—added an elastic waistband of red, white and blue stripes.

Harold Bowman, a rep from Wilson, said, "I've been in this business for thirty years, and for a long time I've thought someone ought to do something to dress up baseball uniforms, something that would hit the spectator in the eye. Now we've got it. Even though a team may be playing bad, at least it will look good."

The color palette—"mod" was the term most often used for any color other than red or blue—exploded. In the 1970–71 season, six teams in the National Hockey League began wearing colored skates. After a century of black skates in hockey, suddenly the Los Angeles Kings were skating out shod in purple and gold.

Color television, in the words of sports fashion historian Paul Lukas, "changed everything in terms of uniforms, and it really mirrored what was going on in civilian clothing. A lot of it had to do with new fabrics and the increased use of polyester which allowed for a wider range of dyes to be used. And of course in the '70s, sort of coming on the heels of the '60s, with the counterculture and LSD and all sorts of psychedelic things became part of youth culture. And then hand in hand with that we also saw the rise of color TV, which certainly led to greater use of color in uniforms."

•

It wasn't just the uniforms and hairstyles that were being modernized. So were the stadiums. This was, in the main, a welcome change, with city after city building new stadiums, and fans spared the indignities of splintered bleacher seats, obstructed views, and cramped corridors. It made a difference for players as well. Chuck Noll noted that the opening of Three Rivers Stadium in 1970 coincided with the beginning of the Steelers' renaissance: "It had as much of an effect on the football team as anything we did."

In Dallas and Kansas City, football-only stadiums costing (a relatively economical, in retrospect) $35 million in Dallas in 1971 and $43 million in Kansas City in 1972 changed forever the calculation of what to expect from the environment of a sporting event.

The new stadiums were something more than gleaming palaces espousing the virtues of professional sports. In almost every instance—from Texas Stadium in Irving to the Harry S. Truman Sports Complex in Kansas City to the Superdome in New Orleans (designed to call the Astrodome's bet and raise it, opening in 1975 at a staggering cost of $163 million)—the new structures were reimagined as gargantuan office parks, accompanied by conference rooms, restaurants, and offices that possessed many of the trappings of modern corporate design: spacious meeting and common areas, and carpeted hallways with recessed lighting that evoked the smooth ethos of modern professionalism.

Those stadiums were football-only. In Kansas City, across the parking lot from Arrowhead, was the baseball-only Royals Stadium, built for $70 million, opening in 1973. It transformed the sheer act of going to work. "Having toilets that worked," said John Schuerholz, then an assistant to the general manager. "Pretty much the whole experience. We were all anxious to go, thrilled to go. When you drove up and got your first look at the complex and the back of the scoreboard [modeled after the Royals' crest, with a distinctive crown on top], that took your breath away, and gave you an extra boost of energy to work that much harder."

For all the innovation, many of the new stadiums were plagued with a stultifying sameness. In St. Louis and Cincinnati, Pittsburgh and Philadelphia, stadiums were built in the late '60s and early '70s that were designed to be multipurpose—for both baseball and football—kept most fans far away from the action and wound up being, more than anything else, depressingly generic. "Cookie cutters," they were called, and the *New Yorker*'s Roger Angell referred to Riverfront Stadium in Cincinnati as a "cheerless, circular, Monsanto close."

It was an assessment the players came to agree with. While they enjoyed the carpeted locker rooms and the ability to walk to the field without encountering rats in a dark tunnel, the stadiums all lacked personality. "I stand at the plate in the Vet and I honestly don't know whether I'm in Pittsburgh, Cincinnati, St. Louis, or Philly," said the Pirates' Richie Hebner. "They all look alike."

America had celebrated the first Earth Day in 1970—the same year that the Ad Council started its "Keep America Beautiful" campaign with a melodramatic commercial showing a Native American weeping at the pervasive littering and garbage in his midst. But even as ecology turned into a buzzword, and earth tones became newly ascendant, the society was trying to control nature with central air, wall-to-wall carpeting, and No-Pest Strips that hung outside and repelled mosquitoes. So it should not have come as a surprise that one of the most powerful forces in the sports world in the early '70s was the push toward artificial turf.

The Astrodome was to blame. When the "Eighth Wonder of the World" opened in 1965, it proved inept at growing grass indoors. (Originally the ceiling was covered with panes of glass, but the glare from the panes made fielding fly balls a danger; when the panes were painted black, the grass soon died.) That prompted Monsanto to rename its Chem-Grass product as Astro-Turf and roll it out for the 1966 season.

Perceptions mattered, too. Rainouts in baseball were a nuisance. In football, inevitably, any injuries that occurred on muddy surfaces were blamed on the slippery footing. So when fake grass came of age, it was probably inevitable that it would be marketed for sure footing, quick drainage and increased safety. The rush to artificial turf came quickly in the wake of the AstroTurf in the Astrodome. Franklin Field switched to the turf in 1969. The Orange Bowl was still a grass field on New Year's Day 1970, but had gone to tartan turf by the 1971 Orange Bowl. Tulane Stadium had grass for Super Bowl IV in 1970 but had installed turf by Super Bowl VI in 1972.

Soon, all of the multipurpose stadiums (Riverfront in Cincinnati, Busch in St. Louis, Veterans in Philadelphia and Three Rivers in Pittsburgh) had adopted turf, as did the two football-only edifices, Texas Stadium outside of Dallas and Arrowhead Stadium in Kansas City. The same happened within the space of a few years in college football, as national powers Texas, Arkansas, Nebraska, Ohio State, Michigan, Oklahoma, Alabama and Auburn all adopted the new surfaces.

The industry bragged of playability and safety, and soon it was sweeping through the National League in baseball. By the early '70s, Monsanto was running full-page full-color magazine ads for AstroTurf, and the American Biltrite Rubber Co. was doing the same for its product, Poly-Turf.

There was one problem. The people who actually *played* on the new surfaces almost uniformly hated them.

"Somebody has done a great selling job on this artificial turf, but not to the players," said the Raiders' quarterback Daryle Lamonica. "Every player I've talked to hates it. You have good footing, and maybe it cuts down on knee injuries, but you get terrible burns and the stuff is so hard it's like falling on your living room floor with two 260-pound guys on top of you. That artificial grass is good for the owners and promoters, but they don't ask the players. We have three times as many painful injuries as on real grass."

In Dallas and Kansas City, two Hall of Fame quarterbacks were experiencing similar problems. In Dallas, Roger Staubach's elbow swelled up so badly—the product of an infection from earlier turf burns—that he had to be hospitalized. The Chiefs' Len Dawson suffered blood poisoning when the chemicals used to treat the surface got into his bloodstream. Dawson recalled that the Chiefs' veterans "begged Stram to get some relief from the stuff."

All the more frustrating in Kansas City was the fact that groundskeeper

George Toma—the legendary "Sod God"—was reduced to tending the bristly rug. "The thing I couldn't figure out," said the Chiefs' linebacker Bobby Bell, "is when you've got the best grass guy in the world, they'd go to a carpet. I mean, this guy can grow grass in your *pocket*—and they wanted to get turf."

At Cincinnati's Riverfront Stadium on a blazing hot day, the temperature on the field was 160 degrees, and 134 degrees just above field level. "It's like playing on a shopping-center parking lot on a hot day," said Braves manager Lum Harris.

The idea that it provided surer footing was also a canard. After a 1971 game between the Dolphins and Jets, Miami coach Don Shula reviewed the film and determined that players slipped on the Poly-Turf surface fifty-nine times. (The field was replaced with an updated nylon version of turf in time for the 1972 season.)

The Phillies' All-Star Dick Allen put it best: "If a horse can't eat it, I don't want to play on it."

There was also an aesthetic cost. Games played outdoors on natural grass, whether they be football or baseball, had a texture. You could tell by looking at a picture whether it was the first quarter or the fourth quarter. Just as golf and tennis played outdoors had to deal with elements, so did football and baseball. But with artificial surfaces and, eventually, domes, there were no elements, no variables, no soul.

"Artificial turf has made football look strange," reported Bud Shrake in *Sports Illustrated* in 1972. "Take the foot out of the grass and put it on a carpet, and the game can seem to become an amusement, like the hotel ballroom boxing matches staged for gentlemen in dinner jackets."

•

In the '70s, sports intersected with popular culture in a way that had not applied before. Though the Beatles famously played at Shea Stadium, the band and their music were not really a part of the ethos of sports.

The decade would see pop music insinuate itself into the fabric of the games. At Cobo Hall in Detroit, the Pistons of the early '70s would warm up to the strains of Elton John's "Bennie and the Jets." "The song had the perfect rhythm and rallied the fans," recalled the Pistons' coach Ray Scott, "who would respond by clapping their hands in time and singing along. At one point, Elton John's agent came to a game to thank us for making the song such a big part of our game-time entertainment."

Prior to the '70s, athletes had rarely mixed with the larger streams of popular culture. There were exceptions—Joe DiMaggio marrying Marilyn Monroe—but even the best-known athletes of the '60s, like Frank Gifford and Paul Hornung, were famous in their particular realm, and endorsed largely niche products for men.

But as sports made its incursion into prime time the '70s, so did it begin cross-pollinating with popular culture. Wilt Chamberlain made an appearance (staging a mock fight with Sammy Davis Jr.) on NBC's *Laugh-In*. Johnny Carson, University of Nebraska Class of 1949, returned to Lincoln for the Cornhuskers' homecoming game in 1971. By 1975, Bob Dylan had taken up the cause of incarcerated boxer Rubin "Hurricane" Carter in his song "Hurricane," released that November.

The effect could also be seen in motion pictures. In 1971, Woody Allen used Howard Cosell for a widely praised spot in *Bananas*, and that same year Billy Dee Williams and James Caan co-starred in the made-for-TV movie *Brian's Song*, depicting the interracial friendship between the Chicago Bears' running back Gale Sayers and Brian Piccolo. Later, Burt Reynolds starred in *The Longest Yard* (1974), and in 1976 Walter Matthau and Tatum O'Neal carried the funny, profane *Bad News Bears* and Sylvester Stallone won best picture for *Rocky*, based loosely on the story of tomato-can Chuck Wepner's longshot title fight against Muhammad Ali.

During the 1976–77 season, the Atlanta Hawks, the team with the lowest payroll in the NBA, adopted the theme from *Rocky* as its fight song, as a way to rouse fans for the full-court pressing defense that Hubie Brown preferred. "Every time the ball went out of bounds, or there was a time-out, we'd play *Rocky* in the building," said Brown.

•

Sports was not immune to the changes coursing through the society. In 1970, the Pirates' Dock Ellis had arrived with the team for a road series in San Diego, and on the eve of a twi-night doubleheader, partied with a friend in Los Angeles. After taking a tab of LSD that night, Ellis recalled, he emerged from his haze the next morning: "I might have slept maybe an hour. I got up maybe about nine or ten in the morning. Took another half tab." When he finally arrived back at San Diego Stadium, he was still tripping, but then attempted to flush acid out of his system by taking Dexamyl and Benzedrine. Naturally, Ellis threw a no-hitter in his start that day.

"Drugs were always available," said Red Sox outfielder Bernie Carbo. "I played eleven years in the big leagues, and there wasn't a day that I played without any drugs. Amphetamines, Dexedrine, Benzedrine, Darvon, Darvocet, codeine, sleeping pills, shots. I was addicted to drugs. Marijuana and cocaine."

In the summer of 1972, the Miami Dolphins were coming off the epic 27–24 double-overtime playoff win over the Kansas City Chiefs, which came on Christmas Day 1971. Miami had a charismatic fullback, Larry Csonka, whose serially broken nose looked exactly like what a novelist might envision a fullback's nose looking like. Csonka and his running back sidekick Jim Kiick were that rarest of things in the '70s, a white one-two running back punch. They had met in 1968 when Kiick was sneaking up a fire escape at four a.m. a few nights before they played the Packers in the College All-Star Game in Chicago. A year later, inspired by the Paul Newman–Robert Redford film, the *Miami Herald* writer Bill Braucher dubbed the pair Butch Cassidy and the Sundance Kid (Csonka was Butch; Kiick was Sundance).

Their off-season *Sports Illustrated* cover in 1972, courtesy of the legendary photographer Walter Iooss Jr., came with the two players dressed in their uniforms under a goalpost. "Those two guys were so stoned," remembered Iooss. "I'll never forget Csonka saying, 'This is the longest walk I've ever made in my life.' They were out of their minds. All they did was laugh, and give me the finger, for the entire session. Obviously these pictures were shown to the managing editor, the art director, and everyone else. No one saw the finger, not even when they looked at the proof. You'd have thought they'd have gotten wise when virtually every picture someone had a finger up. But no one saw it. These things happen."

These things led to Csonka and Kiick on the cover of the August 7, 1972, issue of *Sports Illustrated*, with the former flipping off the camera with his right hand. The Dolphins had the last laugh, going 17–0 en route to a victory in Super Bowl VII.

While it was clear everywhere that the culture was in flux, nothing quite prepared the media or the masses for what developed between the New York Yankees' pitchers Fritz Peterson and Mike Kekich, and their respective wives, Marilyn Peterson and Susanne Kekich.

In the summer of 1972, three years after the release of the partner-swapping film *Bob & Carol & Ted & Alice,* the Petersons and Kekiches attended a party at the home of sportswriter Maury Allen. At the end of the party, around two a.m., the two couples had a long conversation outside of Allen's home, and Mike Kekich went home with Marilyn Peterson, and Fritz Peterson went home with Susanne Kekich. Eventually, those new pairings were declared permanent.

It was called wife-swapping, though that was technically inaccurate. The women each stayed in their home with their children. What was being swapped, in fact, were the husbands.

But when the word leaked out about the new arrangement during the Yankees' training camp in 1973, the press ran wild, interviewing every-one from teammates to Fritz Peterson's mother-in-law to a besieged Susanne Kekich ("most people think it's smutty when it's not. It's simply that we were attracted to each other and we all fell in love. We did not partake in lechery").

In the end, it was unclear whether the most startling thing about the epi-sode was that two active major leaguers willingly traded their marital part-ners, or that two active major leaguers willingly attended a party thrown by a sportswriter.

That athletes had a lot of sex was hardly new, but it took on a different tone in the 1970s, where the relaxed mores combined with the more aggres-sive role of the media made certain stories fair game that wouldn't have been reported in the past.

In spring training in Florida in 1975, the Mets' outfielder Cleon Jones was found and arrested, in the back of a van, sleeping nude, with a woman who was not his wife. The charge was eventually dropped, but the Mets' chairman, M. Donald Grant, vowed "we have to restore the Mets' image." That led to one of the more uncomfortable press conferences in sports his-tory with Jones publicly apologizing for the incident with his wife, Angela, at his side.

But at times, even the owners were complicit in the casual sex. When the Suns' owner Dick Bloch was being deposed in the Oscar Robertson suit, he was asked whether he had entered into any secret agreements that were not part of the standard NBA player contract.

After conferring with his lawyer—a young associate from the firm of Proskauer Rose named David Stern—Bloch agreed to go off the record and explained that the Suns *had* made one contractual agreement not listed in the signed contract. The club had agreed to provide a prostitute before each home game to perform oral sex on star forward Connie Hawkins.

Amid the snickering suits, the owner hastened to clarify the agreement. "This was only for home games," Bloch explained. "Connie was on his own on the road."

For those who aspired to character-building and conflated Cold War readiness with discipline and conformity on the field, the era amounted to nothing less than the great reckoning.

The relaxed mores were no laughing matter to those who still espoused old-school virtues. Speaking at a physical education conference in Pittsburgh in 1973, the Ohio State football coach Woody Hayes addressed what he viewed as the alarming developments.

"If our society goes down the drain," Hayes said, "and there are big signs it might, then historians will report: 'Here is a nation founded on team play that went down because they forgot about it.' If you want to destroy a society, talk down the heroes...Nations are built on the positive approach, just like football teams."

One of the most prestigious honors of the era was being named to *Playboy* magazine's preseason All-America team. The magazine would fly in players and shoot all twenty-two in their uniforms. Hayes disapproved of the magazine ("those people are trashy; I don't go for people like that," he said) and wouldn't allow any of his players—even returning Heisman Trophy winner Archie Griffin—to appear in the photograph.

"He said you can't play football with an erection," recalled running back Jim Otis.

# EIGHT

# I AM WOMAN

IT WAS NOVEMBER 1972, and in the halls of *Sports Illustrated*, on the nineteenth floor of the Time & Life Building in New York City, the magazine's surly, brilliant French managing editor, Andre Laguerre, was on the verge of making a historic decision. The magazine's annual Sportsman of the Year award had traditionally gone to a male athlete, but he had tentatively settled on giving the 1972 honors to two recipients, UCLA basketball coach John Wooden and the Wimbledon and U.S. Open champion Billie Jean King, making her the first woman to ever receive the honor.

But Laguerre had heard some rumors and now was worried. One day, he spotted the writer Frank Deford in the halls.

"What's this I hear," he asked, "about Billie Jean King being a lesbian?"

"Oh, Andre," said Deford with a smile and dismissive wave, "they say that about all women athletes."

Reassured, Laguerre stuck with his decision. And a month later, there was King, sharing the cover with Wooden, on *SI*'s final issue of 1972, as Sportsman and Sportswoman of the Year. Inside, she and Wooden traded viewpoints on sports' role in society.

"Sometimes there are down moments and I feel unimportant," she said. "I think, 'Sport, big deal.' But what is sport anyway? An art, an amusement... an outlet, an expenditure of energy. Not everyone gets that from reading a book or watching a movie. But also it teaches us about daily living. Certain things don't always go our way. Sometimes we have to lose and we all must face it. Ups and downs. Hills and valleys. That's what sport is all about. That's what life is about, too."

King's ascent came at an exciting, if chaotic, period for American women.

For the first time ever, a majority of American women worked outside the home. The same year had seen Title IX legislation passed and the Equal Rights Amendment approved by the Senate and sent to the states for ratification. A month after King's cover appearance, the Supreme Court handed down its decision in *Roe v. Wade*, effectively legalizing abortion. (King had been among the fifty-three prominent women—including writers Nora Ephron and Anaïs Nin and singer Judy Collins—who signed a petition in the spring 1972 preview issue of *Ms.* magazine, whose opening words were "We have had abortions," calling for "a repeal of all laws that restrict our reproductive freedom.")

Amid all those signs of progress there was, inevitably, resistance. If ever there was an apt time for a certain type of American huckster, the early '70s was the perfect time—perhaps even the *only* time—for the peculiar character that was Bobby Riggs.

A tennis champion in the '30s and '40s, he'd been a fringe personality for decades since, noted more for his gambling skills, a tennis equivalent to the golf hustler Titanic Thompson. But in the early '70s, as *All in the Family*'s Archie Bunker became the voice of a certain retrograde portion of American manhood, Riggs emerged as the sporting world's leading revanchist, starved for attention and unabashed about saying whatever needed to be said to get it.

He had been trying since at least 1970 to schedule a challenge match with King, to prove that even a middle-aged male could beat a top female. King recognized there was no upside to it and consistently rejected his proposals. But in 1973, Margaret Court (at that point, ranked number one in the world) finally accepted the offer.

King learned of the match shortly after she'd ended Court's twelve-tournament, fifty-four-match winning streak in the final of the 1973 Virginia Slims of Indianapolis; the two women were riding an elevator when Court broke the news. "You know," said Court casually, "I've decided to play Bobby Riggs. They offered $10,000."

King winced; she had turned down Riggs for the umpteenth time earlier that week.

"Okay, Margaret, if that's what you want to do," King said. "But I'm begging you, please—you *have* to win. You know that, right? This isn't just about tennis. You have no idea how important this is for women's tennis."

King was right. Court had no idea.

Margaret Court was an undeniably great player—she'd won the Grand Slam in 1970, and twenty-two major singles titles by then. She had been one of the first women players to adopt weight training and the London Biomechanics Laboratory had once determined that her arms were three inches longer than the average woman's, one reason that opponent Rosie Casals referred to her as "The Arm." Yet she seemed a breed apart from the other women on the tour, at once aloof and isolated.

For the traditionalist Court, the match signified nothing more than a challenge and a payday; she did not see herself representing anyone but Margaret Court.

"I haven't really taken this match on in a Women's Lib sort of thing," said Court beforehand. "A woman is not supposed to beat a man so I've nothing to lose. To me it's a challenge, I like a challenge."

This perplexed many of her fellow players, who couldn't help but notice that Court herself, with the assistance of her husband Barry, was living a kind of modern feminist dream.

"How can Margaret Court say she's not in the movement," asked King, "when she is the sole wage-earner in the family, her husband travels with her, and takes care of their domestic responsibilities, and her husband is chief baby sitter for their son? Who is she kidding?"

Riggs reveled in the pre-match publicity. With his jogging regimen and daily ingestion of 415 vitamin pills and supplements, he seemed intent on disproving the Fitzgerald line that there are no second acts in American lives. The Raiders' forty-three-year-old George Blanda had his storybook spell of game-saving kicks and passes in the fall of 1970, but Riggs was nearly a decade older, reshaping the boundaries of what constituted one's athletic prime.

The Riggs–Court match, played in a budding residential development outside of San Diego, generated a good bit of curiosity, and CBS broadcast it live on Mother's Day, 1973.

The day's omens were not good for Court. Her year-old son dunked her only pair of tennis shoes in the hotel bathroom toilet the morning of the match. Preparing for her moment in the spotlight, she agreed to show up in a bright canary yellow tennis dress whose large collar (sporting "MARGARET" in green all-caps) was designed by Ted Tinling. It was the first time in her career she'd ever worn anything other than a white tennis dress.

During the introductions—in which both players marched down the aisle from the stands and onto the court—Court looked exquisitely uncomfortable. When Riggs was introduced, he greeted Court at the net with an echo of mid-century decorum, presenting a bouquet of roses to the mother on Mother's Day. Frozen for a second at the gesture, Court curtsied in response.

When she lost the first two points of the first game, a tennis writer leaned over to her husband, Barry Court, and asked, "Is she nervous?"

"Really bad," Court replied, which was an understatement.

Riggs' gamesmanship and elaborate variety of spins and lobs and drop shots left his opponent frazzled. "The Mother's Day Massacre" ended with Riggs routing Court, 6–2, 6–1, and receiving a winner's check from John Wayne.

King hadn't watched the match. She'd won a tournament in Japan the night before and was flying back to the United States with the other women on the tour. On a stopover in Hawaii, they were able to pick up a report on Rosie Casals' portable radio providing the emphatic final score.

"Oh, shit," said King. "I'm going to have to play him now."

•

The negotiations started that week, but at King's insistence, the match couldn't be announced until after Wimbledon.

In late April, the USLTA and the Virginia Slims tour finally reached a peace in which the USLTA agreed to recognize and sanction the Slims tournaments and scrap their own tour. That meant that all the best women players would be playing together on the Slims tour.

But on the men's side, the 1973 Wimbledon championships came amid more controversy, as the nascent Association of Tennis Professionals, the men's pro association, voted to boycott Wimbledon in support of Niki Pilic, the Yugoslavian pro who was suspended by his country's tennis federation, and thus barred from Wimbledon, for missing a Davis Cup match.

It was another chapter in the continued battle for control of the tennis universe between Wimbledon, the ILTA and USLTA, Lamar Hunt's World

Championship Tennis circuit, and the men's collective bargaining group, the ATP.

Just as the women had held center stage at the U.S. Open in 1971 (when the World Championship Tennis players were barred from the tournament), they would be the main attraction at Wimbledon.

In the midst of the fortnight, Billie Jean King was frantically taking meetings. She was working with her husband, Larry, to drum up interest in their idea for World Team Tennis, set to launch the following year. More urgently, during a siege at the Gloucester Hotel in London, King persuaded sixty-five fellow pros to vote for the formation of the Women's Tennis Association, an important step in standardizing the professionalization of women's tennis. It was the same step that the men had taken in 1972 when the ATP formed. (When King had offered the women's support to the ATP, she never received a response.)

At Wimbledon, King was vying for her fifth singles title and Riggs was shadowing her throughout the fortnight, scouting his next opponent for the as-yet-unannounced showdown. Averaging about four hours of sleep a night, she still managed to sweep three Wimbledon titles that year: the women's singles, the women's doubles with Casals and the mixed doubles with Owen Davidson. In each of her victories, she was listed on the Wimbledon scoreboard as "Mrs. L. W. King."

The King–Riggs match was finally announced four days later, at the Town Tennis Club in Manhattan. The buildup would mark the return of Hollywood art patron/producer/rainmaker Jerry Perenchio onto the sports scene. He and Jack Kent Cooke had been spectacularly successful with the first Ali–Frazier fight, and along with Norman Lear, Perenchio turned *All in the Family* into one of the top-rated shows on American TV. With Riggs–Court as a prelude, and the cultural conversation stirred up by the result of that match, Perenchio knew the ensuing battle between King and Riggs would be a different order of magnitude.

At the press conference, both contestants toed their party lines, Riggs every bit the grating uncle who prided himself on his chauvinism, and King making the point that she'd never wanted the match until Court had done such a "miserable" job. (Riggs and King would make a few other appearances together in the months leading up to the match, and even did a TV commercial for the Sunbeam Mist-Stick Curler Styler.)

"The Ali–Frazier fight was 'The Fight,'" Perenchio said. "This is 'The Match.'"

The cavernous Astrodome paid $300,000 to host the event with the prospect that it would attract the largest crowd in the sport's history. Perenchio then offered the rights to the networks for a prime-time telecast on September 20. Early in those negotiations, Roone Arledge had asked Donna de Varona what she thought of the commercial appeal of a King–Riggs match. "Absolutely!" said de Varona. "It's not just about tennis. It's the dialogue—how valuable are women athletes compared to a man? And can a woman ever beat a man?"

Other networks were skeptical. "Would CBS have ever bought that event, put it on prime time?" said CBS Sports producer Kevin O'Malley. "Not on your life. No chance at all. So we didn't respect the event, let's put it that way. And were we wrong about that? Probably."

Arledge and ABC Sports snapped it up for $750,000, while still viewing it as more of a made-for-TV pseudo-event.

"We didn't really think of Riggs–King as a sports event, per se," said Jim Spence, the program planning vice president for ABC at the time. "We looked at it as a fun sporting event, you know—Riggs, who was kind of crazy, against this superstar tennis player, Billie Jean. Prime time, live, a fun event. Were there ramifications in terms of the women's movement, of course, but we did not look upon it—and did not commit to do it—based on its connections to the women's movement and what that would mean if she lost or won or whatever."

For women in the world of sports, especially those who'd been on the front lines in establishing the Association for Intercollegiate Athletics for Women, the match was hardly a "fun event," but rather amounted to a highly symbolic battle occurring in the midst of the larger struggle for equality for American women. ABC might have guessed as much when, within a day of signing the deal, it sold out fifteen minutes of commercial time at $80,000 per minute.

That August, King finally spoke with Court about the Mother's Day debacle. "She said she didn't remember a whole lot about the match, which I could understand," King recalled, "but one thing she did tell me was that Riggs couldn't hit through his backhand very well. That is, he couldn't hit over the ball with much power from that side and so had to rely on placement almost entirely."

As the pressure mounted, and the interest in the match rose, so did King's edginess. Plagued with chronic knee pain, she'd pulled out of three events and then, at the U.S. Open, in ninety-six-degree heat, sequestered out on Court 22, she was felled by a virus and had to default her third-round match to Julie Heldman in the midst of the decisive third set. Documenting the Virginia Slims tour for her book *A Long Way, Baby,* writer Grace Lichtenstein observed in early September, "For the past four weeks, Billie Jean had been behaving like a paranoid bitch. She had shut herself off almost completely from the press, refusing nearly all requests for private interviews on the grounds that what counted was what she did on the court."

Then, just like in the run-up to a heavyweight title fight, King went into seclusion, training at a resort on Hilton Head, South Carolina. Larry King was there, along with a small coterie that included the King Enterprises secretary Annalee Thurston, Hilton Head financier Dick Butera and King's personal secretary at the time, the former hairdresser Marilyn Barnett.

A fan of *Soul Train* and the R&B and soul it featured, King was one of the first players to train to music, hitting out to songs like Elton John's "Take Me to the Pilot" and the soundtrack to *Jesus Christ Superstar.* She trained with Pete Collins, the resident pro at Hilton Head, and lifted weights, focusing on her legs, to be prepared to run for five sets if necessary.

She'd also spent time scouting film of the Riggs–Court match with her challenge-match coach, the teaching pro Dennis Van der Meer (who'd also worked with Court ahead of her match with Riggs).

On September 15, the Saturday before the match, King was at the Hilton Head resort while a TV was showing the nationally telecast Stanford–Penn State game. During halftime, the Stanford marching band performed Helen Reddy's "I Am Woman," the number one hit from the previous December. And as King watched, the Stanford marching band moved into a new formation, spelling out three initials:

B J K

"My God!" King said as she stared at the screen.

When King and her small entourage embarked to go to Houston, "I swear, it was like we were all going to off to war or something. It was very upbeat, but very eerie, too, like we were going someplace we might not return from. I really didn't know what to expect."

•

While King had been in seclusion, Riggs had been—really since his Mother's Day triumph over Court—living some kind of aging bachelor's desperate fever dream, a midlife crisis disguised as a renaissance. He was bouncing between the Playboy mansion and TV appearances, running up a string of romantic dalliances and drinking like a middle-aged couch potato. In his spare time, he was in talks with producers; word was that Mickey Rooney was eager to make a film about Riggs' life.

In the summer of 1973, *Time* put him on its cover and writer Roland Flamini, after following Riggs for a week, mused, "He was so blatantly chauvinistic that I began to suspect that he was really the Women's Liberation movement's secret weapon."

Nora Ephron, previewing the match for *New York* magazine, also spent a few days with Riggs, heard his myriad gibes and japes against women and the movement, and finally asked, "And what do you *really* know about women's liberation?"

"You're not going to believe this," said Riggs. "Nothing."

Down in Houston, where 300 writers and television reporters requested credentials, and many of Perenchio's friends and clients flew in from Hollywood, the week took on the hyper, frenzied tone of a political convention.

In the Tarzan Room of the Adventurers' Suite of the Astroworld hotel, Robert Larimore Riggs was holding forth, courting the press, entertaining a string of females, and worrying his nominal coach, Lornie Kuhle.

"You know how much he's practiced for this thing?" Kuhle said two days before the match. "Zero…he practiced much harder for Margaret Court. I think he's overconfident. Of course, maybe he knows something. He hasn't been wrong yet."

Before the match, there was also the added obligation that so many women would have recognized. Even as she traveled to Houston to face Riggs in this defining battle, hoping to lay down a historic marker, King still had to do her regular day job, which was to compete in the Houston Virginia Slims tournament going on the very same week. She had committed to play in the tournament months earlier, and she was still the biggest draw on the Slims tour. She was able to arrange playing both her first- and second-round matches that Tuesday, giving her the next day to rest and focus on the Riggs match Thursday evening.

King and Riggs hardly saw each other that week, but Larry King and Riggs did cross paths. For months, when Riggs would stop by one of the Virginia Slims tour stops—to scout Billie Jean and drum up more publicity for an event that didn't need any additional hype—the one person he could hit with was Larry King, who felt as though they were fairly evenly matched. But on that Wednesday, on the eve of the Battle of the Sexes, in the practice bubble outside of the Astrodome, Riggs played Larry King again, spotting him four games and routing him, 6–4.

The convincing loss left Larry King anxious about the match the next night. "Suddenly, the whole aura about Riggs, the quintessential con man, the guy who never lost a hustle, began to affect me," he said. His wife didn't want to hear about it.

King had talked the Adidas shoe company into a new design of blue suede tennis shoes for the occasion. ("We're on color TV," she reasoned, "let's do something that stands out.") Her dress proved a more problematic matter. She had agreed to let her friend, the peripatetic designer Ted Tinling, design it. Two days before the match, he'd presented a brilliant multicolored concoction, in what he would describe as "opalescent cellophane stitched in wavy stripes onto thin nylon net...its rainbow shades shimmered like an oil slick in the sun." King looked at it and loved it. But when she tried it on, the fabric was scratchy, and she realized the very act of wearing it in competition would be a distraction for her.

"I am so sorry, Ted," she said. "I'm afraid I can't play in this."

"No worries, Madame Superstar," said Tinling, who had also designed a simpler backup dress, in mint green, with a cutaway collar and blue-paneled bodice strip, that complemented the blue-suede shoes.

King modeled that dress and loved it, though Tinling would spend much of the next day glamming the dress up, finding sequins and rhinestones, which he sewed into the fabric, completing his handiwork at 3:55 the after-noon of the match, just minutes before King left for the Astrodome.

There was one other subplot: In the days leading up to the match, there had been a standoff over ABC's announcing crew. King was adamant that she wouldn't participate if Jack Kramer, who'd been so dismissive of the women's tour, was the color commentator. Finally, less than forty-eight hours before the match, Arledge relented, Kramer went back to LA (where he presided over the same Pacific Southwest Open that had caused the women to embark on the Virginia Slims tour three years earlier), and the pro Gene Scott took his place.

At the Astrodome that night, the gravity of the moment was suffocating. But as the Steelers' head coach Chuck Noll used to say, "Pressure is what you feel when you aren't prepared." Billie Jean King was prepared, and her heart was full. She had a cause, Riggs had only a shtick. King had requested the vis-itors' locker room in the Astrodome, where four days later her brother Randy Moffitt and the San Francisco Giants would be visiting. She changed in the visiting manager's room, and then tacked a note onto the locker she was told Moffitt would occupy. It read, "Hi, Randy—BJK."

ABC spent several minutes in its opening segment explaining why Kramer wouldn't participate, airing a prerecorded interview with Kramer about bowing out, then doing the same with Larry King, who articulated Billie Jean's objections to Kramer's involvement.

Then there were the inevitable pre-match interviews and, striving for a simulacrum of journalism with Billie Jean, the tuxedoed Frank Gifford asked the timeliest of questions in the most '70s way imaginable: "The feminist thing, how important is that, Billie?"

"The women's movement is important to me as long as it stays practical," she said. "I think the women's movement is really about making a better life for more people than just women."

Soon King and Riggs entered the arena, got off their respective modes of transport, traded the gag gifts (Riggs presented King with a twenty-six-pound all-day sucker from his corporate sponsor Sugar Daddy; King pre-sented Riggs with a baby piglet she'd named Robert Larimore Riggs II) and began warming up.

Howard Cosell, presiding over the match for ABC, didn't mention King's many accomplishments in major tournaments, but instead unintentionally offered the most backhanded of compliments. As King was carried into the arena, Cosell said, "Sometimes you get the feeling that if she ever let her hair to her shoulders and took off her glasses, you'd have someone vying for a Hollywood screen test."

At courtside, the heavyweight champion George Foreman was there, sitting next to Jim Brown. Glen Campbell was in attendance, wearing the inevitable rhinestone blazer, along with Ken Howard and Blythe Danner of TV's *Adam's Rib*, and Perenchio client Andy Williams, as well as his estranged wife, Claudine Longet, the latter cheering for Billie Jean.

There was a breathless quality to the competition—the sense of the unknown leaving both competitors tight. King had played men before, but never in a traditional match, and never in front of the largest tennis crowd ever assembled. Cosell, for his part, sensed the gravity of the occasion. "They tell us there's a big movie on against us," he said early in the broadcast (CBS was premiering *Bonnie and Clyde* on television that night), "but you can see a movie any time."

The first three games found each player holding serve. But then, on the changeover after the third game, Riggs—drenched in sweat—finally took off the Sugar Daddy windbreaker.

Larry King often couldn't bear to watch his wife's matches, and he'd had his head ducked for much of the early proceedings, but watching Riggs now, he got an eerie sense of déjà vu. "He looked exactly the way I looked the night before," said Larry King. "Overwhelmed. Unprepared."

In the ABC booth, Cosell played the unusual role of peacemaker as Rosie Casals and Gene Scott traded barbs like a recently divorced couple striving to one-up each other at a cocktail party. The totems of big sports events were all around—there was Jimmy the Greek, the University of Houston marching band (playing snatches of *Jesus Christ Superstar*) and even the inexplicably ubiquitous sports artist Leroy Neiman, who during a third-set interview with Gifford stressed that he'd spent much of his time drawing a portrait of King's mother, as well as the backside of the female linesman stationed closest to him.

Throughout the night, Riggs looked like what he was—a slightly overweight middle-aged man who'd just discovered that he was not in as good a shape as he'd believed. King, meanwhile, was an athlete in the zone. She didn't smile, barely spoke and even on the changeovers was a deeply focused study in athletic concentration. Riggs broke King's serve three times on the night. Each time, she broke him back the following game. Her training on overheads paid off and Riggs had no answer for her superb court coverage. There were a half-dozen points where King earned standing ovations by getting to balls that seemed unreachable, then rallying to win the point. She won the first set, then started a run of five straight games to win the second set and go up 2–0 in third. At 4–2 King in the third set, Riggs asked for a medical break because of a cramp in his hand. It was granted, but the outcome by then was inevitable. King closed out Riggs in the third set when, after a long rally, he put his weak backhand into the net. In that moment, six months of pressure melted away, and King threw her racket up in jubilation.

Somehow, the weary Riggs had enough energy to jump over the net and congratulate his conqueror. "I underestimated you," he told her.

As the hangers-on and officials flowed onto the court, King moved to her husband and greeted him with a relieved kiss.

"When I was young, I thought it was a sport just for the rich and white," she said later. "There were a lot of non-tennis people who saw tennis for the first time tonight. You know I believe in spectator participation so a lot of my dreams came true tonight."

When King saw Grace Lichtenstein at the post-match press conference, she asked, "Did ya win a lot of money, Grace?"

"Yes, thank you, Billie Jean," said Lichtenstein, who'd been in a consortium of women journalists who'd put together $500 to beat Riggs out of $800, with Nora Ephron holding the cash. "But it's not the money, it's the pride."

"Right on!" said King.

After filing her sidebar for the *New York Times*, Lichtenstein returned to the hotel for an impromptu party among many of the women journalists who covered the event. "It was the first time I ever felt there was actually sort of a fraternity of females in and around a sporting event," said *Sports Illustrated* senior editor Sarah Ballard. "Most of these people weren't actually in sports, but the fact that we had someone—that I wasn't the only one, for once—made it great."

It would be difficult to find any athlete in any sport at any time who'd performed under more pressure than King did that evening. Years later, she would wake in the middle of the night fearing that she still had to play Riggs before blinking into cognition that she'd already done so.

In fighting for equality, King didn't merely inspire millions of girls and women. She also transformed sports for boys and men. The ratings for the Battle of the Sexes would come in a few days later. Forty-five million people watched, and in so doing offered more proof that sports could succeed on prime-time television before a broader audience.

"What I remember is that everyone I knew watched—I mean *everybody*," said the AIAW's first president, Carole Oglesby. "And it was like euphoria, it was Mardi Gras, for all the women in the sports world."

Not quite everybody. On that very evening, the eighteen-year-old tennis superstar Chris Evert was not in attendance, nor even watching the match with friends. She had made a sudden decision earlier in the day and made a declaration of independence of sorts, leaving home without informing her parents, and jumped on a plane to Los Angeles to meet her boyfriend, Jimmy Connors. "I knew how important the match was for women's tennis," she'd recall later, "but at eighteen years old, I didn't feel I had any part in it."

"She didn't know any better," said Lichtenstein of Evert's initially blink-ered worldview. "She was just a Catholic girl from Florida, how could she know?"

It wasn't her fight yet. But it would be in time.

•

There was a lot of crow to be eaten on the night of September 20, 1973. It wasn't just the wagers that Riggs lost. In Cincinnati, the conservative columnist William F. Buckley was giving a speech to a group of women voters. At the beginning of his speech, searching for a topical opening, he told the women that they had "been summoned at this hour by the *Cincinnati Enquirer* no doubt in order to reduce the total number of women available to witness the forthcoming humiliation of your sex at Houston." By the end of his talk, the King–Riggs match was final. The women, remembered Buckley, "were good-natured about my chauvinist exposure, but palpably exhilarated by the liberating news."

At the Los Angeles Tennis Club, the men on the tour were late for some of their matches in the Pacific Southwest Open. Jack Kramer had to order them onto the court because they were gathered around the television watching Riggs and King. After the first game, Arthur Ashe sensed that King had come to play. "She's too good," he said to some of the other male pros. "She hits the ball like a man." That night, Ashe put his money on King and won $70.

In living rooms, grocery stores, tennis clubs, and country clubs, played out in millions of little vignettes that Thursday night, women were not merely delighted but spiritually leavened by the result. Ground zero of the reaction might have come that evening in New York City, where there was a raucous party, chock full of *Ms.* magazine staffers and the architects of second-wave feminism, held at the condo on West Fifty-Seventh Street shared by city councilwoman Ronnie Eldridge and her husband, the columnist Jimmy Breslin. Gloria Steinem was in attendance, watching perhaps her only sports event of the year. Fellow *Ms.* magazine founder Letty Cottin Pogrebin was there, along with the congresswoman and feminist icon Bella Abzug, *That Girl* star Marlo Thomas, and dozens of other bastions of the movement. Thomas sat in front of a TV and announced that the match that was about to commence was one of the most important moments in her life.

For the feisty, boisterous crowd, the match amounted to a kind of catharsis. For Pogrebin and the other founders of *Ms.*, "competition was unfeminine when we were growing up. And competition was de-feminizing. It de-sexed you, literally. Sweat was masculine. Power was de-feminizing, muscles were associated with lesbians, ugliness. And now here we were."

Pogrebin had been part of a generation denied any sporting activity. Her mother even forbade dodgeball, fearing that "the ball might hit my chest or my belly, and then I couldn't have children. So the people gathered in that room, then, we were young, but we were raised on that ethos. And so when we were cheering for Billie Jean, we weren't just cheering for Billie Jean. We were cheering for an absolute break—not just a crack, but a break—in the wall and the ceiling about women's physicality, about women in sports in general. It was huge. It wasn't just, we wanted to win because we want her to win. We wanted *us* to win. That was a real victory."

Afterward, the group sent a telegram to King, which read: "From all of us who have been forced to grow used to defeat, thank you from the bottom of our hearts for showing us victory. We will never again settle for less."

As the partiers toasted deep into the night in New York City, a smaller celebration was taking part a continent away, in Santa Rosa, California.

Charles M. Schulz, creator of *Peanuts*, the most popular comic strip in the world, was busy that week. His empire continued to expand, there was work being done on a new line of plush dolls and he was about to get married for the second time just two days later to Jeannie Forsyth. But he'd been waiting for the Battle of the Sexes for weeks, and even highlighted "BJK–Riggs Match" on September 20 in his calendar. That evening in Santa Rosa, sitting with his bride-to-be, Schulz cheered for King while watching the match on his new color television.

"Sparky" to anyone who knew him, Schulz might not have described himself as a feminist, but for years he'd found common cause with the women athletes he followed. His Midwestern sensibilities blanched at the crass male chauvinism of Riggs. (Earlier in 1973, Schulz penned a Sunday strip where an enraged Lucy sat down to write a letter, in the wake of the Mother's Day Massacre, which read: "Dear Bobby Riggs, You were lucky!")

In his more than two decades of drawing *Peanuts*, Schulz had sketched out the most famous loser in the history of American culture, the hard-luck, no-talent Charlie Brown. Now, as he watched Billie Jean King trouncing Riggs, Schulz was jubilant. He and Jeannie shared a toast, and Schulz sensed that the match signaled a change in American life in which more women would become involved in sports. It was a prospect that Schulz loved as sports had shaped his worldview, hardened his resilience, helped define his moral universe.

"In a single tennis match, Billie Jean King was able to do more for the cause of women than most feminists can achieve in a lifetime," wrote the *New York Times* editorial page.

And yet the true impact of King's victory—even as it was covered on the front page of newspapers and magazines around the country (it was the lead news item in the next week's issue of *Sports Illustrated*, with the headline "There She Is, Ms. America") was not yet fully appreciated.

No one—not King or any of the commentators, not the *New York Times* or the *Washington Post* or *Time* or *Newsweek* or *Sports Illustrated*—mentioned any connection between what happened on the tennis court in the Astrodome and the piece of legislation signed into law by President Nixon a year earlier, Title IX, the clause in the National Education Act.

King had changed millions of minds and inspired millions more, but the greater change—the seismic, disruptive one that would shake the country itself—had yet to register.

•

As all of this was going on, the Association for Intercollegiate Athletics for Women was making remarkable gains. Women's college basketball, freed from the shackles of the six-on-six game, was growing all over the country. The first AIAW basketball power was an unlikely one, tiny Immaculata College thirty miles outside of Philadelphia. With head coach Cathy Rush (whose husband was Ed Rush, the pro basketball referee), the Mighty Macs reversed a 32-point late-season loss to powerful West Chester to win the first of three straight AIAW titles (each accompanied by the fervent cheers of the school's nuns, bashing garbage cans in raucous support) in 1972.

But the AIAW was also coping with the realities of bringing its idealized vision of pure amateurism into the modern American world. The catalyst for that reckoning was a woman named Fern Lee "Peachy" Kellmeyer who, in 1957, had been a teenage debutante at the U.S. Nationals. At the University of Miami in the '60s, she became the first woman to play on a major-college men's tennis team. After her competitive career, she became the athletic director at Marymount College, an AIAW school in Boca Raton. In the fall of 1972, the tennis team was declared ineligible for the AIAW tennis championships because it offered scholarships, putting Marymount in the same category as Tennessee State's stellar track and field team, the Tigerbelles, who were banned from the AIAW track and field national championships (a meet that, with multiple Olympians on the roster, Tennessee State likely would have won).

Kellmeyer was persuaded by a tennis-playing friend—a lawyer named Ted Hainline who agreed to take the case on a pro bono basis—that the ban constituted discrimination. Marymount, and a public college, Broward Community College, sued not just AIAW, but also DGWS, AAHPER, and the National Education Association. The lawsuit cited Title IX, arguing that since male scholarship athletes were allowed to compete in the NCAA, the AIAW's policy was actually discriminating against women. (By the time the lawsuit was filed, Kellmeyer had started working for Gladys Heldman as the director of the Virginia Slims tour, and before the end of 1973 she'd be the first employee of the Women's Tennis Association.)

Carole Oglesby, the first president of the AIAW, had been spreading the organization's anti-scholarship gospel around the country and was summoned to Washington for a meeting with the AAHPER and DGWS representatives and legal counsel.

"So the AIAW people came to this meeting, prepared up to the teeth to how we were going to fight this lawsuit, and feeling we could beat it back," said Oglesby. "And we barely crossed the threshold into the offices to have this meeting, and the AAHPER and DGWS people had already had meetings and decided they were not going to fight this, the decision was already made. So AIAW was going to have to let schools offer scholarships…we felt so abandoned and shocked in thinking that this was a rock-solid principle, that DGWS stood for us forever. The rug was just pulled out from under us."

In the short term, what this meant was that AIAW could no longer bar schools that offered scholarships from championship competition. But even then, the full implications of Title IX and what it would mean to women's athletics weren't fully understood.

That changed in early November 1973, barely six weeks after King's landmark win, at the first AIAW Delegate Assembly, in which representatives hammered out policy, discussed strategy, and charted their course for the future. It was the historic first meeting in which a quorum of the 278 AIAW schools gathered.

The site where they gathered, the suburban Kansas City enclave of Overland Park, Kansas, was centrally located. But it was also a somewhat audacious and pointed choice, located only minutes from the NCAA headquarters in Mission, Kansas. Tom Jernstedt, NCAA Director of Special Events, visited the assembly on behalf of the NCAA.

The grudging concession by many of the AIAW leaders on scholarships underscored the schism that remained among the women's ranks. There was almost universal agreement that AIAW didn't want to go down the same path of bloated, commercialized, hyper-competitive athletics as the NCAA. But while one faction felt that scholarships should be a last resort, and then limited to tuition and books only, another faction felt that competition was not just inevitable but also necessary and healthy for women athletes and coaches alike. For this group, of which Charlotte West at Southern Illinois had been a staunch proponent since the early 1960s, women had as much right to full-ride scholarships as men, and the prospect of athletics as an avenue to a free education could only encourage more young women to dedicate themselves to their sport of choice.

That philosophical disagreement had been going on for a while and would continue through the decade, but what was clear by the end of the AIAW's first delegate assembly is that the vision of a sporting utopia free from all of the temptations and trappings of big-time collegiate sports would be practically impossible.

The epiphany came the morning of the first day of the assembly during a speech by Marjorie Blaufarb, representing AAHPER. She arrived from Washington to outline the ways in which the Department of Health, Education and Welfare (HEW) would oversee the implementation of Title IX and the ways in which college athletics would be under that umbrella.

In her speech, titled "Solomon's Judgment on Women's Sports," Blaufarb offered a bracing slap of reality to both sides of the debate. "There are still men around saying that no matter what the women say, the fact is that they need more than women," said Blaufarb. "More money, more and better facilities, and so on. And there are still women saying they don't believe in competitive athletics for girls except in specially sheltered situations because the men's experience has shown them to be commercial, unjustly exploitative, and so on. On both sides of this argument there is deep feeling and absolute sincerity. But it has become an argument to which Congress for good or ill has provided the answer."

Blaufarb went on to stress that the initial interpretation of the education amendments was that Congress would "not subsidize sexual inequality...and they will not subsidize sexually segregated or unequal educational programs."

Blaufarb stressed that men could no longer assume preferential treatment "in the provision of equipment, supplies, scheduling of games and practice times, travel and per diem allowance, award of athletic scholarships, opportunity to receive coaching and instruction, and so on. This will end the practice of passing on old, out-of-date facilities to the women, and of giving the women's hockey teams the old football jerseys to play in."

The gathering already offered an oasis of hope for women in intercollegiate sports; now, energized by the news from Blaufarb, the women of the AIAW returned to their campuses around the country emboldened.

"This was a meeting of women who loved sport, who had been denied their fair opportunity in sport, and who realized that they were being given an opportunity to be in on a revolution," said Christine Grant, the women's athletic director at the University of Iowa, who—along with Peg Burke and the administrator Bonnie Slatton—was building one of the best women's programs in the country. "It was electric."

Returning to Iowa City, Grant and Burke spent the entire ride discussing the implications, the potential, the sheer universe of possibilities that had been opened up and, in Grant's words, "we never stopped talking for another month after that."

In the immediate aftermath of the assembly, the women of the AIAW—along with, very quickly, the men of the NCAA—were still reconciling the broad impact of the thirty-seven words of Title IX. Less than five miles away from where the women of the AIAW had their first assembly, Walter Byers, the head of the NCAA, was still in his office when Jernstedt returned to report on what he'd heard in the assembly and share the crux of Blaufarb's address.

Once Byers knew, the entire apparatus of collegiate athletics would be informed. It was the sort of alarming news that spread quickly.

Fresh off Billie Jean King's epic victory and Marjorie Blaufarb's bracing message, the women who'd been so long on the margins sensed a moment of glorious potential.

The men who'd for so long had the fields and courts to themselves sensed a threat.

And the battle lines were drawn.

# NINE

# FOUR STARS

THE SPRING OF 1973 had been dominated by Secretariat's dramatic chase to become the first Triple Crown winner in twenty-five years, while the summer witnessed the extended buildup to the King–Riggs match. Through it all, there was the constant presence—day by day, at bat by at bat—of the grandest quest in the American sports record book, Henry Aaron's epic pursuit of Babe Ruth's iconic career mark of 714 home runs.

By the 1973 season, Aaron was thirty-nine years old and yet somehow newly emergent, a long time co-star thrust into a leading role. Coming out of the contentious end of the '60s —with pro- and anti-war polarization, "Black Power" and the "Silent Majority"—there was a perception in some circles that race had become a less divisive issue or that the "melting pot" of American culture had finally and successfully assimilated Black Americans.

But the question of race, and the hyper-awareness of it, was perhaps best illustrated by the juxtaposition of that distant, mythic figure of 714—so long associated with the immortal Babe—suddenly being approached by the very human, very contemporary, decidedly un-mythic Henry Aaron.

In 1952, the lanky, soft-spoken Aaron, eighteen, had gone from a Mobile, Alabama, high school to a contract with the Indianapolis Clowns of the rapidly dying Negro Leagues, leaving home with two sandwiches, two dollars and two pairs of pants. Aaron soon landed a minor league contract with an affiliate of the Milwaukee Braves. It was Aaron who in 1953 received the thankless, psychologically daunting task of integrating the South Atlantic League—the Sally League—and its network of small and mostly small-minded cracker southern towns. Enduring a year of racial epithets as the star of the league-leading Jacksonville Braves, Aaron prospered and, in 1954, was brought up to the majors.

Though he was shy by nature, it was a significant mistake to assume that Aaron was timid or guileless. Over the years, even as he'd remained a reserved, self-contained product of the Jim Crow South, Aaron made it clear that he recognized his own inherent value. In 1955, the Milwaukee Braves had asked the outfielder Aaron to fill in at second base as the light-hitting Danny O'Connell had pretty much stopped hitting altogether. Following another sterling season (27 homers, 106 runs batted in), Aaron received a contract over the winter with the scantest of raises. He called the Braves general manager Bob Quinn and asked, "Hey, Mr. Quinn, did you send me Danny O'Connell's contract by mistake?"

Throughout the '60s, as Aaron toiled in Milwaukee and then Atlanta (when the Braves moved to the Deep South in 1966), he established a metronomic consistency of excellence even as he remained in the shadow of the more spectacular Giants' outfielder Willie Mays. But Aaron passed Mays on the all-time homer list in 1972 and, after hitting 119 homers in the first three years of the decade, he greeted the beginning of the 1973 season just 41 shy of Ruth's mark, once thought to be unassailable.

Because Ruth was white and Aaron was Black, the chase took on a larger meaning, and in the process exposed the deep fault lines of America's long reckoning with race. Though the America of Aaron's adulthood was far more tolerant than the segregated land of his childhood, Aaron once said that there was not a single day in his life that he wasn't reminded, in one way or another, of the color of his skin.

Those reminders intensified in volume and tone in the summer and fall of 1973 as he moved closer to breaking Ruth's record. That year, Aaron received 930,000 pieces of mail; only President Richard Nixon received more. The letters were fielded by Aaron's personal secretary and a vast majority were positive. But an alarming, dispiriting percentage were hateful and threatening: "Dear Nigger, Everybody loved Babe Ruth. You will be the most hated man in this country if you break his career home run record." Another read, "Listen Black Boy, We don't want no nigger Babe Ruth." Then there was, "Dear Mr. Nigger, I hope you don't break the Babe's record. How do I tell my kids that a nigger did it?" The hate mail was almost entirely in that same narrow vein.

The letters—and the publicity surrounding them—was perhaps the most significant instance of America catching an elusive reflection of itself. "It bothers me," said Aaron in the summer of 1973. "I have seen a president shot and his brother shot. The man who murdered Dr. Martin Luther King is in jail, but that isn't doing Dr. King much good, is it? I have four children and I have to be concerned about their welfare."

By the fall of 1973, the sobering fact of Aaron's hate mail had become a story in itself. Response to the news of it had included a broad letter-writing campaign of encouragement. Charles Schulz, in his *Peanuts* strip, found common cause by having Snoopy on the verge of breaking Ruth's record before Aaron does and absorbing the same pushback. ("We don't like your kind," read one letter.)

Throughout that 1973 season, the questions were constant, increasing as he neared the mark. "Babe. Babe. Babe. Babe," said Aaron. "Babe Ruth. I never made a study of the man, but I know an awful lot about him. It seems that everybody I talk to tells me a little bit more."

Aaron's sense of grievance went beyond hate mail. Throughout the end of the 1973 season, the city of Atlanta's support for Aaron was pitiable. With Aaron sitting at 712 home runs and returning to Atlanta for the season's final home stand, the Braves drew crowds of 10,211, then 5,571 for a pair of weeknight games before 17,836 turned out for the season's penultimate game, when Aaron homered off the Astros' Jerry Reuss for number 713. The next day, the final day of the regular season, the Braves drew 40,517, but still nowhere near a sellout. Aaron went 3-for-4 that day, without homering. The chase would go on, into the beginning of the '74 season.

The off-season was pregnant with expectation and a raft of appearances. In October, Aaron became the first active player to throw out the first pitch at a World Series. He was on *Hollywood Squares* and *The Flip Wilson Show*. With his new wife, Billye (a trailblazer in her own right, the first African American woman to host a television show in the Deep South), he cooked on Dinah Shore's show.

In Aaron's ascendance there was a lesson that cut against many of the more revered notions of sports. Ruth was, even while playing, a larger-than-life figure, the gargantuan Bambino, a man whose power was as great as his appetites. Those who had anointed Mays or Mickey Mantle as Ruth's heir were doubtless swayed by the physical brilliance of both men as well as the extra attention the players derived from playing in New York (which carried over for Mays even after the Giants moved to San Francisco).

Would Aaron have been worn down by being the feature headline subject in 500 editions of New York tabloids? It would never be known, but it was his constancy, the way he slipped beneath the radar, the way he approached 600 home runs before anyone started routinely *asking* him about the pursuit of Ruth that would be a decided advantage.

As he eclipsed Mays and Ruth came into range, there was a renewed awareness of Aaron's particular genius. He used to sit in the dugout, put his cap over his face, and look through one of the small air vents in the crown of the cap to focus on the opposing pitcher. At the plate, he was superb at empathizing with any pitcher's particular mindset. "Hitting," he once said, "is mostly *thinking.*"

Even as he neared his fortieth birthday, Aaron was still potent. The Pirates' Steve Blass had found him through much of the late '60s to be "virtually unpitchable," spraying balls to all fields. But as his reflexes slowed slightly and the record neared, Aaron became a more traditional pull hitter.

Through it all, Aaron had earned respect not only for his accomplishments, but for the way his lack of grandstanding communicated an underlying respect for the game.

"It was all in the way he circled the bases and returned to the dugout," said the Reds' manager Sparky Anderson. "He never did anything out there to embarrass the pitcher. He never gave anyone a slap shake."

•

With Aaron's historic chase on hold for one more off-season, America's sports fans turned their attention to the gridiron. The Miami Dolphins were coming off their perfect season, hoping to defend their title in the fall of 1973. But the most celebrated athlete in the sport wasn't Larry Csonka or any of his teammates, but instead a running back in isolated upstate New York, plying his trade with one of the smallest-market teams in all of professional sports, the Buffalo Bills.

As the decade began, Orenthal James Simpson might have felt like he'd stepped into an alternate universe. The celebrated Heisman Trophy winner from Southern Cal was so revered that when the *Encyclopedia Britannica* chose to use two pages of color photographs to illustrate the sport of football in its 1970 volume, it chose the 1969 Rose Bowl game in which Simpson strafed Ohio State for 171 yards. But after being selected first overall by the Buffalo Bills in the 1969 draft, he was suddenly a prominent professional player on a very bad team, better known for his nickname (Orange Juice) than his accomplishments. For his first few pro seasons of the '70s, he toiled in obscurity as the losses mounted. The Bills' games were rarely seen outside of upstate New York and Simpson's profile waned.

But then came the 1972 season, when the Bills' new coach Lou Saban retooled the offense around Simpson. A year later, when Simpson ran for 157 yards and scored two touchdowns in a midseason *Monday Night Football* win over Kansas City, he set his sights on Jim Brown's single-season rushing record of 1,863 yards.

Simpson was a sleek, slithering, darting revelation. His style did not mimic the bruising physicality of Brown's bull rushes. Instead he was elusive, seemingly always running toward the open field, changing directions, the ball cradled in one hand while the other was often raised at a jaunty angle to maintain balance for his next cutback. He even made stars of his offensive line, which had been nicknamed the Electric Company, because "we turn on the Juice."

But it was Simpson's off-field persona that solidified his broad popularity. At the time, Simpson represented the great assimilationist dream. Tall, handsome, gracious (and often described, in the coded vernacular of the era, as "articulate") and never abrasive, he was adept at the simple skill of being consistently likable.

In a mid-'70s poll of grade-schoolers, commissioned by *Ladies Home Journal*, Simpson was voted the nation's most admired figure by both boys and girls. Many Americans found Muhammad Ali and baseball slugger Reggie Jackson to be too brash and, in their eyes, insistently Black; Aaron, forty years old by the time he completed the 1974 season, was already a distant saint. As his teammate Dusty Baker put it, "Hank was kind of like your dad. [He] goes to work and you know work's not always rosy, but dad never tells you about it."

By contrast, Simpson came across as more affable and approachable, someone that a certain sector of white America could view as a handsome man who *happened* to be African American.

"He was very, I'm not gonna say humble, because he wasn't that, but he was very cordial," said Ted Koy, traded to the Bills in 1971. "O.J. was comfortable and very accommodating with everybody; it could be a guy down the street or corporate America. He had that deep, booming voice, and he'd love to go in a restaurant and just *take over*."

There also was a sense of unobtrusive style in his persona, a frictionless charisma that was at once captivating and superficial. Even his showmanship seemed somewhat tempered; midway through the 1973 season, Simpson started wearing white game shoes. Soon, some of his teammates started sporting them as well, a fact that pleased Simpson. "We got players now who want to be fly in what they do," he explained to a reporter. "Wearing those white shoes, that telling the people in the stands, 'Look at me. I ain't just like everybody else on the field.'"

Going into the final game of the 1973 season, at Shea Stadium against the New York Jets, Simpson needed 61 yards to break Brown's single-season record. He'd reached that by the end of the first quarter, galloping through a snowstorm and the aging Jets' defense. Both Simpson and his teammates wanted more—to reach the unthinkable 2,000-yard mark. When his last carry of the day pushed him to 2,003 yards, Koy was on the sideline. "We were ecstatic, and even the Jets fans were ecstatic," Koy said. "Here we are, grown men, working in our profession, and we were almost giddy about it. I remember I got a picture with O.J. after the game and had him sign it."

In the postgame press conference in the bowels of Shea Stadium, Simpson brought with him his entire offensive line, wide receivers and backfield mates, stressing the point that his individual achievement was a group effort. "These are the cats who did the job all year long."

It was a different sport, and a different record, but those who watched Simpson chase down Brown's mark couldn't help but notice the lack of pushback he experienced, the sense of widespread public support, the absence of anything approaching the controversy that had accompanied Aaron's record chase. Then, too, there was the fact that the record Simpson was breaking was that of another Black man.

•

As teams reported for spring training in 1974, the focus returned to Aaron. The Braves' schedule in 1974 called for them to open the regular season on the road, playing a three-game series in Cincinnati before a ten-game homestand. Soon there was speculation about whether the Braves would hold Aaron out of some or all of the series in Cincinnati so that he could break the record in front of the home crowd.

Presiding over all of this, and coordinating baseball's response to it, was the decidedly distant, consistently tone-deaf figure of Bowie Kuhn. When Aaron hit his seven hundredth home run in 1973, he received hundreds of telegrams, but none from the commissioner of baseball. It had vexed Aaron at the time, but Kuhn promised him that he would be there for Aaron's record-breaking homer.

During spring training in 1974, Kuhn imposed himself on the lineup question, ordering Braves manager Eddie Mathews to play Aaron. This only served to alienate the Atlanta fan base from Kuhn.

The season opened April 4, the five-year anniversary of the slaying of Martin Luther King Jr. Players on both teams expected the milestone would be recognized in pregame ceremonies, and Aaron had made a request to the Reds to do so. It was ignored.

In his first swing on Opening Day, Aaron homered off Cincinnati's Jack Billingham, tying Ruth at 714 homers. After the game, downbeat about the Reds' walk-off win, Aaron said he and his teammates "were all very disappointed" that King's anniversary was ignored. At that point, Billye Aaron interceded to go a step further than her husband had, noting, "It should not have been necessary to ask. The stature of the man demanded it."

Aaron sat out the second game at Cincinnati and failed to homer in the third. As the Braves made their way back to Atlanta, what worried the Braves PR man Bob Hope most was not a racist assassin—the Braves had beefed up their security—but rather a random streaker, disrobing at the key moment and besmirching the setting of baseball's most hallowed record. This was an entirely plausible concern. Ray Stevens' novelty single "The Streak" had been released that February and was working its way up the pop Top 40 charts, and just six days before the Braves' home opener, David Niven had been interrupted while preparing to introduce Elizabeth Taylor at the Academy Awards show by a mustachioed streaker dashing across the stage behind him. In Cincinnati, on the day of the opener, a man in the bleachers stripped down and was seen signing autographs before police escorted him out.

There was also the question of how television was going to cover the historic moment, given the unpredictable nature of its timing.

NBC had an exclusive contract with Major League Baseball and the Braves' home opener against the Dodgers would be the season premiere of *Monday Night Baseball*. But if the record wasn't broken during that contest, NBC planned to cut into regularly scheduled programming to show every at bat live until Aaron reached 715 (raising the disquieting prospect of an extended slump dragging out the big moment for weeks).

Which meant that, as the Braves prepared for their home opener on Monday, April 8, 1974, all anyone knew for sure was that the game against the Los Angeles Dodgers would be the only full prime-time broadcast of a full Braves game for that week. More than 400 writers were there that night, hoping to cover the eclipse of American sports' single most famous record.

The Braves had turned the pregame ceremonies into a live version of *This Is Your Life*, with a large map of the United States painted into the outfield and a group of close friends and dignitaries, like Atlanta mayor Maynard Jackson and Georgia governor Jimmy Carter, sitting behind home plate. Sammy Davis Jr. was in attendance, Pearl Bailey sang the national anthem and a national television audience tuned in.

Throughout his career, Aaron had possessed a strange prescience. Earlier that day, he told his teammate Ralph Garr, "I'm gonna break it tonight. I'm tired. I'm going to break the record so we can get down to serious business."

At 9:07 p.m. that evening, in the bottom of the fourth inning, in front of a rare Atlanta sellout crowd of 53,775, with the Dodgers leading 2–0 and a runner on first base, Aaron struck. The Dodgers' Al Downing hung a high fastball and Aaron's wrists rotated into the swing, the bat connecting to the ball with a loud report. It sailed toward left center and kept sailing.

Aaron never saw the ball clear the fence. He'd never seen any of his previous 714 home runs, either. "That's not what I'm supposed to do," he explained once. "I've seen guys miss first base looking to see where the ball went." Aaron did see Braves first base coach Jim Busby leaping with joy as he rounded first, and he heard the roar, which would continue uninterrupted for ten minutes. After he rounded second base, he was congratulated by two seventeen-year-old fans, Britt Gaston and Cliff Courtney, who'd run onto the field simply because they wanted to pat the back of the baseball hero they admired. Fans storming the field was not uncommon in the '70s, but the ease with which the two made it onto the field suggested that there were still some holes in the Atlanta security force.

Because the historic event took place in front of a live prime-time national TV audience, the moment also resonated in a way that was unprecedented, even for the erstwhile national pastime. Curt Gowdy, Tony Kubek and Joe Garagiola were calling the game for NBC's *Monday Night Baseball*, and Milo Hamilton was in the play-by-play booth for the Braves radio network. But it was Vin Scully, calling the game for Dodgers fans, who put it best: "What a marvelous moment for the country and the world! A black man is getting a standing ovation in the Deep South for breaking a record by an all-time baseball idol."

That put it just about right, but left a little bit more to the imagination. Aaron had seen a portion of America at its worst—and now he represented America at its best. He was greeted at home plate by his Braves teammates and soon thereafter his father, Herbert, and mother, Estella. Interviewed after the game, Aaron simply smiled and said, "Thank God it's over."

Western Union estimated that, on the night he broke the record, Aaron received more telegrams than any athlete in any single day in history, about 20,000 from across the country.

The historic moment in baseball was not witnessed by its commissioner. Bowie Kuhn was in Cleveland for the Indians' home opener. Instead, he sent Monte Irvin, the one executive of color in MLB's office.

Especially given Kuhn's earlier promise, Aaron later noted, "I was deeply offended that the commissioner of baseball would not see fit to watch me try to break a record that was supposed to be the most sacred in baseball. It was almost as if he didn't want to dignify the record or didn't want to be part of the surpassing of Babe Ruth."

Two nights after breaking the record, with the all-time home run champion playing at home, the Braves drew a crowd of 6,426.

What did Aaron's chase say about sports in America and race in America? Jimmy Wynn of the Dodgers might have summarized it best, talking to Aaron's biographer Howard Bryant. "It wasn't about numbers," Wynn said. "It wasn't even really about Babe Ruth. It was about him breaking a white man's record. Everything he went through was happening because he put himself in a position to break a white man's record. You see, that record, it *belonged* to them, and in a lot of ways, to them, the ones who wrote those letters and said those things, Henry Aaron was taking it from *them* and giving it to *us*. He was giving us a little something more than what we had, something that we'd never had."

•

While Henry Aaron was chasing Ruth, Muhammad Ali was striving to remain relevant, in both boxing and cultural circles.

After the loss to Frazier in 1971, there was only the inevitable long procession of fights to get back to the top. In 1972, he fought in Stateline, Nevada, on the shores of Lake Tahoe, against the light-heavyweight champion Bob Foster.

At the weigh-in, Ali seemed philosophical and subdued. "I'm not excited about fighting anymore," he said. "You people are the ones who're excited, not me. It's like a pilot flying through a storm. The passengers are scared, but the pilot knows what strain the equipment can take. I've been fighting since I was twelve. To me Foster is a joke, Frazier is a joke, fighting is a joke. It's just another night to jump up and down and beat up somebody." The Foster fight ended in the eighth, after Ali had knocked him down seven times.

Shortly thereafter, Ali was at the Las Vegas Hilton for an Elvis Presley concert—they were mutual admirers—and Presley gave him a specially designed robe inscribed with the motto "The People's Choice," which he'd wear for his fight with Joe Bugner on Valentine's Night, 1973, a lackluster twelve-round unanimous decision. But Ali's tepid comeback was derailed a month and a half later by a broken jaw and a split-decision loss to the former Marine Ken Norton. By then, the heavyweight landscape had changed.

As Ali was working his way back to Frazier, the champion was making a grievous miscalculation. Against the protestations of his manager Yancey "Yank" Durham, Frazier agreed to fight George Foreman, the undefeated

1968 Olympic gold medalist (he'd waved a small American flag in the ring ten days after John Carlos and Tommie Smith's Black Power salute on the podium), on January 22, 1973, in Kingston, Jamaica. This was the ambush forever immortalized by Cosell's ringside declamation, "Down goes Frazier! Down goes Frazier!" as the underdog Foreman destroyed the champ with six knockdowns before the fight was stopped in the second round.

It would go down in boxing lore that the champion Frazier invited a peripheral figure with him to the fight that night. He was an ex-convict numbers runner named Don King, who'd served three years and change for a manslaughter conviction. King was a man of massive will and a fuzzy sense of loyalty. He walked into the arena in Jamaica as part of Frazier's entourage. After the fight, King left the arena in George Foreman's limousine. "I came with the champion," King would later boast, "and I left with the champion."

At a time when other mushroom cloud afros were carefully tended and manicured, King's was a radical departure, an unruly avalanche of upward thrust, a gravity-defying work of art that would in the coming years compel a hundred white sportswriters to use the identical line: that he looked like a man who'd stuck his finger into an electrical socket.

But as it transpired, his shock of hair was one of the less interesting things about King. Prolix and grandiloquent, he was a streetcorner fabulist whose view of the American dream was expansive enough to include even himself. "I transcend earthly bounds," he once explained. "I never cease to amaze myself; I haven't yet found my limits."

King wasn't all bluster; he also was a shrewd student of the human condition. And he understood, in currying favor with Ali's camp, an angle he could use with Ali's manager, Herbert Muhammad (the son of the Black Muslim leader Elijah Muhammad). The Black Muslims placed a priority on Black industry. King would be able to deliver on a promise that the more established, more reputable white promoters could not: He could keep it Black.

Over the coming years, King authored a grand, audacious, corrupt, imaginative, dishonest, and innovative series of promotions. In Ali, he found a source of inspiration and revenue that brought out his best and basest instincts. In other instances, like ABC's notoriously corrupt sanctioned fight series later in the decade, King became just another numbers runner, a fixer who could not and would not respect the game enough to make it honest.

But with Ali, he was a visionary of promotion, someone who could call and raise Ali's bombast.

After avenging his loss to Norton, then earning a decision over Joe Frazier in their 1974 rematch at Madison Square Garden, Ali was poised for another shot at the title. Just as he needed to beat Foreman to regain his crown, Foreman needed to beat Ali to solidify his standing as a great heavyweight champion. King emerged as the one man who could get them together. After persuading Ali's camp that they should go with a Black promoter, it wasn't too large a step to argue that the event—the legendary former champ fighting the young champion—should take place in Africa, the Motherland. In truth, King would likely have placed the fight in any country that offered the sum of $10 million, split equally between the two fighters. In the event, it was the totalitarian nation-state Zaire (the once and future Democratic Republic of the Congo), under the autocrat Mobutu Sese Seko, that made the offer.

Ali may have passed his prime as a fighter, but his boastfulness reached a kind of art form in the buildup to the "Rumble in the Jungle," with echoes in the mythic folklore of the African American tradition.

"I done something new for this fight!" he proclaimed at a New York press conference announcing the fight. "I done wrestled with an alligator, I done tussled with a whale, I done handcuffed lightning, throwed thunder in jail! That's bad! Only last week, I murdered a rock, injured a stone, hospitalized a brick; I'm so mean, I make *medicine* sick!"

Like so much of Black culture, the broad contours of this style were adopted and imitated by whites, invariably losing something in the translation. (The bombast of Bobby Riggs' pre-match boasts and insults before The Battle of the Sexes were a pale echo of Ali's style, and were understood as such—by Billie Jean King, at least.)

The parallels with the Foreman fight and Ali's first title challenge were clear. Just as in 1964, when he challenged Sonny Liston, there was a feeling that Ali was taking on a fighter who was virtually indestructible. Foreman had taken just two rounds each to destroy Frazier and Norton, the fighters who had given Ali the most trouble. And, as then, those closest to Ali were whispering in the days before the fight that they were worried about Ali being seriously injured.

The numerous incidents that took place in the weeks leading up to the fight—well chronicled decades later in the Oscar-winning documentary

*When We Were Kings*—were so diffuse and incredible that they belonged solely to the '70s. Ali's wife, Belinda, showed up in Zaire while he was romancing another woman, the slender ingenue Veronica Porche (whom he would marry in 1977, a year after divorcing Belinda). After multiple arguments, at least one of which led to a physical altercation, Belinda returned to the United States, though not before she was spotted at the Zaire airport sporting a George Foreman button. Foreman was cut by his sparring partner, forcing the fight to be pushed back by a month, and neither fighter was able to leave because Mobutu feared—quite plausibly—that if the combatants left the surreal scene in Zaire, they might never return.

On September 22–24, the accompanying music festival—titled Zaire '74 and featuring James Brown, B. B. King and the Spinners—went on as planned. But then the fighters, the writers and the entourages remained for another full month, until October 30, before Foreman was fully healed and ready to enter the ring. In the interim, Ali interacted with the locals, who revered him and his presence, and often chanted "Ali! Boomiya!" (an admonition for Ali to "kill him" in Bantu) when he made public appearances.

Finally, the night arrived. It was a fight, like many of Ali's, in which he seemed to use chaos to gain clarity. As the two fighters were receiving their pre-fight instructions, Ali started in again. "Boy, you in *trouble!*" he promised. "You're gonna meet the greatest fighter of all time! We here now and there ain't no way for you to get out of this ring—I *gotcha!*"

What everyone seemed to agree on going into the fight was that the aging Ali's lone chance was to dance and elude Foreman. After months of training and weeks of strategizing with trainer Angelo Dundee and his inner circle, this had been Ali's fight plan entering the ring as well. Then the bell rang, and within minutes Ali shifted gears, ignoring his increasingly panicked trainer and handlers and going his own way. Rather than dance, he leaned on the ropes, allowing himself to be caught in Foreman's crosshairs.

It seemed as though he was on a suicide mission. Foreman, striding to the edge of the ring to rain down blows, started savaging the former champ with lefts and rights, rarely connecting with Ali's face, but repeatedly battering his arms and stomach as Ali clinched and evaded. Ali faced the barrage of blows each round, and then a barrage of apoplectic questions and exhortations in his corner, all variations on the question, "What are you doing?"

He had his own plan. In the oppressive humidity of the African night, Foreman's fearsome punches persisted and then, into the sixth and seventh rounds, began to subside, like a respite from a torrential downpour. Suddenly, Ali was talking again, disparaging Foreman while the fight was going on. "Lookatcha, you're not a champ, you're a tramp," he taunted. "You're fightin' just like a sissy. C'mon and *show* me somethin', boy."

And then, come the eighth round, in the middle of the night in a strange land to which Ali felt an ineffable, marrow-deep connection, he responded with a wicked combination—shards of the old genius flashing again into the night—and knocked out the befuddled Foreman with a sharp right.

In the moment of victory and its immediate chaotic aftermath, as the rhythms of African drumbeats echoed across the Zairean countryside, the boxing ring was enveloped in a crush. The restored champion Ali was lifted into the arms of the adoring throng and—even before he could put his warm-up robe back on—he was carried out of the stadium in a frantic, jubilant, waving procession.

Ali rode the wave, as thrilled as his admirers, and perhaps slightly in awe of what he himself had wrought. They carried him out, thundering chants of *"Ali! Boomiya!"* over and over again accompanying the boxer into the pitch-black African night. Has there ever been another mortal who might have more plausibly felt like a god as Ali in the post-fight euphoria of Kinshasa?

There are moments that forever seal a public figure's impact in memory. For Ali, more than the repeated wins over Sonny Liston, more than the transcendent first Frazier fight or the gothic third encounter to come a year later, there was this highly improbable, wholly original performance. Ali had dubbed his extemporaneous strategy the "rope-a-dope" and, in so doing, placed a new idiom into American English.

Looking back at the athletes and their weeks in Africa, it is tempting to conclude that Ali was an egomaniac who reveled in the public's attention, while Foreman was cowed by it in Zaire, but the body of evidence suggests a more complex answer. Decades later, Foreman would also become a popular, even beloved, figure. But in 1974, he hadn't yet been able to reconcile his own idea of himself with the image that the public embraced. Those who could do so had a leg up on sports in the '70s.

So expertly had Ali framed the encounter that from the streets of Detroit to the dusty lean-tos in Zaire, much of the world reacted as if somehow Ali had been fighting for redemption not only for himself but for people of color around the globe.

At one level, this was "just" sports—Ali was the twenty-seventh lineal heavyweight champion, dating back to John L. Sullivan in the 1880s—but it was also so much more. By the fall of 1974, Ali's profile in American popular culture had blossomed into something as resonant as it was complicated. He wasn't just Black America's fighter any longer; now wide swaths of the mainstream white audience—and even people who weren't sports fans—embraced him. Around the world, only the soccer great Pelé could approach his popularity. Ali was many things to many people, but in the process of his exile, return and redemption, his had become a quintessential American drama.

•

As Ali stole the headlines around the world, the other best-known Muslim athlete in the United States continued to ply his trade in Milwaukee, Wisconsin.

For all of Ali's heroics, and Simpson's superlatives, and Aaron's achievements, a case could be made that the most exceptionally talented star in the American sports firmament—and perhaps still, in 1974, the most misunderstood—was Kareem Abdul-Jabbar.

As Nina Simone sang "To Be Young, Gifted and Black," there was Abdul-Jabbar, evoking equal parts awe and resentment by his very existence—his height, his color, his reserved demeanor, misunderstood by many whites as a kind of aloof petulance.

By the time he got to the NBA, he was still not fully comfortable in his own skin, ducking under doorways, folding himself in a modest, almost prim fashion, in an attempt to avoid dominating his surroundings.

After a childhood spent in New York City and four formative years of college in Los Angeles, Lew Alcindor, as the Bucks' rookie superstar, was thrust into a Midwestern environment that seemed alien. As he put it later, "I was in a midwestern city that supported me without sustaining me."

Before the 1970–71 season, he was joined by Oscar Robertson and the

Bucks went from a contender to the team to beat. Robertson invested the team with a shrewd steel and Milwaukee tore through the regular season.

Still, Alcindor remained aloof, and his occasional candor didn't endear him to fans. In the spring of 1971, in a *Look* magazine article, he committed the heresy of admitting that some of the eighty-two games on the schedule could be tedious. "Especially when it's a boring game," he said, "my mind wanders. When I look off into the rafters, Miles Davis or maybe Freddie Hubbard playing 'Suite Sioux' will be going through my head. Or in a rough game, if you see my face screwing up, it's because, man, I just tired of the pushing—this isn't a contact sport."

Robertson knew better. "It *is* a contact sport," he stressed. "It's a game where you never let up regardless of how bad you're beating somebody: you brute them, so next time they won't forget…When this team gets the killer instinct, then we'll really jell."

Bolstered by the acquisition of Robertson, the Bucks marched to the 1971 NBA title, sweeping the Baltimore Bullets in the Finals. That summer, the new champion Alcindor announced that he had changed his name legally to Kareem Abdul-Jabbar. While the news was greeted with perplexity in some circles, there's no doubt that Ali's decision to change his name a decade earlier had made Abdul-Jabbar's transition easier.

But the ground Ali paved also brought a dilemma. "There would also be confusion between my religion and his," Abdul-Jabbar said. "This was very important because Ali's religion was a sham to me, and I took mine very seriously. The Muslims and the so-called Black Muslims have very little in common."

Abdul-Jabbar was at pains to make this distinction, and always did so carefully, so as not to insult Ali, whom he knew and admired, or to anger the Nation of Islam's leader Elijah Muhammad, whom he viewed as a charlatan.

In the meantime, the most gifted player in basketball maintained a kind of ascetic's devotion to the practice. On the first day of the Bucks' training camp in 1972 at Carroll College in Waukesha, the new assistant coach Hubie Brown and head coach Larry Costello were in the basement locker room. As they were preparing for the players to arrive later that day, Brown heard the staccato drumbeat of a basketball on the court above.

Brown pointed up and asked, "Who's here *already*?"

"You'll see," said Costello.

A few minutes later, Brown ventured upstairs onto the Carroll gymnasium floor and saw a solitary figure. It was Abdul-Jabbar, drenched in sweat, working on one of the side courts. He was shooting his hook shot at a basket equipped with a rebound ring so every shot that went in would be ejected out. Abdul-Jabbar would shoot, then hustle over to grab the rebound, then do moves off the rebound, other variations on the skyhook or facing the basket. Brown watched him admiringly; in all his years in basketball, he'd never seen anyone do such a drill.

What Abdul-Jabbar was doing, in addition to refining his rebounding instincts, was honing to perfection the single most dominant, unstoppable shot in basketball history. His version of the hook shot found Abdul-Jabbar using his left arm to shield the defender while he raised the ball over his head and floated the ball toward the basket.

He had been perfecting the shot since high school and at UCLA John Wooden had helped him streamline it further. Earlier in his career, he took a wider arc in launching it, but Wooden told him, "Keep the ball close to your body. I want your hand, your elbow and your knee close and in line. I don't want you any farther than eight or nine feet from the basket, and when you get the ball, go straight up with it."

The shot was a thing of complex beauty with Abdul-Jabbar stepping out in a flowing motion, executing a drop step, extending his arm and then, in a frisson of supple guidance, his slender fingers would catapult the ball toward the basket. The ball, perhaps nine feet off the ground when it left his fingers, would rise above the top of the backboard before nestling into the net.

It was also an inversion of the standards of center play—Wilt Chamberlain's brute force and elbows, Bill Russell's churning lay-ups, Nate Thurmond's futuristic muscles. Only Willis Reed, with his deft, almost delicate, left-handed jumper from the key, could compete with the gentle grace of Abdul-Jabbar's shot. But there was a key difference: Reed's jumper could be blocked; Abdul-Jabbar's skyhook simply could not.

The definitive Abdul-Jabbar hook shot came late in Game 6 of the 1974 NBA Finals against the Celtics, with the Bucks clawing to survive to force a Game 7. Boston Garden was still a fortress then—manic and stifling, seats close to the floor and photographers even closer—with the Celtics hoping to clinch another title. The crowd was a pulsing, threatening thing, and uniformed police officers were behind press row to keep the fans at bay.

Trailing by one point with seven seconds left in overtime, Abdul-Jabbar took the inbounds pass from Robertson and, with defenders bodying him away from the basket, he launched the ball in a majestic arc. Calling the game from the elevated press area in the rafters of the Garden, the Bucks' announcer Eddie Doucette watched the ball come nearly up to eye level, then drop cleanly through the hoop. "The shot seemed to come down from the sky! It was a skyhook!" He had used the term before, but never in such pivotal circumstances.

The Bucks would go home to Milwaukee and lose Game 7, and Abdul-Jabbar's subsequent final season in Milwaukee would be profoundly unhappy. But the nomenclature persisted, and soon everyone was describing Abdul-Jabbar's unstoppable arabesque as a "skyhook."

But Abdul-Jabbar's talent was so substantial that most fans didn't fully appreciate his skills. Nor did most writers, who found him aloof, as he negotiated his way through his postgame routine.

For decades, the postgame interview paradigm had been set. Writers would lodge questions, some highly superficial, and the athlete being interrogated would provide stream-of-consciousness answers, almost always equally superficial. The artless, mostly joyless process did not often add to an understanding of the game, but it allowed writers to have "quotes" for their morning stories.

Abdul-Jabbar was not comfortable with the arrangement and so assumed a more deliberate process.

"I saw it so many times," said Brown, who spent two seasons as a Bucks assistant. "They would ask him a question and he would slowly take his sock off and then he would give a one-sentence answer. Then they'd ask him another question and he'd slowly take the other sock off and then give another one-sentence answer. He would give himself time to think about the answer, and then he would give it."

The deliberate nature of Abdul-Jabbar's answers, plus all of the other elements—his height, his reluctant nature, his sometimes awkward interactions and the fact that he was both smarter and more educated than many of the people interviewing him—created a chasm.

He was quintessentially the *other*. Black, tall, reserved, smart but distant. A generation of coaches and fans didn't know how to start understanding him. Abdul-Jabbar, like Malcolm X, made a spiritual pilgrimage to Mecca. He'd studied Arabic at Harvard, pursuing a graduate degree in Islamic studies. And he purchased a townhouse on Sixteenth Street NW in Washington, DC, to provide a gathering place for his spiritual leader, Hamas Abdul Khaalis and the Hanafi sect to which he belonged.

Meanwhile, Khaalis had grown increasingly critical of Elijah Muhammad. And on a night in 1973, representatives from a Black Muslim sect from Philadelphia ambushed the DC townhouse. Then, in what at the time was the largest mass killing in the history of the District of Columbia, the assailants shot two men and a boy in the back of the head, drowned four children, and shot two women, whom they left for dead (both women survived).

For the rest of the season and into the next, there were security guards and FBI agents shadowing the Bucks. The security detail would increase whenever the Bucks traveled to Chicago, where the Nation of Islam was based.

Abdul-Jabbar, absorbed in his own grief, grew more distant, from both the city of Milwaukee and his teammates.

"I can sense that it bothers him," said Lucius Allen, who had roomed with Abdul-Jabbar back at UCLA. "He carries it around within him. But it's not there on the court. At no time is it on the court."

The respect, the admiration and the affection from fans would come in time, but by the time Henry Aaron and O. J. Simpson were record holders, and Muhammad Ali was restored to his position as champion of the world, Kareem Abdul-Jabbar had decided he wanted out of Milwaukee.

"We knew as players he was never really comfortable here," said teammate Jon McGlocklin. "And then the whole thing went down in Washington, DC, at the home he owned, and people were killed in it. And then that year was a tough year for all of us because there were security and safeguards and all kinds of things around the whole team. And it was tough. And we knew he wanted out." On June 16, 1975, he got his wish, and was dealt to the Los Angeles Lakers, where the unimaginably long second act of Abdul-Jabbar's pro career would commence.

•

One glimpse into America's mindset in the '70s was to look at what sort of endorsement deals each of these four supreme athletes attracted. Abdul-Jabbar, excellent as he was, did little outside of endorsing basketball sneakers. Aaron, finally, at the end of his career, signed a deal with Magnavox, which was built less on his personality than giving the company a few months to tour the country with the bat and ball Aaron used to break Ruth's record before donating it to the Baseball Hall of Fame. Ali, for all his worldwide fame, struggled to find ancillary income. There was the short-lived Muhammad Ali boxing game in 1976, but throughout the decade, his highest-profile American endorsement was for d-CON Four/gone roach spray.

And then there was O. J. Simpson. Simpson pursued acting in the off-season and was no worse than Joe Namath at it, playing a security guard who rescues a kitten from a skyscraper in the 1974 disaster blockbuster *The Towering Inferno,* and starring in *A Killing Affair,* a crime drama and inter-racial love story, opposite *Bewitched's* Elizabeth Montgomery in the made-for-TV movie.

In 1976, the same year that *Ladies Home Journal* poll of adolescents named him the most admired American, Simpson's agent reached out to him, informing him that the Hertz rental car company was mounting a new campaign and they wanted to discuss it with Simpson.

Later that year, Simpson became the first African American to lead a major American corporation's television advertising campaign, running through airports for Hertz, "the Superstar in Rent-a-Car."

The idea that a professional athlete—and a Black one at that—would be the spokesman for a large corporate campaign would have been unthinkable in the '60s; by the '70s, the development reflected the changing attitudes on the part of the American consumer and implicitly recognized the realm of sports as a place to change minds. So it was Simpson rather than any other athlete, and Simpson rather than any established Black entertainer—Sidney Poitier or Bill Cosby, Harry Belafonte or Marvin Gaye, Diana Ross or Diahann Carroll, Stevie Wonder or Flip Wilson—who was selected as the *most* trustworthy, *most* likable, *most* marketable figure.

It may or may not have been true that Americans didn't want to be reminded of race. It was certainly true that American *advertisers* were convinced that Americans didn't want to be reminded of race. In the case of Aaron, Ali and Abdul-Jabbar, the racial manners and mores of the time meant they were fighting to be accepted on their own terms.

Simpson, by contrast, pointedly avoided any declaration of his own race. And that—at least in and around the mid-'70s—was enough to make him, by some measures, the most admired man in America.

# TEN

# THE OUTSIDERS

THE NEWS TRAVELED fast at Holcombe Rucker Park, on the corner of West 155th Street and Frederick Douglass Boulevard, ground zero of the Rucker League, where pro basketball's best turned up each summer to sharpen their steel against one another and the Harlem standouts who never made the pros: Clyde was coming.

Clyde being the Knicks' stellar, stylish guard Walt "Clyde" Frazier, who may or may not have arrived in his Rolls-Royce, depending on whose version could be trusted.

Frazier was Rucker royalty, even though he was never a big scorer like the playground legends Joe Hammond or Earl "The Goat" Manigault, who would routinely drop in fifty points on an opponent in a Rucker League game. But Frazier infused the game with his own distinctly casual coolness.

But on this day, all anyone wanted to ask him about was the *other* piece of news that had made the rounds: the series of one-on-one games that Frazier had recently played up at Kutsher's resort in the Catskills.

They wanted to greet him and to console him on the ordeal he'd reportedly endured.

Recalling it later, Frazier would remember the conciliatory reassurance of the assembled who crowded the chain-link fences that surrounded the court. Despite his loss, "the kids said, 'Well, Clyde, he's taller than you.' Or 'You'll beat him the next time.' Or 'You just probably had an off day.' Others said, 'Clyde is still the best guard. Julius, he's a forward.' Stuff like that."

What no one disputed, even the supremely serene Frazier, was that up at Kutsher's he had been bested by a still relatively unknown player from the ABA, who'd challenged Frazier to a best-of-seven series of one-on-one games, and beat him four games to two.

Soon Julius Winfield Erving II—a gangly six-foot-six with a righteous afro that made him a good half-foot taller—had become a Rucker Park legend himself. And as he dazzled viewers and opponents alike, the announcers strove for a suitable nickname. They tried:

The Claw.

Black Moses.

Houdini.

But finally, after another thunderous dunk had sent the crowd into euphorics and the Rucker PA announcer into paroxysms of superlatives, Julius Erving walked up to the announcer and calmly informed him, "Just call me 'The Doctor.'"

By then, Erving had been traded from the Virginia Squires to the New York Nets prior to the 1973–74 season, where he could do what Kareem Abdul-Jabbar had never been able to do—play his home games just a few minutes from where he grew up.

Within six months, he was a household name, a *Sports Illustrated* cover subject ("What's Up? Doc J"), a coveted basketball card, a popular shoe endorser, and one of the biggest names in all of basketball.

And what made all of the above so unlikely was that none of his regular games as the star forward of the Nets had been nationally televised. Dr. J's exploits were hailed from coast to coast, yet he remained almost entirely unseen, the last truly mythic figure in the history of American sports.

Erving became the decade's preeminent stylistic influencer. With his afro and wispy goatee, sporting the mod stars-and-stripes uniform of the New York Nets, Dr. J was a secret, a wild rumor, an urban legend. His sublime game was a glimpse into basketball's future, the catalyst for the transition from the low-post game dominated by hulking centers of the '60s to one of fluid motion and athleticism, in which graceful, multidimensional players became more central.

Erving's playground artistry developed on the cement courts in Hempstead, Long Island, and then, as a teenager, in Roosevelt, New York, in the '60s. Sitting around after a pickup game one summer day, his friend Leon

Saunders tried to explain what he'd seen to Erving himself. "How you're playing—nobody plays like that," said Saunders. "Flying around like that. Snatching rebounds from the air a couple of feet above the rim. Dunking over guys. You're...a whirlwind. It's a new way of playing. Man, the Boston Celtics don't play like that. The Knicks don't. Nobody."

This truth soon became apparent when Erving reached the pros. He was a player who recognized the fundamentals and mastered them, and then took his game to some mystical realm beyond. "It's all psychological," he said. "If we're down a few points and I'm fast-breaking toward the hoop, I'll sometimes decide that the time has come to get freaky. It gets the crowd up and our team up and it gets me up. Because of the excitement, we'll often start to defend better, to make good plays and to pull ahead."

As an opponent, he presented a nearly unprecedented range of problems. It wasn't just the scoring and the rebounding, it was the effect he could have on the crowd, even on the road. At Kentucky, the head coach Hubie Brown—who seemed almost a savant at feeling the ebbs and flows of a game—ordered his Colonels to foul Erving every time he dribbled toward the lane at full speed.

"We had to stop him even turning a *home* crowd," said Brown, "with the oohs and aahs and the dancing in the aisles with people doing the elbow stuff. Because he would turn your home court into admiring what he was doing."

After seeing Erving dunk over the ABA's supreme shot-blocker, the seven-foot-two Artis Gilmore, Brown vowed to himself, "I would never allow my guys to be embarrassed by that again. It was just something you never saw before: There's Erving, who's six-foot-six and his armpit was up *over the top* of your seven-foot guy, who's a great shot blocker, and he's just throwing it down."

The ABA didn't have a national TV contract. It didn't have many modern arenas. It lacked a sufficient number of large markets. But it did have the incomparable Erving. Which put it well ahead of many of the other upstart leagues of the era.

•

Like the legion of imitators that followed Bob Dylan's success in the music industry—each destined to be an unsatisfying echo of the sui generis original—the success of Lamar Hunt and the American Football League in the '60s spawned a phalanx of would-be entrepreneurs to start new sports leagues, none of whom possessed the wherewithal or resilience of Hunt, but each of whom thought he could capitalize on the apparently unlimited potential of American spectator sports.

That series of audacious undertakings would characterize the decade: new leagues challenging the old order, teams in cities that had never been considered major league in the past, individual sports trying to move to a team sports format, amateur sports determined to provide a pro framework. All of it was done without anything resembling market surveys; each was its own hopeful, sports-minded leap of faith.

The 1970s turned out to be an abysmal time to take financial risk. The postwar boom was faltering. In 1974 alone, wages fell by 2.1 percent and income shrunk by $1,500 per capita. Manufacturing jobs, which had consti- tuted roughly a third of the nation's workforce in the postwar years, would stumble to less than 20 percent by the end of the decade.

Into the teeth of this financial instability, the new leagues seemed to come out of nowhere. The glut of upstarts had begun in 1965 when Dennis Mur- phy, the young mayor of Buena Park, California, joined a group applying for an American Football League franchise in Anaheim. When the AFL and NFL announced their merger in 1966, these prospective owners' hopes for a football team were dashed. "I kept thinking about it, how we had a pretty good group of money people who loved sports and we should do *something*," remembered Murphy. "I thought, 'There's only one basketball league and one hockey league, so why not have another?'"

Basketball was Murphy's favorite sport, so that prompted the formation of the American Basketball Association in 1967. One of his partners was a young California lawyer named Gary Davidson, a would-be wheeler-dealer whose early efforts at takeover—he proposed himself to be the new league's commissioner—were rebuffed on the grounds that he was still too callow. Undaunted, Davidson would be back.

Having a major league franchise was inordinately important to cities in postwar America. As the country became connected via air travel, and as more events made it onto TV, the status offered by a big-league team was sub- stantial. The economic impact would remain vague and ineffable (in many cases, the economic-impact numbers were oversold). But the psychic effect was not; as the mayor of Kansas City, Missouri, once put it, "Without the Chiefs and the Royals, we're Omaha. We're Des Moines."

Through it all, the ABA forged ahead, going from the edge of big markets like Oakland and Long Island to smaller ones like Hampton, Virginia, and Louisville, Kentucky. "We were always traveling on Piedmont Airlines or Mohawk Air, regional flights, tiny seats, and sometimes we have to make three connections to get from, say, Norfolk, to Tampa," recalled Erving. "And about half of the flights on these regional airlines seem to turn around because of equipment malfunctions, fuel leaks, a door being open, whatever. And then we miss our connection and we're killing five hours wandering around an airport in Shreveport."

But consider: The humble, motley ABA was *by far* the most sophisticated and legitimate upstart league of the decade. It was soon joined by the World Hockey Association (1972) and the World Football League (1974), both like the ABA attempting to get people to abandon the leagues and teams they'd grown up with for entirely new franchises. Of course, the hidden agenda of each of these leagues was to survive long enough to force a merger with the older league, just as the AFL had done with the NFL.

Those endeavors, at least, had an identifiable endgame. It was the other enterprises that were truly nervy. Entities like World Team Tennis (1974), which was attempting to convert an individual sport to a team concept, and the International Volleyball Association (1975), which was trying to take a historically amateur sport and make it professional. Both WTT and the IVA were also attempting, each in its own way, to introduce the concept of co-ed professional sports, with men and women competing side-by-side on the same court at the same time.

Meanwhile, limping along after a stuttering start in 1968, and a near collapse in 1969, was the nascent North American Soccer League, which was trying to introduce the world's game to a mostly distracted American audience. The high hopes for nearly all of these new leagues would all be dashed by the end of the decade.

•

After the commissioner debacles with Mikan and Alcindor, and Jack Dolph and the signed contracts, the ABA remained in critical condition, though nominally solvent.

In the absence of attractive markets, a national TV contract and healthy attendance, what the upstart league possessed was a wide-open, entertaining style of play—including the long-range three-point shot adopted from the defunct American Basketball League in the '60s—and a surprisingly large percentage of the best young players in the game.

The red, white and blue ball had been George Mikan's greatest contribution to the cause, an eye-popping alternative to the dark-orange-ish-brown of the NBA basketball. The ABA balls sold in stores seemed somehow springier than the NBA balls. And they were easier to coach with, since they so clearly showed the ball's rotation in flight.

"In some respects, we were a maverick league, but so what?" said Erving. "What was wrong with a red, white and blue ball? What was wrong with the three-point shot or creating a faster tempo so that the little man would have an opportunity to play? What's wrong with a little experimentation and encouraging an individual to excel in a team sport?"

The rules were innovative and the young players in the league were at times brilliant. But the markets were disappointing and the marketing of the ABA was often desperate. In 1968, the Kentucky Colonels put a woman— the five-foot-three-inch, 110-pound female jockey Penny Ann Early, who'd been exiled by the jealous male jockeys at Churchill Downs—in for a game. She checked into the scorer's table wearing a skirt and a turtleneck sweater, inbounded the ball to an open teammate who immediately called time-out, and with that her career was over. But Early was at least an athlete. Another ABA franchise, the Floridians, boasted a four-woman team of beauty queens decked out in bikinis with little effect on attendance (one didn't have to buy a ticket to see women in bikinis in Florida). The Indiana Pacers sponsored cow-milking contests at halftime. None of it felt particularly major league.

Everything the ABA did was on a modest budget. Some teams didn't have assistant coaches, meal money for a time in the '70s was $7 a day ("the big thing was to get a hotel near a McDonald's, a Kentucky Fried Chicken or a

White Castle hamburger joint," said the Pacers' Mel Daniels), players often taped their own ankles.

Hubie Brown would recall getting a taste of the ABA during his first game in St. Louis, when the Colonels visited the Spirits at the Checkerdome. "There weren't 5,000 people in the building," said Brown, "and we're walking toward our bench, and a fight breaks out in the lay-up line with St. Louis. And Fly Williams is getting killed by Joe Caldwell. He's got him on the floor and punching the shit out of him, and I can't believe this because nobody's even breaking it up. The players are just standing there watching it."

Inevitably, the ABA was overlooked, and its players were particularly sensitive to their media coverage. "We felt as if we were in the shadows," said the Squires' Dave Twardzik. "You'd pick up *The Sporting News* and there would be NBA articles all over the place and maybe one column with ABA news. You'd go through Chicago and pick up a newspaper at the airport and you'd be lucky if they ran the ABA standings or the box scores. In the ABA cities, our coverage was usually very good, but just go a little outside that area... forget it. It was as though we didn't exist."

One place the ABA could prove itself was in preseason games, where the younger league held its own with the NBA, edging the senior league seventy-nine games to seventy-six.

"I was an NBA loyalist and wanted to bury them," said Wayne Embry, general manager of the Milwaukee Bucks. "I hated the ball, everything. We thought they were making a mockery of the game. We wanted to show also the NBA was superior."

In some of the smaller markets, like Indianapolis and San Antonio, teams developed fiercely loyal followings. But the lack of a TV contract meant the league was always in a perilous state. The league counsel Mike Goldberg despaired that "we just couldn't get traction. To some degree, I think that was a racial situation. The league was very African American in those days. The afro was a big statement of the ABA. There was a certain swagger. This wasn't *Hoosiers*, if you follow what I mean. This was freedom of movement, freedom of expression, and even our coaches bought into it. The talent was so rich there was no holding these guys back."

In addition to Erving, there was Artis Gilmore of the Colonels, who'd led tiny Jacksonville University to the 1970 NCAA championship game; George

"The Ice Man" Gervin, the slender sharpshooter from Eastern Michigan who built a staunch following in San Antonio; and Len Elmore, the Maryland standout who chose the Pacers over the Washington Bullets of the NBA.

The league was fighting a guerrilla war. The NBA had been amenable to a merger years earlier, but Oscar Robertson's suit put that on hold, and the ABA's continued raiding of underclassmen while the case was working its way through the courts infuriated NBA GMs and owners. Then in late August 1974, during the same week that Oscar Robertson announced his retirement from pro basketball, the Utah Stars announced they had signed the eighteen-year-old high school graduate Moses Malone, making him the first player to go straight from high school to the pros. It was another shot across the bow of the NBA. A year later, in 1975, the ABA won the duel for North Carolina State's national champion David Thompson.

At the same time, the weaker ABA franchises were barely hanging on. The Memphis Pros franchise, transported from New Orleans, launched for the 1970–71 season, but only after Mid-South Coliseum was largely booked for the winter, leaving the Pros to settle for nine Monday nights and ten Wednesday nights on their home schedule. They sold 180 season tickets. After four uneventful seasons with three nicknames—they were also the Tams (under Charles O. Finley) and the Sounds (under Al Bell, of Stax records)—the team moved to Baltimore and was originally named the Baltimore Hustlers, until enough people questioned whether that was an appropriate nickname. They then became the Baltimore Claws, owing to the city's reputation for fine seafood. The entity played three exhibition games in the 1975 preseason, sporting the old Sounds uniforms with a patch of cloth reading "Claws" sewn over the old team name. Five days before the start of the regular season, still behind on the players' per diem checks and owing $500,000 to the Kentucky Colonels, the Claws' franchise was terminated by the ABA.

In the face of it all, the league carried on, buoyed by the presence of Erving.

"We had the Doctor, so we carried that league, because of the Doctor," said Rod Thorn, a Nets assistant in the mid-'70s. "Wherever we went, there was always a crowd because he was like a guy that you've heard about but you haven't seen, we gotta see. And Julius had the personality as well as the game to carry that off."

•

The National Hockey League would have been ripe for an upstart to challenge it in the mid-'60s when there were still only six teams, none west of Chicago or south of New York. But by the time the World Hockey Association announced its formation in 1971, the NHL had fourteen teams and the environment had changed considerably.

And yet, just as in the NFL, Major League Baseball and the NBA prior to the arrival of the ABA, salaries were depressed, the reserve clause was intact and players were ripe for the taking.

There was also the fact that the NHL had put their six new expansion franchises under such onerous conditions that the gap between the established teams and the new ones had only grown. The six expansionists won once out of every 3.6 games against the Original Six in their debut season of 1967–68. In the first half of the 1971–72 season, they were winning only once in 6.6 games.

Enter, once again, Dennis Murphy and Gary Davidson, the tandem that had been around at the beginning of the ABA. Murphy was the idea man who envisioned an entirely new league. Davidson, the closer, had grown more assured in his pitches by 1972. Murphy and Davidson each took a franchise, and sold the other franchises for $25,000 each, then turned around and sold one of their franchises to a group from Quebec for $215,000.

By June of 1972 the upstart league had already signed twenty-two players who'd played the previous season in the NHL, with the big prize being Chicago's slashing scorer Bobby "The Golden Jet" Hull, signed by the Winnipeg franchise—they decided to call themselves the Jets—for a five-year, $1.25 million contract, paid by the Jets' owner, jukebox mogul Ben Hatskin, while each of the other WHA owners chipped in on a $1 million signing bonus.

The presence of a new league gave prized players a leverage they'd never known. When Hull reported to the Black Hawks after an extended holdout in 1969, the team insisted that he apologize at a press conference. "I can never forget what they did to me then," he said. Three years later, the WHA realized the value of one of the biggest names in hockey, and made him an offer he couldn't refuse.

"I thought it was a joke," said Hull. "I pretended to go along with it, just to scare Chicago. Then my agent said, 'Bobby, these guys are serious.' "

But the NHL fought fiercely to invalidate the league-jumpers' contracts. NHLPA executive director Alan Eagleson, who'd coordinated the much-hyped 1972 Canada Cup series between the Soviet national team and a Canadian all-star team, barred any players who'd signed with the WHA from playing in the series. (Eagleson's resistance to an open market for hockey players may, in retrospect, have been one of the first signs that he was not entirely in the corner of the players.)

Hull's signing prompted a skirmish of dueling lawsuits and he missed the first month of the WHA's inaugural season before he was cleared to play.

"The name of the game now," said Hull, "is money."

It was hard to begrudge Hull his riches. He'd been an established star who led the NHL in goals scored on seven occasions. Later that summer, Derek Sanderson—center on the champion Bruins' third line, who'd never scored as many as thirty goals a season—was given a ten-year, $2.65 million contract by the Philadelphia Blazers of the WHA. Sanderson, who'd toiled in Boston very much in the shadows of Bobby Orr and center Phil Esposito, styled himself in the mold of Broadway Joe Namath—complete with the penthouse apartment with circular bed and carpeted walls—though he seemed more self-conscious about it than the original. "I knew I couldn't compete on goal-scoring because of Espy and I knew I couldn't compete on sheer ability because Orr had that, so I had to be colorful." Image was not, as of yet, everything. By the time Hull actually played a WHA game for the Jets, the bloom was already off the underperforming Sanderson, who was much less spectacular with a pedestrian Blazers team than he'd been with the NHL champion Bruins. "The people aren't buying my act," Sanderson concluded. (He wound up playing only eight games with the Blazers. By the end of the 1972–73 season, he was back in Boston, trying to regain his form with the Bruins.)

The WHA used navy-blue pucks, which it claimed were easier to see, and a ten-minute sudden-death overtime period to break regular-season ties. Early returns were surprisingly successful in some hockey-mad cities like Edmonton, Quebec City and Winnipeg. A year later, a WHA franchise, originally awarded to Dayton, Ohio, was established in the unlikeliest of locations, Houston. After the Houston Aeros drafted Mark and Marty Howe, sons of hockey legend Gordie Howe, they coaxed the elder Howe out of retirement.

The Aeros paid the all-time NHL scoring leader a $500,000 bonus and a salary of $125,000 a year.

Howe was philosophical about the money that Houston was offering. "In my scoring-title years and my Stanley Cup years, I couldn't live on my hockey salary," Howe said. "I was the star of the world, and I watched my neighbor, a salesman, take his family and his boat away every Friday night for the weekend at their cottage. There I was, supposedly the star of everything, working a second job to get along."

At its core, the WHA's problem was similar to the ABA's problem. People could argue about the quality of play beyond the highest profile stars, but neither league could muster a national television contract and that meant that the leagues were surviving primarily on the tickets sold. In a competitive market during an economic downturn, it was hardly a recipe for success.

•

As the NFL's popularity rose in the early '70s so did its emphasis on safe, ball-control offense and its own dynastic self-importance. The Super Bowls, commercial hit that they were, had been mostly boring, with only Super Bowl V and its comedy of errors (eleven turnovers, five in the fourth quarter) truly close at the end. There was a feeling in many circles that the NFL had grown stultifying with its success.

And so a new football league was born. It was that man again: Gary Davidson, the young California lawyer who was compared to Robert Redford by numerous writers, apparently on the basis of being young and blond and persuasive. The tanned, smiling Davidson looked like what a dashing young executive was supposed to look like in the early '70s, and proved quite effective at convincing wealthy people that their lives would be immeasurably improved by owning a sports franchise. "I thought he was incredibly charismatic," said the New York Stars' general manager, Howard Baldwin. "I thought he was the kind of guy you became drawn to."

The WFL held its first draft in 1974, a week before the NFL (the WFL's first choice being All-American Kansas quarterback David Jaynes, not a prized prospect among NFL scouts).

The new league vowed to depart from the NFL's stasis by providing more action. There would be no long slog of six preseason games, but the WFL would instead play a twenty-game regular season. The new league inaugurated a series of rule changes that were soon copied by the NFL (sudden-death overtime for regular-season games, goalposts moved to the back of the end zone, missed field goals returned to the line of scrimmage). One rule change wasn't imitated; the league did away with extra-point kicks entirely. Touchdowns were worth seven, not six, points, and the conversion attempt following them ("the action point") would be run from scrimmage.

The WFL football was genuinely butterscotch-colored with stripes the color of orange traffic cones. The league would go hard into modern colors and singular nicknames. There was the Portland Storm, the Southern California Sun (sporting magenta game pants), the Chicago Fire and the Philadelphia Bell.

But the best way for upstart leagues to draw attention was by signing stars from established leagues to rich contracts. That spring, Toronto Northmen owner John Bassett, heir to his father's beer fortune, decided to go after the stars of the reigning Super Bowl champions.

After winning their second straight Super Bowl at the end of the 1973 season, the stars of the Miami Dolphins had fame and adulation and couldn't buy a drink anywhere in south Florida. What they didn't have was financial security. Larry Csonka's body was already starting to break down and his backfield mate Jim Kiick was perpetually injured. The team's star wide receiver Paul Warfield was in his thirties. All of which is to say that they were ripe for the approach of a new owner with a new team in a new football league.

Along came the engaging Bassett, who in the spring of 1974 announced the most shocking deal of the decade, a $3 million joint package for Csonka ($1.4 million), Warfield ($900,000) and Kiick ($700,000) for three years. All three players were still under contract to the Dolphins in 1974, so they wouldn't get to the new league until 1975.

In July 1974, the same month of the WFL debut, the NFL players went on strike, arguing for more benefits. Suddenly the stage for football belonged exclusively to the new WFL, which, unlike the other start-up leagues, did have a TV contract of sorts (through a syndication deal with the independent network TVS). By the time the league drew 60,000 fans for its first game, in Jacksonville, with a respectable 16 percent share of the TV audience, Gary

Davidson was arguing that franchises would be priced at $4.2 million the next season, and he expected to have franchises in Mexico City and Tokyo by then.

The league had about it the whiff of the new, and there was authentic interest in cities that had never had major-league sports franchises before. Arnold Palmer made a small investment in the Charlotte franchise and frequently attended games. In Memphis, where Bassett's Toronto franchise migrated after fights with the Canadian government, Elvis Presley went to most of the home games. One night, Charlie Rich struggled through the national anthem before returning to his seat next to Presley.

"That's a hard song," said Elvis, by way of consolation.

"It ain't no 'Behind Closed Doors,'" Rich agreed.

Even with the exposure from TVS and the modest amount of money, all parties agreed that the key to the league's survival that first year wouldn't be TV, but would come from the gate. Optimistic figures said that the league could break even averaging 35,000 fans a game.

But within weeks, the WFL's "papergate" was exposed. Philadelphia's crowd of 120,000 from their first two games turned out to have mostly been freebies. Teams were soon hemorrhaging money and some franchises were leaving in the middle of the night. The New York Stars soon became the Charlotte Stars (the "NY" in their helmet logo covered by a C sticker). The Houston Texans were scheduled to play one of the nationally televised WFL games, but by the time the game was telecast they'd uprooted and moved to Louisiana, to become something called the Shreveport Steamer.

When the NFL settled with the players in August, the nation's football fans turned their attention back to the real thing. By the time the first WFL championship game—the "World Bowl"—was played in November, the new league was on life support. The WFL's three co-MVPs wouldn't agree to appear at halftime of the World Bowl unless they were being paid in cash. And so the presentation came with a wheelbarrow featuring stacks of one-dollar bills.

The two final teams were limping to the finish with creditors nipping at their heels—the Florida Blazers, who hadn't been paid in ten weeks, faced the Birmingham Americans, who had their uniforms repossessed immediately after winning the league championship.

When the league met at the end of its first season, six of the twelve franchises no longer had owners, and the commissioner Davidson had been ousted by popular acclaim and replaced by Chris Hemmeter, co-owner of the league's Honolulu franchise, the Hawaiians.

The WFL returned for its second season with a plan to give all players a percentage of the gate receipts. The league's brain trust, trying to capitalize on the public's fascination with the nuances of football strategy, briefly considered color-coordinating game pants by position. Defensive linemen would be in blue pants, linebackers in red pants and defensive backs in yellow pants. Quarterbacks and kickers would be in white pants, offensive linemen would wear purple pants, wide receivers orange pants and running backs were in green pants, with black piping, that called to mind nothing so much as Rudolf Nureyev playing a court jester. The experiment ended when Csonka, Kiick and Warfield sent a telegram to the league office reading, in its entirety: "WILL NOT WEAR CLOWNLIKE PANTS."

Hemmeter and the league staked their reputation on getting Joe Namath to jump to the new league, but when that gambit failed, the end was inevitable. The World Football League had begun its inaugural 1974 season with TVS having assembled a network of 100 affiliates. By the end of the season it was down to sixty, and even fewer started the 1975 season, which ended after twelve weeks in a flurry of recrimination and unpaid bills, the league having lost $30 million in two years, and shutting down on October 22, 1975, with $15 million more in debt.

•

More Americans than ever before were playing and watching tennis, the boom sport of the decade. In 1970, 10.9 million Americans called themselves tennis players. By 1974, the number had grown to 33.9 million; by 1975, the figure was up to 40.9 million. Partially due to Billie Jean King's victory in the Battle of the Sexes, participation in tennis nearly doubled in the next two years, and a majority of the new players drawn to the sport were women.

By the end of 1975, tennis had developed into a billion-dollar industry; Americans spent $100 million on tennis balls that year, $200 million on clothing, nearly $250 million more on equipment, while more than $400 million was spent on construction of tennis courts and complexes.

There was $10 million in prize money and promotions on the professional tennis tour by then, and that was also reflected in television coverage. In 1971, American TV networks aired parts of seven tennis tournaments; by 1975, they were showing parts of seventy. The King–Riggs match wasn't only important for gender, it opened up the sport to a broader crowd, one that wasn't cowed by the staid country-club manners of tennis' past. *Time* magazine recognized the boom with a curious cover story "Sex and Tennis: The New Battleground" in September 1976, noting the societal dynamics of mixed doubles.

While the popularity of the game continued to grow, the powers fighting for primacy within the game remained at war. Though the USLTA and the Virginia Slims tour made peace in the spring of 1973, the battles between Lamar Hunt's World Championship Tennis and both the USLTA and the ILTA would persist. When the U.S. Open threatened to bar WCT players from the tournament in 1972, there was pushback. Joe Cullman of Philip Morris vowed to pull the $250,000 worth of sponsorship and CBS said they wouldn't televise the tournament unless the best players showed up.

In the midst of the infighting, Hunt's million-dollar gamble on the World Championship Tennis tour was paying off. On May 14, 1972, the final of the second annual WCT championship played in front of a sold-out crowd at Moody Coliseum in Dallas, and a tennis audience of 21 million nationwide, as Ken Rosewall edged Rod Laver in a five-set classic. By 1974, the WCT tour comprised eighty-four players competing for $1.35 million in prize money.

But even the rebels had to deal with rebels. The biggest tennis star on the men's tour didn't play on the WCT tour in 1975. One could see the shock of the new in the persona of Jimmy Connors, who'd come up an outsider, playing tennis on the cement public courts in Belleville, Illinois, learning the game from his relentless mother and grandmother.

"We played in Jones Park in downtown East St. Louis," Connors recalled. "We were always at public parks where there was no shade and you had to walk a hundred yards to get a drink of water." Bursting onto the scene as his game matured in 1974, Connors was a kinetic revelation. If Laver and Rosewall's elegant shot-making suggested the fine art of a Cezanne or Renoir, Connors' game evoked something more contemporary, like really artful subway graffiti.

His headlong style ushered in a new era and he revolutionized the backhand, becoming the first to use a two-fisted shot not merely as a resource but a weapon. The game looked and sounded different in Connors' hands. With his tautly strung, steel-suspension T-2000 racket, he led the tennis equipment revolution away from wood into lighter, stronger materials. On the service return, he was a charging bull, reacting to the ball's motion in an instant, hitting it while it was still on the rise. "Serving to him is like pitching to Hank Aaron," said Australian star John Newcombe. "If you don't mix it up, it's going out of the ballpark."

Even his movements were unique; he was prone to nervous tics like blowing into his hands and spinning the racket before receiving serve. Once the ball was in play, he enjoyed off-balance shot-making. While other players exhibited poise and control, Connors seemed forever on the verge of losing control. "I'm flying," he said. "I prefer to hit all my balls on the run, even when I don't have to."

Connors, even more than Billie Jean King or Chris Evert, was a product of the public courts. He claimed to be the first top-ranked men's player to be trained by women. His mother, Gloria (who had once dated Chris Evert's father, Jimmy), had raised him, along with her mother, whom Connors referred to as "Two-Mom." Gloria Connors would thwack balls at young Jimmy, and urge him to get his "tiger juices" flowing. "If your own mother will do this to you," she'd counseled across the net, "imagine what those other players will do!"

Connors shunned the WCT circuit in favor of an independent indoor circuit run by his manager, Bill Riordan. During the times he played WCT players, such as at the U.S. Pro Championships, he was going to war. On the flight up to Boston for the tournament in '73, before his opening-round match against Stan Smith, Connors kept writing notes to himself: "Beat son-of-a-bitch. Beat son-of-a-bitch."

Connors' comportment was also a departure. Because he'd not been raised in the politesse of privilege and courtesy on the courts, he was more combustible (he popularized, for better or worse, the crotch grab in response to a disputed line call).

His time on the second-rate tour meant he rarely faced the world's best players, like WCT mainstays Rod Laver and John Newcombe, some of whom questioned his credentials. After winning the U.S. Open in 1974, Connors walked off the court and muttered to Riordan, "Get me Laver."

That request led to another made-for-TV innovation, "The Heavyweight Championship of Tennis" challenge matches, which carried all the trappings of a title fight and were played in front of a portable grandstand in the parking lot of Caesars Palace.

CBS had moved aggressively into tennis and now paid just under $100,000 to televise the Connors–Laver match on February 2, 1975.

The day before the match, the two sides gathered for a coin flip to determine who would serve first, with Connors winning the toss.

"The bastards won the coin flip," complained someone in the Laver camp.

Connors overheard and responded, "That's *Mister* Bastard to you."

The telecast was watched by 17 million people, who saw Connors win the first two sets before losing the third. Then Connors and Laver tangled in a scintillating fourth set, highlighted by a tenth game in which the thirty-six-year-old Australian fought off five match points. Connors prevailed, though not before he flipped off the comedienne Totie Fields sitting courtside.

The subsequent match—Connors vs. John Newcombe in April, again for the Heavyweight Championship of Tennis (it was one of the few missed opportunities for kitschiness in the '70s that neither Caesars Palace nor Riordan came up with a tennis championship belt)—brought $650,000 in TV rights.

The jaunty Aussie Newcombe possessed the decade's definitive mustache. Not fussy enough to be a handlebar or quite long enough to be a Fu Manchu, it was nonetheless a work of bristly brilliance, so distinctive it was the key part of the logo for Newcombe's apparel line. Connors won again, solidifying his claim to the number one ranking. Later it was learned that the "winner-take-all" portion of the matches were a complete fiction; Connors was guaranteed 47 percent of the net receipts and Newcombe 33 percent of the receipts, win or lose.

(Around the same time, Jack Nicklaus and Johnny Miller had been offered a similar payday for a head-to-head challenge golf match, but Nicklaus refused to participate. "It's bad for the game," he said, "and I will not be a party to it.")

In the midst of this stormy, sprawling period in tennis history, Billie Jean and Larry King chose to launch an entirely new creation, which would inevitably antagonize almost all of the other alphabet entities, while trying to carve out a place on the increasingly crowded tennis calendar. The idea was called World Team Tennis, to begin play in the spring of 1974, bending the sport of tennis into a heretofore unidentifiable shape that could accommodate team competition.

After some initial tweaking, the format that emerged called for five sets to be played in a night: men's singles and doubles, women's singles and doubles, and mixed doubles. There was no-ad scoring and in the event of a 6–6 tie, the set was decided by a 9-point tiebreaker. Scoring was tabulated not by sets but rather by games so a team that won a set 6–1 and lost two sets 6–4 each would be ahead 14–13. Coaches were allowed live substitutions, and cheering during points—even heckling during points—was encouraged.

"I think the team concept and the league are Americana," said King. "Every major sport is built around these concepts."

The league launched on May 6, 1974, when Billie Jean King and the Philadelphia Freedoms (owned by her friend Dick Butera) faced the Pittsburgh Triangles at the Spectrum in Philadelphia. The Kings were on to something; the new format brought more crowd involvement and even appealed to the road-weary players who were able to enjoy a more settled existence for a few months.

"I love doubles and mixed doubles," said the Denver Racquets' Kristin Kemmer. "It was the most enjoyable time of my career. You had a base for three months, it was more familial in my mind, and it was the men and the women playing together."

The first season found King's Freedoms in the championship match against a balanced Denver Racquets team, which included doubles specialist Tony Roche as well as Kemmer, who had been the most improved player on the Virginia Slims tour the previous season.

That first championship was won by the Racquets, with Kemmer and Roche defeating Fred Stolle and Julie Anthony in the decisive final set. The raucous crowd at McNichols Arena cheered them on and the Racquets raised something called the Teflon Cup to celebrate the title. Consistent with the prevailing ethos of every other start-up league in the '70s, the franchise moved to Phoenix shortly thereafter.

But a marker had been laid down, the fledgling cable channel HBO showed some live matches and the crowds had proved gratifyingly boisterous, giving the Kings hope. "Professional sports and entertainment are one and the same," said Billie Jean. "In sports the best way to ensure success is to win, and winning is my concern."

To that end, King got an assist from her friend, the musician Elton John, whom she'd met at a Jerry Perenchio dinner party in Los Angeles. Later in 1974, John—merely the biggest pop star in the world at the time—showed up at a Freedoms match, a charity event in which he out-dueled the comedian Bill Cosby in a preliminary set.

On that trip, he told her, "I want to write a song for you. What should we call it? How about 'Philadelphia Freedom'?"

The ensuing single—which owed a great deal to the Philadelphia sound of the writers Kenny Gamble and Leon Huff, and the producer Thom Bell—did not expressly mention tennis, but it did share the name of King's first WTT team, and the label for the 45 included the message "with love to BJK and the sound of Philadelphia." (The song was released in February 1975. A month later, the Freedoms were moved to Boston, where they became the second incarnation of the Lobsters, and King had been "traded" to New York, where she became the coach and captain of the New York Sets, later Apples.)

By 1975, Chris Evert—who had been the first player selected in the inaugural WTT draft—was finally in the fold, playing for the Phoenix Racquets. That same season, the blond-maned Swedish teenager Bjorn Borg was attracting hordes of teenage fans in Cleveland. The league also came up with a new concept for the court, which included no lines, only multicolored rectangles for each section of the court. The four service boxes, two on either side of the net, were in a checkerboard of alternating green and blue, the doubles alleys were in burnt orange, and the backcourts were in brown. It looked like Mondrian had been put in charge of groundskeeping duties.

•

There were more leagues to come. The International Volleyball Association was the brainchild of filmmaker David Wolper who, while shooting the official film of the 1972 Olympics, became enamored of women's volleyball. The league, which launched in 1975, included a franchise owned by Motown mogul Barry Gordy (who summoned Diana Ross to the opener).

The league qualified as international because it had one franchise on the U.S.–Mexican border, the El Paso/Juarez Sol. Attendance was not good, but the IVA was (along with WTT) a league in which women competed side-by-side with men. The similarities ended there, though. In WTT, women were full partners, and each team was stocked with the same number of male and female players. In the IVA, women (two out of six players on each side had to be female) played only in the backcourt and were viewed by some of the male players in the league as merely target practice. A player whose spike hit a female opponent in the face or head was said to have earned a "six-pack," with his teammates buying him a six-pack of beer for the accomplishment.

Billie Jean King also found time to help bankroll and promote the International Women's Professional Softball Association (IWPSA), which launched in 1976, and was inevitably led by the Connecticut Falcons and their owner/captain/pitcher Joan Joyce (who, in her spare time, earned an LPGA tour card). Joyce went on the golf circuit seeking financial support for the softball league. "Corporations are putting a lot of money into women's sports on the individual level," she said, "but most people, especially in high schools and colleges, play *team* sports."

In the end, what all the upstart leagues struggled with—ABA, WHA, WFL, IVA, NASL, WTT, IWPSA—was the lack of a major network television contract. But the influx of new players, new teams, new leagues, and in the instance of WTT, a sport with an entirely new orientation, was indicative of the sense of possibility that pervaded sports in the '70s.

•

Not all the newcomers were leagues, per se. For sports reporters, sports fans and sports media, February had traditionally been the longest month. Football season was over, baseball season had yet to begin, hockey and basketball were moving through the grind of the last part of their regular seasons.

Dick Button, the 1948 Olympic gold medalist for figure skating, had an idea. Wouldn't it be interesting, Button thought, to bring the best athletes in individual sports and have them compete in a sporting decathlon of sorts? Not the traditional Olympic version, but instead a modified one that tested skill across a range of sports: a sprint, a long-distance run, a bicycle race, a golf tournament, a ping-pong tournament, bowling, weightlifting and base-ball hitting.

Roone Arledge, knowing ABC had lost the NBA contract to CBS after the 1973 NBA Finals, was intrigued with the possibility, and also intent to find programming that could make the NBA regret ever having strayed. And so the first *Superstars* competition—Roone's Revenge, as it was called within the TV industry—took place in early 1973 in a new wetlands development called Rotonda, Florida. The Olympic gold-medalist pole vaulter Bob Sea-gren was the first winner, as the event sparked surprisingly good TV ratings. Curious viewers tuned in to find that the former heavyweight champion of the world, Joe Frazier, was unable to actually swim.

But it was the second year, with competitors like baseball's Reggie Jack-son and Pete Rose, and football's O. J. Simpson and Franco Harris, that ABC truly triumphed, routinely routing CBS's coverage of pro basketball in the ratings.

The second winner had a well-known name, but was hardly a superstar. He was Kyle Rote Jr., American soccer player, whose father had starred for the New York Giants in the NFL and went on to a successful broadcasting career.

The younger Rote was impossibly self-effacing ("I feel almost embar-rassed by winning"), and his win was more meaningful than it might have been for any of the other competitors. He'd made $1,500 in his first year of professional soccer, but earned $53,400 in the *Superstars* competition. His victory brought more attention to the North American Soccer League. And the North American Soccer League needed it.

In the United States, the previous decade had seen the awakening of a sleeping giant. Though some 80 million Americans routinely watched the Super Bowl, five times as many people around the world watched the 1970 World Cup. For the first time ever, the matches were broadcast in color, and the aura surrounding the canary-yellow jerseys of the Brazilian national team was embedded in the consciousness of sports fans almost everywhere in the world, with the exception of the U.S., which still viewed the entire sport with a combination of indifference and suspicion.

That was starting to change, though slowly. The first awakening had come in 1966, with England's victory as hosts of the World Cup. Not one but two upstart leagues began in the U.S. a year later, both nearly extinguishing in the process. By 1969, the merged leagues were down to only five teams, and only the resolute sportsman Lamar Hunt—founder of the AFL and the Kansas City Chiefs, financier of World Championship Tennis, minority owner of the NBA's Chicago Bulls and unrepentant lover of soccer—had kept the league alive.

On June 21, 1970, Hunt rented out the auditorium at his Bronco Bowl entertainment complex in Dallas, to show the closed-circuit telecast of the World Cup final between Brazil and Italy. "Only about seventy or eighty people showed up," recalled Tornado defender Bobby Moffat.

The league had a long way to go, but Hunt was steadfast.

"Believe me, I tried—politely—to talk Lamar out of soccer," said his brother-in-law, Al Hill Jr. "His premise was always the same: 'If it's this popular around the world, it can be this popular here.' I thought that was wrong and I told him that. I said, 'Lamar, look at all the other things that go on in America. In those other countries, there's nothing else.'"

But while not a lot of people were attending Tornado matches, there was something happening on the ground in Dallas. Maybe it was all the English players and the persuasive effects of their accents. (The Scottish star John Best would begin clinics at local high schools by putting a soccer ball between his feet and challenging anyone to take it from him without using their hands, invariably prompting a few big American football players to clumsily try to dispossess him while he dribbled around them.) When the Tornado began in 1967 in the United Soccer Association, a forerunner to the NASL, there were only 300 youth soccer players in the Dallas area. By 1973 there were 45,000. But while attendance was increasing modestly, to a league average of 9,000 a game, the sport hadn't broken through to the national consciousness yet.

It did not, at that point, translate to greater attendance or a television contract and the belief persisted through much of the U.S. that the sport itself was terminally boring. When tickets were $11 for basketball and hockey, and $7 for football, the NASL offered a family format with midfield tickets going for $4 and kids routinely getting in for $1 each.

The NASL's commissioner was Phil Woosnam, a Welsh international who had played for West Ham and Aston Villa in the top flight of English soccer before coming to the U.S. in 1966. He would later be named coach of the year, leading the Atlanta Chiefs to the 1968 title, and a year later was named commissioner of the NASL. Under his watch, it would survive, then begin to thrive, expanding from five teams in 1969 to six in 1970 to eight in 1971 to nine in 1973.

By 1973, Woosnam was telling people, "It's all just about to happen. In six or eight years our franchises will be worth more than those in the National Football League. Right now we offer the best investment in professional sport."

The claim seemed laughable at the time, and would remain equally preposterous when Woosnam passed, forty years later.

But everyone in NASL agreed on one thing: If the league was going to make it big in the end, it needed a superstar. And in the United States in the 1970s, only one superstar in soccer even registered.

The AFL had needed Joe Namath.

The ABA had desperately wanted Lew Alcindor.

Similarly, the NASL recognized that the one man who could save the league was Pelé.

# ELEVEN

# CRITICAL MASS

B Y 1973, WITH Richard Nixon's presidency slowly dying in the Watergate scandal, there were fewer calls from the White House to victorious locker rooms.

Giving the commencement speech at Penn State University that spring, the Nittany Lions' football coach Joe Paterno weighed in on the prevailing political crisis. "I'd like to know," said Paterno, "how could the president know so little about Watergate in 1973, and so much about college football in 1969?"

The twin traumas of Vietnam and Watergate had rendered the country in a kind of fugue state. The Knicks' Bill Bradley would recall a game at Chicago Stadium early in 1973, when the cease-fire and return of prisoners of war was announced on the arena's PA system: "There was none of the catharsis of a V-J Day. It was as if people had forgotten the war."

It was a long goodbye; the last U.S. combat troops had left Vietnam in late March 1973, and it would be seventeen more months before Nixon finally resigned, and another eight more before the last American chopper scrambled out of Saigon on April 30, 1975, marking the definitive end of the disastrous misadventure in Vietnam.

Back home in the United States, the country turned inward. How much the end of these two disastrous chapters contributed to the nearly simultaneous rise of sports in American broadcast and print media in the mid-'70s is hard to pinpoint, but what's clear is that in the aftermath of Watergate and Vietnam, sports offered a kind of reassurance and took on a more central role in the cultural life of the country. Even by the time of Muhammad Ali's upset of George Foreman in 1974, the draft and the long argument about national service felt distant. Indeed, it had been decades since the military seemed *less* relevant in American life.

By the time the country celebrated its Bicentennial in 1976, the growth of spectator sports was widespread: More people attended games, more people watched games on TV, more people listened to games on the radio and more space was devoted to sports in magazines and newspapers.

"One of the happiest relationships in American society is that between sports and the media," wrote James Michener in 1976. "This interface is delightfully symbiotic, since each helped the other survive."

That much was true, but there were other factors. What made spectator sports successful? A variety of things mattered: competitive balance, recognizable stars, insightful and effective rules, compelling games and an enjoyable gameday experience at the stadium or arena. But by the mid-'70s, the one basic truth of American spectator sports was becoming starkly evident: None of those individual factors were so decisive to a sport's bottom line, profile and future as the watchability of its game on television and, by extension, the terms of its television deal.

This could be seen in the spectacular successes enjoyed by the National Football League in the decade, as well as the lesser gains realized by baseball, college football and college basketball. Conversely, virtually all the leagues that died in the '70s shared one failing: the lack of a significant TV deal.

The TV deal had become destiny. Prime time had been terra incognita for sports at the beginning of the '70s, but by the middle of the decade—with *Monday Night Football* a cultural institution, the Olympics providing a quadrennial glut of prime-time coverage, more World Series games in prime time, and the NCAA national championship game moving into prime time—sports was asserting itself, staking its claim to a more central role in American popular culture.

ABC's innovations were beginning to be felt across the industry, as other networks brought in more talent and creativity to compete. CBS's new head of sports, Robert Wussler, had a background in television news (he'd been instrumental in the network's coverage of Apollo missions and political conventions) and brought a different perspective to live sports.

"The mid-'70s is when the competition in sports broadcasting really kicked into high gear," said Geoff Mason, working with Arledge at ABC at the time. "Everything meant something, and there was more money than ever before. We really focused on technology advances, unique replay positions and approaches." All of those developments made sports on TV a more compelling proposition.

There was more money in sports TV advertising, but it was not coming at the expense of print media. Newspapers were expanding the space they devoted to sports pages, and prioritizing more national coverage as fans began to look further beyond their own home teams. (And, significantly, as more people became transplants in different parts of the country, the reasons for broadening coverage became more compelling.) The nation's leading sports magazine, *Sports Illustrated*, was becoming hugely profitable, with thick weekly issues often exceeding 100 pages, while pioneering the increasing use of "fast color," providing color photographs of late-breaking events.

Even the more pedestrian weekly newspaper *The Sporting News* was broadening its horizons, expanding its previously perfunctory coverage of non-baseball sports. Some of the growth in print advertising was directly attributable to the FCC's ban on cigarette advertising on television, but it was also part of Madison Avenue concluding, in a way it hadn't in previous decades, that the audience for sports, sports telecasts and sports magazines was attractive, intelligent and affluent.

As interest grew and national games earned more attention, it became more difficult for a four-minute local sportscast to do justice to the vast landscape of games. "This time limitation, more games, more players and different time zones," noted *Sports Illustrated*, "have combined to make it difficult for television to compete with newspapers and radio as any kind of encyclopedic compendium of sports results."

In response to the heightened interest, a New York enterprise called Sports Phone—offering a minute of the latest sports scores and news for a dime—began to prosper. Located in a building a floor above the legendary Manhattan tavern P. J. Clarke's, the service catered primarily to the subterranean society of gamblers, but also the sporting true believers who were thirsting for the latest update from a midweek playoff game, or a West Coast game that ran late.

The announcer Mike Breen grew up a sports-mad kid in Yonkers in the '70s, and recalled Sports Phone being a kind of lifeline for obsessives. "You would call Sports Phone if you were desperate, like if they played an after-noon game and you missed the game because you had to go to a cousin's birthday party or something. So as soon as you got home, you'd call Sports Phone. It's truly amazing that you had to do those things just to find out if your team won the game."

By the end of 1975, Sports Phone was averaging 65,000 calls per day, and later in the decade would expand into other markets, like Chicago, where it opened a new branch in November 1977. By then, some newspapers were recording a late-scores hotline, just to spare copyeditors the repeated phone calls for scores that fans knew wouldn't be in the newspapers the next morning.

On fall weekends when college and pro football games were coming thick and fast, the calls would increase, and Sports Phone would begin calling press boxes three or four times an hour, so as to provide more frequent updates.

"They'd answer, 'Stanford press table,'" said Sports Phone's operations manager, Fred Huebner. "We'd go, 'Hey, this is Sports Phone in Chicago, can we get a score?' That would be the first time. The next time we'd call, they wouldn't be as nice. The third time, they'd just answer 'Cardinal 38–15,' and hang up."

The clamor for up-to-the-minute scores was a reflection of widespread gambling interest, of course, but something else besides. For serious sports fans, the serial drama of a season meant that every game and every week brought new developments, new twists. A Knicks fan in New York might feel the need to know the score of a Phoenix–Philadelphia game, as it could affect playoff seeding. If Nebraska was climbing the AP college football Top 20, vying for a New Year's Day bowl bid, then the prospect of an upset that would knock Southern Cal down a peg would be a piece of information that a fan in Lincoln desperately wanted before retiring for the night.

•

One major sport was suffering. By the mid-'70s, the National Hockey League was hemorrhaging money, bankrupting teams and becoming ever more marginalized, all while facing competition from another league, as the threadbare World Hockey Association began its fifth season, still existing on the back of big names (the Howes and the Hulls) and previously untapped markets (Houston, Hartford, Edmonton).

But the NHL's biggest problem wasn't the competition from the rival circuit. It was the league's apparent inability or unwillingness to police its own culture of violence.

The violence had become baked in, part of the NHL's own sense of itself. Almost any proposed safety measure was routinely dismissed as somehow impractical. After the Bruins' Ted Green suffered a fractured skull in a preseason game in 1969, there was renewed discussion about requiring all players to wear protective helmets. But many of Green's teammates balked at the idea. "They're uncomfortable," said Derek Sanderson. "They'd probably provoke more stick fights than there are now and they can shatter when hit."

In 1971, the NHL's rules committee implemented a rule that pointedly did not ban fighting but, rather, applied a major fine to the third player to join in a fight. The "Third Man In" rule was designed to prevent bench-clearing brawls but largely had the effect of spotlighting the two-man scuffles. A 1974 rule that penalized the aggressor, rather than both players in the fight, also met with mixed results. The consequence was that the new power in the league was the seven-year-old expansion team the Philadelphia Flyers, who rose on the skating prowess of center Bobby Clarke, the reliable goaltending of veteran Bernie Parent, and an intimidating cast of enforcers and brawlers—dubbed the Broad Street Bullies in the press—that led the league in penalty minutes, serving more than twenty-one minutes per game in the penalty box during their first title run in 1974.

NHL president Clarence Campbell, in the wake of criticism of the champion Flyers, conceded, finally, that action was called for. "Something must be done to control the violence in our game," Campbell said. "I hear ten discipline cases each week. And over the course of a season, I suspect I hear at least ten cases where the civil authorities might think a crime was committed." Those words would come back on him months later.

When the Bruins visited the North Stars on January 4, 1975, Boston's Dave Forbes and Minnesota's Henry Boucha tangled in the first period, and both were charged with seven minutes of penalties. When the time was served, Forbes came out of his box and immediately went after Boucha, using his stick to slash Boucha's right eyelid, which required twenty-five stitches to close. Days later, with Boucha still suffering double-vision, further testing revealed a fracture at the base of the right eye socket.

At the time, the game misconduct penalty—essentially an ejection—carried only a $200 fine in the National Hockey League. The business-as-usual response to the mayhem so enraged Minnesotans that a Hennepin County grand jury indicted Forbes for aggravated assault with a dangerous weapon—his hockey stick—on Boucha. In so doing, Forbes became the first professional athlete in the U.S. to be charged with a felony in court for an act committed during a game.

The problems went beyond violence. In May of 1975, NBC showed Game 1 of the Montreal–Buffalo semifinal playoff series. But the game that hockey fans throughout North America wanted to see was Game 7 of the epic New York Islanders–Pittsburgh Penguins quarterfinal series, in which New York became the first team in thirty-three years to rally from a three-game deficit to win a best-of-seven series. That dramatic deciding game had been played the night before in Pittsburgh, but NBC wasn't able to move it to a time slot in which it could be nationally televised. So the game that everyone in hockey was talking about was the one that almost no one saw.

The league also lacked the marketing sophistication of the most successful sports entities. In 1974, with the addition of the expansion Kansas City Scouts and Washington Capitals, the NHL revamped its divisional structure and renamed its divisions after NHL forefathers Lester Patrick, Conn Smythe, James Norris and Charles F. Adams, and grouped those divisions into two conferences named after the Prince of Wales and Clarence Campbell. The average NHL fan recognized the name Campbell, the league's president, but none other. In addition to the clumsy nomenclature, the new divisions lacked any significant geographical coherence (the three West Coast teams were placed in three different divisions). On top of this, the league added what one writer described as "the most confusing playoff setup in sports history," which eliminated just six of the league's eighteen teams, gave the four division champions byes, and seeded the other eight teams into play-in series to meet the four division-winners in another round of re-seeding.

Hockey remained absorbing to watch in person, and the loyalty of the NHL's fan base made for a raucous atmosphere at most arenas. But the speed and competitive texture of the game was lost on television in the '70s, and most of the attention that hockey got in the decade came from fighting.

When the Philadelphia Flyers beat the Buffalo Sabres in Game 6 of the

1975 Stanley Cup Finals, NBC declined to show the game on national television. The network dropped their contract with the NHL after that season. Ratings had been disappointing in NHL cities, microscopic in the rest of the country. Without a national television deal, the status of hockey as one of the "major" sports would remain tenuous.

By then, it was lost on no one that hockey was generating its own bad publicity. Around that time, the comedian Rodney Dangerfield had worked into his act the line, "I went to a fight last night—and a hockey game broke out."

•

There was a zero-sum outcome to hockey's loss, and the beneficiary was college basketball.

The watershed moment in the growth of the college game occurred during the ACC tournament in 1974. The match-up in the final between North Carolina State and Maryland (ranked first and third in the Associated Press Top 20) would yield only one qualifier, since the NCAA tournament rules limited conferences to only their champion into the tournament. The Wolfpack wound up winning, 103–100 in overtime, leaving Maryland's players so devastated by the loss that they voted unanimously not to accept an invitation to the second-tier National Invitation Tournament. Their season ended that night.

In the aftermath of the game, Willis Casey, the athletic director at North Carolina State, and Wayne Duke, the Big Ten commissioner, began politicking for the tournament to allow more than one team per conference.

"I credit them with actually making the NCAA tournament what it became," said Billy Packer, the Wake Forest alum who was calling ACC games during that period. "They decided this is ridiculous. And they ramrodded through that multiple teams should be eligible."

The idea that more than one team per conference should be able to qualify for the tournament went against the principles of, among others, John Wooden, who argued that a championship tournament should be comprised exclusively of champions. But the case of Maryland's epic loss was so strong that Casey and Duke pushed through the change following the 1974 tournament. In 1975, the NCAA field would grow to thirty-two teams, and teams that didn't win the conference were eligible to be invited.

For just the third time that March, the NCAA Final Four was contested on a Saturday–Monday schedule, this time at the San Diego Sports Arena. In the semifinal, Wooden and UCLA were matched against Louisville and his former assistant, Denny Crum. The Bruins needed a basket by Rich Washington in the last four seconds of overtime to edge Louisville, 75–74. Wooden hadn't been sleeping for weeks. In the locker room, after the game, he told his team that he'd be retiring after the championship game Monday night. The words hung in the air, and his players looked at the floor, greeting the news with what Wooden would describe later as "quietness."

Suddenly Monday night's championship game, matching UCLA and an oversized Kentucky team, offered the drama of the last game in the career of the man regarded as the greatest college basketball coach of all time.

That Monday, Wooden did something he'd never done before: He called a walk-through workout the day of the game. The Bruins walked through their offense at Point Loma College and prepared for Kentucky's zone trap.

There were no Alcindors or Waltons on the team—center Rich Washington and forward David Meyers were the high-scorers—and it lacked the usual depth, as Wooden used only one substitute the entire championship game, center Ralph Drollinger, who grabbed 13 rebounds and scored 10 points. Usually sanguine during games, Wooden was particularly intense on this night, at one point barking out that the referee Hank Nichols was "a crook" when Nichols called a technical foul on Meyers.

In the end, UCLA fought off a second-half rally to win, 92–85, and send Wooden out on top. "The Wizard of Westwood" would leave, but college basketball—on the back of an increased national television profile, more teams in the tournament and increased interest in the sport—would endure.

The dance had gotten bigger, and that would soon make all the difference. The change to the enlarged thirty-two-team field didn't just add eight teams; it brought greater clarity to the entire process. With a thirty-two-team field, all of the first-round tournament games began on the same weekend, meaning teams from obscure conferences like the Southern Conference and the Big Sky weren't being relegated to the little-seen "play-in" games played in the final week of the regular season, but instead were full-fledged members of the tournament.

"It added symmetry and structure to the tournament and was another step in bringing the tournament to all corners of the country, which it really wasn't in before," said Bill Hancock of the Big Eight. "And of course the expansion—someone told me one time and I know it's true, within a half-day's drive of virtually every community in America was a team with a chance to get in the tournament. And that just infused life and growth into the tournament, because instead of it being *their* event it became *our* event."

The networks noticed. Shifting gears from hockey, NBC chose to replace its NHL package with a full schedule of regular-season college basketball games in the 1975–76 season, which also served as a complement to its post-season NCAA basketball tournament coverage. The most regional of all major sports was becoming increasingly national—you could tell it from the added interest in the tournament, increased coverage in newspapers, even the growing ad base and circulation of the sport's definitive annual, *The Street & Smith's College Basketball Yearbook,* from the highbrow publisher Condé Nast.

Soon, coaches like Al McGuire began to leverage their national TV appearances for greater recruiting out of their own region. McGuire understood that he wasn't selling players on just the school or the city, but instead the overall experience of being a college basketball player. Under McGuire, Marquette developed a reputation for innovative, original uniforms. At the NIT in 1971 (after rejecting an NCAA bid that would send them to a regional in Texas), the Warriors wore black uniforms with gold horizontal pinstripes, earning them the "bumblebees" nickname, before the NCAA banned them. In the mid-'70s, Marquette began wearing a uniform whose jersey was designed to hang outside the shorts, a concept created by one of McGuire's own players, the forward Bo Ellis. Beyond that, it was relatively conventional.

Before the 1976–77 season—when Marquette's players took their team picture in tuxes, standing next to a Rolls-Royce—McGuire wanted to expand on Ellis' vision, and reached out to the most creative designer he knew. That was Jule Campbell, the woman who had turned the annual "swimsuit issue" into a money-making institution at *Sports Illustrated.*

Campbell, working with her husband, Ron, the art director at *Fortune,* updated Ellis' original idea and created the most distinctive uniform in college basketball: pale gold shorts with a thick white stripe trimmed in blue on the side, and a white jersey with gold lettering, trimmed in blue, and arrowheads going up the side panels of the jersey. The untucked look caught on, and soon Georgetown, among other teams, copied the idea. (By the early '80s, the NCAA would ban that uniform as well. Rumor was that Walter Byers decided the untucked look was sloppy.)

The year after UCLA's triumphant farewell for Wooden, Bobby Knight's Indiana team completed a perfect 32–0 season by beating conference rival Michigan in the final. In 1977, there was another memorable farewell, as McGuire announced his pending retirement in the middle of the season, and then led Marquette to a run of upsets en route to the title, defeating North Carolina in the final.

The rights fees for the tournament in 1973—the first year of the primetime national championship game—had been $681,000. By 1976, the fee had increased to $2.5 million. Eleven months before the 1977 Final Four at the Omni in Atlanta, the NCAA had received requests for 210,000 tickets for an arena that seated 16,181, and had only 5,341 tickets for public sale.

"The Final Four in '62 was big in Louisville," said the longtime North Carolina coach Dean Smith, "but in '72 it still wasn't real big when we played Florida State in the semis. But then we hit Atlanta in 1977 and found a media blitz, and it was on. I mean, what a change."

There was something in the fervent, cloistered intimacy of college basketball that played particularly well on TV, and allowed college basketball's star to continue to rise. Adding an NCAA basketball package had paid immediate dividends, nearly doubling the ratings NBC had from hockey a season earlier. NBC's college basketball coverage was also earning higher ratings than CBS's NBA broadcasts airing in the same time slot.

•

In the summer of 1975, the North American Soccer League's New York Cosmos finally reeled in the retired legend Pelé, the one soccer player in the world whose name was known to most American sports fans. The signing, announced in a New York press conference at "21," was greeted with media from around the world.

Pelé's debut, in a nationally televised Sunday afternoon match on CBS against the Dallas Tornado, made the front page of the *New York Times* and the cover of *Sports Illustrated*. Yet just beyond the glamour and trappings, there was the always-shaky foundation of NASL. Pelé's nationally televised NASL debut wasn't a league match, but rather a hastily arranged friendly, with the Cosmos playing the Dallas Tornado, an opponent chosen simply because the Tornado had Kyle Rote Jr., who, by virtue of his success in ABC's *The Superstars* competition, was the only American-born soccer player that most U.S. sports fans had ever heard of.

The Tornado had, in fact, played a league match the *night before* the Cosmos game, in San Antonio, against the San Antonio Thunder. The Tornado players flew into New York that Sunday morning and were given sandwiches in the locker room at Downing Stadium on Randall's Island. As they went out for the pregame warm-ups the Tornado's English defender Bobby Moffat saw a groundskeeper spraying green paint onto the bare playing surface.

"What are you doing?" asked Moffat.

"Spraying the grass," he said.

"That's not grass, it's dirt," Moffat pointed out.

"It's grass."

"It's dirt."

"It's CBS," the man said. "So it's grass."

American sports coverage, geared toward time-outs, two-minute warnings, halftimes and breaks between innings, was not yet prepared to deal with the continuous play of soccer. The network was showing an instant replay of another piece of action when Pelé's header equalized the game in the second half.

But now even soccer, often derisively dismissed in America, had a potential foothold. In the two seasons after Pelé joined the league, average game attendance would rise from 7,642 per game to 13,558.

•

By the fall of 1975, Muhammad Ali was a year removed from his electrifying upset of George Foreman. He talked incessantly of retirement, but he still needed the money that boxing brought. There was one last great payday out there, and Don King understood the appeal of a third and decisive Ali–Frazier fight to complete the trilogy.

King—along with the promoter Bob Arum—had arranged for another exotic locale far from the American tax system. Unlike their first two bouts, held at Madison Square Garden, Ali–Frazier III would be staged at the Araneta Coliseum in the Philippines, where Ferdinand Marcos and his wife, Imelda, presided over a country living under martial law. While the hype was nothing on the order of the Foreman fight a year before, Ali made the usual rounds, insulting Frazier's looks, smell, intelligence and fighting skills, all the while promising a "Thrilla in Manila." The proud Frazier, infuriated by Ali's endless stream of insults, was on a quest to destroy his nemesis. "I'm gonna eat this half-breed's heart right off his chest," Frazier vowed to his trainer Eddie Futch before the fight.

The fight was scheduled to start at ten a.m. local time (it started forty-five minutes late), to fit into the closed-circuit schedule back in the U.S. It also, for the first time, offered fans the option of watching at home, on the burgeoning HBO cable system.

Ali was thirty-three, Frazier was thirty-one, but somehow they had both arrived in peak shape. They would need to be. Though the arena nominally had air-conditioning, it was not up to the punishing heat of a sellout crowd packed in on a humid morning.

What transpired in the ring was a primal battle, frightening in its intensity and unceasing in its drama. The upper hand seesawed through the early rounds. Ali rocked Frazier with a right hand in the third round; Frazier responded in kind with a thunderous punch near the end of the sixth.

Coming out for the seventh, Ali said, "Old Joe Frazier! Why, I thought you was washed up."

"Somebody told you all wrong, pretty boy," replied Frazier, and with that the battle resumed. There were passages in the coming rounds where it looked like either fighter might not survive the round, much less the full fifteen. Frazier's incessant body blows and occasional left hook hurt Ali more severely than even in the first Ken Norton fight, in which he suffered a broken jaw. By the eighth round, there was no more dancing for Ali. But as he'd done so many times in the autumn of his career, Ali proved tragically superhuman at taking a punch. Frazier would pummel him; Ali would call and raise, using his superior reach to punish Frazier. In lashing out in the thirteenth round, he completely closed Frazier's left eye.

The new decade as inflection point: *Darrell Royal (above) was carried off the field as his Texas Longhorns were crowned national champions on Jan. 1, 1970; ten days later, Hank Stram (below) was carried off the field as the Kansas City Chiefs won Super Bowl IV; Grambling coach Eddie Robinson (right), friends with both men, was keenly aware of the seismic changes coming.*

*Freedom fighters: Curt Flood (above, left) prepares for an ABC-TV interview with MLBPA executive director Marvin Miller; NFLPA president John Mackey (middle, right) confers with Fran Tarkenton and Roman Gabriel; Oscar Robertson (below, right), preparing to testify with the Knicks' Dave DeBusschere in front of the Senate Antitrust and Monopoly committee, studying the possible NBA-ABA merger.*

*Under the bright lights: Roone Arledge (top, second from left) is joined by the* Monday Night Football *crew of, from left, Don Meredith, Howard Cosell and Keith Jackson before the first game of the series, Sept. 21, 1970, in Cleveland.*

*The Fight: Joe Frazier (middle, left) outpointed Muhammad Ali in their first fight, an event so momentous that Frank Sinatra (bottom, center) served as a ringside photographer.*

The college game: (clockwise from upper left) Walter Byers presided over his NCAA empire; John Wooden, after UCLA won its 61st straight game in 1973; Johnny Rodgers broke free on a crucial punt return in Nebraska's "Game of the Century" win over Oklahoma in 1971; Billie Moore (second row, far left) coached Cal State—Fullerton to the first 5-on-5 women's college basketball championship in 1970.

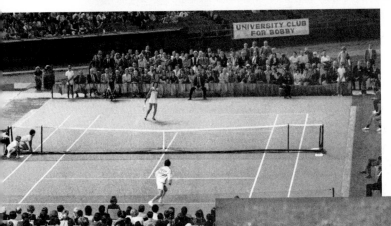

The Battle of the Sexes:
Billie Jean King arrived on a
palanquin (top), defeated Bobby
Riggs in straight sets (middle),
then accepted a trophy from
heavyweight champion George
Foreman (right).

*Four stars: Henry Aaron was greeted by teammates as he touched home plate after breaking Babe Ruth's home run record (above); months earlier, O. J. Simpson broke Jim Brown's single-season rushing record (below)…*

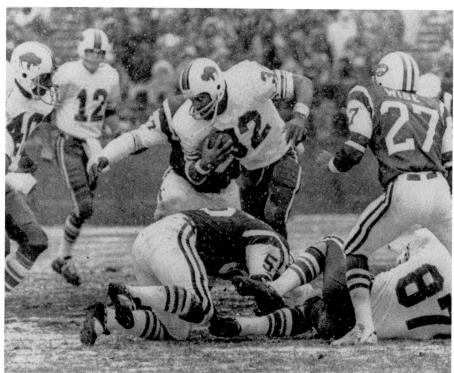

AP IMAGES

*…in the Rumble in the Jungle, Muhammad Ali regained his heavyweight title after shocking George Foreman (above); Kareem Abdul-Jabbar hit a game-winning sky hook in overtime of Game 6 of the 1974 NBA Finals (below).*

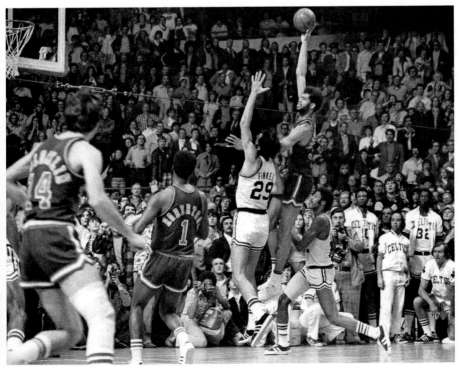

AP IMAGES

*The upstarts: (top to bottom Julius Erving, dunking over Dan Issel, won two ABA titles en route to becoming the last truly mythic figure in American sports; Gordie Howe, at left, came out of retirement to join his sons Mark and Marty on the WH Houston Aeros; Pelé, in his NASL debut, battled for the ball with Tornado defender Bobby Moffat.*

The carnage at the end was frightening to watch, and even more so for those at ringside. "Ali took a beating like you'd never believe anyone could take," said Dr. Ferdie Pacheco, in Ali's corner. "But Frazier took the same beating. And in the fourteenth round, Ali just about took his head off. I was cringing. The heat was awesome. Both men were dehydrated. The place was like a time bomb. I thought we were close to a fatality."

In the other corner after the fourteenth round, Eddie Futch carefully examined his fighter, and made his decision.

"Joe, it's over," he said.

"But I want him, boss," said Frazier in protest.

"You're blind, Joe," Futch said. "You can't see. Sit down. No one will ever forget what you did here today."

Frazier argued further, to no avail, and with that, the last chapter of the epic trilogy was complete; he and Frazier would be bound for the rest of their days.

Adding to the intrigue surrounding the fight was the cornerman Wali Muhammad's assertion that Ali came to his corner after the fourteenth round and told Angelo Dundee to "Cut 'em off," meaning the tape surrounding his gloves. It's nearly impossible to imagine Ali quitting, but he would tell biographer Thomas Hauser later, "Frazier quit just before I did. I didn't think I could fight anymore."

Ali lavished Frazier with praise after the fight. "It was insane in there," he said. "It was like death. Closest thing to dying that I know of."

The third Ali–Frazier fight would instantly be elevated into the realm of legend, at once irresistibly compelling and also horrible to witness. ("THE EPIC BATTLE" read the cover headline in *Sports Illustrated*, which devoted eight pages to Neil Leifer's captivating images.) "I don't like watching that fight," said the writer and boxing scholar Gerald Early. "It bothers me to watch that fight. I think it was kind of the twilight of the gods—there's just this aura of tragedy that surrounds the fight."

Later that night, at a post-fight gathering hosted by the Marcoses at Malacañang Palace, Ali asked the question that so many who cared about him had been asking for years: "You get so tired. It takes so much out of you mentally. It changes you. It makes you go a little insane. I was thinkin' that at the end. Why am I doin' this?"

•

After more than two decades with NBC, Major League Baseball signed a new television contract in 1975 that would, beginning in 1976, split the telecasts between NBC and ABC, with NBC retaining Saturday afternoon broadcasts, ABC Monday nights. In so doing, the network revenues jumped from $18 million per season to $23.2 million per season.

By the end of the 1975 regular season, baseball was enjoying a resurgence, with the three-year dynasty of the Oakland A's ended by a precocious Boston Red Sox team, whose catalyst was rookie of the year and MVP Fred Lynn, who'd become the first player to win both awards in the same season.

Playing in only their second World Series in twenty-nine seasons, the Red Sox faced Cincinnati and its Big Red Machine lineup of heavily favored future Hall of Famers.

In Boston, where the *Globe* was establishing itself as the best sports section in the country, editor Dave Smith talked his bosses into devoting an entire special section to the World Series games, above and beyond the regular daily sports section.

The sublime series offered a panoply of treasures: the gyrating Cuban hurler Luis Tiant (whose father was allowed to leave Cuba to watch his son, whom he hadn't seen in fourteen years), the imposing array of talent on Cincinnati's Big Red Machine, and an authentic umpiring controversy when Cincinnati's Ed Armbrister loitered after his sacrifice bunt, impeding Boston catcher Carlton Fisk's throw to second base, the decisive play in the Reds' extra-inning win over the Red Sox in Game 3.

After five games, the Reds led three games to two, and returned to Boston hoping to clinch it on Saturday afternoon. But the weather prevented that, and three consecutive days of rainouts pushed the Series out of the weekend daytime starts and back into the week, which moved the games to prime time. Suddenly, unintentionally, and for the first time ever, the majority of Series games would be played in prime time.

The sixth game would become the standard against which all previous and future World Series games—and all future World Series telecasts— would be judged. Bernie Carbo's two-out, three-run homer in the bottom of the eighth tied the game at 6 and kept the Red Sox alive. George Foster's throw from left field caught Brian Doyle trying to score from third in the bottom of the ninth to keep it tied. Leading off the bottom of the twelfth, Fisk hit Pat Darcy's 1–0 pitch down the left field line. As it sailed into the chilled New England night, 70 million Americans were still watching, and as the ball struck the pole that indicated the very edge of fair territory, the antiquated Fenway Park erupted in a throaty din. Soon enough, NBC had its built-in promo for the next night's deciding Game 7, as director Harry Coyle showed a replay of the game-winning homer, a shot from a camera inside Fenway Park's scoreboard, showing Fisk urging the ball to stay fair.

The series was a classic in part because of the accident of context, of the rain pushing the final two games into prime time. The Reds and Red Sox would have played to a smaller universe of viewers, to lesser ratings, up against college football and pro football, on Saturday and Sunday afternoons. Instead, after three days of rainouts, the Tuesday and Wednesday night games each drew Nielsen ratings over 30 and viewership shares over 50 in the nation's two largest markets. In the process, it proved convincingly that sports besides football could succeed in prime time.

"I tell you this," said World Series MVP Pete Rose afterward, "if the sixth game of this series didn't turn this country on, there is something wrong. After that show, the Super Bowl had better be up…up…up. It's going to have to be spectacular to compete with what we did in that game."

•

By the middle of the decade, the National Football League was separating itself from all other sports, and all other leagues. Just a year after facing charges that the game was becoming boring, the league responded. The recommendations from the league's Competition Committee—chaired by Tex Schramm and featuring a cross-section of some of the league's brightest and most influential minds, including Paul Brown, Don Shula and Al Davis— soon implemented a series of changes designed to open up the game. One offered overtime in the event of ties in regular-season games, another moved the goal posts to the back of the end zone, to discourage field goal attempts and open up passing lanes in the end zone. (More changes would come in future years, almost all of them leading to an increase in passing.) By 1975, *Monday Night Football* had become a perennial top twenty–rated TV show.

As the league continued to rise, so did the visions of grandeur from some of Rozelle's staffers.

"We imagine pro football as a power grid, pulsating and popularly rooted," said Bob Carey, the president of NFL Properties. "A national promotion guy clamps his wire into the grid and gets the benefit of the power. He uses the popularity of the game to sell his product, and if it's a good product, everybody benefits."

This was not mere hyperbole. By the summer of 1975, Bob Wussler had been in his position as the head of CBS Sports for over a year. He recognized the degree to which the NFL had become not only the biggest property in sports, but a crucial vehicle for promoting the rest of a network's lineup.

As Pete Rozelle had correctly noted years earlier, the NFL was beginning to transcend the long-held boundaries of sport. "We have the advantage of being both news and entertainment, so our word-of-mouth profile is excellent," said Rozelle. "You don't find people telling their parking attendant, 'Wasn't Lassie magnificent putting out that forest fire last night?'"

What that meant was that the games themselves had become so popular, there was an audience that would watch programming related to the event, before and after. Through the early '70s, CBS had a pregame show, called *The NFL Report,* later retitled *The NFL Today.* In its first incarnation, it was a feature show, partially written by Dave Anderson, the Pulitzer Prize–winning sportswriter for the *New York Times,* and recorded on film on Thursdays at the same site where Pat Summerall and Tom Brookshier did their syndicated *This Week in the NFL* tapings with NFL Films. In 1974, CBS executive Bill Fitts wanted to make it a live show, featuring CBS's sage commentator Jack Whitaker. Though he was a master at the flinty thought piece, Whitaker was not stellar live, and the show was relatively unsuccessful.

In 1975 Wussler decided to revamp *The NFL Today,* reimagining it as a live in-studio news show about the NFL—that would treat the day's events in pro football with the same attention and scrutiny that Wussler had pioneered in CBS's coverage of political conventions and Apollo missions.

Instead of Whitaker, Wussler hired the former print reporter Brent Musburger as the host; the two had worked together at WBBM in Chicago. Musburger possessed a garrulous avidity, and was a nimble, quick thinker on live television.

As the off-season planning began, Wussler began a Monday morning meeting saying, "I've met Brent's playmate—she's great."

His staffers exchanged quizzical looks. The possibility that Musburger's co-host would be a woman had not occurred to any of them.

The woman in question was Phyllis George—a Miss Texas and Miss America—whom Wussler had met at a party that weekend. He sensed instantly that the TV audience would take to her, and there would be a bright interplay between her and Musburger. "She knows football a bit," Wussler told his staff.

The prior experience of women announcers on sports hadn't been positive. The announcer Jane Chastain had done some NFL games on CBS the previous year. The audience was clearly not ready for a woman in the booth ("as I recall, we broke the existing CBS switchboard record for negative phone calls," said Musburger, who'd done one of the games with Chastain). But Wussler sensed that there would be less resistance to the presence of a woman in the studio.

That first season, Musburger and George were joined by the former Eagles' defensive back Irv Cross, the first African American to serve as a regular analyst on network TV. What *The NFL Today* ingeniously offered was a large tent with soft features that would bring in women—Phyllis George's sit-downs with stars and coaches brought a disarming intimacy—but also hard news for serious fans, including updates on late injuries, overnight developments and, perhaps most importantly for gamblers searching for an edge, the weather.

The program-opening "whip-around," in which Musburger would go to various stadiums around the country for updates before kickoff, became a staple, and bred Musburger's tagline: "You are looking *live* at…"

This mattered a great deal to the significant subset of viewers who were gambling on the games, as late weather changes and field conditions were elusive elements that often escaped those who placed bets. With *The NFL Today* on the scene, and with halftime highlights from games around the country (beating even *Monday Night Football*'s Cosell-narrated highlight package by more than a day), the show was an instant hit.

CBS had the rights to the Super Bowl that season, and Wussler decided to try something that had never been done before: a ninety-minute pregame show for the Super Bowl. CBS was banking on viewers being so starved and excited about the upcoming event, they would tune in hours before it began just to prepare for it.

Super Bowl X was held in Miami, and on the Friday before the game, Pete Rozelle hosted a reception for the forty writers who'd attended all ten Super Bowls to date. One of them, the *Baltimore News-American*'s John Steadman, was asked which of the games had been the most memorable. "None of them," he responded, and in this he encapsulated the NFL's lone failure in marketing the Super Bowl. The event had become an instant sellout, and was annually the most watched television program of any year, earning increasingly high ad rates. But there hadn't been a great game yet.

The tenth Super Bowl offered promise: the Pittsburgh Steelers defending their crown against the resurgent Dallas Cowboys. It helped that the combatants were two sharply defined teams with loyal followers. Chuck Noll's Steelers, with their vaunted Steel Curtain defensive line, had become the apotheosis of tough, modern football. On the other side were the dashing Cowboys, the league's most visible and most popular team, playing in their third Super Bowl in six seasons.

Riding the wave of the NFL's popularity, and the confluence of events—the success of *The NFL Today*, the glamour of Miami, the high-profile match-up of the Steelers and Cowboys, and the fact that Madison Avenue was realizing that the Super Bowl offered the best mass audience of the year—Wussler felt emboldened to create something new.

The result was a watchable if uneven grab bag called *The Super Bowl Today* that opened with Jack Whitaker's commentary about the big game before moving to Musburger, George and Cross from the dock where they would soon take a yacht around Miami Bay. One of the early segments found Lindsay Nelson and Sonny Jurgensen interviewing Don Shula, in front of a crowd in the lobby of the Fontainebleau Hotel at Miami Beach, before Nelson executed what was known in the business as a "walk-and-talk," in which a remote camera followed him as he walked through the building and interviewed other celebrities about the game. It was likely the first time in history that Raquel Welch, Alice Cooper and Henny Youngman had been in the same sentence, much less the same place. Youngman did his leering shtick: "Raquel, you look tired, go up to my room and rest." As Nelson continued to navigate through the crowd, he passed by a frowning man standing against a wall who would in time become much better known to CBS audiences: Jimmy "The Greek" Snyder, America's best-known oddsmaker and gambling tout, added to the *NFL Today* cast in 1976.

Decidedly light on the pregame analysis, the show featured brief inserts with spouses and children of the players, as well as vignettes from each of the NFL Films' highlight packages for previous Super Bowls. There was also a fashion show and interviews with wives of Cowboys' players.

But a Rubicon had been crossed. A pregame show half as long as the event itself demonstrated further the country's appetite for pro football. Cold weather across much of the country added to the audience as well. Then, too, there was the presence of the Dallas Cowboys cheerleaders, a product of the marketing vision (and old-school sensibilities) of Tex Schramm and the woman he hired to create them, a former model with a master's in English named Dee Brock. The cheerleaders had traveled to Miami for Super Bowl V, but by the time of Super Bowl X, their outfits had been redesigned, with halter tops accompanied by crop-top vests, and white spandex hot pants—Tex Schramm's idea of "sexy but tasteful."

The game was shown live in the U.S., and either live or via tape delay in Canada, Mexico, throughout the Caribbean, Venezuela, the Philippines, Japan, South Korea, Bali, and via closed-circuit in both London and Paris. A minute of commercial time cost $215,000.

It became a certifiable epic, a closely fought, fascinating contrast of styles. On the sun-faded tartan turf in Miami, wide receiver Lynn Swann made four indelible catches, including the go-ahead touchdown on a play where Terry Bradshaw was knocked out cold while making a throw. The Steelers held on to win, 21–17.

But the defining moment of the game came in the third quarter, when Pittsburgh's Roy Gerela missed a tying field goal attempt. As the ball veered away from the goalposts, the Cowboys' safety Cliff Harris patted Gerela on the head in a spontaneous taunt. The Steelers' linebacker Jack Lambert—lanky, gap-toothed, and fanatical about tackling—noticed the hazing just as he was walking toward the sidelines. Lambert turned around, grabbed Harris by the shoulder pads and flung him to the ground. With that small message delivered, the momentum of the game turned.

It would become, for a time, the single most-watched sports event in American history. Significantly, CBS broke even on the rights fees for the Super Bowl game, but made $2 million on the pregame show.

•

By the 1975–76 season, the American Basketball Association was like a battle-weary platoon that had absorbed heavy casualties. "In the ABA, there was always conjecture that the next game might be the last," said Rod Thorn, who became the Spirits of St. Louis head coach in 1975. "There were teams on the precipice constantly. You would be set to go to Utah, and somebody would say, 'Oh, Utah's not gonna make it.' Go to San Diego and, 'Oh, this game may not be played, they're not gonna make it.'"

Shortly after the Baltimore Claws were terminated by the ABA league office, the San Diego Sails ran aground, and then one of the league's flagship teams, the Utah Stars, went under, many of their players migrating to the Spirits of St. Louis, which even then was flirting with a move to Cincinnati.

The league somehow survived through that chaotic 1975–76 season. Because the ABA was down to just seven teams at the time, the ABA All-Star Game no longer matched stars from the East and West Divisions, but instead was a contest between the league-leading Denver Nuggets, at their home court, McNichols Arena, against the All-Stars from the other six teams in the league.

The idea of staging a slam-dunk contest at halftime of the game was the brainchild of the ABA's director of public relations, Jim Bukata, who suggested it in a meeting with Nuggets GM Carl Scheer and the ABA finance director Jim Keeler. "Everybody said, 'Great,'" recalled Bukata. "Then we all said, 'Okay, how do you have a slam-dunk contest?' There had never been a dunking contest before, or at least none of us knew of one. We had no idea about rules or anything like that. So we simply made it up as we went along." In a decade of cheesy made-for-TV events, the one that may stand as the apotheosis of the form was never shown on national television.

When asked to participate, Erving was initially dubious. The timing of the contest meant that the players participating wouldn't get a chance to rest during halftime. But he finally agreed to participate. Denver hedged its bets, adding Glen Campbell and Charlie Rich for a pregame concert.

which Arledge spoke about not as a journalist or documentarian, but rath
as a head of network programming.

Going into the event, he sensed that Nadia Comaneci, the Romania
gymnast, and the American decathlete Bruce Jenner would be the sensation
of the fortnight in America.

"We figured Comaneci would be big for us," he said early in the first weel
"People may be discovering her for the first time, but we've been working he
into *Wide World* for a year or more. And in the second week, [marathone
Frank] Shorter is attractive enough to be big again. We'll go with that. And
Bruce Jenner, of course. He could really come out of this hot. He's charis-
matic. I think he could be another Dorothy Hamill."

# TWELVE

# BATTLE LINES

In THE AFTERMATH of her victory over Bobby Riggs, Billie Jean King became the face of women's athletics in America and, from that position, sensed the unique opportunity of the moment, seizing upon it commercially, politically and organizationally. In 1974, she appeared on the *Gillette Cavalcade of Champions*, a year-end variety show hosted by Bob Hope, which presented $5,000 cash prizes to the most outstanding athletes in sports. That year alone, besides organizing and playing in the first season of World Team Tennis, and competing in the Virginia Slims and the Grand Slam events, King used the cash award from the *Cavalcade of Champions* show to found the Women's Sports Foundation, the advocacy group that would play an increasingly crucial role in the fight for Title IX in the years ahead. With her husband, Larry, she launched *womenSports* magazine, a slick, authoritative monthly devoted to the growing field, in June 1974. She also took time with softball legend Joan Joyce to get the International Women's Professional Softball Association off the ground.

Ratings and prize money for women's tennis and women's golf were on the rise, and women's college basketball was making strides as well. Cathy Rush's Immaculata College, the AIAW's first basketball dynasty, won its third straight title in 1974, the first year that AIAW allowed scholarship schools to compete for championships. Rush and her team had also made an appearance on *The Mike Douglas Show*, and were becoming a national draw. Immaculata played Maryland in the first nationally televised women's basketball game in January 1975, when the independent Mizlou network aired the game to 70 percent of the country. A month later, the women's game made it to Madison Square Garden, when Immaculata beat Queens College, 65–61, in front of a crowd of 11,969.

•

Bernice "Bunny" Sandler continued to advocate for equality for women in her post as the director of the Project on the Status and Education of Women, at the Association of American Colleges. Very early on in the debate, Sandler recognized that while the law was enacted to end quotas—and exclusion—of women in higher education, what piqued the public's interest was not the number of women entering law schools or the number of female professors on fellowships, but instead the degree to which Title IX would change the face of intercollegiate sport.

"Athletics is going to become very important," she told her new second-in-command, Margaret Dunkle. "We need to figure that out."

Figuring that out meant sending Dunkle on a fact-finding mission to uncover the myriad ways women were being discriminated against in inter-collegiate sports, and to suggest remedies. That required an eighteen-month study—there was virtually no data on the subject, and early estimates were that only 1 to 2 percent of college athletic budgets were devoted to women.

That number seemed about fair to the NCAA executive director Walter Byers. As the nascent women's programs were growing, the forces aligned against Title IX were coalescing. Byers had sprung into action shortly after the first AIAW delegate assembly in November 1973, and a year later, spent nearly $1 million lobbying against the Title IX regulations that HEW was drawing up.

"Impending doom is around the corner," predicted Byers from the NCAA headquarters, and he had a chorus of some of the best-known football coaches in the nation endorsing that apocalyptic view.

It was probably inevitable that the prospect of change would be greeted with widespread alarm, even panic, on the part of men's athletic directors and football and basketball coaches. For years, college presidents had fretted over the runaway spending in college sports, at a time when funding went almost exclusively to men's programs. Now, with fears that overall athletic spending would have to double, or else spending on men's programs be cut in half, the rhetoric reached doomsday levels.

"This may well signal the end of intercollegiate athletic programs as we have known them in recent decades," said Michael Scott, a lawyer hired by the NCAA to fight Title IX.

When Darrell Royal was asked about the implications of the new law, he said, "The end result very well could be that we'd have to give up all athletic programs."

In the short term, the unlimited amount of scholarships for football would have to be reined in, and this was done in fits and starts—from an unlimited number to 105 in 1973 (and again, to 95 in 1978).

Soon, the battle was joined in Congress by Texas' Sen. John Tower, a compact man with a pinched face, the son (and grandson) of a Methodist minister, who'd become an Anglophile in college, shopping for his suits on Savile Row, sporting a gold cigarette lighter, and otherwise exuding an air of clipped authority, even as he stood a shade below five-foot-six. One day, Tower was boasting of the relative affordability of the bespoke suit to the Texas congressman Jake Pickle, when Pickle casually asked, "How much would the suit cost in a man's size?"

Among Republican senators in the '70s, Tower was less a power player than a tactical soldier. "When we need his help," said one GOP lobbyist, "it's most often when we want something *not* to happen."

As word began to spread in the aftermath of the AIAW delegate assembly in November of 1973, it turned out a lot of people wanted Title IX not to happen, especially in athletics. Soon, the University of Texas faculty representative to the NCAA, J. Neils Thompson, was meeting with Darrell Royal and Tower to craft the wording for a proposed amendment that would eliminate revenue-generating sports like football and basketball from Title IX calculations. Doing so would have, for lack of a better term, emasculated Title IX and made it thoroughly inconsequential in the world of amateur sports.

On the AIAW side, the organization hired a tough, uncompromising lawyer named Margot Polivy who would become general counsel. For years, she had been the de facto chief of staff of Bella Abzug; Polivy was a forthright woman who grew up smart and iconoclastic, disinclined to treat her colleagues or her adversaries in a deferential manner. She played tennis in college and taught physical education at Hunter College High School. As a lawyer, she was at once indefatigable but also flashy. She favored corduroy pantsuits, and tooled around Washington, DC, in a Datsun 240Z. In short, she was a lot of things that the women in AIAW—and certainly the men in the NCAA—were not at all used to.

"I think I was ahead of the times," Polivy said of those opposed to her manner and sartorial sense. "And they were behind the times."

"She did not fit with some of the people's image of what someone in her position should be," said Peg Burke. "She might come in her combat boots, or however she wanted to dress, and I loved her. And she's quite straightforward. That did not sit well with everyone. But in my view, she was absolutely essential to AIAW, and no one worked harder to preserve it and to preserve the values we were fighting for."

Polivy was experienced in the rough realities of political influence, and became the hub of a broad coalition of Title IX advocates, which formed the National Coalition for Women and Girls in Education in 1975. In the years ahead, Polivy became a vital conduit between these groups and the AIAW, injecting the organization's wide-eyed idealism with a tough-love dose of the realities of the bruising world of politics and the law.

For her part, Polivy soon got a sense of the tenor of the debate when she spoke with Duke University president Terry Sanford, who explained to her, "The problem is that you're thinking in terms of equality for men and women. Well, I'm all in favor of equality for men and women. But it's not just men and women; there's men and women and *football players.*"

The month before Tower brought the issue to the Senate floor, Margaret Dunkle's research report, *What Constitutes Equality for Women in Sport?,* was published and distributed to a mailing list of more than 10,000 people, including every member of Congress. It identified and documented massive inequities, not only of scholarship money and resources, but routine ancillary services that in theory should have been equal.

"It was bake sales [for women's teams] to travel and the guys got the planes," said Dunkle. "The female coach is a volunteer and the male coach is paid...It was 'We can only practice at six o'clock in the morning and eight o'clock at night because the guys use the field.'"

The examples were legion. At Texas Christian University during the 1972–73 school year, the athletic budget was $1.6 million, of which $18,000 was allotted for women. In numerous instances, such as at Ohio State, the women's swim team was only allowed to use the pool when the men didn't want it (from six-thirty to nine a.m., and during the dinner hour). At the University of Maryland, the men's athletic budget was $2.015 million; the entire budget for women's athletics was $19,000.

Tower's first effort to exclude football and basketball from Title IX consideration, in May 1974, met fierce resistance from Title IX advocates. AIAW launched a letter-writing campaign, as did Billie Jean King, who wrote to members of Congress on *womenSports* letterhead, urging them to oppose Tower. When Tower's amendment was eventually dropped less than a month later in a House–Senate conference committee, it marked the first time that Title IX narrowly eluded the thresher. It wouldn't be the last.

On June 18, 1974, HEW secretary Caspar Weinberger announced the publication of draft regulations of Title IX, soliciting comments before the final regulations would be specified. By October, HEW's offices had received 10,000 comments, a majority of them geared toward the implications for athletics. As Weinberger sarcastically put it, "I had not realized until the comment period that athletics is the single most important thing in the United States." HEW asked for more time before the final regulations were established.

The debate would carry on, but a key compromise that summer was an amendment hammered out by New York's Sen. Jacob Javits, as a less onerous alternative to the Tower Amendment. The Javits Amendment, written in the hallways of the Capitol by Polivy—who, lacking a desk, used the back of Rep. Shirley Chisholm to compose the wording—simply stipulated "with respect to intercollegiate athletic activities, reasonable provisions considering the nature of particular sports." In essence, it reassured colleges that they wouldn't have to spend the same money on gymnastic equipment as they did on football equipment, nor have equal event-management budgets for games attended by 100 people as games attended by 100,000 people. It was both obvious and suitably vague ("It was a word salad," said Polivy). In the wake of the Javits Amendment, though, the NCAA's worst fears—that suddenly women's sports would have to be funded at equal levels as men's sports—were baseless.

But the Javits Amendment was also a victory for Title IX proponents because it codified what they'd wanted all along: not the ludicrous claim that softball squads would be required to have as many scholarships as football teams, but rather that athletic departments would offer a rough equality of opportunity, and reasonably similar resources, especially in scholarships.

Even as it was opposing Title IX and the federally mandated growth of women's athletics, the NCAA also was dropping hints that it might want to govern women's sports. As early as August of 1974, Byers suggested that if Title IX mandated equal treatment under the law, eventually it would require a single, unified governance organization.

The leaders of AIAW weren't opposed to that, providing that the AIAW would have equal representation. Byers and the NCAA's position was that an athletic organization nearing its seventieth year of existence was not about to surrender its autonomy to a group of women physical educators who comprised a small division of a larger division (DGWS) of a professional advocacy organization (AAHPER).

In the meantime, Byers was not above subterfuge, a reality seen most vividly in January of 1975 when both the NCAA (in Washington) and the AIAW (in Houston) were conducting their annual meetings.

The AIAW delegate assemblies had become a rollicking annual exercise in lofty ideals and parliamentary procedure, as the people who cared most passionately about women's athletics persuaded and cajoled and argued for hours on end, often well past midnight. Women would fall asleep in their chairs, knocking their ashtrays onto the floor. For Judith "Judie" Holland, the representative from Sacramento State University, the delegate assemblies were tests in endurance, "agonizing in some respects and in some respects very uplifting. You had to really dig deep. It was hours and hours of infighting, but I thought it was exhilarating in many respects."

In light of the gains at both the college and professional levels, the third delegate assembly of the Association for Intercollegiate Athletics for Women started with an atmosphere of extreme optimism, as more than 250 representatives from 238 different colleges and universities converged on the Houston Marriott Hotel in the first week of 1975.

On January 6, 1975, as the AIAW president—the laconic, chain-smoking Southern gentlewoman Leotus "Lee" Morrison—was presiding over the afternoon meeting, an aide slipped her a note marked urgent, to call a reporter in Washington. Forty-five minutes later, there was another message, this one from the first AIAW president, Carole Oglesby, who was also in Washington, attending a symposium in conjunction with the NCAA annual meetings.

The news out of Washington was alarming. The NCAA had just announced an "Official Interpretation," a resolution that hadn't even been on the meeting agenda, to launch a "pilot program" to offer women's athletics under the NCAA banner, to be voted on the next day. This endeavor, which would have circumvented the AIAW entirely, came at the same time that the NCAA was lobbying against HEW's interpretation of Title IX, actively pondering a lawsuit against HEW and when Walter Byers had expressed skepticism about women's sports, noting that the female athletes "would have to prove that this is more than a fad."

On the phone, as Morrison's chain-smoking pace quickened, Oglesby outlined what she had heard in DC, and told her successor. "Lee, you *have* to do something."

In Houston, a plan soon coalesced, and the women sprang into action. Within minutes of the conclusion of the evening session, almost every delegate in attendance marched out of the assembly hall and rushed to the long bank of pay phones in the Marriott lobby. There they queued up five to ten deep in each line and began calling their school's voting reps at the NCAA meeting in Washington, DC—in most cases, the men's athletic director—or, if they knew the school's NCAA rep wouldn't be sympathetic, their university presidents. Calling and re-calling well into the night, they mobilized enough awareness to cause a majority of school presidents to intervene. The next day, the resolution of the NCAA council was rejected. The NCAA would not be interfering in the AIAW affairs for the time being.

But the shot had been heard, and in the midst of their growing movement, the women of the AIAW had been notified of the NCAA's intentions. It was the sort of blatantly naked power move that could jar even the pure vision of an idealist. It also presaged an extended period of profound uncertainty and protracted conflict, a sense that all the work done by generations of women in love with athletics might be scuttled by a single amendment or an arbitrary takeover. There would exist through the rest of the decade a fear by most of the AIAW membership that the governance of women's sports—which the NCAA had expressly professed indifference to in 1969—would soon be overtaken by a group of men who even then were lobbying against Title IX, and who neither sympathized nor really understood the universe of women's athletics.

Meanwhile, as HEW continued pushing toward a final set of regulations, Weinberger felt the need to rebut the NCAA's lobbying effort. Testifying before a House education subcommittee on June 26, 1975, he said, "The NCAA position on this is wrong. I again repeat, the new regulation does not mean equal funding, but the opportunities need to be made available...This does not mean the National Collegiate Athletic Association will be dissolved and will have to fire all of its highly vocal staff."

In the next month, July 1975, Tower reintroduced his amendment as Senate Bill S. 2106, and accompanied by lobbying visits from Royal, Michigan football coach Bo Schembechler and Oklahoma coach Barry Switzer. (By then, Royal's antipathy toward Switzer—whom, he was convinced, was blatantly cheating and paying for athletes—was a matter of record; so the fact that they were allied in this effort spoke to how gravely they viewed the situation.)

"Title IX will bring an end to major-college football," warned Royal.

What shaped up in the aftermath of that was a battle for the future of college sports.

"The battle was about saving football," said Carole Oglesby, the AIAW's first president. "They didn't give a shit about the larger implications for girls and women. It was about saving football, and they just didn't want the federal law to have anything to do with football."

This was not an opinion held only by members of AIAW.

"There was a group of older ADs in our league," said Bill Hancock, then with the Big Eight, "who were set in their ways, who were, at all costs, determined to protect the revenue and the experience from college football, who were upset that Title IX had come through, and then that we were going to have to add women's sports."

And that sense of entitlement was what Polivy seized on.

"It never dawned on the people who were the administrators of colleges that these weren't things that were just given by God," said Margot Polivy. "And they never woke up, until after something happened."

•

At the college level, the egregious imbalance between men and women (in 1974, there were 50,000 male students on athletic scholarships, but fewer than 100 females) was slowly starting to change. After AIAW's pivot in the wake of the Kellmeyer case, many schools began to offer athletic scholarships for women as well. The University of New Mexico added scholarships two days later, though they were no-frills financial aid, which covered only tuition, about $570 per year. Smaller, private schools, like Wayland Baptist—an early AIAW basketball power—were already offering scholarships of up to $1,000 for seven varsity players. Tennessee State's sterling track and field program, the Tigerbelles—which had produced Olympic gold medalists Wilma Rudolph and Wyomia Tyus—also offered eight scholarships.

At high schools and colleges, coaches and administrators were beginning to come to terms with the implications of Title IX. While smaller schools like Wayland Baptist and Immaculata had dominated the earlier years of AIAW sports, now the growth was most pronounced at large state schools. In 1973–74, UCLA devoted $60,000 to women's athletics. A year later it was $180,000 (and Ann Meyers—the younger sister of UCLA's All-American David Meyers—became the first woman offered a full-ride four-year scholarship), and in 1975–76 it was $265,000. Across the country, programs that recognized both the social utility and the practical necessity of Title IX showed similar rapid growth. Others moved more slowly; at the University of Washington, the administrator Kit Green—who'd originally overseen the women's intramural program—was in 1974 given a bare $1,000 to cover the needs of gymnastics, swimming and track programs.

Where there were scholarships and competition, recruiting inevitably followed. At the AIAW, the protracted battle over scholarships had created a philosophical divide.

In 1975, the second year that schools offering scholarships were eligible for AIAW championships, the end to Immaculata's reign came at the hands of Delta State, and their center Lusia "Lucy" Harris, at once amiable and imposing. In the same tournament, Billie Moore's Cal State–Fullerton team advanced to the semifinals, only to lose to the three-time champions.

Moore had come to the conclusion that, even in the rarefied air of "pure athletics" that AIAW fostered, the paradigm was shifting. "We haven't done any recruiting so far," she said at the 1975 Final Four. "In the past, we haven't had to. But the time has come now that if you don't recruit, you'd better go look for a different game to play. We were allowed to give our players a waiver of tuition this year, but our tuition is only $95 a semester, so it didn't amount to much. If the school wants us to continue at this level, it's going to have to contribute more."

•

If there was one university in America that encompassed all of the contradictions and challenges of the coexistence of men's and women's sports, it was the University of Texas in Austin.

It was often said that Darrell Royal could have been a governor or a senator if he'd wanted, because in the nearly two decades he'd been at Texas, he'd brought multiple national championships and created an athletic program as big and powerful as the aspirations of the school's legion of boosters. That ethos of organized competitive excellence had been followed by coaches in other sports—notably Cliff Gustafson in baseball and Harvey Penick and George Hannon in golf—also earning national honors.

Women athletes at UT, on the other hand, were largely invisible, though this was a matter of choice. For decades, the female students who sought physical education or longed for extracurricular athletic activities at UT were all under the guidance and unblinking eyes of their protector, advocate and chaperone, Anna Hiss.

Raised in a moneyed but troubled family in Baltimore, the young Anna Hiss found refuge in scholarship and physical activity. She was thirteen years old when her father, having been ruined financially, took his own life. Hiss set out on her own, far from her family, and forged her own way. She was sixty-one and already an institution at UT in January 1950 when her younger brother, Alger, made national headlines, leading to his later conviction on two counts of perjury for lying to a grand jury about spying for the Soviets.

As always, she lost herself in her work. Hiss had been a proponent of young women engaging in athletics as a way to promote comportment and posture rather than to attain peak athletic performance. She viewed competition— especially intercollegiate competition—as anathema to the development of young ladies.

So Hiss designed the women's physical education program at UT to avoid the corrupting influences of the male gaze and the dreaded beast of competition. To that end, the court to play basketball was purposely built short of regulation length and surrounded by close walls so as to avoid spectators. The pool was similarly built short of competition length, so there could be no intercollegiate meets.

In her decades at UT, Hiss oversaw physical education programs for thousands of young women. One of them was the Texan Waneen Wyrick, who in 1953 was a freshman at UT. Her athletic dreams had already been dashed during her first days in Austin. "I was active in the early '50s and I was not allowed to do anything in athletics," she recalled. "In fact I was told by a professor when I arrived as a freshman at the University that I could not be a teacher and a softball player. Because women softball players were cheap, and smoked, and drank beer, and teachers could not be seen as that kind of lady."

Hiss had an office on the ground level of the Women's Physical Education Building. She kept her door open, the better to supervise the young co-eds. Wyrick had two encounters with Hiss that semester. The first, she was whistling while walking by, and Hiss called her into the office. "Young ladies do *not* whistle when they walk—or any other time, for that matter." Another time, Hiss summoned Wyrick into her office to inform her that, "You are swinging your arms too vigorously; young ladies do not swing their arms that way."

Wyrick didn't stop swinging her arms, but she did stop walking by Hiss' office, choosing instead to regularly detour through the basement to the stairs on the opposite side of the building.

After Hiss retired and the building was renamed in her honor, the Anna Hiss ethos was still embraced, to a great degree, by Dr. Betty Thompson, the head of UT recreation department. Thompson was also a supporter of athletics for its comportment and health benefits. Reserved and dignified, she played squash regularly, either at Gregory Gymnasium or on the ninth floor of Bellmont Hall. And she never, ever kept score. The dozy, prim ethos that characterized women's athletics at the University of Texas was all about to change.

With the prospect of Title IX implementation looming, Royal made it clear that he had no interest in overseeing the women's athletic program at UT. Modest funding of $128,000 was approved for a separate women's athletic department and director of women's athletics. The head of the committee recommending a women's athletic director would be the same Waneen

Wyrick—by now Waneen Wyrick Spirduso—who as an undergraduate had been scolded by Anna Hiss two decades earlier, and was now back at UT, teaching in the kinesiology department.

Spirduso reached out to Carole Oglesby, the first president of the AIAW, for recommendations. One of the women that Oglesby named was an energetic, fiercely competitive woman named Donna Lopiano, only twenty-eight at the time. They'd been on opposite sides for some epic Amateur Softball Association games, Lopiano pitching for the Raybestos Brakettes, Oglesby hitting for the Whittier Gold Sox.

Lopiano's life had already been a refutation of every cliche about women being uninterested in sport. She was an athletic prodigy, dominating the sandlots and the newly opened Mickey Lione Park off of Stillwater Avenue in Stamford, Connecticut. She grew up loving the Yankees—Mickey Mantle of course, but also the pitchers Don Larsen and Whitey Ford. She modeled her wind-up on Larsen's.

Her childhood was marked by the spring day in 1957 when the ten-year-old Lopiano and her friends ventured down to Lione Park to try out for the Little League baseball team. Lopiano's prowess was well known in the neighborhood, and she was among the first players chosen. Later, waiting in line with her new teammates to pick up the team uniforms of shirt and cap, she saw that she'd been assigned to a team with the same midnight blue color as the Yankees—dark cap, pinstripe shirt. She thought happily it was an omen. Just then, a man came up to her—the parent of another player—holding in his hands a Little League rulebook, and showed her the provision that prohibited girls from participating. Tears welling up in her eyes, Lopiano went out of the line and left her friends.

That summer, she just kept crying. Watching games, reading at home, the tears would come without warning. Her parents tried to find her some league—any organized league—in which she could participate. But there was nothing in Connecticut in the mid-'50s for young girls.

Her parents ran Casa Maria, an Italian restaurant named after her grandmother, in Stamford, Connecticut. One evening in 1962, Lopiano's father plied his friend Sal Caginello—a high school baseball coach and regional scout for the Pirates—with Chianti, and persuaded him to get Lopiano a tryout with the powerful traveling softball team, the Raybestos Brakettes.

Caginello was hung over and regretful the next day, but he kept his word. On the day of the tryout, Caginello picked up Donna, but didn't say a word to her on the twenty-five-mile drive up to Stratford, where he introduced the young girl to Wee Debbits, the manager of the Brakettes, then returned to his car. Lopiano proceeded to hit everything, and showed good fielding sense and great promise as a pitcher. It would take her a year to adapt to the underhand delivery. But she instantly earned a spot on the Brakettes.

She'd spend much of the next decade playing softball for the nationally ranked Brakettes team, part of an awesome pitching duo with all-time multi-sport great Joan Joyce. Lopiano would go to Southern Connecticut State University and major in physical education, then got her master's and, later, her PhD from USC. After finishing her coursework, she applied to fifty schools before getting hired—still in her mid-twenties—as the assistant athletic director and women's softball, basketball and volleyball coach at Brooklyn College.

Dark-haired and decisive, there was a headstrong brusqueness to Lopiano, the aura of a woman in a hurry to right past wrongs, and fiercely advocating for her right to a spot at the table and on the field. In her athletic career, she had competed for twenty-three different national championships in four different sports. She didn't need to be told about the value of competition.

She flew to Austin to interview for the women's athletic director job, and was introduced to Darrell Royal at a lunch in the Headliners Club in downtown Austin.

Royal lobbed the prospect an easy pitch: "Donna, do you like country and western music?"

Lopiano, for all her idiosyncrasies, remained an Italian from the East Coast, and one completely unaware that Royal was a regular golfing partner of Willie Nelson.

"No," she explained. "I'm a Yankee, I *hate* country music."

Several people in the lunch party looked down at their plates during the pregnant silence that followed, which was broken soon by Royal's gentle laughter. He took it in stride.

The hiring process soon reached a stalemate. The new president at the University of Texas, Lorene Rogers (a biochemist who'd just become the first female president of a major research university), had asked Spirduso's committee for three candidates, but while the committee had sent her a list of three names, it only recommended one candidate: Lopiano.

Rogers demurred. She had gotten wind of Lopiano's visit and summoned Spirduso to her office to discuss it.

"I don't want to hire Donna Lopiano," Rogers said. "She's harsh and grating, and she'll alienate Darrell. He doesn't like her."

"She's smart and she gets things done," responded Spirduso. "She will learn—and learn quickly—how to navigate."

Rogers grumbled that she would think about it. A few days later, she wrote Spirduso to say she could hire Lopiano.

As it turned out, both women were right. Donna Lopiano *would* alienate Darrell Royal, but she'd also learn how to adapt.

In the process, the noncompetitive philosophy of the Anna Hiss Gymnasium would be wiped out by Lopiano's thirst not merely to compete but to excel on every athletic stage possible.

In the months ahead, Darrell Royal would perfect a certain weary, pained expression. In their talks both before and after Lopiano was hired and moved to Austin, Royal was persistent about one point: He told Lopiano he had no problem with women's athletics, he just didn't want to have any responsibility for it. Royal's position, which Lopiano hadn't heard anyone express before, was narrow-minded but consistent. He did not begrudge women their right to be athletes or to build programs, but as his program accepted no federal funds, he felt that Title IX–mandated programs for women should properly be funded by the departments at the university that did receive federal funds—chemistry and engineering, medicine and biology, departments that were receiving federal grants and working with military contractors.

In late August, Lopiano moved into a spacious but cluttered office in the Anna Hiss building; the floor was covered with sports equipment, pinnie vests from intramurals, whistles and balls.

The budget of $128,000 included Lopiano's own salary, and was required to cover all of the women's athletic expenses, from travel to uniforms, scholarships to office supplies. "It was so stark," said Lopiano, "because there was nothing. Nothing was fixed. There was no plan. It was just waiting to happen."

Basketball, like all women's sports at UT, was essentially a club sport, with coaches coming from the physical education faculty ranks. "I remember looking at the basketball schedule and saying, 'Who the hell are these schools?'" said Lopiano. "It was like Our Mother of the Lakes; there was almost no name I recognized on the schedule." Women's basketball was growing back east and in other pockets, including the Southwest—where Stephen F. Austin and Wayland Baptist were both regional powers—but not at UT. The women's basketball team drew crowds in the dozens—a smattering of roommates and family members. Lopiano spent time that first season teaching people at the concession stand how to dispense Cokes without too much foam.

Under the considerable shadow of Royal and the men's athletic department, Lopiano was trying to gain a foothold. At the same time, she was pushing back against what she viewed as the excessively narrow view of sports maintained by the AIAW. Even as she understood the good intentions that informed this position, Lopiano vehemently disagreed. In her mind, sports could be exactly what male coaches had long said it was—a crucible of fierce competition that taught self-reliance, accountability, toughness and resilience—without having to also embody the worst excesses of the cynical recruiting wars. In Lopiano's view competition, in and of itself, was good. And she felt that female athletes had just as much right as male athletes to sweat and bleed and fight for the brass ring. This made her a revolutionary intent on overthrowing not just one convention, but two.

•

Meanwhile in Washington, Margot Polivy, the National Coalition for Women and Girls in Education, and the women of AIAW were preparing for testimony before Congress to argue against the latest version of the Tower Amendment, S. 2106, which proposed to exclude "revenue-generating" sports, i.e., football and basketball, from Title IX regulations.

At the Office of Civil Rights, the attorney Gwen Gregory had been assigned to oversee the Title IX regulations. She had been among the first people in government to truly grasp the revolutionary implications, and had arranged a meeting with John McKay, whose USC football team had won the national title in 1972. "We went to visit with him," she recalled, "but he wasn't particularly concerned because, he said, 'Well, you know, if it gets too complicated, I'll just go independent like Notre Dame.'"

As HEW began to work on writing up the final regulations, the NCAA was mobilized into action on all fronts.

The original feeling at the NCAA was that athletics couldn't possibly be affected by the legislation, because they weren't mentioned in the law. "The NCAA was never consulted about its formulation," said the organization's executive vice president, Tom Hansen, of Title IX, "and we were completely unaware of the implications."

It was true that athletics was never the main inspiration for Title IX. But very early on, it was also clear to those who would administer the rules inside HEW that athletics—being such an intrinsic part of the American high school and college experience—would be included.

"The reason why athletics stayed in the original proposal and stayed in the regulation is that to those of us who were working on it inside—many of whom were Nixon appointees and what you then would call moderate Republicans—it was very clear that athletics was covered," said Jeff Orleans, one of the lawyers for HEW during that period. "And it was clear, at least to me, for two reasons. One, there was nothing in the statute that said it wasn't covered. And this was modeled on Title VI of the Civil Rights Act, and everybody understood Title VI—because we were in the height of the government's attempt to desegregate southern schools—so everybody was very aware that you had a remedial statute, you're going to construe it broadly. And you weren't going to exempt stuff unless it was clearly exempted."

Hansen later went to Washington, DC, to meet with Gwen Gregory, at HEW. By then, the NCAA's thinking had evolved. Hansen's opening salvo amounted to an offer: "If you exempt to the numbers in football," said Hansen, "then I think we can manage it the rest of the way, baseball and softball and so forth." Gregory informed Hansen that there were presently no plans to exempt football from Title IX regulations.

And that, then, became the battleground. Since major-college football programs at most schools offered more scholarships than all the other men's and women's sports combined, the prospect of football and basketball being excluded would have effectively destroyed the purpose and function of Title IX's effect on college sports.

Lopiano had been at her job at Texas for only two or three weeks when she was invited to testify in Congress. Thrilled to be summoned to Washington, she called and shared the news with her parents and told some friends in UT's women's athletics department.

The day before leaving for DC, she was at home when she received a call.

"Donna, it's Lorene."

Lopiano drew a blank for a moment.

"Rogers," said the caller. Lorene Rogers, the new president at Texas, had herself only been in the job for a few weeks.

"Oh! President Rogers!" said Lopiano, recovering. "I'm so excited to be here. I think we're going to do great things."

"That's good," said Rogers. "I heard that you're going to Washington, DC, to testify before Congress."

Only then did it occur to Lopiano that she might be in jeopardy.

"Are you calling to tell me that's not a good idea?" said Lopiano.

"No," said Rogers. "I'm calling to tell you how to keep your job."

Rogers' request was simple yet comprehensive. When giving her oral testimony, Lopiano needed to begin her remarks by saying that she was there as an expert witness, and was not there as a representative of the University of Texas. Also, when submitting her written testimony, she needed to begin her comment—at the very top of the very first paragraph—by explaining that she was there as an expert witness, not as a representative of the University of Texas. But before she did either of those things, Rogers explained, she needed to pay a courtesy call to the office of Sen. John Tower and explain to him that she was there as an expert witness, and not a representative of the University of Texas.

So on Thursday, September 18, 1975, Lopiano—after a courtesy call to Senator Tower, in which she realized to her surprise that she was a head taller than the senator—testified. In her statement, she outlined the $2.4 million that the men's athletic department had for their seven team sports, as well as the bare fraction—about one-nineteenth—of the $128,000 devoted to women's sports.

"The Tower bill would not only prevent the regulations from being effective," she said, "but would perpetuate the idea that it is necessary to discriminate in order to protect 'profit-making,' big-business sports."

Lopiano's testimony didn't get as much coverage nationally as it might, having occurred on the same day that federal authorities finally caught up with kidnapped heiress Patty Hearst. But it surely got noticed in Austin, where J. Neils Thompson, the chair of the UT Athletics Council—and soon to be the president of the NCAA—walked into Lorene Rogers' office the next day demanding that Lopiano be fired.

•

Around that time, the AIAW's Polivy contacted Donna de Varona and urged her to devote more of her time and energy to defending Title IX. The gold medalist de Varona had already made the rounds in DC, and was a member of the Presidents' Commission on Olympic Sports. Now she joined the forces of the AIAW and others fighting to preserve Title IX against the intense lobbying efforts of the NCAA and its allies.

"We knew we had our work cut out for us," said Charlotte West.

It's possible that Richard Nixon would not have signed the Education Amendments of 1972 if he had been aware of the ramifications. The main early battles over Title IX were fought during the presidencies of a football-mad former end from Whittier College and a former All-American center from Michigan, both of whom were sympathetic to the entreaties of Darrell Royal and Bo Schembechler.

In the face of the challenge to Title IX from the NCAA, John Tower, the American Football Coaches Association, and many of the most entrenched powers in American society, the women of the AIAW along with the National Coalition for Women and Girls in Education and the other defenders of Title IX adopted a sporting strategy: They flooded the zone.

In this, the forces supporting Title IX had the benefit of a nimble, informed, well-connected organization—the AIAW being one of many—that could fight fear with facts, and was able to respond to the challenges. There were regular meetings in the District of Columbia when the forces aligned to preserve Title IX met. With Polivy as the conduit, the women of AIAW were kept apprised of all the latest developments on the Hill.

"There was very effective politicking, from the beginning," said Jeff Orleans, a lawyer working with HEW in the early '70s. "It was bipartisan, it was very well organized. And they were not going to let the administration off the hook. I'm pretty confident that the word would have gotten to the Ford White House, as he thought about reelection, 'This is going to be a close election. You're going to win the South anyway. But you could lose some swing states if you come down on the anti-women side of this.'"

The Tower Amendment was defeated again, but early in 1976, growing increasingly alarmed, Byers had the NCAA take the battle to the courts, filing a lawsuit against HEW, alleging that the regulations "exceed the lawful scope of Title IX in that they purport to govern collegiate athletic programs offered by educational institutions which do not directly receive financial assistance" from the government. It was the Darrell Royal argument.

Everyone lawyered up. AIAW's legal bills had become so substantial that the organization couldn't pay for travel or lodging expenses of the teams that qualified for national championships (a perk that the NCAA could afford for all of its men's championships because of its television riches). Even as the NCAA began searching for other measures of relief, the AIAW remained vigilant, poised, ready to take up the fight.

•

In 1973, Billie Moore had made a career decision. She accepted an offer from Mississippi College of Women coach Jill Upton, to serve as an assistant coach for the U.S. women's basketball team that summer, as they prepared to head to Moscow for the 1973 World University Games. It meant she had to retire from the Raybestos Brakettes, the national power on the ASA softball circuit, where her teammates Joan Joyce and Donna Lopiano were pursuing another national title.

In Cold War Moscow, the U.S. contingent was mindful of not starting an international incident. "The one thing we didn't want to do," said Moore, "was anything that would result in us having to stay there." In the group stage games, Upton sent Moore out to scout the Mexican team, which opened against the Soviets. It was there, for the first time, that Moore got to see in person the most intimidating, unstoppable women's player on the planet, Uljana Semjanova, the seven-foot center who wore a men's size 21 basketball shoe.

Watching the Soviets' 133–12 win over the Mexicans, Moore was hard-pressed to find anything to write on the scouting report. When the Soviets returned for the second half of the thrashing, Semjanova was already in street clothes, having showered at halftime. Later in the group stage, the Americans faced the Soviets, and the USSR took a 35-point lead into halftime, prompting another scene in which Semjanova's efforts ended at halftime.

But the Americans rallied in the knockout stages, and made their way to the gold medal game for a rematch with the Soviets. The cause seemed hopeless. Upton gave the team a talk, and then asked Moore if there was anything she wanted to add.

"Yes," said Moore, staring intently at her players. "Let's make sure Semjanova doesn't get to hit the showers at halftime."

The Americans were tenacious, using their superior dexterity and fitness, managing possessions, and trying to contest the ball. The Soviets led by only 20 points at halftime. When the Soviets came out for the second half—with Semjanova still dressed and still in the lineup—the American bench exploded with cheers.

They headed home with the silver medal and a goal: to qualify for the first women's Olympic basketball competition in Montreal in 1976.

Moore's performance opened up a path of opportunity in international competition. Two years later, she served as an assistant to the Immaculata coach Cathy Rush on the U.S. women's team that finished eighth in the Pan American Games. Later that fall, it was Moore who was tabbed to be the head coach of the U.S. team trying to qualify for one of the two open spots in the first women's basketball tournament in the history of the Olympics.

•

That summer of 1976 would prove a watershed for women's sports. It began with tryouts in Colorado Springs and continued at the U.S. national team's training camp at Warrensburg, Missouri, in Garrison's Gym on the campus of Central Missouri State University.

The women who survived the Warrensburg training camp would, in later years, talk about it in the same way that football players discussed legendarily brutal training camps, like "The Junction Boys" of Bear Bryant's first Texas A&M team, who endured a Darwinian ten-day camp in the Hill Country of Texas, or Sid Gillman's San Diego Chargers, who made it through the infamously spartan Rough Acres training camp to start the championship year of 1963.

It was in Warrensburg where the finest women's players in the country came into contact with a work ethic and coaching style that had led Nancy Dunkle, one of Moore's players at Fullerton, to describe her coach as a "tyrant." Moore worked her charges through a grueling string of three-a-day workouts. "There was nothing else to do there," she reasoned. "So you might as well practice. I knew enough to know from the world championships that, most of these teams we were playing, that was their job."

Moore was a teetotaler, but she knew better than to insist the same from her players. ("Don't make a rule you can't enforce.") If she knew members of her team had been out drinking, though, the next morning's practice would be more intense.

The women were divided into groups, and made to run "suicides," up and back on the court in thirty seconds. If anyone on the team didn't make the thirty-second mark, the whole group was punished by having to run it again. The drills were tough on everyone, but no one more so than the Delta State All-American Lusia "Lucy" Harris.

Harris had grown up the tenth of eleven children, the daughter of sharecroppers, in Greenwood, Mississippi. Bewitched with the game of basketball from an early age, she used to surreptitiously watch games on the family's small black-and-white television until late in the night, throwing a heavy quilt over herself and the TV to block out the telltale light. She loved Oscar Robertson and his quick-release jump shot. At Delta State, Margaret Wade had made Harris the centerpiece of a walk-it-up-the-floor national champion.

But for the U.S. team, Moore had other ideas. Trying to qualify for a tournament with the invincible Soviet team and their star Semjanova, Moore wanted a team that would play to the Americans' strengths of speed, fitness and agility.

So in Warrensburg, Lucy Harris suffered.

"We had to run for Lucy," said Trish Roberts. "We had to run thirty-second suicides, and if anybody in the group didn't make that time, then the whole group had to run. So we were putting pressure on each other—'don't make us run, don't make us run'—and Lucy almost always didn't make her time. I mean, it was a *situation*. But she got to the point where she started making that time. When we started getting towards that line, we were diving over the line."

For Moore, the lessons of her father still held sway. No mercy, no quarter. But she commanded the respect of all her players, from the stars like Harris and Ann Meyers, and the teenage phenom Nancy Lieberman, who won the last spot on the team, and the twenty-four-year-old veteran guard Pat Head, already a head coach of the women's team at the University of Tennessee.

During the period of the Warrensburg camp, the team drove up to Mission, Kansas, to play a scrimmage against some NCAA staffers, in a game arranged by David Berst, the head of the NCAA enforcement division. The NCAA team was full of men in their twenties and thirties who'd had college basketball playing experience, including Berst himself, Kansas State alum Warren Brown, and Tom Jernstedt, an all-around athlete who'd played football at the University of Oregon.

It was a tough, physical game, with Berst aide Jim Delaney, who'd been to two Final Fours at North Carolina, fouling out late in the game, and Brown hitting a jumper from the baseline to send the game into overtime, when the men finally won.

But it wasn't the close loss to the men that earned Moore's ire. After a steal, Ann Meyers and guard Juliene Simpson headed downcourt on a fast break. As they were moving in for the lay-up, Moore scanned the court and saw her front line—Harris, Nancy Dunkle and Trish Roberts—hanging back.

"We just figured she had a breakaway, so the bigs stood back watching," said Trish Roberts. "And then we saw Billie."

The Billie Moore Stare had already become a matter of legend.

"She was not a smiler," said Simpson. "She had this mean stare. I didn't even have to look at her. I *knew*."

Back in Warrensburg that night, a few women wanted to go out for a drink, but Pat Head declined. "Guys, I'm going to sleep—I know we're going to get killed tomorrow."

The next morning, just as Head had feared, Moore worked them through a punishing series of suicides. For forty-five minutes, there wasn't even a basketball on the court. She ran them, and ran them some more.

"It was brutal," said Roberts. "People were throwing up on the sidelines."

Moore had said before she only wanted players who hustled down the court every time; that hanging back or half-measures were not an option.

"My message was that when you've earned the right, you will play," said Moore. "But that there are no shortcuts. It impacts the whole team."

Toughened by the camp in Warrensburg, the U.S. earned an Olympic berth at a qualifying tournament in Hamilton, Ontario. For this accomplishment, they found themselves stranded, since the Olympic village wouldn't open for another week and a half, and the U.S. Olympic Committee hadn't expected the team to qualify, and therefore had made no arrangements for provisional lodging.

With the credit card of U.S. Basketball chairman Bill Wall, the team stayed for ten days in Rochester, New York, the home base of Kodak, an early sponsor of the women's game. Moore would look back on it later and realize how naïve they all were ("we didn't know what to ask for, or who to ask").

When they arrived in the Olympic village, the entire team was put into a cramped suite that left some players sleeping on cots and others sleeping on the floor.

The trappings of the game were still in the rudimentary stage. "There was no film," said Moore. "No scouting report. There was none of that." So in the absence of that, she doubled down on her own philosophy. Like Wooden, she was mindful of not overreaching. "My biggest fear as a coach is that my players would run plays instead of playing the game." The offense was up-tempo and aggressive, the defense was a mixture of player-to-player (they tried to avoid calling it "man to man,") and mixing it up with a 1-3-1 zone that regulated the pace and could create turnovers.

The Soviets were ready as well, and as the USA–USSR game started, it was clear that the Russian women were focused. With Semjanova dominating the inside, and the taller Soviet forwards clogging the passing lanes, the USSR jumped out to a 17–0 lead. At which point Moore turned to her assistant Sue Gunter on the American bench and said calmly, "Just please tell me we will score."

They did, though the final score was 112–77, Soviets. Bill Russell was providing color commentary on all the basketball games for ABC. Afterward, he pulled Moore aside and told her that her only mistake was not sending her eleventh or twelfth player out to the court early to try to injure Semjanova.

Going into the final game of the round-robin format, the USA faced Czechoslovakia knowing a win would earn them a silver medal; a loss would drop them to 2–3 and off the podium. Prior to the game, Moore was adamant that the U.S. needed to win. Not just for the women on the team, but for the future of women's sports.

The game was tied at 37 at halftime when Moore brought in the eighteen-year-old Nancy Lieberman, the youngest player on the team, and switched to a 1-3-1 zone defense. Stirred by another commanding halftime speech and the tactical tweak, the U.S. women dominated the second half, running away with an 83–67 win to earn the silver medal.

Inside the Montreal Forum, the pro-American crowd hailed the USA squad. Simpson's husband had driven from Gallup, New Mexico, to watch. Other friends and family members of players had come just as far.

During a postgame interview, asked what the U.S. needed to catch up with the Soviets, Moore replied, "Ten more inches."

After the American squad stood through the emotional national anthem, Moore gave them the speech, not all that dissimilar from the one she gave to the Cal State–Fullerton women when they won the CIAW title in 1970.

"Don't do anything tonight," she told her players, "that will prevent you from remembering what happened today."

They didn't. But they drank quite a few beers that night. And they stayed well clear of Billie Moore.

For the women on that '76 team, Moore's message endured: *You'll always be the first.*

For Lusia Harris, Annie Meyers, Pat Head (who would be married in 1980 and thereafter known as Pat Head Summitt), Trish Roberts, Juliene Simpson, Mary Anne O'Connor, Nancy Lieberman and all the rest, the summer was an odyssey that stretched from Colorado Springs to Warrensburg to Hamilton to Rochester to Montreal, but in the course of that ordeal, they had achieved something historic.

There had been celebrated American women athletes before, dating all the way back to Gertrude Ederle swimming the English Channel in the 1920s and Babe Didrikson Zaharias excelling at a variety of sports in the '30s and '40s. More recently, fans had thrilled to Peggy Fleming and Billie Jean King and Chris Evert. But in the summer of 1976, American sports fans were exposed to something new and entirely different—a women's *team* that they could root for and rally around. That was unprecedented, and a sign of what was yet to come.

•

As the women's game continued to grow, one of the writers who'd covered women's sports, Jay Searcy, moved from the *New York Times* to the *Philadelphia Inquirer.*

One day, Searcy mentioned an idea to the voluble Mel Greenberg, a Temple grad working on the business desk who'd taken to moonlighting as a writer for women's basketball games around the city.

"What do you think," asked Searcy, "about starting a Top Twenty women's basketball poll?"

Greenberg at first thought it absurd. "Where are you going to get the *scores*?" he asked. "Where are you going to get the voters? Where are you going to get *twenty teams*?"

But Searcy had passed the idea on to the right man. Greenberg was both a tireless worker and a tireless talker and began spreading the word.

In November 1976, the *Inquirer* ran its first preseason women's poll as part of its basketball preview. It featured a photograph of Delta State's Lucy Harris examining the preseason poll results. Within a year, the *Inquirer* poll—which soon became better known as "the Greenberg poll"—was showing up in dozens of newspapers across the country.

Beyond the growth of basketball, a burgeoning respect for and attention to women's sports could even be seen on network television. In 1973, NBC had devoted 365 hours to sports telecasts showing male athletes, but only 1 hour to women, while CBS devoted 250 hours to men, and 10 to women. But with women's tennis leading the way, that drastic imbalance slowly started changing. Even the marquee women's golf event—the Dinah Shore–Colgate Winners Circle tournament—showed astonishingly strong ratings, outpolling the Masters, the U.S. Open and the PGA Championship in 1974 and 1975.

•

With the last issue of 1976, *Sports Illustrated* made Chris Evert its Sportswoman of the Year, the first time that a female was the sole winner of the award. She'd had a truly remarkable campaign, maintaining her number one ranking, extending what would become a six-year, 125-match clay court winning streak, and winning both Wimbledon and the U.S. Open, the first woman since Billie Jean King in 1972 to win both in the same year.

King had recognized the importance of Evert even before Evert herself. And in 1976, mature and composed at just twenty-two, Evert succeeded King as the president of the Women's Tennis Association. As with Jack Nicklaus in golf, Evert was the rainmaker. TV ratings were up when she was in the mix late in a Grand Slam tournament, and she was virtually always in the mix. From the French Open in 1973 through the same tournament in 1983, she would reach at least the semifinals of every major tournament she entered, winning fifteen of them.

Evert—surprisingly, to many—contained multitudes. After being an outcast on the circuit in the early days, she was now the social director of sorts, participating in an endless streak of backgammon games and initiating outings to dance clubs from Los Angeles to London. Evert had the best two-fisted backhand on the tour, and also told the best dirty jokes. Against the backdrop of the contentious debate over the role of women in sports, Evert had established herself as someone who exuded both an air of consummate femininity and also an unyielding competitive fire.

It would even prove to be a point of strain in her on-again, off-again relationship with Jimmy Connors. The couple played some mixed-doubles matches together. For Connors, it was a lark, a chance to spend some time with his fiancée. For Evert, the consummate competitor, it remained another challenge, another chance to prove herself. Connors would remember "she took it very seriously, finding it almost impossible to rein in her competitive spirit."

Evert and Connors had been engaged in 1974, when they won the women's and men's singles title at Wimbledon (they danced the first dance at the Wimbledon ball to the song "The Girl I'm Going to Marry"). But the men's and women's tours rarely intersected, and neither athlete—both at the height of their powers—was inclined to curtail their schedule for the sake of the relationship. What ensued was a long and public breakup (Connors showed up with actress Susan George in the crowd at Wimbledon during Evert's semifinal loss to King in 1975), followed in later years by extensive media coverage of Evert's social life, including relationships with actor Burt

Reynolds, Jack Ford (the son of President Gerald Ford) and then English touring pro John Lloyd, whom she would later marry.

Her maturation could be seen on and off the court. Five years earlier, she'd been sensitive about even being called an athlete. By 1976, she was doubling down, reveling in it and starting to do weight training to maintain her edge. "Chrissie is becoming her own person," said Billie Jean King. "She says she is feeling more like a woman now."

For her part, Evert was coming out of the cocoon of her upbringing. "Billie Jean is so independent I could listen for hours," she said. "It kind of infiltrates my mind and I start to question all the things I've been brought up on."

One thing hadn't changed: The metronomic concentration, so at odds with the frilly ribbons and delicate earrings, remained intact. What America saw was, as with Nicklaus, an attractive athlete who behind the pleasant facade was a fierce, relentless competitor.

In the end, Evert was a competitor first, blessed with a single-minded focus. When Connors called her late one night to call off the wedding, saying they were both too young to get married, she said, "Okay, if that's what you think. I've got a match tomorrow. Not a problem."

# THIRTEEN

# FOLLOW THE MONEY

TWO DAYS BEFORE Christmas 1975, on a chilled, windy day in New York City, the world of professional sports changed forever.

There were no athletes present at the pivotal moment, only MLBPA executive director Marvin Miller, the owners' chief negotiator, John Gaherin, and the seventy-year-old pipe-smoking arbitrator Peter Seitz.

The arbitration case that Seitz was deciding focused on the very heart of the reserve clause. The matter under dispute was whether the owners' reserve clause right to renew the contract of an unsigned player for one more year meant one year *only* or a series of one-year extensions, at the team's discretion, into perpetuity. The Dodgers' surfer-turned-pitcher Andy Messersmith and the Expos' veteran Dave McNally had played the 1975 season without signing a contract. They would be the test case for the Players Association's belief that the reserve clause could be employed by the owners for one year only, and not forever, as the owners interpreted it, and that after that year a player should be free to negotiate and sign with any team.

The sixty-seven-page ruling that Seitz shared with Miller and Gaherin that day was clear in its conclusion: "There is no contractual bond between these players and the Los Angeles and the Montreal clubs, respectively. Absent such a contract, their clubs had no right or power, under the Basic Agreement, the Uniform Player Contract or the Major League rules…" Seitz added that there was nothing in the standard player contract "which, explicitly, expresses agreement that the players' contract can be renewed for any period beyond the first year."

Seitz met with Miller and Gaherin at his office that morning. He handed each man a copy of his decision. Miller turned to the back and saw the verdict. He smiled, took out a pen and signed it. Gaherin also read the verdict, but did not smile. He signed the document as well and then, following his instructions from Bowie Kuhn, handed Seitz an envelope and said, "Peter, I'm sorry. I love you dearly, but you're out."

Seitz had, in a single stroke, changed the power dynamic between players and owners forever. And, in so doing, he'd been fired for his interpretation. (Soon Gaherin—who had urged the owners to settle rather than take the case to arbitration—would himself be fired.)

Later that day, Kuhn declared that the decision was "a disaster for a great majority of the players, the clubs, and most of all, the fans. It is inconceivable that after nearly 100 years of developing a system for the overall good of the game, it should be obliterated in this way." Kuhn would later claim—intending to insult Seitz by the accusation—that the ruling was made with "visions of the Emancipation Proclamation dancing in his eyes."

The repercussions of Seitz's decision were felt instantaneously, from Pete Rozelle's office on Park Avenue to the NBA headquarters in 2 Penn Center above Madison Square Garden, to the NHL offices in Toronto. The fallout might occur quickly or drag out over any number of years (in the NFL's case it would be seventeen more years), but after the Seitz decision, it was inevitable that free agency was coming.

•

When Miller called Messersmith with the news later that morning, the pitcher said, "Great! What do I do next?"

It was a good question. Messersmith would eventually sign a three-year, $1 million contract with the Atlanta Braves and their new owner Ted Turner. But the larger question that would hang over the off-season was what would become of the other 599 major leaguers. Would any player who played out his option be able to sign with another team?

The owners locked the players out of training camp on March 1, pending a collective bargaining agreement. But the owners soon lost their nerve, and camps were opened sixteen days later. After baseball's two attempts to appeal Seitz's decision in the courts failed, the owners returned to the bargaining table; they were not dealing from a position of strength.

Some players like the Dodgers' pitcher Mike Marshall wanted free agency one year after the end of any contract, the "one-and-one" idea. Miller feared that such an arrangement would flood the market, and effectively depress salaries, and he carefully explained his reasoning to the players.

"He was the most important person in all of this," said Sal Bando of Miller. "His demeanor, his knowledge. Not forcing his opinion on anyone, just guiding us through what the negatives would be."

The owners' offer, rejected out of hand, was that only veterans who played out their option after ten years of service would be eligible for free agency, later softened to eight years.

Meeting in New York City with a group of team reps and other players, Miller presented a middle path that he believed would ultimately benefit all players.

"Only your best players make it to six years of service," pointed out Miller. "So your free agents would be the best players. And a rising tide lifts all boats."

That was the deal that was finally reached, and it was another victory for Miller and the MLBPA. What the owners had unwittingly agreed to was a system by which the best players in free agency would set the market, and then younger players—going through the salary arbitration process—would profit from the new market.

By the time free agency came to pass, Miller's credibility with the players was unrivaled.

"Marvin had a gift that no one I have ever seen—including every politician I've ever come across—ever had," said his longtime lieutenant, Don Fehr. "Marvin could take the most difficult concepts, with the most exceptions and the most nuance and requiring the most explanation, and boil it down to seven or eight sentences, so everybody would get it. And what he focused on more than anything else was educating the players: 'I know what they tell you guys, but this is what the facts are. This is what it means. This is how you get from here to there. This is what your rights are under the labor laws, this is what your risks are, if you exercise those rights. This is what the benefits might be, if you're successful going forward. No, the owners won't want you to do it. It's not because they're bad or evil people; it's because they don't want to pay you anything more than they absolutely have to.'"

•

If all professional sports in America were patriarchal, none was more so than the National Football League. The sheer size of rosters meant that any one player was less significant in the overall success of the team than in other sports. Given the complex, interdependent nature of the game, it was the league in which free agency was considered most dangerous to the quality of play. The fear of the unknown ran deep. Whatever one might say about Tex Schramm or Paul Brown or the other influential figures on the league's competition committee, it was true that, to a man, they sincerely felt free agency would ruin their game.

Since 1971, the executive director of the NFL Players Association was the acerbic Wisconsin lawyer Ed Garvey. With Garvey at the helm, the NFLPA struck in 1974, under the slogan, "No Freedom, No Football." But it was jarring to see picket lines—the first occurred on July 3, outside the San Diego Chargers' training camp—populated by healthy professional athletes, and the entire list of NFLPA demands, which totaled fifty-seven, and included an elimination of "psychological and personality testing" and a relaxation of training-camp curfews, were routinely ridiculed in the press.

"Most of the coverage was like: 'Ungrateful,' 'Overpaid,' 'Fat cats,'" said the veteran Bill Curry. "I think our average salary at the time was like $25,000. We didn't think we were overpaid. And when we started staying out of training camp, our wives had those house notes. They didn't think we were overpaid either. So it was a real tenuous time. We were deadly serious, but we just didn't have the guts or the organization to hold it together."

The 1974 strike collapsed late in the preseason, and the players returned to camp, playing without a collective bargaining agreement (CBA). There was nowhere near the consensus of support for Garvey that his counterparts enjoyed in other players' associations. When the Dolphins' Dick Anderson and Steelers' president Dan Rooney hammered out a deal, Garvey scuttled it, persuading the player reps to table a full union vote until John Mackey's lawsuit against the NFL could work its way through the courts.

That meant the players were without a CBA for the better part of three years. Even when Mackey won the decision, ruling that the Rozelle Rule was an illegal restraint of trade, the NFLPA wound up negotiating away many of those gains when the next agreement was reached in March 1977.

By then, many of the players had grown alienated with Garvey's tactics and his lack of effectiveness. "Fire Ed Garvey, that's my opinion," said one Houston Oiler in the fall of 1976. "He's getting $57,000 a year and he's taking us for a ride."

It would be a long time before the NFL would achieve true free agency, but the existence of the wounded WFL at least offered an opportunity for players to get a glimpse of their genuine value and, in certain instances, some negotiating leverage.

Watching all this from afar was a University of California law student named Leigh Steinberg, a tanned beach kid equally intrigued with capitalism and the counterculture. He'd met Jim Morrison and Jimi Hendrix during his time as the Cal student-body president. In the early '70s, he applied for a job as one of ABC's college football sideline reporters, but had lost out to Jim Lampley and Don Tollefson.

Nearing graduation, Steinberg decided he wanted to become a player agent, and reckoned that modern athletes might relate more comfortably to agents closer to their own age. Steinberg also recognized the implicit social compact of the modern athlete and vowed that he would represent only players who promised to donate a portion of their salary to charity. He convinced fellow Cal grad Steve Bartkowski that he could make a better deal for him than any established agent. On January 28, 1975, the Atlanta Falcons made Bartkowski the first pick in the 1975 NFL draft.

The World Football League was gearing up for its second season then, and Steinberg received interest from two WFL franchises, the Chicago Winds and the Shreveport Steamer. Neither of those teams, nor the league they were in, would survive the 1975 season, but his flirtations with them brought the Falcons to the table. Intent on avoiding the embarrassment of losing the top pick in the draft to the rival league, Atlanta eventually paid Bartkowski a four-year, $650,000 deal, the richest contract ever signed by a rookie in the NFL.

As Atlanta news stations cut into regular programming just to track Bartkowski's *arrival* in Atlanta to negotiate, Steinberg saw the outsize impact that even a rookie athlete could have on a major metropolitan area. "I began to understand in that experience how athletes trigger imitative behavior, especially among the young," he said. "One can argue whether they should, or whether they should have the burden of that responsibility, but in point of fact, they do. I realized, by encouraging athletes to give back to the community, I could help make an impact."

Steinberg had launched his career, though not everyone was ready for the new world order. Steinberg's other client that spring was the wide receiver/punter Pat McInally, who was drafted by the Cincinnati Bengals. When Steinberg phoned the Bengals' offices to start his negotiation with Mike Brown—running the club in the wake of his father's retirement—he introduced himself, and Brown said, "We don't deal with agents," and hung up on him.

•

By the time of Seitz's decision, the National Hockey League was in real trouble. The loss of an American TV contract had left the NHL in the lurch, relying on ticket buyers, Canadian television and expansion fees to survive. Two more expansion teams had joined the league in 1974 and one of them, the Kansas City Scouts, was in trouble by its second season, crippled by a historic slump (they won just one of their last forty-four games in the 1975–76 season, then moved to Denver). But even the downtrodden Scouts weren't the NHL's biggest problem. The Pittsburgh Penguins, who'd enjoyed strong community support in Pittsburgh, still wound up broke in the summer of 1975, with the IRS putting a lien on the club for unpaid taxes and padlocking the team's offices at the same time banks foreclosed on $5 million worth of Penguins loans. This came on the back of the league spending over $10 million on the California Golden Seals, Charlie Finley's ill-fated hockey team, who were finally moved to Cleveland, where they became the Barons, and limped along for two more seasons before being absorbed into the Minnesota North Stars.

Free agency in the NHL was similar to the NFL. Though a player who played out his option was a free agent who had the right to negotiate with other teams, there was a proviso in the standard contract that called for the team signing a free agent to make an "equalization" payment to the team losing the player.

In Boston, Bobby Orr played out his contract in the 1975–76 season and waited for his agent, Alan Eagleson, to negotiate a new deal.

Eagleson, like Larry Fleisher of the NBPA, was both a player agent and the head of the Players Association. But there the similarities ended. Even among owners in the NBA, Fleisher was known to be impeccable with his word. Eagleson seemed less transparent and more domineering, but he had gained the trust of a large majority of the NHL's players when he'd negotiated a lucrative deal on behalf of the sixteen-year-old Orr in 1965, ushering in the era of agents in hockey. A year later, Eagleson formed the NHLPA, becoming the organization's first executive director.

In 1976, though his career had been derailed by knee injuries, Orr was still the biggest name in hockey, and there was little doubt that, if he chose to leave the Bruins and test the market, he'd become the highest-paid player in hockey history. Orr was inclined to stay with the Bruins. But as negotiations continued near the end of the '75–'76 season, Eagleson informed Orr that the team didn't seem very interested and didn't value Orr's historic contributions.

When Bruins president Paul Mooney stopped by the locker room to talk with Orr late that season, the injured Orr was on an exercise bike.

"I brushed him off," Orr recalled. "He asked me if I knew the substance of the offer the team had made. I told him that he was trying to drive a wedge between Alan and me and that it wouldn't work. That was the end of the discussion. When I found out what he had wanted to tell me, it was too late."

What Orr never heard, until he'd already signed the five-year, $2.5 million deal with the Black Hawks, was that Boston had offered him a contract that included a 5 percent ownership stake in the entire franchise. (With the Bruins valued at $1.3 billion in 2023, a 5 percent stake would today be worth $65 million.)

It would be the end of the decade before Orr discovered Eagleson's treachery, and another decade more before the agent was exposed for a wide series of episodes of financial malfeasance and embezzlement.

•

By the time of the Messersmith-McNally case, the NBA had been in litigation for so long and in so many venues that the gallows humor around the league office held that the NBA's initials stood for "Nothing But Attorneys." Beyond the extended legal battle of the Oscar Robertson case, the NBA had lost the Spencer Haywood lawsuit, which allowed players to sign pro contracts before their college eligibility was up.

For all their legal firepower and resources aimed at the Players Association, the league kept getting thumped in court, most clearly in the "Valentine's Day Massacre" of 1975, when federal judge (and noted basketball fan) Robert Carter of the Southern District of New York denied the NBA's motion to have the charges dismissed.

That prompted a letter from the league's counsel, George G. Gallantz. In what the lawyer described as "the most serious and important letter I have ever written to" NBA commissioner Walter Kennedy, Gallantz noted, "Although the legality of the present methods of operating professional athletic leagues will ultimately be passed upon by appellate courts—and quite possibly the United States Supreme Court—*it is no exaggeration to say that an adverse result in this case, if not ultimately reversed, threatens the very existence of the NBA…*"

Within months of the letter, Kennedy retired and was replaced by Lawrence "Larry" O'Brien, the consummate dealmaker who had served as John F. Kennedy's postmaster general in the New Frontier. Though O'Brien had been born in Springfield, Massachusetts, the birthplace of basketball, and often played in the YMCA where Dr. James Naismith invented the game, he had no professional background in the league or the sport. The NBA Board of Governors had hired O'Brien to get the league out of court and bring a measure of stability.

Meanwhile, another idea for free agency was offered by ABA commissioner Mike Storen in 1975. Rather than offering compensation to teams losing a player, Storen suggested giving teams the right of first refusal, allowing players to test their value on the free agency market, but giving the original team the option of matching any contract offered.

"Under the system," said Storen, "players would reach their true value instead of the value they negotiated when they came out of college. The better players who deserve more would get more, and the journeymen who weren't worth as much probably would earn less."

The idea intrigued NBPA executive director Larry Fleisher, who had earned the same allegiance from the NBA players that Marvin Miller commanded from major leaguers. In the words of Jim Quinn, his longtime lieutenant at the NBPA, Fleisher was "the ultimate liberal," passionately devoted to progressive causes wherever he found them. In the mid-'70s, when his client Earl Monroe sold Fleisher his used purple-and-silver Rolls-Royce Silver Shadow, Fleisher proudly drove it to his home in the tony suburban enclave of Chappaqua, New York, earning furtive looks from his neighbors. Coming out to observe the new family car, Fleisher's wife, Vasso, inquired if her husband really wanted to keep the "Black Power" decal that Monroe had placed in his rear window.

Fleisher peered at it and replied, "Definitely!"

In the wake of the Seitz decision and Carter's ruling, both sides in the *Robertson* case viewed the pending trial with trepidation.

"The NBA was thinking before this judge, they're going to lose," recalled Quinn. "But our concern is twofold. How long can we keep this up with no money? And if there were a jury, how sympathetic would they be to well-paid, mostly African American ballplayers? Our problem was we didn't have any money, and [the NBA and its lawyers] were bleeding us, so there was pressure on Larry to get a deal."

The two sides remained at a stalemate when Fleisher, in a moment of inspiration, called the Golden State Warriors' player rep, the veteran guard Jeff Mullins, and invited him to come to New York and meet with Robertson and the Celtics' venerable all-pro John Havlicek. Mullins, educated at Duke, was a white, middle-of-the-road presence who brought a fresh perspective and a keen desire for a resolution.

The NBPA was interested in establishing the right-of-first-refusal policy that Storen had espoused with the ABA, while the owners were adamant that, in any free agency, they needed some form of compensation. At one point, Mullins asked Fleisher how long the case would take to work its way through the courts.

"Three or four years," estimated Fleisher.

"Well, then, why don't we let them have compensation for three or four years?"

Thus was born the seeds of an idea—a long-term CBA that would start with a few years of compensation for free agents, but would conclude with the right of first refusal.

It was then left to Fleisher and Mullins to persuade Robertson and Havlicek to consider a compromise that would lead to a settlement. The ABA was in shambles, Fleisher pointed out, and if the NBPA went to court, the other league might perish before the case was settled, leading to the loss of another eighty-four jobs within the industry.

In the end, after a twenty-four-hour negotiation session, Mullins' plan was adopted. The players agreed to a five-year period in which compensation was guaranteed to teams losing players to free agency, with a stipulation that it couldn't be "punitive," in the way that the NFL's Rozelle Rule was. The wording was suitably vague, and the NBA's Russ Granik remembered "there was stipulations about what compensation would mean, and not to be a penalty, which was kind of unclear and made for lawyers to fight about." (A special master would be hired to hear appeals and overturn them if he viewed the compensation as unreasonable.) In turn, the back half of the CBA would include another five-year period, eventually modified to six, in which compensation would go away but the player's original club would have the right of first refusal.

When the agreement was finally reached, also marking the settlement of the Robertson suit, there was little celebrating on either side. There were no lavish dinners on the part of players—Robertson had already retired; Havlicek and Mullins shook hands and boarded planes to return to their teams for the next game. What they had in hand was modest but ultimately historic: The reserve clause was eliminated entirely. The NBA paid $4.3 million in restitution to 479 players, based on the length of their careers. Owners preserving the rights to players in perpetuity ended.

The agreement, signed just one week after Julius Erving's memorable dunk contest victory at the ABA All-Star Game, left open the option for the NBA to end its decade-long war with the ABA and merge with some or all of its teams.

The only person who suffered from the deal, in retrospect, was the man who filed the suit himself. The NBA effectively blackballed Oscar Robertson, one of its greatest players ever, from a career as a coach or team executive.

"I always felt that it was held against him," said Jerry West. "I'm shocked that he was never given an opportunity to be involved as an executive, because he would have brought a real presence to another team. I don't blame him for being bitter."

•

There was one footnote to the McNally-Messersmith case and the Robertson settlement that would resonate across the decades. Even in the midst of all the legal combat, the future of sports labor negotiation was slowly coalescing behind the influential article written in 1971 in the *Yale Law Review* by Ralph K. Winter Jr. and Michael S. Jacobs, entitled "Antitrust Principles and Collective Bargaining by Athletes: Of Superstars in Peonage."

The article posited that the issue of the reserve clause and the draft, and other similar points of contention, weren't truly subject to antitrust violations, but rather were issues between labor and management that were properly settled in collective bargaining. Winter, who later became a judge, built his analysis on a Supreme Court decision in the Jewel Tea case of 1965.

This seemed to benefit the leagues, and they were in favor of this interpretation. Hamilton Carothers, the general counsel for the NFL, viewed it as a key tenet in the league's defense in the Mackey case. "It was the kind of pathbreaking analysis that you would basically have to memorize in order to have a thoughtful discussion with Carothers," said Paul Tagliabue, then a young associate at Carothers' firm of Covington & Burling. "It tilted in the direction of the leagues and clubs in pro sports, surprising a lot of people."

For the NFLPA and MLBPA and NBPA, the response to Winter's article was considerably more tempered. "The issue was whether any of these restrictions had been bargained over, and of course they hadn't because they'd been in place for decades," said Jim Quinn, who spent the '70s working with multiple players' associations. "And because whenever we brought it up, the owners basically said, 'Fuck you; it's not on the table.'"

But the advent of free agency in baseball and basketball meant that the players' associations had more bargaining power. In the meantime, the money would flow.

•

The spectacle of the All-Star Game slam-dunk contest aside, there was a sinking-ship quality to the 1975–76 season of the ABA. By February, the Virginia Squires were teetering on the edge of bankruptcy, with a desperate scheme to sell 100 adverting banners at $5,000 each to put up in their arenas and stay solvent. By then, there were doubts if the team would show up for its games. "We'll definitely have a game," a Pacers spokesman said about the

Virginia–Indiana game slated for a Friday night. "If it isn't Virginia, New York, Kentucky, and San Antonio are available."

With the legal impediment to the merger finally lifted, all that was left were the details, but the ABA was in a much weaker position than it had been five years earlier.

"Our original proposal to the NBA was for six teams to get in, everyone but Virginia," said Jim Bukata, the ABA's marketing and PR director. "But the NBA didn't want Kentucky or St. Louis. Kentucky talked about moving from Louisville to Cincinnati, but that still didn't interest the NBA. St. Louis said it would move to Hartford, but the Celtics went crazy, saying that violated their territorial rights."

The NBA's national television contract was so modest—and so shaky—that no one thought much at the time about the concessions made to one of the disbanded ABA teams, the Spirits of St. Louis. The team's owners, Ozzie and Danny Silna and Don Schupak, agreed to fold the franchise for $2.2 million and one-seventh of a share of the TV money from the four ABA teams—thus, four-sevenths of a team share—in perpetuity. (In time, as each NBA team's annual share of national TV contracts would increase—to $88 million per year in 2023—the Silna brothers' deal would turn out to be far more valuable than their team ever was.)

The Appomattox scene took place in Hyannis, Massachusetts. The ABA had lost $50 million over the previous decade. "The difference between a good negotiator and a bad negotiator," said the Spurs' owner Angelo Drossos, "is that the good one knows when someone has him by the proverbial balls. Well, at our final merger talks in Hyannis, that was how the NBA had us, and we knew it."

NBA commissioner Larry O'Brien, who'd been hired to achieve this outcome, presided over the merger between the NBA and the ABA, accepting four ABA teams, and making arrangements for a dispersal draft to allocate the players on the three defunct franchises.

So the ABA champion Nets were joined by the ascendant Denver Nuggets, who'd had the best record in the ABA, and Indiana and San Antonio, new markets for the NBA but two cities that had shown stalwart growth over the years. They were solid.

"We never called it a merger, by the way," said Russ Granik, responding to the grammatical precision of the NBA's in-house counsel, David Stern. "It was an expansion by four new teams, which is what David always insisted on calling it, as an antitrust lawyer. Everyone else in the world, but he and I, called it a merger."

The deal was signed June 17, 1976, and less than two months later, Judge Carter approved the NBA–ABA–NBPA settlement. Pro basketball would go forward with twenty-two teams.

The arrival of Dr. J into the enlarged NBA was the main storyline heading into the 1976–77 season. Erving was featured with the Celtics' Dave Cowens on the cover of SI's pro basketball preview issue ("The Merger Season," read the headline).

But the NBA's hard-bargained deal turned out to be too demanding for the Nets. Roy Boe, the owner of the team (and also of their Long Island–based hockey brethren, the Islanders), had to pay not only the $3.2 million "entry fee" to join the NBA, but another $4.8 million in indemnity fees for impinging on the territory of the New York Knicks. He wound up doing the unthinkable.

"I didn't have the $3.2 million in liquid cash to get into the NBA and it was due on September 15," said Boe. "I was offered $3 million for Julius from Philadelphia and I took it, because I had no choice. The merger agreement got us in the NBA, but it forced me to destroy the team by selling Erving to pay the bill."

CBS had planned a season-opening prime-time national telecast of the Nets playing at Golden State. When the deal was made two days before the start of the season, CBS canceled the broadcast.

Notified of the trade, the Nets' guard "Super" John Williamson had the same reaction as most of the team's fans: "The season's over for us already." He wasn't wrong; the Nets, without Erving, wound up going 22–60 that year. They truly did resemble an expansion team.

The 1976–77 season would find the ABA teams and players staking their claim, much as the AFL had in the end of the '60s, to reaching parity with the older league. Two of the four ABA refugees, the Nuggets and Spurs, won their division in their first season in the NBA, and the 1977 NBA All-Star Game featured ten former ABA players. Erving, inevitably, wound up as the game's MVP.

•

As television opportunities expanded and purses grew ever larger, it became clear that the right athlete with the right management structure could earn far more off the field of play than on it.

Here again, Jack Nicklaus was setting the pace. In breaking with Mark McCormack and the seminal sports management firm IMG in 1970, Nicklaus had assembled a team that would focus on becoming something of an anti-IMG. Everyone was working to maximize the one client, Nicklaus, and in turn the golfer spent time developing personal relationships with the leaders of each company he was working with. This formula led Nicklaus to become an endorsement monolith, with deals not only for golf clubs, shoes, clothes, and balls, but also everything from suits to lawnmowers.

McCormack, though pained by Nicklaus' exit, and prone to charge that Nicklaus left in part because of jealousy of his original client Palmer, finally concluded in 1975, "As it was, I guess if I were him I would have left me, too."

While many of his competitors worried about where they finished on the annual money-winning list, Nicklaus was intent on leaving his mark on the sport. In 1968, he announced plans to build a golf course in the Columbus area and create a new tournament. The course, Muirfield Village, opened in 1974, and the first Memorial Tournament was held in late May 1976. Beyond that, Nicklaus entered far fewer tournaments than any of the other top pros, dedicating himself to concentrating on the four major tournaments each year, an approach that found him winning eight majors in the decade—one Masters, two U.S. Opens, two British Opens, and three PGAs—and finishing in the top ten during 35 of the 40 major tournaments of the '70s.

In designing golf courses around the world, in flying in his own corporate jet (*Golden Bear One*), Nicklaus pointed a direction in which an athlete could become a brand of his own. Palmer, of course, had been even more important to the sport than Nicklaus, but the difference was what Nicklaus contributed. He envisioned not merely promotions but partnerships.

The sports world was changing to the degree that an athlete could, as Dan Jenkins once put in when discussing Nicklaus, "become his own conglomerate."

•

Before the '76 season began, in response to the Seitz decision, Charlie Finley began off-loading his best players, dealing unsigned stars Reggie Jackson and Ken Holtzman, both entering their option year and likely to seek free agency, to the Orioles. Waiting to decide whether he'd report to Baltimore, Reggie Jackson read the news with avid interest. He finally reported to the Orioles in time for the nightcap of a doubleheader against his former team, the A's, on May 2.

It had seemed for years that Jackson and free agency were meant for each other. The three-time world champion with the A's was immortalized on the cover of *Sports Illustrated* as baseball's first "Superduperstar," and in 1975, offhandedly claimed to the press that, "If I played in New York, they'd name a candy bar after me."

When Major League Baseball grudgingly agreed in the 1976 CBA to a system of free agency for players who'd played out their option year, it set the stage for a raft of veterans to earn salaries that a year earlier would have been unimaginable. The California Angels' Gene Autry signed Don Baylor, Joe Rudi and Bobby Grich for a total of $4.9 million, while the Padres paid $3.4 million to sign Rollie Fingers and Gene Tenace, continuing the dismantling of the A's dynasty.

But of all the free agents, Jackson was the highest-profile name, and the Yankees' new owner, George Steinbrenner, was intent on getting the biggest name.

What free agency meant for the players was more money. What it would mean for the owners was a great deal more visibility. Some were temperamentally uncomfortable with being in the limelight (the AFL founder and Chiefs chairman Lamar Hunt recalled being "horrified" the first time he saw his name in the newspaper). George Steinbrenner had no such qualms. He was a new breed of owner, as patriarchal as his predecessors but possessed of a sense that owners had as much right to be a celebrity as the stars they signed to rich contracts.

On November 29, 1976, the Yankees held a press conference at the Americana Hotel to introduce Jackson as the newest Yankee, whom they'd signed to a five-year, $3 million contract.

Steinbrenner's wooing of Jackson would lead to a new phase, not only in sports economics but also in sports coverage. The highly combustible Yankees team offered a case study in interpersonal dynamics, and New York City's voracious tabloids were happy to devote back-page headlines to every bruised ego, player fine and owner outburst. The team leaders were the the fiery (and possibly alcoholic) manager Billy Martin and the Yankees' irascible team captain Thurman Munson. Neither man got along well with either Jackson or Steinbrenner, two men accustomed to having the largest ego in the room.

The spring training camps in baseball had typically been mostly sleepy and relaxed settings, but the explosion in money and media altered expectations. Even before the Yankees got to New York, two players had been fined for sleeping through one of Steinbrenner's bombastic clubhouse talks, and outfielder Mickey Rivers was fined for missing an exhibition game in Syracuse.

While in Fort Lauderdale, Jackson sat for an interview with Robert Ward, writing for the June issue of *Sport* magazine. When it hit the newsstands on May 23, Jackson's honeymoon period was officially over. "I'm the straw that stirs the drink," proclaimed Jackson in the story. "Munson thinks he can be the straw that stirs the drink, but he can only stir it bad."

In asserting his own leadership skills, Jackson seemed to have completely misread the Yankees' locker room. After the story came out, Munson stopped speaking to him, and both Mickey Rivers and Carlos May moved their lockers away from Jackson's. Someone else left an anonymous message in his locker, advising Jackson to "Suck my ass."

The moment that crystallized the season occurred on an NBC Game of the Week in Boston in June, when Jackson misplayed a fly ball, and Billy Martin subbed him out *during the inning*, sending Paul Blair onto the field in his place.

This most public of humiliations—magnified exponentially by the fact that it occurred on a nationally televised game—understandably made Jackson furious, and by the time he reached the Yankees' dugout, through an avalanche of catcalls from the Fenway Park crowd, he was furious, as was his manager.

"What the *fuck* do you think you're doing out there?!" raged Martin. "Anyone who doesn't hustle doesn't play for me."

Jackson insisted he wasn't loafing, then added, "You never wanted me on this team in the first place. You don't want me now. Why don't you just admit it?"

The scene and its aftermath only left Jackson further aggrieved.

"It makes me cry the way they treat me on this team," said Jackson. "I'm a big black man with an IQ of 160, making $700,000 a year, and they treat me like dirt."

All of the eternal verities of sport that every team tried to observe—unity, sacrifice for the greater good, lack of ego, coherent purpose—were gone from the Yankees' team dynamic. Yet they kept winning. Under Steinbrenner, the team had enough money and enough cushion to survive the internal strife and win their division again. If it meant that Munson, hitting behind Jackson in the order, refused to shake his teammate's hand after Reggie's homer, so be it.

Of course, there had been fractious champions before. The A's of Jackson's era bickered but, in the end, always came together in opposition of the owner Finley. With the Yankees, there was no unity, only enmity. One got the impression that the twenty-five men who were living out millions of fans' childhood dreams were having an awful time in the process.

Coming on the heels of a horrific span of time for New York City—this was the overheated summer of the Son of Sam killings and the blackout that plagued the city—there was something almost inspiring about a bickering Yankees team, regardless of how charmless or strife-ridden it was, rising to the top. That '77 Yankees campaign came in the same year that the city, however bruised, however squalid Times Square had become, was beginning to get a renewed sense of itself. The graphic designer Milton Glaser introduced the I♥NY logo, soon to become an icon.

Jackson's first season in New York had been a colossal miscalculation, his ego ripped bare. Yet there were the Yankees, back in the World Series again (having edged the Kansas City Royals in a second straight gripping AL Championship Series that again came down to the last inning of the fifth and deciding game).

Alienated from many of his teammates, Jackson responded with a 1977 World Series performance for the ages. Seemingly impervious to both the criticism and the pressure, rising to the occasion, Jackson gave New Yorkers a sense of their own resilience. (Within three years, Frank Sinatra's "New York, New York" would start playing after every Yankee win.)

In the clinching Game 6 against the Dodgers, Jackson hit three home runs on the first pitch from three different pitchers to lead the Yankees to their first world title in fifteen seasons.

The third home run—a 450-foot shot beyond the monuments in center field at Yankee Stadium—was accompanied by Jackson doing something that Henry Aaron would never have considered doing: standing at home plate for an interminable few seconds after the ball was hit, admiring his handi-work and the cacophonous din of the Yankee Stadium crowd that greeted it. To Aaron, such an act would be disrespecting his opponent and the game; to Jackson, the long look was simply an act of self-expression, Reggie being Reggie.

"He's answered the whole world," exclaimed a giddy Howard Cosell, call-ing the game for ABC. "What a colossal blow! What are they all thinking now? After all the furor, after all the hassling, it came down to this."

With the Series in the bag and nothing but the record books to chase, nearly everyone in Yankee Stadium—even those who purported to dislike Jackson—were chanting "REG-GIE! REG-GIE! REG-GIE!"

By the end of the game, the crowd was feral. When Mike Torrez caught the pop-up to end the game, Jackson—by this point wearing a batting helmet in the outfield—sprinted from right field toward the dugout, evading the riot of onrushing fans who invaded the field by the thousands, even knocking two or three over during his urgent dash to safety.

That off-season, the millionaire Jackson finally got his wish, as the Reg-gie! bar was brought to market. On Opening Day 1978, everyone in sold-out Yankee Stadium got a free Reggie! bar, and when Jackson homered during the game, the crowd celebrated by throwing thousands of the candy bars onto the field.

The Reggie! bar was not quite the hit Jackson hoped it would be, and was soon off the market.

Catfish Hunter, who didn't seem to like Jackson any more in New York than he had in Oakland, remarked that, "When you unwrap a Reggie! bar, it tells you how good it is."

•

The changes that Peter Seitz enacted—for which the owners fired him immediately—would resonate across the world of sports.

In baseball, genuine free agency would cause an explosion in salaries, which rose from an average of $51,500 in 1976 to $149,000 only five years later.

The patriarchal system that had prevailed for the entirety of spectator sports was changing with alarming speed.

What wouldn't change is that players, coaches and owners alike were striving for a kind of cohesion. Free agency didn't make this impossible, but it made it more difficult.

At the same time, the Ralph Winter piece in the *Yale Law Review* provided the leagues with some solid ground on which to proceed. But what that meant, in the end, was that the owners would have to confront the players across the bargaining table in something resembling good faith.

It was a new world, and the baseball players had no doubt about who was most responsible for making it happen.

"All of that labor unrest—the challenge to the reserve clause—all that was what was going on in our society at the end of the Vietnam War," said Phil Garner, who'd come up to the majors with the chaotic A's of the mid '70s. "It was where people were challenging the norm, the whole reserve clause idea was going to be challenged. And the players were right to challenge it. But you know, as the younger folks in America were rising up to challenge authorities and question what everybody was doing, we were doing that at the same time in baseball. And we had the perfect leader in Marvin Miller, who was a brilliant tactician, strategically talking about what we were going to do in labor negotiations, and he was brilliant with handling the players in the way he educated the players on everything. And so it was the time, it was a good time."

# FOURTEEN

# THE LAST OF THE FIRSTS

GROWING UP IN Jackson, Michigan, Tony Dungy played quarterback in high school while his father, Wilbur, a science professor, was working on his PhD at Michigan State. Wilbur was part of a long line of African American strivers who after the Great Migration out of the Jim Crow South found a new life and less onerous racism in the North. Wilbur Dungy rooted for the Cleveland Browns because they were the first pro football team to integrate after World War II. The Dungys watched Black quarterbacks with keen interest, noting how African Americans like Jimmy Raye at Michigan State, Sandy Stephens at Minnesota, and Jimmy Jones at USC excelled in major-college football.

There was by then a mystique around the position that hadn't always been there. More than anything, it was the work of John Unitas and Bart Starr, later updated with the examples from the American Football League, like Joe Namath and Len Dawson. But as Tony Dungy matured, he soon confronted a painful, inexplicable truth.

"I saw Jimmy Raye move Michigan State to a national championship, and I'm very cognizant of that," said Dungy. "And then I'm watching on Sundays, and then *Monday Night Football* comes in and I'm watching on Monday night. And all these guys that I've seen play in college, I don't see them play in the NFL. And when you're younger, you think, 'Well, it's a different game.' Then as you get a little older, you start to think, 'Why?' I'm like, 'Okay, what happened to Jimmy Raye? What happened to Chuck Ealey?' He never lost a game in college, and he had to go to Canada. Why is he not playing?"

On the recruiting trail, Dungy heard tales from Black players who came to a college expecting to be quarterbacks, only to wind up being moved to defensive back or wide receiver. He was warned at multiple schools to get an ironclad guarantee that he would be able to play quarterback.

Dungy matriculated to the University of Minnesota (where Sandy Stephens had been the first Black quarterback to win a major-college national title in 1960). By his sophomore year, when Dungy won the starting job, a majority of the starting quarterbacks in the Big Ten were African American, including at the two football powerhouses, with Dennis Franklin at Michigan and Cornelius Greene at Ohio State.

By then, Dungy had become acutely aware of the long-entrenched double standards that were attached to the position.

"If you are a white quarterback, okay, we could look at leadership and we could look at different things and we could look at your ability to improvise, if you didn't have everything else perfect," said Dungy. "But if you were a black quarterback, and you're a good athlete, and you can improvise and you do things—well, then you could play another position."

During Dungy's sophomore year at Minnesota, 1974, there were indications—at the most important position—that pro football was finally veering uneasily toward the meritocracy it had long claimed to be.

The Pittsburgh Steelers were coming off two playoff appearances when, during the strike-marred 1974 training camp and preseason, it became clear that Terry Bradshaw (the blond-haired, blue-eyed first overall selection in the 1970 draft) was being outplayed by Joe Gilliam (who'd played for his father at Tennessee State, and had been the two hundred seventy-third selection in the 1972 draft).

It was unthinkable to some that a highly paid, highly coveted blue-chip player like Bradshaw, who'd been on the cover of *Newsweek* his rookie season, could lose his starting job to a little-known Black quarterback from an HBCU in the exhibition season. But Chuck Noll, who played on an integrated team in a sandlot league while growing up in Cleveland, was perhaps as close to color-blind as a white pro football coach could be in the '70s. When he named Gilliam the starter a week before the season, it reverberated through the team and the city.

"The black guys were elated," said the Steelers' cornerback J. T. Thomas. "That was a year that there was a lot of racial tension in the city here. The world is going upside-down. So you look at that role again: The head coach

and the quarterback have a father-son relationship. Suddenly, you know—
*Chuck Noll got a black child.*"

Across the country, in Los Angeles, the Grambling alum James "Shack"
Harris—whom Eddie Robinson had groomed to be Grambling's first quarterback to go on to NFL success—finally got his chance by earning a starting job with head coach Chuck Knox and the Los Angeles Rams. He'd been
released by the Buffalo Bills at the beginning of the 1972 season, but the
Rams' scout (and fellow Grambling grad) Tank Younger had made the case
that Harris deserved a shot. In 1973, Harris served as the backup to NFC
Player of the Year John Hadl, who led the Rams to a 12–2 record.

When the veterans finally got to training camp in 1974, Harris was calling
Robinson frequently. "I wrote him a letter telling him what he needed to do,"
remembered Robinson. "He needed to be the first one to practice and be the
last one to leave. He had to practice hard and run all the plays with fire. I told
him to study all the other quarterbacks…James had to stop worrying that
he was not going to be the starter and just practice like he was the starter."

Five games into the 1974 season, the Rams dealt the thirty-four-year-old
Hadl to Green Bay for a bounty of draft picks, securing the position for Harris. "At the time, I was trying to figure out how I fit in," recalled Harris. "Then
Chuck gave me the news—I'm thinking, *does he know I'm black?*" Harris
would become the clear-cut leader on the team. His Rams teammate Harold Jackson had recognized the innate confidence from the moment Harris
arrived. "At Grambling, there must have been a course in bullshitting," said
Jackson. "They all took it." By the end of the '74 season he had established the
trust of the entire team.

"James Harris clearly stepped up in terms of his ability to execute and
to command real respect in the huddle," said the Rams' all-pro guard Tom
Mack. "And that confidence translated to everybody feeling like, Hey, this is
right. We've got the right people, and we've got the right team. We can make
this play."

The 1974 season found Harris leading the Rams to a second straight division title, a first-round playoff win over Washington, and then agonizingly
close to a Super Bowl trip, only to fall 14–10 to the Minnesota Vikings in the
NFC Championship Game.

•

While Harris was leading the Rams to a division title—and the cursed Gilliam was succumbing to a drug addiction that cost him the starting quarterback job on a team that was Super Bowl–bound—Eddie Robinson was witnessing the price of progress.

The syndicated Grambling highlights show, a staple on American television Sunday mornings, began losing advertisers and then affiliates, and ended after four seasons, hurt in part by the advent of live NFL pregame shows that started crowding out recorded football programs like the Notre Dame and Grambling tape-delayed replays.

By now the Grambling name was known nationwide. When the Tigers played in the Astrodome against Texas Southern in 1973, they were greeted by the third largest crowd in Astrodome history, 53,859, trailing only Billy Graham's 1965 religious crusade and Sandy Koufax's last regular-season game in 1966. In 1975, Grambling faced Southern U. in the second Bayou Classic, the first to be played in New Orleans' just-opened Superdome. A crowd of 73,214 showed up to watch Grambling prevail on the Saturday after Thanksgiving, 33–17.

The challenge for Grambling was no longer the box office but instead recruiting. As segregation ended at Southern football powers like Texas and Alabama and LSU and Arkansas, more blue-chip high school prospects were going to major state schools in the Deep South. Times were changing: In Alabama, George Wallace crowned a Black homecoming queen for the Crimson Tide in 1973, and the next year, 600 Black students matriculated to the university.

Eddie Robinson had no illusions about the importance of recruiting, which he recognized as the lifeblood of college football success. "When a coach thinks he's the reason his team is winning, I think he's silly," he said. "I think you could take the best pro coach in the country and put him at a college with inferior material, and he wouldn't win."

Even as more blue-chip prospects went to large state colleges in the Southeastern and Southwest conferences, Robinson conceded nothing. For his assistant and recruiting coordinator Jerry Hardaway, Robinson's mantra was clear.

"We saw the pace, he knew things were changed," said Hardaway. "But Coach Rob said, 'We will not be denied, we will not be defeated, we will not be outworked, we will not lose our morals, we will not lose our sense of pride.' If LSU wanted a player, we were still going to give it a shot."

Robinson would remain a father figure and a mentor to another generation of young Black student-athletes, but fewer *elite* young Black student athletes.

In 1974, Robinson insisted that his assistant, Doug Porter—whose region included Texas—make a pitch to the top-rated running back in the state. So Porter made dozens of trips to Tyler, Texas. He would go to the small clapboard house where the young running back Earl Campbell lived. Campbell was, even in 1974, a remarkable physical anomaly, running with an intimidating ferocity, combining strength and speed in a way that was nearly unprecedented.

He was being recruited everywhere, but Darrell Royal—fighting hard against the notion that the University of Texas wasn't a comfortable landing spot for Blacks—was pushing hardest of all, with alumni like Frank Erwin and Tex Moncrief urging Royal to make sure he didn't lose this prospect to Oklahoma—a dismayingly regular occurrence over recent years—or anyone else.

On a trip to Tyler in January 1974, Porter pulled up to see a late-model sports car parked in front of the Campbell house. Earl's mother, Ann Campbell, was waiting on the front porch for the Grambling assistant.

"Mr. Porter, I appreciate you coming," she said. "But you don't need to come here no more." Earl Campbell had decided to become a Longhorn.

On that day, Porter got back in his car and drove the 160 miles back to Grambling. It was hard news to give to Coach Robinson, but both men recognized it as a sign of the times.

There was nothing particularly outrageous about Campbell's recruitment; it was similar to that of hundreds of other blue-chip high school prospects in the '70s. While there were a handful of stories about "bag man" assistants who would hand out cash, most recruiting was by the '70s more subtle and sophisticated. At many schools, recruiters and alumni developed an apparatus designed to sidestep the most blatant recruiting practices of the past and avoid the oversight of the NCAA. When Darrell Royal said that UT didn't pay its players and didn't violate any recruiting rules, he was almost certainly telling the truth as he knew it.

But even beyond that, there were agents acting on behalf of universities, nearby bankers who might give loans without collateral to the *parent* of a player, in a way that had no official connection to the university.

"Texas did not buy me," said Campbell later. "Blacks are through selling themselves...or at least I'm not going to sell myself...Texas offered me everything legal, and there was none of this stupid talk of cars and money."

What was clearly true was that the sort of players that Eddie Robinson had been able to court throughout the '60s—those players denied opportunities at large Southern football powers—were now being actively recruited by those same schools, almost all of which had more resources, directly and indirectly, to persuade players to come there.

"It would be real hard for me to tell a boy, living in a shotgun house with five sleeping in one room, to turn down a new house, a car, a better job for his daddy," Robinson said. "I know it's wrong, but it's hard for a man to walk in another man's shoes."

That was only part of it. In an American culture in which integration was becoming more common, many young African American prospects were choosing to venture out onto larger and more prominent campuses.

"I think what had changed the most was integration," said Ron Wolf, the superb personnel evaluator who scouted for the Raiders for much of the decade. "Suddenly, those great players who had been at the predominantly black schools were now at like Alabama. Earl Campbell was at Texas, Ozzie Newsome was at Alabama, Kellen Winslow was at Missouri. You still had a Jackie Slater at Jackson State, Walter Payton and Robert Brazile, but that was right at the turn. Suddenly Ray Donaldson is at Georgia, and Joe Cribbs is at Auburn, Otis Wilson is at Louisville. That was a big change."

All was not lost. On the same day that Earl Campbell signed his national letter of intent to go to Texas, Eddie Robinson did get a blue-chip prospect he wanted. He was a remarkably poised quarterback named Doug Williams, a harbinger of the future of the sport.

•

Meanwhile, the problem of perception was not confined to football, or even to the field of play. Major League Baseball had been in existence for ninety-nine years, and had been integrated for twenty-eight years before a Black man was hired to manage a major league club. When Jackie Robinson threw out the first pitch before Game 2 of the 1972 World Series, he ended his speech by saying how pleased he would be to see a Black man finally hired as a major league manager. By then, the excuses about why such obviously qualified candidates as Bill White, Buck O'Neill, Billy Williams, Elston Howard and Larry Doby couldn't get a job were legion.

Then there were the gallantly patronizing attitudes on the part of the owners. The Cubs' owner, Philip Wrigley, after rehiring Leo Durocher in 1972, was asked about Ernie Banks managing one day.

"Ernie has such a beautiful reputation in baseball, it would be a shame to ruin it by making him a manager," Wrigley said. "Managing is a dirty job. It doesn't last long, and it certainly isn't anything I'd wish on Banks."

The excuses grew ever more elaborate and mystifying.

"There are many blacks qualified in this business," said the Pirates' slugger Willie Stargell in 1973. "All we have to do is hire them! I've always wondered: is it color they hate? Is it a social standard where if you're not part of a group, then you're an outcast? I talk about race more than I used to. My feelings are seeping out little by little. I used to be so upset that I kept it all inside."

After Dick Williams left the two-time World Champion Oakland A's following the 1974 season, Reggie Jackson was hoping that the A's iconoclastic owner Charlie Finley would hire Frank Robinson to be the A's new manager. Jackson had played for Robinson in winter ball in Puerto Rico and believed that the two-time MVP would make an excellent manager. "Frank was from Oakland," Jackson reasoned. "It's a black town, and he's a hero there. Finley does things others don't do. He likes to shake up the establishment. I would have thought he'd have loved to have been a pioneer, the first man to get himself a black manager. But he didn't. He blew the best chance he'll ever have to erase all the harm he's done."

It was Frank Robinson, in 1975, who got the opportunity. Rather than being tabbed to run a perennial contender like the A's, the job he was offered was with the Cleveland Indians, who'd gone through a decade and a half without so much as a second place finish. It was a major league job, and another big step, but observers couldn't help but notice that, without sufficient investment or front-office vision, Robinson was taking over an inferior team, outgunned in its own division, in a job that many managers viewed as a career-killer.

The press assembled for his first spring training game with the Indians, and Robinson was asked what he was thinking of when he filled out his first lineup card.

"I was thinking, 'Hey, this is it—now it's official,'" he said. "And I thought about Jackie Robinson, and the many people, both black and white, who helped me in my lifetime, who made this thing happen. That's all."

Robinson had come to the Indians late in the 1974 season as a designated hitter, and noticed the segregation on the bench, with the white players grouped around manager Ken Aspromonte while the Black players gathered by coach Larry Doby.

In the midst of his first spring training as manager, Robinson would tangle with two of his best pitchers, Gaylord Perry and his younger brother Jim Perry. They had grown up in rural North Carolina and seemed to blanche at the idea of taking orders from Robinson.

Early in spring training, Gaylord Perry objected to the Indians' new conditioning program. "I'm nobody's slave," said Perry. "The way this place is run is really chickenshit."

When Opening Day came, African American players accounted for more than a quarter of all major leaguers, a record. And the thirty-eight-year-old Robinson, given the title of player-manager (and a $200,000 salary), wrote his name into the lineup on Opening Day, one year to the day after Aaron broke Ruth's home run record. The Indians, sporting their new all-maroon uniforms, beat the Yankees, 5–3, with Robinson homering in his first at-bat.

It would wind up being the highlight of his season.

Over the course of his first season, Robinson was greeted with the customary assortment of hate mail and death threats that prominent Black athletes endured during the era.

He wound up trading both Perry brothers during the season. "I was disappointed that Gaylord never tried to make my job easier," Robinson wrote in his diary of the season. "He never came to ask me if there was anything he could do. Instead of helping, Gaylord seemed to go out of his way to make little comments, always negative comments."

But by the end of the 1975 season, when the Indians closed strong, winning twenty-seven of their last forty-two games, Robinson was just glad that the focus was on his performance and not his race. "It's nice to come into a town," he said, "and be referred to as the manager of the Cleveland Indians instead of as the first black manager."

•

The same week Robinson was breaking a color barrier for baseball managers, the golfer Lee Elder was doing the same at the Masters in Augusta, Georgia.

Up until 1961, the Professional Golfers Association was, according to its bylaws, open only "for members of the caucasian race." The clause banning Black players was changed only after a legal challenge from the California state attorney general Stanley Mosk, on behalf of golfer Charlie Sifford. Sifford had dominated on the Blacks-only United Golf Association tour, but didn't earn a PGA card until Mosk's challenge, which prompted the PGA to drop its whites-only clause in November 1961. When that segregationist precept was struck down, there were still only a scant handful of African Americans who had earned their PGA touring card. Sifford, already in his forties, won the Greater Hartford Open in 1967 and the Los Angeles Open in 1969, but never got an invite to the Masters.

Sifford was joined on the PGA tour in 1968 by the thirty-four-year-old Lee Elder. Elder had grown up around Dallas, one of ten children, and caddied at an all-white club in the area before moving to Los Angeles to live with an aunt after both his parents died. After two years of military service, Elder wound up making a name for himself on the United Golf Association tour, winning eighteen of twenty-two tournaments at one point.

It wasn't until 1971 that the Masters announced that any player who won a PGA tour event would automatically earn an invitation to Augusta. On April 21, 1974, Elder won the Monsanto Open in Pensacola and, in so doing, earned an automatic qualification for the Masters tournament, becoming the first Black golfer to do so. After his Pensacola win, the next eleven and a half months were a long buildup to the historic occasion at Augusta. Elder was honored with a testimonial dinner in Washington, DC, which had earlier offered him a key to the city. He played a round with President Gerald Ford. Elder received hate mail in much the same vein that Henry Aaron had received, virtually all of it unsigned.

He teed off on April 10, 1975, two days after Frank Robinson's opening day homer in Cleveland. By that time, Elder had answered thousands of questions about how it felt to integrate the most exclusive—and whitest—golf tournament in the world.

He would shoot 74 and 78 and wind up missing the cut, but when he was walking toward the eighteenth green to finish his second round, he was greeted with an impromptu reception.

"Most of the staff was black, and on Friday, they left their duties to line the eighteenth fairway as I walked toward the green," Elder remembered. "I couldn't hold back the tears. Of all the acknowledgments of what I had accomplished by getting there, this one meant the most."

•

Back at Grambling, Eddie Robinson consoled himself on the loss of Earl Campbell to Texas with the recognition that he had recruited one of the best quarterback prospects in the nation. At a time when the prototype of the pro quarterback was six-foot-four, 220 pounds, with a strong arm and superior smarts, Doug Williams from Zachary, Louisiana, checked all the boxes.

It was not a difficult recruiting job. Williams' older brother had played a few years earlier on the Grambling baseball team. "We always felt pretty good about getting Doug," said Doug Porter. Raised on visits to campus and the Sunday morning televised game replays, Doug Williams had no doubt where he was going to school. "The only thing I knew was Grambling, and I saw them every Sunday morning," he said.

At Grambling, Williams worked for endless hours on his footwork. There was a key play in the Grambling playbook—26 Counter—that required a particularly deft pirouette by the quarterback, who had to spin and navigate his way around a pulling guard, a fullback and tailback both charging forward, and a wingback running by underneath him. Williams would soon master that task of agility and so much more about the Grambling offense. He started as a freshman, and by the time he was a junior he'd been made Black College Player of the Year. Scouts were coming around; the word was out.

Williams, scheduled to graduate ahead of his class, was working on his accelerated education degree when he got a call from Grambling's indefatigable publicity man Collie Nicholson in the summer of 1977, prior to Williams' senior year.

Nicholson was succinct, telling Williams, "I'm going to put you up for the Heisman." That was it.

"Collie did what he wanted to do," recalled Williams. "He never sat down with me."

Nicholson, a unique mix of scholar, scribe and carnival barker, staged a full-court press, leaning hard into Williams' substantial career accomplishments, and also stressing his obvious status as a prime pro prospect. The campaign for the Heisman was probably always going to be a quixotic effort. Only one Grambling game was telecast in 1977, the Grambling–Southern game, which showed on five total stations in and around Louisiana, as a regional alternative to the Army–Navy game (which aired on 222 stations across the country) on November 26. Yet Williams earned plenty of publicity and finished fourth in the Heisman voting, the highest-ever finish for a player from a historically Black college, behind Earl Campbell, Oklahoma State's Terry Miller and Notre Dame's Ken McAfee. Williams also was named the first-team Associated Press All-American quarterback, unprecedented for an HBCU player at that glamour position.

While Williams was excelling at Grambling, his predecessor James Harris was facing the challenges and pressures of being the lone Black starting quarterback in pro football, and doing so in the fickle, football-mad metropolis of Los Angeles, for the mercurial Rams owner Carroll Rosenbloom.

In a city always looking for the Next Big Thing, Harris had prevailed over Hadl in 1974, but found himself, in an injury-plagued season, competing with the popular young upstart Ron Jaworski in 1975, and then both Jaworski and Pat Haden in 1976.

The Rams' coach Chuck Knox would recall attending one of Rosenbloom's dinner parties with his wife, Shirley, at Rosenbloom's estate in Bel Air after the 1975 season. "I think maybe Jonathan Winters and Ricardo Montalban were there," said Knox. "We all gathered in C.R.'s living room. With this spark in his eye, he said, 'Let's play a game. Let's vote on who we want for president this year, and then, just for fun, we'll vote on who we want for Rams quarterback.' So he passed around these little pieces of paper and everybody voted. Shirley and I were the only ones who voted for James Harris." It was that kind of town; it was that kind of team. Before the 1977 season, the Rams dealt Harris to San Diego.

But James "Shack" Harris still found his way back to the Grambling campus a few times a year, and offered Doug Williams encouragement. Talking one day after a practice, he reminded him, "Hey, Doug—they not going to change the field at all. It's still 100 yards long and 50-some yards wide in the NFL. If you can do it at Grambling, you can do it anywhere."

Among the visitors to Grambling's campus ahead of the 1978 draft was Joe Gibbs, offensive coordinator for Tampa Bay head coach John McKay. Gibbs didn't ask to work out Williams; instead, he spent two days sitting in the back of the classroom, watching Williams student-teaching at Shack Harris' old high school, Carroll High School. Gibbs' scouting report noted that Williams possessed "a big-time arm with perfect passing mechanics" and was "a natural leader" who was "very academic and extremely prepared."

In the 1978 NFL draft, Earl Campbell was selected first by the Houston Oilers. But later in the first round, Eddie Robinson's dream came true. With the seventeenth pick in the draft, the Tampa Bay Buccaneers took Doug Williams.

Nearly a decade had passed since Robinson had to fight every step of the way to convince the pros to take a chance on Shack Harris, rebuffing scouts and coaches who would idly speculate that Harris might *really* be good at some other position. With Doug Williams, those discussions didn't occur. And the fact of his selection midway through the first round was a definite sign of progress. By 1978, most pro scouts and coaches had come around to the notion that a successful quarterback could be Black.

And yet, the rest of the 1978 draft also told another story. In the second round, Matt Cavanaugh of Pitt and Guy Benjamin of Stanford were drafted; in the third it was Bowling Green's Mark Miller and BYU's Gifford Nielsen; Missouri's Pete Woods and Maryland's Mark Manges went in the fourth round; USC's part-time starter Rob Hertel in the fifth, small-college prospect Mike Rieker from Lehigh to New Orleans in the sixth round, Arizona State's Dennis Sproul in the eighth round and then, reaching deeper into the barrel of low-upside prospects, Utah State's Keith Myers and Santa Clara's John Hurley in the ninth round; Tennessee's Pat Ryan in the eleventh round. With the penultimate selection in the draft, choice number 333, the Miami

Dolphins selected future journeyman pro Bill Kenney, who would spend all or part of seven years as an NFL starter.

But conspicuously absent was the Black quarterback who had just led the University of Washington to its first Rose Bowl berth in seventeen years, then upset 10–1 Michigan on New Year's Day, while being named the Most Outstanding Player of the 1978 Rose Bowl.

He was Warren Moon. Six-foot-three, 218 pounds, Moon had been the Pac 8 player of the year. His agent was Leigh Steinberg, whom Moon hired in part because it was clear to him that Steinberg would work just as hard for him as he had for the top overall pick Steve Bartkowski.

"He threw a great ball," said Carl Peterson, then pro personnel director for the Philadelphia Eagles. And yet for 334 selections he went unselected. Informed that spring that he likely wouldn't be drafted in the first three rounds, Moon had already signed with the Edmonton Eskimos of the Canadian Football League. But significantly, not a single team in the NFL expended even a twelfth-round choice to reserve his future rights.

By then, Tony Dungy had already been passed over by every NFL team, eventually switching positions and playing with the Pittsburgh Steelers as a defensive back. But he still recalled Moon outdueling him at quarterback during a Washington–Minnesota game in 1976. "We played against each other, and they beat us," said Dungy. "And I'm saying, 'Man, this guy's *really* good.' The next year, he's the MVP of the league, MVP of the Rose Bowl. You can't tell me people didn't know who this guy was. And you couldn't watch him throw and see what type of arm that he had and the skill set that he had? I mean, I saw that from across the field, one game."

Shack Harris agreed: "It's not like, you know, Warren was hard to *evaluate.*"

Moon was not a classic drop-back passer, running ninety-nine times during the season and scoring six touchdowns, while passing for eleven touchdowns. He was more elusive than Williams, with plenty of strength, though not the surface-to-air missile that Williams possessed. But scouts fretted about the system, remarking that Moon had played as a rollout quarterback in college. "To me, that sounded like code for 'We're not ready to start a black quarterback,'" said Moon.

Steinberg, nearly alone, saw the upside. If Moon was as good a quarterback as both Moon and Steinberg thought, he'd prove himself in the CFL and come to the NFL in a few years as a prized free agent.

•

Even in the midst of the progress in the '70s, the issue (and awareness) of race in sports was omnipresent.

"There was so much chatter about it becoming a black league," recalled Spencer Haywood. "And we black players didn't help the matter. We weren't refined. It was like, big fur coats, big fur hats. It was like *Superfly* in the NBA."

As one NBA official put it, in trying to summarize the league's marketing challenges, "It's race, pure and simple. No major sports comes up against it the way we do. It's just difficult to get a lot of people to watch huge, intelligent, millionaire black people on television."

The race question was particularly acute in the NBA, where two-thirds of the players were African American. This made the NBA the most progressive league, but that was not a feature that was easily marketed, and the league's general counsel, David Stern, working behind the scenes, kept pushing for the league to broaden its marketing footprint.

"One of David's great pushes was, 'we've got to be out in the marketplace better,'" remembered Russ Granik. "But we were met, very often, with companies that said, 'Well, we'll send our special-markets person'"—industry euphemism for the urban or black markets—"'to come talk to you.' It wasn't like you could do anything about it."

And CBS continued to treat the NBA as a second-class citizen. In 1976, when the Phoenix Suns met the Celtics in the NBA Finals, Game 3 of that series—the first NBA Finals game ever played in Phoenix—had to begin at ten-thirty a.m. local time, because CBS wanted the brunt of the afternoon to broadcast its third-round coverage of Jack Nicklaus' Memorial Tournament from Columbus.

The 1977 NBA Finals suffered a similar fate, as CBS cut away almost instantly after the Blazers clinched their first league title, to show the Kemper Open. On April 9, 1978, as John Havlicek was playing his last game as a Boston Celtic, CBS left the Celtics–Buffalo Braves game with three minutes remaining to begin coverage of the final round of the Masters on time.

Even the moments of brilliance could be misread. On the final Sunday of that same '77–'78 regular season, the Nuggets' David Thompson poured in 73 points in a valiant bid to overtake George Gervin for the scoring title, only to see Gervin drain 63 points that evening to finish on top. Neither game had playoff implications, yet the image of two players striving for personal glory—perhaps at the expense of the overall good of the team—affected the perceptions of the league.

From one perspective, the 1970s in sports was a long experience of whites—fans, coaches, administrators, athletes—slowly beginning to reach a dim understanding of the difficulties and double standards of the Black experience. Which wasn't the same as solving those problems. Bill Bradley, examining the racial divide in his memoir *Life on the Run,* shared the distance that he'd traveled in the preceding decade: "Generalities about race become unacceptable against the diversity of human traits. And yet I have changed in some ways because of my black friends. It is hard to say exactly how but after witnessing their joys, fears, perceptions, and spontaneous reactions for seven years I am different. I regard authority a little more skeptically than I once did. I am more interested in experiencing life than in analyzing it…But, above all, I see how much I don't know and can never know about black people."

There were gains, but they couldn't mask the larger inequities that remained. For every milestone, there was an asterisk, for every achievement there was a caveat.

The trends in the country were depressingly well known. By 1977, 9 percent of whites and 22 percent of Hispanics lived below the poverty line, but for Blacks—in spite of all the efforts of LBJ's Great Society—the worrying percentage was 31 percent. "We are on the bottom," said the academic Harry Edwards. "If America falls, it will fall on us."

Many of the Black athletes who were stars in the '70s still sensed a double standard. "I'm a black man," said Otis Taylor in 1971. "I can't talk, I can't express myself, I can't do anything." Noting his lack of endorsement opportunities, Taylor added, "I haven't done a dog food commercial, and that's pretty sorry for a guy who'd be so happy to do one he'd eat the dog food."

Bob Gibson noted his lack of endorsement opportunities in St. Louis. Willie Stargell, though popular and beloved in Pittsburgh, and among the most respected players in the game, still sensed the delineation.

"Even today I'm made to feel sensitive about my color," he said. "I don't get television commercials like the white players, although I use the same products they do. The front office has never talked to me about a job with the club when I retire. I watch management favor white players on the team." ("Willie is as good a person as I've ever known," said his manager, Bill Virdon. "He is whiter than most whites. That's just a figure of speech, because I don't think of black and white.")

In regards to commercials, Taylor, Gibson and Stargell were certainly right—that race was a key factor in endorsements was a given by the mid-'70s, to such an extent that some players took it as a simple fact of life.

"Look, if you owned Swanson's Pizza, would you want a black guy to do the commercial on TV for you?" asked the Reds' Pete Rose. "Would you like the black guy to pick up the pizza and bite into it? Or would you want Pete Rose?"

Though Rose's view of things was certainly endorsed by a part of America, there was also another, more complicated, truth. Hertz's campaign with O. J. Simpson was by then in its second, highly successful year, and Simpson had become a commercial powerhouse to rival even Jack Nicklaus.

In January 1977, the eight-part ABC series *Roots* premiered, turning Alex Haley's forefather, Kunta Kinte, into a cultural touchstone. It was a Nielsen hit that would have been unthinkable even a decade earlier, with 130 million Americans—a clear majority of the country—watching at least some part of the miniseries. Haley's book sold 900,000 copies in the space of a month. In one of the supporting roles, there was Simpson in a cameo as the character Kadi Touray, running down Levar Burton's Kunta Kinte.

By that point, Simpson was making as much from Hertz as he was from the Buffalo Bills. Asked to explain the appeal of the campaign, he was—in his own way—as matter-of-fact as Rose: "People identify with me and I don't think I'm that offensive to anyone," he said. "People have told me I'm colorless. Everyone likes me. I stay out of politics, I don't try to save people for the Lord and, besides, I don't look that out of character in a suit."

By 1976, he had signed a $1 million contract with Treesweet orange juice, had his own line of Juicemobile shoes for Hyde Spot-Bilt, was the spokesman for Dingo boots, and had lined up a major movie role in the film *Capricorn One*.

•

All of that was the context for September 13, 1977, and comedian Richard Pryor's visionary, if short-lived, network variety series *The Richard Pryor Show*.

One sketch featured a press conference with Pryor playing the part of the nation's first African American president. A reporter from *Ebony* (played by Tim Reid, who would later star in *WKRP in Cincinnati*), asked, "About blacks in the labor force, I want to know what you gonna do about having more black brothers as quarterbacks in the National Football Honky League?"

Pryor's president sketched out a vision of the future laced with grievances from the present. "I plan not only to have lots of black quarterbacks," he said, "but we going to have black coaches, and black owners of teams. As long as there's gonna be football, gonna be some black in it somewhere, doin' something about it..."

Then, warming to the topic, Pryor's president continued, "'Cause I'm *tired* of this mess that's been goin' down, you know what I mean? Ever since the Rams got rid of James Harris, my jaw been uptight. You know what I'm talkin' 'bout? We gonna get down on the case now!"

In San Diego, Harris' teammates were ebullient, reporting the show to their new quarterback.

"I just really appreciated being part of the skit and that he was even aware of my journey," Harris said.

The journey for African Americans in sport would continue along the promising but rocky path. Doug Williams would have to prove himself over and over again, and would do so. Warren Moon would go to Canada, throw for more than 21,000 yards and win five Grey Cups before returning to the U.S. and a more interested NFL. Before his playing career ended, Dungy would see evidence that there might be room for African American head coaches in the NFL. In Major League Baseball, Dusty Baker—during a playing career that would span two decades—became convinced he had the right stuff to be a good manager.

By the end of the decade, despite all the barriers that remained, there was also a growing sense of potential and possibility. On October 2, 1978, *The Mike Douglas Show* featured entertainer Bob Hope and a young guest who would someday follow Lee Elder to Augusta and make it his own: a two-year-old golfing prodigy named Eldrick "Tiger" Woods.

# FIFTEEN

# GOING TO EXTREMES

By THE TIME they made their fourth Super Bowl trip of the decade—at the end of the 1977 season, for Super Bowl XII, the first that would end in prime time—the Dallas Cowboys had become as identifiable a national "brand" as McDonald's or Coca-Cola. With their sophisticated public relations and their keen use of image, they were—in the words of *Esquire* magazine—"football's richest and stuffiest team."

If Oakland's Raiders were the anti-heroes in black and silver (immortalized by NFL Films' Steve Sabol in his adaptation of Mary Jane Carr's poem "Pirate Wind") and the Pittsburgh Steelers the very reflection of hard-hat resilience of western Pennsylvania, then the Cowboys were an even more clearly defined entity. The team had become a shiny glass skyscraper, the consummate expression of sports superiority for the modern age.

Tom Landry, in his suit and fedora on the sidelines, striding the sun-bleached artificial turf at Texas Stadium, exuded corporate detachment. His quarterback, Roger Staubach, was a daring throwback, known as much for his All-American rectitude as his unscripted scrambling and late-game heroics.

If Paul Brown had treated football as an academic discipline, injecting it with intellectual rigor, Landry reimagined it as an engineering project, which relied on exact specifications (his Flex defense, his modern adaptation of the shotgun formation, endless analysis of opponents' tendencies) and personnel that would carry out the tasks with consistent precision. The Cowboys would miss the postseason only once between 1966 and 1983, and always seemed to be playing either on *Monday Night Football* or in the featured late game on CBS. Their success created the image, and team president Tex Schramm was an expert at burnishing it.

"Tex Schramm took care of the media in a way that I don't think anybody else ever has," said the announcer Verne Lundquist. "He understood how important television and written media could be in promoting his product." At a time when other teams relied on local newspapers and TV to convey their message, the Cowboys had an assured grasp of the media in the Dallas–Fort Worth area and beyond, and also their own newspaper, *The Dallas Cowboys Weekly*.

The image of sophistication was there in the team's uniforms, designed by Schramm a decade earlier to evoke the spacesuits of the Apollo astronauts. It was certainly there in the uniforms of the Dallas Cowboys Cheerleaders, who'd become a cultural phenomenon of their own, with a poster selling over a million copies in 1977 and a made-for-TV movie starring Jane Seymour and Bert Convy. In previous decades, teams sold tickets; by the late '70s, they were selling something more: an image, an experience, a sense of belonging.

•

Since the merger, the NFL draft—or the "Annual Selection Meeting," as it was officially known—had been a fairly simple undertaking, conducted in a hotel conference room a couple of weeks after the end of the Super Bowl. But in 1976, the draft was pushed back to the second week in April, giving coaching staffs nearly three more months to grade film, research, interview, test and scrutinize prospects.

Moving the draft back in the calendar coincided with the beginning of more nuanced forms of personnel evaluation. Aptitude tests like the Wonderlic became routine. The Giants and other teams began to increase the sophistication of psychological testing, employing tools like the Minnesota Multi-Phasic Inventory (MMPI). In this area as well, the Cowboys were viewed as leaders.

The Cowboys' computerized system used a standardized evaluation sheet, in which scouts, based on game films and interviews with coaches and other staff, would evaluate each player on a scale of 9 ("Exceptional Rare Ability") to 1 ("Poor") on the general traits of Character, Agility, Competitiveness, Mental Alertness, and Strength and Explosiveness. Gil Brandt presided over the Cowboys' scouting operation—even as his rivals on other teams insisted that he "never wrote a single scouting report." Brandt was the face of the

Cowboys on college campuses, connecting with coaches and assistants, bringing the NFL Properties catalog around to campuses and offering assistant coaches their choice of Cowboys' apparel.

The rest of the league resented the Cowboys' success and accompanying arrogance. And that was marked by jealousy and of course imitation.

"The whole time in Philadelphia," said Eagles' director of player personnel Carl Peterson, "we measured ourselves by where the Cowboys were, because they were the reigning champions. And each year, our goal was to try to get up to and hopefully eventually surpass the Dallas Cowboys."

The April draft offered further proof of Pete Rozelle's public relations mastery, because it led to yet another off-season news cycle around the sport. Other sports looked on enviously.

"Football was always ahead of us," said the basketball coach Frank Layden. "It was big; it was planned. Football was like, you're invading France every night."

•

There was another component to the Cowboys' popularity, a development in which the team became characterized not just by the gleaming towers and corporate culture of its hometown, but also its religiosity.

In his celebrated, much-debated essay "The Me Decade," Tom Wolfe presaged the counterintuitive trend that swept the '70s, in which the remnants of the New Left and drug culture and communal living prompted a religious reaction—less suburban button-down, more Southern charismatic—and what Wolfe would describe as a third great religious awakening: "Ten years ago, if anyone of wealth, poor, or renown had publicly 'announced for Christ,' people would have looked at him as if his nose had been eaten away by weevils. Today it happens regularly…"

Wolfe had tapped into the broader societal trends at work. The moderate and comparatively liberal wings of American churches—Presbyterian and United Methodist among them—suffered a decline in their parishioners in the '70s, while "born again" or evangelical Christianity exploded—reaching 25 percent of the nation by 1978 and continuing to grow from there. The number of Americans who reported that religion played a growing role in their lives tripled over the decade. After declining steadily from the mid-'50s, weekly attendance at church ticked up from 40 to 42 percent in 1976, and stayed at 41 percent the rest of the decade.

Against the backdrop of the shifting mores of the '70s, there was a back-to-basics revival. The decade that saw the first evangelical "born-again" Christian president, Jimmy Carter, also saw the same movement animate the sports world. Unsurprisingly, Dallas—which at times had been referred to as the "Vatican of American Fundamentalism"—was a hotbed for the movement. Not coincidentally, the two most visible figures on the Cowboys, Landry and Staubach, made a point to cite their faith in public interviews.

At the same time, Staubach's self-possession kept him from being easily typecast. When Phyllis George interviewed Staubach for an *NFL Today* piece, she asked him if his straight-arrow image was a burden. "Everyone in the world compares me to Joe Namath," said Staubach. "You know, as far as the idea of off the field, he's single bachelor swing, and I'm married and family, and he's having all the fun. I enjoy sex as much as Joe Namath, only I do it with one girl. But it's still fun."

Not all teams were comfortable mixing faith with sports, but religious services became more prevalent and organized in the '70s, with the launch of Baseball Chapel (started by the Detroit sportswriter Watson Spoelstra) in the majors in 1973, and pregame chapel services in the NBA. Within teams' chapel services, and through organizations like the Fellowship of Christian Athletes, the believers began networking. Responding to the excesses of the previous decade, but also motivated by the proselytizing of Muhammad Ali and the Black Muslims, many athletes became more forthright about public declarations of faith.

"There was a time when it was like, you don't talk about that—that may be what you believe, but this is your job," said the Steelers' defensive back Tony Dungy, who'd been raised in a deeply religious home. "And this is pro sports, and that should be off limits. But I think it did come out of that time of the '70s when everybody was doing their thing, as we say. And so if they can do their thing, then we as Christians can do it. I think the seventies brought out that kind of freedom of expression in everybody, and the guys of faith then had the sense that, 'You know what?—I can say what's on my mind without offending people, because everybody else has said what's on their mind, right? And nobody's getting offended.'"

In his rookie year in Pittsburgh in 1977, Dungy found a circle of devout Christians. (The Steelers had both a Protestant chaplain, appointed by Athletes in Action, and a Catholic priest, a friend of owner Art Rooney, both of whom presided over pregame Sunday services.) With so much to cut through—Black, white, urban, rural—Christianity was something that could cross barriers of race and socioeconomic class. Other teams, like Seattle, with born-again Christians Jim Zorn and Steve Largent, became known as particularly enthusiastic outposts.

Meanwhile, there were organizations springing up—the Fellowship of Christian Athletes, Athletes in Action, Pro Athletes Outreach—that proselytized on behalf of Christian ideals.

An athlete's religious or political preferences had mostly been off-limits in the previous decade, with some notable exceptions like Sandy Koufax skipping a World Series Game 1 start because it fell on the Jewish holiday of Yom Kippur.

But no team was more associated with religion than the Cowboys. "Texas Stadium has a hole in its roof," said the Cowboys' D. D. Lewis, "so God can watch His favorite team play."

"Well, I think they were always dubbed as the good guys in the white hats, and we were the evil guys in black," said the Steelers' Dungy. "But I think we had the same number of Christian guys. And Coach Noll wasn't as outgoing about his faith as Landry, but it was very important to him."

Throughout the decade, there was a recurring tension between the image of the Cowboys and the reality, a constant sense of sin and salvation sitting side by side. Landry was featured in a Christian comic book in 1973, the same year that *North Dallas Forty*, former Cowboy wide receiver Pete Gent's debauched novel about the Cowboys, hit the bestseller lists. There were strict rules governing the off-field behavior of the Cowboys Cheerleaders. Yet, at the end of the Cowboys' win over Denver in Super Bowl XII, there was Danny White, the Cowboys' backup quarterback, sharing a deep kiss with cheerleader Cynde Lewis. (The pornographic film *Debbie Does Dallas* debuted a year later, over the team's legal objections, starring the actress Bambi Woods, who'd once tried out for the Cowboys Cheerleaders, but hadn't made the cut.)

"They also had their fair share of characters," noted Verne Lundquist. "A lot of guys who were not going to be associated with Sunday attendance in whatever denominational church you choose."

Players were indoctrinated early on, with varying results.

"I had a sense of the image and all that," said Thomas "Hollywood" Henderson, a splendidly talented rookie from Langston College who joined the team for the Super Bowl run in 1975. "I'm not sure I swallowed it, but I was served that up."

Henderson was intent on leading a new generation of Black Cowboys. The warnings, from the assistant coach John Wooten about overstepping the accepted bounds of behavior, went unheeded.

"I ignored it 100 percent," Henderson said. "I could see the veteran African American players knew their place. It was never said out loud, but I could tell, I could see they looked at me like they feared for me. I was jovial and ebullient, and fuck this and fuck that, and I could see the fear in their eyes for me, if that makes sense."

Before the Super Bowl XIII rematch with the Steelers, Henderson went on record that Pittsburgh's Terry Bradshaw "couldn't spell 'cat' if you spotted him the C and the A." The ensuing controversy—and the high visibility of the Cowboys and Steelers—landed Henderson and Bradshaw on the cover of *Newsweek* magazine. The Steelers cemented their claim to be the Team of the Seventies with another narrow win over Dallas, 35–31.

After that 1978 season, an NFL Films producer named Bob Ryan (not the *Boston Globe* reporter of the same name) suggested that the Cowboys' annual highlight film focus on the degree to which the Cowboys had become the league's most popular club. The show was titled *America's Team*, and when it premiered to widespread acclaim—and resentment—in the summer of 1978, the Cowboys had a new nickname.

"That was NFL Films," said Lundquist, "and I must tell you that came with the complete approval of the organization. They thought, *well, that's a nice thing to be called.*"

There was perhaps no way that a society in as much flux as America was in the '70s could reconcile both the earnest rectitude of Staubach and the unvarnished hedonism of Henderson on the very same team.

By Super Bowl XII, Henderson—who'd grown up in a poor family in East Austin—had become a celebrity, dating Anita Pointer of the Pointer Sisters, and also hobnobbing during Super Bowl week with the likes of Marvin Gaye and Richard Pryor. Gaye came to the Cowboys' hotel and hung out with Henderson and the Lions' Lem Barney. "Marvin thought he could play football," said Henderson. "Richard liked me because I was a raw black boy. And he was raw. We were awful for each other, smoking crack, though."

Of the Cowboys of that era, Henderson estimated that just a few players used cocaine, "maybe 20 percent smoked marijuana, and the rest drank alcohol. We were all using something, except for Roger. He had a baby bottle."

Eventually, Henderson's drug use affected his play. Tom Landry finally decided to release Henderson a year later, the day after a Thanksgiving game against Washington during which Henderson was seen on the sidelines waving the "rally towel" that teammate Preston Pearson was hoping to market as Dallas' answer to Pittsburgh's Terrible Towels. Landry called Henderson into his office. It was their first conversation of substance in five seasons.

"By the time I figured out what he was talking about, I went ballistic," said Henderson. "'You haven't said a fucking word to me in five fucking years. And now you call me in here because of some bullshit and you fucking want to fire me? What the fuck is this?' That's kind of how it went. The half a gram of cocaine in the parking lot didn't help the conversation."

Drug use had become more common in American society, and sports was not immune. Later in the decade, the Atlanta Hawks' GM Stan Kasten, discussing the NBA, said he thought "75 percent of the league was using drugs."

"That was a very damning accusation, backed up by I don't know what," said the NBA's Russ Granik. "But it was said by a responsible person at a high level with a team, and quoted endlessly. We always felt that part of the issue—you can't run away from the issue entirely, because I think recreational drugs were a problem—but we always felt that it was exaggerated because the league was predominantly black."

Around that time, an editor at *Sports Illustrated* asked the writer John Papanek, who was covering the pro basketball beat, how prevalent drug use was.

"I said well, you know, there's not that much drugs," said Papanek. "It was just smoking a lot of pot and using a lot of cocaine. Everybody in New York City was using cocaine—you know, everybody I knew. So if you say

75 percent of the players in the NBA used cocaine, that's probably pretty close to true."

Numbers were impossible to prove, but there was enough anecdotal evidence to support the belief that drug use may have peaked in sports during the decade. The athletes of the decade had it all at their disposal.

"So from Woodstock on—I'm talking about the entire United States—marijuana, hallucinogens like acid, orange sunshine, purple haze and the Vietnam War impacted everything," said Henderson. "And that is the '70s, ladies and gentlemen. Even African Americans in white Dallas were having orgies."

•

And yet. At the very same time this was happening, a new generation of athletes was emerging with a different set of sensibilities. The juxtaposition could be jarring. One of the new breed was Ron Johnson, a hard-hitting cornerback from Eastern Michigan. Raised in Detroit, he came up on the cusp of the fitness revolution, and had embraced physical fitness well before he realized he had pro potential. Small but powerful, Johnson began using Nautilus machines at Eastern Michigan, drank sparingly, and closely monitored his nutritional intake and body weight.

In 1978, he was drafted by the Pittsburgh Steelers. On the day Johnson walked for the first time into the carpeted locker room at Three Rivers Stadium, he noticed a cavernous room that was larger, better lit and more lavish than any locker room he'd ever seen in his life. But he also noticed, to his astonishment, a remnant of the past: welded into the floor, just outside of each and every one of the locker stalls in the grand room, were ashtrays.

Johnson had never seen anything like that, either. He couldn't even imagine it. Finally, he asked equipment manager Tony Parisi about it.

"Ron," said Parisi, "you've gotta understand something: These are grown men."

Cigarette smoking had once been common among professional athletes. John Unitas was a smoker, as was Len Dawson (immortalized with a cigarette and a bottle of Fresca in a photograph taken at halftime of Super Bowl I). The Browns' lineman Bob McKay remembered warming up for his first pro game, seeing the veteran Browns' lineman Gene Hickerson leaning against a goalpost smoking a cigarette. Willie Brown of the Raiders similarly took a cigarette with him when he left the locker room before taking the field, often taking one long last deep drag before emerging from the tunnel at Oakland-Alameda County Coliseum at the beginning of games. It wasn't uncommon for Rosie Casals to come off the court in the early '70s and have a cigarette and a beer. For much of the '70s, in fact, there was a cigarette machine (thirty-five cents a pack) in the visitors' locker room at Candlestick Park.

But by the end of the decade, the smokers—like the Pirates' slugger Dave Parker, sneaking a drag in a spring training game—were the exception. The younger athletes, like the Steelers' Johnson, couldn't imagine such a thing.

That generational schism was felt throughout sports by the late '70s, as an old set of conventions and assumptions began to make way for a new order in which athletes were worth more and, in turn, treated differently. It didn't change overnight, and there were outposts of resistance in every quarter, but what steadily occurred was a recalibration in the relationship between athletes and their own bodies.

This went beyond resistance to smoking and adherence to improved diet and nutrition, and soon included the widespread use of year-round strength training. The Universal gym at the Browns' training camp at Case Western Reserve was little used in the early '70s. "All it was was a hanger for people's clothes," said Bob McKay. "I don't think I ever saw anybody use it." When Buffalo opened Rich Stadium in 1973, Ted Koy remembered a weight room. But in his four years with the team, "I never walked in it; I walked *past* it a lot, but never used it."

Meanwhile, on other teams, a revolution was starting. While most teams used free weights sparingly, the beginning of the '70s saw the onset of the strength guru Arthur Jones' Nautilus machinery, which promised a more concentrated strength-building experience and fewer needless reps. Both the Cowboys and Dolphins were early adopters. Dick Butkus was convinced the machines extended his career, and the Bengals' All-Pro defensive tackle Mike Reid swore by them, convinced that they provided relief to his knees.

Even Joe Greene, who'd been notoriously blasé about weight training— he was country strong, and never had much use for it—began to reconsider when he started seeing the results on other players.

"I started to get involved when guys started beating up on me," said Greene. "I had to do something."

As the weight lifting increased by the middle of the decade, so did the use of anabolic steroids in football, a development that would have grave consequences for some of the early adopters, like the Broncos' Lyle Alzado and the Steelers' Mike Webster.

As the money in the sport increased, so did the temptation to find any edge a player could. The '70s was largely unpoliced in pro football, meaning that in addition to steroid abuse, there was widespread drug abuse, with Benzedrine and other uppers readily available.

The increase in television money and the advent of free agency meant that athletes were becoming more valued by teams and leagues, a development that could be seen in ways both obvious and subtle.

Treating players like plow horses started to decline during the '70s. Nolan Ryan was the last major league pitcher to throw 200 pitches in a game (striking out nineteen Red Sox over thirteen innings in a 235-pitch outing in 1974) and soon enough no one would be throwing 300 innings in a season (Wilbur Wood of the White Sox threw 376⅔ innings in 1972, the equivalent of more than forty-one complete games).

In basketball, Kareem Abdul-Jabbar was one of sport's earliest practitioners of yoga, which would contribute to his flexibility during his twenty-two-year career. "Kareem was doing yoga before anybody could *spell* yoga," said Hubie Brown.

While preventative maintenance was becoming more common, so were cutting-edge surgical procedures. In 1974, the orthopedic surgeon Dr. Frank Jobe performed a new operation, transferring a tendon from the pitcher Tommy John's right wrist to the badly ripped ulnar collateral ligament in his left elbow. In pro football and basketball, arthroscopic surgery would turn career-ending injuries into merely season-ending injuries, and in other instances drastically shortening rehab times.

•

The landscape was also changed by the outsized prominence of the owners of the era, and the increased attention on the people spending (and making) all that money. The new breed of owner was much more media-conscious if not

GOING TO EXTREMES | 301

particularly media-savvy, as exemplified by the Yankees' headline-grabbing boss George Steinbrenner, and the Atlanta cable mogul Ted Turner, who owned the Atlanta Braves and Hawks, and also found time to compete in (and win) the America's Cup yacht race in 1977.

Surveying the blizzard of free-agent signings in the late '70s, the MLBPA's Don Fehr saw something different in Steinbrenner's approach: "Essentially, he said two things. One, I can improve my product by investing in my product, and that's what I'm going to do, because I owe it to the fans. Whether he meant that or not, I don't know, but that's what he said. And the second thing is, he turned the players into celebrities. You know, 'I'm paying Reggie Jackson all this money, he must be something special, you should come watch him.' He didn't back away from saying they were worth it at all, ever, under any circumstances. And that created a big change."

Turner, whose mustache and dimpled chin led to some comparing him to Rhett Butler (a comparison that he liked so much he named one of his sons Rhett), hailed from the Egomaniacal School of sports ownership, explaining to one writer in 1978 that "Life is a game, but the way to keep score is money." In the late '70s, the teams he owned —the underpaid and under-performing Braves, and the underpaid and over-performing Hawks—were not strong enough to make much of a dent in the national consciousness. So what Turner became known for was launching the first nationwide Super-Station in sports, as his WTCG-Channel 17 in Atlanta was renamed WTBS, and became a staple of basic cable networks around the country. American sports fans had the novel sensation of being able to turn on a game many more nights than they had in the past.

Beyond that, Turner was known for being brash, impetuous (he appointed himself "manager" of the Braves one day, in the midst of a long losing streak in 1977, before Bowie Kuhn prohibited it) and having little in the way of a filter, as when he remarked to a writer while watching an Atlanta Flames NHL game on his own network in 1978, "God, this hockey is awful. I can't understand why people like this game. It's just as terrible in person as on TV. Something to keep small minds occupied. They say the only reason people go to the rink is because the players are white. Maybe hockey needs blacks. Naw. If it's black, nobody goes. I could buy this hockey team, but the thought alone is so frightening I can't even stand to turn the sound on. That's 40 more miserable nights in The Omni."

As the contracts grew, and the stakes grew, some of the things that athletes endured, both small and large, began to change.

For much of the '70s, the Steelers had a promotion at Three Rivers Stadium with a Chrysler dealership and an array of cars behind the end zone, making for a showroom in the stadium. When, in a 1979 game, a deep Terry Bradshaw pass to Lynn Swann forced Swann, running at full speed, to attempt to leap the trunk of a car, he landed on the other side flat on his back. The scary-looking fall shook up Swann, but could have been much worse. Somewhere, a calculation was made: Whatever revenue teams were getting for selling cars couldn't touch the value of star players and a successful season. By the next season, there were no more cars on the field at Three Rivers Stadium.

•

Amateur athletes were also gaining a greater sense of autonomy. It had started with the Presidential Commission on Olympic Sports, which was formed with the purpose of streamlining the country's Olympic efforts and also regulating the perennial squabbles between the National Collegiate Athletic Association and the Amateur Athletic Union.

The NCAA offered no appeal process in its discipline of athletes, and the AAU, for its part, was prone to its own capricious rulings. When Dwight Stones set a new world record of seven feet, five and three-quarters inches in the high jump at a meet in Madison Square Garden in February 1975, the AAU refused to recognize it as an official record because Stones had neglected to fill out an AAU membership card for that year.

The springboard diving gold medalist Micki King was among the leading voices agitating for a spot at the table. "We're mystery people," said King. "We have our place in the sun once every four years and then we disappear. We're forgotten. Nobody wants to hear from us or about us. People understand Joe Namath, but they just don't understand us—and so they ignore us."

The Presidential Commission chaired by Mike Harrigan began meeting in the fall of 1975, and issued their recommendations in a report to President Gerald Ford on January 13, 1977 (one week before Ford was leaving office). Subsequently, the bill known as the Amateur Sports Act—which included the key points of the committee's recommendations—was introduced, and finally passed in 1978, though without any of the necessary government funding (leading to a byzantine process that took nearly two more years).

The Amateur Sports Act managed to reduce the internecine battles between the NCAA and the AAU, which had often left athletes with the dilemma of how to negotiate the demands of two governing organizations frequently at cross purposes.

That would begin to change with the new law, which also offered a key element from AIAW's playbook: due process for appeals and representation by athletes on the board (neither of which were in the NCAA's bylaws at the time). In the messy process, Harrigan achieved a genuine bipartisan consensus that allowed his group to be, in his words, "one of the few presidential commissions which resulted in exactly what the fuck we recommended."

The act took away much of the AAU's control, and put it in the hands of national governance organizations for each sport; the act called for at least a 20 percent representation on the board of each NGO for athletes who were either active or had been so within the past decade. The importance of this infusion of youth and actual athletic experience was hard to overstate. Where the decisions had largely been made by white men all over the age of sixty, the individual NGOs going forward would have more diversity in age, gender, and race.

"We had a 20 percent seat at the table after the Amateur Sports Act passed," said Donna de Varona. "We had due process for the first time. Harrigan still doesn't get credit for all that he did—he was brilliant."

•

In baseball, the American League approved the designated hitter rule for the 1973 season; this soon extended the careers of aging sluggers no longer fleet enough to play the field. That same season, Charlie Finley ordered the A's to keep the world-record-holding sprinter Herb Washington (who hadn't played baseball since high school) as a "designated pinch runner." Washington made ninety-two appearances in 1974, without once coming up to bat.

The statistic of pitching saves, created by the *Chicago Sun-Times'* Jerome Holtzman in 1959, was finally recognized as an official statistical category by Major League Baseball a decade later. That didn't simply affect newspaper statistics; it eventually helped change the use of pitchers. There had only been three thirty-save seasons prior to the 1970s, but that number more than doubled by the end of the 1972 season. Twelve pitchers recorded 100 saves in the decade, and the Dodgers' Mike Marshall became the first relief pitcher to win the Cy Young Award. But as the decade progressed, pitchers were used differently, often only in the last one or two innings of a game. Marshall threw more than 200 innings when he won the Cy Young in 1974, while Bruce Sutter—whose split-finger fastball made him nearly unhittable—threw half that amount in winning the Cy Young for the Cubs in 1979. That pitch soon spawned a phalanx of imitators, but few ever threw it as well as Sutter, the man who popularized it. "It comes in like a fastball for 55 feet and then it explodes," was how Sutter's catcher, George Mitterwald, described it.

The other developmental change, hastened by the DH in the American League and the popularity of artificial turf in the National League, was a rapid rise in stolen bases, which topped 2,000 for the season for the first time in 1973, and jumped to 3,000 for the first time just three seasons later.

In basketball, the NBA finally approved the three-point shot prior to the 1979–80 season; it came amid plenty of pushback.

"Red Auerbach and the NBA didn't want anything to do with the three-point shot," said George Karl, who'd played in the ABA before coaching in the NBA.

The rule came against the vocal protestations of Auerbach and other basketball purists. (John Wooden once said, "If you're going to give three points for a long shot, we should only give one point for a dunk.") For coaches it was an adjustment, requiring a revamping of a lifetime's worth of endgame strategy.

The first year in the NBA, the three-pointer was used sparingly. "They weren't accustomed to it," said ABA alum Hubie Brown. "Unless you were an ABA guy. Your footwork in the corners took time—there's only three feet there. And the mechanics of getting there and catching the ball without stepping out of bounds, you know, you had to really work at that."

The biggest changes in the evolution of the NBA had less to do with specialization than fluidity, seen most clearly in the gradual relative decline of the omnipotence of the big man. With the evolution of versatile players like Julius Erving, David Thompson and George Gervin, there were more hybrids, as the roles of different positions started to subtly blur.

Asked to measure his own effect on the game, Erving once said, "I've had an effect in three main areas. First, I have taken a smaller man's game, ball-handling, passing, and the like, and brought it to the front court. Second, I've taken the big man's game, rebounding, shot-blocking, and been able to execute that even though I'm only six-foot-six. What I've tried to do is merge those two types of games, which were considered to be separate— for instance, Bill Russell does the rebounding, Cousy handles the ball—and combine them into the same player. The third thing I've tried to do, and this is the most important thing, is to make this kind of basketball a winning kind of basketball, taking into account a degree of showmanship that gets people excited. My overall goal is to give people the feeling they are being entertained by an artist—and to win."

•

The generational shift could be felt in the stands as well. As more modern stadiums opened around the country, there were fewer dilapidated municipal arenas where fans could sneak in under a torn fence or jump an unmanned turnstile.

But there was still ample drinking, and fistfights in the stands were so common that many stadiums cut off beer sales well before the end of games, often at the end of the seventh inning in baseball and at the end of the third quarter in football.

As early as 1972, the Patriots' GM Upton Bell was bemoaning the pervasiveness of the problem. "We've got as many guards, ushers and police officers on duty as any stadium in the country and it doesn't seem to help," Bell said. "We've tried right along to prevent the flow of hard liquor into the stadium, which I feel is at the root of the problem, but we haven't been able to stop it. I guess we're just going to have to try harder because we can't let things continue as they are."

In Cleveland on June 4, 1974, the promotion "10 Cent Beer Night" devolved into a near-riot, with hundreds of drunk fans in an unruly crowd of 25,000 storming the field, and fighting with the Rangers and eventually Indians players. In 1974, Jimmy Connors, in a World Team Tennis match, went into the stands after a fan kept heckling about his relationship with Chris Evert. During the end of 1975 Cowboys-Vikings playoff game in Minnesota, the back judge Armen Terzian was clocked with a bottle that cut his head and required stitches. A year later, four Philadelphia Flyers went into the stands at Maple Leaf Gardens (two were charged with assault), and NBA ref Richie Powers was attacked on the court in Boston by a fan during Game 5 of the '76 NBA Finals.

"What we know is that all kinds of social barriers have been lowered in the last 10 years," said Art Fuss, Major League Baseball's head of security. "In many cases it's just a question of the social ills outside the ballpark coming inside." A Pinkerton security executive agreed, describing the "root problem" as "the tremendous decline that has taken place in standards of public behavior. Sports fans today are wild in ways they never used to be."

But Dr. Arnold Beisser, a behaviorist at UCLA, saw it differently. "The socioeconomic distance is so great between most fans and highly paid athletes," Beisser said, "that the athletes don't seem like real people. So the fans are more apt to be callous towards them."

The crowd could be a feral, unruly organism. Yankees fans stormed the field after Chris Chambliss' walk-off home run to win the 1976 American League Championship Series (he had to fight his way to actually touch home plate), a scene repeated a year later when the Yankee Stadium crowd stormed the field at the end of the World Series. By the end of the night, there were nearly fifty injuries, thirty-eight arrests and a fan hospitalized with a concussion.

The challenge of fan behavior existed in football as well, but Pete Rozelle realized that the game needed the atmosphere of a stadium. To that end, the NFL became very conscious of wanting a full stadium and enthusiastic crowds. "We don't want to become a studio sport," Rozelle said. Several stadiums developed their own raucous fan culture. Pittsburgh had a crowd dominated by blue-collar workers waving their "Terrible Towels"; in Houston, the noise reverberated inside the Astrodome, where the Oilers faithful were fond of endless renditions of the team theme song, usually accompanied by the sellout crowd shaking light blue pom-poms; at Denver's Mile High Stadium, when the Broncos faithful were at a fever pitch, the metal stadium shook so much that the stationary television camera vibrated.

Several pro teams had earlier experimented with mercenary "Superfan" Crazy George, who pounded a drum from San Jose to Dallas to Kansas City as his hairline continued to recede.

But that kind of generic enthusiasm didn't age well. As the games became more entrenched in their communities, and more a staple of television, the more authentic "superfan" emerged. Wilford Jones, an unpaid booster who got nothing beyond a free parking pass and lots of screen time, soon became renowned as "Crazy Ray," patrolling the sidelines at Cowboys games. An airline mechanic named Tim McKernan went to Mile High Stadium for a decade before his brother bet him $10 that he couldn't get on TV. In the midst of Denver's "Broncomania" season, when the defense was nicknamed Orange Crush, McKernan went to the game bare-chested and pantsless, wearing nothing but a barrel held up by suspenders, painted to resemble an Orange Crush can. And so "Barrel Man" became a tradition in Denver.

Even by the mid-'70s, players were noticing the changing nature of their crowds.

"There is a big difference in our relations with the fans," said the A's Sal Bando in 1975. "The diehard fan has gotten older, and the younger one has so much else he can do besides come to a game. How many kids do you see now listening to the game on the radio and keeping score? That type just isn't there anymore."

Teams became more conscious of encouraging a family-friendly atmosphere. That meant more than just shutting off beer sales after the third quarter or seventh inning. At the beginning of the 1970s, the Chicago Bulls had introduced the NBA's first mascot (Benny the Bull, named after the Bulls' longtime PR man Ben Bentley) and the first dance troupe. From there it was a matter of time.

In San Diego, a journalism major at San Diego State, Ted Giannoulas, accepted a two-week gig to dress up in a chicken suit—a three-dimensional cartoon with an orange beak, yellow feathers, purple eyelids, blue hair, and bright yellow chicken legs and webbed feet—and hand out candy Easter eggs at the San Diego Zoo. It being the '70s, Giannoulas went to the San Diego Padres games in his costume and soon became a regular at Jack Murphy Stadium, providing a kind of comic relief that the Padres needed at the time. Soon enough, he was on the payroll.

The Braves' Ted Turner tried to hire Giannoulas away from San Diego in 1977, promising him, "You come with me, and I'll make you bigger than Mickey Mouse." But Giannoulas chose to stay, and soon other teams were looking for their own Chicken alternative.

In Philadelphia, the Phillies decided that Philadelphia Phil and Philadelphia Phillis—two fans in revolutionary-era garb—were not capturing the imagination of the youngsters at Veterans Stadium. Phillies GM William Giles sought out Muppets creator Jim Henson to see if he could design a mascot, and he directed Giles to his longtime collaborator Bonnie Erickson (she had designed Miss Piggy, and the show's crusty Greek chorus of balcony hecklers, Waldorf and Statler). On April 25, 1978, the Phillie Phanatic—basically a large green Muppet with a long snout and sporting a Phillies jersey—made its debut. Mascots had become a trend.

"Red Auerbach once said, 'We'll never need cheerleaders,'" said Frank Layden. "But it's show business, and now we have all that, we have halftime entertainment and dancers, and guys dunking balls on trampolines. It's show business."

•

As sports grew in scope, and the dress codes of the past were relaxed, the jogging suit became an item of casual wear by the late '70s. It was another sign of the running boom sweeping the country. In Oregon, a small company named Blue Ribbon Sports—founded on a handshake deal between the Oregon track coach Bob Bowerman and the young executive Phil Knight—changed its name to Nike in 1971, and continued to diversify its line of "waffle trainer" shoes, which provided enough cushion for distance runners yet, crucially, remained stylish enough for casual wear.

The Nike Cortez soon transcended the sports realm and became a staple of popular culture, worn by Farrah Fawcett in a *Charlie's Angels* episode and Elton John at some of his concerts. Company revenues would go from less than $2 million in 1972 to $700 million within a decade.

By the mid-'70s, the Julius Erving Dr. J model for Converse and Earl Monroe's MVP model for Pony (which also used Bob McAdoo, John Havlicek and David Thompson) showed the shoe wars had begun in earnest. Walt Frazier's low-cut suede Clydes, from Puma, had already broken out of the athletic lane and were becoming prominent in the proto-rap scene of the late '70s. "Brooklyn loved the Puma," recalled the rapper Doug E. Fresh. "Harlem and the Bronx loved the Puma. The Puma was runnin' things."

Golf and tennis were continually in a competition to modernize, with new materials. Graphite shafts and metal club heads were the wave of the future in golf. In tennis, the response to the 1975 Wimbledon final—in which Arthur Ashe and his graphite composite racket out-dueled Jimmy Connors and his iconic steel-suspension T-2000—signaled the rush toward modern materials.

In 1976, the Head-designed Prince Classic came out, an oversize racket that contained a "sweet spot" twice as large as in a typical racket. This was fine for weekend hackers, but even better for elite players, who were able to accelerate the use of extreme topspin shots—their shot paths becoming much more vertical (as in Bjorn Borg's game) and much less horizontal (as in Connors'). There were still wood loyalists, but their years were numbered. (The Frenchman Yannick Noah, winning at Roland Garros in 1983, would be the last player to win a Grand Slam tournament with a wood racket.)

A long-distance runner in Vermont named Lisa Lindahl, frustrated by the painful bouncing of her breasts on runs, sat down with a childhood friend, Polly Smith, a costume designer, and set about creating a prototype of a bra that would provide more support for women in motion. One of Smith's humble prototypes was created by sewing two jockstraps together, but by the end of the project, Lindahl, Smith, and their friend Linda Miller had founded a company—Jogbra, Inc.—and shortly thereafter received a U.S. patent. The sports bra was born.

The effect of the growth of women's sports could be seen in commercial circles. The Virginia Slims tour had given way to an even higher profile sponsor in Avon. Meanwhile, Adidas reported a 63 percent increase in one year on the sale of its women's athletic shoes.

On both levels, the influx of participation was accompanied by a change of perception.

"Women no longer feel that taking part in athletics is a privilege," said Joan Warrington, executive secretary for the AIAW. "They believe it is a right."

•

Football, more than any other sport, embraced change. The NFL became fiendish about specialization, as rosters grew nearly 20 percent in the space of a single decade. That brought the third-down back, the nickel defensive back, the long snapper, and a new distinction between blocking and pass-catching tight ends.

But much of the change had to do with the way the league set its rules and marketed its game. Late in 1976, anticipating the upcoming TV negotiations the following year, Pete Rozelle typed out a confidential letter to Browns owner Art Modell and Chargers owner Gene Klein, of the NFL's television committee.

"The best solution would appear to be 'stacking' the schedule. This would be achieved by pitting strong against strong and weak against weak (based on previous year's standings) for the out of division games... it would ensure a great increase in attractive games for TV, but also give us the strong likelihood of fantastic divisional races with many more teams staying in contention longer."

The "stacked schedule," somewhat modified, was combined with the Competition Committee's vote to expand to sixteen regular season games (and reduce the preseason from six games to four). That came along with more rules from the Competition Committee to liberalize the passing game, and the expansion of the playoffs (adding a fifth team in each conference), to expand the postseason by one week and reward division champions with a week of rest. The changes increased the NFL's bargaining position with the networks, while at the same time accentuating the forces for competitive balance that were at the heart of the league.

"The idea of parity or competitive balance or whatever you want to call it is behind just about everything that the league talked about during the '60s and '70s," said the NFL's vice president Don Weiss.

In addition to expanding the regular season to sixteen games and adding an extra wild-card playoff qualifier in each conference, the NFL added three nationally televised Sunday night games, and a fourth nationally televised Thursday night game, to the schedule.

Armed with excellent ratings, more games, more attractive match-ups in the future and rumors of a possible "fourth network," which would be built around pro football broadcasts, Rozelle was able to negotiate a staggering series of contracts with ABC, CBS and NBC, each of which renewed its previous package. The total value—$576 million over four years—was described by the *New York Times* as "the biggest deal in television history."

Rozelle had become the most powerful man in sports because he understood the marketplace and also the media landscape. Scarcity was a strength in pro football. Even when the schedule grew to sixteen games in the NFL, each game carried the same competitive weight as ten baseball games. Whereas basketball and hockey let in a larger percentage of their teams to the playoffs, the NFL was still stingy. All of that created sizable ratings throughout the season.

"The number one rule in sports," said CBS's Kevin O'Malley, "the postseason is what counts. The regular season isn't worth anything. *Except* in the NFL."

In less than a decade, pro football had gone from being a sport that dominated American weekend afternoons for a largely male audience to the single most prized commodity on network television, the largest gathering place in American popular culture.

The NFL was leading the way, but the rest of sports would, inevitably, follow.

•

As Muhammad Ali's career wound down, he had defeated everyone of consequence. Ali's camp began to stage more of his title defenses on network television, which made for a more certain payday.

On a February night in 1978, in front of a CBS-TV audience, an out-of-shape, overconfident Ali entered the ring with the untested 1976 Olympic gold medalist Leon Spinks (it was only Spinks' eighth pro bout) completely unprepared. Outboxed and out-thought by the younger fighter, he was out-pointed on all the judges' cards, ceding his championship to Spinks.

The rematch six months later was broadcast live by ABC-TV in the States, and watched by an estimated two billion people around the world, and while it was unspectacular, a rejuvenated Ali dominated to regain his title by unanimous decision, becoming the first fighter ever to win the heavyweight title three times.

But the experience itself was flattened by TV, and the Superdome in New Orleans lacked the frontier grandeur and mystery of Kinshasa or Manila.

The three-time champion Ali had by now moved to a different place in the culture. On the same day the fight was taking place, President Jimmy

Carter was meeting at Camp David with Egyptian president Anwar Sadat and Israeli prime minister Menachem Begin. On the night of the fight, Carter and Walter Mondale were guests at Sadat's cottage, and were served tea.

Later that night, back at his quarters, Carter called Ali at one-thirty in the morning to congratulate him on the victory. It was exactly the sort of congratulatory call that Richard Nixon never would have made. And another reason Carter made it.

•

There were still plenty of authoritarian coaches and managers in the late '70s, but the breed was beginning to suffer attrition.

The 1978 season had been a disappointing campaign for Woody Hayes, whose Buckeyes lost to Michigan for the third year in a row (they mustered a total of nine points in those three games). For the first time in Hayes' tenure, Ohio State accepted a bid to a bowl that wasn't one of the four major New Year's Day games, the Gator Bowl in Jacksonville. Ohio State and its fans were not accustomed to playing in second-tier bowl games.

Hayes was a curious case. Resolutely old-school in many respects, he was never particularly bothered by changing hairstyles. A strict purist about what constituted rectitude in sports, he rebuffed an early effort by Nike to offer free shoes to the Ohio State program; Hayes didn't want to be beholden to any outside organization. But his volcanic temper had hurt him in the past, and on a misty night at the Gator Bowl, on December 29, 1978, it would end his career.

The Buckeyes were trailing Clemson 17–15 late in the game but driving to retake the lead, when freshman Art Schlicter's pass was intercepted by Clemson's stocky linebacker Charlie Baumann, who lumbered back upfield before going down near the Buckeyes' sideline.

It marked the downbeat end to a disappointing season, and as Baumann stood up holding the ball aloft, the apoplectic Hayes grabbed Baumann's shoulder pad with his left hand and swung wildly with his right, connecting with Baumann's neck. On the field of the Gator Bowl, it was over in an instant, as Hayes' punch was greeted with a flurry of players intervening from both sides.

"What happens on the sidelines is guys get shoved around and pushed

AP IMAGES/HARRY CABLUCK

*Follow the money: Jack Nicklaus (above), with a crucial putt that helped him win the 1975 Masters, showed the way for athletes as entrepreneurs; arbiter Peter Seitz (left) made the decision that brought free agency to Major League Baseball; by the following year's ALCS, Yankees owner George Steinbrenner (below, left) was already courting marquee free agent Reggie Jackson.*

AP IMAGES

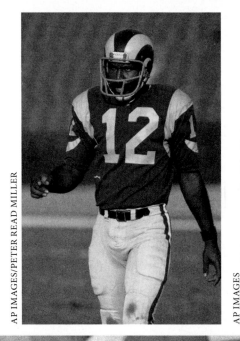

*Milestones (clockwise from top): James "Shack" Harris emerged as a playoff quarterback in LA; fellow Grambling alum Doug Williams found an easier path coming out of college nearly a decade later; Frank Robinson broke the color barrier for Major League managers; Lee Elder teed off as the first African American competitor at the Masters.*

*King of the hill: (top to bottom) Pete Rozelle introduces 1978's top draft choice, Earl Campbell; Terry Bradshaw and the Steelers outdueled Thomas Henderson (56) and the Cowboys in Super Bowl XIII, a match-up of the decade's two dominant NFL teams; Phyllis George and Brent Musburger revolutionized the pregame show with The NFL Today in 1975.*

*Silver lining: (top) Ann Meyers and Pat Head, later Summitt, of the 1976 U.S. women's Olympic basketball team, grappling with the formidable Soviet Uljana Semjonova; Billie Moore (middle) implored her players to a history-making achievement; (bottom) the Americans won the silver in Montreal, becoming the first women's team to capture the imagination of American sports fans.*

*Women's work: Chris Evert (left)—a model of concentration and consistency—celebrating the 1975 US Open, one of her eighteen Grand Slam titles; Charlotte West (below), coach, scholar, professor and, eventually, president of the AIAW; Donna Lopiano (bottom, left) and Jody Conradt charted a new course for women's college basketball at the University of Texas.*

*Dealmakers: Larry O'Brien (top) presided over the merger between the NBA and the ABA; meanwhile, his ambitious lieutenant David Stern (middle) soon began striving to put the NBA on better financial footing, an effort that would eventually bring him to the bargaining table with NBPA executive director Larry Fleisher (bottom).*

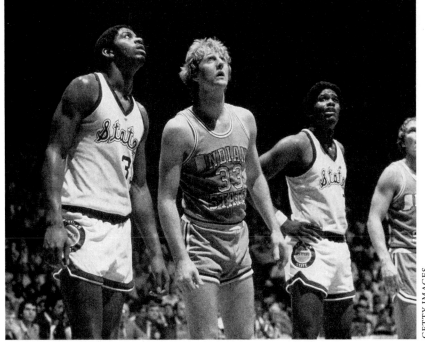

*Gamers: Earvin "Magic" Johnson and Larry Bird (above, from left) played the 1979 NCAA Championship Game, the most-watched college basketball game ever, before revitalizing the NBA; meanwhile in Pittsburgh, Willie Stargell (below left) of the Pirates, and Joe Greene (below right) of the Steelers set new standards of leadership.*

*New era; On September 7, 1979, ESPN took to the air (George Grande, left, and Lee Leonard, co-hosts of the first* SportsCenter)*, filling a void that even some people in the world of sports didn't fully realize existed.*

*Front lines: (clockwise from middle) In a series of comic strips in the fall of 1979 Charles Schulz highlighted the stakes of the battle for Title IX; Gloria Steinem (standing), joined by Rep. Bella Abzug (left) and Rep. Patsy Mink (center) lobbied for a final interpretation that would preserve Title IX; in the summer of 1979, Ann Meyers earned a tryout with the Indiana Pacers, foreshadowing an era when women would have a league of their own.*

around and everything else," said Larry Kindbom, the Buckeyes' graduate assistant then. "There were actually three or four of their players around, and I looked up and saw all these Clemson eyes just watching this whole thing, and I'm thinking, *Oh, no.* It was apparent that this wasn't just a side-line scramble. They saw Woody actually hit the kid."

Hayes had lost his temper before, and he'd even lost his temper on national TV before. He'd once chased *Sports Illustrated*'s photographer Walter Iooss down the sideline, and in 1974 punched a Michigan State fan after the Spartans had upset the Buckeyes. After Ohio State fumbled away the ball late in a 14–6 loss to Michigan in 1976, Hayes punched and kicked an ABC cameraman. But this was prime time, in front of an audience of tens of millions of American viewers.

ABC's play-by-play announcer Keith Jackson didn't see the punch. But America did. And that would make all the difference.

Hayes did not immediately return to the locker room, but even among the staff there was a sense that a line had been crossed. "Some of the people that were there thought, you know, hey, those things happen," said Kindbom. "Everybody knows Woody, he's probably going to get punished for it. But I think deep down inside the coaches kind of knew that's probably it. And because now you take into account all those things that led up to the bowl game and these other things. It was almost like when he decided to be George Patton, for that one moment. And he was certainly a disciple of George Patton."

The next morning, Hayes' twenty-eight-year tenure as Ohio State's head coach abruptly ended, and some wondered if a larger era of the all-powerful head coach might have ended with it.

But power is exerted in different ways. Twelve days after Hayes' meltdown on national TV, the San Francisco 49ers announced the hiring of their newest head coach, who was by then well known to sports fans in the Bay Area. He was Bill Walsh, the cerebral pro assistant who'd come to Stanford in 1976 and revived the Cardinal.

Back in the pros, he was given unusual latitude. On most NFL teams, the head coach was hired by and reported to the GM. But Walsh was doing the interviewing for his own GM, and it was clear who was going to be in charge.

At the Doral Hotel in Miami Beach, the Friday before Super Bowl XIII, the young Giants' assistant GM Ernie Accorsi finished a meeting with Bill Walsh. On his way out the door, he ran into his friend George Young, who was also interviewing to be the 49ers' new general manager.

"The guy's a genius," Accorsi told Young. "I don't know if what he's going to do will actually work, but he's brilliant."

Walsh was a far cry from taskmasters Vince Lombardi and George Allen and Hank Stram. He was equally obsessed with the game, but also understood that a generation of football players who'd come of age in the '70s were bound to be less subservient and more eager to express themselves.

Walsh felt like too much time in football training camps and practices was devoted to "toughening" up players when in fact the daily grind of teammates scrimmaging against teammates only served to wear down an entire squad.

During his first year in the 49ers job, he stressed to his assistants that, heading into training camp, "Each drill must have a direct relationship to a specific action the player would experience in a game."

Walsh was among the modern coaches to observe the unmistakable similarities between head coaches and CEOs. In his time at Stanford, he'd developed some of the principles of communication he'd seen expounded by business leaders and applied them to the craft of coaching.

Sometimes, this was simply calling old things by new names: playbooks became "our inventory of plays," while individual pass patterns became "schematics."

"He wasn't concerned that he didn't sound like an old-school football coach," said Tony Dungy, who after two years with the Steelers was traded to San Francisco and played for Walsh in 1979. "He talked differently. That kind of language was new; you'd never heard a football coach talk about inventory or schematics before." Dungy also noticed the record number of Black coaches on San Francisco's staff, another sign that the times were changing.

Walsh wanted a liaison between the public relations department and players, and wanted a former player to serve in that role, and so the 49ers hired a former Brigham Young player named Brian Billick, himself an aspiring head coach.

Walsh could be as sharp-tongued as any coach, but Billick soon noticed his evolved approach. Walsh didn't yell at players, but instead at assistant coaches.

"When a player ran a route, Bill wouldn't chew out the player, he'd holler at the assistant," said Billick. "Bill would say, 'Can't you teach these guys the right angle on a flat?' The coaches could take it, and the players would notice because their position coach was taking heat on their behalf."

It was a subtle thing but intentional.

"Bill was emphatic that every part of the organization be assigned so that we're prepared to take advantage of when we're good and winning," said Billick.

That approach would bear fruit in the future. In the third round of the 1979 NFL Draft, Tom Landry and the Cowboys went against their vaunted, computer-generated master list, skipping the top available player for the one they ranked second, the tight end Doug Cosbie. Six selections later, when the 49ers draft choice came up, San Francisco took the player that Dallas had passed on.

His name was Joe Montana, and he would help Walsh build a dynasty in San Francisco that would in the coming years topple the Cowboys.

# SIXTEEN

# THE RISING

GROWING UP IN the town of Goldthwaite, Texas (pop. 1,300), Addie Jo Conradt was indoctrinated in a tight-knit community in which sports was as pervasive as religion or brisket. Her father played on a semi-pro baseball team, and her mother played softball one evening a week. At Goldthwaite High School, she was the class valedictorian and the star of the basketball team, scoring 41 points per game her senior season. Her parents were Baptist, so she went to college at Baylor.

When she got to Waco, Conradt discovered that all of her outlets for sports had been denied. Baylor didn't promote competitive athletics for women, but rather the same sort of "play days" that Charlotte West had loathed so much. Competition was frowned on, Conradt would recall, and "winning was actually discouraged." She hadn't counted on how much she would miss sports. So she gravitated to the world of physical education. She graduated, taught at Waco Midway high school and earned her master's degree at Baylor.

By this time, everyone was calling her Jody, and what Jody Conradt realized in those years was that basketball wasn't just a physical impulse; she'd become enamored of the strategy and tactics of the game. She sent away five dollars for North Carolina coach Dean Smith's pamphlet on how to coach the Run and Jump Defense, and began her college coaching career in 1969 at Sam Houston State, before moving to Texas–Arlington in 1973. It was still the dark ages, when women's sports were a marginal, largely volunteer-driven activity. At Sam Houston, there were no women's uniforms available in the school colors, and even getting to road games was a challenge ("If you had a car, you made the team," said Conradt). At Arlington, she dealt with a women's athletic director whose background was modern dance, and who was forever calling Conradt's practices "rehearsals" and referring to her team's uniforms as "costumes." By the time she moved to UT–Arlington, coaching basketball and volleyball, she'd developed a reputation as a hard-driving, no-nonsense coach.

Meanwhile, it had been a bumpy first year for Donna Lopiano at the University of Texas. Like women starting major-college programs around the country, she was pushing against generations of inertia and indifference on the part of male administrators. In addition to the congressional testimony that nearly got Lopiano fired, she ruffled feathers everywhere she went. Most of her coaches for women's sports were physical education teachers, adding to their workload by taking on the coaching duties for a small stipend and one fewer class to teach. Lopiano realized that she needed coaches who were full-time professionals.

Out of the sparse women's athletic budget, Lopiano had about $20,000, to hire two coaches—one for basketball and one for volleyball—and knew that her first hire would be crucial. She interviewed Sue Gunter at the regional power Stephen F. Austin, but she realized she wanted someone more polished, more self-assured, someone who could engage not only with UT's alumni—the well-heeled and often big-bellied "Texas Exes"—but withstand the scrutiny once those alums finally bought in. That brought her to Arlington to interview Jody Conradt.

Owing to her family's restaurant and her Italian upbringing, it was Lopiano's modus operandi to make a big Italian dinner for the person she was interviewing. While that was more challenging in Conradt's case ("I think I actually had to go out and buy pots and pans; Jody wasn't much for cooking"), Lopiano made pasta and pitched Conradt on the job. By the time dinner was complete, Lopiano had offered—and Conradt had accepted—both the basketball and volleyball coaching jobs ("I wanted to increase my chances for success," said Conradt) for a salary of nearly $20,000. At a time when the previous Texas men's basketball coach, Leon Black, had been making $21,000 a year, the hiring amounted to a statement of intent.

It was a match of perfect contrasts. If Lopiano was a headstrong rush of astringent Yankee enthusiasm (viewed as pushiness by many of the Texas men she ran across), Conradt was the composed antidote, elegant in dress and comportment. Upon hearing Lopiano's forceful presentations about what needed to change in athletics, some UT boosters despaired the end of the world as they knew it. But after hearing Conradt deliver her stirring rhetoric of teamwork and cooperation—with the self-possessed poise of a Texas frontier woman—they believed the republic might yet stand.

So in the fall of 1976, Conradt arrived. In Austin, the men were still coming to terms with the implications of Title IX. The two basketball teams shared the humble, cramped Gregory Gym, and the new men's basketball coach Abe Lemons was infuriated when Lopiano had volleyball lines painted on the dark wood basketball court there. That same fall, as the women prepared to begin practice, the men's team was still shooting around, and Conradt had to go tell the guard Jim Krivacs to get off the court. He initially resisted, but that conflict was taken care of quickly. People soon learned that the cordial new basketball and volleyball coach possessed an iron will.

"When the office door was open, she was the sweetest lady ever," said Texas sports information director Bill Little. "But when the door closed, and Jody was serious—look out."

The team wasn't ready for it. Nearly every one of the school's varsity holdovers either quit the team or transferred. Conradt talked two key players, the center Retha Swindell and the senior Cathy Self, into giving her new methods a chance, then she built from there; almost every other player on the team was a freshman. In her first season, Conradt implemented a pressing defense and a fast-breaking offense and went 36–10 (for all its emphasis on academic-athletic balance, AIAW had no limit on the number of games a school could play in a season).

With the women playing games at five o'clock ("the prelim") and the men at seven-thirty, it soon became painfully clear that the Venn diagram overlap of the two audiences was fairly small. "We need our own audience," Lopiano soon realized, "because the people who watch men's sports are different than the people who watch women's sports, and they can't get good seats if they're victims of having to clear out of their seats after the five o'clock game."

"It was going nowhere," said Conradt. Family and friends were urged to attend. But in Conradt's first season, the Lady Longhorns generally played in front of crowds so sparse that the loudest sound in the auditorium was the echoing from the sneaker squeaks on the hardwood. That and Conradt's thundering calls for more pace on the fast break.

From the remnants of that first season came a new way forward for women's sports.

•

In the summer of 1977, Lopiano and Conradt embarked on a series of discussions that led to a revolutionary strategic approach. They were wrestling with an all-encompassing question of their newfound profession: Why do people follow *men's* sports? What was the nature of the sports fandom? Could it be replicated on the women's level?

What they were striving for was more than a theoretical construct; they were trying to identify the DNA of modern American sports fandom. Conradt recognized that one of the key aspects of fandom was that fans identified with the players: "They don't know 'em, they read about 'em, they see 'em, they *feel* like they know them. So how can we reproduce that? We can't reproduce it on television, we can't reproduce it through the media. We've gotta do it one on one."

That realization came with broad implications. Rather than agitating for press coverage that would treat the games as an event, Lopiano and Conradt realized they would have to create the event first, and then trust that the media coverage would follow. They wanted some measure of the same excitement that bubbled through a college campus on the eve of a big men's football or basketball game.

Embedded in that desire was the implicit assumption that many of the trappings of big-time college sports—the pressure, the competition, the recognition, the sportswriters, the school band and, yes, even the cheerleaders—were not inherently bad but actually desirable, provided that academics wasn't an afterthought.

All this was a long way from the message—"Ever soft and gentle as a lady"—on the wall at Wellesley.

The plan called for a person-to-person, door-to-door, day-to-day approach. From Chambers of Commerce to alumni groups, from sewing circles to Lions Clubs, Lopiano and Conradt would go anywhere and speak to any group, and along the way, sell season tickets for $20 per seat. Anyone who bought a season ticket was in turn encouraged to go out and sell more season tickets. The season ticket would include invitations to the postgame

"Fast Break Club," which allowed for dedicated fans to come to a conference room after the game and meet the players, ask them questions and get a better understanding of the strategy and tactics of the team.

There was a kind of simulated intimacy in the world of booster clubs and touchdown dinners that fostered what in the world of advertising was described as brand loyalty. "Start backwards," said Lopiano, on the mindset of fans. "People want to be able to say, 'I talked to coach yesterday.' There was this personal aspect to it. Then they go back to the office and it's bragging rights, either bragging rights because they talked to coach, or bragging rights because they got a season ticket. And so it was in that context that I think that was the only way that we kind of looked at men's athletics for, you know, anything that we tried to reproduce—it was the familiarity, rather than the arm's length distance from people. It was one on one, it was treating everybody as if they were special because they are. Men had gotten so corporate."

The Fast Break Club was a new frontier for the players as well. "Those first few years, they were so shy," said Conradt. "We had to do it with my asking them questions. We put them on a stage. I usually had them introduce themselves those first few games." It was a way to bring the players to the fans, and it also served—in a way that even Anna Hiss might have approved of—as a finishing school of sorts for the players, who became more poised public speakers.

But it didn't stop there. Lopiano and Conradt felt that most college football and basketball programs didn't make sufficient effort to graduate their players. The next full-time women's athletics staffer was the academic advisor Sheila Rice (whose father, M. T. Rice, had been a legendary coach at Waco Midway, and whom Conradt had watched growing up). Rice helped Conradt compile a nearly perfect graduation rate among her players who stayed at UT for the full four years.

"That was about the need for the faculty to understand that women athletes are here to get a degree, to not be 'profiled' the way some of the male athletes are," said Lopiano. "So let's ask the players, 'Is there one professor you would like to invite to a game?' So we started what we called the 'guest coach program.'"

Conradt was aggressively recruiting in Texas and beyond, and Lopiano scheduled lengthy East Coast road trips over the holiday break, where Texas would face traditional powers of women's college basketball.

Meanwhile, Lopiano was talking to "Texas Exes," spreading the message that women's sports had arrived and would no longer be second-class.

"I tried to follow along behind and smooth anything over," said Conradt. "But Donna was totally aggressive and that's one of the reasons she was the right person. Somebody coming in here and not making any waves, and accepting things as they were, was not going to be able to build a program the way Donna did."

As she was plowing forward, Lopiano turned a weakness into a kind of impenetrable strength. "She couldn't read a room," said Conradt. "She would go somewhere, and she would always come back and say, 'It was great!' I mean it was kind of a joke between us: 'Donna, no, they weren't welcoming you with open arms.' That was always one of her traits. She's just oblivious."

But soon enough, the Texas Exes went from opposition and suspicion to a stance of expectation. At one booster meeting in Austin, the benefactor Ed Clark (whom LBJ biographer Robert Caro described as "one of the true masters of Texas politics") raised his hand and put Lopiano on the spot. "Miss Lopiano," Clark asked, "when can we expect the women to win a national championship?"

With that question, Lopiano knew that if she was going to be judged by the same terms as any other athletic administrator, she had already succeeded. She told Clark the UT women would win a national championship in a women's sport within three years, and bet him a bottle of St. Emilion on the proposition.

By 1977–78, Conradt led the Lady Longhorns to a Top Twenty ranking. That fall saw the opening of the new arena, the Frank Erwin Center, dubbed the "Superdrum" by locals. The prelim slots dwindled, and UT's women began headlining for most of the home games on their schedule. By 1979, the campus radio station began broadcasting their road games, and replays of their home games were shown on the local cable access station. The *Austin American-Statesman* assigned a beat reporter to cover the women's games.

The team was consistently winning, and there at the center of the hive of activity was Jody Conradt, exhibiting an array of skills that went beyond mere coaching.

"On the night of the game, Jody has to stop in the Fast Break Club room to say hello to everybody who's coming for dinner before the game," remembered Lopiano. "She goes from there to give a pregame scouting report to three tables of ten. Then she comes out and the team is doing pregame warm-ups. And she's meeting the guest coaches. She's talking to them as the team has gone through their warm-ups and then walked with them into our locker room—they come in pregame, halftime, and after the game. So she's running these three groups and then afterwards, all of those people go to the Fast Break Club. And she puts on the show for the team. She's the moderator. She runs questions. We couldn't have done it without somebody like Jody Conradt who could juggle all of that as if it were nothing and still coach your basketball team. Wow. Phenomenal PR person."

Among the avid core fan base was Ann Richards, then Texas railroad commissioner, still fifteen years away from being the governor of Texas, but already a rising force in Texas politics. She pulled Lopiano aside one day and said, "You're going to be successful here, just as long as you keep using your Yankee smile, and dress like a lady." Soon Richards was joined in the VIP seats by the Congresswoman Barbara Jordan, who made as many games as she could when she was back from Washington.

At the end of Conradt's first season, Richards hosted a reception of politicos for the UT women's program at the Quorum restaurant, and afterward slipped Conradt an envelope of hundred-dollar bills, saying, "This is what we do to express our appreciation for coaches in Texas."

Colleen Matsuhara, who was an assistant under Billie Moore at UCLA, later worked with Conradt at Texas. She was amazed at the way the Fast Break Club operated. Lopiano and Conradt remained in control, always looking out for the overeager fans—"I used to call them 'droolers,'" said Matsuhara—and keeping the team and the questions on message.

And through it all, there was Lopiano. "Donna was a lion," said Matsuhara. "She could outsmart you, she could outtalk you, she could outlast you."

By Conradt's third season, 1978–79, the team was ranked fourth in the country and sported a 37–4 record. Texas was emerging as a new national power, necessitating weekly Sunday calls from the voluble Mel Greenberg, who wanted Conradt's Top Twenty votes, but really wanted to talk to Lopiano about all the other developments in college basketball. "Sometimes Donna would fall asleep with Mel on the phone," said Conradt.

The program was simple but audacious; and the supporters—who felt like they were both going to an event and becoming part of the event—were the lifeblood. In so doing, Texas created a blueprint for what could be accomplished in women's sports.

"They led the way—attendance, recruiting, promotions," said longtime Georgia women's basketball coach Andy Landers. "Anything that touched the sport of women's basketball."

Watching the growth of the Texas program with admiration was Joan Cronan, the athletic director at the College of Charleston before returning to Tennessee in 1983, and helping the Lady Vols and their head coach, Olympic silver medalist Pat Head Summitt, build a dynasty.

"Donna and I were both lucky to have Pat and Jody, whose goals and ambitions were exactly what ours was to have this opportunity," said Cronan. "And so it was great, great timing. But yeah, that team. I went there, and they had Barbara Jordan and Ann Richards there, and there were guest coaches sitting behind the bench. And I said, 'I'm gonna steal that.'"

•

In Houston in November 1977, women came from all over the country for what Billie Jean King would refer to as "the largest gathering of tomboys and ex-tomboys in recent history." It was the first National Women's Conference, part of the United Nations' International "Year of the Woman." More than a pep rally for the cause, it offered a historic gathering of female politicians, academics and speakers. There were 2,000 delegates and nearly 20,000 more attendees. Congresswoman Bella Abzug served as the chair, with three current and former First Ladies—Rosalynn Carter, along with Betty Ford and Lady Bird Johnson—in attendance.

Ahead of the event, a torch relay to Houston originated in Seneca Falls, where Elizabeth Cady Stanton launched the first modern women's movement in 1848. Among the 2,000 runners who joined the 2,600-mile relay were Olympic silver medalist Cheryl Toussaint, Olympic skier Suzy Chaffee, gold medal swimmer Donna de Varona, Boston Marathon trailblazer Kathrine

Switzer, and Carole Oglesby, the first AIAW president, who'd also served as the sports consultant for the International Women's Year commission. The relay wound all the way down to Houston, with a detour through Beaumont, Texas—childhood home of Babe Didrikson Zaharias—and carried in the final miles by more prominent athletes, including Billie Jean King herself, before being delivered onstage to the three First Ladies in attendance.

Gloria Steinem would describe the Houston summit as "a Constitutional Convention for American women. They ratified the existing Constitution by demanding full inclusion in it, and then outlined the legislative changes that must take place if female citizens are to fully enjoy those rights for the first time."

Sports, unsurprisingly, was not a priority at the conference, and this was consistent with what many of the women of AIAW sensed. "The women's movement never embraced Title IX as an athletic position," said Lopiano. "They thought that athletics was a male construct that taught violence against somebody else, inordinate levels of competition—that it was an unhealthy activity for women—and that we were going to follow in the footsteps of men's values, and not the best men's values at all."

Others viewed this as more of a perception than reality. "Those of us working on Title IX realized early on that sports would become the tail that wagged the Title IX dog," said Margaret Dunkle.

But the feeling persisted among women in athletics that the leaders of Second Wave Feminism didn't really understand how important the athletics piece of the movement was.

Donna de Varona was frustrated by what she viewed as a patronizing attitude toward sports on the part of some of the conference leaders.

"They saw it as, okay, women can play, but there's more important issues like equal pay, you know?" said de Varona. "But they didn't connect it. So we went away really frustrated. Because, women athletes, we were an intellectual exercise to them."

King herself had years earlier agitated for a larger role for athletes in the women's movement, only to be dismissed by Steinem, who explained, "This is politics."

To which King responded, "Gloria, we *are* politics."

The meetings in Houston yielded a "National Plan of Action" platform, which made no direct references to sports beyond asking the president to "direct the vigorous and expeditious enforcement of all laws prohibiting discrimination at all levels of education and oppose any amendments or revisions that would weaken these laws and regulations."

One of the most discussed events of the week was a contentious vote to affirm the legitimacy of the lesbians in the feminist movement, which passed after protracted debate. With the win, organizers released hundreds of lavender balloons—emblazoned "WE ARE EVERYWHERE"—into the conference room.

The question of whether any female athlete was or wasn't a lesbian, and the further question of why the answer mattered in the first place, remained a constant in 1977. Some saw the issue as a subtext in the ongoing enmity between some male coaches and administrators in the NCAA and the women's leadership at the AIAW.

"The AIAW had a lot of lesbians in their hierarchy and their coaching," said the longtime AP writer Doug Tucker, who covered the NCAA in Kansas City. "I'm not making a value judgment, I'm just saying that's the way it was. A lot of the men, male administrators and coaches, saw that as a definite negative. And there was a lot of in-your-face posturing from some of the women, and that was unspoken. You never talked about it, you never wrote about it. But it was a definite undercurrent from both sides, from the AIAW side, and from the more conservative men on the NCAA side. That was a factor in the friction; it wasn't a deciding factor, obviously."

But those assumptions and stereotypes were a factor that plagued female athletes who weren't lesbians, as well as the ones who were.

"When two men share a room at the Gloucester hotel for Wimbledon, it's accepted as the buddy system," noted Chris Evert. "Two women try to defray their expenses the same way and the rumor mill starts grinding."

Carole Oglesby had ruefully seen the way perceptions of sexuality colored people's views of sport. "It was very clear to me that there was this general viewpoint," Oglesby said, "that sports somehow was some kind of turning mechanism, that would turn a previously heterosexual woman into a lesbian. I mean, it's kind of bizarre."

So was the double-edged sword that greeted any female athletes deemed to be attractive. The golfer Jane Blalock described as "quasi-pornographic" a photograph featuring fellow pro Jan Stephenson in the LPGA's *Fairway* magazine (the Aussie Stephenson had prompted a minor furor in 1977 after appearing braless on the cover of *Sport* magazine). Billie Jean King pushed back in defense of Stephenson, arguing that women athletes reserved the right to use all their advantages to convert fans, and that male athletes were doing the same.

"It's just a matter of mutual self-interest," King wrote. "Jan Stephenson happens to be very pretty, as sure as she is a very good golfer, and her displaying that beauty is no more a threat to the integrity of golf than is Jim Palmer's 95 percent naked body in underwear ads a threat to the good name of baseball."

•

Through it all, AIAW kept growing, kept evolving, and kept its eyes on a rearguard action by the NCAA. Support for sticking with women's governance was strong. A 1978 survey of AIAW athletic departments found that of those expressing an opinion, nearly 90 percent wanted to stay with AIAW rather than move under the NCAA umbrella.

In 1977, AIAW signed a $1 million contract with NBC, to cover the next five AIAW basketball and gymnastics championships. It was a sign of the growing appeal of women's sports, and while the initial funding was modest, the national exposure promised to raise AIAW's profile further.

The AIAW president-elect, Charlotte West, who handled the TV negotiations, was sitting in her office in Carbondale early in the spring of 1978 when she got a phone call.

"Dr. West? This is David Stern."

It was not immediately apparent why the general counsel of the National Basketball Association would be phoning the president-elect of the AIAW to discuss the latter's upcoming national championship tournament. But as would become clear in the coming years, Stern tended to get involved in everything related to basketball. Through his well-connected sources in New York, Stern knew that 1) NBC would be broadcasting the 1978 AIAW championship game, 2) West was overseeing the television details for the historic broadcast and 3) the network hadn't hired a color commentator yet.

So Stern was calling to tell West that the AIAW should be thinking about the right person for the job. West suggested the authoritative young coach for Tennessee, Pat Head, who'd played on the 1976 Olympic team. When West mentioned the conversation later to AIAW president Judie Holland, by now the women's athletic director at UCLA, Holland was disappointed. "Nobody wants to hear that Southern twang," Holland said.

It wasn't the first, nor the last, time that Holland veered against the ideas of West. In a way, the two women came to embody different interpretations of the same idea. West loved competition and wanted AIAW to grow, but her first loyalty was to the original vision, of women administrators managing women's sports. Holland also loved the original idea, but by the end of the '70s, her first loyalty was to increasing the competition, and finding a way for college basketball to grow bigger, more lucrative and more competitive.

Like Lopiano at Texas, Holland was intent on building a national power. In 1977, disappointed with what she considered an underachieving performance by the UCLA women's basketball team, she fired Ellen Mosher and hired Billie Moore, who left Fullerton to coach at UCLA.

What even her critics acknowledged was that Holland was a brilliant sports event organizer. Since the CIAW days, the national championship in women's basketball had been a sixteen-team, four-day event at one location, with teams playing one game a day. Holland persuaded the AIAW membership that the sport had grown enough for the tournament to be played over two weekends, with the winners of the four regional tournaments advancing to a larger city the following weekend for a women's basketball Final Four.

Holland's motion passed, and the first Women's Final Four, in 1978, would be hosted by UCLA and held at the largest venue yet, the hallowed Pauley Pavilion, where Wooden's men's dynasty was built.

The 1978 Final Four would prove to be Ann Meyers' moment in the sun. The '76 Olympian, the younger sister of the UCLA national champion and first-round NBA draft choice David Meyers, had become a sensation on the court, the sport's first four-time All American. A kinetic dervish, she'd achieved the first quadruple double in college basketball history. She nearly did it again in the 1978 final, totaling 20 points, 10 rebounds, 9 assists and 8 steals, as UCLA avenged its regular-season loss to Maryland, 90–74.

That would be Billie Moore's second national title, but unlike the 1970 championship with Cal State–Fullerton, this one was achieved on national television, in front of a nearly sold-out Pauley Pavilion. There hadn't been a bake sale all season long.

In the wake of the success of the '78 women's national championship, it became clearer that Holland was hoping to lead the AIAW on a path that closely resembled the NCAA's. "There was a huge rift between those that didn't want to proceed quite so fast," said Holland, "and, quote, unquote, didn't want to make the mistakes the men made. And those of us who wanted to plow ahead."

She prioritized viability over unity and in so doing was much more open and receptive to the idea of the NCAA sooner or later taking over women's sports.

The AIAW had historically resisted a Most Outstanding Player award, owing to the philosophy that all the players are equal. Holland pushed to change that.

"I knew early on that Judie was sympathetic to joining the NCAA," said Charlotte West. "Everything the NCAA did, Judie wanted to do. How they did press conferences, everything. She thought how the men did it was how Judie wanted to do it."

•

The gains in women's sports far transcended Title IX's impact on colleges.

In women's golf, the rookie Nancy Lopez—who'd been seen as a promising junior for years—exploded onto the LPGA scene in 1978, winning nine tournaments, including five in a row, a streak that garnered the sort of cumulative attention that Pete Rose's forty-four-game hit streak did that same summer. Lopez was the daughter of a Mexican immigrant and had grown up in Roswell, New Mexico. When her dad wasn't running his auto body shop, he was teaching Nancy golf. She played on the boys' team in high school before becoming the first woman to receive a full athletic scholarship at the University of Tulsa. Her string of titles in '78 landed her on the cover of *Sports Illustrated*.

That same year, Janet Guthrie became the first woman to qualify for the Indianapolis 500. Her arrival at qualifying was greeted by many of the old guard drivers as purely a publicity stunt, and a desecration of the Brickyard's central assumptions. Most drivers weren't welcoming, and the pushback among a significant portion of fans was even stronger: "No tits in the pits!" read the signs. But that year, Guthrie won the award as the top rookie at Indianapolis; a year later, she did the same thing in a stock car at Daytona.

There were also landmark gains for women sportswriters. In 1975, Jane Gross became the first female sportswriter to enter a pro basketball locker room when she covered both the New York Knicks and Nets for *Newsday*. A year later, at the World Series, *Sports Illustrated*'s young reporter Melissa Ludtke was denied access to the locker rooms—even though both teams had given clearance for her to enter—by Major League Baseball. Bob Wirz from the commissioner's office had had her paged during the game to inform her that she would not be permitted in the locker room under any circumstance.

That eventually prompted the lawsuit *Melissa Ludtke and Time Inc. v. Bowie Kuhn, Commissioner of Baseball et al.*, decided in the fall of 1978, when federal judge Constance Baker Motley ruled that the ban on females was unconstitutional. As female reporters were granted access to the Yankees' locker room, the journeyman outfielder Jay Johnstone hung a handmade sign above his locker reading, "U.S. Judge Constance Motley Sucks Ratshit!" Kuhn, on the wrong side of history again, and baseball appealed and lost.

•

By the beginning of 1978, the growth of women's basketball had become so apparent that a promoter in Ohio, Bill Byrne, began seeking investors to launch the Women's Professional Basketball League, which debuted in December of that year, with eight teams. Intent on star power, the new league drafted UCLA's Ann Meyers, Delta State's Lucy Harris and Montclair State's sharpshooter Carol Blazejowski, but none of them signed on for the inaugural season, since all were retaining their amateur status for the 1980 Summer Olympics.

On December 9, 1978, the Milwaukee Does hosted the Chicago Hustle in front of 7,824 at Milwaukee Arena. Amid the promise, the Hustle's star player Karen Logan struck a note of caution. "Everybody says history was made here today," said Logan. "But it's not history unless we're all still here three or four years from now. Everything that happened today is all well and good, but if we're not here next year, what is it all worth?" Logan had already enjoyed a remarkable athletic career. She was an All-American at Pepperdine, played four seasons with the All-American Redheads softball team and two years in the International Volleyball Association. Along the way, she'd beaten Laker legend Jerry West in a game of H-O-R-S-E on CBS's *Challenge of the Sexes* (produced in the wake of the King–Riggs match) and had narrowly finished second to Mary Jo Peppler in the first women's *Superstars* competition.

In addition to playing, Logan had suggested the idea of a slightly smaller ball—28.5 inches in circumference rather than the standard men's size of 29.5 inches. (It would later be adopted in women's college basketball and eventually the WNBA.) The league found legitimate stars, like "Machine Gun" Molly Bolin of the Iowa Cornets—a sharpshooter with Farrah Fawcett bangs—and developed regional rivalries. Attendance was disappointing, but the league finished its first season in May and prepared to expand to twelve teams in 1979–80.

In the summer of 1979, Ann Meyers, still training with the U.S. National Team, got a phone call from Sam Nassi, the new owner of the NBA's Indiana Pacers. He said he wanted to invite her to try out for the team.

Suspicious that it was a publicity stunt, and unsure about whether she'd truly have a chance, she called her friend Julius Erving, whom she'd gotten to know (at an off-season pro-am tennis tournament), as well as her brother Dave, then a starter for the Milwaukee Bucks, who offered a bracing response. "That's really great, Annie," he said. "But there's no one in the NBA who is five-foot-eight and 134 pounds."

Meyers was intrigued with the challenge and decided to take Nassi up on it, traveling to Indianapolis with the quintessential athletic mindset of "anything is possible." The brief footage that existed of her tryout showed her being bodied by a bigger guard in a routine one-on-one drill. She possessed all of the fundamental skills, but physically she was too slight to compete and was not sufficiently quick to make up for the size difference.

"I was not going to be in the starting five," she said. "How much time do those tenth and eleventh players get? That might equal up to about 48 minutes, for the season. I would have been at the end of the bench. It would have been everything else. How would it look to the wives and girlfriends?"

Even those who were rooting for Meyers thought that her case was a distraction from the larger problem. The issue was never whether women could compete directly with men. Simone de Beauvoir, in her seminal 1949 work

*The Second Sex*, anticipated the dispute over women's role in athletics: "In sports," she wrote, "the end in view is not success independent of physical equipment; it is rather the attainment of perfection within the limitations of each physical type: the featherweight boxing champion is as much a champion as is the heavyweight; the woman skiing champion is not inferior to the faster male champion: they belong to two different classes."

Now that she was officially a pro, Meyers remained a highly coveted commodity in the Women's Professional Basketball League, where she eventually signed with the New Jersey Gems. Just as in the ABA and the other upstart leagues, there was a glimpse for serious fans of a genuine league coalescing. Meyers would star for the team—and be named co-MVP of the league in the '79–'80 season—but after full houses for UCLA and the Olympic Games, she found the new league tough going.

"Games were really physical," said Meyers. "But marketing-wise, they didn't really know how to market the league. They put you through an etiquette class, how to wear your hair, go to the hairdresser's, how to dress, and how to act as a woman rather than as an athlete. We were just excited to be playing basketball."

•

Meanwhile, the battle over Title IX and the future of women's intercollegiate sports raged on.

In 1976, the NCAA had filed a lawsuit arguing that the Title IX regulations were unconstitutional, but by 1978, the case was thrown out, with Margot Polivy weighing in on behalf of the AIAW, arguing that neither the legislation nor the preliminary guidelines as written would spell doom for men's collegiate sports.

Later that year, on October 24, 1978, Charlotte West—by now the AIAW president—wrote letters to Byers and J. Neils Thompson at the NCAA, inviting them to a meeting "jointly to discuss future organizational governance structure(s) designed to meet the needs of male and female student athletes and their institutions."

The offered hand wasn't slapped so much as ignored. After receiving no answer, West wrote to Byers again later that year before receiving a terse reply in his inimitable corporate doublespeak a week later: "Your letter of December

29 was reviewed by the NCAA Council at its January 5 meeting," he wrote. "It was the Council's view that present conditions do not augur for a meeting of national college athletic organizations to consider questions of national athletic governance." (Months later, members of the council were surprised to learn that there had been any correspondence between West and Byers— Byers hadn't informed them.)

Ahead of the 1979 NCAA Convention, HEW Secretary Joseph Califano had sent out a thirty-five-page "clarification" letter, noting that the "expenditures on men's and women's athletics be proportional to the number of men and women participating," and that football and basketball would be included in the determination of equality. What that meant is if a college was spending $100,000 on twenty-five male athletes, the per capita spending on female athletes—whether there were five or ten or twenty-five—also had to be $4,000 per person.

With Califano insisting that the final policy interpretation should be handed down in time for the 1979–80 school year, all the interested parties increased their lobbying efforts.

On April 5, 1979, just days after the Three Mile Island nuclear reactor meltdown, the AIAW reps got an audience with Califano. West was joined by Lock Haven's Sharon E. Taylor, Texas' Donna Lopiano, Iowa's Christine Grant, Temple's Kaye Hart, Michigan State's Nell Jackson, and the ever-present Polivy. The women spoke to Califano about how much trouble they were having getting equal access to facilities and travel budgets. What Taylor would remember was Califano sharing his frustration, "explaining to us why he was getting so much pressure."

The women left the meeting with mixed emotions. They sensed that Califano understood the credibility of their grievance—"He could see that, you know, we weren't all raging feminists," said Charlotte West—but they were not at all sure that Title IX would, in the end, survive intact.

"When he heard this other side of it, I think it may have gotten his attention," said Taylor. "But he certainly didn't give us any reason to go out and celebrate that night."

In July, Califano announced that HEW needed even more time to finalize the interpretations. Throughout the AIAW, there was a sense that the hoped-for gains might be slipping away.

Enter the Women's Sports Foundation.

Donna de Varona may not have been there on day one of the Women's Sports Foundation—she and King would continue to differ on who was and wasn't a full-fledged co-founder—but in that period in 1979, the shrewd de Varona, and her Rolodex full of contacts on Capitol Hill, was crucial to position WSF in its advocacy role.

The foundation had been formed and for a time remained at Larry and Billie Jean King's offices in the Bay Area, but eventually moved to New York. The group was buoyed by a 1978 benefit event in Las Vegas, called "All-Star Salute to Women in Sports." In April, WSF established the Wade Trophy— named after Delta State's legendary coach Margaret Wade—given to the best women's basketball player in the country, with Carol Blazejowski of Montclair State named the first winner.

With HEW waffling and Califano giving way in August to his successor, former HUD secretary Patricia Roberts Harris, the WSF joined a final push, and gained a meeting with the president. De Varona was joined at the White House by Janet Guthrie, the golfer Carol Mann and hurdler Lacey O'Neal, for a meeting with President Carter and Secretary Harris.

"We're here as a living statement that we want women to be able to grow up as part of the American tradition of participation in sports," de Varona said after the meeting. "We want to show the president, Secretary Harris, and members of Congress that there is visible grassroots support for Title IX, that's it's not just an issue for lawyers, educators, or people outside the system."

•

By the beginning of the 1979–80 school year, AIAW's membership had increased from 278 charter members to 973. In 1973, colleges had offered 2.5 intercollegiate sports for women and 7.3 for men. By the end of the decade, the average was up to 6.48 for women. And, despite the predictions of doom, it had maintained for men, bumping up slightly to 7.4. Attendance continued to rise in college football and men's college basketball.

All around women's sports, there were signs of progress. The AIAW had originally offered no scholarships, but by the 1977–78 school year, more than 10,000 women at nearly 500 schools were receiving athletic scholarships. In high school, there was an explosion of participation. Only 294,000 girls had participated in organized sports in 1969; seven years later the numbers had grown to 1.6 million. Women's athletics budgets, barely 1 percent of the total in 1972, had grown to 16 percent. It wasn't nearly enough. But it was a start.

In the fall of 1979, as both sides began their final politicking, Charles Schulz took to his drafting board again and penned a two-week long series of *Peanuts* strips championing women's sports and citing WSF research showing massive inequities. Schulz continued to be an advocate, as was ABC's Frank Gifford, who'd always risen above the towel-snapping hijinks of boys in locker rooms.

Finally, more than seven years after it was signed into law, on December 4, 1979, HEW announced its final policy interpretations for Title IX regulations for athletic departments at colleges and high schools would finally go into effect, and there would be no special exception, temporary or otherwise, for football or basketball. Equal meant equal.

At the press conference announcing the final policy interpretations, HEW secretary Harris held up a photograph of the 1885 Wellesley crew team. "For those who believe that women's interest in athletics is new, I would say that it goes back at least until 1885."

What the provisions meant was that, if women came to sports—if they embraced the discipline and the spirit, and the eternal verities that inevitably came with the games—there would be a place for them in college athletics.

In the end, HEW arrived at a three-pronged system for compliance. The first was that athletic participation be proportional to gender enrollment. The second prong required a school to demonstrate a history of expanding its athletic programs to meet the interest and needs of the historically underrepresented gender. The third prong required that the school's programs demonstrate that they had "fully and effectively accommodated the interests and abilities" of both genders.

The finished product neither lived up to the hopes of the women in AIAW nor confirmed the most dire claims of those in the NCAA. In the end—typical of the American political process—the policy interpretations regarding athletics in Title IX became a compromise. But while the proponents didn't get all they wanted, they got what they needed.

Walter Byers, still appealing the summary judgment in the NCAA's earlier lawsuit against HEW, said the policy stipulations "will not stand a legal test nor the test of time." In this, he was wrong. Byers had in the past speculated that women's interest in athletics was little more than "a fad," a position that Lopiano, for one, found laughable. "There's never been a question of enough interest," she said. "If you build it, they will come."

While the AIAW's future remained uncertain, the crucial legal justification for equality among the sexes had been secured, despite all of the efforts of the NCAA, Sen. John Tower and the rest of the old-guard forces that had fought against it.

For Lock Haven's Sharon E. Taylor, the reason was simple.

"We were smarter than they were," she said. "God knows Donna Lopiano was ten times smarter than John Tower ever was." Of course, it wasn't just Lopiano or even only the AIAW that defeated the Tower Amendment, and the other monied interests fighting Title IX in collegiate athletics. It was a broad-based cooperative effort. Others would get more headlines, but at least one observer felt the hidden heroes in the struggle were the tireless Olympic gold medalist and advocate, along with the Republican senator from Alaska who supported preserving the gains won in 1972.

"Title IX was Donna de Varona and Ted Stevens," said Senator Bill Bradley, who witnessed the infighting on the Hill at the dawn of his own political career. "That's how Title IX prevailed, because of her leadership and tenacity, and because of Ted Stevens' commitment to the issue."

So as the 1970s drew to a close, the AIAW had succeeded in winning the nearly decade-long congressional battle for Title IX.

"I hated that you had to have a law to do what was right," said the Tennessee women's AD Joan Cronan. "But you did because sports was such a male-dominated world."

For women athletes, Title IX was the catalyst that launched a new era in sports.

But for the AIAW, it would prove to be a hard-won, short-lived victory.

# SEVENTEEN

# MODERN TIMES

NEAR THE END of the decade, college basketball was asserting itself in ways unimaginable just a few years earlier. It was difficult to pinpoint the launch, but one might place it at South Bend, Indiana, on a fevered Saturday afternoon in January 1974, when the Notre Dame Fighting Irish—decked out in home uniforms of an almost electric gold adorned with a green shamrock—rallied late to end UCLA's eighty-eight-game win streak, 71–70, in front of a national television audience. Two months later, UCLA's string of seven straight NCAA titles was broken in an epic double-overtime national semifinal loss to David Thompson and North Carolina State on the Wolfpack's home floor in Greensboro, North Carolina.

After John Wooden's farewell championship the following season—giving UCLA ten titles in twelve years—the field of contenders opened dramatically. In the four seasons following Wooden's retirement, sixteen different teams occupied the sixteen Final Four spots, and the bracing unpredictability coincided with the college game's surge in popularity.

While professional sports like the NFL and Major League Baseball had a finite, easily identifiable inventory of familiar teams, major-college basketball was a riot of nearly 300 schools, many obscure, from more than two dozen conferences, along with more than fifty independent teams. It created a chaotic landscape of Cinderella schools on the fringe, and occasionally in the midst, of national recognition. In the 1977–78 season alone, the AP Top 20 included entries from the University of San Francisco, the University of Detroit (coached by a voluble gadfly named Dick Vitale), Holy Cross, Illinois State, the burgeoning program at Georgetown (where the former Celtic backup John Thompson had reversed the Hoyas' fortunes), and even the remote outpost of the University of New Mexico, where the ascendant Lobos were directed by coach Norm Ellenberger, notorious for his turquoise necklaces, his team's turquoise uniforms and his inventive work with school transcripts, which eventually got him in deep trouble with the NCAA.

Serious sports fans began following the tournament to an obsessive degree, always intrigued with the shock of the unknown and unseen. Could Iona College, a tiny school in New Rochelle, New York, with a brash coach named Jim Valvano ("the money Namath makes, you say he's ruggedly handsome; the money I make, you say I got a big nose"), actually compete with perennial powers like Louisville and Marquette? Might the burgeoning smaller conference champions like Idaho State and Wichita State actually hang with the UCLAs and Indianas?

The elements that Roone Arledge had focused on in his basketball broadcasts at the beginning of the decade—the confined setting, the manic crowd, the players being close to the cameras and unencumbered with helmets or padding—all led to a more intimate, compelling atmosphere. And when mixed with the frenetic student sections, the increasingly acrobatic cheerleaders and the historic rivalries, the games provided these nearly perfect two-hour packets of televised sports drama.

The sport's growth was prompting new conferences to form, forged out of basketball rather than football alliances. In 1975, there was the Metro Conference, which brought together a half-dozen Mideast independents like Tulane, Louisville and Cincinnati. Four years later, the Providence College coach and athletic director Dave Gavitt organized a new conference comprised of previously independent Eastern schools—most of them private, many of them Catholic. Providence was joined by St. John's in New York, Georgetown, Syracuse, Seton Hall, Connecticut and Boston College.

The conference had no tradition, but it did have an organizing principle: As TV revenues grew in college basketball, the conference schedule for its schools offered a range of appealing matchups, with nearly every school representing a major media market. That summer before the 1979 season, Gavitt and St. John's AD Jack Kaiser consulted with a Manhattan PR firm to come up with ideas for a new name. The suggested titles included:

The Galactic East

The Seaboard Seven

The Empire Conference

The Mayflower Compact

After wisely deciding not to name their conference after the rules of self-government adopted by the Pilgrims exploring the new world, the caretakers of the new league settled on the name the Big East.

Playing as independents, these schools were sometimes overlooked. But assembled together, the whole was greater than the sum of the parts, and the Big East would quickly become one of the most respected basketball conferences in the country.

•

There was one other factor that helped the tournament grow in popularity in the late '70s: the widespread publishing of the NCAA tournament bracket.

Tournament brackets had been around for decades. There was a bracket printed for a thirty-two-team AAU invitational tournament in the March 10, 1921, edition of the *Kansas City Star*. Brackets had been a country-club staple for years, mostly associated with tennis and match-play golf tournaments; Billie Jean King remembered sitting around at the West Side Tennis Club in the days of the U.S. Nationals in the 1960s. "At the time there was also a fifteen-foot-high billboard of the tournament draws, and a person on a ladder would fill in the results as matches were played." The brackets were also popular in the early '70s at the NFL League meetings, where Lamar Hunt—who by then had become the main financier of World Championship Tennis—began drawing up a bracket for the NFL owners' mixed-doubles tennis tournament played during the week of the meetings. The NCAA regional tournament programs included brackets by 1977. But up until the late '70s they'd rarely appeared in newspapers, where tournament schedules had almost always run in a single column in the Scoreboard section of sports pages.

With the advent of the bracket, the shape of tournament coverage changed from a series of lines of agate into something more easily visualized. At a glance, one could easily scan not only the upcoming games, but the path each team had to travel to reach the Final Four, which regions were easiest and most difficult. In 1978, the *Chicago Tribune* published a small graphic of the bracket the day after the field was announced. The feature was so popular that, a year later, the bracket for the forty-team 1979 field graced a quarter of the front page of the *Tribune* sports section. The bracket had arrived. In the following decade, the bracket would launch a million office pools, but at first in the late '70s, it simply offered a compelling clarity to the unruly fandango of tournament play.

In the midst of all this growing interest came the Platonic ideal of a college basketball season. Every campaign in every sport takes on a shape and character. The 1978–79 college basketball season would be defined by the contrasting brilliance of Indiana State's Larry Bird and Michigan State's Earvin "Magic" Johnson.

Bird had been the cover subject for *Sports Illustrated*'s college basketball preview issue the previous season, in the fall of 1977 (because Indiana State played in obscurity, that was the first color photograph of Bird that many sports fans had ever seen), and was voted first team All-America that season. But the undermanned Sycamores lost in an early-round NIT game, and Bird seemed simply a marvelous player on an irrelevant team. By the fall of 1978, Michigan State's sophomore Johnson graced the cover of *SI*'s college basketball preview issue, as part of a feature on a historically strong class of sophomore players. The magazine copied Marquette's gimmick from a couple of years earlier, photographing ten of the "Super Sophs" in tuxedos and tails, and spotlighting the wondrously versatile Johnson.

As the season progressed, Michigan State fulfilled expectations, prevailing in a brutal Big Ten Conference race. But the real surprise came from Bird and Indiana State in the often overlooked Missouri Valley Conference, where a new coach (Bill Hodges had replaced the mainstay Bob King, who suffered from a congenital heart condition) and a team of mostly no-names were elevated by their leader. Bird had decided not to speak with the media during the season. He was sheepish about how much attention he was receiving, which only added to the intrigue. As the wins kept piling up, and undefeated Indiana State moved to the top of the polls for the first time ever in February, Bird—the hardwood Garbo—remained elusive.

NBC scored a montage of Bird game highlights to the sound of the Trashmen's 1963 garage rock hit, "Surfin' Bird." But the number one team in the country was little seen and roundly dismissed as lightweights (another outsider, the University of San Francisco, had risen to the top of the poll two years earlier, only to lose its regular season finale, then get blown out in the first round of the tournament).

Both Bird, the shy white kid from the country, and Johnson, the flashy Black kid from the city, were originals. There were other white stars during this period, but few looked less like an athlete than Bird, who was almost impossibly pale, with narrow eyes and a wispy mustache. Indiana State—undefeated, ranked number one—had never been on a national telecast before, and even its uniform design was unique, with an outline of the state replacing the first "I" in Indiana. Johnson, for his part, was six-foot-nine and a *guard*, which was improbable enough. But like Bird, he also was blessed with a nearly omniscient sense of court vision, which allowed him to diagnose opportunities on the Spartan fast break. Significantly, he exuded a kind of fizzy joy in the moment—sports as, above all else, something *fun*—that proved infectious for teammates and fans alike.

The tournament expanded to forty teams in 1979, and for the first time the NCAA selection committee seeded every team in every region. This meant more teams moving out of their natural region, and a more balanced bracket. "The idea was to make sure that every team that reached the finals had to travel equally hazardous roads," recalled tournament chairman Dave Gavitt. "We didn't realize it at the time, but that set up incredible intersectional matchups. In the second round, you would have a Georgetown playing a Memphis State or a Notre Dame against TCU."

That confluence of events and characters allowed the 1979 tournament to reach an apotheosis. Michigan State rolled through the Mideast Regional, while Indiana State barely survived the Midwest, needing a last-second winner from guard Bob Heaton to vanquish Arkansas in the Midwest Regional final. They would be joined by two surprise semifinalists: unranked Ivy League champions Pennsylvania upset the East's top seed, North Carolina, on the way to the Final Four, while the at-large independent DePaul—shipped out to the West regional to balance the bracket—shocked UCLA in the West Regional.

The four teams converged for the Final Four in Salt Lake City, and Bird, in his first press conference, finally broke his season-long silence, revealing both a wry sense of humor and a frankness that bordered on truculence. "The Final Four means more to my teammates than it does to me," he said. "I thought we should have been here last year. If we win or lose it don't make no difference to me. I'm gonna get my money anyway."

Bird's cavalier words belied his true feelings and intense competitiveness. When Indiana State and Michigan State advanced to the Monday evening championship game, it set up a showdown between the two best players— and two most charismatic personalities—in the game. On that Monday night, Michigan State bottled up Bird and his outmanned teammates on the way to an 11-point win, ending Indiana State's dream season and leaving the disconsolate Bird on the bench, weeping under a towel.

It became (and remains) the most-watched college basketball game of all time. The TV audience didn't witness a great game but did watch two generational talents who would help define the next era in basketball. For all their differences, both Johnson and Bird had well-earned reputations for making their teammates better, for providing an indefinable extra quality, an admixture of leadership and empathy that promoted the eternal basketball virtue of teamwork.

All of which was *exactly* what the National Basketball Association needed at that moment.

•

The NBA was still reeling from an incident the previous season. In Los Angeles, on December 9, 1977, the Rockets were visiting the Lakers in a tight game, when Kevin Kunnert and Kareem Abdul-Jabbar got into it. They'd had skirmishes in the past, and as the Rockets were taking the ball down the court, a whistle blew to kill the action, and prompted another altercation between the two centers. In the midst of the shoving and swinging, Kermit Washington, the Lakers' six-foot-eight power forward, had just tangled with Kunnert and sensed someone coming at him. It was the Rockets' Rudy Tomjanovich.

The punch Washington threw was a blind roundhouse—he would say later he didn't know whom or what he was swinging at, but only saw a flash of red approaching him from behind—that landed with sickening perfection under Tomjanovich's nose.

"I'll never forget that sound," Abdul-Jabbar would recall. "I had turned Kunnert away from Kermit, and suddenly I heard this *crack*, like a melon landing on concrete."

By the time Tomjanovich got to the emergency room at Centinela hospital in Los Angeles, spinal fluid from his brain was leaking into his mouth. It would take him five surgeries and more than eleven months to play basketball again.

The damage to the sport was considerable.

David Stern, the NBA's general counsel who by this time had been promoted to executive vice president, had become Larry O'Brien's most trusted aide. Stern arrived in the league office early the next morning as the gruesome reports came back and recognized instantly that it could harden the perception that the league was out of control.

"This was a monumental event when it occurred, because it appeared to symbolize everything people were saying about us," Stern said. "What this event told us was that we could not, under any circumstances, allow men this big and this strong to square off and swing at one another."

(In this recalibration of how much violence could exist in modern sports, the NBA wasn't acting alone. It was becoming clear that, as players became more valuable and more games made their way into American homes, the games themselves had to become safer. The NFL outlawed Deacon Jones' patented head-slap pass rush move in 1977, and faced more concerns about safety when Patriots' wide receiver Darryl Stingley was paralyzed by a legal hit from the Raiders' Jack Tatum in a preseason game in 1978. Major League Baseball required batting helmets for all new players beginning in 1971, as did the National Hockey League starting in 1979. The NHL, alone among the major leagues, continued to condone fighting as "part of the game," though this was news to every other major hockey league in the world, where it wasn't permitted.)

For the NBA, the bad publicity from the violence further wounded a league that would go on to be slaughtered in the Nielsen ratings the next two seasons with consecutive NBA Finals matchups between the Seattle Super-Sonics and the Washington Bullets. CBS had earned a 12.7 rating for the 1977 Finals between Portland and Philadelphia, but then only 9.9 and 7.2 for the two Seattle–Washington series in '78 and '79. The league's need to police further acts of violence on the court was among the factors that led to the NBA finally inaugurating the three-point shot for the 1979–80 season in an attempt to unclog the action under the net and open up the game.

All of this was context when Johnson and Bird joined the NBA in 1979.

The previous summer, in the 1978 NBA draft, with the modern Celtics a ghost of their dynastic past, Red Auerbach had made one last crafty basketball decision. Bird was eligible for the '78 draft (because he'd sat out a year after transferring to Indiana State from Indiana his freshman year), even though he'd already announced that he'd play his senior year. Auerbach realized that the star was just what the Celtics needed to revive their fortunes and selected him sixth overall, gambling that he could sign Bird in the three-month window between the end of the college basketball season and the '79 NBA draft in late June. That left Bird with more negotiating power coming out of college than any basketball player since Alcindor in 1969. Bird didn't have another league to negotiate with, but if he didn't like the Celtics' offer, he could simply go back into the 1979 NBA draft. With the agent Bob Woolf handling his deal, Bird signed a contract paying him more than any of the Boston veterans, about $650,000 a year. In the '79 draft, Johnson was drafted by the Los Angeles Lakers, with a pick they'd acquired in a trade with the New Orleans Jazz, where he would join Abdul-Jabbar on one of the league's most prominent teams.

The most-watched college basketball game thus also served as an introduction of two dominant personalities that would define the future of pro basketball.

"It carried over," said Brian McIntyre, PR man for the Bulls and later the NBA. "Here's two guys from the Midwest, who battle it out in the NC-two-As, one's white, one's black, one goes to a gritty, old East Coast city, which is one of our two flagship cities for basketball. The other guy goes out to the glitz and glamour of Hollywood, where they start Showtime. Both guys seem to represent their adopted cities perfectly, and they were embraced by their cities. All of a sudden we had two marquee teams to keep putting on TV when CBS didn't want to treat us right."

As the NBA prepared for its thirty-fourth season in the summer of 1979, Larry O'Brien was still nominally the commissioner. But the initiative on almost every issue was being led by his lieutenant, David Stern.

At the 1979 public relations manager meetings in New York City, gathering the PR men from all twenty-two franchises, Stern sat in on the conference, offering ideas, forever impatient, forever pressing his case. From that first exposure, McIntyre sensed a galvanizing force. "He'd come in and just sit down, he introduced himself and spurred the conversation," said McIntyre. "He'd come up with ideas and I remember that first time, when he walked out, I thought, 'man, that guy's got some ideas; this guy's pretty sharp.'"

Stern navigated his influence shrewdly. By the end of the decade, many in the league viewed Stern as the true catalyst, and O'Brien by then as more of a figurehead. "As a commissioner," said the Suns' Jerry Colangelo, "O'Brien made a good postmaster general."

Stern possessed a quality that, among commissioners, had been seen before only in the NFL's visionary Pete Rozelle.

"He understood what it took," said Frank Layden. "He understood that our product was the players, and we had to take care of them. It was like making a great movie. We needed the talent to make the movie work."

In the short term, there were small things. Stern convinced O'Brien to invest in twenty-two three-quarter-inch tape machines, one for each team in the league, and then sent out a directive ordering teams to record telecasts at the source—through the production truck—rather than on VHS tapes off of televisions. It was the dawn of building a library of footage that could be repurposed, the first step toward the launch of NBA Entertainment in 1982.

More importantly, it was Stern who pushed the idea, in the summer of 1979, that the NBA should be the first American sports league to sign a league-wide cable television deal. Individual teams had tentatively moved into cable, but this would be the first league-wide deal offering national cable telecasts.

"David was sort of the driving force behind that," said the NBA's Russ Granik. "I think he had a vision that cable was going to be a bigger thing."

There were only two serious bidders, UA/Columbia, the parent company of the Madison Square Garden Network (which would become the USA Network the following April), and a yet-to-launch aspiring cable network based in Bristol, Connecticut, called the ESP Network, soon to become ESPN.

Stern recognized that cable was poised to explode into American homes, offering an antidote to the hegemony of the three major networks.

The NBA settled on UA/Columbia, the forerunner of the USA Network, for a three-year deal valued at $1.5 million. USA Network would show Thursday night doubleheaders and some early-round playoff games.

"I remember we had a lot of people on our side of the table who had the view that ESPN made no sense," Granik said, "because how could you have a channel that was going to show nothing but sports all day?"

•

The decade's last major innovation, the cable network that would reshape the sports media landscape, was more accident than vision. It was indirectly prompted by another upstart league whose downfall was sealed by the lack of a national television contract. The World Hockey Association never really capitalized on the presence of aging stars Bobby Hull and Gordie Howe. The WHA was already a fading entity when, on May 30, 1978, the Whalers' owner Howard Baldwin called Bill Rasmussen, the team's communications director, and told him he was letting him go.

With only a month of severance pay, Rasmussen and some colleagues began looking around for other opportunities. He envisioned a cable television service that would offer University of Connecticut athletic events and other regional fare to UConn alums and fans in New England. But as he and his son Scott explored the economics of transponder rentals, they realized that the satellite link-up to broadcast the signals would be cheaper if purchased in bulk. Renting a full satellite for twenty-four-hour service was actually less expensive than purchasing specific blocks of time. And because the signal would cover the whole country, they learned that they need not limit their programming to New England.

After securing their satellite license, the father and son continued casting about for a programming formula that would accommodate their full schedule. On August 16, 1978, stuck in traffic on Interstate 84 in Waterbury, Connecticut, the Rasmussens were arguing about what to do with the added time, when Scott—peeved at the ongoing debate with his father—grumbled, "Just show college football constantly, for all I care..."

ESPN would eventually do just that. But in the short term, few people either within the new company or elsewhere in the business envisioned the potential impact. At the 1978 NFC Championship Game in Los Angeles, the announcer Verne Lundquist was standing on the sidelines when an executive from Getty Oil approached him.

"There is a satellite programming network, ESPN, that is available for sale," the exec told Lundquist. "And we're about to invest $15 million in this property, and we're thinking of making it an all-sports channel. What do you think?"

"Just sports?" asked Lundquist incredulously. "Why in the name of all that's holy would you ever think to do that?"

It was a reasonable question. Many in the industry were skeptical about whether there was a market for such a thing. But Rasmussen was on to something. The idea had been a long time in the making, a serendipitous sequence in which a modest idea—broadcast regional sports for zealots— was so well timed, it birthed a larger, much more ambitious endeavor. In the year before going on the air, Rasmussen, after an extended negotiation with Walter Byers, signed a deal with the NCAA to show championships in all NCAA sports besides football and basketball, as well as all manner of recorded regular-season college football and basketball games. Included in the package, with what at the time seemed a modest throw-in, was the opportunity to offer live coverage of the early-round games in the NCAA basketball tournament.

"What we're creating here is a network for sports junkies," said Scott Rasmussen two months before the launch. "This is not programming for soft-core sports fans who like to watch an NFL game and then switch to the news. This is a network for people who like to watch a college football game, then a wrestling match, a gymnastics meet, and a soccer game, followed by an hour-long talk show—on sports."

With the NCAA providing legitimacy, the network hired Chet Simmons from NBC Sports. Simmons insisted on adding his wingman Scotty Connal to handle the production.

On the day the network began broadcasting, Chet Simmons got a call from his former colleague Geoff Mason. "Good luck, friend," said Mason. "What kind of events are you guys looking for?"

"*Long* ones," said Simmons, still dubious about the ultimate viability of the enterprise.

Later that day, Friday, September 7, 1979, at seven p.m. Eastern time, the first broadcast of the cable Entertainment and Sports Network—ESPN— went to 1.4 million homes and about 30,000 viewers.

As the network went on the air, Lee Leonard, formerly of NBC, promised the network would be "Heaven for sports fans." He then turned it over to anchor George Grande, for the first episode of the network's nightly news program, *SportsCenter*.

The lead story on the first news program of the first day of the cable sports network was a sign of the times as well. As college football prepared for its second weekend and the National Football League for its first, as Major League pennant races were heating up, and NBA and NHL teams were reporting for training camp, the lead item was from the U.S. Open in Flushing Meadows. The four-time defending champion Chris Evert had just made it to her fifth consecutive final, defeating Billie Jean King in straight sets.

Then there was the editorial punctuation that followed the score. "Where does B.J. go from here?" mused Grande. "She's had untold knee operations, and to be truthful, she's only a shell of the player she once was. Lou Brock knew when it was time to get out. We hope Billie Jean does. It's always great to watch a star walk off the court—and not limp."

Would a male star have been called out quite so cavalierly? Perhaps not.

At the same time, if anyone at the beginning of the '70s had imagined a twenty-four-hour, all-sports television station would launch by the end of the decade, they would not have guessed that the first news item from the first show would be about a tennis match between two women.

The sports revolution *would* be televised.

•

In the wake of *The Superstars'* success, networks moved aggressively to find the commercial potential in almost any kind of sports event. This led to an era of what was derisively dubbed trash sports—hackneyed imitations of the Riggs–King match and *The Superstars*.

CBS was not immune to this. When independent producer Eddie Einhorn joined the network as a producer for the *CBS Sports Spectacular*, the network veered toward more marginal fare, contrivances such as a boxing match featuring the Cowboys' fearsome defensive lineman Ed "Too Tall" Jones and a competition called "Battle of the NFL Cheerleaders." When *Sports Spectacular* finally bested *Wide World of Sports* in the ratings, Einhorn explained the success by saying, "Our crap was better than their crap."

There was, admittedly, an initial novelty to seeing TV stars Gabe Kaplan and Robert Stack nearly come to blows over a relay-race rules interpretation in ABC's *Battle of the Network Stars*, but the fascination proved short-lived. As ever, you could fool some of the people some of the time, but the true appeal of spectator sports required elite performers and the gravity of legitimate stakes. Catherine Bach in a dunk tank didn't qualify.

As the '70s drew to a close, there were some last glimpses of unhinged revelry—like Pelé cutting a swath through Studio 54, Chris Evert dancing late into the night after Wimbledon at the private club Tramp—and also a confluence of events that would defy any sort of understanding in future decades: Julius Erving starred with Flip Wilson and Meadowlark Lemon in the incoherent comedy *The Fish That Saved Pittsburgh* (which billed itself, more or less accurately, as "an astrological disco sports extravaganza").

But by the end of the '70s, the Me Decade was slouching toward a reckoning. For the culture at large and for the world of sports, the novelty of always going louder, bolder and more colorful began to dissipate.

Throughout the country, there was a collective fatigue with the constant state of being unmoored. The 1978 midterm elections had seen the lowest turnout since World War II, with only 38 percent of registered voters bothering to cast a ballot. In New York City, election-night coverage ran a distant third behind a rerun of the 1963 Peter Sellers film *The Pink Panther*. A year later, there was the disconcerting visual of President Carter collapsing during a 6.2-mile foot race, just two months after he famously described the country suffering a "national malaise." Inflation reached 13.9 percent, higher than at any point since the end of World War II.

All around, there were signs of retrenchment: On the Top Forty charts, Willie Nelson's *Stardust*—a collection of covers of Hoagy Carmichael songs from the '30s and '40s—reached the Top Thirty in album sales in the spring of 1978, and landed Nelson on the cover of *Newsweek* that summer. After a decade of spandex, fog machines and eighteen-minute drum solos, the more straightforward rock 'n' roll of Bruce Springsteen, Dire Straits, and Tom Petty and the Heartbreakers was beginning to assert itself—intelligent, incisive music, in a traditional format.

A rough parallel could be drawn to similar forces at work in the world of sports. As baseball was just catching up to the wild fashion trends of the '70s, basketball and football were already ratcheting back. At the beginning of the 1976–77 season, the Philadelphia 76ers did a uniform makeover, trading their bold stripes and stars for understated white home and red road uniforms, which read "SIXERS" in block letters. By 1979, several NFL teams, most notably the Houston Oilers, had returned to white game pants for road trips. In Major League Baseball, even the light blue double-knit pullovers were phased out, to be replaced by old-school, button-up gray road uniforms—no longer the heavy wool fabric, but still a look that harkened back to the game's history.

Most significantly, the overwhelmingly negative response to artificial turf forced a reassessment. Miami's Orange Bowl (1976) was the first to return to natural grass, followed shortly by San Francisco's Candlestick Park (1979). For those who loved football and baseball played outdoors on natural grass, this was good news.

•

At the same time, there was a menacing undercurrent to some of the retrenchment. In the first month of 1978, the Bee Gees had the top three singles on *Billboard*'s Top Forty pop chart. But by the summer of 1979, the backlash against disco music—and the thinly veiled accompanying resentment of the Black and gay culture that often went along with it—began gaining steam. By 1979, Steve Dahl, a rock radio DJ in Chicago, had gained notoriety campaigning against disco. As Dahl's profile rose, Mike Veeck, the son of White Sox owner Bill Veeck, suggested the White Sox team up with Dahl for a promotion called "Disco Demolition Night," in which everyone bringing a disco album would get in for 98 cents, then watch the records be blown up between games of a twi-night doubleheader. The Sox had drawn 15,520 the night before, but Disco Demolition Night, July 12, 1979, wound up a sellout, and then some. After the tickets were sold, the unruly mass of attendees—most of them would not be identified as baseball fans—began jumping the turnstiles and climbing up through the portals in the wall on Comiskey's outfield facade.

After the first game, when the promotion was staged, Bill Veeck estimated that about 70,000 fans were in the park. While albums by the Bee Gees and other disco artists bore much of the pyrotechnic animosity, there was something else at work as well. The American music producer Vince Lawrence was a fifteen-year-old usher in Comiskey Park that night and was alarmed to see that many of the records brought in by the crowd—Stevie

Wonder, Marvin Gaye, Parliament Funkadelic—weren't disco records at all, but instead soul and rhythm and blues music. The racial component of the hostility was inescapable.

"As I got older, I recognized this was actually the end of an era," Lawrence said. "It was a book-burning. It was a racist, homophobic book-burning, and the Bee Gees got caught up in that." (So did the baseball. As fans stormed the field after the demolition, the playing surface was damaged and the White Sox had to forfeit the second game.)

In retrospect, the atmosphere that greeted Blacks on Disco Demolition night could be seen as an omen for a larger backlash that would see forces aligned against rap music in the '80s.

The bitter irony of the backlash was that, just as in popular music, the realm of sports—being one of the few arenas in which Blacks entered on anything like roughly equal terms with whites—was shaped and influenced by Black culture and expression.

Homer Jones had spiked the ball after a touchdown for the New York Giants on October 17, 1965. A few years later, the University of Houston wide receiver Elmo Wright began displaying a "touchdown dance"—basically running in place and raising his knees as high as possible—soon followed by Billy "White Shoes" Johnson, whose end zone celebrations were a variation on the rubber-legged wiggle of the Funky Chicken.

In the wake of Julius Erving's legendary performance in the ABA's Slam Dunk contest, the heightened awareness of the different ways to dunk elevated the act into a performance art form. In a 1979 game at Kansas City, the 76ers' young center Darryl Dawkins dunked over the Kings' Bill Robinzine with such ferocity that he shattered the glass backboard, causing a fifty-two-minute delay. The dunk raised the profile of Dawkins and, far from being apologetic about it, he declared later that he'd given the dunk a name, dubbing it the "The Chocolate-Thunder-Flying, Robinzine-Crying, Teeth-Shaking, Glass-Breaking, Rump-Roasting, Bun-Toasting, Wham-Bam, Glass-Breaker-I-Am Jam."

By the time Dawkins shattered another backboard, the NBA announced a fine against breaking backboards (and began intensive research on a basket stanchion that wasn't so fragile). But what Dawkins recognized was that the extraordinary power of the dunks—and the fact that they were replayed around the country on sports reports from nightly newscasts, which were picking up more national video by the late '70s—was giving him notoriety that he hadn't previously possessed, completely out of proportion to his pedestrian 14.7 scoring average.

But even the artfully rendered dunk took a backseat to the main celebratory innovation of the era, pioneered in the most traditional of sports. On October 2, 1977, Dusty Baker became the fourth Los Angeles Dodger to hit thirty home runs that season—he'd been trying to blast one out all weekend—and when he rounded third toward home, his teammate Glenn Burke greeted him not with open palms at waist level but instead with raised palms over his head. Baker, after touching home plate, emphatically raised his own hands to slap Burke's in celebration.

Then Burke homered, and as he reached home and the other Dodgers, Baker greeted him with the same raised hands. The celebration soon gained traction with the other Dodgers. The high five was born.

Within eighteen months, it had become the obligatory congratulatory greeting across the major American professional sports, owing not only to the novelty but to the prevalence of television. From there, it swept throughout Western culture; by 1980, the term "high five" was an official entry in the *Oxford English Dictionary*.

Just over the course of a decade, the rules for personal expression had been revolutionized. The theatrical dunk, the ingenious end zone celebrations, the high five, all moved sports into a theater of self-expression.

•

For all the gains Blacks were making in the realm of sports, race remained a sensitive, charged subject, as some schools, businesses and neighborhoods stubbornly continued a policy of near-total segregation. Just as integrated units in the military had conclusively shown that Blacks and whites could relate and coexist, sports teams provided the same proof. In sports locker rooms, where integration was common, the tension was dissipated, and the topic was more easily discussed, even grist for kibitzing.

When the five-foot-ten white infielder Phil Garner, who'd gone to college at the University of Tennessee, was acquired by the Pirates from the A's in a nine-player deal in 1977, he was indoctrinated on his first visit to the

Pirates' clubhouse. As he walked among the six-foot-five Jim Bibby and six-foot-seven John Candelaria, the six-foot-five Dave Parker surveyed the new arrival and, without so much as saying hello to Garner, bellowed, "What's going on? We trade six brothers for this one little old gray boy?"

The ethos of a clubhouse full of thick-skinned players with a rollicking sense of humor meant that almost nothing was out of bounds. "You've got so many personalities from so many different socioeconomic backgrounds," said Garner. "So the clubhouse was, what's the word? Raucous. It was raucous. You could get things off your chest, but you stay within certain boundaries. And we set those boundaries, and they were pretty broad."

Willie Stargell—the captain, the veteran, the distinguished "Pops"—was also the Pirates' de facto social director and DJ. The culture of the team was ecumenical and freewheeling. Since the early '70s, the Pirates' clubhouse was characterized by a loose affiliation of kidding and earthy humor, which transgressed racial boundaries.

"If Willie Stargell said we were going to have some yardbird and jungle plum, we knew he meant chicken and watermelon," said Steve Blass. "We used to laugh at the way they did their hair, and they used to laugh at us for what we did to our sideburns."

Stargell regularly hosted a team party at the All-Star break. He would fill up a plastic garbage can with every type of alcohol he could find, and then mask it with grape juice. He dubbed it "Purple Passion."

"And then he would stir it," said Blass, "with one of his bats."

At spring training in 1979, Stargell started handing out gold stars for his teammates to affix onto their modern-retro "pillbox caps," a remnant of the National League's centennial season in 1976.

"I saw the football helmets with buckeyes all over them for intercepted passes, downfield blocking, special-team tackling," Stargell would explain. "Baseball just said, 'Nice going.'"

"We fought for those stars," recalled Pirates teammate Bill Robinson. "To get those stars from your leader and captain was special."

Stargell could change minds with a raised eyebrow, and the sum of his leadership that season was to focus a talented team that had underperformed into a tightly knit squad that maximized its potential.

During a rain delay in June, Stargell, Parker and gangly relief pitcher

Kent Tekulve were sitting in the dugout, watching the rain and listening to the Sister Sledge hit single "We Are Family" over the stadium loudspeaker.

"You like this song?" Stargell asked.

"Yeah, that's nice," said Parker.

"We're gonna make this the team song," said Stargell. "I like what it says."

And so "We Are Family" became the team's unofficial theme song, played in heavy rotation during postgames (win or lose, at manager Chuck Tanner's behest). No one was demolishing any disco records around the Bucs' clubhouse.

"We could lose a game," said Rennie Stennett, "and if you came in there ten minutes after the game, you would think we won because we had such a loose club."

The Pirates, just 40–38 on July 8, caught fire and never looked back, going 58–26 down the stretch to win the NL East, then swept their nemesis Cincinnati in three games in the National League Championship Series, sending them to the World Series for the first time since 1971, where they would again face the Baltimore Orioles.

On the morning of the fifth game of the World Series, with the Pirates trailing the Orioles three games to one, Tanner's mother died. Meeting with the team before the game, Tanner said, "She knows we're in trouble, so she went upstairs to get some help." Stargell chimed in with the message that "All we need is three one-day winning streaks."

Two wins sent the Series to a seventh and final game in Baltimore. Midway through the game, as the Pirates were trying to solve the quirky delivery of Scott McGregor, Stargell turned to Dave Parker and said, "If McGregor throws me another fastball, I'm gonna get him."

In the sixth inning, with a runner on, McGregor threw Stargell that fastball, which he launched over the wall in right field to give the Pirates the lead for good. Pittsburgh would go on to win, 4–1, and Stargell would be named the World Series MVP.

By the end of the decade, Stargell had become a beloved figure, both in Pittsburgh and around the majors. There wasn't a racial milestone here—Stargell wasn't the first-Black-this or first-Black-that—but it was a sign of the decade's long journey that he had become the unquestioned team leader, not merely for what he did on the field, but for his manner, his consistency, and his sense of character.

"The biggest thing I regret in all my career is that I didn't get a chance to play with a Willie Stargell earlier," said Tim Foli, a teammate on the '79 Pirates. "Because if I would have, I wouldn't have been an aggressive hothead. Willie played the game properly. He worked his butt off. He got disappointed if he didn't do something, but you never saw it. He'd just go up there and take his best shot and win or lose. You know, he'd come back and say, you know, we've got to do better tomorrow. He had a rapport with everybody. And you respected him the way he played and the way he conducted himself."

•

Despite the doomsday predictions by Kuhn and owners at the advent of free agency, Major League Baseball had set another attendance record in 1979, with more than 43 million tickets sold. Eight of the league's twenty-six teams drew more than 2 million fans.

The baseball world was expanding in ways unforeseen even five years earlier. Free agency didn't just make players richer. It changed the way games would be followed, understood and experienced. The immediate effect of free agency was to keep baseball in the news well past the end of the World Series, thus extending the "hot stove" season far beyond the trades and rumors that accompanied MLB's annual winter meetings.

The most quantifiable of games, the one most calibrated by statistics, Major League Baseball also was the one in which statistics were most jealously guarded. A wry, ruminative man named Bill James, who'd been an English major at the University of Kansas, and later found work as a night watchman at a Stokely Van Camp plant in Lawrence, Kansas, pondered these questions between his rounds at the factory. Convinced that much of the sport's conventional wisdom was either misguided or outright wrongheaded, James took to thinking more deeply about the game. Was baseball really "75 percent pitching," as some said? Did the out a team surrendered in sacrificing a runner from first to second really make sense? Did the Green Monster at Fenway truly hurt right-handed hitters? Armed with the box scores in copies of *The Sporting News,* and the annual *Baseball Guides* with official statistics compiled by the Elias Sports Bureau, James studied these topics and began writing up short treatises. Finally, at the end of 1976, he put several of these together in a publication. He took out a one-inch advertisement in the back of *The Sporting News.* It read:

THE 1977 BASEBALL ABSTRACT
CONTAINS 18 STATISTICAL CATEGORIES
YOU CAN'T FIND ANYWHERE ELSE, AND A NEW
TABLE BASEBALL GAME
$2.50 PLUS 50¢ POSTAGE AND HANDLING
BOX 2150 LAWRENCE, KS 66044

That original publication, sixty-eight mimeographed pages dense with statistics and single-spaced essays, sold only seventy copies. James, disappointed with what he perceived as the slipshod quality of the first edition, compiled a second one in 1978, which sold moderately better but left him exhausted. "At the time, it was a job on top of my job, and I wasn't making any money on it, and in November of 1978, I was ready to say, 'All right, I just can't do this again.' That's when Dan Okrent's letter arrived."

Okrent was by then a well-known name in the book business, a literate, thoughtful editor and writer and a lifelong baseball geek. As a loyal Tigers fan and longtime devotee to the tabletop strategy game Strat-O-Matic baseball, he was the bullseye of the target audience for James' publication, and he was galvanized by James' findings.

"Ballpark effect," said Okrent. "It just floored me. It had never occurred to me; it was like the heavens had opened up. Why are batting averages so much lower in Oakland? It's because there's so much foul territory, and pop-ups into the stands elsewhere are pop-ups to the first baseman or third baseman or catcher's glove in Oakland. I mean, this was revolutionary." It was also the product of rigorous intellectual scrutiny, of James bringing to bear the same elements of skeptical inquisitiveness that serious scholars brought to other fields.

By the fall of 1979, Okrent and James had become friends. They went to a game together that fall—Minnesota at Kansas City, September 11, 1979, just four days after ESPN had gone on the air—and later Okrent pitched *Sports Illustrated* on a profile of James and his findings.

It was initially rejected because of minor factual inaccuracies. "He was pointing out that Gene Tenace was a much better player than people gave him credit for, and that he had an on-base percentage of .414," remembered Okrent. "Well, according to Elias it was .412. And this was used as proof that this guy doesn't know what he's doing. Well, what they left out was the fact that Elias would not give Bill access to their statistics." (Okrent's story would finally run, in 1981, and make James an overnight sensation of sorts.)

James had written to Major League Baseball, to each major league team, and to Elias directly, requesting access to official statistics for research purposes. But the game's numbers in the 1970s were the exclusive province of Seymour Siwoff, and he refused to share any of the game-by-game data that would have allowed James to verify the painstaking granular calculations he was doing through old box scores and baseball annuals.

"I see Seymour Siwoff as one of the great villains of the era," said Okrent, "for his unwillingness to see anything but what he had been seeing since he first put his nose in a stat sheet thirty years earlier."

Meanwhile, the intellectually vibrant Okrent was as consumed as James with the game of baseball. Okrent was working in the books division of *Texas Monthly*, flying once a month from Hartford to Austin to spend a week going over ideas.

One of the ideas he'd grown fascinated with was an inversion of the table-top strategy games like APBA and Strat-O-Matic. In the age of free agency, where Pete Rose could leave the Reds for the Phillies, and Rod Carew could leave Minnesota for the Angels, there was for the first time an open market in which the relative value of players might be compared. Okrent was also frustrated with what he viewed as the hidebound and illogical moves made by his favorite team, the Detroit Tigers.

"There was a huge amount of envy involved," he said. "I felt, *Damn it, why do they get to own baseball teams?* They don't know any more than we do. They just happen to be rich because they inherited it or they fell into something. We could do it, too, and we could do it just as well."

Okrent pursued the idea of assembling real-life players based on their perceived value, and using their statistics during the season to create a kind of parallel competition. That November of 1979, Okrent pitched the idea to a few of his Austin friends, over brisket at The Pit barbecue restaurant in East Austin.

His friends didn't get it.

"I do remember Dan arriving with this idea," said Greg Curtis, the long-time editor of *Texas Monthly*. "I remember just not getting the whole idea, and also thinking it would involve more money than I wanted to gamble."

Undaunted, Okrent returned to his monthly lunch at La Rotisserie

Française restaurant in New York City, and pitched it to a group of stathead writers and editors. And Rotisserie Baseball was born.

The seeds had been planted. James' innovative analysis and sabermetrics would form the foundation for the analytics revolution in sports (decades later, when the writer Michael Lewis profiled Billy Beane in *Moneyball*, Beane would insist that the inspiration for his baseball philosophy came from reading James' work). Okrent's keen insight into watching sports through a GM's lens would not merely launch Rotisserie Baseball and hundreds of offshoots and imitations, it would be the genesis of a fantasy sports industry that by 2022 was generating $8.8 billion dollars annually.

James' impact would be felt in the short term, as well. On November 19, 1979, the Angels' Nolan Ryan signed a historic free agent deal with the Houston Astros, becoming the first player in American team sports to agree to a contract guaranteeing more than $1 million per season.

Ryan's headlining deal reset the market for pitching, and as the players and owners went into arbitration hearings later that off-season, one could begin to see the effect. Here was where the combination of the new riches available to players joined forces with James and his research. Among the first sports agents to grasp the significance of James' work were the Houston brothers Randy and Alan Hendricks, who hired James to help with arbitration cases. A staple of the MLB collective bargaining agreement since 1973, the arbitration process was salary negotiation brinksmanship in which the team and the player would each submit a proposed salary figure and then each have one hour to make a case (and a half-hour to rebut the other side's case) about why their figure was justified.

For years, these arguments were based on the crudest of numbers—batting average, pitching wins, home runs—but in James' work, there was a concerted effort to break the game down to its constituent parts. It wasn't merely ballpark effects, or the importance of getting on base; James was at that point years ahead of many general managers' understanding of the game. The Astros had offered pitcher Joe Sambito a $143,000 contract, while the Hendrickses submitted a figure of $213,000. James was the expert witness brought in to bolster Sambito's case.

"That moment was hugely significant in my life," said James. "I had been teaching myself for years to place the true value of a player in a context relative to other players, that's what I did every day. And every day, in my perception, every day for several years, people told me that what you do isn't interesting, or it's interesting but not really relevant, or it's just playing with numbers. And we get into a room with lawyers. And all of a sudden everybody's trying to do *exactly* what I do every day. And they didn't have a chance. I mean, all of a sudden everybody was playing my game. So the Astros had hired these guys who were trying to do what I do. And they were trying to do it, but they had never done it. So it was just totally a shock to them to find somebody who was way ahead of them. It was a shock to me to discover that I was in the place where this stuff mattered."

Sambito won the case and, in so doing, ushered in an era that would bring fans a deeper understanding of the game, and players greater rewards. As Marvin Miller had years earlier predicted, the stars set the market. So when Ryan signed a contract that paid $1 million a year, the corollary was that a pitcher nearly as good as Ryan would deserve $750,000, and so on.

Free agency in baseball, as it would in all of the sports eventually, changed the way everyone—teams, general managers, players and fans alike—perceived the relative merits of players. It would force them to judge performances with increasingly sophisticated tools of discernment. James' methodology and Okrent's game would change the way baseball was watched and followed. Eventually, those factors would also change the way the game was played.

•

While baseball players were setting the pace in salary, football players were becoming the biggest stars, and their greater exposure led to more endorsement opportunities. One day in 1978, Joe Greene got a call from his lawyer, Lester Zittrain. Coca-Cola was looking to do a commercial with a famous football player. They had considered Hollywood Henderson and Roger Staubach, Randy White and Tony Dorsett, and even Jack Lambert. But they decided who they wanted was Joe Greene.

"I don't know," said Greene. "I'm not an actor."

"How can you turn it down?" argued Zittrain. "It's one of the most popular companies in the world."

Greene said he'd think about it. He never did say yes, but he finally relented and agreed to fly to New York and give it a try.

There, on the concourse of a baseball park in Pelham, New York (whose billboard included signage for Pepsi), Joe Greene filmed the Coca-Cola commercial that would forever change the way he was perceived.

The spot, produced by McCann-Erickson, features a bruised, limping Greene—helmet off—leaving the field through a stadium tunnel, when he is approached by a young boy (played by Tommy Okon) who offers to share his Coke with Greene. At first reluctant, Greene eventually accepts the soda, and drinks the whole bottle (Greene would remember drinking at least nineteen and perhaps as many as twenty-four bottles of Coke during the shooting of the sixty-second spot). As the young boy trudges back to his seat, a revitalized Greene calls out, "Hey kid—catch," and throws his jersey to the boy, who replies, "Thanks, Mean Joe!"

The commercial debuted in the fall of 1979, during the baseball playoffs, at a time when Greene's reputation was largely based on his nickname and his fearsome performances in three previous Super Bowls. The ad was a fair distance from the starry-eyed optimism of Coke's early '70s "I'd Like to Teach the World to Sing" spot. But the depiction of the giant Black man and the small white boy communing over Coca-Cola was indelible. The commercial won a Clio award, and the exchange also served to accelerate the commodification of "authentic," game-worn memorabilia, which would explode in the following years.

In the potent iconography of the era, the commercial crystallized the central role of football players in the culture by showing their human side. They were the gladiators, with a tough shell and a kind heart. With the wide exposure of athletes and games in prime time, players weren't merely behemoth sports heroes anymore. They had attained the rarefied status of movie stars or rock gods. Along the way, at least some of the stereotypes about race were slowly being torn down.

The commercial altered Greene's reputation, but also changed the way he interacted with the public.

"You know the little kids were there, but there was more of them," Greene said. "But what was different was people's mothers, people of that age. You know, I think that's what made me a nicer person. More approachable. As a football player and a guy that did not like to be noticed, didn't want to talk. That changed a lot of things."

•

When Visa pioneered its computerized authorization system in 1973, credit card spending was at $14 billion per year. In less than a decade it exploded, reaching $66 billion by 1982.

In the face of inflation and gas shortages (in June 1979, more than half the nation's gas stations were closed due to a lack of fuel), television viewership continued to climb. The number of men living by themselves doubled over the course of the decade, and the number of people under thirty-five living alone increased by over 200 percent, meaning that by 1980, a quarter of all households consisted of people living alone. There was a lot of time to watch TV.

There was another factor that led to the rise of more national sports coverage. Between the beginning of the 1950s and the start of the 1980s, the interstate mobility rate doubled, meaning more people were moving away from their hometowns and home states. It left a generation of Yankees fans in Florida and Cubs fans in Arizona, but also Steelers fans in Charlotte, Lakers fans in Houston, and Cowboys fans, well, pretty much everywhere.

As the decade drew to a close, excitement was already building for the sports year ahead. The Winter Olympics would return to the U.S. for the first time in twenty years, and the Summer Olympics—triumphantly wrested away from ABC by NBC in a huge bidding war—would be held in Moscow, to be anchored by the team of Donna de Varona and Bruce Jenner.

It was Christmas Eve 1979 when the reports started coming through to the State Department that the Soviet Union was embarking on a major invasion of Afghanistan, with more than 100,000 troops flooding across the border.

In the White House, Jimmy Carter was presented with the eternal Cold War conundrum: Any direct military response could lead to a Third World War, and anything short of that could be seen as ineffective.

After days of meeting with his top aides, Carter saw one significant weapon at his disposal. With the 1980 Summer Olympic Games scheduled to be held in Moscow, he could lead a boycott of NATO nations and other Western states.

But at the U.S. Olympic Committee and around the country, there was a sense—for hundreds of athletes who'd devoted much of the previous four years of their lives for a chance at Olympic glory—that their efforts would be in vain.

On January 14, the White House made the announcement: President Carter would consider advising the USA to boycott the Moscow Games if the Soviets did not pull out of Afghanistan within a month. With that, the sickening countdown came for the athletes, knowing that the U.S. had painted itself into a corner, without the necessary support among the allies or the IOC. One did not have to be a student of Russian history to realize the futility of such a threat.

# EIGHTEEN

# ALL SPORTS ALL THE TIME

THE GLIMPSE OF the future of American sports arrived early in the new decade, on January 6, 1980. The American Football Conference Championship Game pitted the defending champion Pittsburgh Steelers in the eleventh hour of their dynasty, seeking their fourth Super Bowl in six seasons, against their charismatic division rivals, the Houston Oilers, with the formidable Earl Campbell and the resolutely old-school coach Bum Phillips, sporting his trademark cowboy hat (which he abandoned for home games at the Astrodome because "my mama told me not to wear a hat indoors").

In the third quarter at frozen Three Rivers Stadium, with the Oilers trailing by 7, Houston's Dan Pastorini hit wide receiver Mike Renfro in the back of the end zone for what looked to be the tying touchdown. But there was no signal; both officials in the back of the end zone looked at each other, each hoping the other had a better angle on the contested catch. Ultimately, the officiating crew ruled that Renfro hadn't been in bounds when he caught the ball, and so the pass was ruled incomplete, forcing the Oilers to settle for a field goal.

But even as the Houston special teams unit was trotting onto the field, NBC was running replays that showed Renfro was in bounds. "This might be a spot," mused NBC's Dick Enberg, "where instant replay would be important." After watching the replay, Enberg declared, "It is a touchdown. It was not called one but there's no doubt that was a Houston touchdown...of course, the officials do not have the luxury that we enjoy of seeing the instant replay."

The technology and coverage of football had come a long way in the seven seasons since Franco Harris' astonishing "Immaculate Reception" had given the Steelers a 13–7 playoff win over Oakland. There wasn't a single camera that covered the full sequence of the play that was later named the greatest in NFL history. That wouldn't happen again, as networks added more cameras, and more still for playoff games. Officials had missed calls before, but rarely in games of such consequence, in front of a television audience this large. And—significantly—in an era when the shots that proved the missed call would be repeated over and over again, on local and national news and sports shows.

The Steelers won, 27–13, but the controversy overshadowed the accomplishment. "I don't feel quite like celebrating," said Joe Greene after the game. "I hate to call the win tainted, but that's the only way you can call it. I don't get much satisfaction out of it. I'm going to have to find some way to deal with it."

So would the league. In the immediate aftermath, Rozelle displayed an uncharacteristic lack of candor. "Electronic technology has advanced so much now," he said two weeks later during Super Bowl weekend. "No one ever questioned the officials' calls like this in the old days. We must learn to live with it."

That process would involve years of league representatives warning that implementing instant replay would cost as much as $40 million, since networks wouldn't allow their own feeds to be used. In the end, of course, the network feeds *would* be used. (For one thing, the video replay review offered additional opportunities for commercial breaks.)

In the intervening years, the coverage of the NFL would only grow more comprehensive, with more and better television cameras, and more clarity in slow motion. It would be another twenty years before instant replay was implemented for good, but from the moment the officials finally signaled that Renfro's catch was incomplete, instant replay was inevitable. The era of "incontrovertible visual evidence" had dawned.

•

By the end of the '70s, some people were asking if hockey was still a "major sport." After a dozen knee injuries, Bobby Orr's days of length-of-the-ice rushes were long gone. Early in the 1978–79 season, he announced his retirement; he'd managed to play in only twenty-six games over three seasons with the Black Hawks. The Montreal Canadiens won their fourth straight Stanley Cup title that season, though none of those series had been shown on American network television, where the NHL had lacked a national deal since the

Flyers' 1975 title. (ABC had agreed to show a potential seventh and deciding game of the Canadians–Rangers series in '79, but Montreal raised the Cup after five games.)

Later that summer, the World Hockey Association folded, with four teams absorbed into the NHL. The merger was in many ways as tortured as the NBA/ABA endgame, with a deal not coming through until Molson Breweries, which owned the Canadians, felt the effects of boycotts in three of the cities where WHA teams were seeking entry into the NHL.

But an enlarged NHL still faced the same problem. "There are only 20,000 fans in each city," went the joke. "And they go to all the games." The league leaned into its Eastern and Canadian redoubts that had kept it alive. The Canadians' dynasty would soon give way to another, of the New York Islanders. But their growing popularity was a distinctly regional phenomenon. Around the country, very few people would have known who goaltender Glenn "Chico" Resch was, or why he'd become a folk hero to Islanders fans in and around Long Island.

In the fall of 1979, the Penguins—having been bailed out by a consortium of Pittsburgh business interests—faced the Edmonton Oilers, who'd acquired the teenage phenom Wayne Gretzky a year earlier from the burning ship that was the Indianapolis Racers, for cash and other considerations. "They said he wasn't a very good skater," said the Penguins' veteran Rick Kehoe. "I thought, *he looks pretty good going past me*. With Wayne, his hockey IQ was so much higher than everyone else; he knew where the puck was going to go before it went there. Other guys couldn't do that."

In Gretzky, the NHL had the generational player who could inherit Orr's crown. With the relentless expansion of the previous ten years, it also had the markets. What it didn't have was a national TV contract in the U.S. Gretzky's exploits were seen sporadically, but there wasn't the serial presence that builds loyalty, fascination and involvement. Hockey retained a largely Canadian player base, and performed best in the Northern and Eastern markets, and was increasingly viewed as a regional sport.

Yet for a fortnight in the winter of 1980, none of the above mattered, and America fell in love with hockey. The United States hockey team that went to the Winter Olympics in Lake Placid, New York, was young and unproven, a team made up mostly of collegians, none of whom had signed a professional contract. Their naïveté showed when they were routed 10–3 by the powerful Soviet squad in a pre-Olympic warm-up, four days before the Olympics started.

The Olympic hockey competition separated the twelve teams into two six-team groups; after the preliminary round-robin competition in the group stage, the top two teams in each group advanced to the final round. After the USA tied Sweden and then stunned Czechoslovakia in its opening group games, Roone Arledge sensed a growing fascination with the earnest, energetic Americans. His lieutenant Jim Spence of ABC then negotiated a provisional agreement with the Lake Placid Olympic Committee that, in the event that the U.S. advanced to the medal round, its first game—potentially against the mighty Soviet Union—would be moved from a five p.m. start to eight p.m., so it could be shown in prime time in the U.S.

After the Americans advanced with a 4–2 win over West Germany, the Olympic Committee informed ABC they couldn't move the start time—the Soviet Union wouldn't agree to a later start, because the time shift would move the game into the middle of the night in Russia. ABC offered $125,000 to the Soviets to move it, but the bid was rejected.

On the afternoon of Friday, February 22, 1980, just thirteen days after being routed by the Soviets, the same team of American amateurs skated out to face the world champions from the Soviet Union. Spurred on by a rousing pregame speech from coach Herb Brooks, and a fervent pro-American crowd, the U.S. achieved an astonishing 4–3 victory.

That seismic moment in American sports history, though, was shown on tape-delay later that evening (ABC, expecting a Soviet win, had been editing down its tape of the game even as the event progressed, and wound up showing only parts of the first and second periods). The telecast culminated in Al Michaels' iconic closing call—"Do you believe in miracles? Yes!"—and sent Americans out into the streets, singing and honking horns, to celebrate a win that had occurred hours earlier.

The result tapped into a renewed sense of patriotism—coming in the midst of the Iranian hostage crisis—that hinted at a breaking of Jimmy Carter's "national malaise," and perhaps even the Reagan revolution to follow. But it also showed something more. Sports continued to resonate in the larger public imagination.

What didn't change was hockey. Several stars of the American team signed pro contracts after the gold medal ceremony and were rushed through the minors onto NHL teams, and yet the "Olympic bump" that the NHL had hoped for was negligible. Americans may have revered goaltender Jim Craig and center Mark Johnson, but those players could not conjure up the magic of Lake Placid in Saturday afternoon games in Atlanta. Meanwhile, Gretzky was embarking on a historic career in Edmonton, but Americans were seeing almost none of it. There was still no national TV contract, and hockey continued to move to the margins of the American sports landscape.

•

By the time Jimmy Carter made his fateful decision to urge the U.S. Olympic Committee to boycott the Moscow Olympics, the role of sports in American society had already changed. But in Carter's decision came the tipping point, a moment in which the games attained a kind of social relevance that proponents of sports had ostensibly avoided, without much success, throughout the history of the modern games. Carter did not want to be privy to a propaganda celebration. "It is absolutely imperative that we and other nations who believe in freedom and who believe in human rights and who believe in peace let our voices be heard in an absolutely clear way, and not add the imprimatur of approval to the Soviet Union and its government while they have 105,000 heavily armed invading forces in the freedom-loving and innocent and deeply religious country of Afghanistan," Carter said.

In Carter's vision, sports was a sacred space, to be enjoyed among nations not actively at war. He could not reconcile how the political world could censure the Soviet invasion of Afghanistan while the sports world proceeded with business as usual. Asked if the IOC would consider moving the games, IOC president Michael Morris, Lord Killanin, said, "There is no alternative besides Moscow anymore. It's Moscow or nothing."

Even the U.S. Olympic Committee resisted the call but, by mid-April, by which time Carter was threatening legal action to enforce the boycott, the USOC relented and went along with it.

The CIA analyst David Kanin viewed Carter's actions as a response to the sense of powerlessness Americans felt with hostages being held for over a year in Iran. "The boycott was part of the effort, at least to show we're doing something," Kanin said. "After Iran, where it seemed nothing was happening, I don't think anybody, especially in an election year, could afford to be perceived as doing nothing. The Olympics were coming. It was a highly publicized event the Soviets cared about. It gave us a target."

While allies like West Germany and Japan went along with the boycott, the United Kingdom and France both wound up sending delegations. In the spring, Carter sent Muhammad Ali as an emissary to Africa to shore up support for a boycott in four African countries, an endeavor that *Time* magazine described as "the most bizarre diplomatic mission in U.S. history."

The initial groundswell of public support for the boycott (which approached 75 percent) in January and February wouldn't survive the summer. Carter had miscalculated. Americans didn't presume that we could use sports to influence the Russians' bellicose foreign policy. It was enough, to most Americans, to simply beat the Soviets in sports.

As Carter's biographer Jonathan Alter put it, "The Soviet Union and East Germany won more than half of the medals, in what Carter described as a 'farce.' By that time, the shock of the Soviet invasion had worn off, and most Americans felt sorry for the athletes—nearly half of whom would never get another chance to appear in the Olympic Games—and sorry for themselves they had no Olympics to watch on TV in the summer of 1980. They blamed Jimmy Carter."

(The decision was one of many that led to Carter's defeat in the 1980 presidential election, but perhaps his moral calculation was ahead of its time. Forty-two years later, when Russia invaded another sovereign country, the world was much quicker to follow suit. The IOC—belatedly, in the mind of many in the Olympic community—finally banished Russia, and FIFA disqualified the Russians from soccer's World Cup.)

•

The comedian George Carlin once said that in its early years, ESPN's programming consisted primarily of "cross-country bowling and Australian rules dick-wrestling." While there were indeed plenty of minor sports on show, it wasn't quite that grim. As part of the deal with the NCAA, ESPN was able to provide live coverage of the first-round games in the enlarged, forty-eight-team 1980 tournament, at the perfect moment when interest in those games was growing.

A week before the 1980 tournament field was set, an ESPN production manager called the new ESPN announcer Bob Ley and told him they were going to do a show about the tournament selection. There was no remote link-up to the selection committee in Mission, Kansas, no remotes to other schools that were on the bubble. Instead, Ley stood by an ESPN fax machine on Sunday afternoon and waited for the tournament pairings to come in. By this point, the NCAA tournament brackets were appearing in many newspapers. But this allowed fans to survey the field on Sunday afternoon, rather than waiting for Monday morning. Those games, and the avid viewership, provided proof of both the growing interest in the tournament and the viability of the nascent network.

Bob Costas, still early in his broadcasting career, had watched the early months of the network and saw the *SportsCenter* show struggling for an identity. But then came March.

"The first time I thought they had anything going was the first time they were doing the early round NCAA games," said Costas. "It was amazing to me. I'm sitting in St. Louis and I'm watching some game—I forget the teams—but it was amazing to me that I could see these games. It was like you had snuck into a network's control room and you could see anything. I remember thinking, *Okay, this is what ESPN was made for.*"

Later that month, for its coverage of the later rounds of the 1980 tournament—a year before MTV went on the air—NBC used Kenny Loggins' 1979 hit "This Is It," set to a musical montage on the closing credits of their telecasts. While NFL Films had used orchestral music to great effect in the '70s, this was something different, the use of a contemporary American popular song as a thematic keynote to a montage of tournament highlights. It was another example of the future writ large, a full melding of sports and entertainment, a logical extension of the promise hinted at on *Monday Night Football* at the beginning of the '70s. Music was used as a mood-setter, and the events of the game were being distilled not to provide a digest—the highlight snippets weren't in chronological order—but rather to evoke a feeling, strip-mining the most emotional, most exciting and most decisive moments of a game into a new form that told a different story.

NBC had realized higher ratings while gradually increasing its NCAA tournament coverage, but in March of 1981, the network came to an impasse in its negotiations with Byers on the contract for the tournament, which it had held since 1969.

CBS got a chance to pitch Byers, and they did so by offering to increase the number of games they'd show—including carrying the regional semi-final games on Thursday and Friday nights during the second week of the tournament. CBS was also smart enough to recognize and emphasize the bracket. "The Road to the Final Four" would wind its way through the various permutations of the bracket.

All that was innovative and appealing, but what really clinched the deal was the payout—$16 million per year, well above the $9 million that NBC had been paying. So Byers moved away from NBC and into CBS, where Wussler went to his go-to man, Brent Musburger, to direct traffic and deliver highlights.

"What we proposed to do is to show the fans the whole of the tournament, and that it's a road that you go from the beginning to the final," said CBS's Kevin O'Malley. "And that the road that you take is the bracket, the bracket is the star, the bracket has to be everywhere. And NBC never went out of their way. All they did was 'Oh, UCLA could get to play Notre Dame two weeks from now.' They just talked about the big teams, the big name and they should have figured it out in advance is, when you got teams from 27 states going into a tournament, your affiliates in 27 states are going to be happy."

The NCAA Tournament needed CBS to maximize its potential. But it also needed the nascent ESPN to prove—in a way that network executives might not have believed on their own—that there was a dedicated audience, even for opening-round games with obscure colleges that had never before been seen on national television.

The coverage of the tournament had grown—from fourteen hours a year in 1973 to twenty-one hours in 1981. But when CBS took over the coverage in 1982, it started off with twenty-six hours, and by 1990 was covering forty-seven hours a year. That number would continue to grow, an index of the explosion of popularity of the tournament. By 1987, the NCAA was making $43 million a year from their basketball tournament, and CBS had become synonymous with March Madness.

The rise of college basketball's popularity coincided with a larger trend, in which major sports became more major and minor sports became more minor. As viewers had more options, the anthology shows like *Wide World of Sports* and the *CBS Sports Spectacular* became marginalized.

"The television world changed," said the longtime ABC sports executive Dennis Lewin. "The things that got you the biggest ratings—*Wide World* got humongous ratings, but it was in a much smaller universe. And once the universe started expanding, and once you started siphoning off the viewers, things changed. When people had less choice on a Saturday afternoon you could give them the Harlem Globetrotters, you can give them Evel Knievel, you could give them ski jumping, you could give them horse racing, you could give them whatever."

•

With the growth of college basketball, a dramatic expansion of the NCAA's enforcement division, and the ongoing fight over Title IX, it is possible that Walter Byers may have been distracted somewhat from the growing resentment building among major-college football schools, who in an age of rising budgetary challenges were increasingly dissatisfied with having their TV revenue limited.

The grumblings had been going on for years, and the increased need for revenue in the wake of Title IX legislation meant that college football powers wanted more exposure.

"I remember a conversation with Joe Paterno, during which he told me that the major schools are going to drop out of the NCAA because of Walter's position, controlling their exposure and revenue," said ABC's Jim Spence. "And I remember calling Roone and I said, 'We've got to talk to Walter and see if we can get him to change his course.'"

The ensuing conversation between Byers and the ABC brass was unproductive. Byers refused to relax the NCAA TV regulations that stipulated "no institution may appear more than five times during...[a] two-year period under any circumstances." What that meant to a school like Oklahoma was its television exposure and payouts were limited almost exclusively to its two traditional rivalry games, against Texas and Nebraska, each year. Byers' offer to ABC was to add a few more games—with either minor conferences or weaker teams from major conferences—but not any more of the major powers.

"Walter, no!" said Spence. "All you're doing there is watering down the scotch."

The schools had agitated repeatedly for more freedom, and Byers' old lieutenant Chuck Neinas, since 1971 the commissioner of the Big Eight, had repeatedly hinted to his former boss that the NCAA needed to loosen the strictures for major-college schools or face the threat of a direct challenge to the NCAA's control of regular-season telecasts.

On February 2, 1980, Neinas left the Big Eight and was named the first executive director of the College Football Association, an amalgam of major football schools (save NCAA loyalists the Big Ten and Pacific Eight) that would ramp up efforts to acquire more control over regular-season telecasts of college football.

The forces allied with Neinas included Father Theodore Hesburgh of Notre Dame, as well as major schools in the Big Eight, Pacific Eight, Southwest and Southeastern Conference. The chairman of the board of directors of the CFA was the University of Georgia president Fred Davidson, whose influence would continue to grow. When the Neinas hiring was announced, one Big Eight athletic director said, "I don't know where it is going, but I know a lot of people are tired of the way the TV money is being split up." This had been an issue for years.

By 1980, ABC was paying $31 million annually for the football package, with $600,000 per team for each of the twelve national games, and $426,779 for each of the forty-six regional telecasts. The NCAA collected a 3½ percent portion from all TV monies, which was used to cover the travel and lodging expenses of all student-athletes competing in each of the NCAA's championship tournaments.

Faced with the increasing costs of recruiting and the coming pressures of Title IX compliance, the largest programs in college football were growing increasingly disenchanted. It wasn't merely that Byers and the NCAA were leaving too much money on the table; the athletic directors and presidents of many schools had concluded that the NCAA was exerting control over a property—the game broadcasts—that should rightly belong to the schools.

Arledge and Spence's last-ditch intervention was met with Byers' intransigence. "We told him he ought to have a special convention to change the ground rules and allow the haves—the Ohio States and the Southern Cals—to have greater exposure and revenue," said Spence. "But he wouldn't budge. And then that led to the Supreme Court."

It would be another year before Oklahoma and Georgia finally decided to file the historic suit *Georgia and Oklahoma v. NCAA*. "It was clearly a cartel," said Kent Meyers, one of the lawyers who argued for the plaintiffs. "And nobody had ever challenged it, because it would run them afoul of Walter Byers."

But the ensuing lawsuit would go to the Supreme Court, which in 1984 found that the NCAA had effectively been engaging in restraint of trade. That ruling would shape the future of college sports, increasingly controlled by the larger schools and the commissioners of major conferences, who would soon chart the path to the modern incarnation of the game, in which nearly every major-college football game of consequence was televised nationally every week of the season.

•

The wisdom of Bill Rasmussen's audacious foray into cable television was soon apparent. In 1970, there were only 4.5 million subscribers to cable TV systems in the country. By 1979, that number had more than tripled, to 15.5 million, and it would continue to grow.

It turned out to be an excellent time to launch a twenty-four-hour sports channel. The dial-in score service Sports Phone was by now averaging 100,000 calls a day in New York, and could get up to 300,000 during the early rounds of the NCAA tournament. In 1980, the parent company signed an agreement with AT&T to bring the service national, and offer one-minute updates accessed from anywhere in the country for fifty cents. Within a year, Sports Phone had 50 million calls. On Sundays when NFL games were going on all across the country, Sports Phone had four different announcers updating the service every two minutes, providing temporary fixes for both the gambling addicts and the superfans.

In April 1980, ESPN broadcast the NFL Draft. Prior to 1980, it had been done without particular fanfare or public involvement, at a hotel in New York City. When Rasmussen approached Rozelle for the rights, the commissioner was frankly baffled by the interest; eventually, he allowed ESPN to broadcast the proceedings free of charge.

But by 1980, America's most committed and observant sports fans recognized the importance of the draft to the competitive environment of the NFL. Rasmussen, in turn, recognized the thirst in football fans for any kind of news in the middle of the off-season. The first broadcast, from the Sheraton Hotel in New York City, included Bob Ley reporting from Bristol.

On the floor, ESPN did an interview with the *New York Times* stellar sports columnist Dave Anderson, who offered a glimpse of sports journalism's future. "I've always said the draft was the last of the great newspaper stories, but that no longer holds now that ESPN is here," Anderson said. "For years, our offices would get more calls, during the day of the draft, than almost any other story that goes on all year. But now at last it's on television, so good for you."

The network also interviewed the editor John Walsh, the merry chief of *Inside Sports*, which was then using the *Washington Post*'s backing to challenge *Sports Illustrated*. Walsh, decked out in a satin jacket and ball cap, looked around the floor with genuine amazement. He mentioned meeting a man who'd come from Vermont at four in the morning to watch the draft. "I think this is a lot more important than some people have been led to believe," he said. "People are really crazy about this." (Within four years, Walsh would be hired by ESPN as its "editor," and he would infuse the network with the same journalistic principles that had earned him a reputation as a visionary magazine editor.)

By the end of the summer, the impact of ESPN—and the early days of sports talk radio—became apparent. The Royals' perennial All-Star third baseman George Brett had become used to some additional media responsibilities when Kansas City was on the road. His locker was usually in a prime spot, with an empty locker next to it, so the assembled reporters had room to gather.

On August 17 in Kansas City, Brett hit a double to complete a 4-for-4 day, and the scoreboard in center field showed that his batting average was at .401, with six weeks left in the season. No one had hit .400 for a season since Ted Williams in 1941, so Brett's challenge became a daily story. The next day, in Arlington, Texas, multiple stations in the Dallas–Fort Worth area did a live cut-in from their local news shows to document Brett's chase. Suddenly, newspapers around the country were sending columnists and writers to chronicle Brett's chase of the .400 mark. ESPN was running quotes from him nearly every night.

The Royals' director of public relations, Dean Vogelaar, consulted with the Yankees, who'd had previous experience with media onslaughts. Brett started doing a half-hour press conference before every game and another half-hour after every game.

He would wind up five hits short of .400—hitting .390 on the season—but the media coverage was unprecedented. The new age had arrived.

•

For the women of the AIAW, the jubilation of the Title IX victory in early December 1979 was tempered only a month later when the NCAA began to move in on women's sports, voting to offer national championships for women at the Division II and Division III levels.

Suddenly, the NCAA and the AIAW were in the same business, now fighting for schools, which had to decide which tournament they would attend.

"When the budget for women was ten thousand dollars, no one cared how it was spent," said Margot Polivy. "When we added two zeros, it became a power issue."

Already, the changes prompted by Title IX could be seen around the country. In the spring of 1979, the University of North Carolina chancellor Bill Coby called on UNC's men's soccer coach, a young law student named Anson Dorrance, to escort him to a field—beneath the law school library—to watch the UNC women's club soccer team. Dorrance had intended to pursue a law degree so he could work for his father's oil company, but he discovered that he loved playing and coaching soccer more than any other discipline.

Dorrance announced himself surprised and impressed with the women's team—they were fit and well organized.

"Anson, if you'll coach the women's team as well, I'll make your part-time men's position full-time." They agreed, and a few months later, Dorrance confided to his wife, M'Liss, that he wanted to quit law school, only a few classes shy of his degree, to focus on coaching full-time.

She approved. "You love this stuff," she said. "Let's just be happy; we don't have to be rich."

So in that 1979 season, Dorrance ushered the club team to a varsity level. He had no full scholarships to offer, only four "room" slots, which didn't cover North Carolina's tuition or books.

Dorrance's office was a broom closet inside Carmichael Auditorium, where Dean Smith's dynastic Tar Heels were playing their basketball games. On a shoestring, they made it work, and the women Tar Heels earned a 10–2 record.

In the spring of 1980, months after HEW handed down regulations, UNC's head of athletic fundraising, Moyer Smith, spotted Dorrance in the halls.

"Anson, what's the limit on the number of scholarships that you could offer for women's soccer?"

"As many as eleven," said Dorrance.

"Well, you got 'em now."

And with that six-second conversation, Dorrance suddenly could recruit. After North Carolina traveled for an unsanctioned national women's soccer tournament in Colorado Springs (won by a SUNY–Cortland squad that had to make the forty-hour road trip to the tournament in a van), Dorrance decided to petition AIAW to stage a national soccer championship, which North Carolina volunteered to host.

Visiting the 1981 delegate assembly in Detroit, Dorrance made his pitch: "There's a a a big parade of unbelievable young female soccer players, and we have an opportunity to lead the parade." AIAW approved the first women's soccer national championship tournament that spring. North Carolina beat the University of Central Florida in the final, and a women's soccer dynasty was born.

•

In the summer of 1980, the University of Iowa hosted an unusual seminar. It was billed as the AIAW Presidential Review, gathering all nine of the organization's presidents, as well as the president-elect, Donna Lopiano of Texas.

Throughout the three-day meeting, the old schisms were still apparent. The old-school anti-scholarship supporters were there. During her presentation, Lee Morrison—who described herself as "an optimist who is often disappointed"—emphasized that she still wished basketball was played six-on-six, just so more women could participate, a view that Iowa's Peg Burke parried a day later by reminding Morrison and the assembled crowd that, in the six-on-six game, "three of the women on each team are just observing."

There were deeper, more contentious issues, and extended debate on the road the organization had taken. But it was a forum that would have been unthinkable on the men's side—a generation of the sport's leaders gathering to revisit their victories and defeats, offer mea culpas and alibis (more of the former rather than the latter), and in the spirit of inquiry, chart the next steps forward.

The implicit subject of the conference was the organization's fate, and the possibility that women's sports would soon be ruled by the same people who'd spent the past seven years arguing strenuously against Title IX. It was the Illinois State Women's AD, and seventh president, Laurie Mabry, who was the first to say that at some point in the future, a union with the NCAA seemed likely.

"What if I had to choose," asked the ninth president, Carole Mushier, "between Title IX surviving or the AIAW surviving?" She pointed out that the choice wasn't hers and ought not to be mutually exclusive anyway. But she decided, in the end, that she would choose Title IX surviving intact over the survival of AIAW.

By the end of the week, nine of the ten presidents signed a joint statement vowing solidarity in fighting the NCAA. Only UCLA's Judie Holland declined. By then, she'd already initiated a series of back-channel meetings with the NCAA.

By the January 1981 NCAA convention at the Fontainebleau Hotel in Miami Beach, the writing was on the wall. On the docket was the proposal to have the NCAA offer championships for Division I women's sports, along with the knowledge that doing so would, sooner or later, likely kill the AIAW. It was left to Iowa's Christine Grant—who had become the embodiment of the purity of AIAW's vision of women governing women's athletics—to make the final impassioned argument to try to persuade the NCAA to let the AIAW remain the sole governing body for women's intercollegiate athletics.

"I believe our institutions and students will suffer in the coming years in the loss of a viable option to NCAA governance," Grant said, in her steady, lucid Scottish lilt. "I am not angry at what has occurred; I am profoundly sad... You have bought your way into women's athletics with the lure of money and other luxuries, but you have not bought it from those most directly affected... The AIAW is a governance organization, but it is also an idea. While I can't know what the future may hold for that organization, I do indeed know that idea will never die."

But by then, both the fact and the idea of the AIAW had been outflanked. Judie Holland—who, along with Pepperdine's Ruth Berkey and Linda Estes of New Mexico, had staged some back-channel meetings with the NCAA unbeknownst to the AIAW leadership—used the rhetoric of inclusion. "What we're asking for is simply a choice," she said. "We are trying to allow more options for women, the same type of opportunities men have."

In September 1980, Berkey had been named as the NCAA's liaison to women's sports, with an eye to building the first Division I women's NCAA basketball championship. In his 1997 memoir *Unsportsmanlike Conduct*, Byers took pains to mention Berkey's hiring, but not that she shortly thereafter became his third wife.

That relationship was still a rumor on the date of the vote, January 14, 1981. An earlier vote had narrowly missed, by a single vote, the majority needed to begin conducting women's championships that year. But on the final revote of the day, with the NCAA executives sitting in the front of the hall, the NCAA voted to begin conducting women's championships with the 1981–82 school year.

"When the vote was announced that it had carried, Walter and Ruth both jumped up and hugged each other, and kissed on the lips," said Doug Tucker, who covered the NCAA for the Associated Press. "And that was when everybody knew that, yes, they are an item, what I've heard is true. And not long after that they got married." (Then some years later, as with all of Byers' other marriages, they were divorced.)

But the vote was a final defeat in a day full of defeats for women's governance of intercollegiate sport. "This marks the death knell of the AIAW," said one of the convention delegates after the vote. "The NCAA has just taken over, probably for good."

Shortly thereafter, the AIAW filed a lawsuit, charging that the NCAA's takeover was an antitrust violation. At the time, the NCAA showed annual revenues of $20.2 million, with $12.9 million coming from television contracts. AIAW had revenues of $772,000 for the same year, with $219,000 in TV contracts. In that context, the NCAA's offer to pay for all travel and lodging expenses for its women's championships, while not raising membership dues, was a step that AIAW couldn't possibly match.

"It became a personal battle between Donna and Walter Byers," said Jody

Conradt. "He wasn't accepting of a woman who was the way she was. Donna became obsessed with him, and I think he had somewhat the same feeling about her, because he was the one individual that was keeping progress from happening." Lopiano and the AIAW filed an antitrust suit against the NCAA on October 9, 1981, but by then the defections had already begun.

Money begets pragmatism. A majority of Division I schools chose to go with the NCAA. A sizable minority—including Texas and several major state schools like Wisconsin, Minnesota and Colorado, as well as many holdover women's powers, like Delta State and Wayland Baptist—stayed for the 1981–82 season with AIAW. That spring of 1982 saw Women's Final Fours run by two different organizations on the same weekend. Tennessee had bolted quickly, and the Volunteers under their still young coach Pat Summitt made it to the NCAA semifinals, before losing to Louisiana Tech, which in turn beat Cheyney State in the finals. Meanwhile, in the AIAW Final Four, Rutgers edged Texas, 83–77.

After the tournament, Conradt sat down with Lopiano and they conferred. Out of loyalty, Conradt had supported staying in the AIAW, but as a coach, she desired the competition of the NCAA.

But by then, the battle was over.

"It was a takeover," said Lopiano. "It wasn't a merger."

"It wasn't even a takeover," said the historian Diane Williams. "It was an annihilation."

On June 30, 1982, the AIAW closed its doors. All the member schools received a letter from the final AIAW president Merrily Dean Baker, who wrote, "The sense of sadness and frustration so many of us feel in this June of 1982 cannot, and should not, be denied, but neither should it catalyze us into inertia nor prevent us from continuing to strive for that in which we believe. Our work is far from finished and we need to regenerate the commitment and determination we have shared to perfect the imperfections in our small sphere."

The larger vision—of women having the opportunity to pursue their athletic dreams—had undeniably been realized. But in the process, a generation of visionary women administrators were losing their autonomy. "When women's athletic departments were merged with men's," observed Iowa's Christine Grant, "in almost all instances, a man was chosen as 'the' athletic director and a woman may have been retained in a subordinate position."

The evidence for that was everywhere. When the two athletic departments at the University of Washington merged, the experienced administrator Kit Green found herself reporting to the men's AD, Mike Lude. At a meeting to discuss organizational plans for the new school year, Green asked Lude about her duties on UW football game days, when Husky Stadium was filled with 72,500 fans. Lude, after briefly considering the question, advised Green she should "patrol the ladies' bathrooms."

As they forged ahead, for administrators and coaches alike, the nagging, unanswerable question remained. Could it have happened any other way? Did the NCAA *have* to take over women's sports?

"It had to happen because of the visibility and because it gave us credibility," said Conradt. "I think the sense that there was not even an iota of compromise was what was hard about it. We had established the protocol and a set of rules that made a lot of sense. And it just seemed, Why should we jump into this system where it's all about money?"

•

Something that was not at all clear in 1973 was true by the end of the decade: America was ready to accept a woman—even an outspoken woman—as an athlete.

The country was not, as of yet, prepared to accept a woman athlete as a lesbian.

It was April 30, 1981, when Billie Jean King's affair with her former personal secretary, Marilyn Barnett, was exposed. Two days later, she called a press conference, with her parents and her husband, Larry, at her side (they would divorce six years later, but remain close), acknowledging the event. Billie Jean's handling of the Barnett suit, described aptly by the historian Susan Ware as "a model of both candor and obfuscation," was to acknowledge every aspect of her relationship with Barnett, yet treat it as an "isolated" experience.

None of the revelations were a surprise to veterans of the tour. But it was shocking to the public at large, and also to the business community that had embraced King. A large endorsement deal for a clothing line with the Wimbledon brand fell through, and King would estimate that the endorsements that she lost in the next year cost her more than a million dollars, among them a deal with Charleston Hosiery, whose chief executive, according to King, called her a "slut" in the letter informing her of her dismissal. Instantly, the other women on the tour were hounded with questions wanting more details.

The feminists who'd come to appreciate the importance of King's work were there for her. Gloria Steinem wrote a letter to King, which read in part, "It breaks my heart to see you suffering or penalized in any way for living in a still unenlightened time, but please know your troubles have probably hastened a better understanding for everyone."

The better understanding would take time.

But in the midst of the furor, Chris Evert stood by and supported her friend. The legacy of the '70s would involve not only King's journey but also the evolution of Chris Evert. "I'll never feel for any of the others the way I do for her," King once observed of Evert. "It'll always seem a little more painful when she loses, for she became some part of me on the court, and no matter who won, each of us needed the other, because you're more of a player, not just for winning, but for beating someone special. And we always understood that, both of us."

In a way, Chris Evert's journey was just as telling. The daughter of a strictly conservative family came to terms with her identity as an athlete. And the conflicted Catholic who was raised to avoid even the subject of sexuality learned to accept her competitors as friends, and many of her friends as lesbians. Her serial battles with Martina Navratilova would go down as one of history's great rivalries.

•

At the end of the '70s, the perception prevailed that the NBA was a league built on selfishness and statistics. The signal brilliance of both Magic Johnson and Larry Bird was that their contributions were not easily summarized in box scores; each was the rare player who clearly made the players around him better.

CBS's coverage of the NBA in the 1979–80 season began with Magic making his pro debut in the Lakers' opening game against the San Diego Clippers. When Abdul-Jabbar won the game with a basket in the final seconds, Johnson exploded in jubilation and jumped into his arms. Abdul-Jabbar would later describe himself as slightly embarrassed by Johnson's rapturous response ("such a public display, so little cools"), but he grew accustomed to the younger man's effervescent presence.

"If Earvin had any effect on me, it was because he helped the team win and reminded me just how good that made me feel."

CBS still didn't quite know what they had with the 1980 NBA playoffs. Of the two conference final series, CBS showed only three games live, and three more on tape delay, completely ignoring four others.

The Finals showdown was a classic: the revived Lakers with Abdul-Jabbar and Johnson, against the Sixers, paced by the incomparable Dr. J, and a team full of talented shooters.

The Lakers led 3 games to 2 going to Game 6 back in Philadelphia, but Abdul-Jabbar was out, sitting back home in Los Angeles with a bad ankle sprain. CBS gave their affiliates the option of showing the game live or on tape delay after the local news. The only three major markets to show it live were Philadelphia, Los Angeles and Seattle (the previous season's champ). Like Arthur Ashe's upset of Jimmy Connors in the '75 Wimbledon final, Tom Watson outdueling Jack Nicklaus in the '77 British Open, and the USA hockey team upsetting the Soviet Union in Lake Placid, the game being shown on delay created a kind of cognitive dissonance. Serious fans were forced to "go dark," and others with less obsessive tendencies just assumed the game wasn't on television.

What they missed in the moment was one of the definitive NBA Finals performances ever, with the point guard Johnson playing at center in Abdul-Jabbar's place, scoring 42 points to lead the Lakers to their first title in eight seasons. Ten years after the first NBA Finals series to be broadcast entirely live, this would be the last NBA Finals game to be broadcast on tape delay. The Nielsen rating for the series was a collective 8.0, ahead of the previous year's Washington–Seattle series but still well behind the '76 and '77 Finals series.

•

The early '80s was a long slog for labor-management relations in sports leagues. The reserve clause had been struck from baseball in 1976, and its demise was written into the 1976 NBA–ABA merger agreement and settlement of the Oscar Robertson case. But in each of three major professional leagues, owners were not yet ready to concede the inevitable. On December 31, 1979, the collective bargaining agreement between Major League Baseball and the Players Association expired. Over the previous decade, few hands were strengthened more clearly than that of the players. The average MLB player salary was up to $113,558. Salaries continued to rise and, just as Miller had predicted, the increased money also flowed to the owners, who remained resolutely opposed to the control they were losing, but not the increased revenue they were gaining.

That led to the midseason baseball strike of 1981—which lasted nearly two months and forced the cancellation of more than 700 games. In the end, the players realized more concessions, and the owners complained further about how they were doomed to failure.

"You're just a goddamned communist!" Astros owner John McMullen told player rep Phil Garner in 1982. By which McMullen meant, of course, that Garner was just a goddamned capitalist.

Ed Garvey led the NFL players on a fifty-seven-day strike in 1982, forcing the cancellation of nearly half the season. The NFL players were picketing for 55 percent of the gross revenues of NFL teams. That seemed patently unfair to some, but what really rankled was Garvey's idea that salary levels would be uniform, based solely on a player's position and number of years in the league. The idea was criticized by no less than Billie Jean King, who, when she crossed paths with Garvey, criticized him for what she viewed as an inherently socialist disincentive. "Sports is about performance," she insisted. "If you play better, you should get more."

Uniform salaries for all third-year left tackles was not really a cause that captivated the imagination.

"Ed didn't get it," said Jim Quinn. "Ed never fought hard for free agency. He didn't believe in it. He thought the union should be like the steelworkers— you play so many years, you get this amount of money. He really believed that. It wasn't until Gene Upshaw came along that you had a leader who was going to fight for free agency."

By failing to make player free agency a priority, Garvey guaranteed an intractable ownership, a belligerent players' association and two crippling player strikes in the '80s. It was then left to Upshaw, the Raiders' Hall of Fame guard who later became the executive director of the NFLPA, to hammer out a collective bargaining agreement with genuine free agency, with the new commissioner, Paul Tagliabue, who succeeded Rozelle in 1989. Significantly, the 1993 agreement called for a salary cap—and a salary floor—that ensured competitive balance.

But in 1982, the future was murky. And as the NBA's owners met with Fleisher and the Players Association, in the wake of damaging strikes in baseball and football, the mood seemed particularly grim.

"At the end of the decade, and in the first couple of years of the '80s, there were a number of teams that were having significant financial issues," said Quinn. "Of course, they were blaming the players, and saying they were making too much money, and there was also the drug issue, and a feeling that the league was too Black, and all these different issues were swirling around in the late '70s and early '80s."

Fleisher had seen the collateral damage of strikes, and knew the NBA players didn't want to do that.

"I remember asking my father once, 'Why did you make a deal here instead of striking?'" said Marc Fleisher. "He said, 'Marc, you know, my players are not willing to hang in there on a strike anywhere near as long as the baseball players.'"

So the NBPA had gone back to court. When the NBA signed the cable deal with the USA Network in 1979, Fleisher filed a lawsuit, headlined by NBPA president Bob Lanier, arguing that the players had not specifically negotiated away rights for the cable deal.

It was a critical time for the league, which had been bolstered by the arrival of Bird and Magic, but still carried a perception of being a second-class sports league.

At the NBA offices, the NBA's executive vice president, the driven young lawyer David Stern, was arriving at an unconventional conclusion. Stern by now was the agenda-setter at the NBA offices. "There was no question that, at the end of O'Brien's term, Stern was going to be elected commissioner, whether O'Brien wanted to stay or not," said Jeff Mishkin, the NBA's in-house legal counsel. "David was the person who had the concept, and he clearly did have the vision. He was clearly more committed to the NBA than to anything else in his life, there's no doubt about that. And I apologize to his wife Diane and his two sons, but that was the case."

Considering the pro football strike, and the NFLPA's demands for 55 percent of the NFL's revenue, Stern had an epiphany. If the NBA players were partners, and guaranteed a percentage of the gross, then that would also in turn guarantee the owners—who had careered recklessly through the previous two decades in damaging salary wars that left several clubs on the brink of bankruptcy—a measure of stability. The percentage to be attained would amount to a salary cap.

Fleisher had a cordial, even warm, relationship with Larry O'Brien. But as he saw O'Brien being edged out by David Stern, his relationship with the NBA grew more contentious.

In 1982, with the two sides far apart, the NBPA called the owners' bluff and asked the NBA to open their books, to prove that their finances were in the dire straits they claimed. It was a rote move—unions typically asked management to open their books; management typically declined—but O'Brien and Stern conferred with the owners and responded that they would be glad to do so.

What they saw shocked the NBPA leaders. After having the financials audited by an accounting firm, Fleisher confided in Jim Quinn that the entire league "might be beyond help."

The summary showed that only a handful of teams (the Knicks, Lakers, SuperSonics, 76ers and Mavericks) were making money, while most teams were in the red. Several franchises—Kansas City Kings, San Diego Clippers, Cleveland Cavaliers and New Jersey Nets—were in serious danger of going under.

"We were convinced," recalled Quinn, "that unless players made certain concessions, the NBA might collapse."

It was then that Stern, effectively leading the NBA's negotiation despite O'Brien still holding the title of commissioner, offered the prospect of a flexible salary cap, tied to the league's overall revenue. Larry Fleisher didn't like the term, but he liked the deal.

Fleisher adamantly didn't want to call it a salary cap. When the new plan was announced in March 1983, to go into effect with the 1984–85 season, it was known as "guaranteed compensation plan" in the NBA press release, and a "player revenue sharing agreement" at the NBPA, but the effect was the same.

"I learned how you characterized something was very important," said Mishkin.

The settlement guaranteed the players 53 percent of the "defined gross receipts" taken in by the teams and the league office. By pressing their case with the Bob Lanier suit in the wake of the NBA's cable deal, Fleisher and the NBPA essentially guaranteed themselves a steadily growing slice of a pie that would only keep getting larger. It was also clear, in Fleisher's mind, that he was stabilizing the National Basketball Association.

This would become a point of contention between the two union bosses, Miller and Fleisher.

"My father and Marvin Miller were not particularly close," said Marc Fleisher. "I think Marvin felt that my father hadn't come from the old labor laws side like he had with the steelworkers."

After the deal was announced, there was an interaction between Miller and Fleisher that aides to both men would remember. Marvin Miller viewed any salary limits as inherently ruinous and exploitative. Fleisher, after seeing the books of NBA owners, and facing the possibility of a shrinking league and a shrinking players' union, had concluded that healthy sports leagues needed to offer owners and players alike some kind of stability cost certainty.

Going over the terms of the deal shortly after it was signed, Miller was dismissive of the entire plan. "That's stupid," he told Fleisher. "You should never, *never* have a salary cap."

"It's not stupid," countered Fleisher, who argued that as the league's revenue grew, the 53 percent that the players were guaranteed would automatically grow with it. Fleisher also sensed that his adversary Stern—who would be named the NBA's commissioner a year later—would continue to innovate to broaden the NBA's coffers. It was a variation on the counsel that Miller himself had given the baseball players back in 1976: The rising tide lifts all boats.

For all his brilliance, Miller couldn't see it. He had been fighting management so long, he couldn't really conceive of a system of partnership that wasn't inherently exploitative of labor. Miller, the revolutionary figure, was right about so much in the world of sports, but in this one matter, history would prove him short-sighted.

The indexing of salaries to a percentage of a sport's overall gross revenues didn't merely guarantee players in basketball (and, eventually, football and hockey) a larger percentage of the revenue than they'd had before. It also provided an apparatus through which the players truly were partners with the owners; it meant that the arguments in further CBAs were necessarily on the margins (stadium and arena revenue, a percentage of the licensing income, healthcare, etc.) rather than starting each new negotiation with labor trying to get all it could get and management trying to keep all it could keep.

A salary cap accompanied by a salary floor guaranteed relatively similar payroll resources for each team and allowed the players to share in any revenue gains their leagues enjoyed. "The salary floor was crucial," said Quinn, who would serve as outside counsel a decade later when Paul Tagliabue, commissioner of the NFL, and Gene Upshaw, executive director of the NFLPA, agreed to a salary cap with an accompanying salary floor. As Upshaw would explain in the '90s in justifying the NFLPA signing on to a system with a salary cap and salary floor, "Somebody's got to play in Cincinnati."

"Competitive balance is often oversimplified or misunderstood," noted the NBA's Jeffrey Mishkin. "The ideal is not that every game is going to end in a tie. Instead, it's the idea of promoting the uncertainty of outcomes, that when every game starts you don't know who's gonna win. That's why people watch." While the salary cap and floor were new, the paradigm still contained familiar elements. Though challenged at various times by every players' association, the annual college or amateur drafts remained intact, as an integral part of each league's quest for competitive balance. In truth, the system hadn't evolved much from the system Bert Bell had suggested to the NFL in 1936. Pro leagues thrived on competition, and there was no better way to guarantee the *possibility* of competitive balance than giving the teams that had finished worst the previous season the first choice of players in the upcoming season.

It would be another decade before the NFL joined in, and another decade still for the NHL to join, but a new age had dawned. When the deal was announced, in April of 1983, the Milwaukee Bucks' Steve Mix, the secretary of the players' union, greeted David Stern of the NBA with the salutation, "Hi, partner."

# EPILOGUE

By THE CONCLUSION of the '70s, one could squint and make out the broad contours of what sports would become in the twenty-first century. All the elements that would hasten the explosion in popularity and prominence in America were taking root: Television executives had begun to grasp the value and desirability of the sports audience, and cable offered more outlets for struggling leagues like the NBA and NHL to find national broadcast outlets that could consistently reach their audience. That gave fans the opportunity to actually *watch* much more of the months-long postseason in those leagues, instead of being limited to watching only a game or two each weekend. Players had begun to gain more autonomy over their careers, and were in turn earning money more commensurate with their true value. The expanding media coverage, increasingly national in scope, rapidly filled the vacuum that had existed a decade earlier. Suddenly, sports were everywhere. The essence of what drew people to the games remained the same. But the increase in exposure—from the bare trickle at the beginning of the '70s to the steady flow that accompanied the end of the decade—allowed people who loved sports to more fully absorb themselves in that universe.

For ages, people had lived lives defined by politics, or business, or the arts. Now it was possible to live a life steeped in sports. In Florida, there was a Superfan, a self-professed sports junkie, who kept close tabs on each and every week's wire-service poll, and made it to his beloved Ohio State games four or five times a year. He used to stump his friends at bars by asking them what Ty Cobb's jersey number was (he'd let them guess for a while before slyly informing them that Ty Cobb didn't *have* a jersey number). He found that the lessons he'd learned in sports served him well in all aspects of his life. Though he was a family man who had made a fortune in the business world, he had come to view and understand life through the prism of sports. In this case, the fan was like tens of millions of other American sports fans.

Though in one sense, he was very much not like those other fans. His name was Jack Nicklaus.

The first year that Nicklaus played the U.S. Amateur, he made his way around the links with a portable radio so that he could listen to the Ohio State–Michigan game. By the early '70s, transplanted to Miami, he'd became a regular at the Orange Bowl for Dolphins games. He would load his family into the station wagon on Sundays and drive to the games. "One thing about it—you can't deny the hold pro football has," said Nicklaus in 1973. "Look at me, a regular Dolphin nut. And the coverage it gets. The sportswriters, television. They can't stay away."

When ESPN arrived, and NBA games started appearing regularly on the USA Network, as well as on superstations like TBS, suddenly sports had spilled into the week, and was available at any hour. Watching the first quarter of an NBA game one night, Nicklaus was joined by his wife, Barbara, who said to him, "Why are you watching this now? It's all going to come down to the last five minutes of the fourth quarter anyway."

He looked at her evenly. "Barbara," he said, "do you just catch up with me on the fifteenth hole?"

So Barbara Nicklaus took his point and started watching entire games as well.

By then a lot of Americans, whether they were superstar athletes or not, had come to view sports as a metaphor, a way to understand the larger world.

It was the same with Henry Aaron. He still remembered the words of Martin Luther King, whom he had met in Atlanta in the '60s. Aaron asked what he could do to help the cause, and Dr. King was very clear: "The best way you can help us is to keep doing what you're doing." Sports was the forum, the great equalizer, the shining light on what happened when Blacks received a fair chance. Games started 0–0. So many things in life did not.

Aaron took up tennis in the '70s. Even as he was aging and moving more slowly, he continued playing the game, and excelling at it. An avid tennis fan, in retirement he became even more involved, reveling at the serial victories of Venus and Serena Williams.

He had been a Cleveland Browns fan since the early '50s, and in fact had a season ticket in Cleveland Municipal Stadium, where he used to wear a disguise and regularly attend games in the late '80s and early '90s. "Many days I sat over there in the Dawg Pound and had great fun," Aaron said. "I'd catch a flight, come up and watch the team play and fly right back. I wasn't rowdy; I didn't throw any bones. I'd just sit there and watch the game. I could analyze and come to my own conclusions about what was happening."

Aaron befriended fellow Mobile native Ozzie Newsome early in Newsome's Hall of Fame career and switched his allegiance to the Ravens when the franchise and Newsome moved to Baltimore.

When the Ravens made the Super Bowl in January of 2001, Newsome—at the time the Ravens director of pro player personnel—invited Aaron to attend and sit in a luxury box with him and other VIPs.

"No," said Aaron. "If I'm going, I'm going to watch the game."

"Well, that may not be as easy as it sounds," said Newsome. But they worked it out. On the occasion of Super Bowl XXXVII, Aaron, his wife Billye, his manager, Allan Tanenbaum, and Aaron's son-in-law Victor Haydel had four seats on the fifty-yard line behind the Ravens' bench. The seats directly in front of them, and directly behind them, and seats in either direction to the left and to the right, were left empty, with security guards stationed at the outer edges of each corner of the empty block of seats, so that Henry Aaron's entourage was able to watch the game in peace.

For Aaron, and tens of millions of people like him, sports had become something more than a pastime. It had become a lifestyle. Nicklaus and Aaron and so many other stars of the '70s—Abdul-Jabbar, Robertson, Greene, Erving, Evert—remained sports fans long after they stopped being sports stars. By the twenty-first century they were living in a world that they had helped to create.

•

One does not have to be living in the past to find a piquant purity to the way sports emerged during the '70s. Even among people who are lifelong, avid sports fans, the decade had a special character—different from all that went before and all that followed—in which the games became more pervasive, more resonant, more important.

"The '70s were the golden age," said the writer Gerald Early. "It's more diffuse today, but back then, it was so accessible. It was prime-time television, and anybody could watch it—you know, all you've got to do is buy a television and plug it in. All of a sudden, TV was giving sports a sense of order and rationality. There was a narrative structure and a sense of drama to the seasons, and you followed it like you were following the narrative of a TV series. There came a point where it felt like it was almost better to watch it on television than to go in person, because you were getting the close-ups, and the instant replays. It didn't get any better than that, than in the '70s—some of my most enjoyable memories of big sports moments, from Billie Jean King to Muhammad Ali, were on television in the '70s. It was just beautiful."

The events would still resonate generations later: Ali–Frazier. Aaron's 715th. The Battle of the Sexes. Nebraska–Oklahoma. Steelers–Cowboys. Reds–Red Sox. Willis Reed at the Garden. Magic and Bird. The icons remained with us, though their meaning in the culture changed drastically with time. O. J. Simpson—perhaps the most popular and well-liked athlete of the '70s—had become something else entirely, a pariah whom most Americans regarded as a murderer. Muhammad Ali, a man once so controversial that a large swath of Americans refused to utter his name, had gone from an iconoclastic outcast to a kind of civic saint, consecrated in all his frail, tremulous humanity when lighting the torch to begin the 1996 Summer Olympics in Atlanta. Others had evolved, growing with age—Kareem Abdul-Jabbar had become a respected man of letters; Chris Evert not only a legend but also, in her rivalry and friendship with both Billie Jean King and Martina Navratilova, a model of tolerance and acceptance.

So in the '70s, sports did a lot of growing up, and began to realize its potentialities and resonances. One would blanch at calling it a more innocent time—the ritual violence, widespread recruiting corruption and routine sexism would prevent that. But it was, at the very least, a less self-conscious era, perhaps more honest in both its motivation and distractions. Athletes walk differently today, a product in part of seeing themselves constantly, on phones, computers, TVs and fifty-foot high screens in the very stadiums and arenas where they perform—even while they're performing.

But before the new generation of cable-wired, all-sports-all-the-time programming worked its way into a majority of American homes, and before *USA Today*'s 1982 debut as a de facto national daily sports page, there was a winnowing. By the end of the 1970s, many of the aspirations and assumptions about sports had been revealed as illusions—the markets were deep, but they weren't infinite. The World Football League had folded in 1975, bringing about the demise of the butterscotch football (the exact shade of a million fondue pots). The American Basketball Association was gone a year later, its iconic red, white and blue basketball left as a remnant of the era. By 1979, the World Hockey Association collapsed, along with its vulcanized blue rubber puck. The rise of cable television came too late to save World Team Tennis (at least as an avenue for the top ten men's and women's players to work into their schedules) and the International Volleyball Association.

At the start of the decade, virtually anything had seemed possible; but by 1980, everyone from fans to TV networks to investors understood that the American sports universe had matured; there was no longer a need for a constant influx of more leagues; the die was cast. In the next forty years, a rival baseball league, hockey league or basketball league never materialized. Football was the exception, but never again would another league operate (as the AFL had) directly in the NFL's lane in the fall. All the upstart leagues that would follow—from the United States Football League to the World League of American Football to the Arena Football League to the XFL to the Alliance of American Football—would attempt to flourish in the spring and summer. Almost all of them failed quickly; building the sort of enmity that animates genuine rivalries takes time. The North American Soccer League— which became a case study in how not to manage a sports league—collapsed in 1984, to be replaced twelve years later by Major League Soccer, a less flashy domestic league in a more compressed, manageable form.

As the cable age brought a myriad of choices to American homes, and the VCR became a standard part of American life, the cultural hegemony of the three major networks began to splinter and multiply. A country of individu- alists with more choices than ever before about what to watch, what to read and what to listen to found that the one area that remained staunchly mass- market was the world of sports.

While other sports waxed and waned, football continued to grow in pop- ularity, and by the end of the decade no one seriously questioned its position as the most popular American sport.

"Football was always king; there was never any doubt about that during the decade," said Bill Hancock, by now the executive director of the College

Football Playoff. "Basketball became of interest in places like Oklahoma, where it hadn't been as much, right? You began to start to see the unfortunate decline of interest in track and field, and swimming, and even wrestling. And I do think that's unfortunate, and no one's to blame for it."

Pro football's dominance continued beyond the '70s, but it was firmly established by the end of the decade. Sunday after Sunday, Monday after Monday (and, eventually, Thursday after Thursday), fans turned out to watch the national games. An Eagles–Giants game appealed to fans in Kansas City and Los Angeles in the way that a Mets–Phillies or Knicks–Sixers game simply couldn't.

In 1981, more than 70,000 people descended on New Orleans for Super Bowl XV—2,000 of them with media credentials for the game—with Count Basie playing the commissioner's party on the Friday night before the game. The Superdome was wrapped with a giant yellow ribbon, with a bow thirty feet high and eighty feet wide adorning it, to celebrate the freeing of the Iranian hostages.

At one point that weekend, at the NFL's hotel, the New Orleans Hyatt, the longtime college football loyalist Beano Cook and the Colts' GM Ernie Accorsi surveyed the entirety of the scene from their elevated floor looking out on the atrium.

Observing the throng in the lobby, Cook turned to Accorsi and said, "It's now passed Easter. It's second only to Christmas."

It would only continue to grow from there. In pro football, at the end of the '60s, a rabid pro football fan could watch about three dozen AFL or NFL games over the course of a season. By 2022, the same fan could watch 100 games over the course of a season. By 2022, there were more college football games telecast in a single day than could be seen in an entire season in the 1970s.

And then there were the riches. In 1970, each of the twenty-six NFL teams received $1.25 million in annual television revenue. By 2022, each of the thirty-two NFL teams received $320 million per year, as part of an eleven-year, $113 billion package. That same year, 82 of the 100 most watched television programs in America were football games, and another seven were other sports events. There was no baseball or hockey, but there were three World Cup matches, two college basketball games, a Kentucky Derby and a night at the Winter Olympics.

•

The explosion of TV money eventually filtered to the athletes. Fifty years after he first made the point, Larry Fleisher's vision—that athletes were entertainers and should be paid as such—had been realized.

At the beginning of the '70s, the best athletes made good money. Fifty years later, the premiere athletes of the day were capable of earning what the Chiefs' quarterback Patrick Mahomes accurately described as "generational wealth."

"All professional athletes to a large degree can thank Roone for the money he was willing to pay for sporting events like *Monday Night Football*, and the Olympics," said Dennis Lewin. "He changed the formula. And yes, players finally got their rights, in baseball through Curt Flood, free agency in the NFL, collective bargaining, all those things changed in the '70s. But the money that was there through television changed because of Roone. And the money that was there through television feeds the beast today, in every regard."

The millions—by now billions—were hard to comprehend. For the survivors of the '70s, the athletes who remained around to witness the riches of succeeding generations, there was a mixture of bemusement and envy and, yes, resentment.

When the writer Sam Smith was reporting on his 2017 book *Hard Labor: The Battle that Birthed the Billion-Dollar NBA*, about the seminal Oscar Robertson case and the way it opened the doors for free agency, he interviewed one of Robertson's teammates, and co-plaintiffs, Jon McGlocklin.

"Why are you writing this book, Sam?" he asked.

"So the current generation of players will understand what went before."

"Sam!" said McGlocklin incredulously. "Who's going to *read* it to them?!"

Would the average NBA player know Oscar Robertson's significance? Would the average baseball player appreciate Curt Flood? How many NFL players would recognize John Mackey?

For the superstars of the '70s, who made $100,000 a year, it could be difficult to watch players they considered marginal making tens of millions of dollars, even more annoying to see the new generation often seeming oblivious to the trials and contributions of those who came before. Eventually, some made their peace with the possibility that they'd been born too soon.

"Space and time," said Joe Greene, sitting in his handsome home in a gated community in Flower Mound, Texas. "I guess I pacify myself with, if I had been paid $5 million when I was twenty-one years old, I probably wouldn't be here today. Bad things would have happened to me. I don't complain about it."

•

One of the eternal verities of modern American sports is of fairness, of the same rules applying to all competitors. The idea of the "level playing field" is so ingrained as a concept in sports that it has transcended the games, and the phrase has become a shorthand for basic fairness in other realms of American society.

It is through this prism that racism and sexism is put into such stark relief. It was perhaps easier to overlook unfair access or racial bias in other aspects of society, but once the issue was brought to the forefront in the sporting realm, it could not easily be ignored. The issues that roiled the '70s in sports—whether women should have as many opportunities in sports as men did, whether there were too many Blacks in basketball, whether Blacks could excel at quarterback in football, whether women reporters should be allowed into locker rooms—were all trending toward the only possible outcome, because of the nature of sports, which offered a merit-based equality of opportunity.

It would be nearly another decade before Doug Williams' circuitous journey would take him from Tampa Bay to the Oklahoma Outlaws of the short-lived United States Football League to the backup quarterback of the Washington Redskins—whose head coach was his old offensive coordinator in Tampa, Joe Gibbs—to the starting job, to the most valuable player in Super Bowl XXII, where Williams became the first Black quarterback to win the title. Eddie Robinson, watching the culmination of his dreams, wept with joy.

It was longer still before an NFL team saw fit to hire an African American head coach (Art Shell, 1989, by the Raiders), and even longer before an NFL team would hire an African American general manager (Ozzie Newsome, promoted in 2002 by the Ravens).

But the changes that began in the '70s would irrevocably lead to those outcomes. By 2007, Tony Dungy had retired from his playing career and was on his second NFL head coaching job. The Colts won Super Bowl XLI, making Dungy the first Black coach to lead a team to a Super Bowl victory, defeating another African American coach, Chicago's Lovie Smith.

Sixteen seasons later, on February 12, 2023, Patrick Mahomes of the Kansas City Chiefs took the field against Jalen Hurts of the Philadelphia Eagles in Super Bowl LVII, the first ever to match two Black starting quarterbacks. It would become the most-watched telecast in American history, with an American audience estimated at 115 million. The scintillating game—a 38–35 Chiefs win—was played just days after Tom Brady announced his retirement, and confirmed Mahomes as not only the heir apparent to Brady, but as the new face of the league.

Two weeks earlier, on the day of the AFC and NFC Conference Championship games, it had been Doug Williams' turn to cry. "I had tears of joy in my eye because I had an opportunity to witness this," he said. "Sit there, and just look at it, and say to myself, 'Man, we got two Black quarterbacks playing in the Super Bowl.'"

After Mahomes' MVP performance, he made it a point to note those who had gone before him and Hurts.

"It showed that the black quarterback, like we've always been able to do, can go out and have success on the world stage in the biggest game of them all," Mahomes said. "We're standing on the shoulders of Doug Williams, Warren Moon, Shack Harris, all these greats, and the guys that didn't get the chances, they gave us this platform. Hopefully, we can inspire some kids to follow their dream and be a quarterback in the future, whenever we're sitting on the couch watching the Super Bowl."

The wait for the first African American NFL majority owner would last longer.

•

For the women who'd worked so tirelessly and heroically at the AIAW—like Charlotte West at Southern Illinois, Christine Grant and Peg Burke at Iowa, Donna Lopiano at Texas—the takeover by the NCAA was initially devastating. The demise of their own governance organization, and the takeover of women's athletics by the very people who spent the decade in opposition to Title IX presented a humbling, potentially embittering, almost physical hurt.

Because these same women had been shaped by sports, because the ethos of sports informed their worldview, surrender was never an option. So they persevered. "We were all devastated in a way," said West. "But, you know, there was only one thing to do when we lost AIAW, and that was to make the NCAA a better organization. That was our mission."

West began serving on an NCAA committee in the fall of 1982. Grant took longer to come around, but she would do the same. It would take decades, but both women would eventually see changes they pushed implemented within the enlarged NCAA.

In so doing, the women active in intercollegiate athletics tapped into a larger trend. Northwestern University professor Donna Leff began decades of extensive research on minorities in American newsrooms in the 1970s. The takeaway from her research was at once simple and profound: The mere fact of having women and people of color in the newsrooms and on editorial boards changed the assumptions made in those rooms, changed the nature of those conversations, and the topics that were and weren't up for debate.

The same thing happened when women administrators began asserting their voices in the NCAA. In 1982, Charlotte West joined the powerful NCAA Council, where Walter Byers was still calling the shots. Byers remained Byers—"I worked with him and I appreciated his intellect," said West, "but he was a czar"—but there were signs that even his views on women's athletics began to evolve once the NCAA took control.

Byers also came to recognize West's clarity of vision. At one of her first council meetings, West made a point that was largely ignored by the other members of the council. The discussion continued, bouncing around for the next sixty minutes, when someone else on the council offered a comment.

"You guys," scolded Byers. "This is the same thing Charlotte said an hour ago."

Some of the key components that were part of the AIAW framework—due process for student-athletes, minority representation on every committee, at least one student-athlete on each committee, more checks and balances on academic work—all eventually worked their way into the NCAA bylaws.

While women athletes did not magically gain equality, they gained a viability and a visibility in the NCAA that had been elusive in AIAW. By 2021, 74,173 women were attending American colleges on athletic scholarships, which neared parity with the 77,784 men attending college on athletic scholarships. Today, the NCAA conducts twenty-six championships—thirteen in men's sports and thirteen in women's sports.

Along the way, the key players of the AIAW prevailed. In 1985, Jody Conradt led Texas to the first undefeated season in the history of NCAA women's basketball. In 1992, Donna Lopiano became the president of the Women's Sports Foundation. Today, at NCAA headquarters in Indianapolis, NCAA administrators often meet in the Christine Grant Ballroom and the Charlotte West Conference Room.

·

For the true measure of the distance traveled, all roads lead back to Billie Jean King. In fighting for equality throughout the decade, King would become nearly as well known for her political activism as for her tennis. The example she set would resonate across generations.

On Sunday, November 13, 1994, the athletic goods manufacturer Spalding hosted a roundtable on women's sports at the company's headquarters in Chicopee, Massachusetts. Among the guests were Billie Jean King, basketball star Carol Blazejowski, the softball coaching legend Sue Enquist and a young U.S. Women's National Team soccer player named Julie Foudy. The women in attendance had been invited by the Spalding exec Anne Flannery (formerly of the Women Sports Foundation) to discuss the continued quest for sporting parity in America.

During the meeting, King related her story of the launch of the Virginia Slims tour, the battle with the United States Lawn Tennis Association, and the $1 contracts that made them, for a time, the pariahs of tennis.

At the time, Foudy—just two years after graduating from Stanford—had been a women's national team member for seven years, sharing the leadership role with the generational talent Mia Hamm, the midfielder Kristine Lilly and the veteran captain Carla Overbeck, and they were facing a double-bind. Their pay was meager, and they were subsisting on a per diem of $10 a day meal money. But the training was so rigorous, and the schedule was so active that the women were finding it almost impossible to hold down any kind of second job.

When the roundtable finished, Foudy got a moment alone with King and said, "Holy shit! That's *our* story. This is what we're going through right now.

I don't know what to do. We've tried to bring it up to the [U.S. Soccer] Federation, and they just blow us off."

King looked at Foudy and demanded, "Foudy—what are *you* doing about it?"

"What do you mean?" asked Foudy. "I mean, we're trying, we've gone to the federation, we're—"

"No, *you!*" said King, pointing at Foudy. "You as players, *you* get the players together, you sit them down, and you tell them, 'Enough!' What do you want for the next generation? It's a blank canvas out there, but it's not about what you get. It's about what you want the sport to look like for the next generation. What are you gonna fight for? *You* have the power."

Foudy was unprepared for King's reply at the time ("I was reeling"), but over the next twenty-four hours, it began to sink in.

The next day she flew to the next USWNT training camp, as the team began preparations for the 1995 Women's World Cup. On the flight to California, King's words stuck with her.

"And I remember thinking, *Oh, my God, she's so damn right. We do have the power. Oh, my God, why have I never realized that?* We don't have to sign this effing contract. Why are we doing this? We can say no. And mind you back then we hadn't had the Olympics, we hadn't had the '99 World Cup. So we didn't feel like we had a lot of leverage. Because we weren't that popular. We were still kind of unknown. And Billie empowered us to say, 'No, this is not okay.'"

Foudy called a team meeting the day she arrived, and rallied the troops.

"I was like, oh, *hell* no; I got the team together, it was like, 'We are not signing this contract. I was just with Billie Jean King.' I started rattling off all the things she was talking about. And everyone, of course, because we were all feeling it, we're all on the same page. And we were like, 'Yeah, we're not signing this contract.' So that was our first real confrontation with U.S. Soccer."

That protracted battle would be a story for another time, but the subtext was clear: The gains from Title IX would have to be fought for again and again. But the early victories of the '70s would prove crucial in the long run.

Women's college basketball raised the hope, but it was soon joined by soccer. America in the late twentieth century was already geared toward team sports. "Until team sports are accepted the same way they are for men," said Billie Jean King, "we haven't arrived. Everyone talks about our success; all I can think about is, we haven't even started."

There were two watershed moments in the growth of women's team sports in America. The first occurred in 1996, when the U.S. women for the first time won more medals than the men at the Summer Olympic Games in Atlanta. The breakout hit of the fortnight was the U.S. Women's Soccer Team—Hamm, Foudy, Overbeck and the rest—which played to sellout crowds at Sanford Stadium in Athens.

That led Marla Messing, the organizer of the 1999 Women's World Cup, to double down on the bet on the appeal of the team and the tournament, moving many of the key games—including all the U.S. games—out of small venues and into large football stadiums. The gamble paid off handsomely. On July 10, 1999, in front of a sold-out crowd of 90,000 at the Rose Bowl, the U.S. battled China in a tense World Cup final that went to extra time. Across the continent, in Newport, Rhode Island, on the occasion of the International Tennis Hall of Fame induction ceremonies, Billie Jean King was inducting her old mixed-doubles partner Owen Davidson. But during a break in the schedule, she rushed back to her hotel room and sat on the edge of the bed, engrossed in the nerve-shredding ordeal of the USA women and China locked in their 0–0 draw. "I just screamed and watched it, and then of course it went down to penalty kicks." When Brandi Chastain's kick sealed the victory, and Chastain tore off her jersey in jubilation, there were mass celebrations across the country. For Billie Jean King, sitting on the edge of her bed at the Viking Hotel, it was a culmination of something that moved beyond "the thrill of victory" and into the realm of something like redemption. This vision she'd had decades earlier—of American sports fans not merely following but *embracing* women athletes in team sports—had come to pass.

A new era had dawned. It wasn't just that women were playing in football stadiums, and big ones. And it wasn't just that the crowd was at capacity. It was *who* was watching. Families. Girls, of course. Women. And men. So many mainstream American sports fans who had, for the first time in their lives, avidly bought in to cheering for a women's sports team. They came with painted faces, decked out in Mia Hamm jerseys, exhibiting the exact same behavior that they'd displayed for an NBA Finals or a Super Bowl or a

World Series. The longtime sports entrepreneur and avid soccer fan Lamar Hunt called the promotion the greatest marketing campaign in the history of sports.

The seeds of the U.S. Women's National Team's success, both on the field and in the stands, had been planted in the '70s. "It wouldn't have happened without Title IX," said Anson Dorrance, whose North Carolina dynasty formed a backbone of players on that '99 U.S. women's national team. "I still owe the leaders of AIAW a huge debt. That's what real leaders are; they didn't wait for an algorithm to tell them it was something they should do. They knew we were right and they just did it."

•

Of all the changes that transformed sports in the '70s—the riches that accompanied the rise of sports on network television, athletes getting a greater sense of their own autonomy, integration becoming more the rule than the exception—the most resonant was the unprecedented involvement of women in all sectors of the sporting world. As the writer Kathryn Jay put it, "Sports had become too important to American society to exclude half the population."

"A big part of this story," said Bill Hancock, "is how hard the women had to push, how kind of nasty some of them had to be. That is a really important part of the story of the '70s. Some women were so strong and fearless and unafraid to tick off people. And thank goodness. A lot of them were nasty, but it was because they *had* to be."

Spending the better part of a decade fighting for access left scars on all of them. Sharon E. Taylor—who directed Lock Haven State College to six national championships in field hockey—was on the front lines, but fifty years later, she is not bitter.

"The lessons learned in sport," said Taylor. "I mean, everybody thinks, *oh, it's just for fun*. Well, no, it isn't fun sometimes. There were times that we all just wanted to get together to hold each other up and cry. But honestly, there was not a bit that wasn't worth it. I've met some of the greatest people I've ever known in my life through those channels, and that's a friendship that will forever be forged in a way that nothing else could do. It was not easy, and you had to be committed."

It was a rough ascent, with many casualties along the way. In the end, the

AIAW vision, for all its purity, needed the rocket-booster of NCAA riches to realize its true potential. The world wouldn't have been changed quite so rapidly in a hermetically sealed arena in which women administrators and athletes ignored the marketplace. The revolution could start—but not maintain itself nor ever truly flourish—in a small gymnasium in Wellesley. It would eventually need the lights, the notoriety, the exposure, the pressure and, yes, even the temptation, of the alchemy of big-time sports.

"To be successful, you have to be competitive," said Joan Cronan, who along with Pat Summitt helped build a women's basketball dynasty at Tennessee. "I think athletics is a tool to teach you to be competitive. And that's why I was upset we didn't have that opportunity, because if you went around and asked males who were very successful in the business world the key to their success, they'd say, 'I learned teamwork and accountability and other things from sports.' Women didn't have that opportunity. I think that's why we're seeing right now so many women excelling at the highest level of life, in the business world or as a physician or a lawyer. They've had that opportunity to learn to compete, and learn to be on a team."

A recent Women's Sports Foundation study discovered that, among women in C-suite positions for Fortune 500 companies in the United States, 94 percent had a background in organized athletics.

So much changed in the decade, and so much changed *because* of the decade. The exposure. The money. The integration. But what changed the most was inclusion. At the beginning of the 1970s, in American high schools, only one out of every twenty-seven girls competed in organized athletics. Within the next generation, it was one in every three. By the time the U.S. women won their second straight World Cup in 2019, it was two out of every five.

That statistic hinted at not only a change in sports, but a far-reaching and seismic change in the way the rest of the world saw American women, the way American men saw American women, and the way, most significantly, American women saw themselves.

•

The men who ran sports in the beginning of the '70s didn't think of themselves as opposed to progress. Rather, they loved sports and wanted to protect what they had. The irony, in looking back on the decade, is that while they were guarding their turf against the proponents of Title IX, what they were actually fighting against, unknowingly, was their own salvation.

This was true of sports' venture into prime time. Without women, *Monday Night Football* could not have succeeded, opening the way for so many other sports in prime time. It was also true in a larger sense. For sports to become what they would become—the last broad cultural common ground, the last remaining "big tent" in the increasingly balkanized, narrowcast landscape of American culture—women had to be part of it. For the games to resonate, they had to resonate for all. That was true off the field as well, where fully 40 percent of the NFL's and NBA's audiences were female.

At the beginning of the '70s, the idea that women would play such a vital and central role in American sports was unthinkable. By the end of the decade, thanks to Title IX and the AIAW and Billie Jean King, it had become inevitable.

The way modern spectator sports embodied so much of the twin pillars of American life—community and competition—would be fully absorbed into the entire country, not just half of it. In the process, it wasn't merely American sports that had changed. America had been transformed as well.

# Acknowledgments

Shortly after I reached an agreement to write this book, my daughter Ella asked me what my next project was going to be. When I explained to her it would be a broad social history about sports in the 1970s, she winced and said, as tactfully as she could muster, "Um, Dad, it might help if you write about something that happened, like, less than a million years ago."

Her editorial instincts may yet prove sound, but I was convinced then—and am more certain now—that the events of that decade were crucial in shaping how spectator sports emerged as a central part of American culture in the twenty-first century. Trying to tell that story has been daunting, and I could not have done it without substantial help.

I'd had a notion to write this book for some time, but without the tough love and guidance of my agent, Sloan Harris of CAA, it never would have happened. The book was originally acquired by Gretchen Young at Grand Central Publishing, who believed in the story I wanted to tell. After Gretchen moved on from GCP, the book was inherited by Sean Desmond—another empathetic editor with a deep appreciation for sports. Sean and his assistant Zoe Karimy have been wise, supportive and exceedingly helpful throughout. The gifted designer Phil Pascuzzo, consulting with GCP creative director Albert Tang, devised the striking cover. Senior production editor Carolyn Kurek tamed the unruly manuscript, then Roxanne Jones, Staci Burt and Ivy Cheng in publicity and Tiffany Porcelli in marketing helped spread the word.

In trying to assemble the mammoth amount of secondary material on the decade, I relied on the yeoman work of my indefatigable research assistant, Alexa Klyap, as well as—in the later stages—Abbie Steuhm at the University of Iowa. Research is generally more accessible in the age of the internet, but there are many things that still aren't reachable with a few keystrokes. Guiding me through the morass of hard-to-locate books, out-of-print magazines, and obscure congressional testimony was Missy Nelson, the ninja reference librarian at the Perry-Castañeda Library at the University of Texas. Special thanks as well to Margaret Schlankey, head of public services, and Marisa Jefferson, reference intern, at the Dolph Briscoe Center for American History at the University of Texas. I also spent a considerable amount of time at the H. J. Lutcher Stark Center for Physical Culture and Sports on the UT campus, where Jan Todd, Cindy Slater and Kim Beckwith directed me to many hard-to-find treasures.

Photo acquisition for books has become something of a chore, but I've been blessed in this book with people who made the process much easier. At the Associated Press, Tricia Gesner was helpful and responsive, as was Katie Walker at Getty Images. Thanks to Joe Amati at the NBA for helping me acquire some key photographs, to Neil Leifer for giving me a lead on a wayward photographer, and to Marc Fleisher for directing me to a wonderful picture of his dad. Thanks as well to the great Rod Hanna, Rosa Gatti and Mike Soltys at ESPN, Jeannie Schulz and Jackie Rader at the Charles M. Schulz Museum and Research Center, Rebecca Taylor in George Kalinsky's office, Jennifer Shults at the University of Texas, as well as Cec Ponce and Cal State–Fullerton, Cory Mueller and UCLA, and Tom Weber and Southern Illinois University.

Every book is a learning experience. The part of this story I initially knew the least about was the growth of women's sports during the decade, and all the obstacles encountered along the way. Sally Jenkins pointed me in the right direction, and I relied greatly on the memories of several key players, including Charlotte West, Donna Lopiano, Peg Burke, Carole Oglesby, Margot Polivy, Sharon E. Taylor, Merrily Dean Baker, Judie Holland, and scholars like Margaret Dunkle, Susan Ware, Diane Williams, Jaime Schultz, Candace Lyle Hogan and Grace Lichtenstein. My grad school classmate, Jen Miller, former director of special projects at the Women's Sports Foundation, provided some crucial direction early on in the project.

Several people supplemented my research with their own papers. Besides West, Dunkle, Oglesby and Taylor, I also received important materials from Mike Harrigan, Jim Foley, Brian McIntyre, Sue Scheetz, Ed Krzemienski and Ted Koy. A special thanks to Amy Wilson for sharing the 25 DVDs from the AIAW Presidential Review of 1980, and for longtime NCAA vice president Tom Hansen for sharing a decade's worth of NCAA television committee reports. Thanks to Jessie Mayfield at the Eddie G. Robinson Museum, and

Glenn Lewis at Grambling, for allowing me to view the seminal documentary *Grambling College: 100 Yards to Glory*. At NFL Films, the historian Chris Willis proved particularly helpful once again. Ann Meyers Drysdale, Liz Galloway McQuitter, Joe Posnanski, Joe Gordon, Ced Golden, Bob Moore and Sam Mellinger helped me track down some key interviews. Thanks as well are owed to Taylor Damron, Sloan's assistant at CAA, for logistical support.

Writing a book is a lonely endeavor, and I remained energized because of my circle of dear friends, including Rob Minter (to whom I kvetch almost daily), Kevin Lyttle, Chris Brown, Tony Owens, Arlyn Owens, Adam Moses, Steve Bosky, Steven Wilson, Josh Cole, Mark "Jonno" Johnson, David Joiner, Matthew Aucoin, Sam Ulu, Bola Lamidi, Philip Tam, Jacqui and Declan Dunleavy, Neil Atkinson, Anne Rodgers, Kirk Bohls, Ced Golden, Mark Rosner, Peter Blackstock, Doug Miller, Michael Barnes, Patrick Taggart, Kirby Moss, George McMahon, Ryan Cox, Russell Smith, David Zivan, Jeff Zivan, Brian Hay, Lesley McCullough McCallister, Tim Shanley, Brian Shanley, Eric Pils, Aaron Cooper, Francesca Tripoli, Travis Farley, Natalie Hocharoen, Melissa and Scott Harrington, Adrian Healey, Rich Moffitt, Jennifer Harrison, Ross Lillard, Jay Rivard, Greg Emas, Trey Gratwick, Tim and Janice Martin, Brad Garrett, Shekar Sathyanarayana, Steve Riad, Ben Meers, Denise Lieberman, Don McLaughlin, Arika Cannon, Shannon McCormack, Kristin Elizondo, Angie Russo, Dodie Jacobi, Jo Brown, Candace Hastings, Chuck Culpepper, Wright Thompson, Seth Wickersham, Tony Mansell, W. J. Monagle, Yvonne Delnis, Wayne and Cheryl Chapman, Stan Webb, Loren Watt, Larry Johnson and Hal Cox. I remain grateful for mentors Donna Leff and Abe Peck, who've both become friends in the intervening decades.

I'm indebted to my inner circle, including my mother, Lois MacCambridge, my children, Miles and Ella, my sister and brother-in-law, Angie and Tom Szentgyorgyi, as well as our friends Nicole and James Stubbe, Earl Summers, Roger and Leslie Williams, and Riza Rafi. Thanks also to Rusty Kutzer, Brian Martens and Dr. Linda Pak for keeping me reasonably fit, and thanks always to Reggie Givens for his kinship and sense of wonder. I'm particularly grateful for the regular and rejuvenating talks with Laura Pfeifauf, Susan Reckers and Katherine Rivard—the three friends to whom this book is dedicated— as well as the absorbing conversations with my longtime confidant Akin Owoso.

Thanks as well to all those who offered shelter on my travels, including

Todd and Anissa Everett (who provided safe harbor during Austin's epic Snowpocalypse of 2021), Roger and Leslie Williams, Jane and Jonny Girson, Peter and Debbie Moore, Vahe and Cindy Gregorian, Susan and Mark Reckers, Paul and Audrey Boden, Jessica Boden, Lisa Boden, and Muriel Boden and Glenn Wynn.

Near the end of the project I asked some friends and trusted sources to read over portions of the manuscript. Charlotte West, Carole Oglesby, Sharon E. Taylor and Margaret Dunkle all reviewed in exacting detail the chapters I sent—it was like being back in college with really good professors. The comments from John Walsh, Ernie Accorsi, Michael Hurd, Michael Butterworth, Kirk Bohls, Chris Plonsky, Alexander Wolff, Mark Rosner, Cliff Drysdale, Allan Tanenbaum, Donna de Varona, Julie Foudy and Gerald Early were invaluable. Thank you as well to sharp-eyed friends Pat Porter, Larry Schwartz and Bob Jacobi, each of whom fact-checked and proofread substantial portions of the manuscript. They saved me from numerous errors. The mistakes that remain, of course, are all of my own doing. If you see any, please reach out to me at maccambridge@mac.com, and I will endeavor to correct any errors in future editions of this book.

Finally, I am indebted to my partner and partner-in-crime, Carrie Boden, a brilliant scholar whose own life was substantially leavened by Title IX (she went to college on a volleyball scholarship). No one understands the vortex of book writing quite like a fellow writer, so I am grateful for her support and understanding along the way. It was fun going to work and also fun reaching the end of the workday.

Between my childhood and the writing of this book, I figure I've now spent at least twelve years living in the 1970s, and I am well ready to get back to the present. But to my daughter I would say: It sure doesn't *feel* like a million years ago.

—MJM, Austin, June 2023

# Source Notes

EPIGRAPHS

viii **"That which we"**: Ralph Ellison, *Shadow and Act* (New York: Vintage, 1995), p. 199.

viii **"It all happens"**: Ray Cave, quoting Laguerre, in *George, Being George: George Plimpton's Life as Told, Admired, Deplored, and Envied by 200 Friends, Relatives, Lovers, Acquaintances, Rivals—and a Few Unappreciative Observers*, edited by Nelson W. Aldrich (New York: Random House, 2008), p. 163.


PROLOGUE

1 **The fans came:** Billie Jean King int.; scenes culled from ABC broadcast, You-Tube, https://www.youtube.com/watch?v=qqB3yi8MVbQ; *Billie Jean*, by Billie Jean King, with Kim Chapin (New York: Harper & Row, 1974), pp. 164–186; Billie Jean King, with Frank Deford, *The Autobiography of Billie Jean King* (St. Albans, Hertfordshire, UK: Granada, 1981), pp. 20–21; Billie Jean King, with Johnette Howard and Maryanne Vollers, *All In: An Autobiography* (New York: Knopf, 2021), pp. 237–259; Pete Axthelm, "The Battle of the Sexes," *Newsweek,* Sept. 24, 1973, pp. 50–53.

1 **Though the event:** Associated Press, "Nixon Files Tape Response," *Chicago Tribune*, Sept. 20, 1973, p. 3; Bill Anderson, "Detroit a Bit Slow at Thinking Small," *Chicago Tribune*, Sept. 20, 1973, p. 18.

2 **The event came:** Susan Ware, *Game, Set, Match: Billie Jean King and the Revolution in Women's Sports* (Chapel Hill: University of North Carolina Press, 2011), pp. 1–14.

3 **By the time:** Selena Roberts, *A Necessary Spectacle: Billie Jean King, Bobby Riggs, and the Tennis Match That Leveled the Game* (New York: Crown, 2005), pp. 115–136.

4 **"Americans still find"**: Bruce J. Schulman, *The Seventies: The Great Shift in American Culture, Society, and Politics* (Cambridge, MA: Da Capo Press, 2002), p. 145; Peter N. Carroll, *It Seemed Like Nothing Happened: America in the 1970s* (New Brunswick, NJ: Rutgers University Press, 2000).

5 **While the 1960s:** David Maraniss, *When Pride Still Mattered: A Life of Vince Lombardi* (New York: Simon and Schuster, 1999), pp. 470–472; Michael

MacCambridge, *America's Game: The Epic Story of How Pro Football Captured a Nation* (New York: Random House, 2004), pp. 247–251.

7    **No sport was:** Phil Pepe, *Talkin' Baseball: An Oral History of Baseball in the 1970s* (New York: Ballantine, 1998), p. 4.

10   **Or as Joyce:** Joyce Carol Oates, "Muhammad Ali: The Greatest Second Act," in *ESPN SportsCentury*, edited by Michael MacCambridge (New York: Hyperion 1999), p. 207.


**CHAPTER 1: 1969: THE GATHERING STORM**

11   **The first glimpse:** Bob Gibson with Lonnie Wheeler, *Stranger to the Game: The Autobiography of Bob Gibson* (New York: Viking, 1994); Curt Flood with Richard Carter, *The Way It Is* (New York: Trident Press, 1970); Bob Broeg, "Fans Want Baseball, Not Salary Records," *St. Louis Post-Dispatch*, March 23, 1969, p. 1; Bob Broeg, "Gussie Tells It Like It Is—and Players Concur," *The Sporting News*, April 5, 1969, p. 3; Dal Maxvill int.; Mark Tomasik, "Why Cardinals Were Offended by Talk from Gussie Busch," RetroSimba, March 15, 2019, https://retrosimba .com/2019/03/15/why-cardinals-were-offended-by-talk-from-gussie-busch/.

12   **As early as:** MacCambridge, *America's Game*, p. 5.

13   **"It is ridiculous":** Bob Adelman and Susan Hall, *Out of Left Field: Willie Stargell's Turning Point Season* (Lawrence, MA: Two Continents, 1976), p. 140.

13   **Negotiations were more:** Jon McGlocklin int.

13   **The raises, when:** Sal Bando int.

13   **Even standout athletes:** Bobby Bell int.; Steve Blass int.; Johnny Unitas int.; David Halberstam, *The Breaks of the Game* (New York: Hachette Books, 2015), p. 115; Chanel Stitt, "New Book 'Attacking the Rim' Details Dave Bing's Triumph over Obstacles," *Detroit Free Press*, Nov. 13, 2020.

13   **Coaches had learned:** Michael MacCambridge, *Chuck Noll: His Life's Work* (Pittsburgh: University of Pittsburgh Press, 2016), p. 145.

14   **In every sport:** Phil Berger, *Miracle on 33rd Street: The N.Y. Knickerbockers' Championship Season* (New York: Simon and Schuster, 1970), pp. 40–41.

14   **The regular season:** Jon McGlocklin int.; Jim Foley int.; John Devaney, *The Champion Bucks* (New York: Lancer Books, 1971), pp. 156–157.

14   **"Our pregame meal":** Steve Blass int.

14   **A glimpse into:** Bill Bradley int.; Bill Bradley, *Life on the Run* (New York: Vintage Books, 1995), p. 13.

14   **In 1968, when:** Bill Bradley int.; Pat Williams int.; Bob Ryan int.; Berger, *Miracle on 33rd Street*, pp. 40–41; Bradley, *Life on the Run,* p. 146.

15   **Each league was:** Hank Stram int.; Lamar Hunt int.; Jack Steadman int.

15   **For all the:** Pat Williams int.; Brian McIntyre int.

16   **There was little:** Pat Williams int.

17   **The adjustment from:** Kareem Abdul-Jabbar, *Coach Wooden and Me: Our 50-Year Friendship On and Off the Court* (New York: Grand Central Publishing, 2017), pp. 73–75.

17   **Confident and keenly:** Jerry Colangelo int.; Jim Foley int.; Jim O'Brien int.; Terry Pluto int.; Pat Williams int.; Terry Pluto, *Loose Balls: The Short, Wild Life of the American Basketball Association as Told by the Players, Coaches, and Movers and Shakers Who Made It Happen* (New York: Fireside, 1990), pp. 191–193.

18   **Lew Alcindor grew:** Kareem Abdul-Jabbar with Peter Knobler, *Giant Steps: The Autobiography of Kareem Abdul-Jabbar* (Toronto: Bantam Books, 1983), p. 5.

18   **"Big Al" Alcindor had:** Abdul-Jabbar with Knobler, *Giant Steps*, pp. 6–11; Abdul-Jabbar, *Coach Wooden and Me*, p. 33.

18   **That week in:** Abdul-Jabbar with Knobler, *Giant Steps*, pp. 190–194.

18   **On March 24:** Jim Foley int.; Jim O'Brien int.; Terry Pluto int.; Jerry Colangelo int.; "$1.4 Million Dollar Baby," *Sports Illustrated*, April 7, 1969, p. 11; Lew Alcindor with Jack Olsen, "A Year of Turmoil and Decision; My Story, Part 3," *Sports Illustrated*, Nov. 10, 1969, pp. 35–46; Harvey Aronson, "The Sports Commissioners: Czars or Muzhiks?," *Sport*, Feb. 1973, pp. 24–28.

19   **After a moment:** Abdul-Jabbar, "A Year of Turmoil and Decision."

19   **Mikan walked down:** Terry Pluto int.; Jim O'Brien int.; Pluto, *Loose Balls*, pp. 192–193.

19   **"You dumb sonofabitch!":** Pluto, *Loose Balls*, p. 192.

19   **Alcindor would later:** Abdul-Jabbar, "A Year of Turmoil and Decision"; Bob Fowler, "ABA Goes to Court After Lew Nixes Bid Set at $3.25 Million," *The Sporting News*, April 12, 1969, p. 60.

20   **"A bidding war":** "$1.4 Million Dollar Baby."

20   **It was also:** Michael MacCambridge, *'69 Chiefs: A Team, a Season, and the Birth of Modern Kansas City* (Kansas City: Andrews & McMeel, 2019), pp. 33–38.

20   **"I told everybody":** MacCambridge, *'69 Chiefs*, p. 38.

21   **Billie Jean Moffitt:** Billie Jean King int.; King with Howard and Vollers, *All In*, p. 12; Jason Gay, "A Sibling Rivalry for the Ages," *Wall Street Journal*, Oct. 10, 2021.

21   **Billie Jean was:** King with Deford, *The Autobiography of Billie Jean King*, p. 19.

21   **She found solace:** King with Howard and Vollers, *All In*, pp. 80–81.

22   **Tennis was still:** Cliff Drysdale int.; Ware, *Game, Set, Match*, p. 30.

22   **While Billie Jean:** Larry King int.

22   **So by training:** Larry King int.; "Billie Jean King: The Pioneer," in MacCambridge (ed.), *ESPN SportsCentury*, p. 223; Ware, *Game, Set, Match*, pp. 25–27.

23   **Within a year:** Larry King int.; Billie Jean King int.; Judy Dalton int.; Peachy Kellmeyer int.; Rod Humphries int.

23 **The most famous:** Thomas Hauser, *Muhammad Ali: His Life and Times* (New York: Simon and Schuster, 1991), pp. 234–238.

23 **Still in boxing purgatory:** "Notes for an Autobiography," Scorecard, *Sports Illustrated*, Jan. 19, 1970, p. 9; Gerald Early int.; Jonathan Eig, *Ali: A Life* (Boston: Mariner Books, 2017), pp. 275–278; Peter Wood, "Return of Muhammad Ali, a/k/a Cassius Marcellus Clay Jr.," *New York Times Magazine*, Nov. 20, 1969, p. 32; Hans J. Massaquoi, "The Unconquerable Muhammad Ali," *Ebony*, April 1969, p. 168.

24 **The simulated bout:** Brad Schultz, *Lombardi Dies, Orr Flies, Marshall Cries: The Sports Legacy of 1970* (Lanham, MD: Rowman & Littlefield, 2015), p. 18; "The Super Fight," *Time*, Jan. 19, 1970, p. 59.

24 **Meanwhile, as his:** Martin Kane, "Welcome Back, Ali!," *Sports Illustrated*, Sept. 14, 1970, p. 20.

24 **With his generosity:** Gerald Early, "Introduction: Tales of the Wonderboy," in *The Muhammad Ali Reader*, edited by Gerald Early (Hopewell, NJ: Ecco Press, 1998), p. xi.

25 **In the words:** Stephen E. Ambrose, *Nixon: The Triumph of a Politician* (New York: Simon and Schuster, 1989), p. 456.

25 **Earlier in 1969:** Mark Mulvoy, "Oh, Prez, Where Is Thy Ring?," *Sports Illustrated*, Aug. 31, 1970, p. 42; "Fan No. 1," *Newsweek*, Dec. 22, 1969, p. 70.

25 **Presidents had been:** Hunter S. Thompson, *Fear and Loathing on the Campaign Trail '72* (San Francisco: Straight Arrow, 1973), p. 61; MacCambridge, *America's Game*, p. 300.

25 **In October 1969:** Michael Weinreb, "Tricky Dick's Trick Play," Grantland, June 18, 2013, https://grantland.com/features/texas-arkansas-face-president-richard -nixon-1969/; Nicholas Evan Sarantakes, "Nixon Versus Paterno: College Football and Presidential Politics," *Pennsylvania History: A Journal of Mid-Atlantic Studies*, Vol. 73, No. 2, 2006; Roy Reed, "In the South, Football Is a Religio-Social Pastime," *New York Times*, Oct. 6, 1969.

26 **There may have:** Bob McKay int.; Ernie Koy int.; Bill Little int.; Kelli Stacy, "Remembering Texas and Arkansas' 1969 'Game of the Century,' from Three Guys Who Played the Game," *Athletic*, Dec. 6, 2019.

26 **There were protesters:** United Press International, "Nixon Gives Texas Number One Plaque," *Boston Globe*, Dec. 7, 1969.

26 **During its halftime:** Chris Schenkel int.; Bill Little int.; Ernie Accorsi int.; Texas at Arkansas game program, Dec. 6, 1969; ABC broadcast, YouTube, https://www .youtube.com/watch?v=ORAFBpWrNZ8; Dan Jenkins, *Saturday's America: The Chronic Outrage and Giddy Passion of College Football* (Boston: Little, Brown, 1970), pp. 253–268.

26 **Alcindor's pro debut:** Bill Bradley int.

27 **For twelve years:** Bob Posen, "Cards Get Allen; McCarver, Flood Go," *St. Louis Post-Dispatch*, Oct. 8, 1969, p. 4E; "Flood Announces He Is Retiring," *St. Louis Post-Dispatch*, Oct. 8, 1969, p. 4E.

28 **In the coming:** Gerald Early int.

28 **Talking privately with:** Gibson with Wheeler, *Stranger to the Game*, pp. 217–222.

28 **By December, Flood:** Schultz, *Lombardi Dies*, p. 18.

28 **But Flood remained:** Curt Flood with Richard Carter, "My Rebellion," *Sports Illustrated*, Feb. 1, 1971, p. 24; Dal Maxvill int.

29 **"Does anything about":** Schultz, *Lombardi Dies*, pp. 17–18.

29 **Carl Yastrzemski of:** Schultz, *Lombardi Dies*, pp. 17–18.

29 **In a Christmas Eve:** Curt Flood letter to Commissioner Bowie Kuhn, Dec. 24, 1969; "Flood Tide," *Newsweek*, Jan. 12, 1970.

29 **Kuhn was still:** "Flood Tide."

29 **His friend Bob:** Gibson with Wheeler, *Stranger to the Game*, p. 218.


CHAPTER 2: THE WHITE HOUSE IS CALLING

31 **Most political grievances:** Bob McKay int.; Ted Koy int.; Kirk Bohls int.; Bill Little int.; Bud Shrake int.

31 **Royal had lived:** Jenna McEachern int.; Dan Jenkins int.

32 **"If Coach Royal":** Bob McKay int.

32 **The process of:** Bob McKay int.; Ted Koy int.; Bill Little int.; Darrell Royal with Blackie Sherrod, *Darrell Royal Talks Football* (Englewood Cliffs, NJ: Prentice-Hall, 1963).

32 **All the elements:** Bill Little int.; Darrell Royal papers, The Dolph Briscoe Center for American history, University of Texas at Austin.

32 **Royal's speech was:** John Anders, "Royal Treatment," *Dallas Morning News*, Dec. 26, 1976.

33 **But even kicking:** Robert Hilburn, "Waylon Jennings: An Outlaw Breaks Out," *Los Angeles Times*, July 25, 1976, p. 271.

33 **By the time:** Bill Little int.

34 **In so many:** "PreGame, Halftime," Cotton Bowl Classic 1970 Texas vs. Notre Dame game program, p. 53.

35 **"You played like":** Dick Moore, "UT No. 1? Hmmm, Says Irish," *Fort Worth Star-Telegram*, Jan. 2, 1970, pp. C1–C2.

36 **That created an:** Willie Lanier int.

36 **The players both:** Jack Rudnay int.; Bobby Bell int.; Jan Stenerud int.

37 **The Vikings entered:** Tex Maule, "Wham, Bam, Stram," *Sports Illustrated*, Jan. 19, 1970. "The decade of the '60s was the decade of simplicity," said Stram the week of the game. "During the '60s the good teams—the Green Bay Packers,

for example—came out almost all the time in the same set and ran the play. In effect, what they said was here we come, see if you can stop us. Well, the '70s will be the decade of difference—different offensive sets, different defensive formations. What we try to do is to create a moment of hesitation, a moment of doubt in the defense." Stram would never win another postseason game, but wasn't wrong in his prediction of pro football's growing multiplicity.

37  **"Hey, Lenny, come":** MacCambridge, '69 Chiefs, p. 172; Joe McGuff, *Winning It All: The Chiefs of the AFL* (Garden City, NY: Doubleday, 1970), pp. 1–9; Len Dawson with Lou Sahadi, *Len Dawson: Pressure Quarterback* (New York: Cowles, 1970), p. 219; Larry Bortstein, *Len Dawson: Superbowl [sic] Quarterback* (New York: Grosset & Dunlap, 1970), p. 179.

38  **Amid the bustle:** Peaches Sellers int.; Doug Porter int.; Eddie Robinson with Richard Lapchick, *Never Before, Never Again: The Autobiography of Eddie Robinson* (New York: St. Martin's Press, 1999), pp. 125–127; Warren Rogers, "Grambling College: Where Stars Are Made," *Look*, Dec. 16, 1969, pp. 72–75.

38  **Robinson was the:** Robinson with Lapchick, *Never Before, Never Again*, pp. 9–26.

38  **Robinson's recruiting pitch:** James "Shack" Harris int.

39  **That and the:** Doug Porter int.; Bill Little int.

39  **But Robinson had:** Doug Porter int.; Michael Hurd int.

39  **It was Jones:** Robinson with Lapchick, *Never Before, Never Again*, p. 147.

40  **Though he lacked:** Shack Harris int.

40  **As Robinson left:** Doug Porter int.

41  **"That was a":** Doug Porter int.; Jerry Hardaway int.

41  **Stram knew that:** Lloyd Wells int.; Bill Nunn int.

41  **"We have to":** Shack Harris int.; Doug Porter int.

41  **Harris was Robinson's:** Doug Porter int.

41  **At one of:** Shack Harris int.

42  **"James was extremely":** Doug Porter int.

42  **That fall of:** James Toback, "Longhorns and Longhairs," *Harper's*, Nov. 1970, pp. 70–73.

43  **At the end:** Dr. Harry Edwards, "The Sources of the Black Athlete's Superiority," *Black Scholar*, Vol. 3, No. 3, Nov. 1971, pp. 32–41; Martin Kane, "An Assessment of: 'Black Is Best,'" *Sports Illustrated*, Jan. 18, 1971, pp. 72–83; Sam Smith, *Hard Labor: The Battle That Birthed the Billion-Dollar NBA* (Chicago: Triumph Books, 2017), p. 165.

43  **"You didn't want":** Pat Williams int.

43  **Much of the racism:** Wayne Embry int.; Jackie MacMullen, Rafe Bartholomew, Dan Klores, *Basketball: A Love Story* (New York: Crown Archetype, 2018), p. 53.

43  **On the eve:** Jim O'Brien int.; Sam Heys, *Remember Henry Harris: Lost Icon of a Revolution: A Story of Hope and Self-Sacrifice in America* (Atlanta: Black Belt

Press, 2019), pp. 129–135; Jim O'Brien, "The '70s Were Something Else!," *Street & Smith's Official College, Pro, Prep Basketball Yearbook, 1980–81*, pp. 57–58.

44 **The remnants of:** Marty Schladen, "How the 1966 NCAA Championship Changed the World," by *El Paso Times*, March 19, 2016; Curry Kirkpatrick, "Crazy Cat and His Curious Warriors," *Sports Illustrated*, Jan. 25, 1971, p. 32.

44 **"There are so":** Berger, *Miracle on 33rd Street,* p. 152.

45 **But the racial:** Pat Putnam, "No Defeats, Loads of Trouble," *Sports Illustrated*, Nov. 3, 1969, pp. 26–27.

45 **"Nobody wants to":** Pat Putnam, "End of a Season at Syracuse," *Sports Illustrated*, Sept. 28, 1970, pp. 22–23.

45 **For the athletes:** Julius Erving with Karl Taro Greenfeld, *Dr. J: The Autobiography* (New York: HarperCollins, 2013), p. 102.

46 **In the third:** Tyler Kepner, "A Lineup of Color Made History, Even If It Felt 'Routine,'" *New York Times*, Aug. 30, 2021, p. D-7.

46 **Even when the:** Lacy J. Banks, "Black Football Players in the White South," *Ebony*, Dec. 1970, pp. 131–141.

46 **"Black parents and":** Banks, "Black Football Players in the White South."

## CHAPTER 3: THE WORKING PRESS

47 **By that time:** Bob Ryan int.; Bob Ryan, "Frazier Leads Knicks to First NBA Title," *Boston Globe*, May 9, 1970, p. 21.

47 **Instead, ABC set:** ABC broadcast, YouTube, https://www.youtube.com/watch?v=Vzt1hYfDqFE.

48 **The real reason:** Roy Blount, Jr., "Talking Baseball. Language! Language!," *Take Another Little Piece of My Heart Now* (blog), Nov. 5, 2022.

48 **"One thing I":** Joe Posnanski, "I: Uh: Correa: What?," *Joe Blogs Baseball* (blog), Dec. 21, 2022

48 **The reason print:** Ernie Accorsi int.

49 **"Print was number":** Bill Hancock int.

50 **The announcer Gil:** William Leggett, "Hello, There, TV Sports Fans," *Sports Illustrated*, June 26, 1972, pp. 36–45.

50 **Even the scores:** Berger, *Miracle on 33rd Street,* p. 179.

50 **Much of the:** Larry Bird with Bob Ryan, *Drive: The Story of My Life* (New York: Bantam, 1990), pp. 34–35.

51 **Bird was hardly:** Michael Corcoran, *The Game of the Century: Nebraska vs. Oklahoma in Football's Ultimate Battle* (Lincoln, NE: University of Nebraska Press: 2004), p. 100.

51 **No one understood:** Ernie Accorsi int.

51 **In Boston, where:** Dave Smith int.

51 **Within almost every:** Dave Smith int.; George Solomon int.; Ed Storin int.

52 **"I'm developing a":** Michael MacCambridge, "More than a Game," in *A New Literary History of America*, edited by Greil Marcus and Werner Sollors (Cambridge, MA: The Belknap Press of Harvard University Press, 2009); Michael MacCambridge, *The Franchise: A History of* Sports Illustrated *Magazine* (New York: Hyperion, 1997), p. 891.

52 **In the meantime:** Dan Jenkins int.; Bud Shrake int.

52 **In 1970, the aging:** Ed Storin int.; Dave Smith int.; George Solomon int.

53 **There was an:** Bill Hancock int.

53 **"How you hittin'":** Bill Little int.; Denne H. Freeman, *Hook 'Em Horns: A Story of Texas Football* (Huntsville, AL: Strode, 1973), p. 177.

53 **When the formidable:** Freeman, *Hook 'Em Horns*, pp. 177–178.

54 **A year earlier:** Bill Little int.; Mickey Herskowitz int.

54 **Implicit in all:** Darrell Royal Oral History, Darrell Royal papers, Dolph Briscoe Center of American History, University of Texas at Austin.

54 **But even the:** Dave Smith int.

55 **"Look here," said:** Berger, *Miracle on 33rd Street*, p. 88.

55 **The journeyman pitcher:** Jim Bouton, *Ball Four*, edited by Leonard Shecter (New York: Dell, 1970); Michell Nathanson, *Bouton: The Life of a Baseball Original* (Lincoln, NE: University of Nebraska Press, 2020), pp. 129–142.

55 **The book was:** Mark Armour, "Ball Four," Society of American Baseball Research, https://sabr.org/bioproj/topic/ball-four/.

55 **Nowhere was the:** "Absolutely Clear," Scorecard, *Sports Illustrated*, July 6, 1970, p. 7.

55 **That marked perhaps:** Nathanson, *Bouton*, pp. 143–155.

56 **The dividing line:** Allen Barra, "One Man Out," in *Rolling Stone: The 70s*, edited by Ashley Kahn, Holly George-Warren, and Shawn Dahl (Boston: Little Brown, 1998), p. 18.

56 **But it went:** George Solomon, "For the 33 Years Before the Nats' Arrival, D.C. Didn't Have a Team, Much Less a Winner," *Washington Post*, Oct. 19, 2019.

57 **But in the:** Mike Breen int.; Dan Epstein, *Big Hair and Plastic Grass* (New York: Thomas Dunne, 2010), p. 108.

57 **Though the televised:** From ABC broadcast, YouTube, https://www.youtube.com/watch?v=n_uAJlWP0lQ.

57 **NBC's broadcast of:** From NBC broadcast, YouTube, https://www.youtube.com/watch?v=PGKPMkTo-fU.

58 **The man who:** Roone Arledge, *Roone: A Memoir* (New York: HarperCollins, 2003), pp. 1–10; Phil Patton, *Razzle-Dazzle: The Curious Marriage of Television and Professional Football* (Garden City, NY: Dial Press, 1984), pp. 59–64; Ron Powers, *Supertube: The Rise of Television Sports* (New York: Coward-McCann, 1984), pp. 125–138.

58  **A fanatic about:** Dennis Lewin int.; Geoff Mason int.

59  **"Arledge taught us":** Geoff Mason int.

59  **Those who knew:** Anne Marie Bratton int.; Joe Browne int.; Paul Tagliabue int.; Ernie Accorsi int.

60  **By that point:** MacCambridge, *America's Game*, pp. 276–277.

60  **His commercial instincts:** C. C. Johnson Spink, "TD for Monday Night TV," We Believe, *The Sporting News,* June 6, 1970.

61  **In late August:** "Goodby, Howard," Scorecard, *Sports Illustrated*, Dec. 7, 1970, p. 9.

62  **The game announcers:** From ABC broadcast, YouTube, https://www.youtube .com/watch?v=n_uAJlWP0lQ.

62  **Reed strode to:** Jeff Greenfield, "Willis Reed: The Art and Agony of a Gentle Giant," *Sport*, Feb. 1973, pp. 72–83.

63  **On September 21:** Erika Berlin, "50 Years of Monday Night Football's Memorable Theme Music," *Mental Floss*, Sept. 21, 2015.

63  **"Of course, Weeb:"** From ABC broadcast, YouTube, https://www.youtube.com /watch?v=0zPj6lFuzL4&t=279s.

64  **"When the games":** Dennis Lewin int.

64  **Don Meredith's charge:** From ABC broadcast, YouTube, https://www.youtube .com/watch?v=0zPj6lFuzL4&t=279s.

64  **"We knew that":** Dennis Lewin int.; Robert H. Boyle, "TV Wins on Points," *Sports Illustrated*, Nov. 2, 1970, p. 14. Boyle reported theater owners describing Monday nights as a "disaster," and restaurants reported business dipping by as much as 25 percent.

64  **Instantly, the ABC:** Geoff Mason int.

65  **In Oakland, the:** John Madden int.

65  **"If you were":** Ernie Accorsi int.

65  **"Wherever I was":** Joe Greene int.

66  **"ABC has lost":** Edwin Shrake, "What Are They Doing with the Sacred Game of Pro Football?," *Sports Illustrated*, Oct. 25, 1971, pp. 96–108.

66  **"Sport is a":** Cait Murphy, *A History of American Sports in 100 Objects* (New York: Basic Books, 2016), p. 166

66  **He wasn't finished:** Frank Gifford int.

66  **One measure of:** *The Bob Newhart Show*, "Don't Go to Bed Mad," aired Nov. 11, 1972, IMDb, https://www.imdb.com/title/tt0789361/.

67  **Almost all of:** Powers, *Supertube*, pp. 140–141.

67  **Rozelle was among:** William Oscar Johnson, "You Know You're Not Getting Maudie Frickert," *Sports Illustrated*, Jan. 26, 1970, pp. 30–37.

67  **Even as print:** "Red, White and Blue Ballgame," Scorecard, *Sports Illustrated*, Jan. 5, 1970, p. 6.

## CHAPTER 4: DOWN TO BUSINESS

69 **In the 1970:** Ernie Accorsi int.; Sheila Mackey int.; Bill Curry int.

70 **"I never met":** Ernie Accorsi int.

70 **He understood that:** Bill Curry int.

70 **"What the *hell*:":** Bill Curry int.; Tex Schramm int.

71 **"We thought if":** Bill Curry int.

71 **At the time:** Joe Jares, "The One-Night Season," *Sports Illustrated*, Aug. 10, 1970, pp. 8–11.

71 **At heart:** John Mackey int.; John Mackey with Thom Loverro, *Blazing Trails: Coming of Age in Football's Golden Era* (Chicago: Triumph Books, 2003), p. 179.

71 **But they did:** "Second Strike," Scorecard, *Sports Illustrated*, Dec. 21, 1970, p. 11.

72 **"The idea that":** Jim Quinn, *Don't Be Afraid to Win: How Free Agency Changed the Business of Pro Sports* (New York: Radius Book Group, 2019), p. 11; Jim Quinn int.

72 **While many old-school:** "The Flood Case," Scorecard, *Sports Illustrated*, June 1, 1970, p. 6.

72 **As the case:** John Schuerholz int.

72 **What they were:** Marvin Miller, *A Whole Different Ball Game: The Sport and Business of Baseball* (New York: Birch Lane Press, 1991), pp. 11–18; Don Fehr int.; Jim Quinn int.; Steve Blass int.

73 **When, in an:** Gerald Astor, "Are Sports Salaries Too High?," *Sport*, Oct. 1972, p. 52.

73 **Historically, the culture:** Matthew Futterman, *Players: How Sports Became a Business* (New York: Simon and Schuster, 2016), p. 118.

73 **"The owners called":** Ralph Garr int.

73 **Around the world:** Bill Curry int.

73 **Though Flood would:** Leonard Koppett, "Hall of Famers Go to Bat for Flood," *The Sporting News,* June 6, 1970, p. 5; Epstein, *Big Hair and Plastic Grass*, p. 10.

73 **But the layoff:** Pepe, *Talkin' Baseball*, p. 22.

74 **Throughout, Major League:** "Absolutely Clear," Scorecard, *Sports Illustrated*, July 6, 1970, p. 7.

74 **In the end:** Schultz, *Orr Flies*, p. 19.

74 **In the days:** Miller, *A Whole Different Ball Game*, p. 205.

74 **"I'll never forget":** Steve Blass int.

75 **After the strike:** Miller, *A Whole Different Ball Game*, p. 213.

75 **On April 1:** Miller, *A Whole Different Ball Game*, p. 215.

75 **The strike ended:** Robert H. Boyle, "And on the 10th Day They Played Ball," *Sports Illustrated*, April 24, 1972, p. 18.

75 **For baseball's owners:** Gerald Astor, "Are Sports Salaries Too High?," *Sport*, Oct. 1972, p. 52.

75 **Throughout the '60s:** Earl Lawson, "A Writer Probes for Real Big O," *The Sporting News*, March 15, 1969, p. 29.

76 **As Marvin Miller's:** Jim Quinn int.; Don Fehr int.; Marc Fleisher int.

76 **"It was unbelievable":** Smith, *Hard Labor*, p. 93.

76 **Fleisher realized that:** Jim Quinn int.; Russ Granik int.; Jerry Colangelo int.

76 **That's when Fleisher:** Oscar Robertson, *The Big O: My Life, My Time, My Game* (Emmaus, PA: Rodale/St. Martin's, 2003), p. 213.

76 **Robertson was the:** "Cage Merger? It's Up to Congress," *The Sporting News*, July 4, 1970; Phil Elderkin, "Cage Merger Awaits Okay of Congress," *The Sporting News*, July 25, 1970, p. 52.

77 **Dolph did get:** Pluto, *Loose Balls*, pp. 194, 201; Bill Simmons, *The Book of Basketball* (New York: Ballantine Books and ESPN Books, 2010), p. 113*n*.

78 **After he stormed:** Pluto, *Loose Balls*, p. 424.

79 **"Black players, who":** Bradley, *Life on the Run*, p. 108.

79 **"Anything that had":** Joe Greene int.

79 **And so those:** Jim Quinn int.

79 **The political scientist:** Schulman, *The Seventies*, p. 49.

80 **Ali's comeback was:** Mark Kram, "Smashing Return of the Old Ali," *Sports Illustrated*, Nov. 2, 1970, pp. 18–19.

80 **Ali's entourage for:** George Plimpton, "Watching the Man in the Mirror," *Sports Illustrated*, Nov. 22, 1970, p. 80; Eig, *Ali: A Life*, pp. 290–296.

80 **That night also:** Edwin Shrake, "Bundini: Svengali in Ali's Corner," *Sports Illustrated*, Feb. 15, 1971, p. 32.

80 **Ali showed rust:** "The Return of an Exiled Champ," *Newsweek*, Nov. 9, 1970, p. 56.

80 **There was one:** Mark Kram, "A Muddle, and Then a Zinger," *Sports Illustrated*, Dec. 14, 1970, p. 26; "Two Down, One to Go," *Time*, Dec. 21, 1970.

81 **Joe Frazier often:** Mark Kram Jr., *Smokin' Joe: The Life of Joe Frazier* (New York: HarperCollins, 2019), pp. 1–37; Peter Wood, "In This Corner: The Official Heavyweight Champ," *New York Times Magazine*, Nov. 15, 1970, p. 26; Perry Deane Young, "The Fraziers' Time," *Harper's*, Feb. 1972, p. 72.

81 **While Frazier was:** Martin Kane, "The World Champion Nobody Knows," *Sports Illustrated*, Nov. 16, 1970, p. 36; David Amram, "Joe Frazier, 'Singer and Champ,'" *Vogue*, May 1970, pp. 148–150.

82 **The top bid:** Michael Arkush, *The Fight of the Century: Ali vs. Frazier, March 8, 1971* (Hoboken, NJ: Wiley, 2007), p. 115.

82 **Perenchio had lived:** Jerry Kirshenbaum, "Sport's $5 Million Payday," *Sports Illustrated*, Jan. 25, 1971, pp. 20–23; Richard Sandomir, "Jerry Perenchio, Entertainment Mogul Who Advised 'Think Big,' Dies at 86," *New York Times*, May 25, 2017; "The Purse Snatchers," *Time*, Jan. 25, 1971, p. 65.

82 **"This one transcends":** Eig, *Ali: A Life*, p. 308.

82 **"Once Jerry put":** Arkush, *The Fight of the Century*, p. 118.

82  **It was the:** Aldrich, *George, Being George*, pp. 257–258.

83  **While he was:** Robert Lipsyte, "'I Don't Have to Be What You Want Me to Be,'" Says Muhammad Ali," *New York Times Magazine*, March 7, 1971, p. 24; Lacy J. Banks, "The Biggest Fight in History," *Ebony*, March 1971, pp. 134–142.

83  **"If you want":** Gerald Early int.

83  **On the eve:** Arkush, *The Fight of the Century*, p. 165.

83  **On the night:** Peter Guralnick, *Careless Love: The Unmaking of Elvis Presley* (Boston: Little, Brown, 1999), p. 432.

83  **And at Madison:** Lacy Banks, "The Winner, The Loser, the Crowd," *Ebony*, May 1971, pp. 133–142; "Now There Is One Champion," *Newsweek*, March 22, 1971, p. 72; Hauser, *Muhammad Ali*, p. 226.

84  **The fight itself:** Budd Schulberg, "The Loser," *Saturday Evening Post*, Fall 1971, pp. 57–58, 107, 159; the *New Yorker* provided five different firsthand reports of Ali–Frazier's first battle in its Talk of the Town section, "The Fight," *New Yorker*, March 20, 1971, p. 32.

84  **The fight had:** Mark Kram, "The Battered Face of a Winner," *Sports Illustrated*, March 15, 1971, p. 16.

85  **The unanimous decision:** Maurice Berube int.; Maurice Berube, "The Defeat of the Great Black Hope," *Commonwealth*, March 26, 1971, pp. 54–55; "Now There Is One Champion," *Newsweek*, March 22, 1971, p. 72; Norman Mailer, "Ego," *Life*, March 19, 1971, p. 18.

85  **And at the:** Eig, *Ali: A Life*, p. 321.

85  **In the aftermath:** Robert Markus, Along the Sports Trail (column), *Chicago Tribune*, March 9, 1971.

85  **"End of the":** Cover, *Sports Illustrated*, March 15, 1971; Pete Hamill, "The Disintegration of a Folk Hero," *Harpers Bazaar*, May 1971.

85  **Ali's case had:** "Ali Wins by a Decision," Scorecard, *Sports Illustrated*, July 5, 1971, p. 6; Winner If Not Champ," *Time*, July 12, 1971; "Decision for Allah," *Newsweek*, July 12, 1971, p. 61.

85  **In this, too:** "Don't Call Me Champ," *Nation*, July 19, 1971, p. 37.

85  **Somehow, Frazier, for:** Kram Jr., *Smokin' Joe*, pp. 207–209.

86  **Things did not:** "Say It Ain't So," Scorecard, *Sports Illustrated*, June 7, 1971, p. 13; Kram Jr., *Smokin' Joe*, pp. 208–209.

86  **"If there had":** Arkush, *The Fight of the Century*, p. 192.

86  **"Do you think":** Billie Jean King int.; Arkush, *The Fight of the Century*, p. 199.

## CHAPTER 5: A WOMAN'S PLACE

87  **"Half the human":** Elizabeth Janeway, "The Subordinate Sex," *Saturday Review*, Oct. 11, 1969, p. 27.

87 **As the new:** "The Rage of Women," *Look*, Dec. 16, 1969; "The New Feminists," *Nation*, Feb. 24, 1969; "The Retreat from Masculinity," *Saturday Review*, Aug. 16, 1969, p. 52.

87 **Women in prominent:** "For Women, a Difficult Climb to the Top," *Business Week*, Aug. 2, 1969, pp. 42–46, which quoted a *Harvard Business Review* study from the mid-'60s, noting, "In the case of both Negroes and women, the barriers are so great that there is scarcely anything to study: Nor can one easily observe the process of breaking down the barriers, since this occurs so rarely"; "The Retreat from Masculinity"; "Woman's Changing Role in America," *U.S. News and World Report*, Sept. 8, 1969, pp. 44–47; Kathryn Jay, *More Than Just a Game: Sports in American Life Since 1945* (New York: Columbia University Press, 2004), p. 164.

87 **But throughout the:** Carroll, *It Seemed Like Nothing Happened*, pp. 23–24.

87 **"We have suddenly":** Carroll, *It Seemed Like Nothing Happened*, pp. 23–24.

88 **"I had gotten":** Peg Burke int.

88 **The revolution began:** Stephanie Mansfield, *The Richest Girl in the World: The Extravagant Life and Fast Times of Doris Duke* (New York: G. P. Putnam's Sons, 1992); Jason Thomas and Pony Duke, *Too Rich: The Family Secrets of Doris Duke* (New York: HarperCollins, 1996); Bob Colacello, "Doris Duke's Final Mystery," *Vanity Fair*, March 1994.

88 **On one of:** Hope Smith, "The First National Institute on Girls Sports," *Journal of Health, Physical Education, Recreation*, Vol. 35, 1964, p. 32.

88 **A half million:** Margaret Dunkle int.; Charlotte West int.; Amy Wilson int.; Carole Oglesby int.; Sharon E. Taylor int.; Thelma Bishop, "Second National Institute on Girls Sports," *Journal of Health, Physical Education, Recreation*, Vol. 37, No. 2, Feb. 1966.

89 **Billie Moore might:** Billie Moore int.; Charlotte West int.

89 **The Fourth Institute:** *Proceedings: Fourth National Institute on Girls Sports* (Washington, DC: AAHPER, 1968), pp. 3–32; Charlotte West int.; Billie Moore int.; Carole Oglesby int.; Jane Betts int.

89 **On the basketball:** Charlotte West int.; Jane Betts int.; Billie Moore int.; David Michaelis, *Schulz and* Peanuts: *A Biography* (New York: HarperCollins, 2007), pp. 223, 335; Schulz described the character thusly: "Peppermint Patty, the tomboy, is forthright, doggedly loyal, with a devastating singleness of purpose, the part of us that goes through life with blinders on" (*TV Guide*, Feb. 23–29, 1980, p. 24); "Peppermint Patty," *Peanuts* Wiki, https://peanuts.fandom.com/wiki/Peppermint_Patty.

90 **One of the:** Charlotte West int.

90 **Both women found:** Charlotte West int.; Billie Moore int.

90 **For Moore, the:** Charlotte West int.

91 **"I remember being":** Billie Moore int.; Vicky O'Hara, "Women Athletes Don't Eat Steak," *Southern Illinoisan*, Jan. 7, 1974, p. 3.

91 **This was reflected:** Bil Gilbert and Nancy Williamson, "Sport Is Unfair to Women," *Sports Illustrated*, May 28, 1973, p. 88; Margaret Dunkle, "What Constitutes Equality for Women in Sport?: Federal Law Puts Women in the Running," Report from the Project on the Status and Education of Women (Washington, DC: Association of American Colleges, 1974); "Working Women Making It in Sports," *Ladies Home Journal*, Oct. 1974, p. 63.

91 **Historically, female physical:** Carole Oglesby int.; Waneen Spirduso int.

92 **Women in high:** Charlotte West int.

92 **In 1970 in:** Amy Wilson int.

92 **Such was the:** Charlotte West int.

92 **Governance for women's:** DGWS would change its name, in 1974, to the National Association for Girls and Women in Sports (NAGWS). Shawn Ladda, "The National Association for Girls and Women in Sport: 110 Years of Promoting Social Justice and Change," *Journal of Physical Education, Recreation & Dance*, Vol. 80, No. 7, Sept. 2009, pp. 48–51.

92 **Among the women:** Carole Oglesby int.; Katherine Ley, "A Philosophical Interpretation of the National Institute on Girls' Sports," in *Proceedings: First National Institute on Girls Sport* (Washington, DC: AAHPER, 1965), p. 3.

93 **By 1969, CIAW:** "Affidavit of Donna A. Lopiano, *AIAW v NCAA*, in the United States District Court for the District of Columbia," Oct. 9, 1981, p. 22; National Invitational Collegiate Women's Basketball Tournament, tournament program, March 20–22, 1969.

93 **The women's game:** Charlotte West int.; Billie Moore int.; Joan Cronan int.; Carole Oglesby int.

93 **"Oh, I thought":** Peg Burke int.

93 **The "six-on-six":** Not-for-attribution int.; David Tatel email, Feb. 2, 2023.

93 **There were other:** Jennifer Stanley int.; Cec Ponce int.; Marie Ballard int.; "Women Aren't So Fragile," *Science Digest*, Dec. 4, 1969, pp. 53–54.

94 **Of course, there:** Charlotte West int.; Marie Ballard int.; Jennifer Stanley int.; Billie Moore int.

94 **At the Hollinger:** Charlotte West int.; Marie Ballard int.; Jennifer Stanley int.; Billie Moore int.

94 **The women on:** "Rammette Dribblers Win Nationals; End Season Undefeated," *Quad Angles* (West Chester State College student newspaper), undated (1969).

94 **Later that year:** Billie Moore int.; Cec Ponce int.; Sue Sims int.

95 **When Moore got:** Billie Moore int.; Charlotte West int.

95 **The goal was:** Billie Moore int.

95 **In mid-March:** Billie Moore int.; Cec Ponce int.; Sue Sims int.

95   **The next morning:** *Boston Globe*, March 16, 1970; *Los Angeles Times*, March 16, 1970.

96   **Yet even here:** King with Howard and Vollers, *All In*, p. 171

96   **By the fall:** King with Howard and Vollers, *All In*, pp. 165–171; Grace Lichtenstein, *A Long Way, Baby: Behind the Scenes in Women's Pro Tennis* (New York: William Morrow, 1974), pp. 26–28.

97   **The retired tennis:** Lichtenstein, *A Long Way, Baby*, pp. 26–28.

97   **Heldman was an:** Julie Heldman, *Driven: A Daughter's Odyssey* (Julie Heldman, 2018), pp. 15–18; Roberts, *A Necessary Spectacle*, p. 76; Ted Tinling with Rod Humphries, *Love and Faults: Personalities Who Have Changed the History of Tennis in My Lifetime* (New York: Crown, 1979), p. 259.

97   **Heldman agreed to:** United Press International, "Billie Jean King Leads Revolt of Women Tennis Players," *Muncie Star*, Sept. 24, 1970, p. 22; Billie Jean King int.; Julie Heldman int.; King with Howard and Vollers, *All In*, pp. 172–173.

97   **With Cullman handling:** Heldman, *Driven*, pp. 77–79; King with Howard and Vollers, *All In*, pp. 176–177.

97   **The irony of:** Billie Jean King, int.; Larry King int.; King with Howard and Vollers, *All In*, p. 179.

98   **The mere existence:** Judy Dalton int.

98   **"To our great":** Tinling with Humphries, *Love and Faults*, pp. 265–266.

98   **Tinling sensed, in:** Lichtenstein, *A Long Way, Baby*, p. 137.

98   **There were no:** Billie Jean King int.; Larry King int.; Judy Dalton int.; Peachy Kellmeyer int.; Julie Heldman int.; King with Deford, *The Autobiography of Billie Jean King*, pp. 43–54; Ware, *Game, Set, Match*, pp. 15–39; King with Howard and Vollers, *All In*, pp. 9–42.

99   **Which is why:** Arnold Hano, "Billie Jean King: 'This Is Not A Good Life,'" *Redbook*, Oct. 1971, pp. 86, 233, 235.

99   **King finally pushed:** Bob Di Pietro, "Billie Jean Proves a Point, Scales $100,000 Peak," by *The Sporting News*, Oct. 23, 1971, p. 56.

99   **"Hello, Mr. President":** Bob Di Pietro, "Billie Jean Proves a Point, Scales $100,000 Peak," *The Sporting News*, Oct. 23, 1971, p. 56; King with Howard and Vollers, *All In*, pp. 199–200.

99   **While King's earnings:** Billie Jean King, int.; King with Howard and Vollers, *All In*, p. 200.

99   **Evert (even then:** Chris Evert (Lloyd) with Neil Amdur, *Chrissie: My Own Story* (New York: Simon and Schuster, 1982), p. 38.

100  **Evert burst onto:** Roy Blount Jr., "More Joan of Arc Than Shirley Temple," *Sports Illustrated*, Sept. 20, 1971, pp. 30–31; Larry Keith, "Happiness Is Six Hours a Day with Your Eye on the Ball," by *Sports Illustrated*, July 26, 1971, p. 58.

100  **Evert was stoic:** Billie Jean King, int.; Judy Dalton int.

100 **At one point:** Billie Jean King int.; King with Howard and Vollers, *All In*, pp. 192–196.

100 **Asked in the:** Frank Deford, "Love and Love," *Sports Illustrated*, April 27, 1981, pp. 68–84.

100 **In the event:** Julie Heldman, "Chrissy [*sic*] and Evonne: The Fairy Tale Tandem," *Seventeen*, Aug. 1972, p. 276.

101 **In the summer:** Frank Nicklin, "Goolagong in the Altogether," *Sun*, June 26, 1972.

101 **Thanks largely to:** Bil Gilbert, "Hanging in for Women's Lib," *Sports Illustrated*, July 13, 1970, p. 49.

102 **At the Army–Navy:** Peter Carry, "To a Stripper, Boyer's Hipper," *Sports Illustrated*, July 20, 1970, p. 47.

102 **In 1970, *Sports*:** "Triumph for Good Form," *Sports Illustrated*, March 30, 1970, pp. 20–21.

102 **In baseball, major:** Roy Blount Jr., "Curtain Up on a Mod New Act," *Sports Illustrated*, April 19, 1971, p. 30.

102 **Ever since its:** Margie S. Hansen, "Katherine Ley, 1919–1982," *Journal of Physical Education, Recreation & Dance*, Vol. 54, No. 4, April 1983, p. 11; "Affidavit of Donna A. Lopiano," pp. 2–25; Charlotte West int.

102 **"No, ladies, we":** Charlotte West int.; Tom Lamonica, "Dr. Charlotte West's Love-Driven Journey Raised the Bar for Women in Sports," MVC-Sports.com, July 15, 2022, https://siusalukis.com/news/2022/7/15/general-dr-charlotte-wests-love-driven-journey-raised-the-bar-for-women-in-sports.

102 **And so the:** "Affidavit of Donna A. Lopiano," p. 22–23.

103 **The women who:** Amy Wilson, "A 'Saga of Power, Money, and Sex' in Women's Athletics: A Presidents' History of the Association for Intercollegiate Athletics for Women," PhD diss. (Iowa City, IA: University of Iowa, 2013); Mark Bechtel, "A League of Their Own," *Sports Illustrated*, June 2022, p. 38.

103 **"She was one":** Carole Oglesby int.

103 **Carole Oglesby had:** Carole Oglesby int.

104 **The AIAW's bylaws:** Diane Williams int.

104 **Its official statement:** Susan B. Craig, "Sports Scholarships for Women," *Sportswoman*, Spring 1973, p. 21.

104 **A later AIAW:** "Affidavit of Donna A. Lopiano," p. 27.

104 **The first complaint:** Not-for-attribution interview; Megan Elise Chawanksy, "Getting the Girl: Female Athletes' Narratives of the Recruiting Process," PhD diss. (Columbus, OH: Ohio State University, 2008), pp. 33–35; "Policies on Women Athletes Change," *Journal of Health, Physical Education, Recreation*, Vol. 44, No. 7, 1973, p. 51.

105 **When Roberta Gibb:** Amby Burfoot, "At the Boston Marathon, Leading the Way for Women Fifty Years Ago," *New York Times*, April 16, 2016; Kathrine

Switzer, "The Real Story of Kathrine Switzer's 1967 Boston Marathon," excerpted from *Marathon Woman: Running the Race to Revolutionize Women's Sports* (Cambridge, MA: Da Capo Press, 2017); Kathrine Switzer, "The Real Story of Kathrine Switzer's 1967 Boston Marathon," Kathrine Switzer (personal website), https://web.archive.org/web/20230302123555/https://kathrineswitzer.com/1967-boston-marathon-the-real-story/.

105 **The notion of:** "No Place for a Lady," Scorecard, *Sports Illustrated*, Jan. 5, 1970, pp. 7–8.

105 **Women were even:** "Asking for Trouble," Scorecard, *Sports Illustrated*, April 13, 1970, p. 19.

105 **Chris Evert's father:** "Long Live Ms. King, but Tennis Hails a New Queen," *People*, Feb. 3, 1975, p. 4.

106 **Evert remained conflicted:** Michael MacCambridge, "Chris Evert: A Whole Woman," in MacCambridge (ed.), *ESPN SportsCentury*, pp. 256–257.

106 **Billie Jean King:** "Women Lobbers," *Newsweek*, May 3, 1971.

106 **"Women's lib can":** Ware, *Game, Set, Match*, pp. 150, 153.

106 **Within the Education:** Margaret Dunkle int.; Jen Barton, *Bernice Sandler and the Fight for Title IX* (Washington, DC: Magination Press, American Psychological Association, 2022), pp. 1–24; Bernice Resnick Sandler, "Title IX: How We Got It and What a Difference It Made," *Cleveland State Law Review*, Vol. 55, 2007, p. 473; Alison Neumer, "Birch Bayh Revisits Title IX Victory," *New York Times*, July 5, 2002, Bernice Sandler, "'Too Strong for a Woman'—The Five Words That Created Title IX," bernicesandler.com; Katharine Q. Seelye, "Bernice Sandler, 'Godmother of Title IX,' Dies at 90," *New York Times*, Jan. 15, 2019; Rachale Bachman, "Thank Edith Green for Title IX," *Oregonian*, Jan. 17, 2010.

107 **That Friday evening:** Ware, *Game, Set, Match*, p. 150; Sandler, "Title IX," p. 478. In 2007, Sandler noted, "I recently checked my original testimony for Title IX in 1970, and there is no mention whatsoever of sports, simply because we did not know at the time that there was any discrimination in sports."

## CHAPTER 6: AMATEUR ACTS

108 **The NCAA offices:** Doug Tucker int.; Chuck Neinas int.; Phyllis Tucker int.; Tom Hansen int.; David Berst int.; Walter Byers with Charles Hammer, *Unsportsmanlike Conduct: Exploiting College Athletics* (Ann Arbor, MI: University of Michigan Press, 1997), pp. 129–133; Jack McCallum, "In the Kingdom," *Sports Illustrated*, Oct. 6, 1986, pp. 64–78.

108 **Nor, for that:** David Berst int.; McCallum, "In the Kingdom."

109 **But for Byers:** Byers with Hammer, *Unsportsmanlike Conduct*, p. 152; McCallum, "In the Kingdom"; *120 Years of American Education: A Statistical Portrait,*

edited by Thomas D. Snyder, Center for Education Statistics (Washington, DC: US Department of Education, 1993), p. 65.

109 **Byers sported sideburns:** Jim Host int.

109 **"I think he":** Tom Hansen int.; Phyllis Tucker int.

110 **After two decades:** Byers with Hammer, *Unsportsmanlike Conduct*, p. 152.

110 **By that time:** Byers with Hammer, *Unsportsmanlike Conduct*, p. 90.

110 **It was Byers:** Byers with Hammer, *Unsportsmanlike Conduct*, p. 40

111 **Faced with the:** William Johnson, "A Legal License to Steal the Stars," *Sports Illustrated*, April 12, 1971, pp. 34–41.

112 **As the decade:** Dan Jenkins, "Two Gods Too Many," *Sports Illustrated*, Nov. 9, 1970, pp. 14–17; Joe Posnanski, "Who's No. 1: The History of the Polls," in *The ESPN College Football Encyclopedia*, edited by Michael MacCambridge (New York: ESPN Books, 2005), pp. 1124–1127.

112 **Sunday sections in:** Dave Smith int.; Ed Storin int.; George Solomon int.; Jenkins, *Saturday's America*, pp. 3–23.

112 **The first NCAA:** Byers with Hammer, *Unsportsmanlike Conduct*, p. 84.

113 **With ABC, the:** Byers with Hammer, *Unsportsmanlike Conduct*, p. 84.

113 **So Byers was:** Chuck Neinas int.; Jim Spence int.; Tom Hansen int.; Doug Tucker int.

113 **Despite the pending:** Dan Jenkins, "Eating High on the Hogs," *Sports Illustrated*, Sept. 21, 1970, p. 22.

114 **The Huskers and:** Blair Kerkhoff, "The Legend Lives On," *Oklahoman*, Nov. 9, 2008.

114 **As the Oklahoma–Nebraska:** Corcoran, *The Game of the Century*, p. 123.

114 **The buildup to:** "Irresistible Oklahoma Meets Immovable Nebraska" (cover), *Sports Illustrated*, Nov. 22, 1971; "Football Frenzy at Nebraska and Oklahoma" (cover), *Life*, Nov. 26, 1971.

114 **When it finally:** Corcoran, *The Game of the Century*, pp. 133–177.

115 **Afterward there was:** Corcoran, *The Game of the Century*, p. 174.

115 **Jenkins wrote the:** Dan Jenkins, "Nebraska Rides High," *Sports Illustrated*, Dec. 6, 1971, pp. 22–25.

115 **Dave Kindred, writing:** Dave Kindred, "Oklahoma–Nebraska: Bottle It and Stamp It Vintage Football," *Louisville Times*, Nov. 26, 1971.

115 **At the time:** Ira Berkow, "The Grapes of Wrath at Oklahoma," *New York Times*, Feb. 18, 1989, p. 49.

115 **The Big Eight's:** "Little Ten," Scorecard, *Sports Illustrated*, Oct. 19, 1970, p. 11.

116 **The new Big:** Chuck Neinas int.; "All Together: One-Two-Three," Scorecard, *Sports Illustrated*, Jan. 17, 1972, p. 10.

116 **ABC would become:** Dick Snider, "Reliving the Toughest Hour in Network Television," *Topeka Capital Journal*, Aug. 21, 1995.

116 **The college hardcourt:** Eddie Einhorn with Ron Rapoport, *How March Became Madness: How the NCAA Tournament Became the Greatest Sporting Event in America* (Chicago: Triumph Books, 2006), p. 29.

117 **Even as the:** *The ESPN College Basketball Encyclopedia* (New York: Ballantine Books, 2009), pp. 767–872.

118 **There had been:** Billy Packer int.; Frank Layden int.

118 **"How can you":** Seth Davis, *Wooden: A Coach's Life* (New York: Times Books, 2014), pp. 98–99.

118 **Yet in the:** Einhorn with Rapoport, *How March Became Madness*, p. 16.

119 **Even in the:** Billy Packer int.

119 **Those fears would:** "Sellout of Sellouts," Scorecard, *Sports Illustrated*, April 16, 1973, p. 21.

119 **In major-college:** In the much more diffuse world of college basketball, the regular-season games were out of the NCAA's hands—and in the hands of regional marketers like C. D. Chesney and Eddie Einhorn—and the NCAA owned only the rights to the national championship tournament at the end of the season.

Chesley had the rights to the most prestigious conference in college basketball, the Atlantic Coast Conference. But his syndicated network was built up almost exclusively in that region—from the tip of Maryland down to the base of South Carolina. The broadcasts were produced in tandem with the talented Frank Slingland, whose day job was directing *The Huntley-Brinkley Report* on NBC. With a technical staff of camera and sound operators primarily gleaned from the University of North Carolina Radio, Television, and Broadcasting department, Chesley's crisp, low-budget productions were hits throughout the ACC area, but those teams were rarely seen outside that region. (Chesley had a broader sense of ambition with football, where he produced a weekly series of Notre Dame football replays during the season, which would reach 144 markets during the 1970s, hosted by Lindsay Nelson and Paul Hornung.) Chesley's nominal competitor was the Northwestern alum and television packager Eddie Einhorn, a driven raconteur who set up a series of regional networks of major-college conferences, allowing Big Eight games to be broadcast in the Midwest, Big Ten games in the Mideast, and Pacific Eight games on the West Coast. Einhorn had produced the epic UCLA–Houston matchup in 1968. Jack Hilliard, "The Man Responsible for Transmitting The Madness," A View to Hugh, edited by Stephen Fletcher, University of North Carolina, March 9, 2016, https://blogs.lib.unc.edu /morton/2016/03/09/the-man-responsible-for-transmitting-the-madness/; Daniel M. Haygood, "Viewpoint: ND, ACC Share TV History," *South Bend Tribune*, Oct. 8, 2014.

120 **Arledge—aware that:** Geoff Mason int.

121 **The generation gap:** David Halberstam, *The Breaks of the Game*, p. 115.

121 **The chaos at:** Frederic J. Frommer, "50 Years Later, the Chaotic End of a U.S.-U.S.S.R. Basketball Game Still Stings," *Washington Post*, Sept. 8, 2022.

121 **Beyond the basketball:** Rick Telander, "A Voice for Those Long Silent," *Sports Illustrated*, June 30, 1975, p. 62.

122 **The *Los Angeles*:** Jim Murray, "The Man Who Missed His Golden Moment," *Los Angeles Times*, Feb. 14, 1990.

122 **Coming back from:** Donna de Varona int.

122 **Later that year:** Mike Harrigan int.

123 **Harrigan was uniquely:** "Solution," Scorecard, *Sports Illustrated*, March 26, 1973, p. 11.

123 **It would take:** "Fact Sheet: The President's Commission on Olympic Sports," April 16, 1975, Gerald Ford Library Museum.

123 **College football was:** Pat Ryan, "A Grim Run to Fiscal Daylight," *Sports Illustrated*, Feb. 1, 1971, p. 18; Sandy Padwe, "Big-Time College Football Is on the Skids," *Look*, Sept. 22, 1970, p. 66.

124 **"The mandate to":** "Turmoil in the Big Ten," Scorecard, *Sports Illustrated*, June 12, 1972, p. 16.

124 **Even Michigan, one:** "Turmoil in the Big Ten."

124 **"The enforcement was":** Chuck Neinas int.; David Berst int.

124 **Of his recruiting:** Byers with Hammer, *Unsportsmanlike Conduct*, p. 107.

125 **As the competition:** "UVA Football—Random Musings: Quotable Quotes," HoosFootball.com, 2008, https://hoosfootball.com/Random_Musings/Quotable_Quotes.html.

125 **"I don't remember":** Bill Hancock int.

CHAPTER 7: STYLE AND SUBSTANCE

126 **On Friday, October:** Hubie Brown int.

126 **The clothing revolution:** Rod Thorn int.; David Vance int.; Hubie Brown int.

126 **"Chuck's rule when":** Joe Greene int.

127 **Sports had always:** Abdul-Jabbar with Knobler, *Giant Steps*, p. 248; Jim Prime, "Bill Lee ('Spaceman')," Society for American Baseball Research, https://sabr.org/bioproj/person/bill-lee-spaceman/; Epstein, *Big Hair and Plastic Grass*, pp. 287–288; Pepe, *Talkin' Baseball*, pp. 230–238.

128 **The Steelers had:** Marty Bell, "With Frenchy Fuqua," *Sport*, Dec. 1973, pp. 20–24.

128 **Around that time:** Robert Wilonsky, "Just a Few of the Many Wonderful Columns That Frank Luksa Wrote During His Time at the *Dallas Morning News*," *Dallas Morning News*, Oct. 23, 2012.

128 **The following year:** Bob Daly, "The Infamous Duane Thomas Interview," Pro Football Daly, http://profootballdaly.com/the-infamous-duane-thomas-interview/.

129 **Namath's 1969 autobiography:** Joe Namath with Bob Oates, *A Matter of Style* (Boston: Little, Brown, 1973), p. 11.

129 **So it was:** Walt Frazier and Ira Berkow, *Rockin' Steady: A Guide to Basketball & Cool* (Hoboken, NJ: Prentice-Hall, 1974; reprint edition Chicago: Triumph Books, 2010), pp. 20, 77.

129 **Namath and Frazier:** "The Ecstasy of Being Joe Namath—The Agony of Having His Knees," *People*, Sept. 19, 1974, p. 6; Paul Zimmerman, *The Last Season of Weeb Ewbank* (New York: Farrar, Straus and Giroux, 1974), pp. 15–20; Frazier and Berkow, *Rockin' Steady*, p. 20; "People," *Sports Illustrated*, Aug. 31, 1970, p. 36.

129 **In *A Matter*:** Namath with Oates, *A Matter of Style*, p. 57.

130 **Writing about the:** Ian O'Connor, *Arnie and Jack: Palmer, Nicklaus, and Golf's Greatest Rivalry* (Boston: Houghton Mifflin, 2008), pp. 93–94.

130 **The selfless act:** Jack Nicklaus with Ken Bowden, *Jack Nicklaus: My Story* (New York: Simon and Schuster, 2007), p. 256.

131 **In the months:** Jack Nicklaus int.; John Underwood, "A Heavy Comes to Light," *Sports Illustrated*, Feb. 19, 1973, pp. 70–82.

131 **Nicklaus had never:** Nicklaus with Bowden, *My Story*, p. 259.

131 **His wife, Barbara:** Underwood, "A Heavy Comes to Light."

131 **The Nicklaus makeover:** Underwood, "A Heavy Comes to Light."

132 **He wasn't the:** Jack Olsen, "Sportsman of the Year: Bobby Orr," *Sports Illustrated*, Dec. 21, 1970, pp. 36–44.

132 **Hair was growing:** Epstein, *Big Hair and Plastic Grass*, pp. 172–173.

132 **"Well, he didn't":** Sal Bando int.

132 **Soon Jackson had:** Epstein, *Big Hair and Plastic Grass*, p. 107.

132 **Even some of the coaches:** Willie Lanier int.; Hank Stram int.

132 **When a reporter:** Freeman, *Hook 'Em Horns*, p. 143.

133 **There were still:** Ray Didinger, "Tim Rossovich, A Wild Man Burning to Make a Difference," Philadelphia Eagles (website), Dec. 9, 2018, https://www.philadel phiaeagles.com/news/didinger-tim-rossovich-a-wild-man-burning-to-make-a -difference.

133 **"All I know is":** Dan Jenkins, "Another Nightmare for the Year Ahead," *Sports Illustrated*, Sept. 14, 1970, p. 46; Wayne Fuson, "Cozza's Problem," *Indianapolis News*, Dec. 3, 1970.

133 **The next year:** Epstein, *Big Hair and Plastic Grass*, p. 104.

133 **Harold Bowman, a:** "Couturier," Scorecard, *Sports Illustrated*, April 17, 1972, p. 17; "Cold Colors," Scorecard, *Sports Illustrated*, Oct. 5, 1970, p. 10.

134 **Color television, in:** Paul Lukas int.

134 **It wasn't just:** MacCambridge, *Noll: His Life's Work*, p. 156.

134 **The new stadiums:** Michael MacCambridge, *Lamar Hunt: A Life in Sports* (Kansas City: Andrews & McMeel, 2012), pp. 223–226; MacCambridge, *America's*

*Game*, pp. 304–307; Joe Nick Patoski, *The Dallas Cowboys: The Outrageous History of the Biggest, Loudest, Most Hated, Best Loved Football Team in America* (New York: Little, Brown, 2012), pp. 259–267; Peter Golenbock, *Cowboys Have Always Been My Heroes: The Definitive Oral History of America's Team* (New York: Warner Books, 1997), pp. 468–472; Peter Finney, "Superdome: New Orleans' $163 million Igloo," *The Sporting News*, Aug. 17, 1974, p. 45.

134 **Those stadiums were:** John Schuerholz int.

135 **For all the:** Epstein, *Big Hair and Plastic Grass*, p. 51.

135 **It was an:** Epstein, *Big Hair and Plastic Grass*, p. 48.

136 **"Somebody has done":** Edwin Shrake, "Just Call Him Super Daryle," *Sports Illustrated*, Jan. 5, 1970, pp. 36–45.

136 **In Dallas and:** Len Dawson int.; Carlton Stowers, *Staubach: Portrait of the Brightest Star* (Chicago: Triumph Books, 2010), p. 75; MacCambridge, *America's Game*, pp. 304–307.

136 **All the more:** Bobby Bell int.; MacCambridge, *America's Game*, p. 307.

137 **At Cincinnati's Riverfront:** Associated Press, "Fosse Still Feels Effects from 1970 All-Star Game Collision," *Sports Illustrated*, July 9, 2015, https://www.si.com/mlb/2015/07/09/ap-bbo-all-star-game-fosses-moment.

137 **The idea that:** "Rug," Scorecard, *Sports Illustrated*, Oct. 18, 1971, p. 18; "Turf Made of Grass," Scorecard, *Sports Illustrated*, Nov. 13, 1972, p. 20; "New Rug," Scorecard, *Sports Illustrated*, April 24, 1972, p. 9.

137 **The Phillies' All-Star:** Epstein, *Big Hair and Plastic Grass*, p. 55; "They Said It," Scorecard, *Sports Illustrated,* May 25, 1970, p. 16.

137 **"Artificial turf has":** MacCambridge, *America's Game*, p. 307.

137 **The decade would:** Ray Scott with Charley Rosen, *The NBA in Black and White: The Memoir of a Trailblazing NBA Player and Coach* (New York: Seven Stories Press, 2022), p. 129.

138 **But as sports:** Larry Keith, "The Week," *Sports Illustrated*, Oct. 25, 1971, p. 62.

138 **During the 1976–77:** Hubie Brown int.

138 **Sports was not:** Donald Hall with Dock Ellis, *Dock Ellis: In the Country of Baseball* (New York: Simon & Schuster, 1989), p. 317.

139 **"Drugs were always":** Pepe, *Talkin' Baseball*, p. 175.

139 **In the summer:** Matt Schudel, "Butch & Sundance," *Orlando Sentinel*, Dec. 2, 1989.

139 **Their off-season *Sports*:** Walter Iooss Jr. int.; MacCambridge, *The Franchise*, p. 185.

140 **In the summer:** Pepe, *Talkin' Baseball*, pp. 103–107; Epstein, *Big Hair and Plastic Grass*, pp. 181–183.

140 **But when the:** Phil Pepe, "Pressure Is Off Now, Says Susanne Kekich," *New York Daily News*, March 7, 1973.

140 **In spring training:** *Big Hair and Plastic Grass*, p. 162.

141 **Amid the snickering:** Quinn, *Don't Be Afraid to Win*, p. 39.

141 **"If our society":** "Word from Woody," Scorecard, *Sports Illustrated*, Jan. 22, 1973, p. 12; Don Kowet, "Dr. Strangehayes," Sport Talk, *Sport*, Oct. 1972, p. 12; Larry Kindbom int.

141 **One of the most:** "Woody Hayes," *ESPN Classic SportsCentury*, YouTube, https://www.youtube.com/watch?v=p8X7iWRLuN0.

**CHAPTER 8: I AM WOMAN**

142 **"What's this I":** King with Howard and Vollers, *All In*, p. 224.

142 **"Sometimes there are":** Curry Kirkpatrick, "The Ball in Two Different Courts," *Sports Illustrated*, Dec. 25, 1972, p. 28.

142 **King's ascent came:** Schulman, *The Seventies*, p. 161; Jodie Tillman, "'We Have Had Abortions': 1972 Petition Changed Abortion Rights Movement," *Washington Post*, May 16, 2022; "Tennis: A Triumph for Women's Lob," *Newsweek*, June 26, 1972, pp. 56–63.

143 **He had been:** "War of the Rackets," Scorecard, *Sports Illustrated*, March 5, 1973, p. 13.

143 **King learned of:** King with Howard and Vollers, *All In*, p. 224.

143 **King winced; she:** Gwilym S. Brown, "Chips, Chops, Drops and Lobs," *Sports Illustrated*, Jan. 18, 1971, p. 60.

144 **Margaret Court was:** Peachy Kellmeyer int.; Judy Dalton int.; Lichtenstein, *A Long Way, Baby*, p. 45.

144 **"I haven't really taken":** Richard Muscio, "How Billie Jean, Bobby, and Blindness Begat Tolerance: The Greatest Tennis Match of the 20th Century Changed America, and the Life of a Young Boy, Forever," So What's Your Play?, https://sowhatsyourplay.com; *The Mother's Day Ms. Match*, short film, directed by Richard Muscio, So What's Your Play?, https://sowhatsyourplay.com.

144 **"How can Margaret":** Carol Kleiman, "Billie Jean Works at Her Tennis," *Chicago Tribune*, Sept. 19, 1973.

144 **The day's omens:** Curry Kirkpatrick, "Mother's Day Ms. Match," *Sports Illustrated*, May 21, 1973, p. 28.

145 **During the introductions:** From CBS broadcast, YouTube, https://www.youtube.com/watch?v=E1Ueec50rVw&t=169s.

145 **When she lost:** Sue Denner, "Court Defeated Court While Riggs Gets the Credit," *Sportswoman*, Summer 1973, pp. 4–5; Neil Amdur, "Ramona: It Sang Out a Different Song of Love," *World Tennis*, July 1973, pp. 90–93.

145 **"Oh, shit," said:** Billie Jean King int.; Billie Jean King with Kim Chapin, *Billie Jean* (New York: Harper & Row, 1974), p. 164.

145 **In late April:** "Editorial: The USLTA Women's Pro Circuit: 1974," *World Tennis*, June 1973.

145 **But on the:** Cliff Drysdale int.; Rod Humphries int.

146 **At Wimbledon, King:** Lichtenstein, *A Long Way, Baby*, p. 113.

146 **The King–Riggs:** Nora Ephron, "Bobby Riggs, the Lady Killer," *New York*, Sept. 10, 1973, pp. 49–53.

147 **"The Ali–Frazier":** Roberts, *A Necessary Spectacle*, p. 93.

147 **The cavernous Astrodome:** Donna de Varona int.; Jim Spence int.

147 **"Would CBS have":** Kevin O'Malley int.

147 **"We didn't really":** Jim Spence int.

147 **For women in:** Ephron, "Bobby Riggs, the Lady Killer," p. 53.

147 **That August, King:** King with Chapin, *Billie Jean*, p. 168.

148 **As the pressure:** Lichtenstein, *A Long Way, Baby*, p. 22.

148 **On September 15:** King with Chapin, *Billie Jean*, pp. 172–174; King with Deford, *The Autobiography of Billie Jean King*, pp. 20–21.

149 **When King and:** King with Howard and Vollers, *All In*, pp. 178–179.

149 **In the summer:** Roberts, *A Necessary Spectacle*, p. 107.

149 **"You're not going":** King, *The Autobiography of Billie Jean King*, p. 14; Ephron, "Bobby Riggs, the Lady Killer."

149 **"You know how":** Robert Markus, "Riggs: Calm Eye in Hectic 'Lob' Storm," *Chicago Tribune*, Sept. 19, 1973.

149 **Before the match:** Billie Jean King int.; Lichtenstein, *A Long Way, Baby*, p. 229–239.

150 **King and Riggs:** King with Deford, *The Autobiography of Billie Jean King*, pp. 128–129; Larry King int.

150 **King had talked:** King with Howard and Vollers, *All In*, pp. 202, 245–246; Tinling with Humphries, *Love and Faults*, pp. 290–291.

150 **"I am so":** Tinling with Humphries, *Love and Faults*, pp. 290–291.

150 **King modeled that:** Tinling with Humphries, *Love and Faults*, pp. 290–291.

151 **There was one:** King with Chapin, *Billie Jean*, p. 14.

151 **At the Astrodome:** Lichtenstein, *A Long Way, Baby*, pp. 231–232.

151 **ABC spent several:** ABC broadcast of King–Riggs match, YouTube, https://www.youtube.com/watch?v=qqB3yi8MVbQ&t=5s. Lichtenstein later noted that her friend, the writer Nora Ephron, "saw through it all," making this point the week of the match: "This isn't even the battle of the sexes. This is show business. This is a prime-time television variety show starring the two biggest hams in tennis." See Grace Lichtenstein, "'Battle of the Sexes' Tennis, Triumph, Trauma," NYCityWoman, undated, https://www.nycitywoman.com/battle-of-the-sexes-tennis-triumph-trauma/.

151 **Howard Cosell, presiding:** Roberts, *A Necessary Spectacle*, p. 120.

152 **At courtside, the:** Roberts, *A Necessary Spectacle*, p. 115.

152 **Larry King often:** Larry King int.

152 **In the ABC:** Bud Collins, "We Remember You, Billie Jean," *World Tennis*, Dec. 1973, pp. 34–42.

153 **Somehow, the weary:** Roberts, *A Necessary Spectacle*, p. 131.

153 **"When I was":** Robert Markus, "Best Man Loses," *Chicago Tribune*, Sept. 21, 1973.

153 **When King saw:** Lichtenstein, *A Long Way, Baby*, p. 238.

153 **After filing her:** Grace Lichtenstein int.; Sarah Ballard int.; MacCambridge, *The Franchise*, p. 177; "The Hustler Outhustled," *Newsweek*, Oct. 1, 1973, pp. 63–64.

154 **In fighting for:** Ware, *Game, Set, Match*, p. 6.

154 **"What I remember":** Carole Oglesby int.

154 **Not quite everybody:** Evert with Amdur, *Chrissie*, p. 90; "Chris Evert: When I Was Seventeen," by Sarah Palfrey, *Saturday Evening Post*, Winter 1973, pp. 63–65, 202.

154: **"She didn't know":** Grace Lichtenstein int.

154 **There was a:** William F. Buckley Jr., "Reflections on the Phenomenon," *Esquire*, Oct. 1974.

154 **At the Los:** Jeff Pugh, "It's Only a Game," by *World Tennis*, Dec. 1973, p. 68.

155 **In living rooms:** Grace Lichtenstein int.; Letty Cottin Pogrebin int.; Letty Cottin Pogrebin, "A Woman's Touch," *Sport*, Dec. 1973, p. 35.

155 **For the feisty:** Letty Cottin Pogrebin int.

156 **Charles M. Schulz:** Jeannie Schulz int.

156 **"Sparky" to anyone:** Charles M. Schulz, *The Complete Peanuts, 1973–1974* (Seattle: Fantagraphics Books, 2009), p. 84.

156 **In his more:** Jeannie Schulz int.

156 **"In a single":** Ware, *Game, Set, Match*, p. 2.

156 **And yet the:** Curry Kirkpatrick, "There She Is, Ms. America," *Sports Illustrated*, Oct. 1, 1973, pp. 30–37.

157 **As all of:** Carole Oglesby int.; Peg Burke int.; Bonnie Slatton int.; Charlotte West int.; Sharon E. Taylor int.

157 **But the AIAW:** Peachy Kellmeyer int.; Jeff Orleans int.

157 **Kellmeyer was persuaded:** Peachy Kellmeyer int.; Ying Wushanley, *Playing Nice and Losing: The Struggle for Control of Women's Intercollegiate Athletics, 1960–2000* (Syracuse, NY: Syracuse University Press, 2004), pp. 62–75; Women's Tennis Association newsletter, Aug. 1, 1973.

158 **"So the AIAW":** Carole Oglesby int.

158 **That changed in:** Charlotte West int.; Peg Burke int.; Wilson, "A 'Saga of Power, Money, and Sex.'"

159 **In her speech:** Marjorie Blaufarb, "Solomon's Judgment on Women's Sports," speech to AIAW delegate assembly, Nov. 4, 1973; Charlotte West int.; Peg Burke int.

160 **The gathering already:** Mark Wimarski, "Convention Here Studies Women's Collegiate Sports," *Kansas City Times*, Nov. 6, 1973.

160 **"This was a":** Josh O'Leary, "How Christine Grant Changed the Game," *Iowa Magazine*, Feb. 15, 2022.

160 **Returning to Iowa:** Peg Burke int.; Christine Grant speech, 1980 AIAW Presidential Review, Tape 1 and Tape 2, July 17, 1980, University of Iowa Library.

160 **In the immediate:** "Sex Discrimination and Intercollegiate Athletics: Putting Some Muscle on Title IX," *Yale Law Journal*, Vol. 88, No. 6, May 1979, p. 1264.

160 **In the immediate:** "Sportswomanlike Conduct," *Newsweek*, June 3, 1974, pp. 50–55.

CHAPTER 9: FOUR STARS

161 **In 1952, the:** Howard Bryant, *The Last Hero: A Life of Henry Aaron* (New York: Random House, 2010), pp. 29–58; Henry Aaron with Lonnie Wheeler, *I Had a Hammer: The Henry Aaron Story* (New York: HarperCollins, 1991), pp. 183–185; Henry Aaron with Furman Bisher, *Aaron* (New York: Thomas Y. Crowell, 1974), pp. 10–16; Paul Hemphill, "Hank Aaron Sounds Off: 'Baseball Has Become Too Specialized,'" *Sport*, June 1972, pp. 42–44, 40; William Legett, "Hank Becomes A Hit," *Sports Illustrated*, Aug. 18, 1969, pp. 11–13.

162 **Though he was:** Aaron with Bisher, *Aaron*, p. 55.

162 **Those reminders intensified:** Aaron with Wheeler, *I Had a Hammer*, pp. 230–231.

163 **The letters—and:** William Leggett, "A Tortured Road to 715," *Sports Illustrated*, May 28, 1973, p. 30.

163 **By the fall:** Schulz, *The Complete Peanuts, 1973-1974*, pp. 97–98.

163 **Throughout that 1973:** Leggett, "A Tortured Road to 715," p. 29.

163 **The off-season was:** Aaron with Wheeler, *I Had a Hammer*, p. 256.

164 **As he eclipsed:** "Henry Aaron, Superstar," *Reader's Digest*, April 1974, pp. 183–197.

164 **Even as he:** Steve Blass int.

164 **"It was all":** Melvin Durslag, "He Who Struts Runs Big Risk," *The Sporting News*, Oct. 25, 1975, p. 20.

165 **In a mid-'70s:** Epstein, *Big Hair and Plastic Grass*, p. 94; Cheryl McCall, "Even for O.J., the Dreams Are Big, and He's No Man to Keep Them Under His Hat," *People*, Oct. 17, 1974; Margaret Carroll, "Kids Put O.J. First on List of 50 Heroes," *Chicago Tribune*, July 20, 1976, p. 1.

166 **"He was very":** Ted Koy int.

166 **There also was:** Joe Marshall, "Now You See Him, Now You Don't," *Sports Illustrated*, Oct. 29, 1973, pp. 30–42.

166 **Going into the:** Ted Koy int.

166 **In the postgame:** Ron Fimrite, "Vintage Juice, 1864," *Sports Illustrated*, Dec. 24, 1975, pp. 26–29.

167 **In his first:** Bryant, *The Last Hero*, pp. 385–386.

167 **Aaron sat out:** Bryant, *The Last Hero*, pp. 362–364; Associated Press, "Streaker Unawed by Aaron Homer," *New York Times*, April 5, 1974, p. 42.

168 **Throughout his career:** Bryant, *The Last Hero*, p. 231.

168 **At 9:07 p.m.:** NBC broadcast of game, and Vin Scully call of Aaron's 715th home run, YouTube, https://www.youtube.com/watch?v=QjqYThEVoSQ&t=10s.

168 **Aaron never saw:** Epstein, *Big Hair and Plastic Grass*, p. 124.

169 **Because the historic:** NBC broadcast of game, and Vin Scully call of Aaron's 715th home run.

169 **That put it:** Bob Nightengale, "40 Years Later, Hank Aaron's Grace a Beauty to Behold," *USA Today*, April 7, 2014.

169 **Western Union estimated:** Jonathan Fraser Light, *The Cultural Encyclopedia of Baseball*, 2nd ed. (Jefferson, NC: McFarland, 2005), p. 924.

169 **Especially given Kuhn's:** Epstein, *Big Hair and Plastic Grass*, p. 125, Aaron with Wheeler, *I Had a Hammer*, pp. 267–277.

170 **What did Aaron's:** Bryant, *The Last Hero*, p. 394.

170 **At the weigh-in:** Edwin Shrake, "Live! Booze! Girls! Ali! This Is Fighting?," *Sports Illustrated*, Dec. 4, 1972, p. 30.

170 **Shortly thereafter, Ali:** Trina Young, "When Muhammad Ali Called Elvis Presley 'the Greatest,'" Elvis Presley Biography, Jan. 25, 2019 https://elvisbiography.net/2019/01/15/when-muhammad-ali-called-elvis-presley-the-greatest/; Guralnick, *Careless Love*, p. 488; A. S. (Doc) Young, "Is Muhammad Ali All Washed Up?," *Ebony*, July 1973, p. 83.

171 **It would go:** ABC broadcast of Foreman–Frazier fight, YouTube, https://www.youtube.com/watch?v=eICak7r0bi4; Eig, *Ali: A Life*, p. 343.

171 **But as it:** Eig, *Ali: A Life*, p. 137.

172 **"I done something":** *When We Were Kings*, directed by Leon Gast (Polygram Filmed Entertainment, 1996).

172 **The numerous incidents:** Eig, *Ali: A Life*, pp. 388–389.

173 **On September 22-24:** "It Takes a Heap of Salongo," *Newsweek*, Sept. 23, 1974, p. 72; "Violent Coronation in Kinshasa," *Time*, Sept. 23, 1974.

173 **Finally, the night:** Early (ed.), *The Muhammad Ali Reader*, p. 136.

174 **He had his:** "Playboy Interview: Muhammad Ali," edited from original version, *Playboy*, Nov. 1975. Early (ed.), *The Muhammad Ali Reader*, p. 137; George Plimpton, "Breaking a Date for the Dance," *Sports Illustrated*, Nov. 11, 1974, pp. 22–29; "Ali—You Gotta Believe!," *Newsweek*, Nov. 11, 1974, p. 70; "Muhammad on the Mountaintop," *Time*, Nov. 11, 1974, p. 84.

174 **There are moments:** Charles L. Sanders, "Muhammad Ali Challenges Black Men," *Ebony*, Jan. 1975, p. 120.

175 **After a childhood:** Abdul-Jabbar with Knobler, *Giant Steps*, pp. 266–271.

176 **Still, Alcindor remained:** Paul Wilkes, "Milwaukee Is Basketball's Best, But:," *Look*, April 6, 1971, p. 68.

176 **Robertson knew better:** Wilkes, "Milwaukee Is Basketball's Best, But:."

176 **But the ground:** Abdul-Jabbar with Knobler, *Giant Steps*, p. 235.

176 **In the meantime:** Wayne Embry int.; Hubie Brown int.

177 **He had been:** Abdul-Jabbar, *Coach Wooden and Me*, p. 106.

178 **Trailing by one:** Eddie Doucette int.

178 **"I saw it":** Hubie Brown int.

179 **He was quintessentially:** Jon McGlocklin int.; Eddie Doucette int.; Wayne Embry int.; Gerald Early int.; Abdul-Jabbar with Knobler, *Giant Steps*, pp. 255–269.

179 **Meanwhile, Khaalis had:** Peter Carry, "Center in a Storm," *Sports Illustrated*, Feb. 19, 1973, pp. 16–19.

179 **"I can sense":** Carry, "Center in a Storm."

179 **"We knew as":** Jon McGlocklin int.

180 **In 1976, the:** "The Main Squeeze," Scorecard, *Sports Illustrated*, Aug. 9, 1976, p. 10.


CHAPTER 10: THE OUTSIDERS

182 **Recalling it later:** Frazier and Berkow, *Rockin' Steady*, p. 29.

183 **But finally, after:** "Doctor's Orders," *Time*, Feb. 11, 1974.

183 **Within six months:** "What's Up? Doc J: New York's Julius Erving" (cover), *Sports Illustrated*, Jan. 14, 1974.

183 **Erving's playground artistry:** Julius Erving with Karl Taro Greenfield, *Dr. J.: The Autobiography* (New York: HarperCollins, 2013), p. 88.

184 **This truth soon:** Michael MacCambridge, "Julius Erving: Doctor's Orders," in MacCambridge (ed.), *ESPN SportsCentury*, p. 225.

184 **As an opponent:** Hubie Brown int.

184 **After seeing Erving:** Hubie Brown int.

184 **Like the legion:** Mark Speck, *Wiffle: The Wild, Zany and Sometimes Hilariously True Story of the World Football League* (Haworth, NJ: St. Johann Press, 2015), pp. 9–26; Gary Davidson with Bill Libby, *Breaking the Game Wide Open* (New York: Atheneum, 1974), pp. 3–26.

185 **The 1970s turned:** Jefferson Cowie, *Stayin' Alive: The 1970s and the Last Days of the Working Class* (New York: The New Press, 2010), pp. 13–17; David Frum, *How We Got Here: The 70's: The Decade That Brought You Modern Life—For Better or Worse* (New York: Basic Books, 2000), pp. 19–21; Carroll, *It Seemed Like Nothing Happened*, pp. 117–119.

185 **Into the teeth:** Pluto, *Loose Balls*, p. 39.

185 **Having a major:** Emanuel Cleaver II int.; Michael MacCambridge, "'Without Them, We're Wichita,'" *The Sporting News*, Aug. 11, 1997, pp. 37–40.

186 **Through it all:** Erving with Greenfield, *Dr. J.*, pp. 201–202.

186 **Those endeavors, at:** Larry King int.; Billie Jean King int.; Karen Logan int.; Mick Haley int.

186 **Meanwhile, limping along:** Lamar Hunt int.; Bobby Moffat int.; Dick Hall int.; Mike Renshaw int.

187 **"In some respects":** Pluto, *Loose Balls*, p. 30.

187 **The rules were:** Associated Press, "Refs Keep Florida's Ball Girls Hopping," *Chicago Tribune*, Dec. 25, 1971; Pluto, *Loose Balls*, pp. 329–330; "Penny Anne [sic] Early," NBA Hoops Online, undated, https://nbahoopsonline.com/History /Leagues/ABA/Players/Early-Penny_Anne.html; "Penny's Pro Basketball Career Lasts One Second," *Louisville Courier-Journal*, Nov. 28, 1968, p. D-1.

187 **Everything the ABA:** Pluto, *Loose Balls*, p. 65.

188 **Hubie Brown would:** Hubie Brown int.

188 **Inevitably, the ABA:** Pluto, *Loose Balls*, p. 32.

188 **"I was an":** Wayne Embry int.; Wayne Embry with Mary Schmitt Boyer, *The Inside Game: Race, Power, and Politics in the NBA* (Akron, OH: University of Akron Press, 2004), p. 211.

188 **In some of:** MacMullen et al., *Basketball: A Love Story*, p. 140.

189 **The league was:** Robertson, *Big O*, p. 306.

189 **At the same:** Pluto, *Loose Balls*, pp. 390–394; "Baltimore Hustlers/Claws," Remember the ABA, http://www.remembertheaba.com/Baltimore-Claws.html; Paul Hemphill, "How to Not Run a Pro Franchise," *Sport*, Sept. 1972, pp. 48–50; Peter Carry, "You Make the Most with What You Got," *Sports Illustrated*, Jan. 24, 1972, p. 59.

189 **"We had the":** Rod Thorn int.

190 **There was also:** Mark Mulvoy, "See the Pucklings Wobble In," pp. 20–21.

190 **Enter, once again:** Davidson with Libby, *Breaking the Game Wide Open*, pp. 119–140.

190 **By June of:** Mark Mulvoy, "Hockey's Turn to Wage a War," *Sports Illustrated*, June 19, 1972, pp. 26–27.

190 **The presence of:** Mulvoy, "Hockey's Turn to Wage a War."

190 **"I thought it":** Larry Schwartz, "Hull Helped WHA into Hockey Family," SportsCentury, ESPN.com, https://www.espn.com/sportscentury/features/0001 4266.html.

191 **"The name of":** Mulvoy, "Hockey's Turn to Wage a War."

191 **It was hard:** Jeff Greenfield, "Derek Sanderson and First Prize, Five Years in Philadelphia," *Sport*, Dec. 1972, pp. 46–47, 124–128; Mark Mulvoy, "The Golden Jet Is Earning His Gold," p. 96-97.

192 **Howe was philosophical:** Mark Mulvoy, "Put Them All Together, They Spell Money," *Sports Illustrated*, pp. 59–60.

192 **And so a:** Davidson with Libby, *Breaking the Game Wide Open*, pp. 245–274; "The Brilliant Closer," *Time*, July 1, 1974; "The Defection Deal," *Time*, April 15, 1974; Joe Marshall, "Full of Sound and Fury," *Sports Illustrated*, Feb. 11, 1974, pp. 16–19.

193 **In July 1974:** "Why Those WFL Owners Expect to Score Profits," *Fortune*, Sept. 1974.

194 **"That's a hard":** William Oscar Johnson, "The Day the Money Ran Out," *Sports Illustrated*, Dec. 1, 1975, pp. 84–94.

194 **When the NFL:** Joe Marshall, "World Bowl in Crisis," *Sports Illustrated*, Dec. 16, 1974, pp. 20–23; "WFL: A Tax Shelter That Is Full of Holes," *Business Week*, Dec. 21, 1974, p. 28; "The Brilliant Closer," *Time*, July 1, 1974; Tony Kornheiser, "The Florida Blazers Are Dead, But the Memories (& Debts) Linger," *Sport*, July 1975, pp. 87–93.

195 **The WFL returned:** Charlie Vincent, "Here Lies Expansion Binge—Slain in Detroit," *The Sporting News*, Feb. 22, 1975, p. 26; Kelso F. Sutton, "Letter from the Publisher," *Sports Illustrated*, Sept. 4, 1978, p. 6.

195 **More Americans than:** Futterman, *Players*, p. 106; "Sex & Tennis," *Time*, Sept. 6, 1976, pp. 34–43.

196 **There was $10 million:** Joel Drucker, "After the Gold Rush," *Racquet*, March 7, 2018; "Sex & Tennis."

196 **While the popularity:** Cliff Drysdale int.; Lamar Hunt int.; Rod Humphries int.; "Here Comes World Championship Tennis Every Sunday," advertisement, *World Tennis*, June 1973, p. 58.

196 **In the midst:** Lamar Hunt int.; Cliff Drysdale int.; Rod Humphries int.; Kim Chapin, "Lamar Hunt, the Backyard Player Who Made Big-Time Tennis," *Sport*, Sept. 1972, pp. 32–34; "Around the World," *World Tennis*, Nov. 1973, p. 84; Joe Jares, "Now She Plays for Green Stamps," *Sports Illustrated*, March 12, 1973, pp. 28–29.

196 **"We played in":** Michael Segell, "Jimmy Connors: The Games He Plays," *Rolling Stone*, Sept. 4, 1980.

197 **His headlong style:** Michael MacCambridge, "Jimmy Connors: The Art of War," in MacCambridge (ed.), *ESPN SportsCentury*, pp. 226–227.

197 **Even his movements:** Peter Ross Range, "Match of the Year," *New York Times Sunday Magazine*, June 23, 1974, pp. 28–38.

197 **Connors, even more:** Frank Deford, "Raised by Women to Conquer Men," *Sports Illustrated*, Aug. 28, 1978, p. 90; Jimmy Connors, *The Outsider: A Memoir* (New York: HarperCollins, 2013), pp. 13–24; King with Howard and Vollers, *All In*, p. 63.

197 **Connors shunned the:** Range, "Match of the Year."

197 **His time on:** Connors, *The Outsider*, p. 137; Joe Jares, "Battle of the Ages," *Sports Illustrated*, Sept. 16, 1974, pp. 22–25.

198 **That request led:** Murray Janoff, "Las Vegas a New Tennis Hub?," *The Sporting News*, Feb. 8, 1975, p. 30.

198 **"The bastards won":** Joe Jares, "A Two-Armed Bandit Hits the Jackpot," *Sports Illustrated*, Feb. 10, 1975.

198 **The jaunty Aussie:** Barry Lorge, "Match Hype Disturbed Newcombe," *Washington Post*, May 9, 1977.

198 **(Around the same:** Joe Jares, "Jackpot for Jimbo," by *Sports Illustrated*, May 5, 1975, pp. 12–15.

198 **In the midst:** Greg Hoffman, *The Art of World Team Tennis* (San Francisco: San Francisco Book Company, 1977), pp. 1–19; Ware, *Game, Set, Match*, pp. 99–103; Billie Jean King int.; Larry King int.; Kristien Kemmer int.

199 **"I think the":** Ware, *Game, Set, Match*, p. 99.

199 **The league launched:** "Editorial: 'World Team Tennis' Shakes Up the Tennis World," *World Tennis*, Oct. 1973, p. 14; "World Team Tennis: 1st Player Draft–August 3, 1973," *World Tennis*, Oct. 1973, p. 92; Linda Riggins, "Can Even Billie Jean King Save World Team Tennis?," *Sportswoman*, Sept.–Oct. 1974, pp. 25–27.

199 **"I love doubles":** Kristien (Kemmer) Shaw Ziska int.

199 **But a marker:** Riggins, "Can Even Billie Jean King Save World Team Tennis?"

200 **On that trip:** King with Howard and Vollers, *All In*, p. 277.

200 **By 1975, Chris:** Hoffman, *The Art of World Team Tennis,* pp. 40–46.

201 **The league qualified:** Curry Kirkpatrick, "The Newest Kids on the Block," *Sports Illustrated*, June 5, 1975, pp. 26–28, Karen Logan int.; Mick Haley int.

201 **Billie Jean King:** Candace Lyle Hogan, "League on Upswing," *New York Daily Record*, Oct. 11, 1977.

201 **Dick Button, the:** Futterman, *Players*, pp. 63–67; Dan Levin, "You Got to Have a Gimmick," *Sports Illustrated*, March 5, 1973, pp. 20–23.

202 **Roone Arledge, knowing:** Levin, "You Got to Have a Gimmick."

202 **The younger Rote:** "The Rotunda Follies," *Time*, March 11, 1974, p. 95.

202 **In the United:** Don Kowet, "The Cosmos: The Cosmic Sport Invades the U.S.," *Sport*, Sept. 1973, p. 85.

203 **On June 21:** Lamar Hunt int.; Bobby Moffat int.

203 **"Believe me, I":** Al Hill Jr. int.

203 **But while not:** Lamar Hunt int.; Bobby Moffat int.; Dick Hall int.; "Inflation Sport," *Forbes*, Aug. 15, 1974.

203 **"It did not":** "Inflation Sport."

204 **By 1973, Woosnam:** Gwilym S. Brown, "Quick, Somebody, a Pele," *Sports Illustrated*, May 7, 1973, pp. 101–104.

CHAPTER 11: CRITICAL MASS

205 **Giving the commencement:** Nicholas Evan Sarantakes, "Nixon Versus Paterno: College Football and Presidential Politics," *Pennsylvania History: A Journal of Mid-Atlantic Studies*, Vol. 73, No. 2, 2006.

205 **The twin traumas:** Bradley, *Life on the Run*, pp. 65–66.

206 **"One of the":** Travis Vogan, "Introduction: ABC Sports and Network Sports Television," *ABC Sports: The Rise and Fall of Network Sports Television* (Oakland, CA, 2018; online ed., California Scholarship Online, May 23, 2019), https://doi.org/10.1525/california/9780520292956.003.0001, accessed May 18 2023.

206 **ABC's innovations were:** Richard Goldstein, "Robert J. Wussler, CBS Executive and Aide to Ted Turner, Dies at 73," *New York Times*, June 13, 2010.

206 **"The mid-'70s":** Geoff Mason int.

207 **As interest grew:** "Hello, There, TV Sports Fans," by William Leggett, *Sports Illustrated*, June 26, 1972, p. 36-45.

207 **In response to:** Neil Best, "Remembering Sports Phone and 976-1313: When Sports Info Was a Phone Call Away," *Newsday*, July 31, 2015.

207 **The announcer Mike:** Mike Breen int.

208 **"They'd answer, 'Stanford'":** Phil Rosenthal, "40 Years Ago, Sports Phone Broke New Ground for Fans," *Chicago Tribune*, Nov. 17, 2017.

209 **The violence had:** "Head on His Shoulders," Scorecard, *Sports Illustrated*, Jan. 5, 1970, p. 7.

209 **In 1971, the:** "Dave Schultz Is Hockey's Mr. Misdemeanor," *People*, March 25, 1974.

209 **NHL President:** Mark Mulvoy, "Hockey Is Courting Disaster," *Sports Illustrated*, Jan. 27, 1975, pp. 26–27.

210 **At the time:** Tom Fitzgerald, "Bruins Romp 8–0 as Blood Flows," *Boston Globe*, Jan. 5, 1975; Mulvoy, "Hockey Is Courting Disaster."

210 **The problems went:** "On the Rocks," Scorecard, *Sports Illustrated*, May 5, 1975, p. 7.

210 **The league also:** Gary Mueller, "Divisions Finally Given a Name," *The Sporting News*, Oct. 19, 1974, p. 59; "Hockey 1974–75: Off the Line and into the Chips," *Sports Illustrated*, Oct. 21, 1974, pp. 40–41.

211 **By then, it:** Quoted in Barry Popik, "I Went to a Fight and a Hockey Game Broke Out," The Big Apple, Nov. 24, 2011, https://www.barrypopik.com/index.php/new_york_city/entry/i_went_to_a_fight_and_a_hockey_game_broke_out.

211 **"I credit them":** Billy Packer int.

211 **The idea that:** Billy Packer int.

212 **For just the:** Curry Kirkpatrick, "What a Wiz of a Win it Was," *Sports Illustrated*, April 7, 1975.

212 **That Monday, Wooden:** Smith Barrier, "Last NCAA Crown for the Wizard of Westwood," *The Sporting News*, April 19, 1975, p. 43.

212 **There were no:** Dwight Chapin, "Wooden's Swan Song: UCLA Victory March," *The Sporting News*, April 19, 1975, p. 45.

212 **"It added symmetry":** Bill Hancock int.

213 **Soon, coaches like:** Todd Rosiak, "Marquette's Uniforms Have Long Been Trendsetters," *Milwaukee Journal-Sentinel*, Feb. 5, 2009, https://archive.json line.com/sports/goldeneagles/39180482.html/.

213 **Before the 1976–77:** Jule Campbell int.; MacCambridge, *The Franchise*, p. 277.

214 **The rights fees:** C. C. Johnson Spink, "College Basketball Booming," *The Sporting News*, April 24, 1976, p. 12; Mike Douchant, "Crowd Records Tumble at College Cage Games," *The Sporting News*, Jan. 31, 1976, p. 5.

214 **"The Final Four":** Billy Packer with Roland Lazenby, *Fifty Years of the Final Four: Golden Moments of the NCAA Basketball Tournament* (Dallas: Taylor Publishing, 1987), p. 11.

214 **There was something:** "NHL Plans Cup TV, Seeks New York Audience," *New York Times*, March 23, 1976, p. 26; Jack Craig, "Dinah Shore Event Tops Tube," *The Sporting News*, April 24, 1976, p. 32.

214 **In the summer:** Jerry Kirshenbaum, "Curtain Call for a Legend," *Sports Illustrated*, June 23, 1975, pp. 18–21.

215 **The Tornado had:** MacCambridge, *Lamar Hunt: A Life in Sports*, pp. 240–241.

215 **"What are you":** Bobby Moffat int.

215 **But now even:** Melissa Ludtke, "Soccer Is Getting a Toehold, "*Sports Illustrated*, Aug. 30, 1976, p. 66.

215 **King—along with:** Eig, *Ali: A Life*, p. 426.

216 **Coming out for:** Rick Norsworthy, "Thrilla in Manila," in *Frontlines: Snapshots of History*, edited by Nicholas Moore and Sidney Weiland (Harlow, UK: Pearson Education Limited, 2001), pp. 182–186.

217 **The carnage at:** Thomas Hauser, "The Unforgiven," *Guardian*, Sept. 3, 2005.

217 **In the other:** Eig, *Ali: A Life*, p. 430; Kram, *Smokin' Joe*, p. 253.

217 **"You're blind, Joe":** Norsworthy, "Thrilla in Manila."

217 **Ali lavished Frazier:** Murphy, *A History of American Sports in 100 Objects*, p. 320.

217 **The third Ali–Frazier:** Mark Kram, "Lawdy, Lawdy, He's Great," *Sports Illustrated*, Oct. 13, 1975, pp. 20–27; Gerald Early int.

217 **Later that night:** Kram, "Lawdy, Lawdy, He's Great."

218 **After more than:** William Leggett, "Say It Ain't So About Joe," *Sports Illustrated*, April 7, 1975.

218 **In Boston, where:** Dave Smith int.; George Solomon int.

218 **The sixth game:** Pepe, *Talkin' Baseball*, pp. 200–210; Epstein, *Big Hair and Plastic Grass*, pp. 166–170.

219 **The series was:** Lowell Reidenbaugh, "Drama, Disputes Mark Red Triumph," *The Sporting News*, Nov. 8, 1975, p. 35.

219 **"I tell you":** Wells Twombly, "'75 Series—It's One to Savor," *The Sporting News*, Nov. 8, 1975, p. 32.

220 **"We imagine pro":** Bil Gilbert, "Gleanings from a Troubled Time," by *Sports Illustrated*, Dec. 25, 1972, pp. 34–36.

220 **As Pete Rozelle:** William Oscar Johnson, "After TV Accepted the Call, Sundays Were Never the Same," *Sports Illustrated*, Jan. 5, 1970, pp. 20–29; William Oscar Johnson, "You Know You're Not Getting Maudie Frickert," *Sports Illustrated*, Jan. 26, 1970, pp. 30–37.

221 **As the off-season:** Brent Musburger int.; Kevin O' Malley int.

221 **The woman in:** Kevin O'Malley int.

221 **The prior experience:** Brent Musburger int.

221 **That first season:** Rich Podolsky, *You Are Looking Live! How the NFL Today Revolutionized Sports Broadcasting* (Guilford, CT: Lyons Press, 2021), pp. 36–49.

222 **Super Bowl X:** John Steadman int.

222 **The result was:** *The Super Bowl Today*, CBS Sports, NFL Films Archives, video.

223 **The game was:** Red Smith, "Super Sunday," *New York Times Magazine*, Jan. 12, 1975, p. 79.

224 **It would become:** Kevin O'Malley int.

224 **By the 1975–76:** Rod Thorn int.; Jim O'Brien, "Claws' Exit King-Sized Foul-Up," *The Sporting News*, Nov. 8, 1975, pp. 25–26.

224 **The idea of:** Michael Murphy, "The ABA Way: For Pure Entertainment, American Basketball Association was a Slam Dunk," Remember the ABA, http://www.remembertheaba.com/abaarticles/murphyarticleaba.html, originally published in *Houston Chronicle*, 1996; Pluto, *Loose Balls*, pp. 25–26.

225 **Then came Erving:** Pluto, *Loose Balls*, p. 27.

225 **An excited murmur:** Broadcast of 1976 ABA Slam Dunk Contest, YouTube, https://www.youtube.com/watch?v=tNTgdcBDqJ4; Pluto, *Loose Balls*, pp. 25–29; Erving, *Dr. J*, pp. 290–293.

227 **"We figured Comaneci":** Frank Deford, "High Wide and Handsome," *Sports Illustrated*, Aug. 2, 1976, p. 14.

## CHAPTER 12: BATTLE LINES

228 **In the aftermath:** She was even mentioned by Charles Schulz in a *Peanuts* comic strip, which in the '70s was syndicated in seventy-five countries and read by an estimated 355 million readers. Peppermint Patty, scolding her bespectacled sidekick, claimed, "Marcie, has anyone ever told you that when you're mad, you look just like Billie Jean King?" King with Howard and Vollers, *All In*, p 297.

228 **Ratings and prize:** Joe Marshall, "On and Up with the Mighty Macs," *Sports Illustrated*, Feb. 3, 1975, p. 50; "A Garden of Well-Versed Women," Scorecard, *Sports Illustrated*, March 3, 1975, p. 12.

229 **"Athletics is going":** Margaret Dunkle int.

229 **"Impending doom is":** "Counting Down," Scorecard, *Sports Illustrated*, July 1, 1974, p. 11.

230 **"This may well":** Gerald Eskenazi, "Title IX Rules Issued for Equality in Sports," *New York Times*, July 4, 1975, p. 29.

230 **When Darrell Royal:** *Giant Killers: The Story of the Lady Longhorns*, documentary, directed by Chip Reves (ESPN/LHN Films, 2022).

230 **Soon, the battle:** Griffin Smith Jr., "Little Big Man," *Texas Monthly*, Jan. 1977.

230 **Among Republican senators:** Smith, "Little Big Man."

230 **As word began:** Alexander Wolff, "Winning at Political Football," *Sports Illustrated*, May 7, 2012, p. 59.

230 **On the AIAW:** "Interview with Margot Polivy," from *A Forgotten History: The Women Who Brought Us Title IX*, interviewed by Julia Lamber and Jean Robison, July 11, 2006, Maurer School of Law Digital Repository, Indiana University Bloomington; Margot Polivy int.; Peg Burke int.; Charlotte West int.; Margaret Dunkle int.; Sharon E. Taylor int.

231 **"I think I":** Margot Polivy int.

231 **"She did not":** Peg Burke int.

231 **For her part:** Margot Polivy int.; Ware, *Game, Set, Match*, p. 55.

231 **The month before:** "What Constitutes Equality for Women in Sport?," Report from the Project on the Status and Education of Women (Washington, DC: Association of American Colleges, 1974); James Michener, in his tome *Sports in America*, highlighted the Dunkle report ("anyone wishing to pursue the matter in depth should use this work as a source").

231 **"It was bake":** Lisa Antonucci, "Fifty Years Later, Title IX Slogan 'Give Women a Sporting Chance' Still Propels Advocates," sportsengine.com, May 31, 2022, https://www.sportsengine.com/basketball/fifty-years-later-title-ix-slogan-give-women-sporting-chance-still-propels-advocates.

231 **The examples were:** Testimony of Margy Duval for the Intercollegiate Association of Women Students before the Subcommittee on Education of the U.S. Senate Committee on Labor and Public Welfare on the proposed Tower Amendment, S.2106, Sept. 16, 1975, opening remarks written with Margaret Dunkle and Margie Chapman, pp. 10–12, https://files.eric.ed.gov/fulltext/ED136136.pdf.

232 **Tower's first effort:** Tower's first effort, described in the *Congressional Record* as "amendment No. 1343," never made it out of committee, *Congressional Record—Daily Digest*, May 20, 1974, p. D 388; Billie Jean King int.; Larry King

int.; Margaret Dunkle, "College Athletics: Tug-of-War for the Purse Strings," *Ms.*, Sept. 1974, p. 114.

232 **On June 18:** Cheryl M. Fields, "Fear of Effect on Athletics Delays Sex-Bias Guidelines," by *Chronicle of Higher Education*, March 18, 1974; Ware, *Game, Set, Match*, p. 57.

232 **The debate would:** Margaret Dunkle int.; Margot Polivy int.; Karen Blumenthal, *Let Me Play: The Story of Title IX: The Law That Changed the Future of Girls in America* (New York: Atheneum Books for Young Readers, 2005), p. 68.

233 **The AIAW delegate:** Judith Holland int.; Charlotte West int.; Sharon E. Taylor int.; Carole Oglesby int.; Peg Burke int.; Jon Gold, "Trailblazers," Bruin Athletics, UCLA, March 31, 2020, https://uclabruins.com/news/2020/3/31/bruin-athletics-trailblazers.aspx.

233 **On January 6:** Candace Lyle Hogan, "NCAA & AIAW: Will the Men Score on Women's Athletics," *womenSports*, Jan. 1977, pp. 46–49; "Official Minutes of the Executive Board and Delegate Assembly Meetings, Association for Intercollegiate Athletics for Women," Marriott Hotel, Houston, TX, Jan. 4–11, 1975.

234 **The news out:** *Giant Killers.*

234 **On the phone:** Carole Oglesby int.

234 **In Houston:** Tom Hansen int.; Charlotte West int.

235 **Meanwhile, as HEW:** Eskenazi, "Title IX Rules Issued for Equality in Sports"; Roberts, *A Necessary Spectacle*, p. 164; Therese Pasquale and Margaret Dunkle, "An Upset Victory for Women," *Women's Agenda*, June 1976, p. 7; Margaret C. Dunkle, "Title IX: New Rules for an Old Game," *Capitol Hill Forum*, July 28, 1975.

235 **In the next:** Senate Bill S. 2106, referred to the Committee on Labor and Public Welfare, Ninety-Fourth Congress, First Session, July 15, 1975; Bill Little int.

235 **"Title IX will":** Roberts, *A Necessary Spectacle*, p. 157.

235 **"The battle was":** Carole Oglesby int.

235 **"There was a":** Bill Hancock int.

235 **"It never dawned":** Margo Polivy int.

235 **At the college:** "Working Women Making It in Sports."

236 **At high schools:** Eskenazi, "Title IX Rules Issued for Equality in Sports."

236 **Moore had come:** Sarah Pileggi, "New Era for the Delta Dawns," *Sports Illustrated*, March 31, 1975, pp. 67–68.

237 **Women athletes at:** Waneen Spirduso int.; Donna Lopiano int.; Chris Plonsky int.

237 **Raised in a:** "Anna Hiss Papers," H. J. Lutcher Stark Center for Physical Culture and Sports, University of Texas; Donna Lopiano int., Waneen Spirduso int., "Dr. Anna Hiss," DKG International Society for Key Women Educators, https://www.dkg.org/DKGMember/About_Us/Anna_Hiss.aspx.

238 **In her decades:** Waneen Spirduso int.

238 **Hiss had an:** Waneen Spirduso int.

238 **After Hiss retired:** Donna Lopiano int.

238 **With the prospect:** Waneen Spirduso int.

239 **Spirduso reached out:** Waneen Spirduso int.; Carole Oglesby int.

239 **Lopiano's life had:** Donna Lopiano int.; "Donna Lopiano Oral History Interview," Nov. 16, 2011, part of the Shirley Bird Perry University of Texas Oral History Project, Dolph Briscoe Center for American History, University of Texas at Austin.

239 **Her childhood was:** Donna Lopiano int.

240 **She'd spend much:** Donna Lopiano int.

240 **Royal lobbed the:** Donna Lopiano int.; Waneen Spirduso int.

240 **The hiring process:** Waneen Spirduso int.

241 **In late August:** Donna Lopiano int.

241 **The budget of:** Lopiano would note that the annual telephone bill for the men's athletic department was larger than the entire women's athletic budget when she arrived. Jay, *More Than Just a Game*, p. 170.

241 **Basketball, like all:** Donna Lopiano int.; *Giant Killers*.

242 **Meanwhile in Washington:** *Hearings Before the Subcommittee on Education of the Committee on Labor and Public Welfare, United States Senate, Ninety-Fourth Congress, First Session on S.2106, to Amend Title IX of the Education Amendments of 1972* (Washington, D.C.: U.S. Government Printing Office, 1976).

242 **At the Office:** Julia Lamber, "A Forgotten History: The Women Who Brought Us Title IX," interview with Gwen Gregory, audio, Maurer School of Law Digital Repository, Indiana University Bloomington, https://www.repository.law .indiana.edu/ohtitleix/13/.

243 **The original feeling:** Tom Hansen int.

243 **"The reason why":** Jeff Orleans int.

243 **Hansen later went:** Tom Hansen int.

244 **"Donna, it's Lorene":** Donna Lopiano int.; *Giant Killers*.

244 **So on Thursday:** Donna Lopiano int.; *Hearings Before the Subcommittee on Education of the Committee on Labor and Public Welfare, United States Senate, Ninety-Fourth Congress, First Session on S.2106, to Amend Title IX of the Education Amendments of 1972* (Washington, DC: U.S. Government Printing Office, 1976), pp. 105–121.

244 **"The Tower bill":** "Statement of Donna A. Lopiano Before the Subcommittee on Higher Education, Committee on Labor and Public Welfare, S. 2106," Sept. 18, 1975, pp. 46-92, https://files.eric.ed.gov/fulltext/ED136136.pdf; Bill Choyke, "Lopiano Attacks Tower bill," *Austin American-Statesman*, Sept. 19, 1975.

244 **Lopiano's testimony:** Waneen Spirduso int.; Donna Lopiano int.

245 **Around that time:** Donna de Varona int.; Margot Polivy int.

245 **"We knew we":** Charlotte West int.

245 **"There was very":** Jeff Orleans int.

246 **The Tower Amendment:** Ken Rudnick and Alice Hartman, "N.C.A.A. Suit on Title IX Rules," *Kansas City Times*, Feb. 18, 1976, pp. 1A, 4C.

246 **In 1973, Billie:** Billie Moore int.

246 **In Cold War:** Billie Moore int.

247 **"Yes," said Moore:** Billie Moore int.

247 **The women who:** Trish Roberts int.; Ann Meyers int.; Lusia Harris int.; Billie Moore int.

248 **It was in:** Ron Rapoport, "A Happy Coaching Change," *Los Angeles Times*, March 1, 1977, p. 28; Billie Moore int.

248 **Moore was a:** Billie Moore int.

248 **Harris had grown:** Lusia Harris int.

248 **"We had to":** Trish Roberts int.

249 **During the period:** David Berst int.; Trish Roberts int.; Ann Meyers int.; Billie Moore int.

249 **"We just figured":** Trish Roberts int.; Dave Dorr, "U.S. Girls Gunning for Olympic Cage Berth," *The Sporting News*, June 19, 1976, p. 69.

249 **"She was not":** Juliene Simpson int.

249 **"It was brutal":** Trish Roberts int.

250 **"My message was":** Billie Moore int.

250 **With the credit:** Billie Moore int.; Ann Meyers int.; Mary Anne O'Connor int.; Juliene Simpson int.

250 **The trappings of:** Billie Moore int.

250 **At which point:** Billie Moore int.; Ben Bolch, "Billie Moore, Olympic and UCLA Coach Who Won Championships, Dies at 79," *Los Angeles Times*, Dec. 15, 2022.

250 **They did, though:** Billie Moore int.

251 **During a postgame:** Donna de Varona int.; Billie Moore int.

251 **"Don't do anything":** Billie Moore int.; Juliene Simpson int.; Mary Anne O'Connor int.

251 **There had been:** Donna de Varona int.

252 **One day, Searcy:** Mel Greenberg int.

252 **Beyond the growth:** "Working Women Making It In Sports."; Jack Craig, "Dinah Shore Event Tops Tube," *The Sporting News*, April 24, 1976, p. 32.

252 **With the last:** Sarah Pileggi, "Sportswoman of the Year," by *Sports Illustrated*, Dec. 20–27, 1976, pp. 42–50; Cutler Durkee "A Player for All seasons: Chris," *super-tiebreaker: World Team Tennis Official Magazine*, 1977, p. 11.

253 **It would even:** Connors, *The Outsider*, p. 105.

254 **Her maturation could:** Nancy Faber, "Long Live Ms. King, but Tennis Hails a New Queen," *People*, Feb. 3, 1975, pp. 4–5.

254 **In the end:** Connors, *The Outsider*, p. 134.

CHAPTER 13: FOLLOW THE MONEY

255 **The arbitration case:** Miller, *A Whole Different Ball Game*, p. 238-253; Ed Edmonds, "Dave McNally and Peter Seitz at the Intersection of Baseball History," in *The National Pastime: A Bird's-Eye View of Baltimore* (Phoenix: SABR, 2020), Society for American Baseball Research, https://sabr.org/journal/article /dave-mcnally-and-peter-seitz-at-the-intersection-of-baseball-labor-history/; Roger Abrams, "Arbitrator Seitz Sets the Players Free," by *Fall 2009 Baseball Research Journal* (Phoenix: SABR, 2009), Society for American Baseball Research, https://sabr.org/journal/article/arbitrator-seitz-sets-the-players-free/; "Indignation and Reality," Scorecard, *Sports Illustrated*, Jan. 5, 1976, p. 5.

255 **The sixty-seven-page:** Associated Press, "Baseball bosses Irate as Andy Awaits Bids," *Spokane Spokesman-Review*, Dec. 24, 1975; Associated Press, "Panel Frees Messersmith, McNally," *Chicago Tribune*, Dec. 24, 1975.

255 **Seitz met with:** Murray Chass, "A Pink-Slip Thanks for a Major Decision," *New York Times*, Aug. 22, 2013, p. B-16; Al Neal, "MLB's Historic Fight Over Free Agency," Grandstand Central, Dec. 5, 2018, https://grandstandcentral .com/2018/sections/culture/mlb-free-agency-history/.

256 **Later that day:** Associated Press, "Kuhn Delivers Terse Remarks," *Spokane Review*, Dec. 24, 1975; Roger Abrams, *Legal Bases: Baseball and the Law* (Philadelphia: Temple University Press, 1998), p. 132.

256 **When Miller called:** Miller, *A Whole Different Ball Game*, p. 252.

256 **Some players like:** Phil Garner int.; Sal Bando int.; Don Fehr int.

257 **"He was the most":** Sal Bando int.

257 **"Only your best":** Phil Garner int.; Sal Bando int.

257 **"Marvin had a":** Don Fehr int.

258 **Since 1971, the:** Tommy Craggs, "Fate of the Union: What the NFLPA Can Learn from the Fight of '77," *Sports Illustrated*, June 18, 2019, https://www .si.com/nfl/2019/06/18/nflpa-players-union-cba-negotiations-work-stoppage -ed-garvey-free-agency-1977.

258 **"Most of the":** Bill Curry int.

258 **The 1974 strike:** Larry Felser, "NFL Strike Takes Big Turnstile Toll," *The Sporting News*, Aug. 17, 1974, pp. 46, 50; Wells Twombly, "A Pox on Both Labor, Bosses in NFL Strike," *The Sporting News*, Aug. 17, 1974, p. 44; Furman Bisher, "What a Break for Baseball," *The Sporting News*, Aug. 24, 1974, pp. 2, 4.

258 **By then, many:** "Rancor in the Ranks," Scorecard, *Sports Illustrated*, Sept. 13, 1976, p. 13.

259 **Watching all this:** Leigh Steinberg int.

259 **As Atlanta news:** Leigh Steinberg int.; John Weyler, "Just Don't Call Him an Agent: Sports Attorney Doesn't Fit Huckster Image of His Peers: Leigh Steinberg," *Los Angeles Times*, June 9, 1990.

260 **Steinberg had launched:** Leigh Steinberg int.; Mike Brown int.

260 **By the time:** "Thin Ice," Scorecard, *Sports Illustrated*, June 30, 1975, p. 15.

260 **Free agency in:** Nathan Gabay, "Free Agency Before 1995—On 'Equalization,'" Nathan Gabay.com, https://nathangabay.com/free-agency-before-1995-on-equalization/.

260 **Eagleson, like Larry:** Coles Phinizy, "The Eagle and His Fat Flock," *Sports Illustrated*, Oct. 21, 1974, pp. 56–72.

261 **Orr was inclined:** Stan Fischler, "Would Orr Right Cooke's Boat?," *The Sporting News*, April 3, 1976, p. 18; Stan Fischler, "Bobby Orr Makes Sad Departure," *The Sporting News*, May 1, 1976, p. 39; Stan Fischler, "Team Player? Bobby Orr's Image Nosedives," *The Sporting News*, May 29, 1976, p. 42.

261 **"I brushed him":** Bobby Orr, *Orr: My Story* (New York: Berkley, 2014), p. 199.

261 **By the time:** Jeffrey Mishkin int.; Jim Quinn int.; Russ Granik int.

262 **That prompted a:** Charles Maher, "Pro Leagues Under Heaviest Legal Attacks Ever," *Los Angeles Times*, Sept. 9, 1975, p. III-1.

262 **"Under the system":** "Breakthrough?," Scorecard, *Sports Illustrated*, Jan. 20, 1975, p. 10.

262 **The idea intrigued:** Jim Quinn int.; Marc Fleisher int.; Russ Granik int.; Alexander Wolff, "NBA Players Counsel Larry Fleisher Wears a Second Hat as an Agent," *Sports Illustrated*, Feb. 11, 1985, pp. 208–212.

263 **"The NBA was":** Jim Quinn int.

263 **The two sides:** Jim Quinn int.; Jeff Mullins int.

263 **"Three or four":** Halberstam, *The Breaks of the Game*, p. 349.

264 **In the end:** Russ Granik int.; Jim Quinn int.

264 **When the agreement:** Jeff Mullins int.; Jim Quinn int.; Russ Granik int.; Jeffrey Mishkin int.; Robertson, *Big O*, pp. 313–314.

264 **"I always felt":** MacMullen et al., *Basketball: A Love Story*, p. 62.

265 **There was one:** Michael S. Jacobs and Ralph K. Winter Jr., "Antitrust Principles and Collective Bargaining by Athletes: Of Superstars in Peonage," *Yale Law Journal*, Vol. 81, No. 1, Nov. 1971, p. 1.

265 **This seemed to:** Paul Tagliabue int.

265 **For the NFLPA:** Jim Quinn int.

265 **The spectacle of:** "Oscar NBA Suit Settled, Pro Merger to Follow," *Indianapolis News*, Feb. 3, 1976, p. 20.

266 **"Our original proposal":** Pluto, *Loose Balls*, pp. 428–429.

266 **The NBA's national:** Dave Vance int.; Jim Quinn int.; Wayne Embry int.; Jerry Colangelo int.

266 **The Appomattox scene:** Pluto, *Loose Balls*, p. 429.

266 **"We never called":** Russ Granik int.

267 **"I didn't have":** Pluto, *Loose Balls*, p. 434.

267 **Notified of the:** Curtis Harris, "New York, New York: Julius Erving, the Nets-Knicks Feud, and America's Bicentennial," Pro Hoops History, Sept. 17, 2013, https://prohoopshistory.wordpress.com/2013/09/17/new-york-new-york-julius-erving-the-nets-knicks-feud-and-americas-bicentennial/.

268 **Here again, Jack:** *Sports Illustrated*, April 3, 1972.

268 **McCormack, though pained:** Ray Kennedy, "On His Mark and Go Go Going," *Sports Illustrated*, May 12, 1975, pp. 80–98.

268 **In designing golf courses:** Jack Nicklaus int.; Nicklaus with Bowden, *My Story*, pp. 187–188.

268 **The sports world:** Dan Jenkins int.

269 **Before the '76:** Ron Fimrite, "He's Free at Last," *Sports Illustrated*, Aug. 30, 1976, pp. 14–17.

269 **It had seemed:** Brian Kachejian, "History of the Baby Ruth Bar and Reggie Bar," ClassicNewYorkHistory.com, May 18, 2020, https://classicnewyorkhistory.com/history-of-the-baby-ruth-bar-and-reggie-bar/.

269 **What free agency:** Lamar Hunt int.

269 **On November 29:** Pepe, *Talkin' Baseball*, p. 263.

270 **The spring training:** Pepe, *Talkin' Baseball*, p. 277.

270 **"I'm the straw":** Pepe, *Talkin' Baseball*, p. 277.

270 **In asserting his:** Epstein, *Big Hair and Plastic Grass*, p. 204.

270 **This most public:** Epstein, *Big Hair and Plastic Grass*, p. 205.

271 **"It makes me":** Epstein, *Big Hair and Plastic Grass*, p. 205.

272 **"He's answered the":** ABC broadcast of Game 6 of the 1977 World Series, YouTube, https://www.youtube.com/watch?v=p_QiPpMzclk.

272 **Catfish Hunter, who:** Epstein, *Big Hair and Plastic Grass*, pp. 252–253.

273 **In baseball, genuine:** Futterman, *Players*, pp. 140–141.

273 **"All of that":** Phil Garner int.

## CHAPTER 14: THE LAST OF THE FIRSTS

274 **Growing up in:** Tony Dungy int.

274 **"I saw Jimmy":** Tony Dungy int.

275 **"If you are":** Tony Dungy int.

275 **It was unthinkable:** Roy Blount Jr., "Gillie Was a Steeler Driving Man," *Sports Illustrated*, Sept. 23, 1974, pp. 20–21; Bill Rhoden, "Black Quarterbacks: One Foot in the Door," *Ebony*, Nov. 1974, pp. 166-182.

275 **"The black guys":** MacCambridge, *Chuck Noll: His Life's Work*, p. 200.

276 **When the veterans:** Shack Harris int.; Robinson, *Never Before, Never Again*, p. 133.

276 **Five games into:** William Rhoden, *Third and a Mile: The Trials and Triumphs of the Black Quarterback* (New York: ESPN Books, 2007), p. 107; Steve Wulf, "All Hell Broke Loose," *ESPN the Magazine*, Feb. 3, 2014.

276 **"James Harris clearly":** Rhoden, *Third and a Mile*, p. 119.

277 **The syndicated Grambling:** Michael Hurd, *Collie J: Grambling's Man with the Golden Pen* (Haworth, NJ: St. Johann Press, 2007), pp. 169–170; Robinson, *Never Before, Never Again*, pp. 149–153.

277 **By now the:** Terrance Harris, "Memorable Superdome Moments, No. 31: Grambling Wins First Bayou Classic in Dome," *Times-Picayune*, July 18, 2015, nola.com, https://www.nola.com/sports/memorable-superdome-moments-no -31-grambling-wins-first-bayou-classic-in-dome/article_ce296077-9e62-5c52 -9928-bebe6a84fe93.html.

277 **The challenge for:** Schulman, *The Seventies*, p. 54.

277 **Eddie Robinson had:** "Candor," Scorecard, *Sports Illustrated*, Jan. 8, 1973, p. 8.

278 **"We saw the":** Jerry Hardaway int.

278 **On a trip:** Doug Porter int.

279 **"Texas did not":** Freeman, *Hook 'Em Horns*, p. 360.

279 **"It would be":** Byers with Hammer, *Unsportsmanlike Conduct*, p. 155.

279 **"I think what":** Ron Wolf int.

280 **"Ernie has such":** "Time Out with Editors: Baseball's Shame," *Sport*, Feb. 1972, p. 96.

280 **"There are many":** Adelman and Hall, *Out of Left Field: Willie Stargell's Turning Point Season*, p. 50.

280 **After Dick Williams:** Reggie Jackson, *A Season with a Superstar* (Chicago: Playboy Press, 1975), p. 75.

280 **It was Frank:** Frank Robinson with Roy Blount Jr., "I'll Always Be Outspoken," *Sports Illustrated*, Oct. 21, 1974, pp. 31–38.

281 **"I was thinking":** Ron Fimrite, "Jaunty Stride into History," *Sports Illustrated*, March 24, 1975, pp. 18–19.

281 **Early in spring:** John Rosengren, "Crossing the White Line: As Baseball's First African-American Manager, Frank Robinson Furthered Jackie Robinson's Legacy but Failed to Fully Integrate the Game," *History Channel Magazine*, May–June 2007.

281 **When Opening Day:** Epstein, *Big Hair and Plastic Grass*, p. 149.

281 **He wound up:** Frank Robinson, "How a Pair of Perrys and One Blue Moon Left Cleveland," *Sport*, May 1976, pp. 56–66.

281 **But by the:** "Insiders Say," *The Sporting News*, Oct. 24, 1975, p. 4.

282 **Up until 1961:** Lee Elder with Phil Musick, "Lee Elder's Masters Journal," *Sport*, July 1975, pp. 64–74; "Blacks on the Greens," *Time*, Feb. 14, 1969, p. 54; "Golf Pays Debt to a Real Pro," *Ebony*, April 1969, pp. 44–50.

282 **It wasn't until:** Richard Goldstein, "Lee Elder, Who Broke a Golf Color Barrier, Dies at 87, *New York Times*, Nov. 29, 2021.

283 **He teed off:** Jerry Kirshenbaum, "Long Countdown to Augusta," *Sports Illustrated*, March 10, 1975, pp. 24–29.

283 **"Most of the":** Goldstein, "Lee Elder, Who Broke a Golf Color Barrier, Dies at 87."

283 **It was not:** Michael Hurd, *Black College Football, 1892–1992: One Hundred Years of History, Education and Pride* (Virginia Beach, VA: Donning, 1993), pp. 117–118; Doug Porter int.; Doug Williams int.

283 **Williams, scheduled to:** Collie Nicholson int.

284 **"Collie did what":** Doug Williams int.

284 **The Rams coach:** Wulf, "All Hell Broke Loose."

285 **But James "Shack" Harris:** Shack Harris int.; Doug Williams int.

285 **Among the visitors:** Rhoden, *Third and a Mile*, pp. 145–150; Jason Reid, "Lamar Jackson Joins Small Club of Black Quarterbacks Drafted in First Round," Andscape, April 26, 2018, https://andscape.com/features/lamar-jackson-could-join-small-club-of-black-quarterbacks-drafted-in-first-round/.

286 **He was Warren:** Warren Moon int.; Leigh Steinberg int.; Ron Wolf int.; Ernie Accorsi int.; Art Rooney Jr. int.; Carl Peterson int.

286 **"He threw a":** Carl Peterson int.

286 **By then, Tony:** Tony Dungy int.

286 **Shack Harris agreed:** Shack Harris int.

286 **Steinberg, nearly alone:** Leigh Steinberg int.; Warren Moon int.

287 **"There was so":** Eddie Pells, Associated Press, "Fights, Drugs, Racial Tension: '70s Spelled Trouble for NBA," *San Diego Tribune*, Dec. 16, 2021.

287 **As one NBA:** Mark Jacobson, "The Passion of Doctor J," in *Basketball: Great Writing About America's Game*, edited by Alexander Wolff (Boone, IA: Library of America, 2018), p. 196.

287 **"One of David's":** Russ Granik int.

287 **And CBS continued:** Brent Musburger int.; Kevin O'Malley int.; Russ Granik int.

287 **The 1977 NBA Finals:** "Memorable finale for Havlicek…but TV fans missed the ending," *Boston Globe*, April 10, 1978, p. 25.

288 **From one perspective:** Bradley, *Life on the Run*, p. 140.

288 **The trends in:** Carroll, *It Seemed Like Nothing Happened*, p. 252.

288 **Many of the:** Vahe Gregorian, "On the Hall of Fame Case for Otis Taylor, Vital Not Just to KC Chiefs but Pro Football," *Kansas City Star*, July 1, 2022.

289 **"Even today I'm":** Adelman and Hall, *Out of Left Field: Willie Stargell's Turning Point Season*, p. 24.

289 **"Look, if you":** Epstein, *Big Hair and Plastic Grass*, p. 296.

289 **In January 1977:** Schulman, *The Seventies*, p. 77; Carroll, *It Seemed Like Nothing Happened*, p. 297.

289 **By that point:** Rona Cherry, "Hertz Is Renting O.J. Simpson and They Both Stand to Gain," *New York Times*, Nov. 22, 1976.

290 **One sketch featured:** "The First Black President," sketch, *The Richard Pryor Show*, 1977, YouTube, https://www.youtube.com/watch?v=gFWhoDdnb2k.

290 **"I just really":** Justin Tinsley, "Richard Pryor Told America About the Struggle of Black Quarterbacks," Andscape, Jan. 16, 2020, https://andscape.com/features /richard-pryor-told-america-about-the-struggle-of-black-quarterbacks/.

290 **By the end:** Tiger Woods's first national television appearance, *The Mike Douglas Show*, YouTube, https://www.youtube.com/watch?v=6XupL9h0DOc.


CHAPTER 15: GOING TO EXTREMES

291 **By the time:** "Cowgirls," *Esquire*, Oct. 1977, p. 80.

291 **If Oakland's Raiders:** Steve Sabol int.; Mary Jane Carr, "The Autumn Wind (Pirate Wind)," quoted on Schoolhouse by the Sea, https://www.schoolhouse bythesea.com/students/poems-and-verses/autumn-wind-is-a-pirate/.

292 **"Tex Schramm took":** Verne Lundquist int.

292 **The image of:** Bruce Newman, "Gimme an 'S', Gimme an 'E', Gimme...", *Sports Illustrated*, May 22, 1978, p. 18.

292 **The Cowboys' computerized:** Tex Schramm int.; Gil Brandt int.; Ron Wolf int.; Ernie Accorsi int.; Art Rooney Jr. int.; Bill Nunn int.; William Barry Furlong, "What Is a Punter's 'Hang Time'? Why Does a Receiver Seem to Run on Glass? How High is a Cornerback's I.Q.?", *New York Times Sunday Magazine*, Jan. 10, 1971, pp. 30–41.

293 **"The whole time":** Carl Peterson int.

293 **"Football was always":** Frank Layden int.

293 **"Ten years ago":** Tom Wolfe, *The Purple Decades* (New York: Farrar, Straus & Giroux, 1982), pp. 265–293.

293 **Wolfe had tapped:** Schulman, *The Seventies*, pp. 92–93, 121–122; Carroll, *It Seemed Like Nothing Happened*, pp. 246–247.

294 **Against the backdrop:** James Michener, *James Michener's USA*, edited by Peter Chaitin (New York: Crown, 1981), p. 226.

294 **At the same:** Footage of Phyllis George's interview with Roger Staubach, Facebook, https://www.facebook.com/watch/?v=577355486224994.

294 **Not all teams:** Sal Bando int.; Phil Garner int.; Jon McGlocklin int.; Tony Dungy int.

294 **"There was a":** Tony Dungy int.

295 **But no team:** Todd Brock, "Blowing up God's Peephole: The 10-Yr Anniversary of Texas Stadium's Demise," Cowboys Wire, April 11, 2020, https://cowboy swire.usatoday.com/2020/04/11/texas-stadium-implosion-10th-anniversary/.

295 **"Well, I think":** Tony Dungy int.

295 **Throughout the decade:** Peter Gent, *North Dallas Forty* (New York: William Morrow, 1973); Sarah Hepola, "The Photo the Dallas Cowboys Never Wanted the Public to See," *Texas Monthly*, Dec. 31, 2001; Sarah Hepola, "Sex, Scandal, and Sisterhood: Fifty Years of the Dallas Cowboys Cheerleaders," *Texas Monthly*, Sept. 2022.

295 **"They also had":** Verne Lundquist int.

296 **"I had a":** Thomas Henderson int.

296 **"I ignored it":** Thomas Henderson int.

296 **Before the Super:** Patoski, *The Dallas Cowboys*, p. 406.

296 **After that 1978:** Golenbock, *Cowboys Have Always Been My Heroes*, p. 644.

296 **"That was NFL":** Verne Lundquist int.

297 **Gaye came to:** Thomas Henderson int.

297 **Eventually, Henderson's drug:** Thomas Henderson int.; Golenbock, *Cowboys Have Always Been My Heroes*, p. 653.

297 **"By the time":** Thomas Henderson int.

297 **Drug use had:** Simmons, *The Book of Basketball*, p. 143.

297 **"That was a":** Russ Granik int.

297 **"I said well":** John Papanek int.

298 **"So from Woodstock":** Thomas Henderson int.

298 **And yet. At:** Ron Johnson int.; John "Frenchy" Fuqua int.

298 **"Ron," said Parisi:** Ron Johnson int.

298 **Cigarette smoking had:** Len Dawson int.; Bob McKay int.; Ted Koy int.; Ron Johnson int.; Joe Greene int.; Dick Young, "Young Ideas," *The Sporting News*, June 6, 1970, p. 16; Pat Putnam, "Bubbles and Bounces," *Sports Illustrated*, Jan. 26, 1970, p. 10. Putnam's story noted that Ralph Doubell's prep on the eve of an eight-hundred-meter race included "four bottles of German beer, one Bloody Mary, three glasses of rosé, and 237 pages of *Portnoy's Complaint*."

299 **The Universal gym:** Bob McKay int.; Ted Koy int.

299 **Meanwhile, on other teams:** Barry McDermott, "Exercise You Later, Alligator," *Sports Illustrated*, April 21, 1975, pp. 36–42.

300 **"I started to":** Joe Greene int.

300 **As the weight:** Charlie Getty int.; Bob McKay int.; Jon Kolb int.

300 **In basketball, Kareem:** Hubie Brown int.

301 **Surveying the blizzard:** Don Fehr int.

301 **Beyond that, Turner:** Curry Kirkpatrick, "Going Real Strawwng," *Sports Illustrated*, Aug. 21, 1978, pp. 70–82.

302 **For much of:** Joe Gordon int.; Ed Bouchette int.; Art Rooney II int.

302 **The NCAA offered:** "Next Case," Scorecard, *Sports Illustrated*, May 12, 1975, p. 15.

302 **The springboard diving:** Rick Telander, "A Voice for Those Long Silent," *Sports Illustrated*, June 30, 1975, pp. 60–63.

303 **That would begin:** Mike Harrigan int.; Donna de Varona int.; "Amateur Sports Act Alters Domestic Coordination," *NCAA News*, March 8, 1979.

303 **"We had a":** Donna de Varona int.

303 **In baseball, the:** Andrew Means, "Remembering the Career of Herb Washington, the A's 'Designated Runner,'" Cut4, MLB.com, June 28, 2017.

303 **The statistic of:** Epstein, *Big Hair and Plastic Grass*, p. 216.

304 **"Red Auerbach and":** MacMullan et al., *Basketball: A Love Story*, p. 183; Jim O'Brien, "NBA Cool to Three-Point Basket," *The Sporting News*, July 17, 1976, p. 52.

304 **The rule came:** Hubie Brown int.; Wayne Embry int.

304 **The first year:** Hubie Brown int.

305 **Asked to measure:** Jacobson, "The Passion of Doctor J," p. 194.

305 **But there was:** "Mayhem-Minded Fans," *The Sporting News*, Jan. 24, 1976, p. 14.

305 **As early as:** Will McDonough, "Bell Admits Schaefer Rowdies Proving Tough Foe for Pats," *Boston Globe*, Nov. 12, 1972, p. 108.

305 **In Cleveland on:** Peter S. Greenberg, "Wild in the Stands," *New Times*, Nov. 11, 1977, pp. 24–30, 62–64; Dick Schaap, "Met Mania," *Sport*, Dec. 1973, p. 15.

305 **In 1974, Jimmy:** "Sports Fans' Greatest Hits," *New Times*, Nov. 11, 1977, pp. 24–30, 62–64; Parton Keese, "Celtics Outlast Suns, Fan Attacks Referee," *New York Times*, June 5, 1976, p. 41.

306 **"What we know":** Greenberg, "Wild in the Stands"; Clark Whelton, "Take Me Out of the Ball Game," *New Times*, Nov. 11, 1977, p. 27–30.

306 **But Dr. Arnold:** Greenberg: "Wild in the Stands."

306 **The challenge of:** Pete Rozelle int.; Jim Kensil int.; Don Weiss int.

307 **But that kind:** Paul Schwartzman, "Roll Out the Barrel Man: Denver Pitchman Delivers Good Cheer," *New York Daily News*, Jan. 15, 1999; Golenbock, *Cowboys Have Always Been My Heroes*, pp. 299–300.

307 **"There is a":** Ron Fimrite, "Going to Bat for the Game," *Sports Illustrated*, April 7, 1975, pp. 35–36.

307 **In San Diego:** Fred O. Rodgers, Ted Giannoulas (San Diego Chicken), sabr.org, https://sabr.org/bioproj/person/ted-giannoulas-san-diego-chicken/.

307 **The Braves' Ted:** by Eric D. Williams, "A Look Back at the 'Grand Hatching' of the San Diego Chicken," ESPN.com, June 28, 2018, https://www.espn.com/mlb/story/_/id/23934188/the-grand-hatching-san-diego-chicken.

308 **In Philadelphia, the:** Lauren Amour, "How the Phillies Phanatic Came to be America's Favorite Sports Mascot," Inside the Phillies, FanNation, *Sports Illustrated*, Dec. 15, 2021, https://www.si.com/mlb/phillies/opinions/how-phillie-phanatic-came-to-be-americas-favorite-sports-mascot-mlb.

308 **"Red Auerbach once":** Frank Layden int.

308 **As sports grew:** Murphy, *A History of American Sports in 100 Objects*, p. 197.

308 **By the mid-'70s:** Jonathan Abrams, *The Come Up: An Oral History of the Rise of Hip-Hop* (New York: Crown, 2022), p. 103.

309 **A long-distance:** Allison Keyes, "How the First Sports Bra Got Its Stabilizing Start," *Smithsonian Magazine*, March 18, 2020; National Inventors Hall of Fame (website), https://www.invent.org/inductees/lisa-lindahl#:~:text=Lisa%20Lindahl%2C%20Hinda%20Miller%20and,and%20launched%20a%20global%20industry.

309 **The effect of:** "Comes the Revolution," *Time*, June 26, 1978, p. 54.

309 **"Women no longer":** "Comes the Revolution."

310 **"The best solution":** MacCambridge, *America's Game*, p. 331.

310 **"The idea of":** MacCambridge, *America's Game*, p. 332.

310 **Armed with excellent:** William Wallace, "NFL Is Said to Engineer $576 Million Deal," *New York Times*, Oct. 26, 1977; David Harris, *The League: The Rise and Decline of the NFL* (New York: Bantam, 1986), p. 279.

311 **"The number one":** Kevin O'Malley int.

312 **Later that night:** Jonathan Alter, *His Very Best: Jimmy Carter, a Life* (New York: Simon and Schuster, 2020), p. 410.

312 **"What happens on":** Larry Kindbom int.

313 **Hayes had lost:** Larry Kindbom int.; Jim Spence int.

313 **Hayes did not:** Larry Kindbom int.

314 **"The guy's a":** Ernie Accorsi int.; George Young int.

314 **During his first:** David Harris, *The Genius: How Bill Walsh Reinvented Football and Created an NFL Dynasty* (New York: Random House, 2008), p. 79; Tony Dungy int.; Brian Billick int.; Bill Walsh int.

314 **"He wasn't concerned":** Tony Dungy int.

315 **"When a player":** Brian Billick int.

315 **"Bill was emphatic":** Brian Billick int.

CHAPTER 16: THE RISING

316 **Growing up in:** Jody Conradt int.; "Jody Conradt Oral History Interview," July 7, 2011, part of the Shirley Bird Perry University of Texas Oral History Project, Dolph Briscoe Center for American History, University of Texas at Austin; Helen Thompson, "A Whole New Ball Game," *Texas Monthly*, March 1994.

317 **Meanwhile, it had:** Donna Lopiano int.; Waneen Spirduso int.; Bill Little int.; Alexander Wolff, "Prima Donna," *Sports Illustrated*, Dec. 17, 1990, pp. 74–82.

317 **Owing to her:** Donna Lopiano int.; Jody Conradt int.

318 **So in the:** Donna Lopiano int.; Jody Conradt int.; Retha Swindell int.; Cathy Self Morgan int.; Bill Little int.

318 **"When the office":** Bill Little int.

318 **With the women:** Donna Lopiano int.; Scrapbook, 1976–77 Season, Jody Conradt papers, Stark Center for Physical Culture and Sports, University of Texas.

318 **"It was going":** Jody Conradt int.

319 **In the summer:** Jody Conradt int.; Donna Lopiano int.

319 **Conradt recognized that:** Jody Conradt int.

319 **The plan called:** Jody Conradt int.; Donna Lopiano int.; Missy McCullough int.

320 **"Start backwards," said:** Donna Lopiano int.

320 **The Fast Break:** Jody Conradt int.; Missy McCullough int.; Chris Plonsky int.

320 **"That was about":** Donna Lopiano int.

320 **Conradt was aggressively:** Donna Lopiano int.; Bill Little int.; Missy McCullough int.

321 **"I tried to":** Jody Conradt int.

321 **As she was:** Jody Conradt int.

321 **But soon enough:** Donna Lopiano int.

321 **By 1977–78, Conradt:** Jody Conradt int.; Donna Lopiano int.; Mel Greenberg int.; Joan Cronan int.; Scrapbook, 1977–78 Season, Jody Conradt papers, Stark Center for Physical Culture and Sports, University of Texas.

322 **"On the night":** Donna Lopiano int.

322 **Among the avid:** Jody Conradt int.; Donna Lopiano int.; Chris Plonsky int.; Bill Little int.; Bria Felicien, "Barbara Jordan, Devoted Women's Basketball Fan," Black Sportswoman, June 17, 2021, https://www.theblacksportswoman.com/barbara-jordan-devoted-womens-basketball-fan/; Thompson, "A Whole New Ball Game."

322 **At the end:** Jody Conradt int.

322 **Colleen Matsuhara, who:** Colleen Matsuhara int.

322 **And through it all:** Colleen Matsuhara int.

322 **By Conradt's third:** Jody Conradt int.; Mell Greenberg int.; Scrapbook, 1978–79 Season, Jody Conradt papers, Stark Center for Physical Culture and Sports, University of Texas.

323 **"They led the":** *Giant Killers.*

323 **"Donna and I":** Joan Cronan int.

323 **In Houston in:** Ware, *Game, Set, Match*, pp. 147–148; Schulman, *The Seventies*, p. 186; Lorraine Boissoneault, "The 1977 Conference on Women's Rights That Split America in Two," *Smithsonian Magazine*, Feb. 15, 2017, https://www.smithsonianmag.com/history/1977-conference-womens-rights-split-america-two-180962174/.

323 **Ahead of the:** Jill Lepore, *These Truths: A History of the United States* (New York: W. W. Norton, 2018), p. 660; Anna Quindlen, "Women Relay the Movement's Torch From Seneca Falls to Houston," *New York Times*, Oct. 7, 1977.

324 **Gloria Steinem would:** Ware, *Game, Set, Match*, p. 148.

324 **Sports, unsurprisingly, was:** Donna Lopiano int.; Donna de Varona int.; Margaret Dunkle int.; Charlotte West int.; Margot Polivy int.; Carole Oglesby int.

324 **Others viewed this:** Margaret Dunkle int.

324 **"They saw it":** Donna de Varona int.

324 **King herself had:** King with Howard and Vollers, *All In*, pp. 209–210.

324 **The meetings in:** Ware, *Game, Set, Match*, p. 448.

325 **One of the:** Carroll, *It Seemed Like Nothing Happened*, pp. 289–290.

325 **"The AIAW had":** Doug Tucker int.; Tom Hansen int.; Chuck Neinas int.

325 **"When two men":** Evert with Amdur, *Chrissie*, p. 168.

325 **So was the:** Barry McDermott, "More Than a Pretty Face," *Sports Illustrated*, Jan. 18, 1982, pp. 30–37.

326 **"It's just a":** King with Deford, *The Autobiography of Billie Jean King*, p. 137.

326 **In 1977, AIAW:** "Affidavit of Donna A. Lopiano," pp. 30–31; Charlotte West int.

326 **The AIAW president-elect:** Charlotte West int.

326 **So Stern was:** Charlotte West int.; Judie Holland int.

327 **What even her:** Judie Holland int.

327 **The 1978 Final:** Judie Holland int.; Charlotte West int.; Billie Moore int.; Ann Meyers Drysdale int.

328 **In the wake:** Judie Holland int.

328 **"I knew early":** Charlotte West int.

328 **In women's golf:** Murphy, *A History of American Sports in 100 Objects*, pp. 211–212; Frank Deford, "Nancy with the Laughing Face," *Sports Illustrated*, July 10, 1978, pp. 24–31.

328 **That same year:** Ryan McGee, "Janet Guthrie Outraced Insults to Make History," espnW, ESPN, Feb. 19, 2013, https://www.espn.com/espnw/news-com mentary/story/_/id/8963949/espnw-janet-guthrie-outraced-insults-make-auto -racing-history.

329 **There were also:** Melissa Ludtke int.

329 **That eventually prompted:** Melissa Ludtke int.; Epstein, *Big Hair and Plastic Grass*, p. 285.

329 **By the beginning:** Karra Porter, *Mad Seasons: The Story of the First Women's Professional Basketball League, 1978–1981* (Lincoln, NE: University of Nebraska Press, 2006), pp. 1–11.

329 **On December 9:** Karen Logan int.; Porter, *Mad Seasons*, pp. 18–21.

330 **In addition to:** Karen Logan int.; Liz Galloway McQuitter int.; Porter, *Mad Seasons*, pp. 93–95.

330 **In the summer:** Ann Meyers Drysdale int.; Ann Meyers Drysdale with Joni Ravenna, *You Let Some Girl Beat You?: The Story of Ann Meyers Drysdale* (Lake Forest, CA: Behler Publications, 2012), pp. 1–15.

330 **Suspicious that it:** Ann Meyers Drysdale int.; Drysdale, *You Let Some Girl Beat You?*, p. 6.

330 **"I was not":** Ann Meyers Drysdale int.

330 **Even those who:** Simone de Beauvoir, *The Second Sex* (New York: Alfred A. Knopf, 1953), p. 373, quoted in Ware, *Game, Set, Match*, p. 173.

331 **"Games were really":** Ann Meyers Drysdale int.

331 **In 1976, the:** *National Collegiate Athletic Ass'n v. Califano*, 444 F. Supp. 425 (D. Kan. 1978).

331 **Later that year:** Charlotte West int.

331 **The offered hand:** Walter Byers letter to Charlotte West, Jan. 1979; "Affidavit of Donna A. Lopiano," p. 24.

332 **Ahead of the:** John Underwood, "An Odd Way to Even Things Up," *Sports Illustrated*, Feb. 5, 1979, pp. 18–19; Cheryl M. Fields, "As Criticism Continues, U.S. Prepares Final Policy on Sex-Bias in Sports," *Chronicle of Higher Education*, March 19, 1979, p. 4.

332 **On April 5:** Charlotte West int.; Sharon E. Taylor int.; Donna Lopiano int.; "LHSC's Taylor Talks Sports with Califano," *Lock Haven* (PA) *Express*, April 1979.

332 **The women spoke:** Sharon E. Taylor int.

332 **The women left:** Charlotte West int.

332 **"When he heard":** Sharon E. Taylor int.

333 **Enter the Women's:** Donna de Varona int.

333 **Donna de Varona:** Ware, *Game, Set, Match*, pp. 97–98.

333 **The foundation had:** Ware, *Game, Set, Match*, p. 94.

333 **With HEW waffling:** Joan Ryan, "Crisis Time for Equality," *Washington Post*, April 20, 1979, p. D1; "Rally Slated Today Supporting Title IX," *New York Times*, April 22, 1979, p. S-11; Nancy Scannell, "Carter Meets with Women on Title 9," *Washington Post*, Sept. 14, 1979.

333 **"We're here as":** Scannell, "Carter Meets with Women on Title 9."

333 **By the beginning:** "Affidavit of Donna A. Lopiano," p. 23.

333 **All around women's:** "Comes the Revolution," *Time*, June 26, 1978, p. 54; "Affidavit of Donna A. Lopiano," p. 24.

334 **In the fall:** Billie Jean King int.; Frank Gifford int.; King with Howard and Vollers, *All In*, p. 298.

334 **At the press:** Nancy Scannell, "Title 9 Policies Issued," *Washington Post*, Dec. 5, 1979.

334 **In the end:** Ware, *Game, Set, Match*, pp. 66–67.

334 **Walter Byers, still:** Donna Lopiano int.; Margaret Dunkle int.; Scannell, "Title 9 Policies Issued"; *Giant Killers*.

335 **"We were smarter":** Sharon E. Taylor int.

335 **"Title IX was":** Bill Bradley int.

335 **"I hated that":** Joan Cronan int.

CHAPTER 17: MODERN TIMES

336 **After John Wooden's:** "The Annual Review," *The ESPN College Basketball Encyclopedia* (New York: Ballantine Books and ESPN Books, 2009), pp. 823–872.

337 **Serious sports fans:** Tony Kornheiser, "Jimmy Valvano Went Home to Long Island to Get the Kind of Players Who'll Turn Iona into a National Power," *Street and Smith's Official College, Pro and Prep Yearbook, 1977–78*, p. 149.

337 **The sport's growth:** Larry Albus int.; Dan Gavitt int.

337 **The conference had:** Dan Gavitt int.

338 **Tournament brackets had:** Blair Kerkhoff, *Tournament Town Kansas City: Where the Basketball Madness Began* (Kansas City: Kansas City Star Books, 2011), p. 25; King with Howard and Vollers, *All In*, p. 59; Lamar Hunt int.; Don Weiss int.

338 **With the advent:** "NCAA Tournament Pairings" infographic, *Chicago Tribune*, March 6, 1978, Sec. 6, p. 2; "1979 NCAA Basketball Tournament," infographic, *Chicago Tribune*, March 5, 1979, Sec. 6, p. 1.

339 **Bird had been:** "College Basketball's Secret Weapon: Explosive Larry Bird" (cover), *Sports Illustrated*, Nov. 28, 1977; "The Super Sophs: Michigan State's Classy Earvin Johnson" (cover), *Sports Illustrated*, Nov. 27, 1978.

340 **The tournament expanded:** Packer with Lazenby, *Fifty Years of the Final Four*, p. 12.

340 **The four teams:** Larry Keith, "They Caged the Bird," *Sports Illustrated*, April 2, 1979, pp. 16–19.

341 **Bird's cavalier words:** NBC broadcast of 1979 NCAA national championship game, YouTube, https://www.youtube.com/watch?v=DlG7oSYL3Os&t=242s.

341 **The NBA was:** Chris Cobb, "The Punch: Tomjanovich and Washington Both Still Feel the Pain from That Terrible Moment," *Los Angeles Times*, Jan. 28, 1985.

341 **"I'll never forget":** John Feinstein, *The Punch: One Night, Two Lives, and the Fight That Changed Basketball Forever* (New York: Back Bay Books, 2003), p. 6.

342 **"This was a":** Feinstein, *The Punch*, pp. x–xi.

342 **In this recalibration:** Not all sports reacted similarly. It would be eight more years before the World Boxing Association would change their championship fights from fifteen to twelve rounds.

342 **For the NBA:** Simmons, *The Book of Basketball*, p. 139.

342 **All of this:** Halberstam, *The Breaks of the Game*, p. 367.

343 **"It carried over":** Brian McIntyre int.

343 **At the 1979:** Russ Granik int.; Brian McIntyre int.; Jerry Colangelo int.

344 **Stern navigated his:** Jerry Colangelo int.

344 **"He understood what":** Frank Layden int.

344 **In the short:** Jerry Colangelo int.; Jeff Mishkin int.; Russ Granik int.

344 **"David was sort":** Russ Granik int.

344 **There were only:** John Ourand, "Cable Vision: TV Pioneer Kay Koplovitz Saw the Future of Sports Networks," *Sports Business Journal*, March 6, 2018.

344 **The NBA settled:** Simmons, *The Book of Basketball*, p. 140.

344 **"I remember we":** Russ Granik int.

345 **The decade's last:** Bill Rasmussen, *Sports Junkies Rejoice!: The Birth of ESPN* (Hartsdale, NY: QV Publishing, 1983), pp. 20–67.

345 **After securing their:** Rasmussen, *Sports Junkies Rejoice!*, pp. 76–79.

345 **"There is a":** Verne Lundquist int.

346 **"What we're creating":** Paul Rouse, "How ESPN Went from Hurling Highlights to Conquering the World," by *Irish Times*, May 7, 2021; James Andrew Miller and Tom Shales, *Those Guys Have All the Fun: Inside the World of ESPN* (New York: Little, Brown, 2011), pp. 3–48.

346 **On the day:** Geoff Mason int.

346 **As the network:** Footage from first *ESPN SportsCenter* broadcast, courtesy ESPN.

347 **In the wake:** Madeleine Blais, "Every Body a Winner," *Washington Post*, June 20, 1979; Einhorn with Rapoport, *How March Became Madness*, p. x.

348 **As the '70s:** *The Fish That Saved Pittsburgh* trailer, YouTube, https://www.youtube.com/watch?v=sv5W7XRhvfY.

348 **Throughout the country:** Carroll, *It Seemed Like Nothing Happened*, p. 211.

349 **At the same:** Pepe, *Talkin' Baseball*, p. 359; Epstein, *Bad Hair and Plastic Grass*, pp. 240–244.

349 **After the first:** *The Bee Gees: How Can You Mend a Broken Heart*, directed by Frank Marshall (HBO Max/PolyGram, 2020).

350 **"As I got":** Vince Lawrence, quoted in *The Bee Gees: How Can You Mend A Broken Heart*.

350 **In the wake:** Fred Bierman, "In the Distance, the Sound of 'Chocolate Thunder,'" *New York Times*, Feb. 4, 2007.

351 **But even the:** Jon Mooallem, "The History and Mystery of the High Five," *ESPN The Magazine*, Aug. 8, 2011.

351 **When the five-foot-ten:** Phil Garner int.; Dave Parker int.

352 **The ethos of:** Phil Garner int.

352 **"If Willie Stargell":** Steve Blass int.

352 **"I saw the":** Epstein, *Big Hair and Plastic Grass*, p. 114.

352 **"We fought for":** Epstein, *Big Hair and Plastic Grass*, p. 114.

353 **"You like this":** Dave Parker int.

353 **"We could lose":** Pepe, *Talkin' Baseball*, pp. 371–374.

353 **On the morning:** "Baseball Legend Chuck Tanner, Who Led Greatest World Series Comeback, Dies Aged 82," *Daily Mail*, Feb. 12, 2011, https://www.dailymail.co.uk/news/article-1356328/Baseball-legend-Chuck-Tanner

-led-greatest-World-Series-comeback-died.html; Epstein, *Big Hair and Plastic Grass*, p. 309.

353 **Two wins sent:** Dave Parker int.

354 **"The biggest thing":** Tim Foli int.

354 **Despite the doomsday:** Epstein, *Big Hair and Plastic Grass*, p. 289.

354 **The most quantifiable:** Bill James int.; Daniel Okrent int.

355 **The 1977 Baseball:** Michael MacCambridge, "Following Baseball: In the Abstract and Far Beyond," *The Sporting News*, July 7, 1997, pp. 15–19.

355 **That original publication:** Bill James int.

355 **"Ballpark effect," said:** Daniel Okrent int.

355 **By the fall:** MacCambridge, "Following Baseball: In the Abstract and Far Beyond."

355 **It was initially:** MacCambridge, *The Franchise*, p. 365.

356 **James had written:** Jerry Kirshenbaum, "His Word Is the Law of Averages," *Sports Illustrated*, Aug. 18, 1969, pp. 28–31; Bill James int.

356 **"I see Seymour":** Daniel Okrent int.

356 **"There was a":** Daniel Okrent int.

356 **"I do remember":** Greg Curtis int.

357 **Ryan's headlining deal:** Steve Fehr int.; Bill James int.

357 **For years, these:** Bill James int.; Steve Fehr int.; John Helyar, *Lords of the Realm: The Real History of Baseball* (New York: Ballantine, 1995), p. 312; Edmund P. Edmonds, "Astros Players Arbitration Results," NDLScholarship, Notre Dame Law School, May 10, 2018, https://scholarship.law.nd.edu/cgi/viewcontent.cgi?article=1001&context=baseball_arb_team_player_results.

357 **"That moment was":** Bill James int.

358 **"I don't know":** Joe Green int.

359 **The spot, produced:** Tim Nudd, "The Enduring Charm of Coke's Mean Joe Greene Ad," Muse by Clio, Feb. 4, 2022, https://musebycl.io/super-bowl-classics/cocacola.

359 **"You know the":** Joe Greene int.

359 **When Visa pioneered:** Schulman, *The Seventies*, p. 135.

360 **In the face:** Schulman, *The Seventies*, pp. 140, 181; Carroll, *It Seemed Like Nothing Happened*, p. 280.

360 **On January 14:** Ralph Ray, "Olympic Boycott Gathering Steam," *The Sporting News*, Feb. 9, 1980, p. 46; Furman Bisher, "Put the Heat on Russia—Call off the Olympics," *The Sporting News*, Feb. 9, 1980, p. 46; Ralph Ray, "China, Japan Add Muscle to Boycott Push," *The Sporting News*, Feb. 16, 1980, p 23.


CHAPTER 18: ALL SPORTS ALL THE TIME

361 **The glimpse of:** Barry Tramel, "Bum Phillips Gave the NFL Charm and Charisma Topped by a Stetson," *Oklahoman*, Oct. 20, 2013.

361 **In the third:** Paul Zimmerman, "Hitting a Wall of Steel," *Sports Illustrated*, Jan. 14, 1980, pp. 14–18.

361 **But even as:** Scenes from NBC broadcast of 1979 AFC Championship Game, YouTube, https://www.youtube.com/watch?v=bw4by31W24g.

361 **The technology and:** Jace Evans, "'Immaculate Reception' by Steelers' Franco Harris Named Greatest Play in NFL History," *USA Today*, Sept. 20, 2019.

362 **The Steelers won:** Randy Harvey, "Even Steelers Call It a Tainted Win," *The Sporting News*, Jan. 19, 1980, p. 15.

362 **So would the:** Jack Craig, "TV Replay Hassle Just Won't Fade Away," SporT-View, *The Sporting News*, Feb. 9, 1980.

363 **In the fall:** Rick Kehoe int.

363 **Yet for a:** E. M. Swift, "The Golden Goal," *Sports Illustrated*, March 3, 1980, pp. 16–20.

364 **The Olympic:** Jim Spence int.

365 **By the time:** "Irrevocable or Not," Scorecard, *Sports Illustrated*, March 3, 1980, p. 11; John Lohn, "What a Waste: How the Moscow Olympics Boycott Unnecessarily Crushed Dreams," *Swimming World*, Jan. 19, 2023; Jimmy Carter, "Remarks to Representatives of U.S. Teams to the 1980 Summer Olympics," March 21, 1980, The American Presidency Project, https://www.presidency.ucsb.edu /documents/remarks-representatives-us-teams-the-1980-summer-olympics.

365 **In Carter's vision:** Nicholas Evan Sarantakes, "Jimmy Carter's Disastrous Olympic Boycott," *Politico*, Feb. 9, 2014.

365 **The CIA analyst:** Roy Tomizawa, "The 1980 Moscow Olympics, Part 1: The American Boycott," The Olympians from 1964 to 2020, July 19, 2020, https://theolym pians.co/2020/07/19/the-1980-moscow-olympics-part-1-the-american-boycott/.

366 **While allies like:** Alter, *His Very Best*, p. 493.

366 **As Carter's biographer:** Alter, *His Very Best*, p. 547.

366 **The comedian George:** Live performance, "A&O Board Presents George Carlin," Cahn Auditorium, Northwestern University, Oct. 17, 1985; Stan Isaacs, "The 24 Hours of Plainville," *Sports Illustrated*, Jan. 7, 1980, p. 43.

367 **A week before:** Bob Ley int.

367 **"The first time":** Bob Costas int.

367 **Later that month:** Seth Davis, *When March Went Mad: The Game That Transformed Basketball* (New York: Times Books/Henry Holt, 2009), pp. 204–206.

368 **CBS got a:** Kevin O'Malley, "How CBS Snared the NCAA Tourney Rights from NBC 40 Years Ago—in a Competitive World of 3 Networks," by *Sports Broadcast Journal*, April 4, 2021.

368 **"What we proposed":** Kevin O'Malley int.

368 **The coverage of:** Jack McCallum, "In the Kingdome of the Solitary Man," *Sports Illustrated*, Oct. 6, 1986, pp. 64–84.

369 **"The television world":** Dennis Lewin int.

369 **"I remember a":** Jim Spence int.

369 **The ensuing conversation:** *1979 NCAA Television Committee Report* (Mission, KS: NCAA, 1980), p. 19.

370 **"Walter, no!" said:** Jim Spence int.; Chuck Neinas int.; Tom Hansen int.

370 **The forces allied:** Joe McGuff, "CFA Takes Positive Step Forward with Neinas," Sporting Comment, *Kansas City Star*, Feb. 3, 1980; Chuck Neinas int.; Bill Little int.; DeLoss Dodds int.; Vince Dooley int.; Joe Paterno int.; Bobby Bowden int.

370 **By 1980, ABC:** *1980 NCAA Television Committee Report* (Mission, KS: NCAA, 1981), pp. 7–8.

370 **Arledge and Spence's:** Jim Spence int.

371 **It would be:** Barry Tramel, "OU, Georgia Changed College Football with Its Lawsuit Against the NCAA," *Oklahoman*, Dec. 23, 2017; Gene Wojciechowski, "Judgment Call: How a Supreme Court Decision Led to the Birth of the BCS," in MacCambridge (ed.), *The ESPN College Football Encyclopedia*, pp. 29–32.

371 **It turned out:** Joe Delessio, "That Was a Thing: Sports Phone, the 1980s Way to Get Real-Time Scores," Grantland, Feb. 24, 2015, https://grantland.com/the-triangle /that-was-a-thing-sports-phone-the-1980s-way-to-get-real-time-scores/.

371 **In April 1980:** Pete Rozelle int.; Jim Kensil int.; Don Weiss int.

372 **On the floor:** Broadcast of 1980 NFL Draft, ESPN.

372 **By the end:** George Brett int.

373 **"When the budget":** Ware, *Game, Set, Match*, p. 68.

373 **Already, the changes:** Anson Dorrance int.

373 **"Anson, if you'll":** Anson Dorrance int.

374 **In the spring:** Anson Dorrance int.

374 **Visiting the 1981:** Anson Dorrance int.; Donna Lopiano int.; Charlotte West int.; Merrily Dean Baker int.; Gloria Averbuch, "North Carolina Is Part of the Roots and Growth of Women's Soccer," by *New York Times*, Dec. 3, 2000.

374 **In the summer:** Charlotte West int.; Donna Lopiano int.; Peg Burke int.; Sharon E. Taylor int.; Merrily Dean Baker int.; Carole Oglesby int.; Judie Holland int.; Laine Higgins, "Women's College Sports Was Growing. Then the NCAA Took Over," *Wall Street Journal*, April 3, 2021.

374 **Throughout the:** 1980 AIAW Presidential Review DVD Morrison, Tape 1, July 15, 1980; 1980 AIAW Presidential Review DVD Burke, Tape 1, July 16, 1980, University of Iowa.

375 **The implicit subject:** 1980 AIAW Presidential Review DVD Mabry, Tape 3, July 15, 1980, University of Iowa.

375 **"What if I":** 1980 AIAW Presidential Review DVD Mushier, Tape 3, July 17, 1980, University of Iowa.

375 **By the January:** Gordon S. White Jr., "NCAA Is Warned by Women," *New York Times*, Jan. 15, 1981, p. D-24; David Moffit, "Christine Grant, Director of Women's Athletics at Iowa And…," United Press International, Jan. 14, 1981, https://www.upi.com/Archives/1981/01/14/Christine-Grant-director-of-womens-athletics-at-Iowa-and/4795348296400/.

375 **"I believe our":** "NCAA Convention Minutes, Final Business Session, January 14, 1981," p. 179; Gordon S. White Jr., "NCAA Is Warned by Women," *New York Times*, Jan. 15, 1981, p. D-24.

376 **But by then:** Byers with Hammer, *Unsportsmanlike Conduct*, pp. 245–246.

376 **In September 1980:** Doug Tucker int.; Judie Holland int.; Charlotte West int.; Byers with Hammer, *Unsportsmanlike Conduct*, p. 247.

376 **"When the vote":** Doug Tucker int.

376: **But the vote:** John Feinstein, "NCAA Opens Its Doors to Women," *Washington Post*, Jan. 14, 1981.

376 **"It became a":** Jody Conradt int.

377 **"It was a":** Donna Lopiano int.

377 **"It wasn't even":** Diane Williams int.

377 **On June 30:** Merrily Dean Baker int.; Merrily Dean Baker, "An Open Letter to All Who Have Been Associated with AIAW," June 29, 1982.

377 **The larger vision:** Christine H. B. Grant, foreword to C. Terry Walters, *The Lost Haven of Sharon Taylor: Casualties in the Battle for Equality in Women's Sports* (East Pennsboro Township, PA: Terremoto Grande Publishing, 2016), pp. 1–9.

378 **The evidence for:** Sharon E. Taylor int.; Margo Polivy int.; Charlotte West int.; Carole Oglesby int.

378 **"It had to":** Jody Conradt int.

378 **It was April:** Ware, *Game, Set, Match*, p. 186.

378 **None of the:** King with Howard and Vollers, *All In*, p. 340.

379 **The feminists who'd:** King with Howard and Vollers, *All In*, p. 337.

379 **But in the:** King with Deford, *The Autobiography of Billie Jean King*, p. 170.

379 **CBS's coverage of:** Abdul-Jabbar with Knobler, *Giant Steps*, p. 314.

380 **"If Earvin had":** Abdul-Jabbar with Knobler, *Giant Steps*, p. 314.

380 **What they missed:** Simmons, *The Book of Basketball*, p. 140.

380 **The early '80s:** Pepe, *Talkin' Baseball*, p. 382; Epstein, *Big Hair and Plastic Grass*, p. 286.

381 **"You're just a":** Phil Garner int.

381 **Ed Garvey led:** Billie Jean King int.; King with Deford, *The Autobiography of Billie Jean King*, pp. 145–146.

381 **"Ed didn't get":** Jim Quinn int.

381 **By failing to:** Gene Upshaw int.; Paul Tagliabue int.; Jeffrey Pash int.; Jim Quinn int.

382 **"At the end":** Jim Quinn int.

382 **"I remember asking":** Marc Fleisher int.

382 **At the NBA:** Jeffrey Mishkin int.

383 **Considering the pro:** Marc Fleisher int.; Jim Quinn int.; Russ Granik int.; Jeffrey Mishkin int.

383 **What they saw:** Jim Quinn int.; Russ Granik int.; Jerry Colangelo int.

383 **"We were convinced":** Jim Quinn int.

383 **It was then:** Jim Quinn int. Quinn would remember Bob Lanier, the president of the NBPA, coming out of a negotiation session and concluding that the deal on the table was the best that they could get, even though it would limit the top salaries that elite players like Moses Malone could make. Walking down the streets of Manhattan, Lanier said to Larry Fleisher, "Well, fuckin' Moses is just going to have to live off two million a year."

383 **Fleisher adamantly didn't:** Associated Press, "Sonics' Payroll One of Five Frozen," *Spokane Statesman-Review*, April 1, 1983.

384 **"I learned how":** Jeffrey Mishkin int.

384 **"My father and":** Marc Fleisher int.

384 **Going over the:** Jim Quinn int.; Marc Fleisher int.; Don Fehr int.; Russ Granik int.

385 **A salary cap:** Jim Quinn int.; Paul Tagliabue int.; Gene Upshaw int.

385 **"Competitive balance is":** Jeffrey Mishkin int.

385 **It would be:** Sean Deveney, "Covid-10 Pushes 37-Year NBA Player-Owner Partnership to the Extreme," *Forbes*, May 31, 2020.


EPILOGUE

386 **For ages, people:** Jack Nicklaus int.

387 **The first year:** Underwood, "A Heavy Comes to Light," *Sports Illustrated*, Feb. 19, 1973, pp. 70–82.

387 **When ESPN arrived:** Jack Nicklaus int.

387 **It was the:** Allan Tanenbaum int.

387 **Aaron took up:** Allan Tanenbaum int.

387 **He had been:** Ernie Accorsi int.; Allan Tanenbaum int.; Maria Ridenour, "Hank Aaron, a Die-Hard Cleveland Browns Fan Who Would Sneak into the Dawg Pound," *Akron Beacon Journal*, Jan. 22, 2021.

388 **When the Ravens:** Ernie Accorsi int.

390 **"Football was always":** Bill Hancock int.

391 **In 1981, more:** Gerald Eskanazi, "70,000 Football Fans Make New Orleans Throb with Super Bowl Mania," *New York Times*, Jan. 25, 1981.

391 **Observing the throng:** Ernie Accorsi int.

392 **"All professional athletes":** Dennis Lewin int.

392 **When the writer:** Jon McGlocklin int.

393 **"Space and time":** Joe Greene int.

394 **Two weeks earlier:** Doug Williams int.; Adam Zagoria, "Doug Williams Shed Tears of Joy After Learning Patrick Mahomes, Jalen Hurts Would Be First Black Quarterbacks to Meet in Super Bowl," *Forbes*, Feb. 4, 2023, https://www.forbes .com/sites/adamzagoria/2023/02/04/doug-williams-shed-tears-of-joy-after -learning-patrick-mahomes-jalen-hurts-would-be-first-black-quarterbacks-to -meet-in-super-bowl/?sh=2cdcacfb335c.

394 **"It showed that":** Tyrell Feaster, "'Standing on the Shoulders of All These Greats': Patrick Mahomes Pays Homage to African American Quarterbacks of the Past in Doug Williams and Warren Moon Following His History-Making Showdown with Jalen Hurts in the Super Bowl," *Daily Mail*, Feb. 14, 2023.

395 **Because these same:** Charlotte West int.

395 **In so doing:** Donna Rosene Leff, "How Far We Haven't Come," Annenberg Washington Program Communication Policiy Studies, Nov. 1993; Donna Rosene Leff, The "Angry Voices: Black Journalists and the *Washington Post*," Annenberg Washington Program Communications Policy Studies, March 16, 1992.

395 **The same thing:** Charlotte West int.

395 **Byers also came:** Charlotte West int.

395 **While women athletes:** Chrstina Gough, "Number of College Sport Scholar-ships Available in the United States in 2020/21, by Gender," statista.com, Sept. 23, 2021.

396 **Along the way:** Amy Wilson int.

396 **On Sunday, November:** Billie Jean King int.; Anne Flannery int.; Julie Foudy int.

397 **King looked at:** Billie Jean King int.; Anne Flannery int.; Julie Foudy int.

397 **"And I remember":** Julie Foudy int.

397 **"I was like":** Julie Foudy int.

397 **Women's college basketball:** Christine Terp, "A Whole New Ball Game," *Christian Science Monitor*, May 22, 1981.

398 **That led Marla:** Billie Jean King int.

399 **The seeds of:** Anson Dorrance int.

399 **"A big part":** Bill Hancock int.

399 **"The lessons learned":** Sharon E. Taylor int.; Sharon E. Taylor, "The AIAW," personal memorandum Lock Haven State College, April 8, 1982.

399 **"To be successful":** Joan Cronan int.

400 **A recent Women's:** Tara Chozet, "Female Executives Say Participation in Sport Helps Accelerate Leadership and Career Potential," by espnW, ESPN, Oct. 9, 2014.

400 **So much changed:** Amy Wilson int.; Susan Ware int.; Margaret Dunkle int.

401 **At the beginning:** Ware, *Game, Set, Match*, p. 69.

# Bibliographic Essay

This book is the product of two years of research and more than three hundred hours of interviews, as well as revisiting dozens of interviews I've conducted for earlier projects. There are numerous paths one could take to understand American sports in the '70s, and I have chosen to focus primarily on the most popular team sports, as well as key figures in individual sports, like Muhammad Ali, Billie Jean King and Chris Evert. I'll be the first to grant that there are other paths one could have taken to tell the same story. So what follows is an overview of my particular path.

For those trying to understand the universe of American sports in that era, there are the three leading publications of the decade: the invaluable and exceedingly well-written weekly magazine *Sports Illustrated*; the less well-written but equally invaluable weekly newspaper *The Sporting News*; and the monthly magazine *Sport*. Back issues of *Sports Illustrated* are available online at https://vault.si.com. *The Sporting News* is generally elusive, but a membership in the Society for American Baseball Research includes free access to the online archive Paper of Record, which has reproduced the entire history of *The Sporting News* digitally. *Sport*, urbane and surprisingly progressive, was edited by the great Dick Schaap for much of the '70s, but back issues remain hard to find. In the past, I've had to go to the Library of Congress in Washington, DC. For this project, I was fortunate to find a complete collection of *Sport* from the '70s at the H. J. Lutcher Stark Center for Physical Culture and Sports at the University of Texas.

The changes in television in the '70s were captured episodically by the TV/Radio column in *Sports Illustrated* (usually by William Leggett), the SporT-View column in *The Sporting News* (written by Jack Craig, who also covered the beat for the *Boston Globe*), and in the pages of *TV Guide* (usually by Marvin Durslag). Among book-length treatments, there was William Oscar Johnson's *Super Spectator and the Electric Lilliputians*, a distinctively '70s book title if ever there was one (New York: Little, Brown, 1971), Phil Patton's

*Razzle-Dazzle: The Curious Marriage of Television and Professional Football* (Garden City, NY: Dial Press/Doubleday, 1984) and Ron Powers' *Supertube: The Rise of Television Sports* (New York: Coward-McCann, 1984). Among the most notable participants, Roone Arledge's *Roone: A Memoir* (New York: HarperCollins, 2003) is far more candid and insightful than either of Howard Cosell's self-glorifying books, *Cosell* (Chicago: Playboy Press, 1973) and *Like It Is* (Chicago: Playboy Press, 1974). There's plenty of detail in Jim Spence's *Up Close & Personal: The Inside Story of Network Television Sports* (New York: Atheneum, 1988). More recently, Rich Podolsky's *You Are Looking Live!: How* The NFL Today *Revolutionized Sports Broadcasting* (Guilford, CT: Lyons Press, 2021) takes the measure of *The NFL Today*'s personalities and impact. For the dawn of ESPN, there is the rollicking oral history *Those Guys Have All the Fun: Inside the World of ESPN* (New York: Little, Brown, 2011), by Jim Miller and Tom Shales, as well as ESPN founder Bill Rasmussen's own memoir, *Sports Junkies Rejoice: The Birth of ESPN* (Hartsdale, NY: QV Publishing, 1983).

Varying accounts of the ongoing battle between labor and management can be found in Sam Smith's *Hard Labor: The Battle That Birthed the Billion-Dollar NBA* (Chicago: Triumph Books, 2017), Oscar Robertson's *The Big O: My Life, My Time, My Game* (Emmaus, PA: Rodale/St. Martin's, 2003), Marvin Miller's *A Whole Different Ball Game: The Sport and Business of Baseball* (New York: Birch Lane Press, 1991), John Mackey's *Blazing Trails: Coming of Age in Football's Golden Era* (Chicago: Triumph Books, 2003), Curt Flood's *The Way It Is* (New York: Trident Press, 1970), and John Helyar's *Lords of the Realm: The Real History of Baseball* (New York: Ballantine Books, 1995). The veteran labor lawyer Jim Quinn's memoir *Don't Be Afraid to Win: How Free Agency Changed the Business of Pro Sports* (New York: Radius Book Group, 2019) also offers valuable insight. Joshua Mendelsohn's *The Cap: How Larry Fleisher and David Stern Built the Modern NBA* (Lincoln, NE: University of Nebraska Press, 2020) focuses on the events leading up to the NBA's salary cap. These developments were also covered extensively in the pages of the *New York Times* and the *Washington Post*, among the first papers to take seriously the idea of athletes' rights.

In the discussion of race relations and integration within sports in the '70s, the work of Lacy J. Banks in *Ebony* is consistently strong. Michael Hurd has written the definitive *Black College Football, 1892–1992: One Hundred Years of History, Education and Pride* (Virginia Beach, VA: Donning, 1993), and his biography of Collie Nicholson, *Collie J: Grambling's Man with the Golden Pen* (Haworth, NJ: St. Johann Press, 2007) provides insight into the brilliant career of Grambling's town crier. Eddie Robinson's own *Never Before, Never Again: The Autobiography of Eddie Robinson* (New York: St. Martin's, 1999), with Richard Lapchick, is impressionistic but engaging. William Rhoden's *Third and a Mile: The Trials and Triumphs of the Black Quarterback* (New York: ESPN Books, 2007) is a crucial oral history, following the paths of many Black quarterbacks who were denied a chance at the NFL, and the absorbing stories of those who, finally, were given the chance to succeed. Jason Reid's recent *Rise of the Black Quarterback: What It Means for America* (Los Angeles: Andscape, 2022) contextualizes the struggle to include more recent developments.

For the impact of Title IX, there is a wide and rewarding literature. I relied mostly on historian Susan Ware's *Game, Set, Match: Billie Jean King and the Revolution in Women's Sports* (Chapel Hill: University of North Carolina Press, 2011) and Selena Roberts' *A Necessary Spectacle: Billie Jean King, Bobby Riggs, and the Tennis Match That Leveled the Game* (New York: Crown, 2005), to put the King–Riggs Battle of the Sexes into larger historical context. In addition to those, Amy Wilson's excellent dissertation "A 'Saga of Power, Money, and Sex' in Women's Athletics: A Presidents' History of the Association for Intercollegiate Athletics for Women" (Iowa City, IA: University of Iowa: 2013) is required reading, as is her work at the NCAA, where she is the managing director of Inclusion, and has written progress reports on the fortieth and fiftieth anniversaries of Title IX. For a contemporaneous account of where things stood at the dawn of the Title IX era, Margaret Dunkle's highly influential study "What Constitutes Equality for Women in Sport?: Federal Law Puts Women in the Running" (Washington, DC: Association of American Colleges/Project on the Status and Education of Women, 1974) is a clear look at just how arduous the road ahead was going to be. Late in the '70s, Carole Oglesby and 12 contributors published *Women and Sport: From Myth to Reality* (Philadelphia: Lea & Febiger, 1978), keenly addressing the challenges and the sensibilities of the period, some of which still remain 45 years later. A more recent historical survey is offered by Jaime Schultz's

*Qualifying Times: Points of Change in U.S. Women's Sport* (Urbana, IL: University of Illinois Press, 2014). Among the literature on the changes wrought by Title IX, there are two young-adult titles that are particularly well-written. One is Karen Blumenthal's readable, informative *Let Me Play: The Story of Title IX; The Law That Changed the Future of Girls in America* (New York: Atheneum Books for Young Readers, 2005), which won the Jane Addams Children's Book Award in 2006. There's also Jen Barton's *Bernice Sandler and the Fight for Title IX* (Washington, DC: Magination Press, American Psychological Association, 2022), a chronicle of Sandler's life and outsized impact. The University of Maryland and the University of Iowa both have a rich trove of documents from the AIAW's decade of change.

Among the key figures in the *The Big Time*, Billie Jean King has written not one, not two, but three autobiographies, and while the recent bestseller *All In* (New York: Knopf, 2021), with Johnette Howard and Maryanne Vollers, is clearly the best, both *Billie Jean*, with Kim Chapin (New York: Harper & Row, 1974), and *The Autobiography of Billie Jean King*, with Frank Deford (St. Albans, Hertfordshire, UK: Granada, 1981), are worthwhile memoirs. Chris Evert has only two autobiographies, but she still has time to catch Billie Jean. *Chrissie: My Own Story*, with Neil Amdur (New York: Simon and Schuster, 1982), finds her contemplating the length of her career, while *Lloyd on Lloyd*, cowritten with her then husband John Lloyd, as well as Carole Thatcher (New York: Beaufort Books, 1986), describes the challenges of a relationship between two touring pros on two different tours.

The life of Henry Aaron has also been documented extensively. His first autobiography, *Aaron* (New York: Thomas Y. Crowell, 1974), with Furman Bisher, was not as good as his second autobiography, *I Had a Hammer: The Hank Aaron Story* (New York: HarperCollins, 1991), with Lonnie Wheeler. The definitive version is still Howard Bryant's *The Last Hero: A Life of Henry Aaron* (New York: Random House, 2010).

Julius Erving tells his own story well in *Dr. J: The Autobiography* (New York: HarperCollins, 2013), with Karl Taro Greenfield. Perhaps the most interesting evolution in American sports is that of Kareem Abdul-Jabbar. His book *Giant Steps: The Autobiography of Kareem Abdul-Jabbar* (Toronto: Bantam Books, 1983), written with Peter Knobler while he was still an active player, was a revelation. Since then, he's written numerous books, including the excellent *Coach Wooden and Me: Our 50-Year Friendship On and Off the Court* (New York: Grand Central Publishing, 2017).

There are vivid accounts of the Virginia Slims Tour in Grace Lichtenstein's *A Long Way, Baby: Behind the Scenes in Women's Pro Tennis* (New York: William Morrow, 1974) and Ted Tinling's *Love and Faults: Personalities Who Have Changed the History of Tennis in My Lifetime* (New York: Crown, 1979), written with Rod Humphries. Jimmy Connors' *The Outsider: A Memoir* (New York: HarperCollins, 2013) is also readable, if inevitably self-serving. And Julie Heldman's self-published memoir *Driven: A Daughter's Odyssey* (Julie Heldman, 2018) is a candid, at times harrowing, take on the challenges of mixing family with profession.

In pro basketball, there is no better index of the time than two classics: David Halberstam's *The Breaks of the Game* (New York: Hachette Books, 1981) and Terry Pluto's *Loose Balls: The Short, Wild Life of the American Basketball Association as Told by the Players, Coaches, and Movers and Shakers Who Made it Happen* (New York: Fireside, 1990). But there are other rewarding depictions from the decade. Bill Bradley's *Life on the Run* (New York: Vintage Books, 1995) is one of the most insightful athlete's memoirs. Both Phil Berger's *Miracle on 33rd Street: The N.Y. Knickerbockers' Championship Season* (New York: Simon and Schuster, 1970) and John Devaney's *The Champion Bucks* (New York: Lancer Books, 1971), follow title-winning teams over the course of a season with an intimacy and access that will be striking to twenty-first-century readers (to say nothing of twenty-first-century sportswriters). There's also sublime material in Bill Simmons' bestseller *The Book of Basketball* (New York: Ballantine Books and ESPN Books, 2010), as well as in Theresa Runstedtler's more recent *Black Ball: Kareem Abdul Jabbar, Spencer Haywood, and the Generation That Saved the Soul of the NBA* (New York: Bold Type Books, 2023), which has an audacious subtitle to live up to, and just about pulls it off.

In pro football, there continues to be no better chronicle than Roy Blount Jr.'s vivid, perceptive *About Three Bricks Shy of a Load: A Highly Irregular Lowdown on the Year the Pittsburgh Steelers Were Super but Missed the Bowl* (Boston: Little, Brown, 1974), about the 1973 season with the Pittsburgh Steelers. The emerging specter of the Dallas Cowboys is captured in Joe Nick Patoski's *The Dallas Cowboys: The Outrageous History of the Biggest, Loudest, Most Hated, Best Loved Football Team in America* (New York: Little, Brown, 2012) and Peter Golenbock's *Cowboys Have Always Been My Heroes: The Definitive Oral History of America's Team* (New York: Warner Books, 1997). Among general texts on the decade, there is the wonderfully eclectic *Pro Football Chronicle* (New York: Macmillan, 1990), by Dan Daly and Bob O'Donnell. For arguably the biggest star in football in the '70s, there is surprisingly little written about O. J. Simpson prior to the Bronco chase that would define his legacy. But *Sports Illustrated* covered him frequently in the '70s and, in retrospect, they got no closer to who he actually was than anyone else. (As his teammate Ted Koy once said, "If you told me about what happened that night in Brentwood, and said one of my teammates did it, O.J. would have been the very last person I would have guessed.") For a more impressionistic take on pro football in the '70s, one can turn to the two best-selling novels of the early '70s, Dan Jenkins' *Semi-Tough* (New York: Atheneum, 1972) and Peter Gent's *North Dallas Forty* (New York: Morrow, 1973).

In baseball, Jim Bouton's *Ball Four* (New York: Dell, 1970) started all the trouble, and Mitchell Nathanson's *Bouton: The Life of a Baseball Original* (Lincoln, NE: University of Nebraska Press, 2020) takes a deep dive into the life of the man who changed the way sports were covered in America. The best writing about the decade's trends and evolution can be found in Bill James' *The New Bill James Historical Baseball Abstract* (New York: Free Press, 2003) and of the defining personalities of the decade in Joe Posnanski's *The Baseball 100* (New York: Avid Reader Press, 2021). The two best books to focus solely on baseball in the '70s are Dan Epstein's *Big Hair and Plastic Grass* (New York: Thomas Dunne, 2010) and Phil Pepe's oral history *Talkin' Baseball* (New York: Ballantine, 1998).

In boxing, Muhammad Ali dominated the decade, and his exploits are captured in Jonathan Eig's *Ali: A Life* (Boston: Mariner Books, 2017), Thomas Hauser's oral history *Muhammad Ali: His Life and Times* (New York: Simon and Schuster, 1991), as well as *The Muhammad Ali Reader*, edited by Gerald Early (Hopewell, NJ: Ecco Press, 1998). One should not miss Joyce Carol Oates' recounting of Ali's most eventful decade in her essay "Muhammad Ali: The Greatest Second Act," from the *ESPN SportsCentury* book (New York: Hyperion, 1999). Mark Kram Jr.'s well-researched *Smokin' Joe: The Life of Joe Frazier* (New York: HarperCollins, 2019) sheds light on Ali's antagonist and their complex relationship.

For the decade in college sports, Walter Byers' book with Charles Hammer, *Unsportsmanlike Conduct: Exploiting College Athletics* (Ann Arbor, MI: University of Michigan Press, 1997) is regarded by some as a mea culpa, by others as revisionist history. Regardless, it provides valuable insight into the NCAA's role as viewed by the man who essentially created the organization.

Among the college game, Michael Corcoran's *The Game of the Century: Nebraska vs. Oklahoma in Football's Ultimate Battle* (Lincoln, NE: University of Nebraska Press, 2004) is the best account of the titanic 1971 Nebraska–Oklahoma game. Essays by Chuck Culpepper, Dan Jenkins, Beano Cook, Mark Wangrin, Bud Withers and Andrew Bagnato from *The ESPN College Football Encyclopedia* (New York: ESPN Books, 2005) deftly capture the spirit of the times.

In college basketball, Seth Davis' *Wooden: A Coach's Life* (New York: Times Books/Henry Holt, 2014) is the ideal place to start, and his *When March Went Mad: The Game That Transformed Basketball* (New York: Times Books/Henry Holt, 2009) shows the college game at its moment of ascendance. But the best index of the growth of the sport throughout the '70s can be found in the *Street & Smith's* annual basketball guides, edited by Jim O'Brien, which capture both the heady rise of the sport and the droves of teams, coaches, conferences and personalities. Few American sports have ever possessed the rollicking, slangy texture of college basketball in the '70s.

Among the upstart leagues, besides the previously mentioned and definitive ABA book *Loose Balls*, there is Mark Speck's *Wiffle: The Wild, Zany and Sometimes Hilariously True Story of the World Football League* (Haworth, NJ: St. Johann Press, 2015), an exhaustively researched analysis of that gridiron hot mess. Ed Willes' *Rebel League: The Short and Unruly Life of the World Hockey Association* (Toronto: McClelland and Stewart, 2005) does the same for the short-lived hockey league. For World Team Tennis, the hard-to-find *The Art of World Team Tennis* (San Francisco: San Francisco Book Company, 1977) by Greg Hoffman is a house organ that is nonetheless authoritative. Karra Porter's *Mad Seasons: The Story of the First Women's Professional Basketball League, 1978–1981* (Lincoln, NE: University of Nebraska Press, 2006) is the best chronicle of that enterprise. It is hard to find a history of the International Volleyball Association or the International Women's Professional Softball Association (though Andrew Crossley's website Fun While It Lasted [https://funwhileitlasted.net/] is a good place to start, for both leagues).

Among the general histories of the decade, Bruce J. Schulman's *The Seventies: The Great Shift in American Culture, Society, and Politics* (Cambridge, MA: Da Capo Press, 2002) and Peter N. Carroll's *It Seemed Like Nothing Happened: America in the 1970s* (New Brunswick, NJ: Rutgers University Press, 2000) offer measured takes on the unappreciated decade.

Beyond those sources, I would be remiss if I didn't mention the consistently funny, consistently profane Twitter account @super70sSports, run by Rickey Cobb, which exudes the shaggy spirit of the decade. Also, there's Tim Hanlon's podcast about departed teams and leagues, *Good Seats Still Available*, which covers many of these sporting leaps of faith.

For all the scholarship, oral history and nostalgia that exist, there are still elements of sports in the 1970s that defy both context and explanation. In Billie Jean King's second autobiography there's a picture of her from the mid-'70s, not long after the Riggs victory. She's on a television soundstage...dressed in what looks like *Little House on the Prairie* frontier-era period clothing...sharing a dance...with *Penthouse* magazine editor Bob Guccione Jr....on *The Sonny & Cher Comedy Hour*. That one, I will admit, still leaves me perplexed. It is fair to say that there was more living than thinking done during the '70s.

# Author Interviews

Ernie Accorsi, Larry Albus, Eva Auchincloss, Merrily Dean Baker, Marie Ballard, Sal Bando, David Berst, Maurice Berube, Jane Betts, Brian Billick, Steve Blass, Bill Bradley, Anne Marie Bratton, Mike Breen, Cindy Brown, Hubie Brown, Alexandra Buek, Peg Burke, Michael Cardozo, Jerry Colangelo, Jody Conradt, Bob Costas, Joan Cronan, Bill Curry, Judy Dalton, Donna de Varona, DeLoss Dodds, Anson Dorrance, Eddie Doucette, Ann Meyers Drysdale, Cliff Drysdale, Tony Dungy, Margaret Dunkle, Gerald Early, Wilbert Ellis, Wayne Embry, Don Fehr, Steve Fehr, Anne Flannery, Marc Fleisher, Jim Foley, Tim Foli, Julie Foudy, Marti Fuquay, Phil Garner, Ralph Garr, Rosa Gatti, Dan Gavitt, Joe Gordon, Russ Granik, Mel Greenberg, Marcia Greenberger, Joe Greene, Mick Haley, Dick Hall, Bill Hancock, Tom Hansen, Jerry Hardaway, Mike Harrigan, James "Shack" Harris, Lusia Harris, Thomas "Hollywood" Henderson, Candace Lyle Hogan, Judith "Judie" Holland, Jim Host, Bill James, Rick Kehoe, Peachy Kellmeyer, Blair Kerkhoff, Larry Kindbom, Billie Jean King, Larry King, Ted Koy, Frank Layden, Dennis Lewin, Bob Ley, Grace Lichtenstein, Bill Little, Karen Logan, Donna Lopiano, Dorothy "Dot" Lovett, Melissa Ludtke, Paul Lukas, Verne Lundquist, Sylvia Mackey, Geoff Mason, Colleen Matsuhara, Dal Maxvill, Missy McCullough, Jenna McEachern, Jon McGlocklin, Brian McIntyre, Bob McKay, Liz Galloway McQuitter, Jane Miller, Jeffrey Mishkin, Bobby Moffat, Billie Moore, Cathy Self Morgan, Jeff Mullins, Brent Musburger, Chuck Neinas, Jack Nicklaus, Jim O'Brien, Mary Anne O'Connor, Kevin O'Malley, Carole Oglesby, Daniel Okrent, Jeff Orleans, Billy Packer, John Papanek, Dave Parker, Jeffrey Pash, Carl Peterson, Chris Plonsky, Terry Pluto, Letty Cottin Pogrebin, Margot Polivy, Cec Ponce, Doug Porter, Jim Quinn, Steve Richardson, Trish Roberts, Art Rooney Jr., Art Rooney II, Kyle Rote Jr., Bob Ryan, Sue Scheetz, John Schuerholz, Jaime Schultz, Jeannie Schulz, Peaches Sellers, Donna Shavlik, Juliene Simpson, Sue Sims, Bonnie Slatton, Dave Smith, George Solomon, Jim Spence, Waneen Spirduso, Jennifer Stanley,

Jan Stenerud, Ed Storin, Judy Sweet, Retha Swindell, Paul Tagliabue, Allan Tanenbaum, David Tatel, Sharon E. Taylor, Rod Thorn, Doug Tucker, Phyllis Tucker, Holly Turner, David Vance, Susan Ware, Julie Heldman Weiss, Rick Welts, Charlotte West, Diane Williams, Doug Williams, Pat Williams, Amy Wilson, Ron Wolf, Kristien (Kemmer) Shaw Ziska.

Additional interviews conducted during previous projects and used for this book: Sarah Ballard, Bobby Bell, Bobby Bowden, Gil Brandt, Mike Brown, Joe Browne, Joel Bussert, Jule Campbell, Emanuel Cleaver II, Al Davis, Len Dawson, Vince Dooley, John "Frenchy" Fuqua, Charlie Getty, Frank Gifford, Joe Gordon, Mickey Herskowitz, Al Hill Jr., Rod Humphries, Lamar Hunt, Walter Iooss Jr., Dan Jenkins, Ron Johnson, Jim Kensil, Jon Kolb, John Mackey, John Madden, Archie Manning, Wellington Mara, Al Michaels, Art Modell, Ozzie Newsome, Collie Nicholson, Chuck Noll, Marianne Noll, Bill Nunn, Joe Paterno, George Plimpton, Mike Renshaw, Pete Rozelle, Jack Rudnay, Steve Sabol, Dick Schaap, Chris Schenkel, Tex Schramm, Edwin "Bud" Shrake, Don Shula, John Steadman, Pat Summerall, John Unitas, Gene Upshaw, Bill Walsh, Don Weiss, Lloyd Wells, Paul "Tank" Younger.

# Index

# About the Author

**Michael MacCambridge** is an author, journalist, and TV commentator, whose books have included the acclaimed *America's Game: The Epic Story of How Pro Football Captured a Nation* and *Chuck Noll: His Life's Work*. For eight years a columnist and critic at the *Austin American-Statesman*, MacCambridge was later a contributor to *A New Literary History of America*, and his work has appeared in the *New York Times*, the *Wall Street Journal*, the *Washington Post*, *Sports Illustrated*, and *GQ*. The father of two children, Miles and Ella, he lives in Austin.